PN511W627Y65

THE BIT BETWEEN MY TEE

WILSON

APR 5 '69			
APR 9 '69			
MAR 4 '75			
AUG 3 1 1979	:		
JUL 1 5 1981			

WITHDRAWN

 PRINTED IN

THE BIT BETWEEN MY TEETH

BOOKS BY EDMUND WILSON

The Bit Between My Teeth

A Literary Chronicle
of 1950–1965

BY

EDMUND WILSON

FARRAR, STRAUS AND GIROUX
NEW YORK

Copyright © 1939, 1940, 1947, 1950, 1951, 1952, 1953, 1956, 1957, 1958, 1959, 1960, 1961, 1962, 1963, 1965 by Edmund Wilson

The essay on John Peale Bishop appeared first as the introduction to *The Collected Essays of John Peale Bishop,* edited by Edmund Wilson. Copyright 1948 Charles Scribner's Sons. Used by permission.

All rights reserved

Library of Congress catalog card number 65–23978

First printing, 1965

Published simultaneously in Canada by
Ambassador Books, Ltd., Toronto
Printed in the United States of America

A Modest Self-Tribute first appeared in the *Griffin*; *John Peale Bishop* as an introduction to a volume of Bishop's prose, published by Charles Scribner's Sons; *"The Country I Remember"* and *The Ghost of an Anglophile* in the *New Republic*; *James Branch Cabell: 1879–1958, Oo, Those Awful Orcs!, Mycophile and Mycophobe, Legend and Symbol in "Doctor Zhivago"* and *Donmanship* in the *Nation*; *W. H. Auden in America, Words of Ill-Omen, A Postscript to Fowler* and *More Notes on Current Clichés* in the *New Statesman*; *Everyman His Own Eckermann* in the *New York Review of Books*; and the memoir of Max Beerbohm in *Encounter*, which also reprinted from the *Nation*, *Legend and Symbol in "Doctor Zhivago."* All the rest first appeared in *The New Yorker*. The Swinburne essay has been previously reprinted in *The Novels of A. C. Swinburne*, published by Farrar, Straus; and *The Vogue of the Marquis de Sade*, *The Pre-Presidential T.R.* and *The Holmes-Laski Correspondence* in a volume called *Eight Essays*, published by Doubleday Anchor Books.

It will be seen that a few of these articles antedate 1950. The pieces on George Ade and Trumbull Stickney and the second piece on Logan Pearsall Smith were not collected in book form earlier because I had intended to incorporate them in a work on American literature after the Civil War and through the early years of this century; but what I ended by writing was a book on the literature of the Civil War, which included a number of these later writers, so I have sprinkled these others in here.

CONTENTS

THE BIT BETWEEN MY TEETH

A MODEST SELF-TRIBUTE

I SUPPOSE THAT the primary key in my reading to my work as a literary critic is my finding in my father's library, at some point when I was about fifteen, the brilliant translation by H. van Laun of Taine's *History of English Literature*. I was fascinated by the chapters on the novelists of the eighteenth and nineteenth centuries, whom I was then in process of reading. The opening of the section on Sterne, a great favorite of mine at that time, further stimulated my interest in him: "Imagine a man who sets out on a voyage equipped with a pair of spectacles that magnify things to an extraordinary degree. A hair on his hand, a spot on the tablecloth, the shifting fold of a coat, all will attract his attention; at this rate, he will not go far, he will spend his day taking six steps and will never get out of his room." And I was thrilled by the dramatic opening of the chapter on Jonathan Swift: "In 1685, in the great hall of the University of Dublin, the professors who had assembled to confer bachelor's degrees were confronted with a singular spectacle: a poor scholar, awkward and queer, with hard blue eyes, an orphan without friends, who depended on the charity of an uncle and had barely enough to live on, and who had already been refused his degree on account of his ignorance of logic, presented himself for a second time without having condescended to read the subject up"; and the equally

dramatic close of the chapter on the Restoration dramatists: "In their midst, a great poet, blind and fallen on evil
days, ever brooding on the miseries of the time, thus
painted the tumult of the infernal orgy,"—with its quotation from *Paradise Lost,* that, so placed, acquires a new
meaning; the description of "the sons of Belial, flown
with insolence and wine." Later on, I read Taine in
French, and on one occasion, when living in New York, I
became so absorbed by the *coup de théâtre* at the end of
the final chapter by which Taine evokes Alfred de Musset in order to contrast him with Tennyson and leaves
Musset with the moral advantage, that I continued to
read it on the street all the way to some engagement. But
in the meantime, while still at school, I had thus come
under the influence of French criticism, and my whole
point of view about literature was affected by Taine's
methods of presentation and interpretation. He had created the creators themselves as characters in a larger
drama of cultural and social history, and writing about
literature, for me, has always meant narrative and drama
as well as the discussion of comparative values. I had also
an interest in the biographies of writers which soon took
the bit in its teeth. This interest has not been, as is sometimes assumed, derived from the essays of Sainte-Beuve,
of which I doubt if I have read a dozen, though I have
undoubtedly been influenced by writers—such as Arnold
and Henry James—who were influenced by Sainte-
Beuve, as well as by Leslie Stephen, whose *Hours in a
Library* I read in the school library. My natural proclivity
in this direction is shown by the fact that, when I got to
the point of writing about Sterne at school (in the *Hill
School Record* of April, 1911), what came out was not a
critical essay but a story about Sterne's last visit to London, in which I depicted him wretchedly dying, apparently as a result of his social excesses and neglected by his

fashionable friends. That I was already taking account of a certain irreconcilability between the ideals of ordinary life and the special hazards of art is indicated by the final paragraph: "Thus the book that made Sterne, and sent his name down through the ages, was his ruin as a man. We should never have heard of him if he had not written the book which became so popular, but if *he* had not become so popular, he might have continued to be the quiet, eccentric, kindly parson of York."

As for "the discussion of comparative values," I did not read Matthew Arnold's essays till about 1922, when I was setting up in practice as a critic. My function in this department has, I think, been to make an effort to concentrate synoptically, as they say of the Gospels, to bring into one system, the literatures of several cultures which have not always been in close communication, which in some cases have been hardly aware of one another. There have been many examples of Englishmen who have read widely in the literature of the Continent, and several notable ones of continentals like Taine who have been well-read in English literature; but few European critics have known much about the literature of the United States, and even fewer—Maurice Baring and Melchior de Vogüé have been almost unique in this respect—have known anything at firsthand of Russian. For an American today it is natural to range freely in all these fields, and for anyone who wants seriously to understand the problems of the larger world with which we must now try to deal, it is important to acquire some knowledge of the literature of Marxism, that great international department of thought which, outside the Marxist movement, has, except for its influence on Bernard Shaw, till recently been hardly suspected by the general reading public of Western Europe and the United States. Now, I am far from an authority on any of these subjects, but, out of volatile curiosity and an appetite for varied entertainment, I have done some reading in all of them; and I have been working, as a practicing critic, to break down the conventional frames, to get away from the academic canons, that always tend to keep literature provincial. The educated man of the future will certainly read less intensively in any national literature, but will range over a much greater area. The courses in the world's great books that include both the *Iliad* and *War and Peace,* which have recently become a feature of the curriculums of most universities, are an obvious sign of this. We shall be able to look beyond our own systems and to assign our own suns and their planets to their places in a larger constellation, in which perhaps only the suns will count. Already in the last generation, with its wandering cosmopolitanism and its polygot cultural elements, it was becoming quite common for Americans to look for their literary models to the continental countries of Europe instead of, as had earlier been inevitable, exclusively or primarily to England. Already Greek and Latin have ceased to be taught as a cut-and-dried "disciplinary" survival from the antiquated Renaissance education, and so are beginning to present themselves as an attraction to able students of specifically literary interests, so that the classics are today, I should say, being read to much better purpose than they were in the days when everybody was obliged to have a certain amount of drill in the declensions and conjugations but rarely got to the point of finding out what the ancient writers had written. We are even—in a strangely belated way—discovering our own literature, which as recently as thirty years ago was hardly recognized by the English departments of most of our universities. The falling-off, as a result of the World Wars and the fascist and Nazi regimes, of Italian and German studies has been compensated to some degree, in a number of schools and colleges, by the inauguration of Russian studies. Departments of Comparative Literature, unheard of in my own time in college, have begun to appear in the bigger universities. My own worst disqualification as a critical synoptic eye has been my lack of Portuguese and Spanish and my almost complete ignorance of the literature of Latin America; but a number of accomplished students, critics, translators and teachers have recently been cultivating this field, and it is no doubt true, as they say, that the Hispanic and Anglo-Saxon cultures of South and North America, both now so mixed with other elements, will fertilize one another. In the meantime, I may claim for myself, since nobody, so far as I know, has ever yet claimed it for me, that I have tried to contribute a little to the general cross-fertilization, to make it possible for our literate public to appreciate and understand both our own Anglo-American culture and those of the European countries in relation to one another, to arrive at a point of view from which we may be able to deal with systems of art and thought that have previously seemed inaccessible or incompatible with one another.

1952

JOHN PEALE BISHOP*

JOHN PEALE BISHOP at the time of his death had been planning to bring out a volume of his selected essays, and some notes among his papers show that he had meant to include at least nine of the pieces here reprinted. I have added a number of others which seem to me of equal importance. The result is not a series of literary critiques—though there are some admirable studies of literary subjects—but a set of discourses on various aspects of contemporary civilization: literature, painting, moving pictures, architecture, manners, religion. In the graphic arts Bishop had a special interest, for his father had studied art before he had studied medicine and had taught the son to paint when he was still a child of four. Later on, during a boyhood illness which had prevented him from using his eyes, his attention was diverted to the books that were read to him and he gave up painting for poetry; but there was always in Bishop's poetry a large element of color and plastic form, and he occasionally in after-life went back to the brush again. Of the problems of the moving pictures he had acquired some special knowledge through working for a time, in 1924, in the titling department of Famous Players-Lasky. I have not reprinted here any of his papers on costume and cooking,

---

* Written as an introduction to *Collected Essays*, a volume of Bishop's prose.

6

though he occasionally wrote on these subjects. His interest in ornithology, which had also been stimulated by his father in childhood and which was revived in his later years when he went to live on Cape Cod, that great natural laboratory for bird watchers, played a considerable part in his poetry but is represented here only by his review of *Audubon's America*.

Along with his more elaborate essays, I have included a selection from his reviews. The notes on the young novelists of the twenties have seemed to me worth preserving as conveying the spirit of that era and bringing to bear on it a sounder taste than its exponents were always able to exercise. The discussions of Southern novelists show the same kind of discrimination in a field in which Bishop worked himself. I have reprinted all of his reviews of poetry written after his college days. We have been fortunate in this country during the last twenty-five years in having had at one time or another several poets of distinction regularly reviewing poetry. Bishop was one of these: from the beginning of December, 1939, to the middle of February, 1941, he had first choice of all the poetry at the *Nation*, and he contributed a number of other reviews to *Vanity Fair*, the *New Republic* and *Poetry*. I have not hesitated to put in, also, some of his aphorisms and notes on literature—especially since Bishop was aware that he often wrote more effectively in coining his thoughts into epigrams and paragraphs than in developing them as organized essays, and not long before his death spoke to me of publishing some of these. I have added, at the end, four pieces from his unpublished or uncollected fiction— the first two of these characteristic of the more sensuous vein of his youth, with its fantasy and its dandiacal elegance; the two others, of the mood of his later years, more sober and sometimes macabre. The second piece—*How Brakespeare Fell In Love With a Lady Who Had Been*

Dead For Some Time—is an episode from an unpublished novel on which Bishop spent a good deal of work. This book—called *The Huntsmen Are Up In America*— was finished in 1926. It deals with the childhood and youth of a boy named Brakespeare More-O'Brien, the son of a Virginia lady and a rich Irish-American businessman, who—as the result of the unfaithfulness and elopement of his mother—is brought up by his father, in Virginia, in an exclusively male household, under the influence of an eighteenth-century grandfather, so that he has to discover late for himself both women and modern America. The criticisms of F. Scott Fitzgerald and of the publisher to whom Bishop sent the novel had the effect of discouraging him with it; but, though the book does have serious weaknesses—he does not seem ever to have been very clear as to what destiny he intended for his hero, and the last chapters suffer from this—he put into it so much charming description and so much amusing commentary that one regrets that he should not have worked longer on it and given the ending more drama or point. The story has also an autobiographical interest—not, so far as I know, because it records actual facts of Bishop's life, but because it reflects the influences which had gone to form his tastes and his temperament. By imagining his characters on a Virginia estate and in terms of the culture of an earlier time, he is able to reconstruct the rather special intellectual dwelling from which he first looked out at the American world.

John Peale Bishop was born May 21, 1892, in Charles Town, West Virginia, in the Shenandoah Valley, and his people were mainly Virginian, though the family of his paternal grandfather had come from New London, Connecticut. A little treatise called *Colonel Cameron: His Ancestors and Descendants,* composed by John in his boyhood and carefully written out in a blank-book, shows how proud he was of his mother's lineage, full of ancient and noble Scotch names. He went to day school at Hagerstown, Maryland, which is not very far from Charles Town, to boarding school at Mercersburg, just across the boundary in Pennsylvania, and to college, in 1913–17, at Princeton—so that the whole of his youth was passed within a very small area of the East, where the South shades into the North, and in old-fashioned and countrified places, where one was little aware of modern industry. In a note on Bishop's literary generation at Princeton in the *Princeton University Library Chronicle,* Dean Christian Gauss has written that "even as a freshman John had a self-possession and self-mastery which gave him the poise and bearing of a young English lord." Yet he was also sometimes shy and sometimes crude amid the monied proprieties of Princeton. Later on, in the days after the First World War, when one saw him in his handsome dressing gown amid the Japanese screens and Renaissance beds of his friend Townsend Martin's apartment, which he inhabited during the latter's long absences, one felt about him that he was something like a Wycherley who had adapted himself to the nineties. What was not at all *fin de siècle* was the touch of eighteenth-century coarseness that was still country-bred and Southern and that was not in the least inimical to his fastidious taste and intellect but the soil out of which they grew and which gave them a solid base such as one did not ordinarily find in the more Puritanical Northern aesthete. It was a type, too, that sometimes had aspects of the fabulous bucks of the Regency of whom he delighted to read at that time and about whom, in *The Death of a Dandy,* he wrote one of the most brilliant of his longer poems; but he was also a romantic poet, not of the feverish or the ethereal kind, but in a vein in which purity of style gave refinement to emotions strongly sensual. And it was for poetry that he chiefly lived. He had no interest at all in politics, little in personalities; he very rarely read history or fiction and did not care to discuss general ideas. To quote Mr. Gauss again: he had at twenty-one come to Princeton "with a more carefully thought out and more accomplished mastery of the technique of English verse than any other undergraduate." Later, when he lived in New York and had a job on *Vanity Fair,* of which he eventually became managing editor, his poetry made heavy demands on him, and he would exhaust himself working through the weekends or in the evenings after returning from the office, and would try out, the first thing in the morning, reciting them while he made his toilet, the lines he had composed the night before, with an enthusiasm which to some of his college friends seemed almost Elizabethan, to others quite outlandish, but which, in any case, was perfectly spontaneous. At this time, he liked to quote a poem of Yeats's called *Adam's Curse* (the passage occurs twice in his essays):

> Better go down upon your marrow bones
> And scrub a kitchen pavement, or break stones
> Like an old pauper, in all kinds of weather;
> For to articulate sweet sounds together
> Is to work harder than all these . . .

Bishop had in common with Yeats a quality of feeling and phrasing that was naturally, not conventionally noble. His verse was neither, like Wallace Stevens's, the voice of a helpless pierrot imprisoned in a functioning businessman; nor, like Eliot's, a halting strain that was constantly being turned self-conscious by interruptions from an ignoble actuality. It was Bishop's native mode of speech, that was as much in evidence in the letters that one had had from him during the war and in the frivolous unsigned sketches that he wrote to order for *Vanity Fair* as in the poetry that he wrote for himself.

Bishop's weakness was in allowing himself to be influenced by the idioms of others. At college, it had been Shelley and Swinburne; in New York, it was Yeats and Pound. But in these years he had every appearance of progressing with the normal growth of a writer of first-rate talent: one felt that he was already mastering an idiom of his own. When, after his marriage to Margaret Hutchins, he went to Europe, in the summer of 1922, this development seemed somewhat slowed-up. He chastened and tightened his romantic style, but, now echoing Pound and Eliot, he lost much of his early élan. He improved his Italian and French; he studied ancient Provençal and took to translating the troubadours. He had never lived in Europe—had had, in his army days, no more than a glimpse of France; and he came to it with a lively appetite. Yet one regretted his absence from America, where one imagined that the literary revival would have continued to be stimulating for him. When, however, he returned to New York in 1924, he seems to have found America intolerable. He had no gift for advancing himself; he did not much enjoy the excitement of the twenties. The whole environment seemed a great deal more alien to him than Italy and France had been. And his failure in adapting himself prevented him from finishing his novel—since he had planned to have his hero go abroad and then come back to America—in any effective way. Brakespeare was to have revelled in his native land. John Bishop, in fact, rejected it. The Bishops returned to France in 1927 and bought the Château de Tressancourt at Orgeval, Seine-et-Oise, a rather imposing structure supposed to have been originally built as a hunting lodge for Henry of Navarre but enlarged in the eighteenth century, where they lived until 1933. Here Bishop tried again to do something in prose fiction with the country in which he had been born and toward which he still turned, and worked on *Many Thousands Gone,* a book of short stories, and *Act of Darkness,* a novel, both of which took place in the South. They were quite different from the early novel: more realistic and better thought out, but they were lacking in the kind of brilliance which Brakespeare had shared with his poetry.

When Bishop brought his family back to America—he now had three sons—in October of 1933, he went at first to live in Westport, Connecticut, and then in South Harwich on Cape Cod, and he began to occupy himself with the history of the New England branch of his family, about whom he wrote his poem *Beyond Connecticut, Beyond the Sea.* He had changed much since his first years in New York. In some ways his horizons had widened. He now read fiction, biography and history, and he reflected on historical problems. He had begun writing those thoughtful essays in which he makes an attempt to trace the effects on culture of the rise of the middle class—a phenomenon of which in his youth I do not believe he was even aware—and to expound, as an antidote to these, the virtues of the Southern tradition, as well as to justify the practice of the arts as activities respectable in themselves against what seemed to him a dangerous pressure in the direction of propaganda. And he resisted not only propaganda but journalism. No one was ever less of a journalist than Bishop, and his essays are seldom polemical. They illustrate themselves what they preach; and though he was less a master in prose than in verse, a little lacking the sure sense of the unit that he had for the stanza or the poem, one finds in these papers the purity of tone, the intellectual elegance—as well as sometimes the sensuous images—that are characteristic of his poetry. They flash, besides, at their most inspired, with a rare kind of imaginative fire, when the felicitous or witty phrases keep pace with rapid spurts of insight. Brought together, they will, I believe, like his poetry, make a very much stronger impression than— many of them scattered in periodicals of limited circulation—they did when they were published first. Some— like so much of his verse—have never before been published. He had got into a queer habit of hiding his work or of preventing it from being well known. It was partly that he never thought it good enough and was always holding it back for improvements, partly that he had not the same boldness that had distinguished his early career, when, as at Princeton, he had not hesitated to publish and defend poems that shocked Philistine opinion. He was now shy about his writing. His first collection of poems since a volume of mixed prose and verse published in 1922, to which I had also contributed, was published only in 1933, and his next, in 1935, was brought out in a limited edition of one hundred and fifty copies, so that few except his friends ever saw it. Besides these, there had been only *Green Fruit,* which he published when he was just out of college.

In the meantime, along with the broadening of his intellectual life, he had been growing somewhat more conventional at the same time as more "sophisticated" in the then current sense. His years in France had given him something of the detachment and the addiction to the amenities that are characteristic of American expatriates. His health, which had been frail in his boyhood, failed him also in later life, and he was incapable of the nervous effort, which even at the time had taxed him, of his days at *Vanity Fair.* One tended to assume with sorrow that his passion for poetry had also lapsed; yet, as one gradually saw more of his work—a volume of *Selected Poems* came out in 1941—one realized that this

was not the case. His vein had gone partially underground, but it was still alive and still uncorrupted. His
echoings of other poets seemed now scarcely more important than catchphrases and intonations picked up in
conversation, which do not affect one's opinions or the
quality of one's personality. Though he had dressed in a
variety of fashions, like the dandy that he always was, he
now could be seen unmistakably as a writer who had
always been something in himself and who had held on
to what he had. He had never exploited his gifts or
abused them in any way. At most, his Muse had sometimes been daunted, sometimes discouraged, sometimes
bored; but she had gone on expressing in her beautiful
speech discouragement, dismay or ennui—as well as her
persistent delight in colors, textures and shapes. And she
had laid up for her poet a treasure.

The Bishops in 1937 built a house at South Chatham
on Cape Cod, where Bishop lived, with occasional
absences for visits or lecture trips, all the year around. His
place, to which he gave the name Sea Change, looked out
on a stretch of salt marshes and the quiet coast of the bay.
The house itself, a special creation of Bishop's old Princeton friend, the architect William Bowman, had something of that lofty splendor which Bishop always managed to summon. You ate on Dutch marquetry chairs at a
long Louis Treize table in a high coral-pink room with
Venetian cupboards in the corners and windows on three
sides that opened on the white-wicketed lawn and gave a
view of the pale blue water. At that time he liked to play
on the phonograph Mozart's flute and harp concerto and
the medieval plain-chants of the monks of Solesmes
Abbey (both invoked, I find, in these essays); but when
he spoke to me of the sadness with which the joyousness
of Mozart was tinged and of the thin resignation of the
plain-chant—as if life at that low point in the Middle Ages

had been almost about to stop—I did not realize that it was anything but a mood. Yet he had sunk so far below his old self, his old responses even to the things that were still most important to him, that I remember being startled one day, when I had said something approving about Robert Frost—about whom, except for a few short poems, I did not myself much care--to see him brusquely aroused for a moment into something of his old interest and insolence and to hear him treat Frost *de haut en bas* in the tone of Byron on Wordsworth. In 1941 and 42, Bishop spent almost a year in New York as Director of Publications of the Bureau of Cultural Relations of the Council of National Defense. He studied Spanish and translated some Spanish poems. The fall of France was a terrible shock to him: one was astonished at the tragic character of John's reaction to it. It was as if he had relocated in France that "good society' which he liked to imagine and which had faded from modern Virginia. His friend F. Scott Fitzgerald had died suddenly of a heart attack on December 21, 1940, and John, while still in New York, wrote the elegy called *The Hours,* which set him off, when he returned to the Cape in the spring after his months of office work, on a whole fresh burst of activity which—flowing on into his Phi Beta Kappa poem and others of his later pieces—seemed to commence a new phase of his poetry. He went to Washington in November, 1943, to take a post in the Library of Congress which had been offered him by Archibald Mac-Leish, but he already had a leaking heart complicated with other disorders, and he was obliged to return to Cape Cod, where he died in the Hyannis Hospital on April 4, 1944. Even through these last days, when his life was running low, he had continued to work on his unfinished poems.

1948

SHEILAH GRAHAM AND
SCOTT FITZGERALD

CYRIL CONNOLLY, in writing about F. Scott Fitzgerald seven years ago, noted that, "apart from his increasing stature as a writer, Fitzgerald is now firmly established as a myth, an American version of the Dying God, an Adonis of letters born with the century, flowering in the twenties, the Jazz Age which he perfectly expressed and almost created, and then quietly wilting through the thirties to expire—as a deity of spring and summer should—on December 21, 1940, at the winter solstice and the end of an epoch."

The transformation of Fitzgerald into a vegetable god had gone further even than Connolly could have known. The writer of the present review, who had known Fitzgerald since his college days, edited, after his death, two volumes of his uncollected or posthumous writings and, as a result of this, found himself for years the recipient of a flow of letters of a very curious kind. It was evident that it was not merely, or perhaps primarily, as the author of *The Great Gatsby* and *Tender Is the Night* that Fitzgerald interested these correspondents but that he had become the object of a cult which had gone beyond mere admiration for the author of some excellent books. He had taken on the aspect of a martyr, a sacrificial victim, a semi-divine personage. People would beg me to see them simply in order that they might have had the privilege of beholding and speaking with one who had looked upon and spoken with Fitzgerald. Of course I avoided such contacts; I realized that it would be quite impossible for such worshippers to form any realistic idea of what Scott Fitzgerald had been like, and that they might better be left with their myth. One lady was sure that she had crossed with Fitzgerald at a time when he had been travelling incognito—not, I gathered, without tender passages—and would not be disillusioned when I wrote her that Fitzgerald had always travelled with his family and that he had made no trip to Europe at the time she believed she had seen him. She sent me for verification a letter she was certain she had had from him—so banal in its penmanship and style that it was difficult to know how anyone who had ever read a line he had written could have credited it to Fitzgerald. But this lady may very well still be convinced that she has played shuffleboard or walked the deck with an angel unawares. I had to recognize that my gifted but all too human old friend had been cast, just as Connolly had said, in the role of Attis-Adonis—the fair youth, untimely slain, who is ritually bewailed by women, then resuscitates, as Fitzgerald did, after perishing in the decline of his reputation, when his books were republished and more seriously read than they had usually been during his lifetime and when his legend became full-fledged and beyond his own power to shatter it.

This transformation into Attis-Adonis of a certain type of poet has been a recurrent phenomenon in literature (as well as in other fields), and it evidently repeats a pattern that springs from some instinctive need, some inevitable primitive imagery. There has been a strong element of this in the attitude of their admirers toward several of the Romantic poets. Shelley, who wrote of Keats as "Adonais," is himself one of the most obvious examples. The

passing of Attis-Adonis was, as I say, traditionally la-
mented by the women attached to his cult, and the same
has been true of these poets. Their devotees were sometimes called Maenads, and they seem to belong to the
same family as the Maenad-Bacchantes of the cult of
Dionysus, who tear to pieces a male sacrificial victim. You
get all this in Shelley's case—the emotional fragmenta-
tion among several women, the drowning when the *Don
Juan* went down, the burning of the body on the beach,
the snatching of the heart by Trelawny (there are always
a few male admirers). The poet Elinor Wylie was one of
the devotees of Shelley for whom realistic insight was
hardly possible, and in her novel *Orphan Angel* she
effected a ritual resurrection by bringing him to life in
America and providing him with a further career. D. H.
Lawrence is an even more striking example. He, too, has
been worshipped, bewailed and torn to bits by his feminine celebrants. And the late Dylan Thomas seems also to
be undergoing this transformation. There is always in
these cases an element of the feminine in the Attis-Adonis himself. It was the theory of the German scholar Böt-
tiger—I learn from Smith's classical dictionary of 1844—
that Attis, the beloved of Cybele, symbolically combined
in himself both the masculine and the feminine principles of nature. I do not mean by this to suggest that
there was anything effeminate about Scott Fitzgerald. An
effeminate personage would never do to represent the
force of fertility. But he readily in his fiction—from the
flappers of his early stories to the young girls through
whose eyes, in *Tender Is the Night* and *The Last Tycoon,* so much of the action is witnessed—performs a
kind of feminine ventriloquism, just as Lawrence in *Lady
Chatterley* and so many of his other stories is writing
from the woman's point of view. The woman reader finds
a feminine self-identification in such a writer and she

identifies herself with him. It is only such a poet as this—not the warrior or the builder or the abstract thinker—who can fully represent life's renewal.

This is all by way of a prelude to a book that is not at all typical of the Attis-Adonis celebrant—Sheilah Graham's recent memoir of Fitzgerald. Sheilah Graham is much too down-to-earth British, too close to the practical struggle for life, to perform with the timpani and cymbals. The resurrection does indeed take place, but—like one of Dr. Zhivago's—it takes place in the familiar ignoble world, in flimsiest Hollywood, among massacred scripts and dropped options. It is not a ritual matter, but a renewal in enduring if unfinished production, and the paeans of jubilation, like the chants of lament, are soon curbed.

But since this memoir, *Beloved Infidel*—written by Sheilah Graham in collaboration with Gerold Frank—is not merely a book about Scott Fitzgerald but, as its subtitle indicates, an account of The Education of a Woman, we must begin, as the author does, at the beginning of the story of her life, which she has here for the first time made public.

Sheilah Graham, she tells us, was originally Lily Sheil—a name which "to this day horrifies me to a degree impossible to explain," which she has not pronounced for twenty years and which she has "written here for the first time since my childhood." She was born in London's East End; her mother was "a cook in an institution," and she never knew very much about her father, who died when she was eleven months old. Her mother, when Sheilah was six, put her into an orphanage and left her there for eight years, during the first six of which, for hygienic reasons and to make her easily recognizable if she ran away, she had always to have her hair cropped. When she emerged from this institution, she was employed at first as a housemaid, then demonstrated a new kind of tooth-brush, then worked for a Major Gillam, who dealt in miscellaneous "fancy goods." Eventually, she married the major, who was twenty-five years older than she. He taught her correct table manners and English and got rid of her cockney accent. He even had her presented at Court. But she wanted to go on the stage, and got a job as one of "Cochran's Young Ladies." She played in Noël Coward's revue *This Year of Grace,* and she won a silver cup as the "most beautiful chorus girl" in London. She began to have smart admirers and be invited to smart parties. In the meantime, she had adopted her present name, invented a past for herself with a family background in Chelsea and a finishing school in Paris, and equipped herself with bogus family photographs.

One day, when she had gone to St. Moritz with the Mitfords, a lady with whom she was skating remarked, "You're an adventuress, aren't you?," and, after a brief pause, she answered, "Yes, I am." She was aware that, in her present situation, she could not go on putting herself over in England, so, leaving her husband behind, she emigrated to the United States, where she imagined it would not matter so much where you came from or who you were. She had already attracted some attention by her articles in the London popular press, and in New York she very soon succeeded in making a modest reputation as a journalist. In time she was given a job doing a syndicated gossip column, and this has been her occupation ever since. She was persistently pursued over here—having divorced her husband in England—by a playboy Marquess of Donegall, who did a society column for a London daily, and she was evidently ready to marry him when—her suitor having returned to England—she found that she had set off vibrations in the romantic sensibility of Scott Fitzgerald, who, lonely and in eclipse, his wife in a mental institution and his daughter soon to enter college, had come out to Hollywood in the hope of making money to pay his debts.

Fitzgerald took over Sheilah and set out to complete her education. When he discovered that she was tongue-tied among his friends because she could not speak their language or take part in their clever games, he read her poetry and taught her history, laid out for her a whole course of study. She told him her real story—in spite of her youthful impostures, she strikes one as fundamentally an honest person, perfectly realistic and not given to deceiving herself—then waited with apprehension to see whether his manner toward her would change. It is obvious that Fitzgerald was fascinated. She could have done nothing better calculated to stimulate his interest and sympathy. Having lived so extravagantly beyond his means, having strained so to meet the standards of the rich people of St. Paul and Chicago among whom he had had to grow up without ever having the money to compete with them, he was well qualified to put himself in Sheilah's place. She had already exercised upon him a kind of spell which she could not at first have understood. She was afterwards to find their relationship transposed into fictional terms in the story of Kathleen and Stahr, in his unfinished Hollywood novel, *The Last Tycoon*. Stahr is attracted to Kathleen by a fancied resemblance to his dead wife, as Fitzgerald had been attracted to Sheilah by a blond beauty that resembled Zelda's. This sort of thing is likely to happen after the loss of a woman still loved, and it may lead to mistaken appraisals—a species of optical illusion—that seem strange to an outside observer. But in this case the fundamental difference of Sheilah Graham's character from Zelda's that lay behind the former's glamor turned out to be extremely fortunate. Where Zelda had the charm of a sophisticated child—imaginative, amusing, capricious—and the lack of inhibitions of an Alabama belle, Sheilah Graham was quite mature: sober and self-controlled. If the fairies had been tipsy at the christening of Zelda (as Stevenson said in another connection) and had heedlessly squandered upon her, with a minimum of the stabilizing qualities, choice gifts that were squandered by herself, Sheilah Graham had had to learn slowly and to make herself a place in the world. Where Zelda would have flown away with any topic of conversation, no matter how little she knew about it, and enchanted—though she occasionally exasperated—the company with her opalescent fancies, Sheilah Graham would sit in silence, or, if she should hazard an inept remark, at once become aware of her error and be deeply embarrassed by it. When Fitzgerald set out to instruct her, she mastered what he had to teach with an accuracy that gave her in Hollywood a reputation of being exceptionally well informed. So not only did she rouse in him the sense of romance without which he could not flourish; she was able, with her affection and her common sense, to do everything a woman could to console him, to keep up his morale and to provide him with the necessary conditions for work—all of which meant making it possible for Fitzgerald to insulate himself from the distracting and, for him, the humiliating life of the moving-picture world. And she was admirable in her relations with Fitzgerald's daughter, at the time she was in her late teens and at Vassar, when her motherless relations with her father were evidently something of a problem, since Fitzgerald's imagination accompanied his daughter to college and pursued her in his letters and precepts with a commentary on her career there that became as much of a fiction taking flight from the actuality as any of his professional work.

Scott Fitzgerald, of course, failed as a Hollywood writer. Though he tried to take a hopeful view of the possibilities of the cinema and to acquire its peculiar techniques, he could not help despising its people and parodying and otherwise insulting them with the invincible Irish mockery that was likely to take possession of him when he was trying to induce himself to perform some uncongenial task. And he was not used to being rewritten or to working with other people. His incapacity to function under Hollywood conditions drove him, finally, back to his fiction. He succeeded, in *The Last Tycoon,* in identifying his own predicament with that of his hero, a brilliant producer, an old-fashioned American individualist, with ideals of artistic excellence, who has always been in the habit of doing everything for himself in his own way but is eventually to be destroyed by the crass uncreative elements which are converting the moving pictures into a big mechanical industry that has no regard for persons or for quality. "It occurred to me," says Sheilah Graham, "that I was of some value to Scott, for I could never tell him too much about Hollywood." She is too modest; if it had not been for her, we should undoubtedly have had no *Last Tycoon* at all. Not only did she bring him the gossip; she provided him with the base and supported him with the confidence that gave him the heart to return to his serious work, and anyone concerned with Fitzgerald must feel a special satisfaction that it has been possible for Sheilah Graham, with little vanity and no sentimentality, to do herself this overdue justice. It was impossible, while Zelda was alive, for Fitzgerald to marry Sheilah, and it was impossible, after his death, for a biographer or editor to acknowledge her help. In the biography by Arthur Mizener, Sheilah Graham is not mentioned by name, and this episode of his final years, so important but then difficult to deal with, had to be given too scant attention.

This hiatus in the story has now been filled, and the memoir by Sheilah Graham turns out to be the very best portrait of Fitzgerald that has yet been put into print. Zelda Fitzgerald's novel *Save Me the Waltz* was merely a reflection of the fantasy that he and she lived together; Arthur Mizener had never known Fitzgerald and did not in certain respects perhaps very well understand him; Budd Schulberg did know him briefly and in his novel *The Disenchanted* was able to reproduce quite faithfully the way Fitzgerald talked and behaved when, confronted with something that frightened him, he went to pieces and took to clowning (though some of the lines quoted in reviews of the play made from this would have given poor Fitzgerald gooseflesh). But Sheilah Graham shows us Fitzgerald at both his worst and his best, and, never having been fused into the Fitzgerald fantasy, has been able to put together a picture which, though intimate, is objective and calm. We are a long way here from Attis-Adonis.

When Sheilah Graham first knew Fitzgerald, he had for some time been safely on the wagon; in Hollywood, he went out to few parties, and, when he did, would remain in the background and usually get away early, before the heavy seas began. But his regime was upset by a trip to Chicago, where Sheilah was to make a broadcast. She had not yet got the hang of radio and was somewhat nervous about it, and Fitzgerald went along to give her moral support, but was evidently nervous, too. Before starting, he resorted to the bottle, with the inevitable consequences of chaos and farce. Having helpfully rehearsed her before they left, he insisted, at the actual rehearsal, on sitting in the front row and beating time with an imaginary baton and otherwise distracting her to such a degree that he had to be removed by the stage-hands. These lapses continued at intervals in the course of their years together, and for Sheilah, who had never before had to contend with the maniacal American spree—in her better circles in England she had merely heard of people being "tiddly"—this presented a dismaying problem. The series of these aberrations was to culminate in a terrible crisis, which forced her to call the police and to refuse to see Fitzgerald for weeks.

This episode, shocking though it is, has so much dramatic significance that—from the long-term point of view—I do not think that Sheilah Graham, in including it, is guilty, as some feel, of bad taste. Fitzgerald threw back at her with sneers, and even threatened to proclaim to Hollywood, what she had told him about her origins. It was the familiar phenomenon of impotence—Fitzgerald must have felt powerless in Hollywood either to do work that met his own standards or to succeed on Hollywood's terms—that, with alcohol, breaks out into frenzied aggression, of self-hatred that seeks for relief by directing its fury against someone else. But Sheilah, as a result of this scene, had a rather welcome interval of freedom, when she was able to go out with other men and to circulate in a normal way: his possessiveness had been a tyranny, preventing her, on one occasion, from putting up a woman friend who had come on a visit to Hollywood and, on another, from seeing the head of her syndicate, who was making the rounds of the newspapers to which his features were sold.

But when Fitzgerald had well recovered—his recoveries were long and arduous—he turned to Sheilah again, and she found that she could not reject him. They rented two apartments in the same building, one above the other. He knew now that he had a bad heart, so lived on the bottom floor. He was working on *The Last Tycoon,* and this reviewer, who sorted out his manuscripts, can testify to the scrupulous discipline he was able to impose on himself. He had revised the early chapters again and again, had calculated the value of every touch. One day when, Sheilah says, he had been reading the papers and eating chocolate bars, when he had been telling her that if his book were successful he would take her back to the East and then they would travel together—"if ever I get out of this mess, I'll make it up to you, Sheilo"—he suddenly got up from his chair, clutched the mantelpiece and fell dead on the floor.

This whole story I have found very moving. The book fully justifies, it seems to me, all of Sheilah Graham's revelations about both herself and Scott. They have both of them—she despite the pretenses of her youth, he despite his neurotic divagations—too much dignity at the core of their characters for this memoir to have anything sordid, and Sheilah Graham saw Scott Fitzgerald, as few even of his close friends did, when he was serious, self-exacting, hard-working; she had the best of his humor and charm, his imaginative consideration; and she has done well to leave this record.

To the reviewer, the whole thing seems so far away, so much part of an already classic tale, that the question of scandal can hardly arise. It may be that the intervention of Sheilah Graham's collaborator has something to do with this. No collaborator can quite get away from the conventions of the popular magazine, which act as a non-conductor, which put us at a muffling remove from the emotions of the actual experience. But the story is skillfully told; it has undoubtedly, from this point of view, profited somewhat from Mr. Frank's handling, and, though ironed out, it never sounds false. It almost seems to take its place as a part of Fitzgerald's work, which has become, only eighteen years after his death, already so much an established thing—left intact when the dreams and disorders which it embodies have themselves died away, and we see it from a bleaker world.

> But, tell, shall he, the tourist, find
> Our isles the same in violet-glow
> Enamouring us what years and years—
> Ah, Ned, what years and years ago!

January 24, 1959

MENCKEN THROUGH THE WRONG
END OF THE TELESCOPE

"THE IRREVERENT MR. MENCKEN," by Edgar Kemler, is a workmanlike and readable biography, which has been checked for accuracy by Mencken himself. Undertaken on a modest scale, it hardly even attempts literary criticism but concentrates on Mencken as a public figure and tells the story of his political polemics, of his battles with the New York Vice Society and the Boston Watch and Ward, of his vicissitudes as a newspaperman in Baltimore and his role in the Scopes Monkey Trial.

The book makes a curious impression on a reader who got out of college in the second decade of the century, when Mencken was at his best as a journalist and when his first important books were appearing; who witnessed, without quite the same enthusiasm, his apotheosis during the twenties; and who has derived a good deal of pleasure from his subsequent autobiographical writings and from the supplemental volumes of *The American Language*. The main facts about Mencken are here; all the aspects of his career are accounted for; but a big "value" has been omitted: the excitement and the effect of brilliance of the days when the later *Smart Set* (rather than the *American Mercury*) was one of the great stimulants to ferment. One realizes, as one had already done in connection with certain other studies of celebrities of the pre-crash period by writers of a later era, that such writers are looking at the twenties as if through the wrong end of our telescope and see things perhaps more clearly but also much smaller than we do. The veteran may be well aware of the vulgarities and bad thinking of that period, of its pointless prodigality and catastrophic recklessness, and yet find himself taken aback by the apparent obliviousness of the post-depression writers to the creative and liberating spirit that seemed to him so dazzling a phenomenon.

The alumnus of the lean thirties—Mr. Kemler was born in 1916—is not dazzled when he looks back at Mencken. He does not find at all infectious the audacity and verve of the *Smart Set,* a magazine which Mr. Kemler describes as a product of the "interaction between Nathan's aesthetic snobbery and Mencken's resurgent clownishness." He is not much amused by their jokes, and you feel that he is rather relieved when they move in among the shaded lights and the Oriental rugs of the Knopf office and are made to "understand that in such decorous surroundings their buffooneries would no longer be tolerated." Not that it is not a good thing to have Mencken written about in a different style from that of the ebullient De Casseres. Not that one would have Mr. Kemler give us a romantic biography in the vein of Gene Fowler. If the twenties were always a little drunk, this book has the merit of sobriety. It is instructive to learn that the *Smart Set* was a dubious publishing venture which had at first to be kept alive by other frankly trashy magazines such as *Parisienne* and *Snappy Stories,* that it was only for six years self-sustaining, and that it was going broke in 1922, when its editors were at the height of their vogue. Yet, after all, if Mr. Fowler had not written *Good Night, Sweet Prince,* the folklore and the fumes of John Barrymore's life would never have been bottled in book form. And, though the glamor and murk of the twenties have certainly obscured what went on then, one discovers, when these have been cleared away, that something vital has been left out of the picture.

Mr. Kemler gives a reliable account of what he calls "the Battle of the Books" of the years just after World War I, in which the issue was drawn between the movement led by Mencken and the forces of the genteel-academic culture that had done so much to discourage original American writing from about 1880 on, and he suggests some interesting reflections to the veteran of that battle when he shows how the "shock troops," as he calls them, of the movement for liberation made it a point of honor not to associate themselves with academic institutions or with anything that was official or accepted. The writers who matured in the depression years, when both journalism and money were ebbing low, were often glad to get jobs as professors, and some of the intransigents of the twenties have since allowed themselves to be elected to the American Institute of Arts and Letters. But not Mencken—and it is a piquant incident, which has come too late for Mr. Kemler's book, that the Institute should lately have announced that it was going to award a medal to the merciless mutineer who ridiculed his friend James Huneker, when the latter, in 1918, accepted his election to the Institute and made a habit of wearing its purple rosette. Mr. Kemler sees also that the whole perspective of literature in the United States was changed after Mencken had made himself heard. But his way of putting this is insidious. He seems to imply (a) that George Santayana and Van Wyck Brooks could have accomplished this feat more respectably if they had only been "more assertive" and (b) that Mencken did not "give them a chance." It is, of course, true that Brooks, in his early books, played a very important role in our reappraisal of our past, as Ezra Pound did in the improvement

of our poetic taste. But Mencken was not merely assertive—he was equipped by his special gifts for this day to
day combat work in a way that Santayana and Pound
were not. He was without question, since Poe, our
greatest practicing literary journalist.

Mr. Kemler makes a serious error when he declares
that William Dean Howells had "laid it down that such
realists [as Stephen Crane, Frank Norris and Mark
Twain] had no place in the American scheme of things."
On the contrary, the excellent Howells, who regarded
himself as a realist, did everything in his power to encourage these non-genteel writers. In his eloquent book
on Mark Twain he described him as "the Lincoln of our
literature," and he actually made the rounds of the bookstores with copies of Stephen Crane's *Maggie* in an effort
to induce them to stock it. But he was not able to do
enough—even for Mark Twain, who was not generally,
in Howells's time, taken as seriously as Howells took him.
The writers he admired, in many cases, Henry B. Fuller
and George Ade, for example, were the same that were to
interest Mencken. But most of Howells's literary journalism was strangely insipid and impotent. He was somehow
rendered inaudible by those femine magazines against
whose standards he sometimes protested but which he
edited and for which he wrote—those magazines whose
unexceptionable editors seem invariably to have worn like
white shirt fronts impressive-sounding triple names (with
a second family name in the middle) that were almost
guarantees of mediocrity. There were Richard Watson
Gilder and Robert Underwood Johnson—and there was
William Dean Howells. It took an ex-newspaperman, who
wrote his name with simple initials and did not shrink
from the inferior paper of a raffish magazine, to denounce
the false reputations that the public had been induced to
believe in during the nineties and the early nineteen-hun-

dreds—the Henry van Dykes, the James Lane Allens, the Thomas Nelson Pages and the F. Hopkinson Smiths (they mostly had these middle names, too, which had become almost as indispensable as Russian patronymics, and some of the women had four: there was a Mary Raymond Shipman Andrews)—and to bring forward the solid and serious work that was then being done in the United States.

It took, also, very special talent—an imaginative polemical style, to which Mr. Kemler does not do justice. In his rather inept foreword, he says that, "except for *The American Language,* the *Days* books, and a few selections" from his other books, Mencken "has produced no works likely to endure." If this were all, it would be a good deal, but the recent collection, in *A Mencken Chrestomathy,* of his miscellaneous writings showed that they, too, hold up well—not as doctrine (Mencken as a thinker is brash, inconsistent and crude) but for a personal rhythm and color that have their dignity as well as their humor. Mencken can be brutal, obtuse; he almost always oversimplifies; but these articles and essays and squibs are none the less literature.

One feels, in fact, in Mr. Kemler's handling of Mencken's whole career, a certain ungenerosity. It is interesting to know the lengths to which Mencken's pro-Germanism went before our entrances into the two World Wars—readers of the Baltimore *Sun,* in which he was expressing himself on the subject of our foreign policy, were much more aware of this than his admirers in other parts of the country. But why choose to end the book with an account of Mencken's visit to Ezra Pound in his Washington sanitarium and the remark that "but for the grace of God, he, too, might have ended in some such hideous predicament"? The biographer's horror, in all this connection, of his subject's unquestionable Prussianism has betrayed him into insufficient appreciation of the sound qualities of Mencken's German heritage and the value of what he owes to the German literary tradition. I do not see how our literary colonialism could possibly have been dynamited at that moment by a man of Anglo-Saxon stock. If the rivalry of Germany with England led Mencken to be unfair to Roosevelt and to show a certain tenderness for the Nazis, it also counted for something in the boldness with which he met head-on the self-conscious Anglophile culture represented by a Barrett Wendell.

Yet *The Irreverent Mr. Mencken* is, by reason of its subject, inspiriting. Since the story is conscientiously and clearly told, the personality of Mencken cannot but come through. It is a gauge of the rapid decline, during the last twenty years or so, of signed journalism in this country that it should already seem astonishing that one independent critic, writing mainly in newspapers and magazines, should have fought so many successful fights and grown to be so powerful a figure. It makes one rather ashamed—in this era of government propaganda, of religious and political pressure groups, and of anonymous processed reporting—to be reminded of all the things that Mencken, who had his own difficulties with timorous editors and owners, with the censors who interfered with the circulation of his magazine, the federal agents who trailed him around Baltimore, and the enraged Tennessee fundamentalists who threatened to run him out of town, had the courage and found the means to say.

May 6, 1950

THE LAST PHASE OF BERNARD SHAW

BERNARD SHAW, at the time of his death, left two books ready for the press. One of these—*Bernard Shaw's Rhyming Picture Guide to Ayot St. Lawrence*—is a thirty-one-page leaflet of photographs, taken by Shaw himself, of the village in Hertfordshire where he had his country place and where, for more than forty years, a good deal of his writing was done. The pictures are explained in a kind of verse which Shaw describes as Hudibrastic. This book, when it appeared last year, got a grim little review in the London *Times,* which treated it as a posthumous work that was hardly worth bringing out. It is obvious, however, that the pamphlet—which sells, in paper covers, for a shilling—was written in the expectation that Ayot St. Lawrence would become a shrine and that visitors would need a Baedeker. Shaw could not resist writing this himself, and he must have enjoyed the prospect of still haunting the town after death, taking the tourists around and explaining what everything was. The book will perfectly serve this purpose. Shaw was far from a master of verse, but the very badness of the rhyming and the raggedness of the meter make the whole thing rather touching and give it a certain charm. Of his garden, for example, he writes as follows:

Though of my floral treasures no great gem it is
Note how this tree stump clothes itself with clematis . . .

34

These cabbages for my devouring
Cannot prevent the trees from flowering.

This is my immemorial yew tree
(In sober fact it's quite a new tree) . . .

Like Shakespear I possess a mulberry
But find its fruit a somewhat dull berry.

Shaw's other new book is a volume of plays containing *Buoyant Billions*, *Farfetched Fables* and *Shakes Versus Shav*. The last of these little pieces is a blank-verse puppet play on the level of the *Rhyming Guide*. "This," the author says in introducing it, "in all actuarial probability is my last play and the climax of my eminence, such as it is." It is to be noted that this ten-minute dialogue allows Shakes to top Shav at the end, when, exclaiming, "Out, out, brief candle!," he blows out the "glimmering light" of Shav.

Buoyant Billions, a longer piece, shows this glimmering light at its dimmest. It has one or two amusing moments, but it is rather as if Shaw's ghost were speaking, and it is not perhaps mere coincidence that the author, in his preface, discusses the "communications" that come to mediums through ouija boards. *Farfetched Fables*, though written even later—a product, Shaw says, of "the queer second wind that follows second childhood"—does have a certain eerie interest. It makes almost no attempt at drama but presents, in half a dozen brief scenes, a sort of postscript to *Back to Methuselah*. In the second of these, Western civilization is destroyed, not by atom bombs, but by a new kind of lethal gas that has the advantage of not shattering cities and of lifting when it has done its work. Later successive glimpses into an even more remote future reveal an Anthropometric Laboratory, where people are examined and graded for various kinds of work; a period when diet experiments have led to the total rejection of both meat-eating and vegetarianism and the mastery of a technique by which it is possible for human beings to live solely on water and air; a phase in which procreation is effected by seminal fluids chemically prepared in a laboratory instead of by glandular secretions; and, finally, a period that seems to be placed beyond the furthest reach of *Back to Methuselah*. At the end of that earlier play, the Ancients, who have lived for centuries, announce that they want to shed their bodies in order to exist in a more intense way as vortices of pure thought. In this prophecy, a human race still embodied in flesh and blood is shown existing side by side with the "Disembodied Races" of these vortices, who communicate their wisdom to the earthlings and occasionally incarnate themselves.

There is a preface of some length, in which Shaw discusses, in his usual way, religion, politics and economics. Though he sustains his sharp phrasing, his vehement tone and his readiness with concrete examples, the whole effect is rather blurred. The overemphatic old talker sometimes loses his train of thought. And yet there is something impressive about this final volume of plays, turned out by Shaw in his nineties. It is interesting and satisfying to see evidence that so old a brain can go on thinking with animation almost to the last moments of consciousness. It lends a certain plausibility to Shaw's conception of the discarnate vortices; and it can almost make one believe that the intellect—this is a theme that runs through the whole volume—has, to some degree, mastered already the power of liberating itself from the flesh.

Bernard Shaw so succeeded in stage-managing almost everything that was published about him—revising biographies and memoirs and hypnotizing admiring writers when they came to him for information—that while he lived it was hardly possible to compose an objective account of his character and career. The studies and the scattered reminiscences that have been appearing since his death are already perceptibly different from any of the material that was printed before. Shaw's secretary, Miss Blanche Patch, has written a book about him—*Thirty Years with G.B.S.*—that makes a unique contribution to the subject. For Miss Patch, the daughter of a country rector, Bernard Shaw was not the brilliant public man who dazzled almost everyone else. "I can honestly say," she writes, "that when I started working for [him] I knew nothing of his writings, or of the literary and theater world in which he was such an outstanding figure." When friends who disapproved of his ideas reproached her for working for him, she would answer that she typed his writings and attended to his correspondence just as, in her earlier days as a pharmacist for country doctors, she had made up the prescriptions they sent her, "though I might at times think they were not treating their patients in what I thought the most suitable way." How far she is still from Shaw's world may be judged from her blank lack of interest in some caricatures by Max Beerbohm that Shaw left her. It appears from the caption she quotes that one of these was the drawing of H. G. Wells in the series called *The Old and the Young Self*. Not recognizing Wells, she mistakes it for a caricature of Beerbohm himself and comments coldly on the ineptitude of the caption.

That Miss Patch did, however, touch Shaw at one point is shown by her account of her early life. She was a practical independent woman, who had known and admired Mrs. Sidney Webb and had set out, at an early age, like a typical Bernard Shaw heroine, to earn her own living. It is obvious that she and Shaw respected and liked one another, but without any stimulating interaction. Her memoir of her distinguished employer is entirely prosaic and flat. It is not that she did not enjoy his plays or come to understand his ideas, but that they did not very much excite her. She points out the contradictions in his thinking of various periods in the same matter-of-fact way that she tells you he was color-blind and could not distinguish blue from green; that, for all his reliance on statistics, he often made mistakes in the calculations with which he tried to prove his arguments; or that, compelled to take liver extract during an illness of his later years and reproved by the vegetarians, he irascibly thumbed his nose at them, retorting that "it was not their business to bother about what he ate or what he did not eat."

Reading Miss Patch on Shaw's household habits is like meeting an actor off the stage with all his makeup removed. The great exhibitionist, she tells us, was "essentially a shy being who shrank from people." He was in private life not a talkative but in general a taciturn man, who ate with his wife in silence (though after dinner he played the piano and sang her Italian opera) and who insisted on turning on the radio whenever guests came to dinner, in order, Miss Patch believes, to prevent them from talking to him. He sometimes annoyed her by behaving as if she were not there, and on occasions when she had had the flu and returned to work after a week in bed would not ask her about her health or, apparently, notice that she had been away; yet, even in his extreme old age, he would always rise when she entered the room to offer her the better chair. He made very little contact, she says, with the people of Ayot St. Lawrence and hardly knew the names of his neighbors. He did not care much for children and did not know how to get on with them. Mrs. Shaw, who had refused to have any, once said to Miss Patch about babies, "Who could like them? Disgusting little things!" Though Shaw joined a wild-fowl protection society and regularly fed the birds, he never stayed to see them eat: "The cat might have got [them] for all he knew." Though opposed on principle to charities, he sometimes broke down in specific cases. He never observed anniversaries and worked on Sundays as on other days. He very rarely lost his temper and his profanity never went further than such phrases as "Damn his impertinence!" He easily got over illness by a capacity for total relaxation. "His scorn for money extended to the things which money buys: his indifference to material possessions was complete," yet he suffered in old age from a morbid fear—carried over, perhaps, from the poverty of his youth—that he was living beyond his means and that the capital levy would ruin him. He allowed himself the luxury, however, of having his socks specially made for the right and the left feet.

Shaw "looked upon the production of a play as a duel between actors and playwright," but was inexhaustibly tactful and patient, rehearsing "again and again." We know from other sources that he did not get along well with stars, who sometimes had their own ideas about what they wanted to do with his parts, and that he walked out, during the rehearsal of *Pygmalion,* on Beer-bohm Tree and Mrs. Patrick Campbell. Anyone who has seen the productions directed by Shaw himself will re-member how completely the actors were subordinated to the author. He did not think it important that the per-formers should understand the play, but acted out the characters himself and imposed his conceptions on them. One gets from Miss Patch's account the impression that, in Shaw's later years, when he had ceased to be active as a vestryman or as a member of the Fabian Society, this exercise of dominating actors represented, aside from his wife and the admirers who came to see him, his only direct relationship with other human beings.

Miss Patch supplies some curious details on the relations of Shaw and his wife with Einstein, Nehru, Sir Roger Casement and Lawrence of Arabia, and includes extensive quotations from unpublished letters and speeches. She has presented her testimony with sobriety, discretion and common sense, and produced a readable book that is also a useful document.

June 2, 1951

A MISCELLANY OF MAX BEERBOHM

ON THE AFTERNOONS of March 15 and 16, 1954, I was taken to call on Max Beerbohm by S. N. Behrman, the New York dramatist, who was then writing a book about him. Max was living in his villa at Rapallo, taken care of by Miss Elisabeth Jungmann, who for years had been the secretary of Gerhart Hauptmann. Miss Jungmann was intelligent and highly educated and, though German, she spoke and read English perfectly. She had specialized in men of genius and had been a godsend for Hauptmann and Max Beerbohm, who had known her when Hauptmann lived at Rapallo. I was told by Sam Behrman that Max had once said to her that if his wife should die, he did not know what would become of him. She had answered—Hauptmann died in 1946—that she would come to him wherever he was, and gave him an address that would reach her. He had put it in a book and forgotten about it and, after his wife's death, had not been able to find it; but she heard about him and immediately came to him. She was devoted to him and now took care of him, running the villa with one maid.

The Villino Chiaro was pleasant and simple. It hung high above the blue water and had a terrace from which one looked down on the sea and a tower room that Max used for a library and studio. We came in through a hall-way, on the wall of which one recognized the harlequin inn sign which is described in the *Words for Pictures* section of *Yet Again*. At the feet of the harlequin, who looked rather like Max, lay a mask on a tambourine, which so much resembled a bearded face that one took it at first for a decapitated head like that of John the Baptist in *Salomé*. (We were later shown a harlequin dressing-gown sewn together like a patchwork quilt from bits of material of different colors.) On the walls of a sort of anteroom hung a miniature of Max's father—who had been known, Sam Behrman told me, in his youth in Paris, on account of the magnificence of his style of living, as—a pun on his name—"*Superbe-homme.*" On the same wall as the miniature were portraits of Max's grandparents on the continental side—both with a half-smiling look, the grandmother "*l'oeil espiègle.*" They had a recognizable resemblance to Max, but seemed so much like the idealized characters of an eighteen-century opera that I almost suspected Max, with his inveterate love of hoaxes, of having invented these grandparents himself; but when I met him the moment after, I felt that he must indeed have behind him a tradition of wit and elegance.

He had just had an attack of flu and received us sitting in a chair in front of a little fire. He was eighty-two—it was two years before his death—and he was suffering from an inflammation which had encircled his round blue eyes with red rings. But his appearance surprised me by a kind of impressiveness which I had not expected to find. He always liked to represent himself in his caricatures with an almost cherubic head and a frail and wispy figure, the extremities also diminishing; but he was actually rather taller than he looks in these, and his head was larger and stronger than I had imagined even from his photographs. There was something rather Germanic about his nose and jaw and his blond mustache. He struck me as both very

Edwardian and as rather continental than English. He was a good deal more positive, also, than his writing would have led me to believe, even a little contentious—though it may be that I stimulated this tendency. His hands were quite astonishing—they seemed unlike any others I had ever seen. Instead of being slender with tapering fingers, the fingers were long and of uniform thickness, almost like the legs of a spider crab, and they were sharpened at the ends like pencils. It was as if they were very large engraver's tools, the instruments of a formidable craftsman. He wore one ring with a green scarab.

I talked about the book on him, very scholarly but rather boring, written in English by a Dutchman, J. G. Riewald, and he was polite about it but obviously not much excited. He had not read "the parts he remembered," but there were many things he found he had forgotten. I asked about certain points in his caricatures which I had never understood. His memory of his drawings was perfect, and he was able to answer at once, in a way that showed how very carefully every detail of these had been planned. Who were the people in the procession of hump-nosed monsters who appeared in his *Fifty Caricatures,* with the simple caption, "Are we as welcome as ever?" Those, he said, were "the friends of Edward VII," and he went on to explain rather slyly that the occasion for this caricature had been the accession of George V. The friends were Sir Ernest Cassel, two Rothschilds, Lord Burnham and Baron de Hirsch. He added, after a second, referring to the new king: "Didn't need to borrow money so often, don't you know?" He said nothing about these friends being Jewish. He was not, as has been sometimes said, Jewish himself, and I think that it was probably his delicacy which had restrained him from making the caption more explicit. He went on, as if

apologetically, to describe how, having started the picture, he had found that his hand went on drawing without his thinking about it—as if he wanted to represent
this caricature as having been executed involuntarily. I
asked him whether the Polish of the question that the
young Conrad puts to the old Conrad, in the series called
The Old and the Young Self, were not a language that
Max had invented. He said it was and repeated verbatim
this imaginary exclamation in Polish.

Why, I asked, weren't his drawings collected? Oh, he
answered, it would be impossible to dig them all up. He
had had periodical exhibitions, and the pictures had been
bought by Tom, Dick and Harry—he had been very glad
to sell them!—but Tom had given his away, and Dick
had left his somewhere, and Harry didn't know what had
become of his. I inquired about Walter Sickert, the only
one of Max's subjects who looks different in almost every
drawing—"He was Protean," Miss Jungmann put in—
and Max gave me an account of Sickert. At first, he had
been completely Whistlerian, his painting was all black
and blue; but he was always having new ideas and deliberately changing his manner, and he would also transform his appearance. At one point, he had his hair
cropped short; at another, he had had made for himself
an enormous top hat—"he must have found an ancient
block"—and wore trousers striped black and white in
some curious way. He was a great linguist, his French
was perfect, and he was able in a few weeks to pick up
the patois of Venice. It was only after the First World
War that his father became Danish, not German. I mentioned Max's drawing of Sickert "explaining away Piazza
San Marco." Why was he explaining it away? He was
always explaining, said Max. Sickert theorized too much;
he would perhaps have made a good critic. The painter
should be "an impassioned eye that sets down what he

sees, or thinks he sees." (But he later went on to complain about painters who set down things "as nobody would see them.") The idea that Walter Sickert was the best English painter of his time was, Max declared, perfectly ridiculous. A question from Behrman brought out that Max thought Wilson Steer was immensely superior.

I found that he much enjoyed having his own jokes fed back to him. When I told Sam Behrman in his presence about his drawings or *bon mots,* he would chuckle without self-deprecation. I spoke of the little hoaxes, intended to upset the scholarly, that he used to let drop in his dramatic articles. "What are you thinking of?" "Well, your statement that Lady Macbeth was originally played by Shakespeare himself." He had forgotten about this and laughed. I told the story I had heard from Isaiah Berlin of his meeting Max somewhere in London and hearing a young lady say that she had just seen Lady——. "How is she?" "Just the same as ever." "I'm very sorry to hear it." He smiled: "Oh, did I say that?" Lady——had a loud voice and came from Chicago, and had married a conventional Englishman, who loathed her, and this was always apparent at their parties. One was accustomed to the situation of the wife's not liking the husband, but the case was somehow different when the husband didn't like the wife.

I said something about his last album of caricatures: Noël Coward and the actors in *Bitter Sweet.* He explained that in this and a series that he had undertaken for the *Spectator,* he found that he was simply doing very careful likenesses that really expressed pity for their subjects—and then he had decided to stop. Pathos (pronounced with a short *a*) was no quality for a caricaturist. I could see that this had been true: the drawing of Noël Coward had brought out a certain weakness but had also made him appealing. He went on to say that something similar had happened in the case of Pellegrini ("Ape"): he had begun, after a certain age, making excellent likenesses which were no longer caricatures. So many of the drawings nowadays were ugly. (He meant artistically ugly. He had made clear in a foreword to a book by Ronald Searle that he regarded Searle's goblins and witches as distinguished exceptions to this.) Now, his own things—"though I am perhaps not the one to say it, and I had nearly left it unsaid"—were very pretty drawings. "I venture to say that even the Milner [which I had told him of having seen in the common room of one of the Oxford colleges] is not disagreeable to have around." At one point, he brought out and showed us a little pink-and-blue watercolor of Edward VII, which I believe he had recently done, and said something like, "Now, that's a pretty little drawing."

I asked about the additional passage for his parody of Henry James, *The Mote in the Middle Distance*, which he had sent to Edmund Gosse and which Gosse had written him of pasting in his copy of the *Christmas Garland*. That, he said, was a new and better ending that he had thought of after the book was published—a more emotional ending, like those of *The Golden Bowl* and *The Wings of the Dove*. He recited a part of the latter: "'Well she stretched out her wings, and it was to *that* they reached. They cover us.' . . . But she turned to the door, and her headshake was now the end. 'We shall never be again as we were!'" This had not impressed me much when I read it, but Max Beerbohm thought it beautiful, and he made it sound beautiful. I quoted the first line of the sextet of the very funny sonnet that he and Gosse, doing alternate lines, had written about Henry James: "How different from Sir Arthur Conan Doyle"— and he went on to recite the rest, making it, too, sound quite beautiful:

You stand marmoreal darling of the Few,
Lord of the troubled speech and single eye.

His sensitivity to language reminded me of the way my
old teacher, Alfred Rolfe, used to read, at school "morning exercises," his fastidiously chosen passages of prose or
verse. I reflected, in connection with this afterwards, that
that kind of fine appreciation of literature was something
that had largely disappeared. Such connoisseurs as Max
Beerbohm and Rolfe experienced the words in an intimate way and seemed to caress the cadences. Max made a
remark that puzzled me in connection with something I
had written about *The Wings of the Dove,* and I asked
him what he thought of the theory that the governess in
The Turn of the Screw was intended to be a neurotic
case, suffering from hallucinations. This aroused him: he
denounced this theory, starting out with a sentence which
began, "Some morbid pedant, prig and fool". . . I explained that this objectionable person was me, and we
argued about the subject a little. We argued, also, about
the new alphabet advocated by Bernard Shaw, which
Max thought was an absurd and outrageous idea. I
pointed out that the abolition of five of the characters of
the old Russian alphabet and certain other spelling reforms had encountered a similar opposition but had made
the language easier and clearer. "When England and
America are communized [he would have spelt it with
an s]," he answered, "they will doubtless have a phonetic
alphabet." He was under the erroneous impression that
Shaw had invented an alphabet and wanted it imposed
by law.

It was evident that he personally disliked Bernard Shaw,
as it was plain that he loved Henry James. He said that
Shaw had "queered his chances" of being buried in
Westminster Abbey by making some démarche to that

end. He had insisted on getting the Webbs buried there, which was entirely "inappropriate." Then in his will he had left instructions that his ashes should be sprinkled in his garden—"a dreadful idea, you know, with dogs and cats about!" I said that I did think it was rather absurd for Shaw to have left as a national shrine his apparently rather commonplace house; but I tried to soften the picture—Shaw has always been a hero of mine—by suggesting that egoism like Shaw's was a disability like any disability—which you had to carry with you all your life. When he was young, it had been amusing, he had carried it off with panache; but it had become disagreeable in his later years, and one saw then that it was compulsive, incurable.

Max described to us in great detail how Shaw had looked when he had first known him in London. He had had smallpox (I do not know whether this is true), which had left his complexion absolutely white, and he had whiskers so straggling that, as someone said, they looked like seaweed on a rock. His eyes were very pale, too pale. Later, his eyebrows grew shaggy and shaded them, which somewhat improved the impression. Shaw perhaps hadn't liked Max's caricatures, but for him any kind of attention paid him was better than none at all. I said that Max had brought out in his caricatures that Shaw had had well-shaped hands. "Yes: he had beautiful hands—the hands of a woman rather than a man." "He had an erect carriage," I said. "Yes, and he moved well. He made a good impression in this way—unless one saw him from the back: the back of his head came straight down and made a line with his neck. At first nights in his early days, he wasn't true to his principles: he wore evening clothes to the theater, but an old suit so shiny that, if you were behind him, you could see your face in it like a mirror. Later he became quite well-dressed. I was rather sorry. I

think people ought to dress according to their . . ." He
left it in the air. He had heard Shaw speak once at a
meeting, at which, after his speech, he had answered
questions and hecklers, with perfect readiness, without
notes. "In a way it was better than what he wrote, you
know. He was a wonderful debater—as [slyly] you see in
his plays."

Max's animus against Shaw appeared, further, in the
laborious pains he had taken to disfigure Archibald Henderson's biography. Miss Jungmann brought out this
volume—it had been given to William Archer, then returned after Archer's death—but I did not think it really
very funny, because it showed too much a jeering hatred
that Max usually kept in leash in his drawings. One felt
that it was not merely a question of kidding the awe-
stricken biographer, but that Max could not stand the
idea that Bernard Shaw had become a great man. He
himself had perhaps a little always felt on the margin of
things, and he was likely to betray irritation in dealing
with great men who took themselves seriously and become public institutions: see his attitude toward Goethe
in *Quia Imperfectum.* He had, in any case, by a cunning
use of ink, turned the photographs of such people as
William Morris and Granville Barker into horrible prog-
nathous gorillas. One felt that he really wanted to degrade Bernard Shaw and everyone connected with him.
The only thing I can remember in his published work
that at all approaches these monsters is his drawing of the
Warden of Merton in his earliest album of caricatures.
The bad little schoolboy in Max Beerbohm was also in
evidence in the doctored books which we were taken to
his study to see. Some of his "misleading title pages" are
reproduced in the Sotheby catalogue for the sale of his
papers and books: a picture of a seasick Victorian couple
in Belloc's *The Cruise of the Nona,* a grinning and

winking cockney in Meredith's *Essay on Comedy,* and villainous-looking Irishman with a gun in an early vc ume of Yeats's poems. There was also Housman's *La Poems,* with a drawing of the cast of a Wagner oper and the title page of a volume of Chesterton's essays w covered with an expanding caricature, in which Cheste ton displayed in his open mouth the printed words "th teenth edition." I found these a little shocking, and whe I came down, I told Max that my nerves had been shake by them. He had operated on such an extensive scale desecrating the books of his friends that it was as if he d not want them approached without their first having bee put in a comic light. Going back to his work after visiti him, I came to recognize that the feelings behind it we somewhat harsher than I had suspected. Henry Jame had been treated with relative tenderness. On the tit page of one of his books, Max had done a little drawir of him, leaning forward and gesturing with his hands, a paroxysm of "getting wound up," as Sam Behrman sai to express some complex impression. I have heard that I was in the habit of pasting unexpected and scandalo words into the volumes of such Georgian poets as Joh Drinkwater, breaking the books at those places and lea ing them for his guests on the bedside table, and I w sorry to hear that none of these turned up for th Sotheby sale.

I was surprised to discover that Max did not care f Virginia Woolf's novels. He had a good word only for h criticism, and he did not seem enthusiastic about that

---

* Since this memoir was published in *Encounter,* Mr. Leon: Woolf has written to the editors to put on record a letter fr Max to Virginia Woolf:

"Dear Virginia Woolf—I can't help this familiarity: I se to know you so well, from *The Common Reader,* a book whi I have read twice, and have often dipped into since, and r

He had just been reading her diary, which he said showed low vitality and was "pettifogging," overanxious about things that concerned herself and not considerate about anyone else. I had somewhat shared this last impression. Leonard Woolf, he said, must have taken very good care of her, and I said that he must have needed patience to talk her over her reviews. "Poor soul!" he added. I said that she had evidently been a peculiar kind of snob—a snob without really belonging to a social group with whom to be snobbish. She had been so extraordinary about Thomas Hardy. It is plain that when she went to see him, she expected to find something like the old gaffers in his novels, and she expressed surprise at his *savoir faire* in offering her husband a whisky and soda. Apropos of Mrs. Woolf's novels, he spoke contemptuously and pettishly about the "stream of consciousness" in general. Everybody had thoughts that went through his head, but it was absurd to try to make a novel of them. He liked to read a *story,* to have characters and see what they did. I stood up for *Between the Acts,* which he had not read, but I did not attempt to argue with him about the stream of consciousness. I was rather dismayed to discover that by the time Virginia Woolf had appeared, Max Beerbohm had got to a point where he was unable to appreciate new excellence in an art he had practiced and loved. I should have thought that for the author of the *Christmas Garland,* with his exquisite sense of style, Mrs. Woolf would have been the writer of the Bloomsbury set in whom he would have felt most interest. But

above any modern book of criticism (rating it thus quite soberly, all unconfused by your habit of going out of your way to be nice about my essays!). . . ."

Any report of a conversation is likely to be somewhat unreliable, since the reported may give way to a mood and the reporter may misinterpret.

he never seemed to have got beyond Lytton Strachey. He had lost the pleasant world of his youth, the world to which he had belonged. The cities were no longer attractive. People in London, he said, were always in a crisis about something—about going somewhere or catching a bus. The old leisurely days were gone. Lytton Strachey had still lived in this world; Virginia Woolf somehow not.

They invited us to tea the next day, and we came at 4:30 instead of 3:30 and did not stay so long. Today he sat up at the table and presided over the tea. His head was sunk between his shoulders, and the hair at the back of his bald domed head was uncut and hung over his collar. He would look up at us as he chuckled in a way that seemed a little deprecatory. We had tea and sherry and an apéritif, with cakes and hors d'œuvres. Max drank a single glass of something from a bottle without a label. While Miss Jungmann was out of the room, he sneaked an extra cigarette, and when she came back and saw it, she commented, "When the Devil . . . !"

He said that he had never been able to caricature Somerset Maugham, had tried it several times, then given it up; but he implied that Sutherland, in his portrait of Maugham, had made up for Max's failure—he had, he said, "carried caricature as far as it would go." After painting Somerset Maugham, Sutherland had written to Max asking him to sit for his portrait, and Max had replied that though he had in his time "made monsters of people" himself, "the bully was always a coward," and that, knowing the portrait of Maugham, he had decided to decline this offer. "Now that I'm old and afflicted-looking, I shouldn't want to be painted anyway, but even in my prime, I don't think I should have wanted to be painted by Sutherland."

I asked him about Sem, the French caricaturist, whose work I greatly admired. Max had caricatured Sem and had known him. He said that Sem had been able to do things that he couldn't do. He was able to make sketches on the spot, which Max never did—sometimes just drawing parts of people: an ear and an arm, etc.—and then would put them together, and there would be a perfect likeness. Sem was extremely good at doing the types at the races and Monte Carlo: *"Tout Paris."* He came to England and drew people at Ascot, and then would ask who they were, and one could always tell him because the likenesses were unmistakable. Max himself could not caricature people unless he had seen quite a lot of them— had heard their voices, caught the tone of their minds. I spoke of the animated album, in which Sem has *Tout Paris* doing the Charleston and the Black Bottom—so wonderful in its imagining of the movements of different bodies and different personalities. Sem's people were always in movement. The loyal Miss Jungmann, at this, produced the recently published volume of R. C. Trevelyan's *Selected Poems*, with its frontispiece by Max of Trevelyan slogging along with a knapsack on one of his long walks. Max had lunched once with Sem at Dieppe, and they had known that people were thinking, "Two caricaturists lunching together: they must be up to something!" Sem was a good mimic, and he had imitated Coquelin, who was also there: *"Je ne parle jamais de moi. Pourquoi? Par-ce-que . . ."* and there would follow a long explanation of why it was characteristic that he should never speak of himself. They decided to send Coquelin a note, saying that they had arranged for a window from which to watch the fireworks that night and inviting him to share it with them. He had not answered. "I think he must have been insulted," Max added with a certain complacency. Sem could caricature women, which Max had never been able to do. I said that he had done well with Zuleika Dobson in his frontispiece to the new edition of the novel. "Oh, that was just a caricature of a pretty girl." I thought the point was—since he had caricatured the women of the Rossetti circle and occasionally imaginary women—that he was too much of an old-fashioned gentleman to be willing to make real living ones ridiculous.

I had said to Sam Behrman that I thought Max's head rather resembled Bismarck's, and Sam now repeated this to him. It was not, it turned out, the first time that this comparison had been made, and he got out a little drawing that he had done of himself as Bismarck—wearing an iron cross which contrasted with his mild dreamy gaze. Bismarck had had, he said, an astonishingly high voice, like a woman's. Hilaire Belloc, also, with his square jaw, his thickset figure and his head set down between his shoulders, surprised one by his high voice. He used to sing French hunting songs in a sweet and exquisite way—"It was rather like a very large nightingale."

I asked him what he thought of P. G. Wodehouse—the enthusiasm for whom of some people I have never been able to understand—and he replied that he could never read more than fifty pages of any of Wodehouse's books. At first he would be entertained by Wodehouse's handling of language—"almost like Cinquevalli" (the great juggler of the last century, of whom Max had once written), but he lost interest after that. It was difficult for him now to read novels: he couldn't believe any longer in the things that were supposed to happen in them. Apropos of George Moore, he said that Dr. Johnson had declared that there were two kinds of talkers: those who talked from a stream, of whom Burke was the example, and those who talked from a tank. Moore talked from a stream, like so many Irishmen. When I mentioned

Compton Mackenzie, he said, "Ah, there's a man who writes from a stream!" *Sinister Street,* he thought, would last. It was wonderful how Mackenzie, in writing of Oxford, had caught with such delicate precision the nuances of the seasons and their moods: Eights Week, St. Mark's Eve, Lent term, Easter holidays, etc. I said that I had just been in Oxford and told him that the traffic there now, on account of the Nuffield works, was as bad as in any big city. Yes, he said, and they could perfectly well have prevented it. Nuffield had kept a bicycle shop when Max had been an undergraduate. Almost nobody rode a bicycle then: it was "the earmark of vulgarity."

I tried to draw him out about the suicides of the nineties and the early years of the present century: Hubert Crackanthorpe, St. John Hankin, John Davidson. I had always wondered about them. Did they lack conviction of their talent? Or did they and the other writers and artists who died relatively young at that time really feel that the *fin de siècle* implied that their world must come to an end? Max did not throw much light on this—whether from discretion in discussing the private lives of men he had known or from a distaste for dwelling on tragedy or from a simple lack of interest, I could not tell. Hubert Crackanthorpe he had known a little. His father had been a successful barrister, and Max had sometimes gone to his parents' house. He had "thrown himself into the Seine and couldn't swim—some sudden fit of insanity, I suppose." His short stories had shown talent, but *"le mot juste* had a way of coming between the lady and gentleman that the story was about." Hankin he had known quite well. He had not been surprised when *he* committed suicide—he was rather a sad man. He was supposed to be unhappily married. Of John Davidson, he said, too, strangely, that he had "thrown himself into the water and couldn't swim." I said something favorable about Davidson's poetry, and Max responded warmly that he was the best English poet of that period. Davidson had been a dominie in Scotland, and had thrown it up and come to London. Once, in the Café Royal, he had set out to sing to Max a translation of the Psalms into Scots and had been told by the headwaiter that he was annoying the other guests. I tried to probe further by asking whether Davidson had been poor and desperate. "Yes," he replied rather vaguely, "but he had enough for himself and his family to live on."

He talked always with natural style—quietly and unemphatically, the words well and easily chosen, always trying to express what he thought, and except for an occasional quaint phrase, with no effort to talk for effect. There is, fortunately, a recording made by Angel of his reading of two of his essays—*The Crime* and *London Revisited*—which preserves the sound of his voice, so casual and conversational even in rendering these carefully-written pieces.

When we left, I told Max that I was going to send him Angus Wilson's *For Whom the Cloche Tolls* and my essay on *The Turn of the Screw*, in a simplified phonetic alphabet, but provided with a key.

In the entrance hall and in one of the rooms, he had painted some murals of his favorite subjects: Chamberlain and Churchill and Balfour, Chesterton and George Moore and Henry James, old friends like Will Rothenstein and Reginald Turner, who had now become rather obscure. He had taken his creations with him, his whole vision of the London world, into the long retirement of his exile. To his villa on the Gulf of Genoa, they still flocked to keep him company. I have spoken of his new watercolor of Edward VII, and I learn that the last carica- ture he drew was still another of George Moore. And seeing them there made me recognize as I had not quite done before the excitement and variety of this vision. Has there ever been anything like it in the realm of caricature? Gillray has his recurrent characters and a grotesque world in which they move, but he is brutal and crude beside Beerbohm. Sem is perhaps the nearest thing; but he does not have Max's historical sense or his intellec- tual insight. Though Max makes all his subjects absurd, though no one is ever idealized except in a comic way, there is a hierarchy of values here: men he despises and men he admires, men that he rejoices in and men that he likes to make ugly. His work as a caricaturist is in general on a higher imaginative level than his stories, his essays and his parodies. Virginia Woolf in her *Diary* quotes him as saying to her: "About his own writing, dear Lytton Strachey said to me: 'First I write one sentence; then I write another.' That's how I write. And so I go on. But I have a feeling writing ought to be like running through a field. That's your way. Now, how do you go down to your room after breakfast—what do you feel? I used to look at the clock and say, 'Oh, dear me, it's time I began my article. . . . No, I'll read the paper first.' I never wanted to write. But I used to come home from a dinner party and take my brush and draw caricature after caricature. They seemed to bubble up from here . . . [he pressed his stomach]. That was a kind of inspiration, I suppose. What you said in your beautiful essay about me and Charles Lamb was quite true. He was crazy; he had the gift: genius. I'm too like Jack Horner. I pull out my thumb. It's too rounded, too perfect."

Yet I read and reread Max Beerbohm as I do not do

any other British prose writer of the period in which I grew up, with the exception of Bernard Shaw. It seems to me queer when I find Max Beerbohm speaking, as he does in some essay, of G. K. Chesterton as "a genius" whose brilliance quite put Max in the shade. The paradoxical epigrams of Chesterton, which became so mechanical and monotonous, are mostly unreadable today. But Max Beerbohm's prose has endured. Since it never asserts itself—except in the comic exuberance of his *Yellow Book* preciosity—one can always forget it and find it fresh.

December, 1963

I went later to the Ashmolean Museum in Oxford to see the Guedalla collection of sixty of Max Beerbohm's drawings. I had seen only a few originals, and I was even more impressed by these than by the imperfect reproductions in the albums. One feels, when one has seen them as he made them, larger in scale and stronger in color, a quite formidable vitality and power. They have the Bloomsbury "significant form" as well as something like creative passion in their rendering of personalities. He has sometimes been carried away by the form-producing imagination as he never is in his prose. The figures, in being distorted, become, not grotesque monsters, but wonderful inspired shapes.

After the papers and books of Beerbohm had been sold at Sotheby's, I bought the manuscript of a set of notes that he had made for an essay on men's clothes. I think it worth preserving, and with the permission of his executor, Mrs. Eva Reichmann, I am reproducing it here.

Men's Clothes
NEAT LOUNGE SUIT

$\left.\begin{array}{l}\text{Rational}\\\\\text{Cheap}\end{array}\right\}$ tailoring — good cut —

Hundreds of thousands of respectably dressed men. Thousands of badly dressed men. A few well-dressed ones.

'Arry and Arriet
loud checks — scarlet
tie — brass horseshoe —
blue and white striped
collar

Boni: "Une sortie de Metro."
Sem: "None one to draw."

No hats,
No gloves,
No sticks,
No overcoats,
No button-holes,
No jewels.
Socks and boots.

No white linen —
No cuffs.
Young Guardsman.
Purple, green, etc.
Laundresses
— grey — torn — lost

---

§ Chorus of Floradora.   Drawing of Christie's Sale.
Top hat sensitive, individual.
Crossing-sweepers.

[scratched out in pencil] One put on top-hat to come up from country —
In August bowler or straw hat.

[Page 2]

Brabazon
Bobbie Spencer
[added in pencil] Sir Edward Sassoon
Ribblesdale — Chaplin.
Clanricarde — Lord Suffield — Lord Cravon.
King Edward — George
Whistler — Oscar —

Liberal M.P.: "More interesting" —
Usually well-mannered. Laughed outright.

Old men used to dress in fashion of their youth.
Stocks.

[struck out
in pencil] Bloomsbury — dismal — unimaginative —

Ruskin on colour. Welcome it.

Frock-coat — fancy-dress.
[struck out
in pencil] Ascot, weddings,
Eton and Harrow

Like golf caddies.

Spiritual tonic of new suit. Dressing for
dinner.

Dinner jacket — Mr. Du Burgh.
I now share his view.
White ensemble.
"Black Tie" — "bare back."

[Page 3]
[struck out   I wish you to visualize me
in pencil]   in evening dress — gardenia.

Conclude: I am wearing neat lounge suit.

Women's clothes better than ever.

Individuality — did not all
follow fashion.   *see* "Old men."
'60's and 70's.
Octavius Hill.

Bad tailoring in '60's.
Lost art. rediscovered in
middle '70's.

D'Orsay.
Mrs. Carlisle. [added in pencil] Lady Ritchie.

[added in
pencil]

Even before The War (unberufen).
    Mechanisation. Pace of life —
    Democracy.

[Page 4]

Immaculate.
Faultless.

[added in   Admiral's
pencil]   Costume

⎰ "Old School Tie"
⎱ Billy Rothenstein

⎰ Man with glasses on brow
⎱ Smoked glasses

Regie's tale: red socks suspenders

⎧ Young men mostly dress badly. wild, seething period.
⎪   Myself — green waistcoat — mother-o'-pearl buttons —
⎪   brown boots
⎨   scarlet tie
⎪ Only later they learn restraint, and what
⎪ suits them.
⎪
⎪
⎪   Birds and other creatures —   [added in
⎩   to attract the female —   pencil]

[Page 5]

⎰ Things which I believe are called
⎱ Plus-Fours
    Trousers — bad — statues —
    But becoming to women —
    Knee breeches —
    Calves required —
    Highland costume —

Grace — incompatible with strength.
Athletes — Sandow — *6

---

§ Top hats —
  Men terrified if taken away —
  In & Out Club —
Evening Parties in 1840's. Callers in '80s —
  Foyers of theatres —
  Houses of Commons & Lords —

Dandies of my day.

[Page 6]
Vice-Chancellor in
flannel trousers.

Shirts all one —
"Faux col" —
Would as soon have worn
  detachable cuffs.
Fell away from grace —
Some men wore ready-made shirts —
Ceased to have boots made for me.

Good figure — *5
Plenty of money.
Taste.

Lady novelist: "Did not go to a
  particularly good tailor, and his
  clothes were often shabby. But
  he had a way of *putting them on,*
  and he always looked very
  distinguished.

Sickert
Pryde
Nicholson
[above
added in
pencil]

Bad dressing throve.
though Cecil, Bernard Shaw,
Orpen, Balfour's hat,
Salisbury's, Lord Cecil,
Augustus John.

"brown paper
parcel" —
(evangelical
waiter),
Cf. Lord
Londonderry.

Evening clothes — upper class —
quite *new.*   Middle class — camphor, etc.

THE PRE-PRESIDENTIAL T. R.

THE FIRST INSTALMENT OF *The Letters of Theodore Roosevelt,* published by the Harvard University Press, is an event of considerable interest, which may do something to restore the prestige of a somewhat staled reputation. The first two volumes of a series that is eventually to run to eight have as subtitle *The Years of Preparation* and cover the period from 1868, when Roosevelt was ten years old, through the Presidential campaign of 1900, when he was elected to the Vice-Presidency on the ticket with William McKinley. T. R. was a prodigious correspondent, and the letters in the whole series will represent a selection of "only about ten thousand" from an "estimated hundred thousand that are available." It has been complained by one reviewer that even this tithe is too many, but it is probably appropriate and inevitable that Roosevelt should be taken in a bulk that corresponds with his enormous energy and the crowding day-by-day business, both personal and official, that he so much enjoyed transacting. The result is, in any case, for one who looks back on the later Roosevelt of 1909-19—unwillingly retired from politics, dissatisfied, blaring and boring—to revive one's respect for the early T. R. and make one feel that, in our recent perspective, he has been rather unfairly eclipsed by Wilson and Franklin D.

Before going on to this subject, however, a word or two ought to be said about the edition itself. It is one of those modern jobs that are the products of collaboration. The title page announces that the letters have been "selected and edited by Elting E. Morison," with John M. Blum as "associate editor" and John J. Buckley as "copy editor," but Mr. Morison's introduction makes it plain that a number of other persons have also made contributions, and the impression is that nobody has adequately coördinated or checked on the work of the various editors. The touch of misplaced coyness in Mr. Morison's introduction suggests an uneasy awareness of this.

The worst feature, perhaps, is the index. Any incomplete index is a nuisance, and this is one of the most incomplete that the reviewer has ever encountered. If you should look up Henry James in this listing, you would not find any reference to a letter of the early eighties in which Roosevelt mentions his first meeting with him at the St. Botolph's Club in Boston; and if you should look up Frank H. Cushing, the anthropologist, a very important man in his field, you would find no reference at all, though Roosevelt twice mentions meeting him. The family of Eleanor Roosevelt come off particularly badly both in the index and in a large chart that undertakes to show the family relationships. There is no mention in either of these of Mrs. Franklin D. Roosevelt's two brothers (she appears in the chart as an only child), though they are mentioned more than once in the text, and the second reference to her in the index is listed by the number of the letter in the series instead of, according to the system adopted, by the number of the page on which it occurs. The circumstances as well as the date of the death of Mrs. Roosevelt's father, Theodore's brother Elliott, though there are several letters about it, are left unexplained in the notes.

These notes are characterized, in general, by a similar incompleteness, combined with an irritating garrulity.

Mr. Morison disclaims any effort to elucidate such well-known names as Mark Twain or Grover Cleveland (though it might have been a good idea to have the latter's terms of office indicated). He says that it is more to the point to throw light on such forgotten topics as Little Egypt and Cahenslyism, but, though he includes a brief mention of this latter subject in a note on Cardinal Gibbons, he does not tell us who Cahensly was or how the movement originated. The notes on literary subjects are full of irrelevant information and gratuitous criticism that is often rather badly expressed. We are told, for example, that Charles A. Dana was an editor of "perverse independence," that Agnes Repplier was "a familiar essayist of rare charm and insight," that John Fox, Jr., married Fritzi Scheff, that the novels of Marion Crawford were distinguished by "a high romance and a kind of baroque glitter," and that the literary activities of Arlo Bates were "all in the genteel and benign tradition." Along with these ineptitudes and this waste of space, one finds a neglect of allusions that really need to be explained. What, for example, is the article by Roosevelt mentioned on page 572? What is the article by Adams (and which Adams?) mentioned on 289? What is the poem of Kipling's on which Roosevelt comments on 909? Nobody's dates are listed, so it is never possible to tell how old anybody is. The chronology of the "principal events" in Roosevelt's life, which does not include his trips to Europe, his early schooling or the birth of his children is, up to his governorship, of an inadequacy that is hardly believable.

Theodore Roosevelt, as these letters show, was fortunate in his early surroundings and the situation to which he was born. The first sections of the correspondence take us into a well-to-do family of the New York of the seventies and eighties, where the adored mother and father and sisters and brother, sheltered by the cozy shrubbery of a house at Sagamore Hill, embraced by its ample piazza, seem multiplied ad infinitum in the world beyond Oyster Bay by innumerable cousins and uncles and aunts. The children are taken abroad, climb Vesuvius and see Karnak in their teens, and at home they learn to ride their ponies, collect ornithological specimens and celebrate the Fourth of July with much popping of firecrackers. "I do not think there is a fellow in College," Theodore writes to his father from Harvard at the age of eighteen, "who has a family that love him as much as you all do me, and I am *sure* that there is no one who has a Father who is also his best and most intimate friend, as you are mine." "It seems perfectly wonderful," he writes at the same time to his mother, "in looking back over my eighteen years of existence, to see how I have literally never spent an unhappy day, unless by my own fault!" And a year and a half later, at the time of his father's death, he addresses his sister Corinne: "My own, darling, sweet, little treasure of a Pussie . . . I do hope you and Muffie are enjoying yourselves. Dear little one, you can hardly know what an inestimable blessing to a fellow it is to have such a home as I have. Even now that our dear father has been taken away, it is such great and unmixed pleasure to look forward to a visit home." To his mother: "I have just been looking over a letter of my dear Father's in which he wrote me 'Take care of your morals first, your health next, and finally your studies.' I do not think I ever *could* do anything wrong while I have his letters." And this early picture seems to merge into that of the son's own household, still at Sagamore Hill, but populated with six children instead of four, where he loves to play bear with them when they are little and read them *Hereward the Wake* when they are older, where he takes them for sails on the Sound, encourages them to camp out at night and is delighted when they name their pets after distinguished Roosevelt ancestors and heroes of the Spanish-American War.

In this matrix, an ideal is conceived of the role of the United States in the world at the end of the nineteenth century and of the role of Theodore Roosevelt as a citizen of the United States. It is the definition of this ideal in relation to pressures and events that makes this first instalment of letters interesting. The slogans of the later Roosevelt—the big stick and the strenuous life, malefactors of great wealth, race suicide and all the rest of it— were to become such journalistic clichés, as the caricaturists' teeth and glasses were to make a cliché of T. R. himself, that it may come as a surprise to find that Roosevelt first met his age as a serious and thoughtful young man who formulated and was ready to fight for a personal philosophy of life. How this age presented itself to him, what he had to contend against, he has stated in his *Autobiography*: "In the reaction after the colossal struggle of the Civil War our strongest and most capable men had thrown their whole energy into business, into money-making, into the development, and above all the exploitation and exhaustion at the most rapid rate possible, of our natural resources—mines, forests, soil, and rivers. These men were not weak men, but they permitted themselves to grow shortsighted and selfish; and while many of them down at the bottom possessed the fundamental virtues, including the fighting virtues, others were purely of the glorified huckster or glorified pawnbroker type—which when developed to the exclusion of everything else makes about as poor a national type as the world has seen. This unadulterated huckster or pawnbroker type is rarely keenly sympathetic in matters of social and industrial justice, and is usually physically timid and likes to cover an unworthy fear of the most just war under high-sounding names."

The elder Theodore Roosevelt, whom the son so much admired, had himself been a businessman, a banker and a glass importer, but, product of a Dutch burgher family long resident in New York, he had interested himself in civic causes and been among the founders of the Metropolitan Museum and the Natural History Museum. In the son, a high sense of noblesse oblige was obviously developed early. At Harvard, he shows a sharp class-consciousness that would hardly at the present time be stated in so bald a way: when writing to his sister that he ranks nineteenth in a class of two hundred and thirty, he says, "Only one gentleman stands ahead of me." He made a point of teaching Sunday school at college—which he found uncongenial work—and he was already studying natural history with something of scientific method. He corrected his physical frailty by resolutely, at the cost of some battering, taking lessons in boxing and wrestling. In a letter to E. S. Martin, the editor of *Life,* written in 1900, he was to explain, in connection with this training, that "In most countries the 'Bourgeoisie'—the moral, respectable, commercial, middle class—is looked upon with a certain contempt which is justified by their timidity and unwarlikeness. But the minute a middle class produces men like Hawkins and Frobisher on the seas, or men such as the average Union soldier in the civil war, it acquires the hearty respect of others, which it merits." In the meantime, he had written to his sister and her husband in 1889, at the time when he was Civil Service Commissioner: "I feel it incumbent on me to try to amount to something, either in politics or literature, because I have deliberately given up the hope of going into a money-making business."

He had further corrected the Manhattan burgher by a dose of the hard-living West. "You would be amused to see me," he writes Henry Cabot Lodge in the summer of 1884, when starting out for the Big Horn Mountains, "in my broad sombrero hat, fringed and beaded buckskin shirt, horsehide chaparajos or riding trousers, and cowhide boots, with braided bridle and silver spurs. I have always liked 'horse and rifle,' and being, like yourself, 'ein echter Amerikaner,' prefer that description of sport which needs a buckskin shirt to that whose votaries adopt the red coat. A buffalo is nobler game than an anise-seed bag, the Anglomaniacs to the contrary notwithstanding." He went to live, after his first wife's death, when he was still in his middle twenties, on a ranch he had bought in Dakota, and tried his nerve against cougars and grizzlies, grappled resolutely with roundups and forest fires, walked up squarely to the insults and ridicule of homicidal saloons and retaliated for the inroads of horse thieves. The opposite of a "gentleman" in New York or Boston was a "mucker" or a "mick." A cowpuncher was something quite different, a free man whom a gentleman Easterner could hardly even call an equal because one had to prove one's equality to *him*. This experience was extremely important to Roosevelt's whole career. It was one of the influences that went to determine his democratic conception of what it meant to be an American, and it enabled him to bring to the Presidency a firsthand sense of the West that no President had had before him.

Toward the new crop of millionaires that had come crowding in since the Civil War and the ostentatious spending they encouraged, the young Roosevelt was patronizing or contemptuous. "The Leiter wedding," he writes, "went off in fine style, and really in very good taste." The Roosevelts had "never liked" the Bradley Martins and declined an invitiation to their pretentious ball of 1897. "We were immensely amused," he later notes when he and his wife meet the Martins somewhere, "by the intense seriousness with which they regard themselves and their ball." But he announces that, as Police Commissioner, he will "have to protect it by as many police as if it were a strike," and declares that the outcry against it has almost made him "retract" his refusal to go. "Do you see," he writes Lodge in 1887, "how the Newport cads have taken up the Duke of Marlborough?" Later, in 1895, when a marriage has been arranged between the Duke and Consuelo Vanderbilt, he exclaims to the same correspondent that "The exhibition of snobbery in regard to the Duke of Marlborough this fall has been loathsome." (None of the names in the above quotations is to be found in the defective index, and a footnote explains erroneously, in connection with the first Marlborough reference in a letter of 1887, that the Duke was then "about to marry Consuelo Vanderbilt"—at a time when she was ten years old!) On Americans such as Henry James and William Waldorf Astor, who went to live permanently in England, he imposed a kind of excommunication, denouncing the novels of the former and declining to meet the latter on the occasion of his return to the States. "I hope you will be presented at court," he writes to his sister Anna. "In your position you ought to be"; but adds immediately, "What snobs the Hays are! They have no business to bring out their daughter abroad. If you see Gussie Jay give him a hint that if he educates his children abroad he will lose all chance of being returned to our diplomatic service, and ought to lose it." On the subject of a correspondent to the London *Times,* he expresses himself with something like fury: "He is more British than the British. He is the kind of man who makes me a ferocious jingo." In the next letter—to Henry Cabot Lodge, on March 13, 1896—the word "Americanism" first occurs.

What did Roosevelt mean by this term? By the end of the First World War, it had become a mere cant word of politicians, brandished vaguely to create the impression that one's opponent was an undesirable foreigner or corrupted by foreign ideas. But Roosevelt had given it a meaning; it was a concept he had had to invent as an antidote to those tendencies in the national life that he found himself sworn to resist.

Americanism implied an ideal of disinterested public service for the benefit of the American community, and an approach to this community that differed from the "alien"-baiting tactics of the later exploiters of the term in insisting on a complete impartiality, a rigorous abstention from prejudice, in dealing with race, color, nationality, religion or social status. These letters are full of expressions that complement the passages quoted above. "There is really a touch of comedy," he writes to Carl Schurz in 1895, when he is Police Commissioner of New York, "about attacking me as an 'illiberal,' 'nativist' and 'know nothing'; I have not got a drop of that kind of blood in me; it is alien to my whole nature. I do not care a rap. Taking the matter of promotions and reductions inside this force, the two last reductions I made were of native Americans who were Republicans, as the local politicians took care to inform me; and to fill their places, and to fill three other vacancies, I promoted five men, all of them, I believe, born in this country, but four of them of Irish and one of German parentage. The four Irish I believe were Catholics. My own only two personal appointments, my secretary and messenger, are both Catholics of Irish parentage." "As you know," he wrote Maria Longworth Storer, "I always treat Catholics and Protestants exactly

alike, as I do Jew or Gentile, as I do the man of native
American, German, Irish or any other kind of parentage.
Any discrimination for or against a man because of his
creed or nativity strikes me as infamy." It is impossible to
go through this correspondence of Roosevelt's early official
life without becoming convinced that he pretty consistently lived up to this principle—though one notes that,
in 1899, when Carl Schurz happens to differ from him
politically, he refers to him invidiously as "that prattling
foreigner."

We see him, also, as Civil Service Commissioner and
as Police Commissioner of New York, doing his best, at
the cost of much obstinate resistance to private pressure
and public abuse, to remove civil service from politics.
His conception of himself was that of a benevolent dis-
penser of justice who rewarded merit and punished
wrongdoing. His insistence on human worth and his
method of dealing man to man were quite natural to him
and not a pose, because handling people of different
kinds—whipping them in a fight, making them like him,
making them do what he wanted—was a sport that he
enjoyed like big-game hunting. The record of his adventures in the state legislature—getting the hang of the
Irish politicians, honest and dishonest; acquiring as his
closest ally a storekeeper from an Adirondacks crossroads;
and in one case defending a bill against "one or two
members of the committee who were pretty rough characters" by flourishing the leg of a broken chair—makes
quite exhilarating reading.

The vicissitudes of Roosevelt's relations with Tom
Platt, the Republican boss of New York, come out in
these letters in a striking way. "Platt's influence is simply
poisonous," he writes in September, 1895, at the time he
is Police Commissioner. "I cannot go in with him; no
honest man of sincerity can." The next March he has

been obliged, in order to attain a certain objective, "to go in with the Platt men. . . . It was of course the only thing to do; but it was very disagreeable having to do it." Yet, in the days of his governorship, he did his best to get along with Platt and to minimize the shock of those policies of which he knew Platt would disapprove by regularly writing or seeing him—he even comes to close his letters with "warm regards to Mrs. Platt." But this formally friendly tone blows up in 1900 with a memorable declaration of independence: "You say that we must nominate some Republican who 'will carry out the wishes of the organization,' and add that 'I have not yet made up my mind who that man is.' Of one thing I am certain: that, to have it publicly known that the candidate, whoever he may be, 'will carry out the wishes of the organization' would insure his defeat. . . . It is not the business of a governor to 'carry out the wishes of the organization' unless these wishes coincide with the good of the party and of the state."

Roosevelt's breakfasts with Platt, which took place quite openly at the latter's hotel and got to be a kind of institution, were reprobated by those whom Roosevelt, writing in his *Autobiography,* characterized as "solemn reformers of the tom-fool variety." One finds in these letters, also, a whole series of retaliatory blasts against editors like Godkin and Villard, who were intransigent in their war against bossism, and Republicans like Carl Schurz and John Jay Chapman, who, disgusted with Republican corruption, ran an independent Good Government ticket. Such attacks are all too often devoid alike of taste and of justice, yet it is impossible, reading these letters, not to sympathize to some extent with Roosevelt in his doctrine of "practical politics," his insistence that the uncompromising kind of reformer, who refuses to yield anything to expediency, can never put through his reforms; that politics is a matter of adapting oneself to all sorts of people and situations, a game in which one may score but only by accepting the rules and recognizing one's opponents, rather than a moral crusade in which one's own stainless standard must put the enemy to shame and rout. Roosevelt's attitude here was akin to his attitude toward expatriates: it was priggish and craven, he thought, to deplore conditions in the United States yet at the same time to raise one's eyebrows at anybody who rumpled his waistcoat by plunging into the plebeian melee. In the United States of that era, one sees, among the noble spirits, so many embittered critics, so many neurotic cranks, that it is cheerful to look on at the spectacle of a well-educated and public-spirited man, not merely attempting to formulate an ideal of Americanism that will discredit the pawnbroker and the huckster but punching it out on their own ground with the sordid political boss, the arrogant millionaire, the bought sena-tor, the exploiter of tenements, the Spanish War profi-teer—all those types from whom so many of his stratum shrank, with whom they refused to contend.

Americanism in foreign affairs had also its definite meaning. The expressions of bellicosity in these letters may antagonize but they will not surprise anybody who remembers T. R.'s fulminations against the peace policy of Woodrow Wilson. "Frankly," he writes in 1889 to Cecil Spring Rice, "I don't know that I should be sorry to see a bit of a spar with Germany; the burning of New York and a few other seacoast cities would be a good object lesson on the need of an adequate system of coast defences," and, in 1895, to Henry Cabot Lodge, at the time of our dispute with England over the boundary of Venezuela, "Let the fight come if it must; I don't care whether our seacoast cities are bombarded or not; we would take Canada." His interpretation of the Monroe

Doctrine was carried to extreme lengths: "I believe," he writes in 1893, "in ultimately driving every European power off of this continent." But what is unfamiliar and more impressive is the first Roosevelt's grasp of world affairs and the scope of his historical imagination, especially as shown in the series of letters to Cecil Spring Rice. I doubt whether either Woodrow Wilson, for whom the history of Europe seems to have figured, like the chronicles of the Bible, as a remote source of moral instances, or Franklin D. Roosevelt, whose comprehensive knowledge of land and sea seems to have been mainly cartographical, would have been capable of such a survey of Europe, America and Russia, past and present and future, as Theodore sends Spring Rice on August 13, 1897. The unexpected feature of these letters is the absence of jingo rant and the freedom from cocksureness of the long-range views.

There is a similar curious contrast between the extreme manifestations of Roosevelt's egoism and his moderate estimate of himself in his soberer moments of self-appraisal. Of his governorship, one finds him boasting to Cecil Spring Rice, "My own business goes on fairly. At any rate, for this year I have had an absolutely honest administration from top to bottom in this State, and an absolutely efficient one, too." And his confidence in his abilities, his exultant satisfaction in his own achievements, completely takes the bit in its teeth at the time of his letters from the Spanish War, in which he really does make it appear that his storming of San Juan Hill (or what he believed to have been San Juan Hill) was virtually the whole of the Cuban campaign. The relentlessly prolonged correspondence with Henry Cabot Lodge and other allies in Washington in his subsequent (unsuccessful) attempt to obtain the Medal of Honor are embarrassing and exasperating. Yet he writes to Andrew D.

White, "Do you know, I have come to the conclusion that I have mighty little originality of my own. What I do is to try to get ideas from men whom I regard as experts along certain lines, and then to try to work out those ideas." Just as in his *Autobiography* one of the most impressive passages is that in which he explains that the "successes" he has "won" are not of the kind due to genius but the products of "hard labor and the exercise of my best judgment and careful planning and working long in advance," and in which he goes on to tell how, in spite of a natural timidity, he had trained himself, by discipline and practice, to face his first self-imposed dangers of bad horses, Western gunmen and large ferocious animals.

Of the demagogue of the later years, the rabid and self-righteous Roosevelt, who diverted attention from his questionable acts by brutal denunciations; of the red-faced and beefy ex-President whom one saw during the First World War pounding his left palm with his right fist and bombarding his hearers with dogmatic opinions, delivered in a high-pitched voice, that no question or objection could touch; of the self-produced mask of the public man, excreted in public debate to protect and fortify himself, to frighten or reassure others—of this crude ventriloquial oracle, there are already some signs in these letters. He early gave in to the habit of accusing his opponents and critics of "dishonesty" and "deliberate falsehoods." He must often, from the start of his career, have had to deal with outrageous examples of both, but it was one of his less amiable traits (somewhat redeemed by the fact that he seems to have been, though a truculent, a not really ill-natured man) that he never gave his critics the benefit of assuming good faith on their part, of admitting that they might be mistaken. "I therefore denounce its statements," he writes in 1891 of an article in the Delphi *Journal* (the editors of the correspondence do

not tell us where Delphi was) that may well have
deserved his indignation, "as mere wanton and malicious
falsehoods, which its editor knew to be wanton and
malicious falsehoods at the time they were written." But
we find him a year later declaring that an article in the
Nation is "so foolish, so malignant, so deliberately men-
dacious and so exultant that it fairly made me writhe to
think of the incalculable harm to decency that scoundrelly
paper, edited by its scoundrelly chief, Godkin, has done."
By 1899, Republicans like Senator Hoar, who happened
to differ from Roosevelt on the subject of annexing the
Philippines, were "little better than traitors." And treason
is now added to his stock accusations. By 1900 we find
him writing, apropos of the election of that year, in
which McKinley ran against Bryan, "I cannot express the
anger and contemptuous indignation with which I regard
the cultivated men from Schurz and Godkin down to the
smaller vermin like Jack Chapman and Erving Winslow
who at this great crisis show themselves traitors to their
country." But these aspects of Roosevelt's character may
be left for consideration till the later instalments of the
letters appear. In the meantime, the general impression of
the pre-1900 Roosevelt is attractive and even inspiring.

                                    October 20, 1951

THE HOLMES-LASKI CORRESPONDENCE

THE CORRESPONDENCE BETWEEN Justice Holmes and Harold J. Laski extended over nearly nineteen years—1916–35. It has been published almost *in toto* in two volumes, comprising sixteen hundred and fifty pages, by the Harvard University Press: *Holmes-Laski Letters,* under the editorship of Holmes's literary executor, Mr. Mark DeWolfe Howe, with a foreword by Mr. Justice Frankfurter. Mr. Howe has supplied careful notes that identify, wherever possible, the innumerable authors and books discussed by the two correspondents, and has added a biographical appendix that gives somewhat fuller accounts of the more important persons mentioned. There is a complete, an ideal index, that runs to a hundred and twenty-three pages.

This reviewer has read the whole correspondence with never-flagging fascination and has found it the perfect resource for railroad trips and bedtime entertainment, but everyone may not feel the same interest in the earlier phases of the "liberal" movement—about which, during the years when Laski was teaching at Harvard and associated with the *New Republic,* before he returned to England in June, 1920, we get a good deal of inside information—nor will everyone, perhaps, care to follow the whole of the detailed record of Laski's inveterate book-hunting, about which he sends Holmes a bulletin in practically every letter. Yet the letters make such easy reading, they are so full of gossip and wit and alert comment on current happenings, and the correspondents are both so extraordinary, that the book may be recommended to anyone with a taste for the informalities of political and intellectual history.

Before going on to discuss the personalities of the two celebrities and their curious relationship, one ought to call attention to one element of unusual interest. Though the exchange between Holmes and Laski deals mainly with law and politics, it is full of incidental observations on all sorts of philosophical and literary subjects. You have Holmes's rediscovery of Melville in 1921—he thought that *The Scarlet Letter* seemed thin beside *Moby Dick*— with his expression of regret that he had not, as a small boy in Stockbridge, "tried to get hold of the (if my memory is right) rather gruff taciturn man that I saw in my father's study." You have his many interesting references to Henry James: "I think," he writes in a letter of 1925, "there was something big in H. James, but I think that with all his preoccupation he wanted something of the gentleman and that it tells in his choice of subjects and sometimes in his writing. This is a thing that I wouldn't say except in confidence and I will not develop it." You have his candid and critical opinions of the Adamses, Charles Eliot Norton and James Russell Lowell. There is a brilliant remark about Santayana in a letter of 1924: "In a general way his thinking more than that of other philosophers coincides with mine. But he has a patronizing tone—as of one who saw through himself but didn't expect others to." This Laski can hardly rival when he writes in his next letter: "For ability to dwell on the heights, to move with sure foot amid great conceptions, I think George Eliot is unsurpassed. Meredith had her quality; but when he tried to express it he was like a man trying to speak with a fishbone deliber-

ately stuck in his throat." In his literary judgments, Laski
is less penetrating and more conventional, for, in general,
he accepted the English canon. Holmes accepted nothing
that he had not examined and approved: "I can't see," he
writes when he is ninety, "why they seem to take the
author of *Walden* (I forget the name) so seriously." One
of the most amusing features of the interchange is the
efforts of both these connoisseurs of literature to understand what it is that the French admire in Racine.
Holmes is still worrying about this at the age of eighty-
six, and Laski is only beginning to get a little light on the
subject when, in a letter written four years later, he tells
Holmes of hearing a Frenchman recite the poet's verses.

These letters, however, are a good deal more than an
entertaining commentary on books and events. They
throw into relief, I believe, certain aspects of Holmes and
Laski in a way that nothing else has yet done, and they
stimulate long-range reflections on the characters and
careers of the two men.

In Harold Laski's case, this revelation brings out some
disquieting problems, which both Mr. Howe in his preface and Mr. Justice Frankfurter in his foreword have had
to handle with tact. These problems are treated with
candor in Kingsley Martin's *Biographical Memoir* of
Laski, and I propose to make use of this excellent book in
this as well as in other connections. The great scandal
about Harold Laski, regretted by all his friends and sometimes used against him by his enemies, was his habit of
unscrupulous romancing. He would freely invent stories
that had often no basis whatever in fact about people he
did not know but whom he claimed to have met and
talked with, exploits that he had not performed, scenes
that had never occurred and books that he had never
read. It is obvious that these falsehoods of Laski's repre-

sented a genuine aberration, because they were entirely gratuitous. Laski *was* on confidential terms with distinguished and famous people; he *did* have a phenomenal memory, and he *was* immensely learned; he *did* have an uncanny knack of picking up unsuspected treasures from the shelves of secondhand-book dealers. From what motive, then, could he have allowed himself to bewilder and trouble his friends, to leave traps for his biographers and editors, and make himself ridiculous in retrospect by providing in his personal letters so much evidence against himself?

More and more, as we read his correspondence with Holmes, it becomes a distracting preoccupation to try to guess which of his stories are false and to check up on his conflicting statements. I would wager, for example, that the following is purely a pat invention: "The outstanding thing was a talk at Shaw's between him and Barrie about the art of the theater; each quite right, and each shouting the other down with grim energy. Shaw insisted that Barrie fled from ideas as though to possess them would defile his virginity; Barrie said that Shaw always shouts sermons at the top of his voice and that if one of his characters seeks to come to life he promptly murders it. Pinero, who was there, amused me greatly; for him the whole art of plays was how you got the actor on and off the stage—and the notion of a function in drama beyond interesting or pleasing situations clearly puzzled him. Half the time he listened as a noble of Louis XIV might have overheard a conversation of two Jacobins." Did Shaw and Pinero and Barrie really consort together? Do celebrities perform in private ever quite so consistently in character? And yet we cannot be sure, and we presently begin to feel that we cannot be sure of anything.

Even Holmes, who was so loyal to Laski, occasionally pounces on him. When he reads about an interview in the course of which his friend, now returned to England, has said that he found Woodrow Wilson "easy to work with," Holmes demands to know "where and what" this was, and Laski is prompt to reply that the interviewer has misreported him. Yet the old man has seemed to swallow without suspicion a good many other dubious statements—perhaps because the inconsistencies, in the early correspondence, at any rate, are usually spaced rather far apart. At one point, Laski tells the Justice that he has just read the complete works of Thomas Hardy, but then, in subsequent letters, he will mention from time to time that he has been reading some novel of Hardy's that he had not known before. He claims in three different years—1926, 1928 and 1929—to have just been completely baffled by Agatha Christie's detective story *The Murder of Roger Ackroyd*. Yet sometimes the contradictions come closer together. In a letter of January 9, 1926, he announces that he has purchased in Amsterdam an engraving of Voltaire by Moreau le Jeune, and in a letter of February 13th that he has bought the same picture "last week" in England. It was certainly careless of Laski, on the occasion of a visit to the Continent, to report a long conversation with Georg von Below, a German historian, whom he describes as a "delightful old man," when von Below, as the editor tells us, had at that time been dead three years. And, in spite of his many reports of conversations with Arnold Bennett, the index to Bennett's diary does not show a single reference to Laski.*

---

* In a review of the Holmes-Laski correspondence by Mr. Kingsley Martin that has appeared, since this was written, in the *New Statesman and Nation* (August 8, 1953), he tells us that, "Most of the anecdotes [Laski] relates were of real events but his own achievements were far more remarkable than those which he related with pride in his letters to America. It was as if he were afraid to be thought boastful if he told the truth, whereas it was only fun if he transformed it into an improbable yarn.

In these letters one gets the impression that Laski became more reckless under pressure of his busier life and
in proportion as Holmes, who was ninety in 1931, grew
mentally less attentive. One of Laski's last efforts to
amuse the old man is an incredible succession of witty
remarks—one of which, only two letters before, he has
attributed to someone else—supposed to have been fired
off by "a young don" at "the high table of Christ
Church." "And all this in one evening," adds Laski, with
one of his circumstantial touches, "from a lad whose
specialty is vector analysis." We finally come to feel that
these letters were composed for a character in a novel,
that they are more or less plausibly concocted for a brilliant young professor of politics with the run of the
London intellectual world, who is supposed to be writing
to a friend in America.

Yet Laski was a real person and a person of some importance. Though his boasting suggests megalomania and
his habit of romancing frivolity, he was actually not only
a well-equipped scholar and an able political thinker but
a fighter for unpopular ideals, whose career as a whole is
an example of singularly disinterested devotion. About
the things that were essential to his subject, he did not
mislead his students, and he did not, so far as I know,
allow any improvisations to get into the text of his books.
He was trying to expound what he thought was the truth,
and he was willing to go to bat for it. From the moment
one recognized this and learned to discount what was
specious, one found, in one's personal relations with
Laski, that he inspired respect and affection—which, in
Holmes's case, he knew how to return with modesty as
well as warmth. Mr. Martin has shown him at his best as

I always knew that Harold was really a friend of Franklin Roosevelt because he did not boast of being one."

a teacher who labored over as well as inspired his pupils and even sometimes helped them out with money; as an adroit and judicial arbitrator who served for twenty-four years on the British Industrial Court that decided disputes between the Treasury and Civil Service employees; and as a political adviser to Labour who was able to play in England a role for which, it would seem, no one else was precisely fitted.

I shall return to this role in a moment, but I want first to advance a theory, also suggested by Kingsley Martin's memoir, that would partly account for Laski's queer incongruities. I had not had any idea, before reading Mr. Martin, of the self-confined character of the Jewish world in which Laski had grown up in Manchester or the struggle he had had to break out of it. His parents had come from Poland, and his father, a successful business-man, was the recognized leader of the Jewish community. The Laskis were rigorously orthodox, and they practiced all the Mosaic regulations about eating and drinking and washing, wearing phylacteries and keeping the Sabbath. Harold was sent to a Gentile school, but this English education ran parallel with his Jewish training without ever being allowed to impinge on it. This must have created a split in his mind, for it eventually gave rise to rebellion. The time came, says Mr. Martin, when Harold said to his father, "I am English, not Polish; an agnostic, not a Jew. I cannot reconcile Maimonides with Mill, nor *Ann Veronica* with the Mosaic Law." He was allowed to go to Oxford, but before he went he had managed, at eighteen, to marry, without telling his parents, a young non-Jewish girl, a lecturer on eugenics and a champion of woman suffrage, who was also at odds with her family. This precipitated a terrible crisis. The two young people were separated. Harold's allowance was stopped till the term began at Oxford, and he was told by the elder Laski that unless he renounced his marriage or persuaded his wife to become a Jew, he would not be given a penny from the moment he graduated. Harold flouted this ultimatum, and when he later emerged from Oxford in 1914, he set out to make a living for himself and his wife, and, physically unfitted for military service, he accepted a history lectureship at McGill University in Montreal. Two years later he went to teach at Harvard, where he remained till 1920. While in America, he studied the United States, made lasting American friends and acquired an American accent. He was undoubtedly one of the foreigners who knew most about this country and understood it most sympathetically, and when he finally returned to England to function for the rest of his life as a professor at the London School of Economics, he never ceased to make the effort to interpret the two countries to one another. Later on, he lectured in Russia and attempted, in a lesser way, the same kind of two-way interpretation between the West and the Soviet Union.

Harold Laski was thus incessantly and in every situation practicing what Stephen Potter calls "clubmanship" —a branch of "oneupmanship" that involves playing one milieu off against another. In Laski's case, he had in his repertoire the English, the Jewish, the American and the Soviet Russian worlds. He was always the informed outsider, full of insight, anxious to be helpful, but not unwilling to score and capable of deadpan mischief. It was also true, I suppose, that he felt he had to out-Oxford Oxford by an exhibition of easy accomplishment. To have known Harold Laski and watched him in action is to find oneself now equipped to appreciate the tone of his letters in a way that would hardly be possible for a reader who had never met him. He was almost elfishly small and looked frail, rather frailer than he really was. With his spectacles and his round black eyes, which defied such a

description as "beady" by force of the high-powered intelligence brought out by the owlish lenses, and which were
usually more lively than the rest of his face, his appearance was perennially youthful, as of a schoolboy who was
stumping his elders or innocently waiting for someone to
pick up one of those buzzing matchboxes that give the
effect of an electric shock. I was told years ago by a friend
who had crossed on a boat with Laski of his method of
dealing with a man who was boring the other passengers
by his pompousness and self-importance. Laski sat down
and wrote this man a note that purported to come from
the captain, apologizing for not having realized before
that there was so distinguished a person aboard and for
not having done him the honors of the captain's table,
and inviting him to dine that evening tête-à-tête in the
captain's cabin. And in Laski's correspondence with
Holmes, he occasionally lets his friend see him in the act
of pulling someone else's leg. "Another," he writes of a
man whom he had met at a dinner of judges in London,
"was, I gather, a great swell in commercial cases; but he
seemed most interested in incomes at the Bar, wherefore I
led him up the garden gracefully. He said that J. Simon
was making sixty thousand a year, so I invented a quite
imaginary Bonville-Smith (don't you think Bonville a
neat touch?) who now makes £100,000 and never appears
in Court. The others nodded solemnly, and the poor
judge was quite persuaded by the third glass of port that
he knew of him vaguely, but had no idea he did so
well."

It is amusing for the present writer to read Harold
Laski's comment on a dinner that was given for him by
the *New Republic* on one of his visits to the States: "I
dined too with the *New Republic* and felt they were as
solemn as a gathering of Baptists met to do justice to the
Scarlet Woman of Washington." I was present at this

dinner, and can testify that the attitude toward Laski was certainly solemn. The old *New Republic* group had found out about Laski's fictions just before he went back to England in 1920—when someone had happened to see Colonel House and learn from him that he did not know Laski, just after the latter had impressed his friends by reporting a long conversation with Woodrow Wilson's advisor—and the dreadful news had been passed along, like the secret of the Glamis Horror, to their successors of the later group. We were constantly suspicious of him, yet we always gave him a dinner when he returned to America, and he had for us a real prestige. It was not the Scarlet Woman of Washington that made the *New Republic* solemn but the splendor and the scandal of Harold Laski. The tiny guest of honor, gleaming through his round glasses, with something of the schoolmaster's manner that overlay the impulses of the schoolboy, would sit plying us affably with questions and evincing a courteous interest, helping us out with the precise figures on some such matter as an ancient plebiscite in some faraway country, which nobody could contradict. When he had claimed, on one of these occasions, to have been told something or other in confidence by a certain Soviet official and was reminded by somebody present that this man had not at that time been a commissar, he ignored the interruption and passed easily on to something else, with an authority one could not challenge.

Paradoxically—incredibly, as it seemed to some—this authority was not a fraud. From what was it derived? First of all, from Laski's undoubted competence as an international critic with a grounding of all-around reading and authentic information. The small boy at a disadvantage, who, puny of physique, had pitted his will against the steam-rollering vested interests of orthodox Judaism, one-hundred-per-cent Americanism and the formidable class structure of the British Empire had made of his intellect an instrument that could analyze and estimate these great social entities as few members of them could do for themselves. He had performed for the liberal press of both England and the United States the service of acting between them as a kind of liaison man, and Mr. Martin makes one feel that for England he performed a unique service in keeping English students of politics in touch with the rest of the world. (I cannot do justice to Laski's books, since I have never done more than look into them.) But the power that Laski exerted had, beyond this, another, an ultimate source—a vision (in the Jewish sense, prophetic) both of the larger forces that were working in the social world and of what he desired that world to become. He not only watched politics intently, he bet on and worked for those movements and groups that he thought would help to realize his vision. He succeeded in maintaining this long-range vision through all the years of the second war as few figures in politics could, and not only brought constant pressure to prevent the abuse of civil rights and to curb the excesses of the censorship but consistently urged that Labour should not be diverted by the national crisis from insisting on social reforms.

Yet in Laski's imagination—for all his considerable shrewdness—lay his weakness as well as his strength. There was always something perhaps not quite sound in his relation to practical realities. His conversational and epistolary inventions were the least important part of this, but they indicated a discrepancy more serious. In some sense, Laski lived in a dream—a dream full of actual data, sustained by a real grasp of history and made vivid with firsthand impressions of a variety of modern societies, but a dream that did not, nevertheless, quite make the right contact with life. One comes to the conclusion, in following Laski through Kingsley Martin's biography, that his steady and considered refusal, up to his later years, to follow the advice of such friends as the Webbs, who wanted him to stand for Parliament or otherwise take a more active part in politics, was prompted by a warning instinct that such a role would impose conditions with which he was unfitted to cope. In his rallying to Soviet Russia at the time when the Stalinist Terror had made the regime least defensible, his capacity for fantasy became quite alarming; and he certainly sometimes behaved in a very unrealistic way when he was Chairman of the Labour Party, after it came to power in 1945. He had by that time become a world figure for the Socialists of Western Europe—an intellectual, a "theoretician," whom the Leftists of the Continent could understand—and he went around abroad making speeches in which he promised a number of things that he and other Leftists wanted but that neither Bevin nor Attlee had any intention of granting, till the latter had to cut him short and rebuke him for his "irresponsible statements."

Mr. Martin takes account of one aspect of this curious performance of Laski's—he was here playing truant to his Party—when he writes in this connection that "no man, however disinterested or clever, can accomplish by letter, conversation and private memorandum the feat of changing the policy of a great party, since that is based not on the wishes or opinions of individuals, but on the interests of classes and groups." It had been unrealistic already, in the heat of the 1945 election, for Laski to sue the *Daily Express* for its story that he had advocated, at a public meeting, "revolution by violence." A denial would have been enough, but Laski insisted on fighting and evidently could not conceive that the verdict might go against him in the event that a jury should fail to grasp the difference between advocating violent revolution and advocating peaceful revolution in order to avert violence. Having always had the freedom of the classroom and of the Left intellectual world, he does not seem to have been aware of how much less secure his position was in relation to the general public, and his losing his case was a terrible shock, for it upset his fantasy about his life. It is probably significant that he specially complains of his feeling that he has been "called a liar." His death less than four years later—when he was still only fifty-six—was probably due partly to this rebuff. But he was sensitive to the force of the shock because, nervously and physically, he had worn himself out in the effort to save the cause of Labour, with which he had associated his vision. He had stoutly stood up to the ordeals of the war, and he now threw away his last strength in travelling about and speaking at innumerable working-class meetings. One finds in Holmes's letters of this period a constant solicitude lest the younger man shall burn himself out. Laski's love of human beings was real, and he was exceptional in class-conscious England by reason of his complete lack of snobbery—for he lived in an unfashionable section of London and he gave to his hundreds of visitors of all statuses, nations and races the same ready attention and patient consideration. He was admirable with his working-class audience. Though he could not help coming to them a little in the role of the fancy Oxford don, he talked to them without constraint, and he knew how to talk to their children. Harold Laski was genuinely kind; one never for a moment had the feeling, as happens with professional politicians, that his electioneering affability was a mask for some hardness or meanness. As for his fantasies, they were no more reprehensible than the commoner kinds of vice that we easily forgive in gifted men and that often do more harm than Laski's, since it was Laski himself who most suffered from his failure in realism. If he had been a poet, like Shelley, instead of a political thinker, his delusions and the croppers they cost him would have been sanctified along with his highest work. Mr. Martin has done well to minimize them and to emphasize that Laski's career was brilliant, courageous and useful, and had behind it a backbone of hard work that contradicted his apparent facility.

But what value and what fascination did this visionary elusive creature possess for old Justice Holmes, who disagreed with most of Laski's premises and thought most of his ideals nonsense, who was scrupulous about every word he wrote, and who did not, till he was over ninety, allow himself the self-indulgence of dropping a book he had once begun? The easy and obvious answer is probably to some extent the right one: Holmes had no children and needed a son, and certainly Harold Laski, who continued to the end of his life to find it a considerable strain to revisit his Manchester family, was badly in need of a father. He even needed a Jewish father, and I believe that Holmes filled this role. But in order to understand how it came about we must go back to Holmes's own beginnings.

The key to a good deal in Holmes is to be found in his experience of the Civil War. How taxing and searching this experience was may be seen from his war letters and diaries, which have been published by Mr. Howe under the title *Touched with Fire*. Holmes went through some of the worst of the fighting; he was wounded three times and constantly expected to be killed; he saw his regiment all but wiped out. In dating his subsequent letters, even in writing to persons whom he did not know well, he seems rarely to have failed to note the anniversaries of the battles of Ball's Bluff and Antietam, at both of which he had been wounded. He had been swept into the struggle on the tide of the New England abolition movement, but his ardor cooled off in the course of the war, and he always remained distrustful of exalted states of mind connected with moral crusades. He mentions this again and again in the course of his correspondence with Laski. At one time when he was thought to be dying, as the result of his wound at Ball's Bluff, he had resisted as weakness an impulse to pray to that traditional God in whose existence, when sound and sane, he had decided he did not believe, and he came out of the Civil War with some very grim and skeptical views, which supplied him with the permanent basis of his social and legal philosophy. He had seen a great political structure disrupted by a social issue and readjusting itself to the needs of war; he had seen the North and the South battering one another down into poverty, scorched earth and chaos; and this revelation of human institutions as provisory and precarious affairs, this spectacle of human nature reduced to its lowest terms in the simple battle for survival, must have had great importance in determining the then unconventional point of view from which he attacked the law— regarding it not merely as a sacred code, which had simply to be read correctly, but as a complex accretion of rules accumulated through more than a thousand years and representing the needs and demands of definite groups of people existing in particular places at particular periods of history. And the methods by which the states had had to settle their quarrel had seriously shaken his faith in the doctrine of human rights and the ideals of democratic government. He had come to believe that the only real rights were those that compelled themselves to be recognized, and he was always insisting that the right to kill, to enforce authority by violent means—even, in time of war, to suppress, as Lincoln had done, subversive or obstructive speech—is of the essence of any sovereign power, and that the function of the law is to put into effect the policies of this power. "The sacredness of human life," he writes Laski on October 26, 1919, "is a formula that is good only inside a system of law." "I repeat my old aphorism," he says on January 14, 1920, "that everything is founded on the death of men—society, which only changes the modes of killing—romance, to which centuries, that is generations, of dead, on the memorial tablets of a great war are necessary." Nor had the war made him more democratic; he was far from having been so favorably impressed by any of the common men with whom he had been thrown in the Army as Tolstoy's Pierre, in *War and Peace,* was by the peasant Karataev. "It's odd," he had written his parents, "how indifferent one gets to the sight of death—perhaps, because one gets aristocratic and don't value much a common life. Then they are apt to be so dirty it seems natural—'Dust to Dust'—I would do anything [for them] that lay in my power but it doesn't much affect my feelings."

It was the paradox of Holmes's career, which lent piquancy to his personality and made him a dramatic figure, that, holding these unpopular opinions, to which he gave frequent expression, he should have devoted himself to the service of the democratic government for which he had fought, attempting to interpret the will of the people in measures which he often disapproved—he speaks somewhere of telling some lady how much, as a private citizen, he detested a good many of the principles which, as a judge, he was bound to uphold—defending the liberties at which he scoffed and finally, being childless, bequeathing his money to the United States. Of the talented "intellectuals" who had taken part in the war and who had then had to function in a climate that did not encourage their highest aims, it was Holmes, perhaps, who succeeded in carrying through most consistently the serious role he had chosen and who came closest to doing justice to his abilities. He had at first been afraid that the law might not turn out sufficiently rewarding in a spiritual and intellectual way. "There were," he told a college audience in 1897, "few of the charts and lights for which one longed when I began. One found oneself plunged in a thick fog of details—in a black and frozen night, in which were no flowers, no spring, no easy joys. Voices of authority warned that in the crush of that ice any craft might sink. One heard Burke saying that law sharpens the mind by narrowing it. One heard in Thackeray of a lawyer bending all the powers of a great mind to a mean profession. One saw that artists and poets shrank from it as from an alien world. One doubted oneself how it could be worthy of the interest of an intelligent mind. And yet one said to oneself, law is human—it is a part of man, and of one world with all the rest."

But working hard and working uphill were natural, perhaps necessary, for Holmes—the result of his Puritan heritage as well as of the discipline of his Army years. He had brought out of the Civil War a character austere and not a little hard, a personality a little bleak, which his humor and his personal charm, his air of being a man of the world, could never entirely embellish. This helped him to survive the Big Money era, whose temptations meant nothing whatever to him and whose demagogueries did not move him. But he suffered from its cultural sterility, and he complains of intellectual solitude. "I must vent a line of unreasoning—rage I was going to say—dissatisfaction is nearer," he writes in 1902 to Sir Frederick Pollock, in connection with the editorials about him at the time when he had just been appointed to the United States Supreme Court. "They are so favorable that they made my nomination a popular success but they have the

flabbiness of American ignorance. I had to get appreciation for my book in England before they dared to say
anything here except in one or two quarters. . . . It
makes one sick when he has broken his heart in trying to
make every word living and real to see a lot of duffers,
generally I think not even lawyers, talking with the
sanctity of print in a way that at once discloses to the
knowing eye that literally they don't know anything
about it. . . . I hope some one of the [legal periodicals]
may have an intelligent word, but you can understand
how at a moment of ostensible triumph I have been for
the most part in a desert. . . . If I haven't done my share
in the way of putting in new and remodeling old thought
for the last twenty years, then I delude myself. Occasionally someone has a glimpse—but in the main damn
the lot of them." And he writes Laski in 1925, from the
country during a summer vacation, "You have a great
advantage in England that you are all so near together
that you can find intellectual companionship on every
side. Whereas here it is nearly solitude outside my wife.
However, one gets a spark here and there. I am afraid
that letters giving one a puff, a natural incident of old
age, hardly take the place of talk with people who keep
you up to the mark. Brandeis is a great comfort in the
winter, but he is not here."

"One gets a spark here and there." For Holmes—
though he was then seventy-three—the prospect had
brightened a little when the *New Republic* was founded
in 1914 and the liberals began to take him up. He speaks
of this in a letter to Pollock of February, 1917, in which
he also introduces Laski: "We had here over Sunday a
youth whom I wonder if you remember: Harold Laski,
an unbelieving Jew with a *spécialité* for church history.
He was distinguished at Oxford, I believe, then lectured
at McGill and now does at Harvard. Beat the American

champion at tennis [this, it seems, was another of Laski's romances], is one of the very most learned men I ever saw of any age, is in his twenties and an extraordinarily agreeable chap. He goes with some of the younger men like Frankfurter and the *New Republic* lot, who make much of your venerable uncle and not only so, but by bringing an atmosphere of intellectual freedom in which one can breathe, make life to him a good deal more pleasant." This late recognition pleased Holmes. His prestige at the Harvard Law School seems steadily to have increased with the years, and he had begun to be accepted by the public, who knew little about his ideas, as a national sage and hero. But there was something else, I think, involved in his *rapprochement* with the "liberal" movement. The tradition of New England idealism, which Holmes had been forced to renounce when he came to discount the abolitionists and to realize the cost of the Civil War, still exerted on him a certain pull and made him feel a certain sympathy with the men of the later era who were working for what they called "social justice." He still hated what Mencken called "the uplift" and what Holmes called "the upward and onward." He shies away when he detects any symptoms that remind him of the fanaticisms of wartime. "He [Bertrand Russell] seems to me," he writes to Laski in September, 1918, "in the emotional state not unlike that of the abolitionists in former days, which then I shared and now much dislike—as it catches postulates like the influenza." Later—October 30, 1930—he writes, of Maurice Hindus's *Humanity Uprooted*, "His account of the Communists shows in the most extreme form what I came to loathe in the abolitionists—the conviction that anyone who did not agree with them was a knave or a fool. You see the same in some Catholics and some of the 'Drys' apropos of the 18th amendment. I detest a man who knows that he knows."

He had already been complaining by the end of the twenties that the *New Republic* was becoming "partisan," and he was later to complain more strongly of its further shift toward the Left. He grumbles and growls to Laski when the latter sends him books by himself or others that put challengingly the case for Socialism—for Holmes's economic views were a combination of Malthusianism with a doctrine of non-interference with what he called "the stream of products." Yet his colleague Louis Brandeis had prevailed on him at least to do a certain amount of reading on the condition of industrial communities, a subject, it seems, he had completely ignored, and one cannot read his correspondence with Laski without feeling that he was not wholly uninfluenced by his contact with him and the liberals. "All my life," he writes Laski on September 15, 1916, "I have sneered at the natural rights of man, and at times I have thought that the bills of rights in Constitutions were overworked—but these chaps [Faguet and Hazlitt, whom he had just been reading] remind me, if I needed it . . . that they embody principles that men have died for, and that it is well not to forget in our haste to secure our notion of general welfare." It is perilous—especially for someone who does not know the law—to explain the motivations of judicial decisions, but one gets, for example, a distinct impression that, between the decisions of Holmes in the Schenck and Debs cases, in which he upheld convictions under the wartime Espionage Act, and his dissent in the somewhat similar Abrams case, his new friends had been working on his conscience. In connection with Debs, he had written to Laski on March 16, 1919, in a vein that is almost apologetic: "The federal judges seem to me (again between ourselves) to have got hysterical about the war. I should think the President when he gets through with his present amusements might do some pardoning." It is clear that the liberals have not been happy about the Debs and Schenck decisions, and Laski greets the Abrams opinion with a veritable paean of joy.

There would be a long chapter to write, for which this is not the place, about the close self-identification with the Jews of the Old Testament that was made by the Puritans escaping from England to what they called the Promised Land, and the profoundly Hebraic elements that persisted in the New England theology and the New England discipline of life. Although this theology had been undermined by the middle of the nineteenth century through the rationalizing of Unitarianism, which had softened the creed of the elder Holmes, the apocalyptic vision of a better world—of America as the country of which Harriet Beecher Stowe says that she used to feel as a girl, after reading Cotton Mather's *Magnalia,* that "the very ground I trod on" was "consecrated by some special dealing of God's providence"—had been revived with ardor on the eve of the Civil War, and it had gone to the head of the youthful Holmes. Its ebb had left him high and dry—high in his moral ideals, dry in the thirst of the spirit. But a reaction against the materialism of the era of unscrupulous millionaires was to bring in time another revival of the traditional American idealism, to express itself in the several varieties of the struggle for a secular "better world," in which the American people were to be rescued—as they had once been from slavery—from poverty and exploitation, from the corruption of machine politics and the debasement of cultural standards, from domestic panics and foreign wars. For Holmes, the expectations of this movement rested on delusions and fallacies, yet he was certainly interested in it and even, one feels, rather stimulated by it. He acquainted himself with its literature (he had already twice read *Das Kapital*); and he came to admit that the tides of society might be setting in that direction, and that if people should want such nonsense as Socialism, they would of course command the means to try it. In July, 1926, he writes to Laski, apropos of a book by R. H. Tawney, *Religion and the Rise of Capitalism,* "I wrote to him this morning and said, as bound, after an appreciative word, that I was an old skeptic and thought capitalism better than anything likely to replace it but that I got more intellectual companionship from you young prophets than from the older orthodox sages." These young prophets included, as is always the case with movements for social betterment, a good many intellectual Jews, and with these it is clear from his friendships—Brandeis and Morris Cohen, Felix Frankfurter and Harold Laski—that Holmes felt a special affinity. Holmes once, in fact, told Morris Cohen that he believed his Dutch Vondal ancestors—who in New England became Wendells—had been Jewish. He had, in any case, in common with his Jewish friends the same background of Old Testament rigor, and they shared—however secular their faith, however practical their professional activity—the conviction that what we do in this world must have the sanction of non-worldly values and be acted in the sight of eternity.

Thus Brandeis and Holmes, though they appeared to differ on fundamental matters, were evidently closer to one another than either was to any other of his colleagues, and Holmes's affection for and interest in Laski seem to have been a good deal more lively than for any of his secretaries. Though Holmes, like his younger admirers, had dispensed with the ancient Jehovah, these latter must have felt that he figured in his field as something of a priest and prophet as well as a man of learning; as, at any rate, a lawgiver and moralist who held himself quite superior to vulgar considerations. In Laski's case—in spite of divergences of opinion that became more and more pronounced—we feel that his attitude toward Holmes is quite that of the loyal disciple of one of the great modern Jewish thinkers or leaders whose position has something of the rabbinical—Marx or Trotsky or Freud, Arnold Schoenberg or Alfred Stieglitz. What dignifies his whole correspondence with Holmes—and not least when, by dint of whatever inventions, he is still trying to amuse the old man, now at ninety too feeble to answer—is its genuine emotion of piety. In this sense, he found in Holmes a father. And on Holmes's side, the veteran of the Civil War, who had continued to serve all his life an ideal that he sometimes questioned, must instinctively have felt at home with the minds of such men as Laski, whose moral inspiration stemmed from the same now remote but still operant source as that moribund New England tradition which, by the era of Calvin Coolidge, could no longer have nourished him much. It may be that even Laski's extravagances, the excitement of a dream that could not become real, were needed to quicken the interest of the stoical old soldier-judge, to reawaken a flush of that fervor for the destiny of human society which had been blighted on the battlefields of the Civil War.

May 16, 1953

GEORGE ADE: THE CITY UNCLE

The Permanent Ade: The Living Writings of George Ade, edited by Fred C. Kelly, is not one of the most satisfactory of the recent volumes of selections from the work of American writers. It includes thirty-one of the Fables in Slang, a few examples of Ade's other fiction and of his essays and newspaper skits, and the texts of a one-act play and of the musical comedy *The Sultan of Sulu.* The specimens of Ade's writings not in slang are probably representative, but they seem rather feeble today. One would rather have had an omnibus collection of the various series of Fables, all now, it appears, out of print. And at this date the libretto of *The Sultan of Sulu* is not particularly exhilarating. One would have preferred to have a chance to look at one of George Ade's more ambitious and non-musical comedies: *The County Chairman* or *The College Widow.*

The Fables in Slang do stand up well. If you first read them in early youth, you may have the same difficulty in bringing to them a detached and mature intelligence that you do with *Mother Goose,* the Bible, or the *Barrack-Room Ballads.* I have sometimes found, in rereading the Fables, that as soon as I started a paragraph, I knew exactly what was coming and could have recited the rest by heart, and this means that a book has become part of oneself. But I have decided that, like the *Barrack-Room Ballads,* the Fables are first-rate popular literature and still more or less alive. It is not merely that they still make you laugh: they command respect on other grounds. George Ade was one of the soundest of our humorists because he was rarely, on the one hand, clownish and never, on the other, sentimental. He was sardonic, steady, shrewd. His tone is so much that of his period—the late nineties and early nineteen-hundreds—that, as you reread him, you can hear intonations of worldly warning and laconic sarcasm that are the echoes of voices remembered from youth. George Ade is like an up-to-the-minute uncle who has been getting on well in the city and who has come back to see the family in the country. He is facetious about the little home town and knowing about the big town, Chicago, which has a good deal in common with the small one. Everybody loves his jokes, but he never cracks a smile when he makes them. He sometimes seems to be jeering at what he does not understand—the "higher" manifestations of "culture"—but he appreciates them more than he pretends. His slang is seldom vulgar, never sordid, and nobody could be more decent or—in an undemonstrative way—more kindly. But he has been up against the poverties of village life and the barbarous free-for-all of the cities, and he knows that if you want to survive, you had better discipline yourself with a calm stoicism and cool sense of the comic. Certain things he will never learn to like—party politics, the smugness of the rich, the exploitation of American patriotism; but he has learned to live among them and to kid them without much indignation. There is nothing romantic about him, as there is about the Southerner O. Henry, who other-wise has a good deal in common with him. George Ade failed to get the girl he wanted—she married a handsome Baptist preacher and went to live in Minnesota (I rely for this and what follows on Mr. Kelly's recent biography, *George Ade: Warmhearted Satirist*); but he never speaks of this: he has merely remained a bachelor all his life. He is as incapable of the moist-eyed meltings with which O. Henry tries to mitigate the stoniness of the urban scene as he would be of O. Henry's Bohemianism. He, too, had once his way to make. George Ade lodged dismally in furnished rooms and ate meagerly at the end of the week. But he soon became a topnotch journalist and a highly successful playwright, and established himself as a solid citizen who built a big place in the country, helped to give his old college a stadium, and could, if he had wanted to, people said, have been Governor of Indiana any day.

George Ade's originality lay in his shifting to slang from academic English in describing American life. The advantages of this were sensational. For Western writers it had come to be a problem to find a language to express their experience. With Howells, who was fascinated by Ade and wrote to him, "I read you morning and night," the primness of the literary medium sometimes seems quite inadequate to the disorderly crudeness of the material. Mark Twain, to get his hands on the resources that he needed to write with color and feeling, resorted, in *Huckleberry Finn*, to abandoning his good but limited English and giving his story to an imaginary character who could talk the vernacular without inhibitions. When we compare George Ade's Fables in Slang with his writings in conventional language, we see at once why his power seems so much increased from the moment when he hit upon the Fables that he seems almost a different writer. The trouble with his non-slangy manner was that it had all come out of books and journalism. He wrote English correctly and soberly, but he expressed himself mainly in clichés, and, except when one of his characters is talking, the effect is always pale. But as soon as he turned his hand to the Fables, the clichés all came to life because they contrasted with the smart made-up phrases and acquired an ironic value. The capital letters which he had written originally in parody of the old-fashioned primer began to be used in a quite different way—as other writers sometimes use quotes: in order to give a special inflection to some phrase that has become so well-worn that it is getting to sound a little ridiculous. Thus when we read in the account of a will in one of George Ade's "straight" short stories, *Getting Sister Laura Married Off*, that "With many literary flourishes . . . it was set forth that no man could be ready to assume sober responsibilities as a property-holder until he had entered into the domestic relation and was the pillar of a home," the whole thing is completely uninteresting, and the story does not hold our interest, though the anecdote is of exactly the same kind as those he used for the Fables in Slang. But when, in the celebrated *Fable of the Two Mandolin Players and the Willing Performer,* he will write: "When they had Concluded there came a Voice from the Outer Darkness . . . Fred and Eustace exchanged Glances. They began to Perceive that they had been backed into a Siding," the stereotyped language of novels takes on a comic flavor, and the picturesque inventions get an additional effectiveness from the contrast. (So much does this irony, once switched on, call attention to the American platitudes among which George Ade lived that, in the last sentence before this of the paragraph, I found that I was obliged to restrain myself from writing "Highly Successful Playwright," "Solid Citizen," "Old College," and "Big Place in the Country.")

Ade's breakthrough with his figurative language did also something queerly creative for the subjects with which he dealt: the people of the Middle Western rural towns and the raw and violent cities. When Howells had

tried to tell about these, he was accurate but quite un-
impressive. Henry B. Fuller succeeded in his delicate
ironic way because he was able to survey this life from a
higher level of intelligence than either Ade or Howells.
But George Ade, with his big capitals and bold metaphors, turned these commonplace people and mediocre
careers into something in the nature of a folk-cycle. The
Preacher who Flew his Kite, the Apprehensive Sparrow,
the Adult Girl, the Regular Customer and the Copper-
Lined Entertainer are remembered like the figures in
fairy tales. George Ade explained in 1900 that his intention in writing the Fables had been merely, as he said, "to
grab a lot of careless money before the reading public
recovered its equilibrium, and then, later on, with bags of
gold piled in the doorway to keep the wolf out, return to
the consecrated job of writing long and photographic
reports of life in the Middle West." That was what
Howells and Fuller had both been urging him to do. But
if he had tried this, it would have been duller than the
fiction of these more distinguished realists. He had done
the thing he could do, and he had done enough, when he
transposed what he knew of life into the anecdotes and
wisecracks of the Fables. They give the accent and the
flavor of their moment better than some of its more ambitious fiction. Their trenchant and compact style may still
afford satisfaction even now that the smart language is
sometimes outmoded; and they always have the merit—to
which Mr. Kelly calls attention—of an admirable objectivity. In his work as a newspaper columnist, George Ade
had never used the first person. "No newspaper man in
that day," he wrote, "ever dreamed of such a thing as a
daily contributor featuring himself. . . . Never, by hint
or suggestion, was it made known to our subscribers that
behind the story department there might be hiding a
human being with thoughts and emotions worth record-

ing. I peered through the camera for seven years and never stood in front of it once." And he continued this method with the Fables, in which the heroes and heroines are not dignified; the villains do not come to bad ends, they are not even particularly hateful; the victims are not sympathetic. The rubes have no hearts of gold to show up the city slickers; the city people derive no prestige from their experience of the world or their money. They are all about equally oafish, all about equally ridiculous. That was how they looked through George Ade's "lens," and, as he said, he never cared to get into the picture.

September 6, 1947

"THE COUNTRY I REMEMBER"

THE APPEARANCE OF VAN WYCK BROOKS's *New England: Indian Summer,* with its only passing mentions of Trumbull Stickney, prompts one to amplify these references in order to pay one's respects to a remarkable American poet whose work is too little read.

Trumbull Stickney (1874–1904) was one of those New Englanders of the last half of the last century who oscillated between Europe and Boston. He was born in Switzerland, in Geneva, was graduated with classical honors at Harvard and went back, as soon as he left college, to Europe, where he spent seven years studying in Paris and afterwards travelled in Greece. He returned to teach Greek at Harvard in the fall of 1903 and died suddenly, a year later, in Boston of tumor of the brain. His brilliance as a scholar was spectacular. He had taken at the University of Paris the only *Doctorat ès Lettres* that had ever been given an Anglo-Saxon. There is an interesting footnote in Brooks, in which he quotes a description by Shane Leslie of Stickney's doctor's examination at the Sorbonne: "With what learning and subtlety he defended himself against their sleight of tongue! How they pricked and tore and tossed his thesis! With his beautiful gray eyes and sad bewildered face, he met them on his own ground and in their own tongue. How carelessly the Greek flowed from his lips, and with what unperturbed French he met all their objections for hour after hour. When the strife was over, they were all polite congratulations." His thesis on *Les Sentences dans la Poésie Grecque* was greatly praised in France. I have heard one of his friends at Harvard, whose experience of American writers and scholars was as wide as that of anyone of his time, declare that Trumbull Stickney was "the most cultivated man" he had ever known.

In the meantime, he had been writing poems. He published in 1902 a volume called *Dramatic Verses,* and his friends brought out after his death *The Poems of Trumbull Stickney* (Houghton Mifflin, 1905), which included this and much unpublished work. Trumbull Stickney was a member of that extraordinary group of writers who graduated from Harvard in the nineties and who included William Vaughan Moody, Robert Herrick and Robert Morss Lovett. The great reputation of Moody always outshone, and still outshines, Stickney's. E. C. Stedman did not include him in his *American Anthology* of 1900; but with time the diligent readers of American poetry began to discover Stickney. Louis Untermeyer gave him considerable space in his *Modern American Poetry;* and Mark Van Doren selected him as one of the limited number of poets to be represented on a liberal scale in his admirable *American Poets.* Van Wyck Brooks, in this second volume, says correctly of Stickney that he suffered in reputation from appearing during the twilight of the New England period, when the attention of the critics was turned elsewhere; and the poets who read him today tend to take him more seriously than they do Moody. It is the purpose of this article to try to make out a clearer case for Stickney's poetry.

Trumbull Stickney had none of the facility of William Vaughn Moody. You may read pages and pages of him and find the verse quite unmusical, even awkward; the color quite conventional and lusterless. Moody's verses slip by as smoothly as some thin ethereal syrup; his colors have the shimmer of a soap-bubble film. You begin by being delighted, but you end by becoming annoyed. With all the sureness of Moody's touch, he has some fundamental deficiency of taste. *The Daguerreotype,* which ought to be moving, goes on and on for so long that it finally begins to sound maudlin. The *Ode in Time of Hesitation,* which ought to be hard-hitting and bitter, is so diluted with conventional rhetoric:

> The proud republic hath not stooped to cheat
> And scramble in the market-place of war, etc.—

that you almost end by sympathizing with the imperialists, because they at least get down to brass tacks. *The Moon-Moth* mirrors Greece in Moody's peculiar soapy iridescence—one of the most successful things in the poem is actually a soap-bubble metaphor—which looks as if it would shatter into dull drops of water if one prodded it with a solid image.

The poetry of Stickney, as I say, has nothing of this false felicity; and there are times when he seems less talented than Moody. One's appetite is baffled by the peculiar aridities of the esthetic American of the nineties, who combines sensuous imagery and sighing emotions with a medium which, for all his efforts, remains basically rocklike and cold; who ransacks the recorded passions of classical antiquity or Renaissance Italy to find only the frustrations appropriate to a novel by Henry James or Edith Wharton. The Greek plays and dramatic monologues of Stickney are just as unreadable as those of Moody. Out of the monstrous brutal myths of Aeschylus he gets only great slabs of blank verse, and from the luxurious crimes of the Papacy little more than an echo of Browning.

But there is a real lyric poet in Stickney. In a poem like the first piece—*In Ampezzo*—of the volume of collected poems, the resisting integument has been broken by an expansion of sensibility that meets, merges into, possesses, some landscape with its atmosphere of a moment. Other poems are rather successful with the cadences of the *fin de siècle,* the accents of the Rhymers' Club. "Be still. The Hanging Gardens were a dream"— which seems to be Stickney's best-known piece, having been trailed through a number of anthologies like the Cynara of Ernest Dowson—is an obvious example of this. But there is something else to the Hanging Gardens, something which gives it more weight than Dowson. We can see the best qualities of Stickney better illustrated in another poem, which is probably not so well known:

It's autumn in the country I remember.

How warm a wind blew here about the ways!
And shadows on the hillside lay to slumber
During the long sun-sweetened summer-days.

It's cold abroad the country I remember.

The swallows veering skimmed the golden grain
At midday with a wing aslant and limber;
And yellow cattle browsed upon the plain.

It's empty down the country I remember.

I had a sister lovely in my sight:
Her hair was dark, her eyes were very somber;
We sang together in the woods at night.

It's lonely in the country I remember.

The babble of our children fills my ears,
And on our hearth I stare the perished ember
To flames that show all starry thro' my tears.

It's dark about the country I remember.

There are the mountains where I lived. The path
Is slushed with cattle-tracks and fallen timber,
The stumps are twisted by the tempests' wrath.

But that I knew these places are my own,
I'd ask how came such wretchedness to cumber
The earth, and I to people it alone.

It rains across the country I remember.

This is in a mood not unlike Verlaine; but it has in it
something stronger and more masculine than *"Il pleut
dans mon coeur"* and the rest. Trumbull Stickney was
less accomplished than Verlaine, and one finds in the
poem a few touches—for example, in the fourth tercet—
of the sentimental conventions and the amateurish style
that afflicted the American poetry of the period. Yet it has
also certain passages in a style not at all characteristic of
that period. *And yellow cattle browsed upon the plain;
We sang together in the woods at night*—the words here
are perfectly plain, there is not a "poetic" word among
them; yet in making a simple statement of seven or eight
words, each of these lines presents a scene and the emotion that is felt in remembering it. This spareness and
accuracy of language that carries a charge of meaning is
quite unlike the decadent romanticism which reigned at
the end of the century.

It is the quality that the Russians admire in Pushkin,
and it is what we occasionally admire in the short poems
of Robert Frost—such as *Stopping by Woods on a
Snowy Evening*—in which words commonplace in themselves, *The darkest evening of the year*, take on a special
color and emphasis. And this was what Stickney could do
that was really authentic and impressive. You find often,
as with Walter Savage Landor, that he will end a blurred
or feeble poem with a sudden clear minting of syllables:

> Through art divine, thou livest—as of old
> Apollo springing naked to the light,
> And all his island shivered into flowers.

Or, better, in one of those sonnets on Greece that are among the best things he wrote:

> To me my troubled life doth now appear
> Like scarce distinguishable summits hung
> Around the blue horizon: places where
> Not even a traveler purposeth to steer—
> Whereof a migrant bird in passing sung,
> And the girl closed her window not to hear.

Or in the curious elegy numbered XXVIII among the posthumous lyrics:

> Leave him, for rest alone can cure—
> If cure there be—
> This waif upon the sea.
> He is of those who slanted the great door
> And listened—wretched little lad—
> To what they said.

What is behind the best poetry of Stickney is a conflict between the desired and the possible which is felt in a more serious way than the usual wistfulness of the nineties. It is evidently one of those New England conflicts such as we get in the heroes of Henry James: the struggle of the appetite to live in resistance to cramped habits and a dead tradition. After confessing in the sonnet about the Hanging Gardens the falsity of romantic literature as a substitute for that "light of life" by which he says he has been blinded like a frightened owl, he resignedly admonishes himself:

> Be still. Thou foolish thing, thou canst not wake,
> Nor thy tears wedge thy soldered lids apart,
> But patter in the darkness of thy heart. . . .

And thus many of Stickney's most effective images—the soldered eyelids, the slanted door, the girl who closes her window, the desolated country of childhood—represent the poet as excluded from some source of vitality or beauty. Trumbull Stickney's real strength lies in his not being content to pretend, as other poets of the period did—the Englishman James Elroy Flecker is a more brilliant example of this than any of the American poets—that the donning of exotic costumes may give one the right to speak in the name of the feelings of their original wearers. Trumbull Stickney is enough of a genuine poet, on occasion, to throw off the costume and speak in his own person; and when he does so, the cluttered and troubled, the all but inarticulate opacities give way to a straight beam of verse—actual, inevitable, distinct. If Stickney had not died at thirty, would he have worked himself clear of the costuming? Would he have learned the free use of his voice? When we can recognize his true style as it appears in these poems, we may reflect that the wit, the poignancy and the homeliness of Heine's lyrics are no more clearly implied in his youthful romantic ballads, nor the Yeats of *The Wild Swans at Coole* in his early Pre-Raphaelite fantasies.

But Trumbull Stickney never arrived artistically, as Yeats and Heine did, at the expression of his full personality; and his conflict remains a deadlock: the door that is closed never opens. But the poet, standing before it, spoke some of the most eloquent words of that dispossessed generation; and then died from a disease of that poor active brain into which he had poured so much Greek.

October 14, 1940

LOGAN PEARSALL SMITH

I. Hannah Whitall Smith

THE PARENTS OF LOGAN PEARSALL SMITH, the essayist and author of *Trivia,* were both prominent Quaker preachers, and Smith's mother, who outlived his father, seems to have been the stronger of the two. The able evangelical woman was an American type of that period, and Hannah Whitall Smith was one of the more attractive examples of it. Her husband lost standing when he became involved in a scandal with a female disciple, and afterward, lost his faith and died disillusioned and bitter. But Hannah, having visited England in connection with her husband's ministry and having made the acquaintance of some titled ladies who had come under the spell of his eloquence, eventually settled there and enjoyed a sort of social success as well as a reputation as the author of Quaker tracts. Her son Logan, when he was writing his memoirs, went over his mother's papers and decided that she was "a most remarkable and brilliant letterwriter." He prepared a selection from her correspondence and wrote a brief introduction for it, but he did not live to bring it out. This has now been done by Robert Gathorne-Hardy, who has contributed a biographical preface (rather deficient in exact information), in a book called *Philadelphia Quaker: The Letters of Hannah Whitall Smith.*

One's feeling on beginning this volume is that Smith

overrated his mother's letters. They at first seem the kind of thing that may be worthwhile to print for the family but that are hardly of general interest. The mind of Hannah Smith was limited; she was neither particularly intelligent nor particularly cultivated. She was unable to appreciate painting and does not seem to have cared much for literature. Of the distinguished people whom she met she has little that is vivid to report. Some of her comments on England and America are amusing and throw light on the state of mind of Americans like the Smiths, who took great pride in their native heritage but found it pleasanter to live in Europe. (Camping trips in the Rockies and the Adirondacks discommoded and bored her.) She is not perhaps a very sharp observer.

Yet as one follows the course of these letters into the cheerful old age of her English years, one finds a personality emerging of unexpected charm and humanity. The prudery of Hannah's upbringing—"When I was young," she writes, "it was considered indecent to have a baby, and I myself was made to feel as if I was a prostitute"—becomes tempered by an amiable worldliness that produces little anticlimaxes not unlike those of her son in the deliberate ironies of *Trivia*. The dear friend of Frances Willard and crusader for the W.C.T.U. deplores the debauched habits of the English aristocracy, but makes a point of going to Ascot. "There certainly *is* a charm," she writes, "about the English upper classes that is indescribable, and I confess I *do* enjoy them exceedingly. For one thing they are far more like Americans than the classes below them." In one letter, she will write to her daughter, Mrs. Bernard Berenson, "I am afraid Willie's continued smoking has so undermined his moral nature that he really does not know right from wrong, poor fellow," and in the next will announce that she is sending her "a belated birthday present—a telescope cigarette holder. Thee need not advertise that it is a present from the author of the *Christian's Secret of a Happy Life!* But I think it may save thee from a little of the poison of thy cigarettes, of which I have a few fears."

Her principles of Quaker non-resistance do not prevent her from rejoicing when the Grand Duke Sergius is assassinated, just as her Protestantism does not prevent her from accepting the education of her grandchildren as Catholics or of confessing that for some kinds of people, who cannot rely on themselves, it is better to go to the priest. Since her instincts have been always humane, her tolerance grows greater and greater. It is all very sweet and droll. Married at nineteen, never in love with her husband, and a champion of women's rights, she does not think much of marriage, but, congratulating her daughter Mary—though evidently with a slight incredulity—on the happiness of her life with Berenson, she advises her to humor and pet him, though not beyond a certain point. She looks forward to death with an eagerness that cannot be insincere. "I had a prophecy from a 'Palmist' the other day, that I am to die at sixty-seven. Of course I place no faith in it, but I cannot tell thee what a real inward spring of joy it gives me every now and then to think— 'Suppose it should be true!' " And she later expresses herself as follows: "My sprees are really over at last. My next spree will be Heaven, and that *will* be a spree worth having!" In her old age, she takes sometimes a humorous turn when she speaks of her relations with God. "I really began to feel," she writes in connection with an importunate admirer, "a sympathy with God for the worship He has to put up with so often." God had meant to her her own sense of life, which had escaped from constraints and conventions and even from the pieties of her cult, to which she did not attach much importance. The most touching passage of these letters is in one of her appeals to her daughter, and the cadences with which it closes again recall the prose of her son: "Thy letter about Carlyle and Emerson interests me very much. It shows that after all your 'top eyes' are not entirely closed, and your spirits are not altogether earthbound. I often and often wonder how it is that people so fundamentally good as you are can be so content without any real link with God, and even, I fear, without any certainty that there is a God to be linked to. My soul was always so full of aspirations, that a God was a necessity to me. I was like a bird with an instinct of migration upon me, and a country to migrate to was as essential as it is to the bird. But you have seemed content to sit on a branch and merely flap the wings that were meant for flying, and to let your horizon be bounded by the fences of one little field, with no longings for the great spaces of the eternities."

II. The Ghost of an Anglophile

AT FIRST GLANCE, Mr. Logan Pearsall Smith seems the type of everything absurd, most vulnerable to the criticism of both worlds, about the American expatriate in England.

A member of a not undistinguished family of Philadelphia Quakers, who combined intellectual and religious pursuits with West Indian commerce and glass manufacture and who included some minor scholars, several evangelists well known in their day and the celebrated head of Bryn Mawr, the late Miss Carey Thomas, he was persuaded by Miss Thomas herself to give up his work in the family business and to go to live permanently with his parents and his sister, who had already settled in England. It was the eighties, when the cultural situation of our post-revolutionary period had been reversed: in the early decades of the century, the American intelligentsia had gone to Europe only in order to plunder the old country of all that could nourish the new humanity, the new literature, art and science of the States; but after the Civil War, when the up-and-coming industrial interests had definitely won the day over the older American farm and village and seemed to be crowding out everything else, many people with the old habits and education became ashamed of the United States and, believing the battle lost, went for training and recognition to Europe. It is a little hard to remember, today, when the culture of such a large part of Europe seems in process either of drying up for lack of vital juices or of being extirpated by rabid nationalists and when the European intellectuals are fleeing for refuge to us instead of the other way around; but it is essential to the understanding of Mr. Smith—as of Eliot and Henry James—to realize that renouncing America could once have presented itself as an exhilarating liberation to a freer and richer life, and could involve an internal struggle in which, for certain sorts of people, the courage did not always lie in deciding to remain at home.

The issue is clearly shown in the remarkable conversation which Mr. Smith reports having had with his cousin, Miss Thomas, in the eighties. "So thee is going into the family business?" asked Miss Thomas; and when the young man replied that he was, "Well," she said, "I'd rather shoot myself." "But," the young Logan protested, "it may be a chance to make a fortune!" "Why make a fortune?" she retorted. "Look at our cousins who have gone into the business; they've all become dull old men before their time. What good has their money done them?" When he asked her whether she really believed that he should do right to "give up America, with its need for culture and cultivated people?" she simply replied,

"Bosh!" She advised him to take up writing, and when he told her that he had no talent, "'Then go and live at Monte Carlo and enjoy thyself,' was the advice of this eminent Quaker to her young Quaker cousin of twenty-one." And the struggle between patriotism and "culture" is exemplified in an even more curious form in the memoirs (*English Years*) of Mr. James Whitall, another cousin of Pearsall Smith's, who tells of how he and his wife, belonging to a younger generation, still arrived at the same great decision; of how, when they came to England, they were mightily awed by "Cousin Logan," who had learned to say "How d'ye do?" casually and curtly like the English; of how, on first meeting Henry James, Mr. Whitall opened the conversation by oafishly blurting out that he had "shaken the dust" of the States "from his shoes," and how the Master gently reproved him by remarking that under the circumstances this might be the only "right thing" to do but that one oughtn't to be too blatant about it.

Mr. Whitall was much younger than Mr. Smith, and he has subsequently returned to the States; but his cousin is still in England and his recent book of memoirs, *Unforgotten Years,* shows him still swimming in anglophilia. It is all too easy for Americans of later generations to expose and to make fun of his illusions. He is, for example, under the impression, one finds, that America has produced nothing "permanent" since Emerson's Essays, *The Scarlet Letter, Leaves of Grass* and William James. He has already described, in an earlier essay, how, finding a map of the United States in the American consulate in Florence, he cried out to an American friend: "Why, good heavens! why, from the point of view of style, that whole continent could sink beneath the waves of the sea, and never leave a ripple!" "Can one

imagine," he asks now in *Unforgotten Years*—and this is
evidently meant also to apply to England—"any one
of the younger literary lions polishing a phrase to make it
perfect, or searching dictionaries for the word he wants?"
—as if there were not going on in some quarters, just as
there was in the nineties, searching and polishing and
little else. And in the meantime Mr. Smith himself—
who is now an expert on English usage and consulted by
the British broadcasters—writes language of such a neutral color as can only be attained by an American who has
stripped away his American colloquialisms and yet must
still handle English turns of phrase a little like a foreign
language, who sedulously but with rather a limping
pulse, must labor to keep up a rhythm which is nonetheless bound to miss the tempo of both English and American speech. Furthermore, with all his talk about good
prose, he frequently produces such writing as this:
" 'That's my class, the class I belong to' she mentioned,
just as a cat might say, 'I am a cat,' or a dog remark that
he belonged to the dog species" (why not, "as a cat or a
dog might say 'I am a cat,' 'I am a dog' "?); "there are two
main methods of attaining excellence in writing, two
ways of attempting to reach the peaks of Parnassus"
(wouldn't any literary schoolboy of Hemingway's generation know enough to throw out the second part of this,
which is the type of many passages in Pearsall Smith?—
wouldn't it have seemed even to James's generation
simply a banal and academic piece of verbiage?); "those
deifications of Shakespeare he regarded . . . as a piece
of German propaganda, having been started by the German romantic writers for the purpose of liberating their
drama from the tyranny of French ideals, thus substituting Shakespeare as a model which would leave them free
to follow their own disorderly instincts and devices" (a
little of the care which Mr. Smith recommends to the

slipshod modern writer of prose would have eliminated some of those participles). And in all his culling and collecting of aphorisms—to which he seems to have devoted a great deal of thought—though he has been through Santayana and Emerson and has rescued the sayings of several little known Englishmen, it has never occurred to him to call attention to the memorable maxims prefixed to the chapters of *Pudd'nhead Wilson*—we may, in fact, assume that he has never read it—or to put together, as Carl Sandburg has done in one of the sections of *The People, Yes,* some of the pungent sayings of Lincoln.

Mr. Smith, with his dear eccentric spinsters with whom he so loves to take tea and about whom, after their deaths, he writes droll but sympathetic memoirs, with his rummaging in old English country houses for hitherto unpublished documents of mild antiquarian interest, is the ghost of James's Passionate Pilgrim, himself a little spectral in his prime, the last and faintest incarnation of Eliot's Mr. Prufrock, who has forgotten even the eagles and the trumpets and the mermaids riding seaward on the waves.

And yet there is something in Pearsall Smith. I always used to think *Trivia* overrated. A certain amount of it, to be sure, seems quite obvious—the style and the sentiment both; and yet there *is* something in it, something dry, independent, even tough. There are things which one took in at a glance when one first picked up the book and looked through it, and yet which ever since have stuck in one's mind. So the first series of *Trivia,* Mr. Smith now tells us in his memoirs, was published in 1902 at the author's own expense and sold about thirty copies; but the book slowly got to be known, and now everybody more or less has read it. The point is that Pearsall Smith, in dealing with incidents frankly infinitesimal, somehow succeeds in being impressively truthful: he has put something or other on record—"I know that my voice is the voice of truth, and my umbrella God's umbrella!" It may be that this marks the moment when the American self-assertion, Whitmanesque, Emersonian, shamefacedly returning to Europe, finds itself self-conscious and comic. It may be the peculiar combination of helpless inadequacy and contemptuous superiority which the artist and thinker must feel in the contemporary bourgeois world. But in any case there is a real personality distinctly and honestly drawn: the pedant, the bore and the snob in him have been delineated by Mr. Smith with the same intentness and precision as the moralist and the esthete. Mr. Smith, as he tells us in these memoirs, became a convert to the heresy of Perfectionism (at one time professed by John Humphrey Noyes, the founder of the Oneida Community), which held that it was possible for the Christian to reach a plane where he was free from sin even while still in this world; and he says that, though he has "undoubtedly done things that were tactless and dishonest, and what the world would consider wrong," he has "never felt the slightest twinge of conscience" or "experienced for one second the sense of sin." One of the most remarkable things about him is the blandness with which he thus accepts himself: "I love money; just to be in the room with a millionaire makes me less forlorn"; "People say that life is the thing, but I prefer reading"; "How can they say my life is not a success? Have I not for more than sixty years got enough to eat and escaped being eaten?" With all this, he is always being carried away by enthusiasms, egoisms, idealisms, which make him, the moment after, feel clumsy and out of place.

These aphorisms are my favorite department of *Trivia*; and I am not sure that the section called *Last Words* isn't the best of all. Logan Pearsall Smith seems to get better as, growing older, he becomes more shameless. This new book, *Unforgotten Years,* is certainly one of the best things he has done. My experience with it was the same as with *Trivia;* when I first read the chapters in the *Atlantic,* they seemed to me rather slight; but then I found afterwards again that the sketches remained in my mind and that I was glad to reread them in the book. About the celebrated people he has known, Whitman, Matthew Arnold, Edith Wharton, Whistler, he does not tell you at any great length; but the anecdotes and traits are selected with exceedingly telling effect and often seen to reveal something important of which one had not learned from any other source. It makes Whistler a great deal more credible to know that "at times there was a touch in him of the loud bar-frequenting American"; it makes tangible the Philistine one had suspected in a great preacher against the Philistines to find out that Matthew Arnold presented himself to the boarders in a Dresden pension, who did not yet know who he was, as "a tall figure in a suit of large checks, with a broad face and black whiskers," marching in "with the jaunty air of an English schoolmaster who, in traveling abroad, assumes what he considers a man-of-the-world deportment"; that he used to regale his fellow boarders "with an account of the very favorable reception he had received at the Saxon court from certain dear princesses who were his especial friends; and that he remarked in an off-hand way that *The Valkyrie* had struck him as 'the sort of thing I should have composed myself if I happened to try my hand at composing music.'" The chapter on Walt Whitman, who used to pay the Smiths long visits when they were living in Germantown and he was in Camden, is unique in performing the same kind of feat for an almost mythical figure, who is here brought before us with humor as well as with admiration in all his homeliness, grandeur and innocence.

The whole of the American half of the book is better than the part about England and France, because Mr. Pearsall Smith is here describing something which he intimately knew and which it is worth while to put on record: the specialized ideas and habits of the well-to-do Pennsylvania Quakers. This seems to have been one of the pleasantest and at the same time not one of the least strange of those cult-circumscribed American worlds; and Mr. Smith has himself brought something out of it—a moral self-sufficiency and integrity which still stands him in good stead at over seventy, after half a lifetime's transplantation in England. Diffident, easily abashed and subject to continual humiliation, as he has presented himself, he may be; but he recovers and retrieves his position by noting quietly his candid judgments.

He seems today to command a respect from the English which is doubtless in proportion to the faltering of their own self-dependent outspoken character. And for us, though his writing somewhat suffers from the pale style and the intellectual sterility which blight the American in Europe, it is impossible, nevertheless, to dismiss him as an old fogey. After all, he has said it first; and he has made us enjoy his company in spite of it.

III. The Narrative of Robert Gathorne-Hardy

THE REVIEWER was once taken to call on the late Logan Pearsall Smith. Mr. Smith, on that occasion, read aloud a little paper by Virginia Woolf on the modern Sir Walter Raleigh. His relish of the malice of this paper did not seem in the least diminished by the fact, revealed in the correspondence between them which Smith himself published after her death, that she had been known to exercise this malice also at his own expense. But he believed that he had devoted his life to the high cultivation of letters and, I suppose, that he had the right to include himself among those of whom Mrs. Woolf says that, in contradistinction to Raleigh, they "never stop thinking about literature. It is kneaded into the stuff of their brains. Their fingers are dyed in it. Whatever they touch is stained in it. Whatever they are doing their minds fill up involuntarily with some aspect of the absorbing question." But was Pearsall Smith really such a one? It seems unlikely, in view of the attitude implied by Mrs. Woolf's letters, that she accepted him as a brother in art. Yet he was not a mere pretender, or, rather, he was not a case of the man who has mistaken his profession, like the speciously brilliant Raleigh. He had some inkling of what the métier was, even if he did not quite have it, and so he could share Mrs. Woolf's sneer, expressed with so much positive eloquence. (It is always a precious experience in the literary world of London to share a distinguished sneer.)

Two recently published books, together with a volume of Virginia Woolf's essays in which the paper on Raleigh appears, have brought this incident back to me and have suggested the above speculations. These are *Recollections of Logan Pearsall Smith,* by Robert Gathorne-Hardy, and *The Golden Shakespeare: An Anthology Compiled by Logan Pearsall Smith.* Mr. Smith was a Philadelphia Quaker, whose parents—his father was a wealthy manufacturer—eventually became evangelists. This took them to England, where they were long associated with well-to-do British Quakers, so that Smith spent part of his boyhood abroad. He went to Oxford after Harvard and finally settled in England. He knew and strongly admired Santayana and Henry James, who do not seem to have encouraged him tremendously. He had the cult of Flaubert and Pater, and consecrated his life to writing, with the self-righteousness and the thrill of excitement that the expatriate of that era felt at rejecting, as Smith had done, an American business career. He wrote little and published less, and took years over everything he did, putting it away and getting it out again, asking advice and revising and revising. He especially loved compiling anthologies, which he described as a "very dainty occupation," and he produced some pretty good ones, such as his volume of selections from John Donne's sermons. The new Shakespeare anthology is also good, though Shakespeare did not need anthologizing as much as the prose of Donne.

For the rest, besides his well-known *Trivia,* of which I shall speak later, he wrote mostly prefaces and essays on fairly obvious subjects—Shakespeare, Carlyle, Milton— about which he rarely had anything new or particularly interesting to say. Nor, in spite of his cult of writing, did he ever become a real master. His prose is rather pale and dead, and in his longer pieces lacking in movement, though it does have a personal accent, not seen at its best in these essays, and it is not exempt from clumsiness and dissonance that mar the smooth surface at which he aimed. One feels that Smith's continual revisions and his talk about "the labor of the file" were due not to a true perfectionism like that of Walter Pater, who knew when he had got what he wanted, but to the fact that he never had the hang of writing good prose at all and always felt that what he had done was faulty, without ever being able to repair it. In the course of his preface to the Shakespeare anthology, he has occasion to quote several passages from the poetry scholar J. W. Mackail, and we find that, in their setting of Pearsall Smith, we experience a feeling of relief at coming upon words that flow readily to the pen and sentences that land on their feet. Mackail was not a great writer, but he was a Scotchman with a natural gift of style, and that is what poor Smith never had. How, then, did he succeed—in England, writing traditional English prose and occasionally producing linguistic studies—in achieving so considerable a reputation and becoming a figure of authority? It was partly, I suppose, simply because he wanted this so much and worked at it with an ambition that was at the same time modest and persistent, and partly—though this, too, was evidently bound up with his desire to put himself on a pedestal—because in his later years he took on a series of secretaries, more or less gifted young men, whom he liked to treat as disciples and whom he sometimes induced to behave as such. Among these were Mr. Cyril Connolly, Mr. John Russell, and the author of the present memoir, Mr. Robert Gathorne-Hardy.

Mr. Gathorne-Hardy, of all of them, must have had the most ungrateful role, as he suffered the most painful fate. For several years, Pearsall Smith, who had a very good income from the family business, supplied the young man with an allowance, on the explicit understanding that he was from time to time to work for his benefactor, helping him with his manuscripts, looking up references and finding him books, and travelling with him abroad in the capacity of companion and courier, but also on the understanding that his protégé should always feel free to pursue his own interests and take time for his own writing. The conditions that Smith had laid down were that Gathorne-Hardy should not get married and that he should not write a best-selling novel. It turned out, however, that the patron was likely to become rather peevish when his young friend would not be summoned from a distance at the cost of his own convenience, and that much less of his time was his own than Smith had apparently intended. It also turned out that Smith was a case of manic depression, the low phases of whose psychological cycles sometimes lasted for months, during which, morose and unable to work, he at best shut himself up alone and read books till he was able to emerge again, but at worst would sometimes develop delusions of persecution and attack with fierce accusations the people to whom he was closest. Mr. Gathorne-Hardy believes that his character had been permanently damaged by his early religious training and his intimate relation with his mother, a passionate and powerful preacher. He had been put, between four and seven, through an agonized religious struggle culminating in an evangelistic conversion.

In his old age, Smith was sometimes quite insane, and Gathorne-Hardy had some horrible experiences—especially on a trip to Iceland in 1938, when recovery from a serious illness had left Smith in a state of derangement, and he accused his young protégé of having kidnapped him and held him for ransom. In the exhilarated phase of his manic cycle, he had been given to practical jokes, which, nasty though they sometimes were—he loved writing anonymous letters and used to make Gathorne-Hardy copy them—have something pathetic about them, as they seem to have been one of his ways of trying to make an impression on people, and evidently correspond to the nagging and insulting charges that characterized his deflated phase. There was also the power of his money, which he liked to make people feel. He had intimated to Gathorne-Hardy that he was leaving the young man his fortune, and if the latter displeased his patron—since he paid for Gathorne-Hardy's companionship, he would not even let him play bridge on their travels—he would threaten to cut him out of his will. When this will came at last to be read—the situation is put obscurely in Gathorne-Hardy's memoir, but what happened is a matter of record—it turned out that, without any warning, he had shifted the expected bequest to another of his protégés, John Russell. It was the last, the most upsetting and the meanest of Logan Pearsall Smith's practical jokes, and the effect was only partly alleviated by the new favorite's generosity in making a settlement of part of his inheritance on his disappointed predecessor. The latter is at pains to tell us that this kindness has prevented his "vision" from becoming "warped and perverted," but his tone all through is aggrieved. Our sympathies for him are somewhat checked by our feeling that he should never have submitted to being bullied and baited so long. He might perhaps have been pleasantly married or have published a successful novel! That he is capable of excellent writing, of a kind more spontaneous than his master's, his descriptions of their travels show.

His memoir, in any case, must be one of the most gruesome ever written, and the horror is protracted at relentless length. We feel that it could only be acceptable if exploited for the theme of a short story by Mr. Angus Wilson. Since it shows Pearsall Smith at his worst, let us remember what he was at his best. His collection of aphorisms called *Trivia* is a delightful and well-written book. Here Logan Pearsall Smith is humorous and truthful about himself and shrewd. Here he impales for us, with cool self-mockery, his old-fogyism, his timidity, his snobbery, his envy, his respect for money, his capacity for being a bore, as well as the touching aspiration, the Quakerish sobriety and purity, of his worship of literature. He shows himself both in his moods of humility in the presence of the universe and in those of proud self-assurance, when he feels that "my umbrella is God's umbrella." It is the portrait of an American of the turn of the century, highly cultivated and too much tamed, who also represents the type of such ill-adjusted people everywhere. This is the daunted but stubborn ego that peregrinates the streets of great cities in which it finds no real function to fulfil, that giggles and holds forth at parties which do not satisfy his longings. It is wistful with immortal longings, but it knows its best achievements are tiny, and it realizes its only dignity in confessing itself, with lightness, with irony, with all the elegance of style it can manage, exactly the creature it is.

It is probable that the small volumes of *Trivia* will keep Logan Pearsall Smith alive—these and *Unforgotten Years,* his volume of reminiscences, with its dry and rather waspish sketches of celebrated people he had known, together with some other such sketches scattered among his writings. He had been publishing, just before he died, some entertaining little storylike portraits, done with more than his usual deftness and delicacy, which represented what was for him a slightly new vein, and these are better to remember him by than the senile and sick moments recorded by Gathorne-Hardy.

January 6, 1951–January 25, 1939–May 27, 1950

ERIC PARTRIDGE, THE WORD KING

MR. ERIC PARTRIDGE, the New Zealand philologist, has become a conspicuous figure. In the course of 1950 alone, four books of his were published in America, as well as a new and enlarged edition of a book that had already appeared over here, and a new book on which he had collaborated. In England, he has published twenty-five books, mostly on linguistic subjects.

Let us begin with Mr. Partridge's most important work. *A Dictionary of Slang and Unconventional English from the Fifteenth Century to the Present Day* first appeared in England in 1936, and a third edition, which adds to the one thousand and fifty pages of the first two editions two hundred pages of fresh material, was published in England in 1948. This new edition has been brought out by Macmillan over here. The dictionary, which aims to cover, as its title page announces, "colloquialisms and catch phrases, solecisms and catachreses, nicknames, vulgarisms and such Americanisms as have been naturalized," is a masterly performance and ought to be acquired by every reader who wants for his library a sound lexicographical foundation. This reviewer has been using it for years, and he does not remember Partridge's ever having let him down. You can find here every kind of slang, from the bizarre inventions of the Elizabethans to the special vocabularies of English public schools and the catch-words of the last two wars. Mr. Partridge also grapples intrepidly with all those terms that nineteenth-century prudery compelled the editors of the great Oxford English Dictionary to slight or to exclude. Not only is the Partridge dictionary a comprehensive work of reference, in which all the information is presented crisply and clearly, but it also makes interesting reading as a picture of English society that brings out strikingly the class stratifications. The low-class language is squalid; most of its humor is ugly or sulky. You get the dreary rhyming slang: "trouble and strife" for "wife," "God-forbids" for "kids," etc. In its grime, the traditional lingo of universities and public schools and the smart slang assigned to "Society" are sprinkled like private codes.

The codes of the criminal groups of both the British and the American worlds have been compiled by Partridge in another work, running to eight hundred pages, which appeared last year in England and here: *A Dictionary of the Underworld,* which includes "the vocabularies of crooks, criminals, racketeers, beggars, tramps, convicts, the commercial underworld, the drug traffic, the white slave traffic, and spivs." This was preceded, in 1948, by *A Dictionary of Forces' Slang: 1939–1945,* which covers the language of the British services. This last has not been published over here, but the Philosophical Library has brought out *Sea Slang of the Twentieth Century*—this, too, exclusively British—compiled by Wilfred Granville, with an introduction and etymologies by Partridge.

As by-products of or supplements to these major works, Mr. Partridge has written also a whole series of books on special subjects. The most ambitious of these are *Slang Today and Yesterday* (the third revised edition of which has now been brought out over here) and *Usage and Abusage: A Guide to Good English*. As a dictionary maker, Mr. Partridge is unrivalled in his liveliness and terseness; as a grammarian and a critic of language, he does not always make so good a showing. Though most of his work in this field is of interest, he is not quite on the same high level as either Mencken or the Fowler brothers. *Usage and Abusage* is less finely discriminating and reasoned, and seems to me less reliable, than the Fowlers' *The King's English* and *Modern English Usage,* which really make this work of Partridge's unnecessary. The book on slang is rather commonplace and sometimes a little tedious when Partridge himself is talking. If, for example, he wants to explain the effects of the First World War on English, he unloads on us a great wad of words that rather obscure than illuminate the subject. But in its function as a history of slang, the book includes an anthology of vernacular writers from the fourteenth century on which makes very entertaining reading, and as a history of the study of slang, it supplies us with the opinions, quoted at length, of the earlier students of the subject, so that the volume stands with Partridge's dictionaries as one of his valuable works.

In connection with these supplemental books, one cannot help having the feeling that Partridge has been overexpanding. His *Dictionary of Clichés* (though it has run into a fourth edition) cannot pretend to be exhaustive and seems of rather dubious utility. This subject, too, has been more tellingly dealt with by Fowler. Mr. Partridge's sense of banality has not prevented him occasionally from succumbing to a cliché himself, as when, in *Slang Today and Yesterday,* he says that those who served in the First World War "claimed a right to eat, drink, and be sexually merry." As for his *Name Into Word,* though it collects some curious etymologies, it, too, seems an unnecessary compilation. What real use is a dictionary of proper names that have been turned into nouns, verbs and adjectives? If you didn't happen to know that a word had been derived from a person or place, you would not look it up in this dictionary, and you would find the proper-name derivation in the ordinary dictionary anyhow. In the case of Mrs. Grundy, Mr. Partridge is actually less satisfactory than the big Funk & Wagnalls dictionary, for all he tells you is that Mrs. Grundy is a character in an eighteenth-century comedy, whereas you learn from Funk & Wagnalls by whom and why apprehension was felt about this lady's opinion. The collection by Partridge of "essays on language," *Here, There, and Everywhere,* is in the nature of linguistic light reading, but it contains several interesting pieces. Mr. Partridge has not much to contribute in his discussion of the humorous inventions of Lewis Carroll and Edward Lear (he does not try to tackle Joyce), but he has written what would seem to be the final word on the British epithet "bloody," the objectionability of which has always presented a puzzle. He concludes that it has nothing to do with the archaic oath "by our Lady," from which it has lately been the fashion to derive it, but that its analogues in other languages suggest that it owes its explosive force to nothing more remote or outrageous than the idea of blood itself, with its implications of cruelty and violence, just as "frightfully" is based on "fright." And there are entertaining papers on euphemisms, on the habit of primitive peoples of naming themselves "the men" or "the people," and on the process by which certain last names give rise to inevitable nicknames, as when a boy at school named Sloan—in memory of the famous jockey—is, or was, immediately known as "Tod."

One of Partridge's lesser books does, however, make a unique contribution to the study of Shakespeare's texts. *Shakespeare's Bawdy: A Literary and Psychological Essay and a Comprehensive Glossary* makes up for the neglect by scholars of one aspect of the poet's work. The timidity or the ignorance of the academic approach to Shakespeare has left some large and awkward gaps in textual elucidation. Falstaff at Mistress Quickly's and Katharine of France learning English have been made to seem even more scandalous through being thrown into naked relief by the commentators' sudden silence. Though Mr. Partridge is here, as always, both courageous and well-informed, he is, as occasionally happens, not always, perhaps, quite intelligent. In looking for Shakespeare's ribaldry, he occasionally, as it seems to me, expands a simple double-entendre to an improbable multiplicity of meanings, while, on the other hand, he misses some obvious tricks. But the book, which steers clear of prurience in repairing the omissions of prudery, is in general based on common sense, and Mr. Partridge deserves praise for having written it.

I have spoken of the class stratifications that appear in the *Dictionary of Slang*. In *Slang Today and Yesterday*, Mr. Partridge points out that since the social compartments began to break down during the First World War, colloquial speech in England has tended to become more uniform. It has always been so in the United States, and the appearance of these books of Partridge's, like that of Mencken's *American Language*, is itself a sign of the increasing invasion by the vernacular of the literary language.

The Language Bar, by Victor Grove, is not a very able or valuable book, but it raises a point that is interesting in connection with this crisis of language. Dr. Grove, another British philologist, contends that it is a good deal more difficult for an Englishman to learn good English than for a German to learn good German or for a Frenchman to learn good French. He ignores the whole question of grammar and does not recognize that the fewness of inflections in English offsets the undoubted difficulties. There is the matter of spelling, of course, upon which Dr. Grove touches. But what worries him particularly is the problem, if one has not had a classical education, of correctly using English words that are derived from Greek or Latin. He says that real literacy in England has been the privilege of the well-to-do minority who have been educated in the universities, and he proposes that courses be given, in the English non-public schools, in which, without the actual study of Greek and Latin literature, the students should be drilled in the Greek and Latin words that give English so many important roots. This is perhaps not a bad idea, but if Dr. Grove had lived in America, he might already have become discouraged by seeing the meanings of so many classical words transformed by illiterate usage; *protagonist, jejune* and *transpire* are among the most conspicuous examples. May it not be that the literary language is rapidly losing ground to a language of streets and motor routes, of office business and mechanical processes, of armed services and criminal rackets, a language in which, except for science, in which the Greek and Latin derivatives lend themselves to international convenience, the derivations do not matter and are going to join the lost inflections? How many of the words and expressions listed by Mencken or Partridge owe anything to a Greek or a Latin that one would have to take a course to master? Opening the *Dictionary of Slang* at random, I do not find many words that are even based on the classical languages, and the *phenomenon* of Mr. Partridge is *a prodigy, a remarkable person;* the *operator,* it seems, is a *pickpocket; tripos* now means *intestines* as well as a degree at Cambridge; and *salubrious, intoxicated.*

August 4, 1951

ANDRÉ MALRAUX:
THE MUSEUM WITHOUT WALLS

MALRAUX IS WELL KNOWN as a novelist, as a fighter for revolutionary causes, and, more recently, as one of the ministers of General de Gaulle. It is not so well known that he began his career as an archeologist, with explorations in Indo-China, and that he became an authority on Khmerian art. Beginning several years before the recent war, he now and then contributed to various periodicals the fragments of a general work on art, which, between 1947 and 1950, was at last brought out in three volumes, under the title *Psychologie de l'Art*. (The whole work is now available in English in the excellent translation by Stuart Gilbert.) It is hard to judge very brilliant books, which may dazzle, deafen and stun when they are detonated under our noses, but, reading these successive volumes, I have finally been brought to the conclusion that Malraux's *Psychologie de l'Art* is not simply one of his best productions but perhaps one of the really great books of our time.

If one should merely look through these volumes without paying attention to the text, turning over the handsome illustrations, one would not get any idea of the originality of the work or of the unconventional way in which these illustrations are used. The original impulse to write the book was given by Malraux's realization that it has now, for the first time, become possible for humanity to take account of the work that has been done in the plastic arts in all ages and all over the world. Hitherto, the limitations of travel and the difficulties of reproduction have prevented the student of art from surveying this whole field. He has known intimately only the work of the region where he happened to live, along with a limited supplement of inadequate copies of foreign work and even fewer imported originals. But with twentieth-century transportation and the perfecting of photographic processes, he is now in a position to bring together and to make a comparative study of all the works of human hands that survive, from the scratchings of the Dordogne caves to the holocausts of paint of the Renaissance; from the anonymous beasts of the steppes writhing on their bronze plaques to the still-lifes and kaleidoscopes of shattered planes, each signed with a known name that has its value on the Paris market; from Alaskan totem poles glaring above the Pacific to the inland serenity of Chinese painting (the only thing, Malraux says, that, rolled up and not put on display, is still rather hard to get at). Greek statues and Roman mosaics, Gothic ornaments and Byzantine murals, Buddhist sculptures and Egyptian mummy cases, Congolese masks and Australasian fetishes, all the show paintings of all the palaces and all the places of worship, all the professional gallery pictures of all the modern schools of art, all the engravings and drawings and the preliminary sketches for paintings, which are sometimes, as Malraux says, more interesting than the paintings themselves, all the movie stills and other photographs, may today be brought together and studied. We can, furthermore, analyze them and pose them as we have never been able to do before. We can get special angles on statues, subject them to special lighting; we can isolate details in a painting and emphasize special values. We are at last in a position to have the run of an imaginary museum that will enable us to find out more about the history of the plastic arts and their meaning to human development than any real one that has ever been assembled. The illustrations of the volumes themselves, many of them in color, show what can be done in this way. They have been chosen with a critical acumen and introduced into the text with an eye for effect that make of *Psychologie de l'Art* certainly one of the most astonishing achievements of André Malraux's versatile genius.

The volume called *Le Musée Imaginaire* (*Museum Without Walls*) of 1947 builds up to a first indication of the writer's principal thesis, which is pursued in the second volume, *La Création Artistique* (*The Artistic Act*) of 1948 but is developed in detail and at length only in the final volume, *La Monnaie de l'Absolu* (*The Twilight of the Absolute*), published in 1950. M. Malraux believes that modern Western art, beginning, as he suggests, with Manet, has a tremendous philosophical and moral importance, because it represents, for the first time, a deliberate declaration by man of his will to master the world, to create it in conformity with his own ideals. The painter is no longer attempting to arrange his relations with God, to attach his existence to another world, or even to celebrate Nature. Nor is he occupied any longer with the problem that so held the attention of European artists between the Renaissance and the modern age—the development of technical methods for reproducing the illusion of the actual. He has come to the end of that and can now leave actuality to the photograph. He can now assert his right as a human being to deal with the world about him in an audacious, even cavalier way, and to conceive—that is, to organize—his environment, his relationships and his destiny in accordance with any system he pleases. The universe is there to be used by him, not he by the universe. With the whole globe and all its schools spread out for his consideration, he can choose from his imaginary museum whatever he finds may serve his purpose—an El Greco or an African carving—and his choices among so many models, which would have appeared to the eyes of an earlier age a grotesquely incongruous assortment, all have it in common that they either give evidence of a tendency on the part of his predecessors to assert, as he himself is now doing, each his right to his special vision, or in some other way encourage him to do so. The Christian or the Buddhist work of art no longer, of course, has for the modern the same meaning that it did for its contemporaries, for whom it was a detail of their cult. He has inherited the "small change" of their absolute, for he can see in the older work only the same affirmation of a human will of which he is the conscious instrument.

The final effect of *Psychologie de l'Art* is not, however, quite so ringingly positive as this account of it might lead one to suppose. The situation in which Malraux finds himself is similar to that in which we left him at the end of the first novel, published during the war in Switzerland, of his uncompleted series, *La Lutte avec l'Ange*. He wishes to justify the human race, to give us courage in our "human condition," but he is obliged to confront some very awkward evidence. As in the novel his affirmation of the stature and the scope of man has had to be made in the teeth of the horrors of tank and gas warfare that he has felt it his duty to describe, so here his declared faith in the high meanings and mission of modern art has to reckon with what must be felt as rather seriously disquieting elements both of primitivism and of decadence. Do the Surrealists' demonology and the abstract patterns of Mondrian speak to us with a proud self-confidence in the role of mankind in the world? Malraux has to face these phenomena as he has had to face the bestiality and the abstraction of modern war. He admits that some aspects of modern art are symptoms of disease and weakness, and this treatise on esthetic history thus presents the same kind of discrepancies that *La Lutte avec l'Ange* did. Yet the discrepancy between faith and evidence—or, rather, between will and obstacle—is what makes the book bracing. Malraux, in this final volume, does go far to convince the reader that modern art, for all its apparent eclecticism, has been forging a new style which denotes a definite victory of humankind over our mortal and earth-bound destiny—though we may have to add the reservation that at the same time it seems to betray a certain grogginess and sulky defiance in its recoil from the hard blank surface that it meets in the industrial age, as well as sometimes a slavish and unattractive imitation of its angles and pipes and wheels.

The second volume of the series, *The Artistic Act,* is mainly devoted to showing how all creative progress in art is accomplished through a transformation of the forms that have gone before. This is rather a familiar story, and I am not sure that this section of the work is quite so satisfactory as the others. One may note, in connection with it, certain dubious—or perhaps, rather, difficult—features of *Psychologie de l'Art* as a whole. As a French writer, André Malraux is an altogether eccentric phenomenon. A great spokesman for the French intelligence, an inexhaustible provider of formulations, he is not a master of exposition. The consecutive and lucid unrolling of smoothly spun-out ideas is something you will not find in *Psychologie de l'Art.* Though Malraux tries to disentangle his argument and to make his main points in some logical order, all the painters and all the periods seem to be trying to crowd into his pages at once, proposing unexpected comparisons and curious observations. His paragraphs and even his sentences become sometimes so

clogged and allusive that one finds them rather hard to
follow. One does not, in fact, quite "follow" them: one
studies them and reads them over in order to canvass their
contents and to analyze them in such a way as to find out
what Malraux is driving at. His style combines, also,
rather queerly, overwriting with elliptical associations. He
sometimes states perceptions or principles in language so
witty and terse that they seem to have the flash of revelation, and at other times he labors at length, and we discover, at the cost of effort, that he has been saying
something rather commonplace in a very strained or
snarled-up way. Though Malraux is always making the
gestures of telescoping gradual processes and plunging for
essential points, one occasionally emerges with the feeling
that he has actually been wasting space by repetition and
confused presentation.

But all of this one is ready to excuse on account of the
variety and richness of the material with which Malraux
deals. What my simplified description above will have
failed to give any idea of is the penetrating survey of
the whole field of art that leads up to the conclusions I
have indicated. Malraux has attempted to treat (though
in some cases he can scarcely more than mention), on a
scale to which one cannot do justice within the limits of a
short review, all the principal phases of visual art—religious, social and personal. You have—to mention only the
larger divisions—India, China, Japan, Greece, Rome, the
Middle Ages, the Renaissance, the Dutch Masters and
modern Paris. This survey is so exciting, shows such an
immense grasp of its subject in its great contours and its
concrete detail, that one is swept by it through snags and
opacities. You have not only extended studies of the most
important schools of art but also picture-by-picture accounts of the careers of certain important painters. Perhaps the most attractive features of the second volume are

the long sections on El Greco and Tintoretto; and Malraux has recently published a separate volume on Goya—*Saturne*—which really belongs with these and which, since the macabre later Goya is particularly congenial to Malraux, seems to me the most remarkable of his studies of individual artists.*

Thus, in scope as well as intention, Malraux's *Psychologie de l'Art* quite transcends the conventional work on art of either the aesthetic or the historical kind. You cannot really characterize Gibbon's *Rome* by describing it as a history, or *Das Kapital* as a treatise on economics, or *War and Peace* as a novel. These great books have taken their place as great books not merely by reason of their literary merit, of the prodigious ground that they cover, of the vast amount of material they digest, but because they are also inquiries into mankind's position and purpose, and, unless I am much mistaken, Malraux's *Psychologie de l'Art* is not out of place in their company.

April 14, 1951

1965. Since this was written, in the same year, 1951, there appeared a new one-volume edition of this work, retitled *Les Voix du Silence,* which has been translated as *The Voices of Silence,* and, being cheaper and more easily manageable than the original three volumes, has had a much wider currency. The presentation here is

---

* I learned later from M. Malraux that, when fighting for the Republicans, he was captured in the Spanish Civil War and imprisoned in Madrid, in Goya's "House of the Deaf Man." He was much struck, in this situation, by the nightmarish and savage murals that Goya had painted there. The huge cartoon of Saturn devouring his children is reproduced on the cover of his book, and the devastations and massacres of the war with the French, the principled executions of the Inquisition, so fiercely and unflinchingly incised on the plates of Goya's etchings, have their counterparts in Malraux's novels.

better; the author has quite drastically reorganized his material. The pictures are not reproduced on so large a scale, and the selection of them is sometimes different. These volumes on painting were then followed by a somewhat similar series on sculpture. *Le Musée Imaginaire de la Sculpture Mondiale* was published in 1952, and supplemented by two volumes, which both came out in 1954: *Le Monde Chrétien* and *Des Bas-reliefs aux Grottes Sacrés.* The photographs in the first of these three make a bizarre and startling collection which can only be understood in the light of Malraux's introduction. This remarkable introduction is perhaps Malraux's most eloquent expression of his hope that the human race, having discarded its old gods, may surpass itself and "try to give a base to its fugitive grandeur by finding in its own nature what would formerly have been called its divine powers." The first volume of a new instalment called *La Métamorphose des Dieux* was published in 1957. This is a kind of recapitulation which was supposed to complete the series and of which the second volume, I am told, was lacking only the last two chapters when the author, then lecturing on art in Venice, was called to take his place as Minister of Culture in the new de Gaulle government.

For one who has been following this series, it is frustrating to be brought up short before Malraux has finished his story, even though this is but another version of the same story he has told us before. *La Métamorphose des Dieux* is full of interesting revelations. This first volume is occupied with tracing the gradual modifications, from the ancient world to the Renaissance, by which the religious conceptions of Europe passed from the phases which Malraux describes as "the sacred"—the statues and temples which are something set aside from time and the appearances of life, as solid symbols of a transcendent truth—and "the divine"—in which the gods of the Greeks are made to take on human forms—through the phases of Christianity from Byzantium to fifteenth-century Western Europe, in the course of which an extra-temporal other world, dominated by a divine Pantocrator, is brought down to an idealized earth with recognizable buildings and landscapes, and a church that was formerly a collective entity is broken up, by way of painting and sculpture, into figures that represent, first, real men and women, then definite individuals, including on occasion the donor. From this it will be only a step to the complete secularization of art. We may assume from *Psychologie de l'Art* that Malraux will be brought by his logic to celebrate the complete dissociation of modern art from either the divine or the sacred; yet we feel, as we finish this volume, that he is approaching the brink of a precipice. He believes that he can see the first manifestations of the independence of modern art in Daumier, when the caricatured types of the latter begin to lose their human idiosyncrasies and turn into pure formal patterns, and when Manet, after making an attempt to represent an historical subject in his canvas of the execution of Maximilian, goes on to do a portrait of Clemenceau in which the artist has "decided to dare to be everything, and Clemenceau almost nothing." (An example of Malraux's clumsy grammar.) But since *Les Voix du Silence* was written, Surrealism, which perhaps at a pinch could be defended on these grounds, has given way to abstractionism, and where does this land Malraux? Abstractionism is, to be sure, not religious, but it looks like an attempt to get away altogether from what Malraux calls the human condition, and not into a realm of transcendent truth, but into a kind of void of floating color and line that has hardly been organized, often mere blots and blobs that seem hardly to form compositions. Surely even the work of

Picasso, with its figures reduced to matchsticks and its women turned to double-faced monsters, does far less toward the vindication of human dignity than even the art of Rome, of which Malraux says disparagingly that it represents a parody of the Greek divinity, but which, in its own inferior way, does aim at an ideal of nobility. In all this, in any case, Malraux seems to disregard the uses of the art of the past and the relative uselessness of the art of the present. Even his having Marc Chagall do a new ceiling for the Paris opera cannot create a demand for the pictorial arts such as that of Greece or the Renaissance. If Manet cannot possibly be considered so great a painter as Titian, it is partly because, in his lifetime, there was so much less demand for his work.

There have been hints in Malraux's recent utterances that he is beginning to think respectfully of "religion," and the tone of this last published volume is so sympathetic toward Christian art that one can almost imagine him reluctant to arrive at the eventual triumph of man that is supposed to be looming as the volume closes. He is said to have been taking an interest in the writings of Teilhard de Chardin, and—though I have found no explicit evidence in his writings—one wonders whether he may not have been influenced by them. But the demands of his official duties have kept him from expressing his views on anything except the great historic role of France, which he is trying to help perpetuate, and his conception of an "Atlantic culture" which includes both America and Europe, with Russia, despite Western leanings, bracing itself to fight Europe off.

I have found that the art experts, in general, detest Malraux's books on art, since they are not, as professional specialists, prepared to consider these for what they are: a kind of huge philosophic prose poem. They regard them as the works of an unscholarly amateur and complain that Malraux not only fails to provide any bibliographies but does not even make any acknowledgment to the authorities upon whom he has drawn. The only full and satisfactory discussion, from the point of view of literature and ideas, that I have seen of Malraux's series is a small volume by William Righter called *The Rhetorical Hero, An Essay on the Aesthetics of André Malraux* (the Chilmark Press, 1964). Mr. Righter tries to come to grips with the curious phenomena of Malraux's prose style and method of presentation, which to his admirers are something of a puzzle as well as something of a trial. These books are absorbing but fatiguing. They are, for example, full of unexplained allusions to works of which no reader but an expert is ever at all likely to have heard. It is true that one may come, in a page or two, on a picture of the work alluded to, with a caption that explains what and where it is; but one may otherwise be left groping. "Several stylistic devices," says Mr. Righter, "are of special importance, two of them consistent features of Malraux's method of comparison: the *startling connection* and the *mysterious ellipsis*. The former is designed to force the mind into movement, to connect the familiar with the remote, the West with the East, the primitive with the sophisticated, and all with the modern. The latter is a simple suppression of the steps by which such connections might be shown, a relying on the imaginative impact of suggestion, rather than the careful tracing of the relation of one detail to another. And as a complement to these two one should probably add the *unspoken implication,* the leaving of a series of suggestions to complete itself, once the imaginative train of reflection is under way." *La Méta-morphose des Dieux* comes perhaps a little closer to fluency than the previous volumes in the series; yet its movement is still much obstructed. Malraux proceeds chronologically, conducting us, age by age, from one phase of Christian art to the next; but this progress is not a straight path. The guide must skip all over Europe from one cathedral to another, and from these to illuminated Psalters and Books of Hours and the works of art in palaces and mansions, and this involves an adroit play of mind which must dart here and there in both space and time to show analogies and point up contrasts. This of necessity rather complicates the exposition; but he seems needlessly to complicate it further by continually going back, with a conjuror's air of discovery, over ground he has already travelled. Instead of establishing one modulation and then moving on to another, he will return to the same idea, adducing further examples and dramatizing them in fresh metaphors.

I do not agree with Mr. Righter, when he says that the effect of Malraux's method in dealing with works of art is "somehow subtly" to "dehumanize" them, that "in the Imaginary Museum, conquests have become collector's items"; that Malraux has isolated himself in a world which, although rhetorical, is abstracted from the world that has produced the art. After all, these are human artifacts and, though Malraux collects and recombines, he does not detach them from their historical contexts. It is precisely with their historical significance as answers to the problems of the human situation that Malraux is chiefly concerned. Nor do I agree with the following passage. "Yet if the act of expression is the act of heroism, this has a curious corollary. Professor [Harry] Levin has remarked that 'André Malraux . . . has been journeying across the world, searching for adventures large enough to exalt the modern intellectual into a tragic hero.' 'Intellectual', not 'artist.' It is precisely the intellectual's personal tragedy that he does query where he cannot answer, discover where he cannot explain, and perceive where he cannot act. The artist stands for him in the world of forms as a substitute creator, inventing images of those perplexities and harmonies, torments and delights that make up his situation. Yet it is inevitably a substitution, and the tragedy of Malraux is in the eternal incapacity of such a substitution to attain the real. True, in Nietzsche's maxim the artist rejects and defies reality. But this in effect commits him to the tragic view. And both as a maker and observer Malraux seems, more than the artists he describes, to be a rhetorical Sisyphus, frenziedly pushing the works of mankind to an unattainable height where they would be more than the works of mankind. Whatever sort of tragic heroism is appropriate to the modern intellectual, the tragedy of Malraux is the tragedy of the will."

I shall return to this point in a moment; but I must first explain that Mr. Righter seems to share with me the premonition that Malraux is approaching a precipice: "Malraux has set out his visual testimony to reassure himself that man is not dead, that his culture has a continuity, and that his presence in the universe is a matter of consequence. But how far does the self-imposed isolation of the testimony conflict with the intended conclusion, and show us instead something abstract and bloodless, with a lack of conviction in its own presence concealed by feverish rhetoric? Cut off by conditions of their own establishment, may not those conquests by means of forms, those arraignments of the world order by the artist's vision, be themselves bypassed by the course of events, and become nothing more than the exotic possession of another sort of academy, a curious anachronism cultivated by a precious minority, ignored and swallowed up in a mass culture?" Yes, and what about "pop art" and "op art" as expressions of human independence? Can the works of Braque, for example, whose recent death Malraux, as Minister of Culture, has made a point of signalizing, stand up to this mass culture? If not, how much less those of Pollock, not to mention Pollock's successors? The finest art, one assumes, must remain: we shall continue to visit museums and buy prints of the pictures in them. Yet the precipice is there, nonetheless; and surely André Malraux must look for salvation from some other source than from the products of modern painting. Yet even in confining himself to the history of an art not his own, he shines as a writer by his own example, which to me is more inspiring than that of such a painter as Braque. I differ from Mr. Righter in his insistence that Malraux here is attempting, with tragic failure, to exalt *the intellectual* by identifying himself with *the artist*. Is not Malraux himself an artist, who, whether working in terms of the history of art or of fiction based on current history, has, by force of imagination, been recreating for us our world?

MARIO PRAZ:
THE ROMANTIC AGONY

SIGNOR MARIO PRAZ is a professor of English literature at the University of Rome, who was previously for ten years a professor of Italian literature in England. He published in 1925 an interesting study of Crashaw and Donne, in which he analyzed the morbid blending, characteristic of the seventeenth century, of erotic with religious imagery, and he has recently brought out two volumes of *Cronache Letterarie Anglosassoni,* a collection of his occasional articles on English and American subjects, which shows an astonishing grasp not only of the England that he knows at first hand but also of the literature of the United States, a country he has never visited. In the meantime, in 1930, he published a remarkable work in the field of comparative literature called *La Carne, la Morte e il Diavolo nella Letteratura Romantica,* which was later brought out in an English translation under the title *The Romantic Agony.* This book is by way of becoming a classic, and two new editions in Italy have now been followed by a reprint of the translation. This latter is in some respects unsatisfactory, for, except for a frontispiece, it does not have the illustrations of the splendid Italian editions, reproductions of paintings and photographs chosen brilliantly by Signor Praz as a sort of chamber of horrors of the mythology of the Romantic Movement; and the new material that the author has

added to the successive Italian reprints has here, for the
purpose of avoiding new plates, been awkwardly tacked
on at the end instead of appearing where it belongs in the
text. A new chapter—of considerable interest to students
of Italian literature but not strictly relevant to the Romantic Agony—on the literary borrowings of D'Annunzio
has not been included at all. Yet the translation by Angus
Davidson—no doubt closely supervised by Signor Praz—
is a sound and distinguished rendering of a book which,
with its idiomatic style and its discussions of exotic
imagery, could not have been easy to handle. We are
fortunate in having in English so accurate and so readable
a version of *La Carne, la Morte e il Diavolo,* which, in its
field of comparative literature, is one of the most truly
original as well as one of the most fascinating works of
our time.

The subject of *The Romantic Agony* is the development from the eighteenth century on, largely under the
influence of the Marquis de Sade, of a literary tradition
of erotic cruelty, hysterical enjoyment of horror and perverse admiration for crime. In the first chapter, called
The Beauty of the Medusa, Signor Praz deals with a
typical Romantic conception—"beauty tainted with pain,
corruption, and death"—which hypnotized the nineteenth-century poets, troubling the mind of Shelley and
settling down inexpugnably on Baudelaire. In the second
chapter, he traces the "metamorphoses of Satan" and
shows how the medieval Devil, a bristling and repulsive
goblin, was transformed into the tragic rebel (invented,
says Signor Praz, not, as we have assumed, by Milton but
by the Italian poet Marino, whom Milton is known to
have read), and eventually, by way of the Gothic novel,
gave way to the Byronic hero, destructive, defiant and
half diabolic, but unmistakably a fallen angel. The chap-

ter called *The Shadow of the Divine Marquis* shows the pervasive though sometimes underground stimulus of Sade to writers as varied as Choderlos de Laclos of *Les Liaisons Dangereuses,* the Shelley of *The Cenci,* Baudelaire and the early Flaubert, and the presence of similar sadistic themes in such writers as Richardson, Diderot, Chateaubriand and Poe. The fourth chapter, *La Belle Dame sans Merci,* investigates the curious transposition—here studied for the first time, so far as I know—by which the tortured and torturing hero-villain of the early nineteenth century was exchanged for an implacable *"femme fatale,"* who, with the difference that she is not usually troubled by feelings of remorse or despair, takes over the destructive role. This is Mérimée's Carmen, Flaubert's Salammbô, Gautier's Cleopatra, Walter Pater's Mona Lisa, Oscar Wilde's Sphinx—the heartless coquette, the cold beauty, the vampire, the cruel queen. Here Swinburne is discussed at length. An enthusiastic admirer of Sade, he consistently celebrated in many forms—from Faustine to Mary Stuart—the imperious, pitiless woman.

In the final chapter, *Byzantium,* the author presents this strange feminine ideal, as well as the other Romantic myths, under the later "Decadent" aspect that they wore at the end of the century. Salome, first exploited by Heine and later a favorite of Flaubert, of Gustave Moreau, of Huysmans, of Laforgue, of Mallarmé, of Wilde, is the most perverse and deadly embodiment of La Belle Dame sans Merci. "We have travelled far," says Mario Praz, "from Delacroix's Sardanapalus, who contemplates with a satisfied air the hecatomb of lovely slave girls: this [the gallery of Moreau's paintings] is a massacre of youths who burn for a kiss from cruel Helen, the majestic Fatal Woman." As the women become more formidable, the men become more drooping and feminine. The sexes, by the end of the century, are blending and have there-

fore ceased to be fertile, but they continue to run true to
the sadistic tradition of tormenting and tantalizing one
another. The impulse to incest—a recurrent theme
through the whole Romantic Movement—which worked
such havoc in its early phase with the heroes of Chateaubriand and Byron, and which figured as one form of their
challenge to conventional law and morals, has now itself
become an insipid convention of the general mood of
impotence. No longer can consanguinity, because of the
taboo against it, be exploited as an incitement to passion;
through substituting a milder relationship for the ordinary sexual one, it has rather become a means of eliminat-
ing passion. You have now Barbey d'Aurevilly, Villiers de
l'Isle-Adam, the Goncourts, Rachilde, Wilde, Beardsley,
Gourmont, Schwob, Barrès, Gide. This decadence was
mainly French. Since its perversities had been largely
cerebral, the fantasies of inhibited men who led quite
unadventurous lives (Sade himself had spent over twenty
years in prisons and insane asylums), it did not have wide
success in Italy, where it was much more natural for
people to act out their desire or violence. Yet from the
"Italia barbara" of the Abruzzi was to spring, Signor Praz
tells us, "the most monumental figure of the Decadent
Movement": D'Annunzio, who greedily devoured, who
unashamedly plundered French and English late Romantic literature, good, bad and indifferent, and who managed to be "a barbarian and at the same time a Decadent,"
with nothing in him of that "temperate zone which, in
the present period of culture, is labelled 'humanity,'" so
that all the now familiar themes—incest, cruelty, the
Black Mass, the disappointing man, the magistral
woman—are reorchestrated in D'Annunzio's work with a
kind of blaring brilliance. But he, too, is an Italian, who
can live his dream, and he is to show himself, says Signor

Praz, in his flying and in his capture of Fiume, the sole
Decadent poet who is capable of becoming a war hero.

Signor Praz explains in his foreword that he has limited
himself in *The Romantic Agony* to writing a chapter of
aesthetic history. He has tried to refrain from critical
judgments. He has often treated second-rate or fourth-rate
figures on the same scale as first-rate ones, and he has
thus—like a fisherman who has raised to the surface a full
net of the fish that are running—brought to light a queer
flapping, squirming mass of helpless but slippery human
dreams that include some disconcerting freaks and suggest
some unexpected derivations. But, except for this kind of
relationship, he is not interested in their natural history
and does not make any effort to account for them in terms
of their time or their habitat beyond characterizing their
century, at the end of his book, as one "which made use
of every kind of exoticism and eclecticism to distract the
restlessness of its exasperated senses and to make up for
its lack of either a profound faith or an authentic style."
In dealing with the criticisms of Croce in a review of the
first edition, he declares that there is no occasion for his
attempting anything more than this. Other writers, he
says, have amply explained how Romanticism and the
"Art for Art's sake" movement represented the attempts
of a Europe that had lost its old system of Church and
State, based on divine authority, to arrive at a new code
of conduct based on the human individual. His aim has
been merely to exhibit one cluster of myths and symbols,
and to show how it proliferated.

This feat Signor Praz has accomplished, and it has
involved him in an unwelcome revelation, in which, I
believe, is to be found the reason for the inept and even
spiteful criticisms that his book has sometimes provoked.
The conventional student of literature had shuddered

away from a demonstration that the doctrine and example of the Marquis de Sade had figured as an influence of the first importance in the literature of the nineteenth century. Though Sainte-Beuve said in 1843 that Byron and Sade were unquestionably "the two greatest inspirers of our moderns—the one advertized and visible, the other clandestine—though not too much so," no scholar, so far as I know, has cared to go into this, and the first reaction of a man like Croce is to protest that Signor Praz has ignored all the generous emotions, the noble libertarian ideals, that were also given expression by the Romantic Movement. But all this is already a commonplace of intellectual history. It has taken Signor Praz to get the Marquis squarely on the map: to show that Baudelaire, Flaubert and Swinburne invoked him with high admiration, and that a number of more unlikely people either evidently, like Shelley, got something from his ogres or, like Richardson and Monk Lewis, were in the habit of dealing with persecuted maidens in a way that was almost as equivocal as that of Sade in his first version of *Justine*, in which he professed to be castigating vice by exposing the castigation of innocence. Signor Praz, so immensely well-read, is, though a professor, essentially unacademic in the ordinary sense of the word, and he is quite free from the Italian tendency—which is likely to seem so antiquated to an Anglo-Saxon—to spin long treatises on literary matters in terms of philosophic conceptions. Signor Praz always gets down to brass tacks; he piles up for you a load of evidence. He has a touch of the morose and the truculent, but also a strong common sense that usually holds in check a certain eagerness to run down his quarry. Not inclined to the rhapsodies of Italian rhetoric, he has a casual curt vein of humor, of which a good example is his use of a passage from the memoirs of a contemporary French actress to show the relative tepidity in practice of some of those mid-century writers, like Gautier, whose work was ostentatiously erotic. Of Paul de Saint Victor, she writes, *"Un rien lui suffisait. Si dans la loge, au théâtre, je me laissais déchausser et je lui abandonnais, durant la représentation, un pied dans sa main, il était au trentesixième ciel."* "Note," Signor Praz adds, "that Paul de Saint Victor went to the theater in the capacity of dramatic critic."

Not, of course, that the cult of the Marquis de Sade has otherwise been lately neglected. He has been having a mad vogue in Europe and is constantly written about. But he interests the French today from a political, a psychological or even a religious point of view rather than from an aesthetic one. This recent preoccupation with Sade is a curious and significant phenomenon, which I shall deal with in a later article.

October 11, 1952

THE VOGUE OF THE MARQUIS DE SADE*

THE INTEREST IN THE MARQUIS DE SADE has been steadily increasing in Europe ever since 1909, when Guillaume Apollinaire published a volume of selections from his work and thus brought him into general currency. Though his influence on the Romantic movement had undoubtedly been considerable, it remained largely unacknowledged, as his books were not openly published and rather surreptitiously read. But the Dadaists, at the end of the First World War, delighted in him as a blaster of inhibitions, and broke down the inhibition against mentioning his name; and the Surrealists inherited him from them and have put him among their prophets. The late war, for reasons I shall discuss in a moment, has brought him again to the fore of the French literary consciousness, and so much has been recently written about him that the subject is in danger of becoming a bore, and he is sometimes, I understand, referred to in Paris as the Marquis de Fade. The most important authority on Sade has been a writer named Maurice Heine, a former Communist of a very ancient vintage, since he was eliminated, in 1923, from the staff of the Communist *Humanité,* when he opposed the suppression of free discussion in the coun-

---

* This essay and the one which follows overlap at certain points, but they are written from different points of view, and the second is based on much new material not available when the first was published.

cils of the Party. Heine's interest in the queer Marquis was evidently partly inspired by this passionate libertarianism, for the Marquis, in his dubious way, was a fierce libertarian, too. Heine virtually devoted the rest of his life to running down and publishing Sade's work and vindicating his reputation. He is said to have reduced himself to penury in buying up Sade's manuscripts. But he did not, unfortunately, live to complete the biography he had undertaken. Some drafts for it and his scattered papers on the subject have, however, been collected in a volume, under the title *Le Marquis de Sade,* by his friend M. Gilbert Lely, who is carrying on the torch and has himself published a volume of selections, *D.A.F. de Sade.* There have been two books on Sade in English, the more recent (1934)—*The Marquis de Sade: A Short Account of His Life and Work*—by that intrepid anthropologist Mr. Geoffrey Gorer, who has made a contribution to the subject by disengaging from Sade's partly pornographic novels his philosophical, religious, political and social ideas.

All three of these books are written with the bias of the Sade cult. The Marquis constitutes, unquestionably, one of the hardest cases to handle in the whole history of literature. He began writing novels to pass the time during his almost thirteen years of imprisonment in Vincennes and the Bastille, and some of them run to Richardsonian length. (His dates are 1740–1814.) They are unique and most uncomfortable productions, which alternate between descriptions of orgies on an impossible multiple scale, which may horrify the reader at first but which soon become routine and ridiculous, and vehement disquisitions, in the vein of the eighteenth-century *philosophe,* which are mostly intended to justify them. The Marquis has, thus, against him that he is often repulsive and often dull, and often both at the same time. He has usually hitherto been ignored by the French in their histories of their literature, and he is not even mentioned by Saintsbury in his work on the French novel.

But the Marquis does have his importance, and to outlaw him thus is unjust—especially on the part of critics who devote considerable space to such a writer as Rétif de la Bretonne, who, if somewhat less improper than Sade, has been also less influential. This unfairness is perceived by the champions of Sade, and they distort the picture the other way in their fanatical attempts to right it. The special difficulty that Sade presents to any-one who tries to arrive at a serious estimate of him is that he was neither quite mad nor quite sane. The perplexed head doctor of Charenton, the insane asylum in which the Marquis was confined during the last eleven years of his life, seems to have put the situation correctly when he explained, *"Cet homme n'est point aliéné. Son seul délire est celui du vice."* The Marquis was a man of strong intellect and a certain amount of literary ability, who in prison had had leisure for enormous reading but who was also what is called nowadays a compulsive neurotic of a violent and incurable kind. To the defense of his impulse to cruelty he brought an inflexible will and a contemptu-ous obstinate pride that moved the Romantics to admira-tion and that still commands a certain respect. But this impulse was a lifelong obsession that gets in the way of his success as both a literary artist and a thinker. Mario Praz has firmly made this point and, as a result, has been treated rather sniffishly by both Heine and Mr. Gorer.

But both Heine and Mr. Gorer—as well as M. Lely—have been betrayed into howling absurdities by their eagerness to explain this obsession away. Their urbane attempts to gloss over the horrid chronicle of Sade's aberrations and the madly inappropriate interpretations that they sometimes try to put on his work have at moments reached the point of high comedy. M. Lely writes tender little poems to Sade and prints on the cover of his book the strange slogan *"Tout ce que signe Sade est amour."* Mr. Gorer tries to give the impression that the Marquis was a sober and luminous thinker, with the good of humanity at heart, in whose mouth butter wouldn't melt. You would never find out from Mr. Gorer's book the real tenor of his subject's life nor suspect the main content of his work. "Although the sexual element," says Mr. Gorer, "is present" in the first published text of *Justine* (a triumph of understatement), it cannot be "considered obscene"—a remark that can be given meaning only if we assume that obscenity must always for Mr. Gorer involve the use of "dirty" words, which, it is true, hardly make their appearance till the rewritten second version. When he comes to explain away the various exploits of Sade that made him an object of concern to the police and nearly cost him his life, Mr. Gorer becomes hilarious if one reads him after examining the courtroom records and the memoranda of the Paris police, which Maurice Heine himself has published. Mr. Gorer represents Sade as a courteous and considerate gentleman—one gets a distinct impression that he has been to an English public school*—persecuted by vulgar harlots. Yet it is plain from these documents and others that the Marquis had for years done his best to enact the elaborate and sinister debauches which

---

* Mr. Gorer was able to score in a protest to the periodical in which this piece first appeared, by writing: "As far as the crack about English public schools is concerned, I spent some years in one of these institutions; it wouldn't surprise me a bit if Sade had been there."

he afterwards described in his novels. In that great age of *"libertinage,"* a good deal must have been permitted to a noble with powerful connections like Sade; still, Sade was always getting into trouble in different places and with different people, and always for the same kind of offense. The various frightened girls who ran to the police about him, declaring that he had tried to poison them or beaten them or tortured them or threatened to kill them, the father who tried to shoot him, had certainly not picked up from his novels the bizarre and deleterious ideas that they accused him of trying to carry out, for these books had not yet been written; and, on the other hand, the persistent recurrence in the fiction he eventually produced of practices exactly similar to those with which he had been charged surely demonstrates a strong predilection. It comes to seem, then, a masterpiece of euphemism when we find Mr. Gorer writing of the episode at Marseille, for which Sade was condemned to death, that the Marquis was "almost certainly exploring conscientiously and practically all possible extensions of sensual pleasure." Yet Mr. Gorer is only improving on a tenet of the Sadist faith established by Maurice Heine: that the allegedly poisoned bonbons offered by Sade on this occasion to some prostitutes, one of whom, the only one who ate them, was at once seized with agonizing cramps, were, in reality, nothing worse than aphrodisiacs. In the literature of the Sade cult, this case is always referred to as *"l'affaire des bonbons cantharidés."* But there is not a shred of evidence for assuming that they were not intended, if not to kill the girls, at least to have painful results, and the behavior of Sade himself, as reported by one of the girls, seems decidedly to show that they were. Why should a dose of cantharides produce convulsive cramps? We know that the heroes of Sade's novels never want to increase their partners' pleasure but always to make them suffer, and that poisoning is one of their specialties.*

No: one cannot blame Sade's family for locking him up. His wife had stood by him through years of this. He had at one time maintained in his Provençal château a harem of both sexes, his reckless experiments with whom became so alarming and troublesome that it was surely not unnatural for the Marquise's mother—not able to avail herself of the resources of modern psychiatry—to have him put away in Vincennes. The defenders of Sade have diverted attention from the propriety of this step by raising the issue of the quite different action of Napoleon, at a later date, in consigning the Marquis to an asylum. This latter was merely an incident of Napoleon's policy of censorship. The real objection to leaving him at large—though he was denounced as an enemy of morals—was that, just having published a scurrilous book about Napoleon and Josephine, he was regarded as a subversive force.†

---

* Mr. Gorer, in 1953, got out a new edition of his book under the title *The Life and Ideas of the Marquis de Sade*. He has added two new chapters, one of them biographical, for which he has had the advantage of new materials but in which he persists, in the teeth of the evidence, in attempting to minimize Sade's misdemeanors; and the other—more valuable, it seems to me—in which he makes what, so far as I know, is a pioneer effort to account psychologically for Sade.

† Since this was written, M. Lely, in his *Vie du Marquis de Sade,* has come to the conclusion that this libel, *Zoloé et ses deux acolytes,* was not written by Sade and had nothing to do with his arrest. It is not mentioned in the papers that deal with this, which record that the necessity for suppressing Sade is due to its having been announced that he is about to follow *Justine* with "un ouvrage plus affreux encore," *Juliette.* The official who wrote this was not aware that *Juliette* had already been published in the ten volumes of which the main title was *La Nouvelle Justine.* M. Lely points out quite rightly that *Zoloé* is an extremely banal work which does not at all sound like Sade.

In the meantime, the Revolution had freed him from the Bastille. His wife would never see him again, but his sons seem to have done what they could for him. He found a mistress whom he appears to have been fond of and who was certainly loyal to him—he was evidently attractive to women—when he got into trouble again. He worked for the Revolution, and he actually served for a time as a judge on one of its tribunals, in which role— doubtless much to their astonishment—he got his mother-in-law and father-in-law off when, in one of the most piquant of confrontations, they happened to be brought before him.* He exercised his influence so often in favor of sparing the accused that the bloodthirsty officials of the Terror began to suspect his revolutionary zeal and had him locked up again for the crime of "moderantism." His behavior had, however, been perfectly consistent. Having had his own head in jeopardy at the time of the Marseille affair, he had long opposed capital punishment on the ground that, since every crime was the result of a "natural" impulse, it was unjust to kill people for committing them. He was now confined in a prison where the guillotine was set up under the windows and where, he writes in a letter, "we buried eighteen hundred in thirty-five days, a third of them from our unfortunate house." His own turn eventually came, and he was saved from

---

* This is another of the legends about Sade to which the researches of Lely have given a somewhat different aspect. The couple were not apparently "brought before him." They were simply on a list of suggested undesirables, and Sade made no comment on them when he could easily have sent them to the guillotine—which may have been due not merely to his foregoing such a revenge on principle but also to a reluctance to refer to them and perhaps set off some train of thought which would lead to the compromising discovery of Sade's own relationship to them.

being beheaded only by the fall of Robespierre the night before his execution was scheduled. Did this frighten the Marquis or disgust him with blood? On the contrary, it probably afforded him a certain satisfaction in confirming his so often declared belief that the destructive lust of humanity represents our essential nature. He is funny in his saturnine way about the moral pretensions of the Revolution: "It is amusing that the Jacobins in the French Revolution should have wished to destroy the altars of a God who talked exactly their language, and even more extraordinary that those who detest and wish to destroy the Jacobins should do so in the name of a God who talks the same language as the Jacobins. If this is not the *ne plus ultra* of human absurdity, I should like to know what is." In a letter from the Bastille, after defending his materialistic philosophy, he ends with the following declaration: "Well, there's a letter that's calculated to prolong my captivity, isn't it? You can tell those prolongers from me that their prolongation is completely futile. They could leave me here ten years and they'd take me out no better, believe me, than I was when I went in. Either kill me or accept me as I am, for Devil take me if ever I change—I've told you that the beast's too old—there's no hope for him any more—the most decent and candid and delicate of men, the tenderest and most indulgent idolater of my children, for whose happiness I'd go through fire, scrupulous to the last degree about not wanting to corrupt their morals or mess up their minds or make them in any respect adopt my ideas, adoring my relatives (my own, I mean)—any friends I still have left, and above all my wife, whom I only want to see happy, and to whom I very much wish to make up for my many youthful indiscretions—because it's true that *one's own wife should not be exposed to that*—I felt this and told her so more than six months before I came here; she is my witness. Those are my virtues—as for my vices—unrestrainable rages—an extreme tendency in everything to lose control of myself, a disordered imagination in sexual matters such as has never been known in this world, an atheist to the point of fanaticism—in two words, there I am, and so once again kill me or take me like that, because I shall never change."

But nobody wants to take him. The conventional people won't touch him, and his defenders, as I say, will not face him. They like to repeat Apollinaire's statement that their hero was "the freest mind that ever existed," though he was certainly one of the most constrained. His peculiar tastes had instigated him to boldness in some directions, but he could never get away from his manias and had to make all his work and his thought eternally revolve around them. Even his pamphlet on the Revolution—anonymously reprinted, it is curious to note, at the time of the Revolution of 1848—turns out to be leading us up to the usual self-justification. One sometimes feels a certain disingenuousness in the attempts of these defenders to whitewash him. They seem to be excited by his atrocities at the same time that they are trying to tell us that Sade was the most charming of men and wouldn't have hurt a fly. M. Lely, for example, is decidedly sentimental in a vein that would have made Sade bellow. The Sadists have even looked up and reverently photographed—as if it were Buddha's Bo Tree—the sordid old iron staircase to the third floor of the house in Marseille where the attempt to poison the prostitutes took place. Among these enthusiasts a certain soft and sly tone prevails. It is characteristic of the cult of Sade that a friend of Heine, M. Georges Bataille, quoted by M. Lely, should refer to Heine as *"ce personnage séduisant,"* assuring us that he was "one of the gentlest and best bred men I have ever known," but remark a little further on that, one day at a political meeting, he "produced a revolver, fired at random and slightly wounded his wife in the arm."

So let us not try to disguise the congenital, the compulsive and inveterate sadism of the life and works of the Marquis de Sade. What, then, is he worth to the world? More than you might expect. His difficulties with his own aberrations made him interested in those of other people, and he brought to this whole so long outlawed subject a certain scientific point of view. He always likes to document himself, and he will tell you in a note that, fantastic though some hair-raising episode may sound, it is based on an actual case that recently came to light in a certain provincial city. He compiled—in *Les 120 Journées de Sodome*—the first systematic catalogue of sexual abnormalities, to the number of six hundred, for he discriminated many nuances; he anticipated Freud in perceiving that sexual constitution was determined at an early age and that a sexual element was present in all family relationships; and he had also the anthropological approach, for he was constantly invoking travel books to show that there is no sort of practice that is not somewhere the accepted thing. He was something of a scientist, something of a philosopher, something of a man of letters, and—if you can stand him at all—he is not without interest in any of these roles. He has even at moments some merit as a writer. Sade's cardinal defect as a novelist was his infantile inability to transpose his erotic fantasies into terms of the real world. The horrors that are perpetrated by his characters are made to take place in a kind of void: they rarely have any of the consequences that they would have in actual life, and that they did, to his sorrow, for Sade himself. Yet it seems to be true, as Heine suggests, that *Les 120 Journées de Sodome* had

beaten all the Gothic novels hollow before most of them
had been written*; and it is true, as M. Lely claims, that
some of its hideous characters—the financier, the bishop,
the duke and the judge, who represent the corruption of
the old regime (Sade was a sharp observer of abnormal
and vicious types)—show a power akin to Balzac's. But
what is most striking about Sade is that, wordy and repetitious, implausible and disgusting though he is, he gives
expression to human malignance in a characteristically
extreme and abstract eighteenth-century way that makes
it forever impossible not to recognize the part it plays in
all fields of human activity.

With the Surrealists and in some other quarters, the
appeal of the horrific Marquis has been that of an up-
setter of conventions and a purveyor of violent thrills. But
there have been other reasons lately for the interest in
Sade and for the curious forms it has sometimes taken. In
Europe, since the Second World War, the professional
intellectual has found himself subjected to unaccustomed
pressures which frighten him: he has had to try in some
way to accommodate—morally, intellectually—in the
world that has been conceived by the ordinary educated
man, the murderous devices for large-scale murder, for
suffocating, burning or blowing up one's enemies, that
the professedly Christian countries have lately been going
in for as heartily as the Odin-worshipping Nazis, the
Emperor-worshipping Japanese or the officially atheist
Russians; and here is a writer, the Marquis de Sade, of
whom one knows that he always insisted that such things
were perfectly normal and who tried to reason about
them. The atrocities he loves to describe do not today
seem so outrageous as they did before. Even writing in

---

* But there is no romantic poetry in Sade and no element of
the supernatural.

1934, Mr. Gorer was able to say truly that "the century and a half which have passed since [the writing of *Justine* and *Juliette*] have more than justified [Sade's] gloomiest prognostications." M. Albert Camus, in a chapter on Sade in his recent *L'Homme Révolté,* points out that Sade's most sickening imaginations are now seen to be well on the conservative side. And there is also the disposition to find the Marquis himself not so bad as he used to be thought. Certain writers have attempted to demonstrate that this man almost all of whose work is a blasphemy was fundamentally or potentially religious, arguing that the recognition of evil leads the way to the love of God and that Sade's lifelong quarrel with the Deity is a proof that he believed in His existence. The result of consulting the work of a professional diabolic to find some way of coming to terms with the forces of destruction that threaten one is, thus, to be moved to attempt to tailor for this diabolic an aspect more acceptable and "human"—that is to say, less psychopathic.*
The Marquis accepted these forces; he had evolved a code of behavior, a proposed set of legislative reforms, a whole system of philosophy based on them. May he not, then, have made some sense? May he not have been an excellent, if embittered, man, who desired to save his own soul, to procure the welfare of the human race?

Now, the Marquis did not make sense; he did not love the human race. But he does have his definite importance in the history of Western thought, and there is a gap if we leave him out. Signor Praz has filled up this gap in the domain of imaginative literature, and he has indicated the role that Sade plays in the politico-philosophical field. In this latter, the Marquis appears as the opposite pole to Rousseau, and if we do not allow him his place, the

---

* Sade, actually, was not a Satanist. He is not preoccupied with the Devil.

picture remains incomplete. To the rebellious but ingenuous mind of Rousseau, it came as a revelation that men
were "naturally" good and that it was only institutions
that had led them astray. To Sade, also nonconformist,
also biassed by abnormality, it seemed obvious that our
crimes and perversions were prompted by tendencies that
we had in common with all the rest of "Nature," and that
the error of institutions was their effort to censor these
tendencies. The logic of Sade, of course, reduces the
argument from Nature to absurdity, but then so does the
logic of Rousseau. We want to put to them both the same
question: Are not our moral and legal codes also the
products of natural instincts? But it was difficult still in
that age to conceive of man as an animal with certain
superior faculties, in the light of which he tries to discipline his so diverse natural instincts for purposes he
strongly feels but is unable to formulate definitively (as
they tried to do with everything in the eighteenth century) since he never can see to the end of them; and in
the meantime the Rousseauist doctrine was in need of a
correction, a contradiction, that it got with a vengeance in
Sade. The utopians of the eighteenth century were eventually to have their complement in the cynical practicality
of Napoleon; and in the interval the two conceptions had
been hopelessly, disastrously, mingled in the sadistic
idealists of the Terror. The Russian Marxists of our own
century have arrived at an even more insidious confusion
of the ideal of human improvement with a gospel of
internecine strife; and the Marquis de Sade still stands as
a reminder that the lust for cruelty, the appetite for
destruction, are powerful motivations that must be recognized for what they are.

But, except for the Surrealist, the connoisseur of horrors, the relisher of sensations for their own sake, it is
difficult to see how Sade can meet any other need. He

tends only toward annihilation. Though he justifies himself by appealing to Nature, he also turns against Nature for having made him what he is: "Is it a being so contemptible, so odious as this that has given me life for no other purpose than to make me take pleasure in what injures my kind?" Nor does he shrink from destroying himself, for, like his characters, he is what is called today masochistic as well as what is called sadistic. He furiously announces again and again that he would like to wipe out the human race, to pulverize the universe: "It is she [Nature] that I desire to outrage. I should like to spoil her plans, to block her advance, to halt the course of the stars, to throw down the globes that float in space—to destroy everything that serves her, to protect everything that harms her, to cultivate everything that irritates her—in a word, to insult all her works." One of Sade's most extraordinary scenes is that in *La Nouvelle Justine* in which the misanthropic chemist encountered on Etna explains that he has mastered a method for producing artificial eruptions, and expresses a strong desire to devastate the whole of Sicily. He will be watching from a mountain, he says, and copulating with the goats. He will not even have to depend on another human being for the pleasure of indulging his lust. The last interest that ties him to others will then have been repudiated. Now, grotesque though this scene may sound, it is quite close to recent states of mind. It is probable that the fascination at present exerted by Sade is due partly to the vertiginous excitement of a destructiveness that is ultimately self-destructive. One had the impression at moments, during the bombings of the last war, that people derived satisfaction from a reckless letting-go of power which might also annihilate the wielder of power. And Adolf Hitler, who presided over the holocaust, had something of Sade's insane chemist. He lived in such alienation from the ordinary natural instincts that he was probably not up to a goat, and he was thinking of himself, in any case, as a character in a Wagner opera; but he had certainly set off Etna when he burned himself up in the bunker. The mad exhilaration in power, the contempt for human life had been there, and he had led many others to share it—men who, unlike himself, might equally well have been more or less amiably associating with their fellows instead of wiping out one another's cities.

To encourage this impulse is the ultimate blasphemy—far more terrible than the Voltairean jeering at theology or the Byronic defiance of law—and it is Sade's queer unique distinction to have declared it with the ultimate audacity.

In Sade's will, one of the most effective things he wrote, he invokes complete oblivion. After explaining that he wants to be buried in a particular copse on his country estate and that there is not to be "a ceremony of any sort," he lays down these specific directions: "As soon as the grave has been filled, the place is to be sown with acorns, in order that thereafter, the earth of the aforesaid grave being overgrown and the copse grown up as it was before, the traces of my tomb may disappear from the face of the earth, as I flatter myself that my memory will be erased from the mind of men, except for the few who have been kind enough to love me till my last moment and of whom I shall carry to the grave a very pleasant recollection." But we have not been able to forget him. We have never been able to shake him off, because we know that he is not wholly mad, not wholly out of touch with reality—that, nauseous and "hipped" though he is, he is harping on an impulse which he has in common with many other human beings who seem to be sane. But let us hope that his moment is passing. That his prestige as a contemporary prophet of human self-immolation to the forces that humanity generates, as well as his old use as a bogy to horrify the bourgeoisie, may already now be declining is suggested by two excellent studies which have been published since 1951: the chapter about Sade in Camus's new book mentioned above, and the long paper by Mlle Simone de Beauvoir (*Faut-il Brûler Sade?*) in the December, 1951, and January, 1952, numbers of Jean-Paul Sartre's magazine, *Les Temps Modernes* (this last perhaps the very best thing that has yet been written on the subject)—in which his ideas are coolly criticized and the man himself brought into the clinic as a special psychological case. They seem to make a new era in the study of Sade.

October 18, 1952

THE DOCUMENTS ON THE
MARQUIS DE SADE

THE WORK OF GILBERT LELY on the Marquis de Sade has gone forward, since my previous piece was written, to an extent that makes it desirable to supplement the above account as well as to correct in footnotes some of the statements in the earlier essay. The two large volumes of M. Lely's *Vie du Marquis de Sade* appeared in 1952 and 1957; and three volumes of Sade's correspondence, all edited by Lely and Georges Dumas (with the announcement of a fourth) have now been published: *L'Aigle, Mademoiselle . . .* in 1949, *Le Carillon de Vincennes* in 1953, and *Monsieur le 6* in 1954. All these are the results of the researches of Lely, building on those of Maurice Heine, who died before his work on Sade was finished, and of the discovery in 1948 of hitherto unexamined papers from the archives of the Sade family. These papers have been released by the present Marquis, Xavier de Sade, who, as an officer in the last war, was captured and tortured by the Germans and so has had some first-hand experience of that side of human nature which the former marquis had emphasized. He is said to take an interest in his ancestor, who seems otherwise to have been an embarrassment to the rather distinguished family to which he belonged. The volumes of Sade's correspondence, though copiously edited, are very unsatisfactory to work with. Each contains only a small number of letters,

and they are all from more or less the same period, that of
Sade's long imprisonment, with no overall arrangement. I
cannot understand why the scholarly Lely should have
allowed them to be published in this form. What is
needed is a *Correspondance Générale,* which would include the group of letters gathered from other sources and
published in 1929, under the editorship of Paul Bourdin,
in the *Correspondance inédite du marquis de Sade, de ses
proches et de ses familiers.* The biography, too, has its
shortcomings. The second volume, for some peculiar
reason, has only an index of the authors mentioned, and
the first volume has no index at all. It is sometimes inconsistent with the volumes of letters because the author
has in certain connections been obliged to revise his
earlier opinions on the basis of better information, and he
has sometimes found himself forced simply to repeat certain statements of Maurice Heine without knowing what
his sources were. I do not know whether Paul Bourdin,
too, is dead, but it is evident that M. Lely is for some
reason unable to consult with him. Lely's account is occasionally marred by those curious *mignardises* and little
outbreaks of lyric sentimentality—mostly reprinted from
the author's earlier writings—which have always been
characteristic of his work on Sade. Yet this biography
seems otherwise a sound piece of work. Though in one or
two cases, the biographer puts some witnesses out of
court, on the ground of overwhelming prejudice, and
even refuses to quote them, M. Lely insists that it is no
part of his purpose to try to "rehabilitate" Sade, and his
chronicle—day by day, so far as the dates are available—
is so scrupulously documented from court, hospital and
prison records, correspondence, official papers and the
memoirs of persons who knew Sade that we can draw our
own conclusions from the evidence. What we get is not
only an account of the career of the aberrant Marquis but

a revelatory picture of various aspects of French society under Louis XV and—since Sade's dates are 1740 to 1814—through the Revolution and under Napoleon. A whole very strange drama emerges: the situations created for the Sades and the family of the Marquis's wife by the existence among them of a man of strong character and considerable intellect who was also an uncontrollable neurotic of a scandalous and dangerous kind. It is a wonder that no Paris playwright has yet exploited this new material.

The biography in certain ways is more interesting than Sade's fiction, since we are dealing here with real people instead of with pornographic fantasies enacted by implausible phantoms. But the writings of Sade are, of course, among the cardinal elements of the story, and without some firsthand knowledge of these, one cannot really understand it. When I wrote about Sade before, I had read mainly books of selections, which make such productions as *Justine* and *Les 120 Journées de Sodome* seem rather more acceptable than they actually are, and a more extensive acquaintance with these books has made my former observations seem inadequate. Though it is true, for example, that the latter of these works has a certain clinical importance and that the horrendous characters involved in it—the financier, the bishop, the duke and the judge, "those leeches" of profiteers who had got rich, as Sade said, while the country was being ruined by Louis XIV's wars—are portrayed with considerable power; it is, nevertheless, one of the most repugnant books that have ever been perpetrated. I am in the habit of reading at breakfast, but I found that *Les 120 Journées* was the only book that I could not face while eating. The almost exclusively anal interests of Sade, which extended to the excremental, figure here, as even his admirers have been obliged to confess, on a scale which is very discouraging from the literary point of view and from the scientific, disproportionate; and it, besides, becomes rather sickening to keep on reading about orgies of torture and murder in which the victims have not even a sporting chance. These debauches take place in a castle in Switzerland which has been rendered unapproachable and impregnable, but the exasperated reader keeps imagining a rescue by the United States Marines, who find a way of scaling the cliffs, or by a parachute attack from above. But, according to the author's plans, the four monsters, with certain of their accomplices, after slaughtering thirty of the company, were to return unimpeded to Paris. For Sade never finished this book, though he had outlined it with the greatest precision. He had a constant preoccupation with numbers which seems a part of his maniacal side, and he had worked out every day of the seventeen weeks of this extraordinary country house party, and projected the description of six hundred perversions, which, in accordance with a graduated system, proceeding from bad to worse, are recounted to stimulate the audience by four foul and evil old women who have encountered them in their lives of sin. The single known manuscript of *Les 120 Journées*, found in Sade's former cell in the Bastille, only carries the full story through thirty days, but there follows a schedule for the rest, with a notation of almost all the case histories. The principles involved here are real, some are probably based on real occurrences; but most of them have been dreamed up by Sade—he likes to dwell on their *"détails delicieux"*—to console himself during his years of imprisonment. A few, out of their context, are amusing. There is the man—a recognizable type—who gets his pleasure out of disappointing people and who contrives for them elaborate traps. There is Number Seventy-nine of the Third Class of Criminal Passions, to be described on the seventeenth of January, who "ties the girl face down on a table and eats an omelet on her behind, at each mouthful stabbing her deeply with a very sharp fork"; and there is Number One Hundred and Twenty-seven of the Fourth Class of Murderous Passions, to be described on the twenty-fourth of February, *un très grand bougre,* who likes to give balls, but there is a ceiling [a floor?] prepared which collapses when a certain amount of weight is put on it, and almost everybody is killed. If he stayed always in the same town, he would be found out, but he changes his town very often; he is found out only the fiftieth time." One can imagine the "delicious details" that might have been filled in by Sade if he had been able to complete his design: in the former case, the beauty of the girl, the superior quality of the omelet; in the second, the arrival of the stranger in one provincial town after another and his charming all the best people. This fantasy, too, however, does represent something we sometimes meet: there are people who do give parties to which they invite persons who do not want to see one another or will not get along together, and who deliberately make their guests uncomfortable. The One Hundred and Forty-eighth and last of the Fourth Class, is scheduled for November 29, but something has gone wrong here: there ought to be a hundred and fifty to make up the round six hundred. "Check why these two are missing," the author reminds himself. This last case is that of a *"grand seigneur, qui se livre à la dernière passion que nous désignerons sous le nom de l'enfer."* He arranges for himself a set-piece of an extremely elaborate kind, like the end of a fireworks display, which involves no less than fifteen girls, between fifteen and seventeen, for whom no less than eighteen pimps have ransacked Paris and the provinces. All of these are tortured simultaneously in protracted and ingenious ways, as the choregus watches from an armchair. This goes on for a long time before the *grand seigneur,* howling, arrives at the desired result, and even then—presenting their rears—two of the pimps have to masturbate him. From this scene and from many like it, as well as from other evidence, it is impossible not to come to the conclusion that the basic trouble with Sade was some kind of psychological impotence. His libertines have the utmost difficulty in attaining any satisfaction, and they resort to the most complicated expedients. The freakishness of Sade consists in his combining a voracious sexuality with some stubborn and infuriating obstruction to having it gratified. A strange letter which he wrote to his wife at the time of his imprisonment at Vincennes seems to indicate that he was able to attain his only solitary pleasure there by flagellating himself. Masochism and sadism, as we know, are closely bound up together, and Sade's novels contain masochistic as well as sadistic scenes. His own ambivalence in this regard is shown clearly by the testimony of the girls involved in the Marseille affair. Geoffrey Gorer, in his book on Sade, points out that, though Sade suffered in prison, he always managed to behave in such a way as to get himself punished again.

This psychological brake on enjoyment makes Sade extremely unattractive as a pornographic writer—especially since the libertines' partners are, as a rule, not allowed to enjoy themselves. His theory about this latter peculiarity is explicitly stated by one of the characters in his *Histoire de Juliette* (which I give in the expurgated version made by Lely for a volume of selections: "[. . .] all enjoyment that is shared is enfeebled. This is a recognized truth; if you try to give enjoyment to the object of your pleasures, you will soon have to recognize that you are doing so at your own expense; there is no passion more egoistic than lechery; there is none that must be served more severely, one must absolutely think only of oneself . . . and never consider the object of which one makes use except as a kind of victim who is destined for the fury of that passion; do not all passions exact their victims?"

And now let us follow the personal history that led to *Les 120 Journées.*

The de Sades were a very ancient family which came originally from Avignon and which figure among the Provençal nobility from sometime in the twelfth century. They had various claims to eminence, especially military and ecclesiastical; and Petrarch's "Laura" was supposed to have been a Laure de Sade.* The Marquis's uncle, a learned abbé, looked up Laure in the family archives and made himself an authority on the subject. He published, in 1767, the results of these researches in a three-volume work, *Mémoires pour la Vie de François Pétrarque, tirés de ses oeuvres et des auteurs contemporains.* Both the abbé and Laure were to play special roles in the life of their outrageous relative.

Donatien-Alphonse-François de Sade was born in Paris in the Hôtel de Condé, where his mother lived as *dame d'honneur* to her relative, the Princesse de Condé. He was baptized by this name by mistake, instead of, as his mother intended, Louis-Aldonse-Donatien, because, with none of his family present, he was taken to the church by two servants, who misunderstood the Provençal name Aldonse and substituted Louis for François. His father was a diplomat, and when his wife accompanied him on one of his missions, the boy was sent to stay with a grand-

---

* This is not known with any certainty: there were other possible Lauras; but the Sade family certainly claimed her.

mother.* An only child, he had already, as he was eventually to write of a character whom he obviously identified with himself, been rendered "haughty, despotic and
irritable" by having "stupidly," he says, been told that he
was connected, through his father, with "all that was
grandest in France" and, through his mother, with all
that was most distinguished in Languedoc. "The too blind
tenderness" of his Languedoc grandmother spoiled him
and made him worse. Between the ages of six and ten, he
was entrusted to the care of the abbé. This uncle had a
reputation for gallantry as well as for learning, and when
he entered the Church, had been greeted by a playful
little poem from his friend Voltaire:

> Ah, tout prêtre que vous serez,
> seigneur, seigneur, vous aimerez;
> fussiez-vous évêque ou Saint-Père,
> vous aimerez et vous plairez:
> voilà votre vrai ministère.
> Vous aimerez et vous plairez,
> et toujours vous réussirez
> et dans l'Église et dans Cythère.

Years later, at the age of fifty, the abbé de Sade was
imprisoned for having taken part with prostitutes in *"une
partie de débauche,"* but, after a few days, was liberated
by the King. The whole of the nephew's career must be
seen in the moral atmosphere of the reign of Louis XV,
who set the fashion in France for profligacy and sexual
excesses just as Victoria was to do in England for domesticity and respectability. The Marquis, when he was later
condemned to many years instead of a few days in prison

---

* Mr. Gorer, who has made, so far as I know, the only Freu-
dian attempt to account for Sade, suggests that his cruelty to
women may have had its prime source in resentment at having
been abandoned by his mother.

and also appealed to the King, was to protest that he had done nothing worse than several other great nobles he could mention.

From his uncle's, Donatien was sent for his studies to the Jesuit Collége Louis-le-Grand, where he remained for four years, and from there, he went straight into a cavalry school. At fifteen, he was a sous-lieutenant and immediately began to serve, continuing through the whole seven years of the Seven Years War of 1756–1763 and being promoted to the captaincy of a cavalry regiment. Of his career as a soldier, he was later to write that "that natural impetuosity . . . that fiery spirit with which nature had endowed me only added a greater degree of force and activity to that ferocious virtue which goes by the name of courage and which is regarded, though no doubt very wrongly, as the only one necessary to man's estate." At one point, he nearly started a fire in the town in which he was quartered by recklessly setting off fireworks in celebration of a victory of the Duc de Broglie's. He apologized to the authorities in a letter of which the tone is more or less facetious. One is reminded of the unfortunate accidents which accompanied General Sherman's early campaigns and which seem to anticipate the incidents of his progress from Atlanta to the sea. The Marquis was twenty-three at the end of the war, and he immediately created for himself, through his gambling and whoring and general disorderly conduct, a bad reputation in Paris. His father, the Comte de Sade, in spite of his extensive estates, had allowed himself to be ruined by bad management and his own extravagance, and the scrapes and prodigality of his son were a serious tax on his resources. He was a pompous and stiff *grand seigneur,* who lived separately now from his wife—she had resorted to a convent—and who could not stand to have anybody about him but his servants. He at one time thought of leaving Paris in order not to have to hear about Donatien, over whom he had no influence whatever; but he knew that the consequences of the boy's behavior would reach him wherever he was, and he decided that the best thing to do was to get the young man married to a rich *parti*. The Marquis was then having a love affair with a Mlle de Lauris of another old Provençal family that Lely says was "one of the most illustrious," and an ancestor of Proust's friend, the Comte de Lauris. One is struck by the un-chaperoned activity in the period of Louis XV of the *jeunes filles à marier* in France. The young man had evidently managed to get himself more or less engaged both to her and to Mlle de Montreuil, the daughter of a President of the Cour des Aides, which decided, under the old régime, on the subsidies provided by "indirect taxation"—that is chiefly by the hated wine and salt taxes—and who would bring him not a bigger dowry but expectations of a large inheritance. He much preferred Mlle de Lauris, to whom he wrote a graceful little poem, in which a Ronsardian rose is made to spring from his mistress's tread; but her father did not approve of him and forbade the marriage. He therefore married Renée de Montreuil at the age of twenty-three. He was to have three children by her. But five months after his marriage, Donatien was arrested for, says M. Lely, "one of those *débauches outrées* of the delights of which his servitude to his family had been depriving him for so long a time" and in order to indulge in which he was maintaining, in Paris and Versailles, five or six *petites maisons,* while the Marquise stayed at home pregnant. We do not know what the charges were, but the police inspector gave orders to the procuress whom the Marquis had been patronizing not to supply him with any more girls. He spent fifteen days in prison in Vincennes. When his father got him out, he immediately returned to his pastimes: prostitutes, actresses and sometimes, also, ladies in the salons of his own class. One of these actresses he entertained in the country at his Château de La Coste, at a time when his wife was away, pretending she was the Marquise's relative. He was now watched by the police when he came to Paris, and an inspector of the name of Marais, who was to make a speciality of Sade and pursue him for many years, announced that "there will soon be more news of the horrors of the Marquis de Sade."

From this point on, Sade's career is a series of arrests and imprisonments. There is the affair of the woman called Rose Keller, a good-looking widow of thirty-six who had had to resort to begging. Sade got into conversation with her, and he offered to rescue her from her poverty by making her his concierge. She accepted, and when she came the next morning to one of his *petites maisons,* he took her around the house and finally led her to the attic, where he told her to take off her clothes. When she protested, he threatened her with a pistol, and when she complied, he flogged her with a knotted whip, cut off pieces of her skin with a pocket knife and poured melted wax on the wounds. He then put ointment on them and locked her up in a room. She tied two sheets to the window and escaped. She laid a complaint against him, which resulted in his arrest. The excuse made by Sade or his friends was that he wanted to test the effects of the ointment. Rose Keller dropped her complaint when she was paid 2400 livres, but Sade spent six months in prison. His family intervened. The abbé came at once to Paris and declared that his nephew was "incapable of the atrocities that public rumor had charged him with," and that "all that he could really be blamed for was a good deal of giddiness and indiscretion." The King was induced to pardon him. He paid a fine of a hundred livres.

After this, Sade returned to the army, but again got

into trouble, in Marseille, where he had gone on what was supposed to be a business trip, and where he engaged in a multiple orgy, which involved a complaisant valet, three girls of from eighteen to twenty-three, a whip strung with pins, and some lozenges which he gave to the girls and by which they said they were poisoned. In the evening of the same day, he visited another girl, who accused him of the same practices and of also having given her lozenges which had resulted in internal pains. All these girls brought charges against him, and he and his valet were condemned by the Procureur du Roi—sodomy was then punishable by death—the Marquis to be beheaded, the valet to be hanged and strangled, and the bodies of both to be burned and their ashes thrown away. But this sentence was only carried out in effigy. The Marquis and his valet had vanished.

But in the meantime, an episode of a quite different kind had commenced for Donatien. He had fallen in love with his wife's younger sister, Mlle Anne-Prospère de Launay, then presumably in her late twenties. (Launay was the family name. The Montreuil title had been acquired when their father bought a baronial estate.) She had visited the Sades at La Coste and had apparently been fascinated by her brother-in-law, who, when at large, was to demonstrate recurrently his power of charming women and even of commanding devotion. He described his sister-in-law in a portrait which may seem surprising if one comes to it from his later writings, for it has obviously been inspired by genuine admiration. He praises Anne-Prospère for her beauty, for her cleverness, for the fineness of her perceptions and for the tenderness of her heart. She is sometimes called a coquette by malicious persons, he says; but actually she is perfectly natural: she pleases without study or art. Now, Anne-Prospère was *une chanoinesse*—that is, a kind of a nun, who had the enjoyment of certain privileges and was not under a perpetual vow. Her headquarters were a convent in or near Clermont-Ferrand, but she evidently came and went as she pleased. That her brother-in-law had been working successfully to dispel the conventual influence is shown by the fact that he commends her for her readiness to be persuaded to divest herself of what he describes as the foolish prejudices with which the Church had "obscured her reason" and taught her "to regard as crimes the sweetest emotions of her soul as well as the sweetest penchants of nature." "The bandage fallen" from her eyes, she has now "avenged the outrage which has been done her." She is entering a new existence, and this is making her prettier. "What a chill has descended on her former pleasures! And with what warmth are her new thoughts imbued!" The world wears a different aspect. The situation was further complicated, in a characteristically eighteenth-century way, by the fact that the abbé uncle also became enamored of Anne-Prospère. He makes her a charming present of a little Corsican horse, for which, addressing him as "uncle," she thanks him sweetly in a letter. A long letter from the abbé indicates that, after she has returned to her convent, she has actually to fight him off. She has begged him not to write her letters which might compromise her reputation, and he replies that he will respect her wishes but regards her as a cold Auvergnate—Clermont-Ferrand is in Auvergne—while he is a hot-blooded Provençal. He addresses her with much eloquence. "The sun whips the blood of a Provençal, the snows retard that of an Auvergnat," and, rather in the vein of his nephew, he declares that "one cannot so easily control the movements of the heart; their vivacity depends on the circulation of the blood, of which we are not masters. I should like to spend my life with you: I shall not see you at all. I burn to go to Clermont: I shall not go. . . . If you want from me anything else whatever that it is in my power to give you, you have only to let me know; but if you want me to keep my word, be careful not to pass the limits that you yourself have imposed. 'Ah, my dear uncle, how I love you!' Is that the style of friendship in Auvergne? I declare to you that I regard that declaration as an incursion into my province. If you continue to go on in that way, I shall no longer be master of myself: I shall concentrate all my fire, I shall go and melt all your snows and I shall make of them a torrent that will inundate you. . . . You wanted my relations with you to be kept on a tone of pleasantry: do you know any better way than this?"

When Anne-Prospère first got news of the scandal in which the Marquis was involved at Marseille, she seems to have been rather resentful; but when Donatien fled for his life, she joined him—the discipline of the convent seems to have been very lax—and spent three months with him in Italy. The whole story seems so bizarre that one wishes one could know something more about the characters of the persons involved. Not the least of its curious features is that the canoness, after her elopement, went back to visit her sister and then, very soon afterwards, rejoined Donatien and spent a few days with him at Chambéry in Savoy, at that time an independent duchy, where he had gone to keep out of French jurisdiction. But his relations with his sister-in-law had now become a public scandal, and her mother, the Présidente de Montreuil, who had now had both her daughters compromised by her son-in-law, was anxious to get the younger one married. An eligible M. de Beaumont was suing for the hand of the canoness, but his family would not allow him to marry her unless the Marquis were permanently locked up. Mme de Montreuil therefore made strong representations to the King of Sardinia, who then ruled Savoy, and the Marquis was incarcerated in a fortress. He escaped, however, after four months, with the connivance of his wife, and went back with her to the Château de la Coste.

But Sade's existence was still precarious. He was still a hunted man. On one occasion, a police inspector from Paris, accompanied by four archers from Marseille and the Marseille mounted constabulary, broke into the château and raised havoc. They did not, however, find the Marquis. He had either to hide at home or to move about from place to place. Madame de Sade and her sister went to Paris together, and the Marquise tried to get the Procureur du Roi to intervene on behalf of her husband. But her mother, la Présidente, was from now on to use all her influence to have her son-in-law restrained from further mischief. The abbé now refused to be helpful. His nephew had gone much too far. He said that, on account of the death sentence, the Marquis was now civically dead; and that, besides, he was mad and should be put away. An appeal was to be presented to the Parliament at Aix, but the President of the Parliament was in no position to be lenient to the Marquis's offenses. We learn from a study of him by Georges Lenôtre that, having begun as a child by sticking pins in live birds, he had gone on, having taken a mistress, to conspire with her to kill his wife. When the latter became pregnant, he had at first sprinkled the stairway with cherrystones, hoping she would have a fall; and then, when this had not succeeded and she was lying in, he had given her poisoned lemonade, which, finding it bitter, she did not drink. He had finally, when all his neighbors had gone out to watch a balloon ascension, cut his wife's throat with a razor. He may well have sat for the horrible judge in Les 120 Journées de Sodome; but at this moment he found it prudent to say that Sade was a dubious character, who "gave himself up to all kinds of excesses with young people of every sex." But while the case was in abeyance, the Sades withdrew to La Coste, where they evidently tried to give the impression of leading a quiet country life. The Marquis attested his morality by refusing to allow travelling players to present in the town a comedy called *Le Mari cocu, battu et content*, tearing down the announcements of it as *"scandaleuses et attentoires aux libertés de L'Église."*

Then his own scandals erupted worse than ever. The Marquis had somehow recruited from Lyon and Vienne five girls, at least one of them very young, provided by a procuress called Nanon, who also came to live at La Coste. Before very long, these girls began running away and making complaints, and at Lyon criminal proceedings were instituted against Sade. It is doubtful how far the Marquise herself was involved in the Marquis's vices. She was very much under his influence, and may have thought that she would rather have him indulge them at home where she could oversee and restrain them. But she was quite unable to control him, and one of the girls testified that the Marquise became "the first victim of a fury which could only be regarded as insanity." She in any case tried frantically to cover up, to prevent the girls from talking—one was sent to a convent—and to buy dismissal of charges from their parents. The little girl who had been most mistreated was—much to the abbé's annoyance—secretly lodged with Sade's uncle, who was threatened into keeping her with him by means of a blackmailing letter, which, on account of its truculent tone, although it was signed by Mme de Sade, seems obviously to have been dictated by her husband and which reminded the abbé of his own misdeeds in passages which the recipient, though he kept the letter, took pains to render partially illegible. "What horrors," the Marquise writes to him, "that creature [the little girl] can say about me!" She, or her husband speaking through her, declares that the girl's leaving the château was due to simple boredom: "She preferred to mind flocks rather than to spin in her chamber"; but the abbé is begged not to let a doctor examine her. Eventually she is sent to a hospital. The Marquis had also got the procuress with child; the baby was put with a wet nurse, but the nurse's milk gave out and Nanon's baby died of starvation.

The Marquis writes in a letter that the women of Avignon "have given out that I am ranging from morning to night through all the neighboring towns and terrifying everybody. I pass for the werewolf here. The poor little chickens with their frightened cries! But why complain? This is the way people behave, and one enjoys taking cognizance of the feeling one inspires." There was a belief in the neighborhood that the Sades had a cemetery on the premises for the girls that the Marquis had murdered; but he himself was always to deny that he had ever killed anyone. In a long letter written from prison, he tries to show that every woman who had been at La Coste had left the place alive, and that some bones which were found in the garden had been brought for a joke by a visiting dancer, who had amused herself by decorating a small room with them. "When the pleasantry, or rather, the platitude, was over," says Sade, "they were deposited in the garden." He nevertheless thought it prudent to disappear from Provence and, under the pseudonym of the Comte de Mazan, he spent the better part of a year in Italy. In the course of these travels, Sade studied Italian and worked on but never finished a work called *Descriptions critiques et philosophiques de Rome, Florence, etc.* At Rome, he commissioned *"un petit docteur"* to supply him with a description of the Vatican and at the same time to make him a collection of stories of unconventional sexual practices to be found both in ancient authors and in the life of contemporary Rome. He enjoyed, of course, such anecdotes for their own sake but it is evident that he is also beginning to take something like an intelligent interest in his own aberrations and in those of others. This was fatal for the little doctor. Sade damaged whomever he touched. A letter to him from Sade on the subject fell into the hands of the Inquisition, and he was consigned to four months in its prisons. A bull of Pius V had authorized the death penalty for anyone who talked about what happened to him at the hands of the Inquisition, so the doctor had had to send his employer a message that he was ill. But when he got out of jail, he wrote that, though he would continue to work on the description of the Vatican, the other project would have to be abandoned. He was surrounded, he said, by spies. When the Marquis went back to France, he brought with him a whole load of *antiquités,* which included medals, marbles, lamps, an amphora, lachrymatory phials, a fine sepulchral urn and a small statue of Hermaphrodite. At Grenoble, he sends word to the family solicitor that he is coming back to La Coste and asks him to procure for him an edition of Martial.

There was now a rumor at La Coste that the Marquis in Italy had become devout. The Marquise did her best to encourage it and said that he had even been to see the Pope. But, in the meantime, the mistreated little girl, who had now been put in the custody of the steward of the Sade estate, had escaped and gone back to Vienne, where she had made a deposition against the Marquis; and the Marquise thought it inadvisable to have her husband return at that moment. Eventually, however, he did, and found everything in the worst possible shape. Donatien, given up to his dissipations, had been an even worse manager than his father. The Sades were now hounded by creditors and could hardly keep up the château. They had no wood, the window panes were broken; the Marquise, who had no warm clothes, took to her bed with, I suppose, what we should now call the flu. Sade's mother-in-law came to the rescue by sending some money to the family *homme d'affaires*, a man named Gaufridy, with orders that it should only be used for the necessities of the château. This made the Marquis furious, because he needed money for the special expenses of getting his new books bound and his new pictures framed. And he immediately created more scandal. He had asked a Père Durand, a member of the Récollet order, to engage for him four servants, and Père Durand arrived one evening with a chambermaid, a kitchen maid, a male secretary and a barber from Paris. All but the kitchen maid left the next morning. The Marquis, after supper, had locked them all up in separate rooms and attacked them during the night. They went back with Père Durand in his carriage. They of course talked about what had happened, and this greatly alarmed the father, a blanket-maker, of the Sade's twenty-year-old cook, whom the Récollet had also provided. The blanket-maker upbraided the priest, who had guaranteed *"l'honorabilité du château"* and who now said that of course he had known about *"Les désordres de M. de Sade, mais que, depuis un certain temps, il le croyait bien guéri."* A month later, however, the worried father came to demand his daughter and when Sade tried to argue with him, fired a pistol at him and fled. The Marquis was not wounded, and the father returned with four companions and fired again into a courtyard where he imagined he had found the Marquis. Sade tried to get the blanket-maker arrested, but the Procureur Général of Aix decided that the behavior of Sade was "horrible in every way" and that Catherine must be

immediately sent back to her father. The girl herself, however, who had evidently been charmed by the Sades or
had managed to adapt herself to the household, remonstrated with her father and refused to leave.

The Sades, taking Catherine with them, now made a
trip to Paris. The Présidente had just announced to
Gaufridy that she was washing her hands of their affairs,
and it is not known whether they wanted to conciliate her
or wished to be with Sade's mother, who was dying. In
any case, a few days after arriving—evidently at the instance of his mother-in-law, who obtained a *lettre de
cachet*—Donatien was arrested by the Inspector
Marais, who had dogged him in his earlier days, and
imprisoned in the *donjon* of Vincennes (a tower, not an
English dungeon), where he remained for sixteen months.
At the end of this time, as a result of his appeal to the
King, he was summoned to appear before the Parliament
of Provence. He was made to pay a fine and pardoned,
but, instead of being released, as he expected, was conducted back to Vincennes. He managed to escape on the
way and quietly returned to La Coste, where, with typical insouciance, he enjoyed thirty-nine days of liberty.
The Marquise was then in Paris and her mother did not
let her know about her husband's having left Vincennes.
When she found out, she wanted to go to him, but her
mother threatened to lock her up, and the poor lady
decided to stay in Paris and try to get the *lettre de cachet*
cancelled. In the meantime, the Inspector Marais had
turned up at La Coste with a squad of ten men and, after
denouncing Sade—addressing him as "*tu*"—for having
committed his various crimes and having the bodies of his
victims on the premises, dragged the Marquis publicly,
garrotted and bound, through his province, where everyone knew him and in which he had just been cleared, to
the prison of Vincennes again.

He was to remain there for five and a half years, and then be transferred to the Bastille, where he was kept for almost five years more, till the outbreak of the Revolution.

Did imprisonment make Sade worse? Was it wrong to keep him in jail so long? He might have said of himself, like Oscar Wilde—as, in effect, he sometimes did—"I am a problem for which there is no solution." What he wrote about was certainly worse than anything he had actually done, and, in the course of fifteen years in prison, he became more and more misanthropic. It is impossible not to sympathize with the victim of a *lettre de cachet,* which, in that era, allowed of no trial, no defence, not even of any charges, and which, involving no definite sentence, could condemn one to confinement for life. To his anguished appeals to know when he will be free, he gets only vague promises which are never kept. And we may sympathize, also, with a man who is driven to erotic fantasies by the privation of solitary imprisonment. But what would have been the hazard of letting him out? Here at least his crimes are all on paper, and the outbursts in his letters were not reassuring. He will tell Mme de Sade that he should always think it proper to keep his life with her uncontaminated by his vices or that if she had only known how to handle him, to accommodate herself to these, he would never have come to this pass; but, after all, he had failed to follow the first of these courses and she had failed to succeed with the second. He sometimes professes contrition and promises complete reform. He writes a letter of this kind to his mother-in-law which must have cost him a prodigious effort of hypocrisy, for he had previously written to a friend that if it were in his power, he would have Mme de Montreuil "burned at a slow fire." He expresses devotion to his wife, especially in the fifty-three months during which he was not allowed to see her. But in the spring before her first visit, he begins to grow jealous of her, and his seeing her in the summer seems to have made it worse. He accuses her of having been unfaithful and having allowed herself to be got pregnant, warns her against staying with a woman friend whom he believes to be a libertine and perhaps a Lesbian. The poor Marquise, to allay his suspicions, took up her abode in a convent. She seems to have done her best for him, supplied him with clean linen, books and sweets; but if his orders are not carried out exactly, he begins to abuse and threaten her: "The biscuit de Savoie is not at all what I asked for: In the first place, I wanted them candied all over, both on top and underneath in the same way as the little biscuits; in the second place, I wanted them with chocolate inside, and there's not the slightest trace of chocolate; they've browned them with the juice of herbs, but there's nothing that can be called the slightest trace of chocolate. The next time you're having things sent, please have them make some of these for me, and try to have someone you have confidence in see to it that there's chocolate in them. The biscuits ought to have the same taste as when you bite into a bar of chocolate. The next time you're sending, then: some biscuits of the kind I say: six ordinary ones, six candied, and two little pots of Breton butter, but good and well selected." When she visits him, he furiously complains about her costume: "Tell me, would you go to Easter services in that get-up that makes you look like a mountebank or a quack medicine peddler?"; or upbraids her for having come to the prison on foot: "Now I understand why you are always so hot, why you are in such a dreadful state whenever you come to see me: it's because you come on foot like a shopkeeper, like a common whore of the streets. And your parents allow it, and your rascally servants don't make any objection! What lowness, what indignity! Listen: I've promised to be calm, I've promised to write this letter as dispassionately as I'm able. So I've only one word to say to you, and that is that if it happens again that you come to me in such a state, I swear to you on all that's most sacred that I shall refuse to see you, that I'll go up at once to my room and that I'll never come down again."

His expressions of affection carry little conviction—he alternates *tu* and *vous,* according to his mood of the moment—and he refuses to pretend that he is other than he is. He can only try to minimize his crimes. He is a libertine, he admits. *J'ai toujours eu un peu de penchant à favoriser le vice,"* he writes to the same woman friend, *"et je regarde comme de grands hommes ceux qui savent y persister avec acharnement";* but he has done very little with married women: "You will hardly find three that I have tried to seduce." *"L'adultère des femmes est sujet à des inconvénients si horribles, il a des suites si funestes et si fatales, que je n'ai jamais pu le tolérer."* So why all this fuss about *"des putains"*? Should he be made to spend years in prison on account of *"le cul d'une putain"*? Suppose he had happened to kill one of these lowest of the low, was that a serious matter? He has more dignity when he admits his abnormality and his powerlessness to do anything about it. To the Marquise, he writes that, when he gets out of jail, he will do his best for her and his children; "But as for me, for me personally, I can't promise you anything. The beast is too old. Please believe me and give up trying to teach him better. . . . There are certain principles of conduct which are too much a part of one's existence, especially when one has imbibed them with one's milk, for it ever to be possible to reject them. It is the same with one's habits: when they have become so prodigiously tied to a being's physique, ten thousand years of prisons and a hundred pounds of chains would only make them stronger. . . . Our *moeurs* don't depend on us, they derive from our construction, from our organization. What depends on us is not to spread our poison beyond us, and to see to it that those who surround us not only do not suffer from it but cannot even become aware of it." This does not of course include *les putains* but only one's own family, who, in Sade's case, had already become all too well aware. "That is the essential, and that is what I promise," he continues when he has made this point clear. "One cannot create virtues for oneself, and one is no more in a position, *in such matters,* to adopt this or that taste than one is to become straight when one has been born twisted, to adopt, in accordance with principle, this or that opinion or to make oneself dark when one has been born redheaded. This is my eternal philosophy, and I shall never have any other.

"However, in 1777 [the year of his first imprisonment in Vincennes], I was still fairly young; the depth of my misfortune then might have prepared me for the task [of reform]; my soul had not been hardened yet, as you have been at pains since to render it inaccessible to good sentiments." One may have one's doubts about this; yet it is not without a sense of tragedy that one watches through these more than a dozen years the lapsing of all human ties. He tries to find out from his wife what has happened to Anne-Prospère, and she refuses to let him know where she is. All he learns, and all we know about these years of her life, is that the canoness has never married and that she has ceased to live with her mother. He asks hopefully whether she and her mother have quarrelled and is told that this is not the case. He was never to see or hear from Anne-Prospère again. She died in 1781 from some ail-

ment of an undetermined nature four years after his
going to jail. He becomes suspicious of a woman friend, a
Mlle de Rousset, with whom he has kept up a correspondence. He tries to exercise some control over his
financial affairs, but Gaufridy, the agent for the family,
has come to dread his letters and either answers them
evasively or ignores them. He becomes convinced—
rightly perhaps—that the Marquise is abetting her
mother, with whom she had before been at odds, and does
not want him to be liberated. He is furious when, on one
of her visits, she is accompanied by a police inspector. He
tells her that her family are far beneath him, only *gens de
robe*—that is, officials—instead of *nobles d'épée,* men of
property, like the Sades; and that he married her only for
money. He threatens her and her family with what he
will eventually do to them. When his elder son enrolls in
an infantry regiment instead of, like himself, in the
cavalry, he can only storm impotently in letter after letter,
and refuses to receive from his boy a New Year's message
which the latter has sent him, expressing affection and
respect and hoping that he can come with his mother to
see him. The father, however, declares that he will not
see the boy or correspond with him till he has shifted to
the Carabiniers, which the young man declines to do.
Sade beats up a jailor, and, as a result of this, they refuse
to enter his cell to shave him or sweep it out, and hand
up his meals through a trap in the floor, "as if I were a
madman." His writings become wholly atrocious. It is
plain from his early verses and his portrait of his sister-in-
law that, with all his compulsive brutalities, he was sensitive to much that was fine, and, in these products of
imprisonment, this is still apparent. The young victims of
the ogres of *Les 120 Journées* are selected for their breeding, refinement and beauty, and the wives of these ogres

are praised for their dignity and the delicacy of their taste; but this is only to enhance the pleasure of outraging them and tearing them to pieces. One of the few touching things that Sade wrote is of a date almost seven years before he began this work. He had been reading his uncle's book on Petrarch. "All my consolation here is Petrarch," he wrote to his wife. "Laure has turned my head; I am like a child about it; I read about her all day and at night I think about her. Hear a dream that I had about her yesterday, while everybody else [outside prison, he means] were amusing themselves. It was about midnight. I had just fallen asleep, with the memoir of her in my hand. She appeared to me all of a sudden. I saw her! The horror of the tomb had not impaired the brightness of her charms, and her eyes had still as much fire as when Petrarch celebrated them. She was enveloped in black crêpe, and her beautiful blond hair was negligently floating over it. It was as if Love itself, in order to make her still more beautiful, wished to soften all the gloomy costume in which she was presenting herself to my eyes. 'Why art thou groaning on earth?' she said. 'Come and join me. No more woes, no more griefs, no more troubles, in the immensity of space I inhabit. Have the courage to follow me there.' At these words, I threw myself at her feet, I said to her, 'Oh, my Mother!' . . . And my voice was stifled with sobs. She held out to me a hand which I covered with tears; and she, too, was shedding tears. 'I used to like,' she added, 'to cast my glance into the future, when I lived in this world that thou dost detest; I multiplied my posterity even to thee, *and I did not see thee so unhappy.*' Then, caught up in my despair and my tenderness, I threw my arms about her neck, to keep her or to follow her, and to water her with my tears, but the phantom disappeared. The only thing left was my grief.

O voi che travagliate, ecco il cammino
Venite a me se'l passo altri no serra.*

"*Bonsoir, ma chère amie,* I love thee and embrace thee with all my heart. And have a little more pity on me, I beg thee, for I assure thee that I am unhappier than thou thinkest. Take into consideration everything that I am suffering, and [that] the state of my soul is as somber as [that of] my imagination. I embrace even those who have a grudge against me, because I hate in them only my wrongs.

"This February seventeenth, at the end of two years of horrible chains." (The chains were rhetorical not real.)

But he was writing her two years later: "Would that you and your accursed family and their base valets might be put all together in a sack and thrown to the bottom of the sea. Then let me be immediately told, and I swear to Heaven that that will be the happiest moment that I shall ever have tasted in my life."

But later on, a new note of pathos is struck in a letter to Mlle Rousset apropos of the chimes of Vincennes: "Since a prisoner refers everything to himself and always thinks that everything people do has some relation to him, and that everything that is said is about himself, I of course got it into my head that those damned chimes were talking to me and that they were saying to me, and very distinctly:

Je te plains, je te plains,
Il n'est plus pour toi de fins
Qu'en poudre, qu'en poudre.

---

* This is the eighty-first poem of Petrarch's *Canzoniere.* Did Sade understand that Jesus is the "friend" of whom Petrarch is speaking and that the lines quoted here are a paraphrase of Matthew XI:28?

"I got up in such a rage as words can't express and wanted to knock the bell-ringer on the head, but then I had painfully to realize that the door of vengeance was closed to me. So I sat down again and took up my pen. I thought I ought to answer that rascal in the same spirit and tone, since I had no way of doing it otherwise, and I said,

> De plaisir, de jouir,
> Il faut donc vous dessaisir,
> Mon âme, mon âme . . ."

He dwells on his sexual privation.

> Ma moitié, ma moitié
> Me rend sans nulle pitié
> Tantale, Tantale.

> Ah, quel sort! ah, quel sort!
> Oh, par ma foi, c'est trop fort!
> J'en crève, j'en crève.

> Le sainfoin meurt sans soins:
> Venez-en chercher au moins
> La graine, la graine.

> Quel martyr! quel martyr!
> Je vois bien qu'il faut souffrir
> Sans cesse, sans cesse.

By the time the Revolution had released the Marquis, the Marquise had given him up as hopeless and was arranging a legal separation. There is no evidence that, after he was freed, he ever saw her again.

M. Lely calls these letters Shakespearean, but they have nothing in common with Shakespeare except that, like *King Lear* and *Timon of Athens*, they contain embittered tirades. There are occasional imaginative exploits in the language of vituperation. Sade is seen at his most horridly exuberant in his letters to a valet and copyist, who was evidently also a crony and whom for some reason he likes to address as *"M. le chevalier Quiros."* The following will give an idea of the Marquis's conception of jovial banter: "Ah, old pumpkin preserved in bed-bug juice, third horn on the head of the Devil, with your great long codfish face and your ears like oysters, you old worn-out slipper of a whorehouse madam, dirty underclothes of the *choses rouges* of Milli [Mademoiselle] Printemps, if I had you, how I'd rub in them your dirty baked-apple snout which looks like burning chestnuts, to teach you to lie to me like that." M. Lely elsewhere declares that Sade, as a literary artist, is comparable only to Shakespeare; he is always referring to his works as *"chefs d'oeuvre."* How do the Sade scholars arrive at such opinions? Sade's books have their psychiatric interest and sometimes their hate-poisoned power, but they are certainly among the curiosities, not the masterpieces, of literature.

Sade wrote a great many plays, in prose and in alexandrines. He was infatuated with the theater, and had loved to put on plays at La Coste. In prison, he was always writing plays, passing them out to his wife and getting her to criticize them, in the hope of having them produced. But even Sade's most fervent admirers cannot find much good to say of these pieces. M. Lely calls the characters of one of his comedies *"d'assez mornes automates."* He cannot here afford to be as indecent as he is in his works of fiction, but the situations on which they depend are as perverse as he thinks he can afford to make them. He protests to his former tutor, the Abbé Amblet, who has criticized one of his scripts: "I am a little of the opinion of Monsieur de Buffon. *Enjoyment* is the only thing that I like and find good in love. Metaphysics is, according to me, the flattest and most monstrous thing there is, and I don't know how to go about it when, in obedience to the exigencies of dramatic art, I have to sprinkle some into my pieces."

By "metaphysics" he meant not philosophy but, one supposes, the reasonings of Racinean morality. He regarded himself as *un philosophe,* and the pornographic episodes of his fiction are made to alternate with long dissertations quite typical of the then booming Enlightenment. Sade's first characteristic work in this line was the *Dialogue entre un Prêtre et un Moribond,* completed in his fifth year of imprisonment. The priest has come to administer the last sacrament, and calls upon the dying man to repent; but the latter replies that the only thing he is conscious of having to repent of is not having enjoyed himself more when he had the opportunity to do so. He does not believe in the doctrine of the Church. If God is what the Church says He is, why has He made man with his corrupt nature? What merit would virtue have, the priest replies, if man were not left free to choose?— But God, since He has made man Himself, must know how the thing is coming out. If the criminal were free *not* to commit the crime—since he knows it will lead to the gallows—he would certainly refrain from committing it. All the crimes are "necessary to Nature" as well as all the virtues. But are we responsible for the side to which she pushes us? No more than the wasp who darts his sting into our flesh.—Then we shouldn't beware of committing crimes?—I don't say that. Let the law, by its menace, do its best to prevent our crimes; but once a crime has been committed, one must not give oneself up to a sterile remorse. And it is reason and reason alone—not the groundless threats of the Church—which can warn us that by injuring others, we can never achieve our own happiness, that contributing to the happiness of others is the greatest felicity that Nature has offered us. All human morality is summed up in this saying: *make other people as happy as*

one desires to be oneself, and never do them more harm
than one would care to suffer. But he is now about to
die, he says, and he mustn't waste his energy preaching.
Six beautiful women, he explains, are waiting in the next
room. Won't his visitor enjoy them with him. Let him
forget about the next world, since it does not exist. "The
dying man rang; the women came in, and the preacher
became in their arms a man corrupted by Nature for not
having been able to explain what a nature corrupted
was."

This contains the whole germ of Sade's philosophy,
which he was later to expound in his novels in innumerable and interminable disquisitions. Why should I love
God when, from the Christian point of view, he has
made such a hopeless botch of me? But God does not
exist, so, for that matter, why should I apologize for myself? There is no God, there is only Nature, and Nature
not only generates; she constantly destroys in the cruellest
way and often on a gigantic scale: earthquakes, volcanic
eruptions; and this preserves a balance that is necessary.
Perhaps the most eloquent expression of this idea—no
doubt because one of the first—is to be found in *Justine*:
"In regard to the crime of destroying one's fellowman, I
can assure you, my dear girl, that it is entirely chimerical;
the power to destroy has not really been granted to man;
at most, he has the power to vary the forms; he does not
have the power to annihilate them: now all forms are
equal in the eyes of Nature; nothing is lost in the immense crucible in which the variations are made; all the
pieces of matter which fall into it are incessantly thrown
up again in different shapes, and, no matter what we do
in this respect [i.e., in destroying], it is not possible for
anyone to outrage her, for anyone to offend her. Our
destructions revive her power; they feed her energy, but
none of them can enfeeble her; she is never impeded by

any of them. . . . Ah, what does it matter to her hand, which is always at work creating, that this or that mass of flesh which today constitutes an individual biped may be reproduced tomorrow in the form of a thousand different insects? Dare one say that the construction of this two-legged animal is more valuable than that of an earthworm, and that she ought to take more interest in it? If, then, her degree of attachment, or rather of indifference, is the same, what difference can it make to her that by the sword of a man another man should be changed into a fly or a weed?" Now, says Sade, in effect, I embody this destructive force, and it is natural to unleash it on women, since Nature has made women inferior; they have always and everywhere, on account of their weakness, been subjugated and scorned by men.

What is unusual in the interchange between the priest and the dying man is the emphasis on promoting the happiness of others. It is true that Sade lays down the principle in his essay on novel-writing that the author should not express himself directly but always make his characters talk, that any character of his who professes this more ferocious point of view is always referred to as "ce scélérat"; but the scoundrels are always given the stronger arguments, the author is on their side. In *Justine,* for example, the virtuous young girl who, though outraged in every other way, manages technically to preserve her chastity and who piously pleads with her tormentors is given a very weak case—made, in fact, a ridiculous figure—in the teeth of the doctrine of "ces scélérats." In the first and milder version, she is eventually rescued and given a home by her more worldly—and criminal—sister; but then falls victim to the destructive force of Nature when she is killed by a stroke of lightning. In the second and nastier version, the highly successful sister, in the company of her equally fiendish friends, laugh at Justine and drive her out. The bulk of the work of Sade is an apology for his own obsessive mania.

Yet he studied current fiction with attention, and though he was not able to publish anything till after his liberation, he had already begun, in prison, to take a quite professional interest in his craft. For *Les Crimes de l'Amour,* a collection of short stories, published in the Year VIII of the Revolution, he composed a remarkable introduction called *Idée sur les Romans,* in which he shows a comprehensive knowledge of the history of European fiction from the Greek romances through Boccaccio, Cervantes, Mme de Lafayette, Marivaux, Richardson and Fielding, to Monk Lewis and Mrs. Radcliffe (who figures as "Radgliffe"). He lays down some excellent principles, all of which he has more or less violated: that the novelist must not depart from what is probable; that he must not interrupt his story with incidents that are either too frequent or not properly related to the subject; that it should never be the author who moralizes but always one of the characters in his novel, and that he ought not even then to be made to except when he is forced to by circumstances. Sade evidently feels some compunction for having insisted on probability, for he indulges, in this connection, in his usual special pleading. He announces that, in the stories that follow, he will "allow himself to take a bold flight"; but "Nature is stranger than the moralists paint and is constantly escaping from the dykes that their systems would like to prescribe for her." He also declares very sternly that one ought not to write for a living. If you do, your work will reflect your needs. You will transmit your weakness to it; it will have the paleness of hunger: other trades are open to you; make shoes, but do not write books.

Yet the Marquis himself was well aware of the fashions, and he knew how to exploit the market. He had two

ways of doing this. One of these was to gratify the appetite for indecency so enthusiastically cultivated in the
eighteenth century. The Marquis carried pornography as
far as it could possibly go, leaving far behind his rivals in
this department, John Cleland and Diderot and Rétif de
la Bretonne, but, by reason of the superior attractiveness
of their merchandise, by no means at a disadvantage. He
first published his *Justine, ou les Malheurs de la Vertu* in
the form in which he had written it in prison, with
scandalous situations but a language that was still fairly
chaste; then he loaded it with obscenities, made the episodes more atrocious, and extended it with the story of
Juliette, the worldly and wicked sister, who stopped at
nothing and prospered from her crimes, travelling
through Europe—her itinerary appears partly to be a perverted reminiscence of his adventures with Anne-Prospère—discovering with the keenest delight all the horrors
committed by sovereigns, monks, governments and feudal
lords, some of them more or less authentic, which the
Marquis was pleased to assemble. The other group of readers he appealed to were more bourgeois and more idealistic.
In the interest of not alienating their sympathies, as well
as otherwise protecting himself, he denied, in *Idée sur les
Romans* and elsewhere, that he had written *Justine* and
Juliette: "it is only the malicious and the imbecile who,
in spite of the authenticity of my denials, can still suspect
me and accuse me of being the author, and henceforth
the only weapon with which I shall combat their calum-
nies will be the most sovereign contempt." He had composed another novel called *Aline et Valcour, ou le Roman
Philosophique,* which, though it had always, as a menace
in the background, an evil demiurge of an incestuous
father, was aimed at the admirers of *Clarissa* and of Rousseau's *La Nouvelle Héloïse.* Like them, it is told in
letters, and it does not offend conventional morality. It is

interwoven with two long narratives in the tradition of picaresque fiction—which M. Lely, in his ingenuous way, has reprinted and described as "masterpieces"—the vicissitudes of two parted lovers. But though both are continually threatened by the regulation Sadean villains, they escape with very little damage, and in the end, they are happily united. One curious feature of *Aline et Valcour* is Sade's unexpected production of a utopia that belongs to the family of Fourier and Saint-Simon. The island of Tamoé has been discovered by a French man-of-war and is ruled by the son of one of its sailors, who fell in love with a native girl and stayed behind when the vessel left. He became the chief of the natives and prepared his son to succeed him by sending him to Europe. The young man was able to see how vile European civilization was and returned with a set of ideas for constructing a better one. Though, wise and deeply respected, he is actually the head of the state and though his people do not have a parliament—which he regards as entirely useless—he will not allow himself to be called king. The society he presides over is classless and everyone is everyone's "equal," in "fortune" as well as in status. The voice of Rousseau is heard when Zamé, the chief, explains that it has been easy to produce this result because his people were "too close to a state of nature to have been corrupted by the false system of social differences." There are communal nurseries, and the houses are the property of the State, which issues them to newly married couples. A husband or a wife can repudiate his or her mate on several legitimate grounds. There is one street in every city, equipped with smaller houses, where the *"répudiés"* and the celibates live. They all worship God without ritual— are in fact eighteenth-century Deists. One of Zamé's most conspicuous successes has been to reduce simultaneously the number of crimes and the number of laws. When a man does commit a crime, he is not sent to prison—which could only make him worse: he is made to repair the injury. We are soon back with the author and his problems. The French visitor to Zamé's island objects that "In certain hearts, there exists a sort of perversity which cannot be corrected at all; there are people who do evil gratuitously; it is recognized today that there are men who give themselves up to evil simply from the charm of infraction." (It is to be explained of Juliette that the very idea of breaking a law or going contrary to a convention is enough to excite her sexually.) How about such human horrors as Tiberius, Heliogabalus and Andronicus? That's a different matter, says Zamé. Such people are very rare. One must not attempt to constrain them. With such people one cannot get anywhere save by sentiment, delicacy and honor. In the meantime, one must just get used to them, as one does to a twisted tree. As for murderers, since in Tamoé they have removed most of the motives for murder, they have hardly any now on the island. But if a murder does occur, a description of the man is sent out and no one is allowed to receive him. He is put into a pirogue with a month's provisions and told to go away. If he returns, he will be executed. "It is the only crime that is punished in that way."

The Marquis, even while still in prison and with no possibility of publishing his work, followed attentively, as I have said, the development of the contemporary novel; and from the time when it was possible for him to publish, showed a jealous sensitivity toward competitors. It is amusing to see Sade and Rétif de la Bretonne snapping and snarling at one another, each accusing the other of purveying filth. Sade uses Rétif as an example of the author who becomes a hack by writing for money and of describing *"des aventures dégoutantes toujours puisées dans la plus mauvaise compagnie."* Rétif detested Sade,

referred to him as *"le monstre auteur,"* and even went
so far as to publish an *Anti-Justine,* which, he said, unlike the work of Sade, did not present "the delights of
love invariably accompanied by the torture and even the
death of the women . . . a book which wives can read
to their husbands," which will make the reader "adore
women, cherish, make love to them, and all the more
abhor the vivisector who has just been brought out of
the Bastille." The lovers in Rétif's novel were, it seems,
a father and daughter. No mention is made by Sade
of the most distinguished writer in his special field. It
can hardly be imagined that he had failed to read
Les Liaisons Dangereuses, which was published in 1782,
but in his *Idée sur les Romans* he says nothing about
Choderlos de Laclos. M. Lely has a theory about this:
he has discovered in connection with it some suggestive
facts. It turns out that Sade and Laclos were kept in
custody together for almost seven month of 1794 in the
same *maison de santé.* M. Lely guesses that they must
have quarrelled and it is for this reason—also, perhaps,
from envy—that Sade omitted his rival's name when,
in 1800, he published *Les Crimes de l'Amour.* We
find, furthermore, among Sade's notebooks a *Plan for a
Novel in Letters,* which sounds very much like *Liaisons
Dangereuses.* M. Lely concludes that Sade wanted to
take over Laclos's pattern and show how much better he
could do with it. But the author of *Justine* and *Juliette*
had not the taste and the balance to bring off such a
masterpiece as Laclos's. The characters in Laclos are real
people, and they are handled with marvellous skill. It
would have been quite impossible for Sade to conceive
the so effective climax of *Liaisons Dangereuses:* to have
the two aristocratic libertines, Mme de Merteuil and M.
de Valmont, who are playing havoc with better people's
lives, at last, by their own logic, set out to ruin one an-

other. The villains and villainesses of Sade do not hesitate to betray one another, but this illustrates no moral
principle as does the débâcle of Laclos's. Because there is
no such real conflict between different moral values, there
is no real drama in Sade.

From beginning to end of his literary career, Donatien
is doing his best, trying first one way, then another, to
justify his aberrations, to put them into some reasonable
relation—since, like other eighteenth-century writers, he
is always talking about "reason"—to the rest of human
society. This makes him very repetitious, and in the long
run the spectacle is painful. If he takes the line that
Nature is destructive and that the forces of destruction
are needed as much as the generative forces, and that a
person who embodies the destructive force should be
allowed to enjoy himself, then why should he reprobate
the people who have put him and are keeping him in
prison? Why should he complain of their "inhumanity"?
If it gives them pleasure to injure him, do they not have
the right to this? And are they not fulfilling the purpose
of Nature? One of the Marquis's favorite imaginings is a
stronghold—a castle in Switzerland or a double-walled
monastery—from which the victims of his libertines cannot escape, so why should he be so indignant at having
been imprisoned himself? One would rather be the tor-
turer than the victim, but why should he judge them
severely? His only resource is to say that his captors are
worse than himself, which involves a moral judgment of a
kind that his system does not admit; and that—what is
more consistent with this system—it will be his turn to
injure *them* when he is eventually at liberty to do so. If
he takes the line that reason and benevolence can produce
an almost ideal society, he is betraying his own belief that
Nature requires a balance between the creative and the

lethal, and is still left with the question of what attitude to take toward his own recalcitrant character, the danger of whose violent acts he makes a point, in *Aline et Valcour*, of having the all-wise Zamé minimize but which he allows to assert itself more and more viciously in most of his other writings.

But at last Donatien is set free, and he finds himself in the midst of the French Revolution. How will he adapt himself? What will he do? What will be done about him? He is now fifty years old.

In the early days of July, 1789, when the rumors were beginning to reach him, in his cell, of the meeting in the tennis court of the Third Estate when the King had turned them out of the great *salle des menus plaisirs du roi* and of the growing excitement of the people, the Governor of the Bastille had his canon loaded and announced that the prisoners were no longer allowed to take their daily walks on the towers. The Marquis flew into a rage and swore to make *"un tapage affreux"* if this privilege were not restored. He had acquired a length of tin pipe and had fitted on to this a funnel in order to make it easier for him to urinate into the moat. He now used it as a megaphone and began to shout through the window. A considerable crowd gathered. He denounced the Governor to them and declared that orders had been given that the prisoners' throats should be cut. As a result, he was roused that night and, hardly dressed and with a pistol at his head, removed to a madhouse at Charenton. A few days later, the Bastille was stormed and its principal officers were slaughtered. A kitchen boy cut off the Governor's head and paraded it on a pike.

The Marquis remained at Charenton nine months in the company of its lunatics and epileptics. His two sons came to visit him there. He had not seen them for fifteen years. When they had told Mme de Montreuil, their grandmother, that they were going to see their father, she said to them, "I hope that he'll be happy but I doubt whether he's capable of it." When the *lettres de cachet* were abolished, she made no effort to prevent his liberation. "It is the only way," she said, "not to have to reproach myself or to be reproached by others." His wife had gone to live in a convent and was arranging a separation. He did, however, succeed in seeing his daughter. To his lawyer, who has apparently remonstrated with him, he writes, "I assure you that *Mademoiselle ma fille* is just as ugly as I painted her to you. I have seen her three or four times since; I examined her very closely, and I assure you that her mind as well as her face are exactly those of a good fat farmer's wife." Whether on this account or on account of her father's reputation, the girl was never to marry. She lived to be seventy-two. Seeing Donatien in these straits, his mother-in-law relented to the extent of supplying him with a few louis but told him that thereafter he would have to depend on getting money from Gaufridy and that she expected him to pay her back. At first, he took a room, where he lived alone. He was completely *dépaysé*. He could not get used to living among men again. In writing to Gaufridy, he inveighs against the Montreuils and describes his present state of mind: "Nobody has any conception of the *infernal* and *anthropophagous* prosecution that I have suffered at the hands of those people. [In his novels, some of his favorite characters are cannibals.] If I had been the lowest creature on earth, no one would have dared to subject me to the barbarous treatment of which I have been the victim; in the course of it, I have lost both my sight and my lungs; I have taken on, lacking exercise, a corpulence so enormous that I can hardly get myself around; all my sensations have been extinguished; I no longer enjoy anything, there is nothing that I like; the world of which I was foolish enough to regret so much being deprived now seems to me boring—sad! There are moments when I am seized with the desire to become a Trappist, and I don't swear that some fine day I may not disappear without anybody's knowing what has happened to me. I have never been so misanthropic as now since I have returned to men, and if I seem to them so strange in reappearing among them, they may be perfectly sure that they produce the same effect on me." The dividing-up of the property that followed the Sades' separation involved long and disagreeable negotiations. The Marquise had made the stipulation that the Marquis should acknowledge himself her debtor for the money received as her dowry, though, instead of demanding it all at once, she allowed him to pay her annual interest. In the meantime, four months after his liberation, the *ci-devant* Marquis had succeeded in attaching to him a young actress under thirty, Marie-Constance Quesnet, who, with a child, had been deserted by her husband. Sade had been haunting the theaters and was even to get two plays produced, and in one case play the leading role. He took a little house in the Rue Neuve-des Mathurins, and there, with some of the furniture from La Coste, he set up housekeeping with his mistress. He must have become less alarming—though what he wrote was, if anything, more ferocious—because he and Marie-Constance seem to have been devoted to one another. It was the only successful relationship in Sade's life.

But his role was now very different. He was no longer a great lord, and what was happening was as frightening to the former Marquis—though, as he says, it did not surprise him—as his own crimes had been to other people. He had registered and had received a card as "active citizen" of the section of the Place Vendôme, later called la Section des Piques, and had been summoned to attend its meetings, in which he played an active part. He was obliged to steer a difficult course. He had to appear a good "patriot," take care not to rouse suspicions; yet he could not help being upset when he heard the news that one of his aunts had been thrown into jail and even more so when his château at La Coste was invaded, wrecked and looted by a mob. His allegiance to the Revolution was probably not wholly due to the desire to save his skin. He might perhaps have escaped abroad, and he was indignant when he found that his name had been included in a list of émigrés. He had suffered enough himself to have some sympathy with the sufferings of the people, and had already, in an episode of *Justine*, made one of his wicked women preach to the virtuous girl a sermon on the text that all human beings have been created by Nature "equal," pointing out to her how wrong it is that the rich should have more than they need and be able to punish the poor for stealing; that the poor should not have any scruples about revenging themselves on the rich. "I confess," he makes Justine say, "that if ever I was shaken at all, it was by the seductions of that clever woman." The Marquis wrote political pamphlets. He rose rapidly in the assembly of his section, and was entrusted with special commissions, including an inspection of the hospitals, where he relieved a shortage of beds when he found that many had to be shared. In April, 1793, he writes to Gaufridy: "I want to tell you two things that will surprise you. Le Président de Montreuil has come to see me." "I can already foresee," he writes later, "the moment when he will ask me to dinner." "—And guess what the other is! I give you one chance in a hundred! I am now a judge, yes, *a judge! Juré d'accusation!* Who would have said that fifteen years ago, my lawyer! who would have said that? You can see that my mind has matured, that I'm beginning to learn wisdom. So congratulate me, and above all don't fail to send money to *monsieur le juge,* or devil take me, if you don't, I'll *condemn you to death!* Spread this news a little in the country so as to convince them at last that I'm a good patriot, because I swear to you that I truly am in heart and soul." He was very soon president of his section and led a delegation to the national Convention with a petition, composed by himself, which that body highly commended and of which it had a thousand copies printed. It was proposed to establish a cult of the Virtues, with hymns and the burning of incense, to be celebrated on the secularized altars.

But Sade did not approve of capital punishment, having narrowly escaped it himself and believing that one ought not to be executed for actions one could not restrain. The meetings of l'Assemblée des Piques became so stormy, in the course of the summer, that he was obliged to defend himself against the violence of his colleagues. He had refused to put to a vote some measure which he describes as *"une horreur, une inhumanité,"* and had resigned his chair of office to the vice president. As the denunciations came thicker and thicker, he seems unobtrusively to have rescued as many of the accused as he could, and when the names of his father-in-law and mother-in-law appeared among those of the suspects, he managed to have them included in a list of those to be cleared. "If I had said a word," he writes Gaufridy, "they would have been in for it. I kept silent; that's how I revenge myself." He opposed the creation in Paris of a special army of six thousand men, on the ground that this was unnecessary because if the city were in danger, "at the first beat of the drum," a hundred and fifty-thousand men would come to its defense, and that the high pay proposed for this body would attract the lazy and the intriguers, who would become a "Pretorian Guard, with the power to put us in chains," and who would violate the principles of the Revolution by constituting a privileged group. It was also whispered against him that he was not a sincere republican, since, in his indiscreet private conversations, he cited instances from the histories of Greece and Rome "to demonstrate the impossibility of establishing a republic in France and converting France into a democracy." His prestige as a victim of the old régime did not save him very long. His past crimes were now being publicized. In a libel against the nobility, "those scoundrels with châteaux, carriages, red heels and red or blue cordons," Sade was named as the worst of the lot and compared to Gilles de Retz. The latter, "though a very great lord and though he lived at a time when the nobility were in a position to commit with impunity the most monstrous crimes, could not escape from justice and was burned alive at Nantes on the twenty-fifth of October, 1450. And now the Marquis de Sade, who has been convicted of the same atrocities, is peacefully living among us." This libel also says that Sade is supporting a rebellion of the actors against certain police regulations. The production of a play of his was stopped on the ground that it was the work of a *ci-devant*. He was arrested on the fifth of December, on a charge of *"modérantisme,"* only a few weeks after presenting his much applauded project for celebrating a cult of the Virtues. Now, shifted from prison to prison, he was to spend more than ten months in jail.

He of course raised a loud complaint. He explained in the most circumstantial way that he was not really noble at all. "We come from a little town of the former Comtat d'Avignon, where my ancestors were farmers and merchants." His title had been thrust upon him, against his will, by "certain slaves of the old regime." He has never

been willing to use it. He is simply a man of letters as his
father was before him. He is going to divorce his wife as
soon as he gets out of prison and marry the daughter of a
tailor, "one of the most excellent patriots in Paris." He
does not know whether or not his sons are émigrés—
he has seen nothing of them for twenty years. If they
have fled abroad, he consigns them "to public execra-
tion, to the national vengeance." He rejoices in the
death of the King—for whom he had formerly professed respect—and congratulates the country on being
delivered from "the most cowardly, the most deceitful
and most unworthy of tyrants." As for Marie-Antoinette:
he declares, after her execution, that "the Austrian
woman has met her just punishment"—though he had
previously written down in his notebook, with obvious sympathy for the Queen, the *Paroles d'Antoinette
à la Conciergerie:* "The ferocious beasts with which I am
surrounded invent every day some new humiliation
which adds to the horror of my destiny; they distil drop
by drop into my heart the poison of adversity, they count
my sighs with delight and, before they feed on my blood,
they quench their thirst with my tears." So Sade's own
victim Justine has wept at the mercy of tormentors entirely invented by himself, when he was all on the side
of the tormentors.

So Sade himself is now at the mercy of the same
"ferocious beasts." With the Terror in full fury, his protestations have no effect. On the twenty-sixth of July,
1794, he was included by Fouquier-Tinville in a list of
men and women to be guillotined, on a charge of "conspiracy against the Republic." Most of these persons were
executed in full view of his place of detention, and
eighteen hundred bodies were buried in what had once
been its fine garden. Sade was afterwards to write of this
experience that it "did him a hundred times more harm

than all the Bastilles imaginable." But he himself by some
fluke escaped. The Tribunals were extremely inefficient.
The many jails were crowded and scattered. It was not
always easy to find the condemned. Then, immediately,
the whole situation changed. Robespierre had just been
arrested, and, the day after the first batch of victims on
the same list as Sade had been executed, at the end of
July, 1794, on the day of celebration of the Supreme
Being, Robespierre and twenty-one other Terrorists were
guillotined to a thunder of applause. In the period of
relaxation that followed, on a petition to the Section des
Piques, Sade received a clean bill of health as belonging
to the category of "patriotic artists devoted to the public
good." Through all this, he had never ceased to correspond with Gaufridy, in the name of *la citoyenne
Quesnet,*" conveying to him detailed instructions about
the management of his estates.

One might think that all this would have given Sade
pause in his literary exploitation of cruelty. But, perhaps
as a result of his increased misanthropy as well as his
indomitable compulsion, he continued in his original
course and even laid the atrocities on thicker. The relatively respectable *Aline et Valcour,* which advocates social
reforms, was announced as *"Par le citoyen S***,"* and
"Écrit à la Bastille un an avant la Révolution de France."
But the anonymous *Justine,* of which the various editions
were supposed to have been printed in Holland, had very
much more success, and it was followed by *La Philosophie
dans le Boudoir,* supposed to be published in London and
announced as *"Ouvrage posthume de l'auteur de 'Justine.'"* Sade decided then to redo *Justine,* making it longer
and more obscene, and to add to it *Juliette.* It is explained
in an "Editor's Note" that the public ought to be informed
that "a disloyal friend" to whom the author had entrusted
the manuscript of his work had not hesitated "to make

from it a miserable extract, very far below the original, which has been repeatedly disavowed by him whose energetic pencil had depicted the Justine and her sister that one will find presented here," with more *boniment* intended to entice the customer. As M. Lely says, this was undoubtedly "a book dealer's speculation based on the general license which reigned during the period of the Directory." This was, in fact, the only period when Sade's works were openly put on sale—they were later suppressed by Napoleon—until the fifties of the present century, when they could be bought in ordinary bookstores, though they were later, under de Gaulle, again suppressed. When *Les Crimes de l'Amour,* which is not obscene though as usual perverse, was introduced as "by D.A.F. Sade, the author of *Aline et Valcour,*" Sade denied that he had written *Justine.* Since everybody knew he had, his position became rather embarrassing. For he considered himself *"un philosophe,"* and he was worried lest his moral misdeameanors might supply the dispossessed clergy with ammunition against those writers whom he regarded as his colleagues of the Enlightenment. *La Philosophie dans le Boudoir* is a very curious work, a series of dialogues which presents the systematic corruption by the usual group of libertines of a young girl just out of a convent but includes a long earnest pamphlet—*Français! Encore un effort si vous voulez être républicains*—an effort to establish a connection between Sade's own rebellious materialism and the idealism of the Revolution.

But though Sade had escaped with his life, he still had the régime against him. His name was on a list of émigrés, and this meant that his property could be seized and that he could be forced actually to leave the country. He sold the château of La Coste; but a part of his income was confiscated, and by the end of 1797, he and Marie-Constance were reduced to such straits that they were obliged temporarily to separate. She went to live with friends and he lodged with a farmer on one of his estates till the latter refused to feed him. He got some sort of job *"au spectacle de Versailles,"* and lived there in a garret with Marie-Constance's son. She brought them food from the house of her friends and, says Sade, went "every day on foot in horrible weather to quiet the creditors and get my name struck off [the list]. This woman is truly an angel sent me by Heaven in order that I may not be entirely crushed by the calamities launched against me by my enemies."

On the sixth of March, 1801, two policemen invaded the offices of the publisher of Sade's books. Napoleon was then First Consul, and till recently it had been thought that the reason for Sade's arrest was a libel against the Bonapartes, *Zoloé et ses deux Acolytes,* supposed to have been written by him. M. Lely, however, has come to the conclusion, from internal evidence and from finding that in the documents relating to the case, no mention is made of this book, that *Zoloé* is not by Sade. In any case, in spite of his public denials, he was known to be the author of *Justine* and was regarded as a dangerous character. He had been watched by the police, who, in their raid on the publisher, found manuscripts in Sade's hand as well as copies of his scandalous books. They also found Sade himself, who had the bad luck to be there. In Marie-Constance's house, they found a tapestry "representing the most obscene subjects, most of them derived from the infamous novel *Justine,"* which was delivered to the *préfecture.* Sade was taken to jail.

He spent two years in the prison of Sainte-Pélagie, in the course of which he wrote in his notebooks: "A phrase to put in my Memoirs: The entr'actes of my life have been too long." Then one of the inevitable incidents oc-

curred. Some young men who had been rioting at the
Théâtre-Français were brought in and put in cells on his
corridor. The starved prisoner incontinently leapt upon
them, and the authorities decided that they would have to
get rid of him. He was moved to an apparently worse
prison at Bicêtre, which, under the old régime, had been
known as *"la Bastille de la canaille."* Charles Nodier, later
to be celebrated as the author of fairy tales and at that
time a young man in the provinces, had published a
rhymed pamphlet that ridiculed Napoleon, and, coming
to Paris, was promptly imprisoned, also in Sainte-Pélagie.
Sade was just being transferred, and Nodier happened to
see him. He has the following description in his memoirs:
"All I noticed at first was enormous obesity which sufficiently hampered his movements to prevent his displaying
any vestige of the grace and elegance the traces of which
appeared in his manners. His weary eyes still kept, however, something fine and brilliant which would come to
life from time to time like the dying spark of an extinguished coal." He had only a glimpse of Sade, he says.
"All I remember is that he was polite to the point of
obsequiousness, affable to the point of unctuousness, and
that he spoke respectfully of everything that is respected."

When Sade had been in jail a year, his family had him
removed to a madhouse at Charenton, where he passed
the rest of his life. But here, too, he became a problem.
The director was an ex-abbé, a gentleman, M. de Coulmier, who made friends with the ex-marquis and allowed
him to organize theatricals, with the patients as actors. He
sometimes wrote the plays himself and on one occasion
composed "an allegoric piece" for M. de Coulmier. He
also presided at balls and various kinds of meetings and
celebrations. *"Les moeurs y étaient fort légères,"* one of the
doctors reports, *"et, à ce qu'il parait, tant soit peu décol-
létées."* Sade even gave private dinners in his own apart-

ment, to which he invited well-known actors and actresses, including the then popular comédienne, Mlle de Sainte-Aubin, whom Lely describes as *"délicieuse."* One evening she found under her napkin a graceful little quatrain composed by *"le galant amphytrion."* But the chief doctor was scandalized and scared by all this. He wrote to the Chief of Police that Sade ought to be removed from the hospital. "This man is not insane. His only madness is that of vice, and an institution supposed to be devoted to the medical treatment of insanity is not the place to control this kind of madness. An individual afflicted with it should be subjected to the severest segregation both to protect others from his furies and to isolate him from all the objects which might excite or maintain his hideous passion. This is impossible at Charenton. M. de Sade enjoys too much liberty there. He is able to communicate with a good many people of both sexes, to receive them in his own rooms or visit them in theirs. He is allowed to walk in the park, and he often meets the patients there. . . . He preaches his horrible doctrine to some; to others he lends books. And the general rumor is that he is living with a woman who passes for his daughter." What had happened was that Marie-Constance had moved into the hospital with him. The doctor then complains about the theater. M. de Coulmier did not, however, agree with him. He said that the theater was therapeutic and that he was very grateful to Sade for the work he was doing. The Chief of Police was ready to send him to jail, but the director and Sade's family prevented this. Sade, on his side, in his threatening and pleading way, was demanding to be taken out of the madhouse and writing appeals to the Minister of Police and to Napoleon, who by this time had made himself Emperor. The latter took up the matter with his privy council and decided not to let Sade be freed. The Minister of the Interior attempted to have him kept in isolation and denied the use of writing materials; but to this order Coulmier replied that the hospital was so crowded that there was no place in which M. de Sade could be isolated, that he was under constant supervision and had no communication with anybody except the servants, and that, in any case, he, Coulmier, "would find himself extremely unhappy to spend his time persecuting a man, guilty enough, of course, but who has seemed for a long time now, by his continued good behavior, to wish to make us forget his faults. . . . My birth, the various posts and dignities with which I have been invested have won me the honor of being made the head of a humane institution, but I should consider myself humiliated to become a jailor." When Coulmier was succeeded by another director, the latter, to his dismay, found Sade enjoying complete liberty and getting the patients to copy his writings and smuggle them out to the printer. This worried him very much, and he wrote to the Minister of the Interior to have Sade taken over by the police, explaining further that the asylum bill had never been paid, as had been promised, by Sade's elder son. But Sade was old and ill now, half-blind, though he never stopped writing—Marie-Constance read to him. He was not sent to prison again, and he died within a few weeks. The last thing he is known to have written is a letter to a farmer on one of his estates, asking whether his instructions have been followed in regard to certain trees that he wanted to have cut down, for the purpose of selling the wood to pay for repairs on one of his châteaux. Three weeks later, he died, after receiving extreme unction. He was seventy-four years old and had been in the asylum eleven years and eight months. A new doctor was with him when he died and has left a short memoir of him. "I used to meet him frequently walking alone, with a heavy and dragging step, very carelessly dressed, in the corridor next to his apartment; I never found him talking with anyone. When I passed him, I would bow to him, and he would return my bow with that kind of cold politeness which discourages any idea of conversation."

He had published one novel at Charenton and left, among other things, an *Histoire Secrète d'Isabelle de Bavière,* about Charles the Sixth's maleficent Queen. He pretended to have discovered a document in the archives of the Pères Chartreux at Dijon—the interrogatory, under torture, of one of the Queen's henchmen—which made her responsible for everything evil that had occurred during her reign. But the library of the Chartreux had, he said, been destroyed at the time of the Revolution. There is no reason to believe, it seems, that this document ever existed. It was simply an excuse for Sade to recreate Isabelle as even worse than she was, as, in fact, one of his own criminal heroines. His principal production, however, had been a huge novel which would have run to ten volumes: *Les Journées de Florbelle, ou la Nature Dévoilée.* It was Sade's elder son who had the sole responsibility for disposing of his father's effects. The younger one had been killed in Napoleon's campaign in Italy. He gave this work to the police to be burned. This, of course, breaks M. Lely's heart, but from the notes for the book that survive one can hardly very much regret it. The author had simply been imagining further sadistic orgies, accompanied by further "dissertations on Religion, on the Soul, on the Creator and on Morals." A group of people who sound rather like those of *Les 120 Journées de Sodome* were to enjoy a series of *"fêtes,"* one of which was to consist of fireworks—perhaps suggested by the author's reckless use of them in his youthful soldiering days—"in which children are blown up by rockets and bombs." How gratified Sade would have been if he could have foreseen the scale on which we were later to indulge in this pastime! Or would he perhaps have been appalled, as he was by the Terror?

Sade left a remarkable will. He makes provision first of all for Marie-Constance, wishing "to demonstrate to that lady, so far as my feeble powers permit, my extreme gratitude for the care and the sincere friendship that she has had for me since the twenty-fifth of August, 1790, up to the day of my death, sentiments to which she has borne witness not merely with disinterestedness and delicacy, but even also with the most courageous energy, since under the régime of Terror she snatched me from the revolutionary scythe too certainly suspended over my head." (Lely says that this can only refer to Sade's getting out of jail, not to his escape from the guillotine and believes that he has misrepresented what actually happened in order to impress his son with his debt to Marie-Constance.) He leaves her twenty-five thousand livres to be derived "from the freest and clearest part of my properties," as well as all his possessions in the hospital, with the exception of his father's papers, which are to be given to his children. There is nothing else about these children except that they are to see to it that Marie-Constance gets her money within a month after his death. To his executor, a notary, in repayment for his services, he leaves a ring worth twelve hundred livres. He gives elaborate instructions for his burial. His coffin is not to be nailed till forty-eight hours after his death. It is to be taken in a cart to a certain wood on one of his country estates and there buried, "without any sort of ceremony, in the first thicketed coppice on the right in the said wood as you enter it on the side of the old château by the great alley that runs through it." Those of his relatives or friends who may wish to may be present, but they are not to wear mourning. "As soon as the grave is filled in, it will be strewn with acorns, in order that, when the ground over the grave will have grown up again and the coppice be thicketed as it was before, the traces of my grave will disappear from the face of the earth as I flatter myself that my memory will be erased from the minds of men, excepting, however, on the part of the small number of those who have been kind enough to love me up to the end and of whom I shall carry to the tomb a very sweet memory."

This was not done, however. Sade was buried, with the regular rites, in the hospital cemetery. A stone cross was put up over the grave, but no name was inscribed to mark it.

Twenty years later, Sade's son, on learning that a "universal biography" was nearing the letter S, wrote to the biographer begging him not to include his father's name.

SWINBURNE'S LETTERS AND NOVELS

THE POETRY OF SWINBURNE is now so out of fashion that it seems to have become very difficult to interest people in him at all. Yet two scholars who are strong admirers have recently done important work on him and made available unpublished materials which fill out one's incomplete picture. One of these is the late Randolph Hughes, who rescued and had printed, between 1942 and 1952, three hitherto withheld manuscripts of Swinburne's, all written, it would seem, in the eighteen-sixties, when the poet was at the height of his powers but, for reasons of propriety, never published (though the second of them mentioned below was privately circulated in an edition of twenty copies). These are six chapters of an Italian romance in mock-Renaissance prose, *Lucretia Borgia: The Chronicle of Tebaldeo Tebaldei*; the opening scene of a play called *Pasiphaë*—intended to supply the loss of Euripides' tragedy on the subject—which contains, in the Nurse's speech, one charming passage of poetry; and—what is of most interest—the novel *Lesbia Brandon,* which, though one of Swinburne's major projects, his friend Theodore Watts-Dunton prevented him from printing. (The two former were published in England by the Golden Cockerel Press, and the third by the Falcon Press.) Hughes had also intended to make available a number of other works by Swinburne which had been circulated only privately, but his death, in 1956, prevented this. It is good news that the publication of these hitherto suppressed writings will be continued by the other great Swinburne specialist, Mr. Cecil Y. Lang, formerly at Yale and now at Syracuse University, who has edited for the first time the whole of Swinburne's extant correspondence. Mr. Lang's edition of this correspondence, which runs to six volumes, presents also, among its more than two thousand letters, a good deal of unpublished material and includes, besides Swinburne's own letters, many others from his family and friends, and from writers such as Browning and Matthew Arnold, Victor Hugo and Baudelaire, with whom he exchanged books and compliments. The correspondence has been supplemented by extracts from obscure memoirs which record impressions of Swinburne at various times in his life.

It is amusing and no doubt inevitable that both Hughes and Mr. Lang should be rather unconventional editors and should have caught, in their different ways, something of the tone of their subject and of the literary atmosphere in which he lived. It is appropriate that their commentaries should remind one of the persistent personal flavor and sometimes bristling attitudes of the early-nineteenth-century scholars, such as Gifford and Dyce, who edited those Elizabethan dramatists to whom Swinburne was so devoted. Randolph Hughes, an Australian, who lectured on French literature at King's College, London, was excessively bellicose and gave vent to his indignation against everyone else who had ever dared to write about Swinburne, in rhetorical denunciations which echo, in a coarser form, the style often adopted by Swinburne himself in detonating against his opponents. In his edition of *Lesbia Brandon,* a hundred and eighty-nine pages of text are enveloped in an enormous commentary of four hundred and twenty-nine pages, which contains a few real insights and some new information but which exhibits Hughes's inability to make any assertion about anything without savagely attacking someone else's assertion or being impelled by his taurine instinct to make a fierce charge at someone who has no real relevance to the subject. His foreword to *Lesbia Brandon* is knee-deep or waist-deep or neck-deep in huge footnotes, the longest of which, occupying the greater part of five pages, consists of a tirade against Ezra Pound. Such an editor resented the intrusion into what he considered his own domain by Mr. Cecil Lang and treated him with the utmost rudeness, which incited Mr. Lang to retaliation. The editor of *Lesbia Brandon* had castigated on every other page the carelessness and incompetence of his predecessors, and Mr. Lang now addressed to the *Times Literary Supplement* a letter that filled almost the whole of a page, in which he listed the misprints, misstatements and inaccurate quotations that had been perpetrated or permitted by Hugues himself in connection with *Lesbia Brandon*. "The arraignment of this book and its author," Mr. Lang concluded with a sigh, "has been a melancholy and tedious task." Hughes replied with his usual fury, but putting forward the very weak excuse—which he would never have accepted from anyone else—that at the time the book was going through the press he had been forced to be absent from London. He quoted Swinburne as having said about William Bell Scott, apropos of the "posthumous falsehoods" of Scott's memoirs, that he had been "insolent, impertinent and presumptuous," and added, "The adjectives apply fully to another case; and let him whom it fits put on the cap and go and stand in the corner."

In the case of Mr. Lang, as with Randolph Hughes, we always feel a personality present, but a much more agreeable one, which asserts itself in an occasional joke or a sprightly informal remark: "Swan seems to have existed and probably had a first name, though all the chroniclers have dropped it somewhere," "Clara Watts-Dunton, who didn't bustle into the picture until years later," "a book of travel that ran (but not very fast) in *Blackwood's*." And this indifference to deadpan scholarship, this sympathetic imagination, only add to the attractiveness of these volumes. We seem to accompany the editor, to participate in his researches—though he sometimes accomplishes feats which make us wonder how they were done. He has performed, really, prodigies in tracking down the innumerable quotations and allusions which are scattered through Swinburne's letters. The poet is likely to assume in these letters, as he is said to have done in his conversation, that everyone else has read all the same books as he and remembers them with the same exactitude, and one is almost driven to supposing that Mr. Lang has held in his head the whole text of these two thousand letters while he carefully went through every book he could imagine that Swinburne knew. It has, I believe, been complained that he has gone too relentlessly far in giving references that everyone must recognize—as when he notes every echo of Sarah Gamp or explains that Ananias is to be found in Acts 5:1–5—but this serves to bring out in a striking way that Swinburne must have known almost by heart the Bible, the Prayer Book, Shakespeare and Dickens, as well as have had an enormous range among lesser writers, famous and obscure. Now and then Mr. Lang takes for granted a knowledge of other matters which might not be possessed by the ordinary reader—as when he says, at the first appearance of Thomas J. Wise, one of Swinburne's correspondents, that "identification is superfluous." Now, that Wise first established a reputation as an infallible and omniscient bibliographer, then was exposed as an unscrupulous rogue, a forger of first editions and a faker of Elizabethan folios is, to be sure, known to all English scholars, but outside this group probably not widely known.

Mr. Lang has collected here, without exclusion or expurgation, every letter of Swinburne's that he was able to track down—including those that Edmund Gosse had believed to be forever unpublishable. Gosse was hampered, when he wrote Swinburne's life and published a selection of his letters, not only by his own Victorian scruples but also—and even more seriously—by the determined obstruction of the poet's relatives. He felt, however, that the gap he had been forced to leave in his account of Swinburne's career laid him under the obligation, as one who knew more about Swinburne than any other surviving friend, to put on record those aspects of his subject which Swinburne's relatives would never have allowed him to reveal—his outrageous and disastrous drinking and his peculiar sexual habits. Gosse, therefore, wrote a supplement to his life, which was bought by the British Museum, and Mr. Lang has now had this printed as an appendix to the correspondence. We must be grateful to him and to Hughes for disregarding both genteel inhibitions and the recent lack of interest in Swinburne. They have expended a great deal of exacting labor—in the case of Mr. Lang, many years—in order to contribute to literature a fuller knowledge of this strange gifted man and his work, and they both deserve citations from the Republic of Letters.

The present writer has, rather to his own surprise, read these six volumes of letters straight through with an interest and an enjoyment hardly ever fatigued. It is true, no doubt, as Mr. Lang says, that Swinburne as a letter writer "is not to be compared with the great masters in English." His intellectual limitations are obvious—not so much in the scope of his interests as in a sort of arrested development in the juvenile preoccupations of his school days, which is felt throughout this long correspondence in a certain repetitiousness and monotony. It was at Eton that Swinburne discovered the Elizabethan dramatists, familiarized himself with them more thoroughly than many boys of that age can have done, and conceived the enthusiasm for them that was to last all the rest of his life; he was still writing about them at the time of his death. It was at Eton that he first also read Hugo and Landor, who were to remain for him supreme heroes, his attitude toward whom was quite abject. The founding of the Second Empire had occurred while Swinburne was at Eton and inspired him with that hatred of Napoleon III which was to cause him later at Oxford to hang upon his wall, opposite a picture of Mazzini—one of his great admirations—a portrait of Orsini, the *carbonaro* who attempted to assassinate the Emperor, and to try to leap up and kiss it, which his slight stature did not quite permit. It was at Eton that he received the floggings which were to remain, also, one of his obsessions and which seem to have conditioned a crippling of the whole of his emotional life. Swinburne's violent republicanism seems also to have been derived very early from his extraordinary old Gallicized grandfather, who—though the Swinburnes, who had been Catholics, were loyal to the Stuarts and fled to the Continent with them—had been a friend of Mirabeau and, by supporting the Revolution, had made himself "liable," as he told the boy, "to be impeached and executed for high treason." (He was born in 1761 and lived to be ninety-nine.) But Swinburne combined, like Landor, an ardent republicanism with a certain lack of enthusiasm for democracy. He makes fun, in his early phase, of Victoria and her consort and, running true to Tory tradition, pretends to scorn the

house of Hanover, but though passionately on the side of
the republicans in the Italian *risorgimento* and the over-
throw of the Second Empire in France, he is later to
write an ode for Victoria's Jubilee which—though he
insists on its essential republicanism—he is very much
pleased to hear has been well received by the Queen, and
at the time of the war in South Africa he becomes quite
ferocious against the Boers. As for Ireland, he begins by
defending the Fenians against the British police, but later
becomes equally ferocious, after the Phoenix Park murders, against Gladstone, Parnell and Home Rule, and
when taxed with inconsistency, writes letters to the
papers asserting that it is all a question of method.
Mazzini, he declares, had never approved of the methods
of the *carbonari*. Swinburne has evidently by this time
forgotten his hero Orsini. Mazzini had always insisted
that the union must be preserved. Swinburne is in fact
quite naïve in his attitude toward political events, as he
never quite is about literary matters. He has not, at any
stage of his life, thought about them realistically at all,
and his rhetorical verse on these subjects has become
today, it seems to me, unreadable.

Yet his hailings of the sunrise of republicanism, his
invectives against its enemies, do not become so boring in
Swinburne's letters as they do in his other writings. Why
is this? He is here reiterating these as relentlessly as anywhere else. But in his odes and his prose essays, he so
often, as his mother once complained, does not know
when to stop. He piles up enormous monuments that can
only impress through their bulk, and he brings to them a
factitious solemnity that can soon become tedious or
approach the burlesque. In his letters, on the other
hand—except in his epistles to the papers, in which he
appears in his public role—he can never go on so long,
and his affectionate and humorous nature prevents him

from becoming a pompous bore. This and his unfailing vivacity. We know that he was often ill, and Gosse tells us that in middle life he had a period of depression and irritability. But there is no self-pity in Swinburne. Though he sometimes mentions indisposition as an apology for not answering letters, though he sometimes becomes enraged over something that has been written about himself or a friend, he never complains about his own afflictions and, though frequently denunciatory, he is rarely ill-natured or peevish. Even his hatreds have a certain exuberance, and his rages all run to rhetoric. Here is a life lived entirely for literature, in which nothing else is really important—and since literature is inexhaustible, a life that is immensely enjoyed. He drank too much when he lived in London, and this made him a volcanic nuisance. He loved swimming and revelled in the Channel and in the seas of Northumberland and Cornwall. He was enchanted by his walking trips with Jowett and Richard Burton. Swinburne never married and after his first disappointment in love, seems to have had no serious love affairs; but, although self-regarding in the sense that his whole life is centered about his own work, his literary enthusiasm is generous and overflows to his favorite authors as well as to the work of his friends. His personality, so eccentric and endearing, comes out in this correspondence as rarely in his formal writings—the combination of signorial dignity, an old-fashioned ceremonial politeness, with schoolboy ribaldry and impish mischief. He is delighted when a man named Robert Browning is arrested for a second offense of running naked at noonday through the Marble Arch and when a man named Matthew Arnold is fined for playing tipcat in the street.

But these letters have another kind of interest. Taken together with certain of his other writings—expecially

Lesbia Brandon—they enable one to recognize as one may not have done before exactly who and what Swinburne was. The poet of *Poems and Ballads,* the retired elfin bookworm of Putney, have, to be sure, been much and well described. The fantastic little man of genius, with his blazing shock of hair, his sloping shoulders and his twitching movements, who skipped and danced as he poured out poetry, sometimes shocking people, sometimes annoying and sometimes exhilarating them, has been created for literary history by Edmund Gosse, Max Beerbohm, Henry Adams and others. Adams described him as "a tropical bird, high-crested, long-beaked, quick moving, with rapid utterance and screams of humor, quite unlike any English lark or nightingale. One could hardly call him a crimson macaw among owls, and yet no ordinary contrast availed." This Swinburne is a legend of Victorian London. But what his life had been like in his youth and how he afterwards came to live is only fully to be learned from these letters, from the results of the special researches of the scholars who have lately been working on him, and from Swinburne's more personal writings, which are also his most unfamiliar—especially his two novels. For Swinburne had a story to tell which he does not tell explicitly in his poetry but which he does partly tell in his fiction, and it is to elements of this personal story, so little brought out by Gosse, that I particularly want to call attention.

The point is that Swinburne was unique among important English writers of the nineteenth century in that he belonged to the top nobility. He describes himself in one of these letters as coming from the same social class as Byron, Shelley and Landor, but actually he must have outranked them. His father, the Admiral, was the second son of the French-born and -bred Sir John Swinburne, whom Algernon believed to have married a Polignac, though his cousin Mrs. Disney Leith says that this is not quite correct; and his mother was the daughter of the third Earl of Ashburnham. Both families were intermarried with the Dukes of Northumberland. The Ashburnhams and the Swinburnes were exceptional in having a good deal of France in their background, in having become incredibly inbred and in being unusually cultivated. Swinburne had grown up among his relatives, and he spent the greater part of his life with them. The pattern of his life after Oxford, except for two early years when he rented a room at the Rossettis', was to live alone in lodgings up to the point when the excitement of London life and the lack of restraining influences would culminate in a fit—he seems to have been an epileptic— or in a complete alcoholic collapse. The city always went to his head. Alone in his lodgings or in company, he would be carried away by transports that sometimes reached the point of paroxysm, and he would consume all the liquor in sight. On one occasion, when dining out, he got into the dining room before dinner and drank up the dessert wine set out there. They found him later, says Gosse, "dancing like a fairy-maenad, round and round the dining-table." Gosse explains that Swinburne was under the impression that he carried his liquor well; he would forget what had happened when he was drunk and deny what people told him he had done because he could not believe that is was possible for a gentleman to behave in that way. This seems obviously confirmed by these letters, in which we never hear of his having a hangover but only of incapacitating illness that has resulted from unexplained or improbable causes. In one case, when he has had to retreat to the country and spend many days in bed, he keeps writing that he has been poisoned at some house where he has stayed from having slept in a room with certain "Indian lilies." Gosse tells us that he "had waked in the middle of the night in a delirium, rousing the household with his shrieks." When things got to this pass, his friends would either ship him off to his parents, or his family would come and get him. Except for a very few weeks, he seems never to have had even a regular mistress; and, with no one to keep him in order, he was obliged to fall back on the Swinburnes, among whom he would sober up, recover his balance and go on with his work.

In London, Swinburne said quite truly, he saw little of the literary world. Most of his close friends—George Powell, John Nichol, Jowett, Burne-Jones, William Morris—he had first known at Eton or Oxford or had this background in common with them (and the Rossettis, too, he knew through Oxford, from the time when Dante Gabriel had come there to do a mural with Burne-Jones and Morris). He can never have known much about London. You get almost as little sense of it from his correspondence as you do from his other writings. Most of his business with publishers was handled by more practical friends, and he was dropped from his only club for stamping one night, in his cups, on all the hats that he found in the coatroom. (Gosse and Swinburne's friend Coulson Kernahan give two different accounts of this. Gosse says that, leaving the club, Swinburne destroyed the hats, after trying them on one by one, in a fury because none of them fitted his disproportionately large head; Kernahan that, coming into the club with a friend, after an evening on the town, when a special committee meeting was being held, and beholding the formidable array of opera hats, silk hats and bowlers hanging on the coatroom pegs, he and his friend were inspired to line them up in two rows on the floor and, hopping on one foot, with the other ankle held in his hand, to compete in a race the objective of which was, stepping on all the hats, to get first to the end of the line. A letter which refers to this incident is distinguished by Swinburne's usual dignity; he seems puzzled by the action of the club and implies that it is merely a question of making the damage good, which he will of course be glad to do.)

During the last thirty years of Swinburne's life, when he lived with Watts-Dunton in suburban Putney, he was guarded by his jealous companion from intruders and friends alike; but even after his father's death, when his mother had sold their two country places and was living in other houses, he pays her long visits in the summers or autumns. He writes Watts-Dunton in 1882 that he has "got again into a delightful groove of quiet family life, and should not"—but for missing Watts-Dunton and his sister and her little boy—"care how long I remained in it." He became more attentive to his mother and wrote his sisters long letters. He is immensely proud of a dear Aunt Ju, who, at ninety-two, walks "slippery" moors and climbs "awkward and rather precipitous banks" with him, and who does not mind being caught in the rain. To his sister Alice he dedicates, with verses of the warmest devotion, one of his later poetic plays and goes to the country to read it to her.

One of the most striking features of Swinburne's family was their interest in literature and the arts. Swinburne's mother taught him French and Italian so early that he was familiar from childhood with the literatures of those languages. His uncle, the fourth Earl of Ashburnham, had collected a valuable library of manuscripts and rare books, and it is evident from Swinburne's letters written after his father's death that the library of the Swinburnes themselves contained rarities and curiosities. The family, including the Admiral—though Algernon less than the others—were also extremely musical; they sang and played the organ and piano. Some of them painted, and Turner was a friend of the family (as was also Leigh Hunt). In the period of his liveliest intellectual life, Swinburne sometimes, during the months when he is staying with his family, complains that he has no one there to share his interests, and he writes to William Rossetti, in connection with Shelley's relations with his father, that he "has no more doubt that it may be said for Sir Timothy that his son was what Carlyle calls 'an afflictive phenomenon' than that I was the same to my father before, during, and since my Oxford time" (he had not been allowed to graduate, for reasons which may be imagined but which have never been made known). He tells Rossetti that he is "sure you can never have felt at that age the irreparable, total and inevitable isolation from all that had once been closest to the mind and thought, and that was still closest to the flesh and the memory, the solitude in which one passes from separation to antagonism (without violent quarrels or open offense, but by pure logical necessity of consequence) the sense that where attraction gradually ends repulsion gradually begins, which many besides Shelley, and as affectionate and faithful by nature and temperament as he, *have* felt at that age." Yet the Admiral from the very beginning offered to pay for the publication of Algernon's books and did pay for that of *Atalanta in Calydon,* and he very much pleased his son by reading the whole of his gigantic *Bothwell,* a blank-verse drama about Mary Stuart. It is quite touching, after the publication of *Atalanta* and the first series of *Poems and Ballads,* which caused so much scandal, to find the father writing to Ruskin, who had been trying to reassure him about Algernon, "It is a great comfort to us to know that he has a friend who understands him so well and can sympathize with him. We all care for sympathy, but he is so far beyond us that it is not easy in his case to give it, at least with reference to his writings: and they contain passages that give us great pain and sorrow, and check the longing desire to be pleased." Yes, Swinburne was in certain ways fortunate. He had in childhood adored Northumberland, from which his family came and where they went every summer and autumn to stay with Swinburne's French grandfather, and he delighted in his summers on the Isle of Wight, where his parents had a country place and where he loved to ride and swim with his brothers and sisters and cousins, and to plunge into the poetry which he read and wrote and in which he swam like the sea.

But Swinburne's immersion in his family had the effect of limiting his emotional life. It is evidently the key to his only real love, to its frustration and to his later inability ever to fall in love again. It is evidently the key to *The Triumph of Time, Les Noyades* and *A Leave-Taking,* the three poems, printed together in the first *Poems and Ballads,* which come out of a crisis in Swinburne's life that has never until very recently been properly understood. Gosse, in his *Life* of Swinburne, asserts that the inspirer of *The Triumph of Time* was a certain girl nicknamed Boo, the adopted daughter of a London physician, who, according to Gosse's legend, laughed in Swinburne's face when he proposed marriage to her. The poet, says Gosse, was "deeply chagrined, and, in a way which those who knew him well will easily imagine for themselves, he showed his displeasure, and they parted on the worst of terms." This, it now appears, could never have happened. The story has been investigated by a Swinburne collector, Mr. John S. Mayfield, and he has discovered that the Boo in question was only a little over ten years old when Swinburne is supposed to have proposed to her.

Mr. Mayfield published his findings in 1953, and Mr. Lang has applied himself further to the problem of the poet's disappointed love. He reread *The Triumph of Time* and discovered that it is said there quite clearly that "the speaker did *not* declare his love, and the Innominata *had no suspicion* of its existence." (*Les Noyades* corroborates this.) It is also quite clear that the lady is now married to someone else but that the speaker will continue to see her. There is no suggestion whatever that they have parted on bad terms. Mr. Lang looked up a rough draft of certain stanzas of the poem which—combined with some stanzas of *A Leave-Taking*—had been preserved in a manuscript in the Yale University Library, and these threw further light on the situation. From these and the poem in its finished form we must conclude that the poet and the lady had written verses and enjoyed music together. Now, we know that Swinburne had a cousin—Mary Gordon—with whom he was extremely intimate, who played the organ, who wrote *bouts rimés* with him and with whom he collaborated on a children's story. Swinburne writes to one of his sisters ecstatically about hearing Mary Gordon play Handel. She was evidently accomplished and attractive, and she and Algernon had been constantly together as children. We know that from the summer of 1863 till early in 1864 he was living with his family on the Isle of Wight, very near the Gordons' place. When the Swinburnes went abroad at the end of the summer, Algernon stayed on with the Gordons from October to February. But Mary Gordon at some point not much later must have had to announce to Swinburne that she was engaged to Colonel Disney Leith. She married in June, 1865. We may imagine that Algernon, then in his middle twenties, was already in love with his cousin but had not yet told her so. When Mrs. Leith wrote an introductory memoir to a collection of his letters to his family, she made a point of denying, in contradiction to a rumor which she says has been circulated, that her relations with Algernon were anything other than those of brother and sister. On the other hand, she tells us that, just before her engagement, Swinburne read her some parts of a novel which was evidently *Lesbia Brandon*. Now, we find in *Lesbia Brandon* a scene between brother and sister which is intensely erotic and extremely moving; and the description in another novel, *Love's Cross-Currents*, of the hero's ecstatic ride with his cousin seems exactly to correspond with Mrs. Leith's account of her reckless country rides with Algernon, in the course of which, as in the novel, they carried on the most animated conversations. From Mary's own point of view, her brilliant cousin, however sympathetic and affectionate, and however erotic in the past their relations had perhaps once been, may well have seemed unimaginable in anything but a brotherly relation. "My marriage," she writes, "in 1865, and subsequent residence for much of the year in Scotland, naturally caused something of a gap in our constant correspondence and intercourse, though he was always the same when we did meet," and they do not, in fact, seem to have corresponded for twenty-five years after this. I agree with Mr. Lang that his theory is confirmed by Swinburne's novels as well as by his late play *The Sisters*—all of them based on the family relationships. (The paper in which Mr. Lang has dealt with this matter appeared in the March, 1959, issue of the *Publications of the Modern Language Association of America*.) The extraordinarily complicated tangles of kinship which sometimes make these works so confusing come to seem less bizarre and more credible when we learn that Mary's and Algernon's mothers were sisters and their fathers first cousins, and that their paternal grandmothers had also been sisters and first cousins of their common maternal grandfather. One can conceive that it may have been as natural for Mary to turn away by instinct from this too protracted inbreeding as it was for poor Algernon—of whom we are told that he was somewhat gauche and distant with women—not to be able to feel any very strong attraction toward anyone but a clever cousin.

Another special feature of Swinburne's family which made him exceptional in Victorian England was the French strain, which gave him what can almost be called a non-English alter ego. He wrote French with facility and elegance, though occasional incorrectitudes, and cherished France as a second fatherland, with which he always kept up close connections. It is a little surprising to see how much of this correspondence is in French—his letters to Victor Hugo, Mallarmé, Vacquerie and others; and there is a letter from Baudelaire, whom Swinburne had discovered with excitement at a time when he was apparently not known in England and had no great reputation in France. Swinburne perpetrated also, in French, a whole series of burlesques and hoaxes, from epigraphs for his poems in imitation Old French to a Hugoesque novel of which over fifteen thousand words survive. Two of his hoaxes were extremely sly attempts to impose on the editor of the *Spectator* with reviews of imaginary French authors, the quotations from whom he concocted himself. One of these was Félicien Cossu, the author of *Les Amours Étiques,* a Baudelairean poet who writes about his mistress in the following vein:

> *Sa voix glapissante a des sons doux et m'attire;*
> *Son rictus morne et flasque est un divin sourire;*
> *Sa crapule a l'odeur fraîche et chaste du lait;*
> *Et son vomissement quelque chose qui plaît.*

The other of the bogus reviews deals with a work called *Les Abîmes,* by an author named Ernest Clouët, a prose counterpart of *Les Amours Étiques*. What is masterly in these burlesques is the contrast between the French decadents letting themselves go and the tone of the English reviewer, with his restrained but superior sarcasm. After quoting an apotheosis of the Marquis de Sade in a poem called *Prométhée,* and noting the regrettable direction which the author appears to be taking, the reviewer concludes complacently: "We who have no inclination that way just now, will take leave of Mr. Clouët with a word of kindly counsel. We recommend him to give up all idea of making headway against the tide of modern morals, even with that Titan-phantom of the Arch-Unmentionable pulling stroke-oar in his boat. We do not believe he is really the sort of man to end in Bicêtre [an insane asylum to which Sade was consigned]. We implore him to think of some honest trade—say of grocery—as an opening in life, feeling convinced that he would sleep warmly and well under protection of the proverbial bonnet de coton; and very heartily wish him speedy repentance, timely silence and compassionate oblivion." The editor refused both these pieces, in the first case remonstrating with Swinburne for the suggestion that the *Spectator* should print anything about an author so vile; in the second, though the article got as far as proof, perhaps suspecting the hoax.

Swinburne wrote also in French two burlesques of a more elaborate kind—a novel called *La Fille du Policeman* and a drama called *La Sœur de la Reine.* He idolized Victor Hugo, and when *L'Homme Qui Rit* appeared defended it against the ridicule the book had provoked by its comic mistakes about English life; but in *La Fille du Policeman* he is undoubtedly to some extent parodying the reckless romanticism of his favorite as well as of other French novelists who have undertaken to write about England. The point of both these jeux d'esprit, which are

also tours de force, is the opposite of the journalistic
hoaxes. Instead of subjecting the French to the com-
placent disapproval of the English, the imaginary French
author here, who is supposed to know nothing about
England save a smattering of the early history of the reign
of Queen Victoria and a few English words and proper
names, which he invariably misunderstands and misuses,
is attempting to impose on the English the conventions of
French fiction and drama. In *La Fille du Policeman,* the
Chartist movement is represented as a popular revolution
à la française. Prince Albert, who wants to establish himself as king in all but the name, pretends to sympathize
with the uprising and is known as *"le prince-prolétaire."*
The mob gathers in *"la grande place Wauxhall"* and
moves on *"Buckingham-Palace"—"le vieux palais goth-
ique"*—which is guarded by the *"Queen's own aldermen."*
But the Prince demoralizes the rebels by throwing open
to them *"les immenses magasins Alsopp-Barclay"* and giving them access to unlimited beer. George Meredith
writes in one of his letters, after Swinburne has read him
this novel: "One chapter, *'Ce qui peut se passer dans un
Cab-Safety,'* where Lord Whitestick, Bishop of Londres,
ravishes the heroine, is quite marvellous." This heroine is
the daughter of a noble policeman who has taken a
leading part in the uprising; John Whitestick is a cynical
prelate who has had the girl doped with opium. This
climactic chapter has disappeared, perhaps suppressed by
someone who found it too shocking. In the play, *La
Sœur de la Reine,* Queen Victoria appears as a debauched and cruel tyrant who vents her passions in long
French *tirades.* She makes a tumultuous scene of jealousy
with Lord John Russell, who has been one of her lovers,
and when he threatens to expose her scandalous life, she
threatens to have him beheaded, as she has just done with
the headmaster of Eton, who has been telling his students

about Messalina. The sister is an illegitimate daughter of the Duchess of Kent, who has spent her early life as a prostitute but has just married the Lord Mayor of London, and who creates a second-act curtain by turning up at court and compelling the Queen to receive her. Only two acts of this drama are known to be extant, but a friend to whom Swinburne had read it has left on record what is evidently a passage from one of the scenes that have been lost. Victoria is confessing to her mother a humiliating love affair: *Ce n'était pas un prince; ce n'était pas un milord, ni même Sir R. Peel. C'était un misérable du peuple, un nommé Wordsworth, qui m'a récité des vers de son 'Excursion' d'une sensualité si chaleureuse qu'ils m'ont ébranlée—et je suis tombée."*

Mr. Lang is soon to publish these pieces in a volume of Swinburne's miscellanies.* They are not only amusing in themselves but are interesting as showing how Swinburne was continually shifting back and forth between an English and a French mentality. I believe that it is probably true, as is suggested by Georges Lafourcade, Swinburne's French biographer, that these pieces imply a longing for an England more passionate and violent than that of the Victorian age. This double point of view is important, as we shall see, in Swinburne's fictions, one of which contains another French parody. The scene is an English household in which the schoolboys are working at their Latin verses while a lady who has come to call is discussing with placid complacency the splendid work that the local clergyman is doing for "those poor women" and another lady is reading aloud from a new French novel called *La Chimère*. The latter two conversations are tangled in the following passage: "And so his wife heard

---

* This book has now appeared: *New Writings by Swinburne,* published by the Syracuse University Press. It includes the two bogus reviews.

of him at the public house, Herbert, and went up to see the clergyman and found him"—"*La tête renversée dans les seins de Cécile, qui haletait comme une moribonde. Cette figure virginale écumait d'amour. La chair de ses joues prenait des tons violacés. On voyait sur la blancheur mate de son cou des taches presque jaunes. Tout son sang battait furieusement. Sa chevelure paraissait s'animer et siffler. Son amant presque pamé ne ralait plus que par moments.*"

Edmund Gosse speaks of Swinburne's "rigidity," and in spite of these alternations it is true that a certain stiffness is one of Swinburne's so queerly mixed traits. It is the cause of his capacity to be boring as well as of the tenacity of his character. Swinburne is hardly mercurial; even his jokes are likely to go on too long; and it is a certain inflexibility which makes his sometimes brilliant literary criticism so relatively difficult to assimilate in comparison with that of almost anyone else of equal importance in this department. These letters are, however, as their editor says, full of excellent literary commentary of a more informal kind, and this is one of the things that make them readable. It is very entertaining and illuminating to hear so un-Victorian a Victorian writer express himself so freely on the subject of his contemporaries, and gossip about the writers of the past, as to whom he knew everything discoverable, down to the last detail of Beaumont and Fletcher's joint household and every tergiversation of every Vicar of Bray in the course of the seventeenth century, as if this were all recent scandal. These letters have sent me to his essays—which I had before found rather unsatisfactory—with the result that I appreciate them more and have come to understand better what it is about them that puts one off. My experience had been that if one read Swinburne's study of—let us say—Thomas Middleton, which made one eager to enjoy this dramatist, and then went on to read Middleton himself, one was sure to be disappointed. Where were the masterpieces which Swinburne had been praising? Yet Swinburne, as a critic, is not undiscriminating; he does not hesitate to say that something is bad, and he knows how, in any given piece, to distinguish between what is good and what is not so good. The trouble is that most of his statements are much too extreme and flat, either in praise or in condemnation. He has been carried away by his subjects as he was in the transports of his conversation, but in writing these exaggerations, he has hardened and stiffened and deadened them. There are here not merely dithyrambs but judgments, and the judgments of an intelligent man, but—as in his poetry—there are no nuances, no ready intuitions, no humanizing touches. Swinburne is indeed rigid, with a rigidity which no doubt derived from his aristocratic origins. In his personal relations with people, as his memorialists all record, except among his family and his intimate friends, he always puts others at a distance. His publisher—as Mr. Lang notes—the cultivated Andrew Chatto, he treats exactly as if he were a tradesman who did not always give satisfaction. Not that he ever, in his discussion of literature, tries to score off the non-U's as a U (though an Ashburnham, it may be noted, had married a Mitford). When he believes that his honor is offended, he is very clear in his mind as to who is and who is not a gentleman, and he merely mentions in passing that Dickens, one of his favorites, did not understand titles and supposed that Sir John Smith's wife could be called Lady John Smith; and his interesting discussion, in his *Wordsworth and Byron,* that spirited retort to Arnold, of the social origins of the English romantics is a simple assigning of them to their origins by someone who knows what those origins are but is incapable of making of them any invidious use. For Swinburne, great literature itself constituted a kind of aristocracy. The poet was ennobled by his genius. But the effect on the poet, seen from Swinburne's position, was also rather peculiar. The riches of English literature are displayed as if among the oak panellings and the high glass-doored cases of the library of some great house. Swinburne, like his Uncle Ashburnham, though on a very much smaller scale, was a collector and loved to show his folios. Such humble fellows as Heywood and Dekker as well as the bricklayer Ben Jonson and the Warwickshire burgess Shakespeare became part of the national pomp and part of the aristocrat's possessions. This, I believe, is what makes Swinburne's criticisms seem so different from anyone else's. The lofty tone and elaborate style, the architecture of the stately and solid sentences, the symmetrical ornamentation of the decorative antitheses and alliterations, the epithets in balancing pairs of a more luxurious Johnsonese have enclosed them in a nobleman's library and sometimes prevent us from noticing—though we know that he is extremely well-informed—how acute and accomplished this nobleman is.

Swinburne's novels take us into the house and let us see the kind of life that is lived there. They are thus unique in English Victorian fiction in dealing at first hand with this life, as they do not in the least, in other ways, resemble any other Victorian novels. Compare them with the usually satirical or at least ironical treatment of the class from which Swinburne came in Dickens and Thackeray and Trollope or with the highfalutin fantasies of Meredith. Swinburne is not at all class-conscious, as these middle-class writers are. He is telling about his own family entirely without constraint—which is impossible for a Dickens or a Thackeray when he is

trying to deal with his. And what Swinburne has to tell,
for the reader habituated to Victorian fiction, is likely to
prove rather startling, as it would have been distasteful or
alien to the Victorian public itself. In these novels no one
has to worry about what the middle class will think or
about the opinion of people above one. The characters
have their own codes and standards, but many things go
on among them that would horrify this middle-class
public. We are brought into a world for which we have
not been prepared by even the smooth lawns of Tennyson
or the great ladies of Coventry Patmore—a world in
which the eager enjoyment of a glorious out-of-door life
of riding and swimming and boating is combined with
adultery, incest, enthusiastic flagellation and quiet homosexuality.

This was the story Swinburne had to tell, and nobody—either in his own world itself or in the middle-class
world he defied (since as a writer he had to face the
public, though his family at home did not)—really
wanted to hear him tell it. His strong impulses and his
recurrent efforts to do so come out very clearly in these
letters; and we now have—together with *Love's Cross-
Currents,* actually published during Swinburne's lifetime
and included in his collected works—the greater part,
presumably, of *Lesbia Brandon,* with fragments, now
printed with it by Hughes, of other similar fictions. They
all deal, though the names sometimes vary, with more or
less the same set of characters, about whom, according to
Hughes, Swinburne was projecting a cycle. But *Love's
Cross-Currents,* the first of these novels, he found great
difficulty in getting published. On the surface it is relatively proper; Swinburne consented to a slight expurgation, but though it was written in 1862, it was not published till 1877, when it appeared in the *Tatler* as a serial,
with the title *A Year's Letters.* Since Swinburne was

dealing with his family, he felt obliged to use a pseudo-nym and called himself Mrs. Horace Manners, and he thus failed to profit by his own reputation. It was not till 1905—his parents were dead—when Swinburne was sixty-eight, that he was able to persuade a publisher to bring it out over his own name. George Meredith and others had praised the book, and it seems to have had a good press, but by this time Swinburne's great reputation had been made as a poet and a critic of poetry; no one expected him to succeed as a novelist, and the book has been entirely forgotten by the historians of English litera-ture. This is one of many examples of the extent to which mere fashion and academic tradition have the power to establish a canon. I am not far from agreeing with Hughes that *Love's Cross-Currents* is a "neglected mas-terpiece," yet copies of the first edition may be picked up today for a dollar. Swinburne's second contemporary novel was begun, according to Hughes, in 1864, immedi-ately after he had finished the first. He had decided now to "give them the works." In a letter to Richard Burton, he describes it as "a scheme of mixed prose and verse—a sort of étude à la Balzac *plus* the poetry—which I flatter myself will be more offensive and objectionable to Bri-tannia than anything I have yet done." This is the work which—though Swinburne never gave it a title—has come to be known as *Lesbia Brandon*. In proportion as it was more audacious, it encountered even more discour-agement than its predecessor had. Some of Swinburne's friends became apprehensive. When he had given it to Watts-Dunton to read, his friend would not return the whole manuscript. In letters to this self-appointed censor, of 1877 and 1878, Swinburne is still begging Watts-Dun-ton to give certain missing chapters back. He did succeed in inducing his publishers to set up the chapters he had, but Watts-Dunton seems further to have obstructed the

project by intercepting the proofs of these while Swinburne was away in Edinburgh. He never restored to
Swinburne the parts he had been withholding but, after
his friend's death, sold all or most of the manuscript to
Thomas J. Wise, the bibliographer and forger mentioned
above, who kept it in a scrambled state. Edmund Gosse—
who had heard Swinburne read aloud, with, as he says,
"his amazing violence," "two long passages, the one a ride
over a moorland by night, the other the death of his heroine, Lesbia Brandon"—declares that in Wise's opinion and
his, "this medley . . . ought never be published." But
Randolph Hughes did reassemble it and explosively bring
it out. One of the chapters, which was missing from
Wise's manuscript, has turned up in the Huntington
Library. The genteel and evasive Gosse says that "Swinburne thought he had completely dropped" this project,
but we know now that the book is brilliant and that the
author took it very seriously. Even as late as 1881, he
writes to a woman friend, herself a novelist, "Some day
perhaps I shall take heart of grace to ask for your frank
opinion on certain crude attempts of my own at novel-
writing—or more properly at studies of life and character
in our own day."

"Studies of life and character in our own day"—this is
what one least expects from Swinburne, yet it is what
one does get in these novels. The mimicry of which he
was a master and which we know from his literary
pastiches and parodies is applied here to social types.
Love's Cross-Currents is told mostly in letters, and the
personalities are admirably conveyed through the vocabulary, the tone and the rhythm of their various epistolary
styles. In *Lesbia Brandon,* the worldly conversation of
the "venomous old beauty" Lady Midhurst and Mr.
Linley, the scholar, collector and wit, with his eyes of

which "the gravity and mockery were alike impressive and repulsive," whose whole face sometimes "bore the seal of heavy sorrow and a fatal fatigue," has something in common with the dialogue of the characters of both George Meredith and Oscar Wilde and seems to show that the latter was exploiting a vein of epigrammatic talk which had already been brought to perfection in the social life of London by the middle nineteenth century. The conversation at cross-purposes quoted above from an unidentified fragment is strikingly anticipatory of Ronald Firbank, who, however, can hardly have read it. There is nothing of this kind, of course, in Swinburne's poetry, and these novels present also an unexpected contrast to Swinburne's writings in verse in their descriptions of people and landscape. He here gets away almost completely from the monotonous vocabulary of his poetry, the rhetorical abstractions and the tiresome alliterations. It is a curious deficiency of Swinburne in his poetry—for a writer so sensitive to style—that he can never surprise or delight by a colloquial turn of phrase, a sharply observed detail, a magical touch of color. He can never, like Tennyson or even Arnold, strike off something actually seen in words at once exact and sensuous. There are sights we remember from the earlier Swinburne—the sunset over the sea in *Hesperia,* Whistler's "White Girl" before her mirror (though if one had never seen the picture, would one ever have known precisely what she looked like?), the *Forsaken Garden* "in a coign of the cliff between lowland and highland,/ At the sea-down's edge between windward and lee,/ Walled round with rocks as an inland island" (one of the very best of Swinburne's lyrics)—but they inevitably tend to be lost in the swathings of the poet's uncontrollable verbosity. And later on he cannot get away from those generalizing visageless monosyllables that mean little and evoke nothing—*love, tears, light, dark, earth, fear, faith, world, wings, song, time, life, death.* Certain passages in these later poems, we learn from his letters, were derived from real places, and yet they always seem to be nowhere. In writing to William Bell Scott, with whom he had visited Bamborough Castle in Northumberland, he says "You will admit the truthfulness" of his description of it in *Tristram of Lyonesse,* and speaks of "the lovely view of the three blue herons on the ledge of a sea-rock to which I remember that I vainly though urgently called your attention, then distracted by sea-sickness." But when one looks this up in *Tristram of Lyonesse,* one finds that, in a Never-Never Land of fairy-tale pre-Raphaelite dream, the blue herons that one had hoped would be breathtaking have been so strung out and diluted that one is almost as little aware of them as of the sea-sickness of William Bell Scott. Their blueness is not made more vivid by being described as "blue as the clear north heaven"; their heads are "bright" and their feet are "bright," and we have, just a few lines before, had "the bright sea's boon." We become exasperated with Swinburne for not knowing that too much brightness will make things dim. He writes to his mother from Putney that he has discovered in "a corner of the neighboring woods or copses . . . the loveliest group of natural arrangement of white and pink or red hawthorns I ever saw anywhere," and later he tells her that the opening of the Arthurian poem on which he is now at work was "inspired by the . . . hawthorns about here which are *too* lovely while they last." But when we look up this opening of *The Tale of Balen,* we do not find the hawthorns at all. From the letter we at least know what color they were; in the poem they are merged with other things as simply "bounteous bloom," and all the rest is "flower and flight," "glad in spirit and sad in soul," "bush and brake and bole," "earth and sea," "blood and breath," "time and death," etc.

But in the novels written long before this, to which Swinburne was never to return, he was able to do something quite different. In *Love's Cross-Currents,* at the beginning of Chapter 3, you are already quite out of the pre-Raphaelite world and in the presence of a recognizable England which the poet has invested with a charm that is never obscured by the wordy blur: "This was a little old house, beautifully set in among orchards and meadows, with abundance of roses now all round it, under the heavy leaves of a spring that June was now gaining fast upon. A wide soft river divided the marsh meadows in front of it, full of yellow flag-flowers and moist fen-blossom. It was a splendid place for children; better perhaps than Ashton Hildred with its huge brick-walled gardens and wonderful fruit-trees blackened and dotted with lumps or patches of fabulous overgrown moss, and wild pleasure-grounds stifled with beautiful rank grass; better decidedly than Lord Cheyne's big brilliant Lidcombe, in spite of royal shooting-grounds and the admirable slopes of high bright hill-country behind it, green sweet miles of park and embayed lake, beyond praise for riding and boating; better incomparably than Captain Harewood's place, muffled in woods, with a grim, sad beauty of its own, but seemingly knee-deep in sere leaves all the year round, wet and weedy and dark and deep down, kept hold of somehow by autumn in the midst of spring; only the upper half of it clear of the clutch of winter even in the hottest height of summer weather, with a bitter flavor of frost and rain in it all through summer. It was wonderful, Lady Midhurst said, how any child could live there without going mad or moping. She was thankful the boy went to school so young, though no doubt his father had picked out the very hardest sort of school he decently could select. Anything was better than that horrid wet hole of a place, up to the nose and eyes in black damp woods, and with thick moist copses of alders and birch trees growing against the very windows; and such a set of people inside of it!" And after this—especially in *Lesbia Brandon*—you get splendid descriptions of swimming and riding that convey the thrill of real experience while at the same time giving the impression that, like Swinburne's fantastic Elizabethans, they are somehow framed and varnished as painted panels in the ornamental country houses in which his characters lived.

I know of nothing else like this in English fiction. It is obvious that Swinburne at this time in his life was attempting to effect a mutation, and it seems tragic that the obstacles he met, the restraining and stunting influences, prevented him from doing this. He would have produced something so much more interesting than the grandiose routine of his verse! How urgent to the end of his life was the need to tell his personal story, to return to those early impressions and emotions which had never been fully described, is shown by his writing at fifty-five a blank-verse play, *The Sisters*—dedicated to the mother of Mary Leith—which is unique among Swinburne's tragedies in taking place in nineteenth-century England. Here we find the same strange snarl of interrelated characters on the same Northumberland estate, the same Reggie—with a surname different from the one he is given in *Love's Cross-Currents*—who is always Algernon himself. But the conventional poetic form to which Swinburne has become accustomed completely destroys the reality and deflects the force of the story. Swinburne is still, to be sure, attempting to do something slightly different from his dramas in the grand manner: "The tragedy of *The*

Sisters," he says in his introductory survey to the collected edition of his poems, "however defective it may be in theatrical interest or progressive action, is the only modern thing I know in which realism in the reproduction of natural dialogue and accuracy in the representation of natural intercourse between men and women of gentle birth have been found or made compatible with expression in genuine if simple blank verse." But it is all too easy for Swinburne here to romanticize his relations with Mary Gordon. Reggie Clavering, like Reggie Harewood in *Love's Cross-Currents,* is in love with one of his cousins, Mabel, and, in this case, she with him, but Swinburne is evidently merging himself with his successful rival, Colonel Leith, who had been gravely wounded in India, by making Reggie a brave soldier who comes back with a wound from Waterloo. The whole play becomes most implausible and artistically most inacceptable when Swinburne confuses and falsifies the family situation by the introduction of Renaissance poisonings. He was also, in another late play, *The Duke of Gandia,* to return to a favorite subject, the Borgias, which he had earlier attacked in the prose work recovered by Randolph Hughes, *The Chronicle of Tebaldeo Tebaldei.* One of the charms of the Borgias for Swinburne was that they gave him an opportunity to deal with incestuous situations, and in *The Sisters* he mixes the two milieux. The young people act a play which has been written for them by Reggie. It is a Renaissance tragedy that takes place in Italy, and the heroine's twin sister Anne, who is also in love with Reggie, enters so into the spirit of the piece that she procures a flask of real poison from a disused laboratory in the house and, after pretending in the action of the piece to poison the character played by her sister, she proceeds, after contemplating suicide, to allow Mabel actually to drink it, apparently under the impression that it is something to cure a cold. Reggie also takes a dose, and he and Mabel die together, forgiving Anne. The situation is further complicated by another cousin, who is one of Reggie's oldest friends but who is also in love with Mabel. The point is that all these young people are so closely bound by kinship and intimacy that it is impossible for Reggie and Mabel ever to extricate themselves to the point of being able to marry one another.

One's enjoyment of the splendor and wit of these novels is, however—for an American reader, at least—likely to be somewhat disturbed by an element which seems to him bizarre and repellent, and this element appears in the correspondence in an even more unpleasant form. As a result of his experience as a boy at Eton, Swinburne had made a cult of the traditional British practice of flogging, and this had become for him inseparable from his capacity for sexual gratification, which seems to have been exclusively masochistic. The pleasure and importance of being flogged are made to figure in all three of these family fictions. In *The Sisters* it is touched upon lightly; in *Love's Cross-Currents* it is dwelt upon at greater length; in *Lesbia Brandon* Swinburne pulls out all the stops, and howls of pain become cries of ecstasy. He wrote some long humorous poems on the subject, known as *The Whippingham Papers,* which Hughes had intended to publish but which perhaps we can do without; the quotations from these poems which he prints in the commentary to *Lesbia Brandon* seem not funny but simply gruesome to anyone who does not share Swinburne's tastes. This is one of the aspects of Swinburne's life that Gosse was obliged to suppress but which are dealt with in his posthumous postscript. He says that Swinburne found a brothel in London which specialized in flagellation, and that Dante Gabriel Rossetti became worried about him and tried to get him to cultivate more normal habits. Rossetti enlisted Adah Isaacs Menken—that strange international charmer from New Orleans, a more or less cultivated woman who wrote poetry, painted and danced, and was much liked by intelligent men but who made a sensation in London by playing Mazeppa at Astley's Theatre and appearing, in flesh-colored tights, strapped to the back of a horse. She and Swinburne grew genuinely fond of one another. The affair became notorious, and a photograph was circulated in London—which Swinburne seems rather to have enjoyed—of him standing and her sitting in a chair so that she does not dwarf his height, with one hand resting affectionately against his frock coat. But at the end of six weeks, she gave him up in despair, reporting to Rossetti, according to Gosse, that "she didn't know how it was, but she hadn't been able to get him up to the scratch. . . . I can't make him understand that biting's no use." But she had become protective about him, as everyone who liked him did. She went on from London to Paris, where she took on Alexandre Dumas *père,* then well along in years; but, after she had left London, fearing that Swinburne was ill, she wrote a worried letter to a common friend of hers and Swinburne's: "She is unable to think of anything but you," this friend passed it on to Swinburne; "she wishes me to telegraph to her if you are in danger, and she will fly on the wings of the wind to nurse you."

This episode occurred in the winter of 1867–68, when Swinburne was thirty-one. Gosse believes that his masochistic impulses had been liberated six years before by discovering the works of the Marquis de Sade, and Swinburne's letters seem to bear out this theory. He had always been interested in Sade and had already written the poem about him which he attributed to the imaginary Félicien Cossu, but he had apparently never read him until his friend Monckton Milnes (later Lord Houghton) lent him a copy of *Justine, ou les Malheurs de la Vertu*. His excitement is evident in his letters. He gives an excellent critique of the deficiencies of Sade considered as a serious writer, but he proceeds, in one of his accomplished French parodies, to exhibit a frank delight which goes on chortling through his correspondence all the rest of his life. Sade becomes one of Swinburne's heroes—though mainly a comic hero—and another of his monotonous obsessions. When you come to a letter to Houghton or Powell—often, too, in his letters to William Rossetti—you may be sure that sooner or later the Marquis de Sade will pop up, that there will be at least a joke about him, and usually a joke that has been made innumerable times before. At first, Swinburne's masochistic outbursts—especially to Monckton Milnes—become extremely embarrassing. Nothing could seem stranger than the juxtaposition of his old-fashioned courtly politeness and his high-pitched political idealism with his childish impersonations of a schoolboy who wants to be flogged. He cannot let the subject alone. He thanks Powell for sending him a birch rod and "desires a sight of the swishing room"; the view of "a fine rapid river . . . winding under fir-woods between banks clothed with broom and wild roses" makes him reflect that there is "birch enough to hand for the bottoms of all Eton." "How could you be at Eton," he is still writing Powell in this vein at the age of thirty-seven—"and not remember to invest for me in at least two of the large photographs of the flogging-block, when you knew how I wanted them and was shy of writing to order them?" He regales his correspondents with anecdotes which Mr. Lang is inclined to regard as fantasies. For example, a young cousin of his had been birched for reading Swinburne's poems: "His tutor confiscated the book under penalties, and the boy of course cribbed it, and was (I am happy to say) caught, as he deserved, studying a most appropriately named and especially prohibited poem—and had what he calls 'such a jolly good swishing' that his elder brother tells me he came out of his tutor's study with his clothes readjusted but the blood visibly soaking through his shirt and the seat of his breeches (these being, providentially, very light) in patches and stripes—to the wild delight of the junior male members of the household, who received him with acclamations. I wish *mon vieux* [Lord Houghton] had been by to hear—it would have made him wriggle and bubble with enjoyment till his teeth came out—a sight profitable for admonition."

Swinburne was no doubt an extreme case, but one gets the impression, in reading these novels, that—in the punitive as well as the proverbial sense—he is letting the cat out of the bag. Such a system as the English one is partly the result of a painful discipline, an enforced submission to authority. In England, they flogged at that time not merely in the public schools but also in the Army and the Navy and as a punishment for criminals; and even today the angry controversies in the British press show that many people are still full of outrage over the recent abolition of these penalities.

There is, therefore, I believe, a certain connection between Swinburne's idealism and dignity and his eagerness for flagellation. He was proud of the exploits of his forebears as crusaders and cavaliers—he claimed Hotspur as one of his ancestors—and had a chivalrous conception of honor. He wanted to prove himself a man, which in some ways his physique made difficult, and I agree with his chief apologist, Randolph Hughes, in supposing that the satisfaction that the Eton boy had taken in his floggings was partly that of having withstood, without unmanly tears, a succession of stiff ordeals. The

more Swinburne was whipped by his tutors, the more he
appears to have respected them. One of his memories of
his school days seems incredible, yet he mentions it
several times in these letters. Already a master of metrics, the boy had handed in a copy of Latin galliambics, a
meter of which the only surviving example is Catullus's
Attis, and though he had never in his school days, he
says, been punished for committing a single false quan-
tity, he was now given a flogging by his tutor on the
ground that galliambics were not a proper meter. To
remember this in afterlife does not seem to make Swinburne indignant but to afford him a certain satisfaction:
though he had appealed from the tutor to another master,
who took a more lenient view of his galliambics, he seems
to assume that the tutor was right. Why? One supposes
that, knowing he was helpless at games but had outdis-
tanced his tutor at classics, he was willing to pay this
price for his pride; and, after all, was he not partly indebted for his proficiency in Latin and Greek to the rigors
of corporeal chastisement with which Eton boys were
constantly threatened? The transmutation of the Samurai
ordeal into a source of erotic enjoyment is shown in a
curious passage in a letter of Swinburne's to Milnes. He
is writing of one of his tutors: "I have known him . . .
prepare the flogging room (*not* with *corduroy* or *onion*
but) with burnt scents; or choose a *sweet* place out of
doors with smell of firewood. *This* I call real delicate
torment. . . . Once, before giving me a swishing that I
had the marks of for more than a month (so fellows
declared that I went to swim with), he let me saturate my
face with eau-de-cologne."

There is actually something quite touching in all this
side of Swinburne. His physical courage was unflinching
as well as his moral courage, and he had to find special
ways of proving himself. His boyhood ambition had been

to have a career as a soldier; he wanted to enlist in the cavalry. He announced this when he was almost seventeen and had just come home from Eton. His parents deliberated three days, then decided that it was impossible, that he would not do as a soldier. Algernon's disappointment was terrible. In one of his letters to Mary Leith—among the undated letters in Mr. Lang's sixth volume—he tells her, on her asking him about a youthful exploit, though he starts off in the third person to avoid the appearance of boasting, how he felt and what he did when his parents gave him their verdict. This letter has the vividness and actuality of the incidents in his novels. The boy "went out for a good hard tramp by the sea" till he found himself at the foot of a steep chalk cliff, almost as unscalable as the cliffs of Dover; "then all at once it came upon me that it was all very well to fancy or dream of 'deadly danger' and forlorn hopes and cavalry charges, when I had never run any greater risk than a football 'rooge'; but that here was a chance of testing my nerve in face of death which could not be improved." His first attempt to scale the cliff failed because he discovered, when he got near the top, that he was stopped by a jutting ledge, "so of course I felt that I must not stop to think for one second, and began climbing down, hand upon hand, till I reached the bottom." He tried it once more, at a different place. "As I began again I must own I felt like setting my teeth and swearing I would not come down again alive—if I did return to the foot of the cliff again it should be in a fragmentary condition, and there would not be much of me to pick up. I was most of the way up again when I heard a sudden sound as of loud music, reminding me instantly of 'the anthem' from the Eton Chapel organ, a little below me to the left. I knew it would be almost certain death to look down, and next minute there was no need: I glanced aside, and saw the opening of a peat hollow in the upper cliff, out of which came swarming a perfect flock of sea-gulls. . . . They rose all about me in a heaving crowd . . . and then scattered. . . . I was a little higher, quite near the top or well within hail of it, then I thought how queer it would be if my very scanty foothold gave way; and at that very minute it did . . . and I swung in the air by my hands from a ledge on the cliff which just gave room for the fingers to cling and hold on. There was a projection of rock to the left at which I flung out my feet sideways and just reached it; this enabled me to get breath and crawl at full speed (so to say) up the remaining bit of cliff." At the top, he fainted; when consciousness returned, he was looking into the nose of a sheep and burst into "a shout of laughter." At home he found the household alarmed; everybody had been out searching for him. "After eating and sleeping I had an interview with my mother, of which I should not care to write except to the daughter of yours. Of course she wanted to know why I had done such a thing, and when I told her she laughed a short sweet laugh . . . and said, 'Nobody ever thought you were a coward, my boy.' I said that was all very well: but how could I tell till I tried? 'But you won't do it again?' she said. I replied, of course not—where could be the fun? I knew now that it could be done and I only wanted to do it because nobody thought it could." He mentions in connection with this that, when swimming off the French coast, he had once been swept out and had fainted when a fishing boat picked him up. His swimming in dangerous waters was another of his testings of strength and nerve. Though slight, he was very muscular, and had powers of tenacity and endurance which were based on a character, says Gosse, "as firm as a twist of iron." But these letters confirm explicitly one's impression that Swinburne's love of swimming, besides providing ordeals, afforded him masochistic gratification. He liked to be pounded and slapped about by the harsh and inexorable "great sweet mother."

The cruel inexorable woman is a figure that towers above everything else in all of Swinburne's writing. She is, in fact, Swinburne's ideal—Dolores Our Lady of Pain; Mary Gordon, who unthinkingly cut him down; the catalogue of perverse and destructive queens in *The Masque of Queen Bersabe;* the Messalina-Victoria of *La Sœur de la Reine;* Mary Stuart, about whom he wrote a huge trilogy and who he insists was not the pathetic victim that her sentimental admirers made her but a woman strong in intellect and passionate, quite ruthless with enemies and lovers alike; Lady Midhurst, the relentless old schemer, who presides over *Love's Cross-Currents* and reappears in *Lesbia Brandon.* Of this character Swinburne wrote in a letter to William Rossetti, when the former novel appeared in book form, "This book stands or falls by Lady Midhurst: If she gives satisfaction, it must be all right; if not, chaos is come again," and he insists that she is entirely his own invention. Lady Midhurst is indeed at the center of *Love's Cross-Currents,* prevailing, persuading, pushing, resorting to blackmail, if necessary—always bringing pressure to bear. Part French, extremely clever, a thorough woman of the world, she enjoys reading French novels and is aware of the irregular relationships in which the members of her family are involved, but she keeps them all under control and in the end she has not a scruple about trapping her young relatives in situations that are sure to make them unhappy but that give them at least the appearance of not violating British conventions. They have been doing what they liked at home but they must not create open scandal. One would not have expected of Swinburne either restraint or psychological subtlety; yet this novel is remarkable for both. Lady Midhurst is by far his most successful incarnation of the dominating merciless woman. Poor old Adah Menken, as Dolores, has a flavor of burlesque vulgarity when put beside this polished and astute old spider. The French element is strong in *Love's Cross-Currents*. Not only has Lady Midhurst French blood; it is evident that the book derives from Laclos's *Les Liaisons Dangereuses*. Both stories are told in letters, and though the incidents and personalities in Swinburne are quite different from those in Laclos, one can recognize that, transposed into these different terms, Swinburne's theme is the same as Laclos's—the manipulation of simple people, regardless of their own real interests, by flexible and steely intelligence. But in Laclos there are two villains, and it is exhilarating when they at last get at odds and begin practicing their tricks on one another. Yet Lady Midhurst has no accomplice with whom she will fall out, to the ruin of their common plans. She is left in the end triumphant, and the upshot of *Love's Cross-Currents* is actually more unpleasant than that of the gratuitous exploits in eighteenth-century wickedness carried out by the schemers of Laclos. Swinburne's obsession with cruelty makes itself felt more sharply in these works than it does in his other writings, because they are made to take place not in a world of history or myth but in Swinburne's own personal world. This is something that is basic to his nature, and the closer we get to the man himself, the more uncomfortable his effect on us becomes. It is not only the nostalgia for floggings that strikes this note in *Lesbia Brandon;* the whole book is shot through with a sinister satisfaction derived from inflicting pain—even to the nasty old ballads which Swinburne has concocted for the purpose of working on his characters' nerves. He can never get away from this, and it is one thing that makes him so limited, in the long run so unsatisfactory. His enthusiasms are exaggerated, seem only half real (though these, too, have their masochistic element), but this masochistic excitement *is* real, and it is hard to be entirely sympathetic with someone who—though only on one side of his nature—longs so much for self-abasement. In his relationship with Watts-Dunton—though he was sometimes impatient with his guardian—he was succumbing to this morbid passivity, and that, too, is a little repellent. An old gentleman of almost sixty, he writes of his friend and himself in terms of "major" and "minor"—Watts-Dunton of course being "major"—as if they were boys at school, and a ramble in the woods, when he is fifty-seven, can still stimulate him to write to his friend as follows: "The day before your minor had (he must confess) broken bounds and played truant in a very Etonian fashion, and came home so torn with brambles and stung with nettles that he felt rather as if he were returning from a subsequent and consequent interview with the headmaster (the birch itself could hardly have stung more, or lacerated the flesh quite so severely). . . . I must take you down a steep grassy dell into a most lovely bit of woodland glen which I then discovered, and along a very high and very steep bank clothed with beeches (no birches to make a fellow feel uncomfortable out of bounds)." It was not in the least, as I have said above, that Swinburne lacked physical courage. He was once in these later years, says Gosse, threatened by a "hulking poetaster half mad with vanity," who "waited for him with a big stick on one of his lonely walks, and proposed to give him a thrashing. The antagonist was a powerful man, his victim a sort of fairy; but Swinburne cowed him by sheer personal dignity, and serenely continued to walk on, with the blusterer growling behind him." (Of this story Coulson Kernahan, again, gives a different and more comic version. The poetaster, Eric Mackay, had written what Swinburne regarded as a "fulsome and offensively flattering letter, in which he expressed the intention of dedicating a book of his own poems to Swinburne." He wrote Swinburne three times but got no reply. Then, after the incident recounted by Gosse, he announced that the book of poems would *not* be dedicated to him, and Swinburne replied that he was "honoured and relieved.") But Algernon could not stand up to Watts-Dunton, the retired solicitor and amateur of letters who had taken him under his wing, who put a damper on his meetings with more amusing people and who seems to have incited him to a derogatory article on his old admiration Walt Whitman and to a somewhat waspish one on the "Ten O'Clock" lecture of his old friend Whistler. Mr. Lang is rather disposed to defend Watts-Dunton against Gosse, and of course it was Swinburne's own weakness that made him lapse into such a relationship, but how one wishes he had had the spirit, when Watts-Dunton had sequestered *Lesbia Brandon* and was refusing to give it back, to throw off his masochistic passivity and go after that respectable solicitor not with a birch but a cudgel. How one wishes that Swinburne had been allowed to make his full contribution to English fiction!

October 6, 1962

EMERGENCE OF ANGUS WILSON

AFTER EVELYN WAUGH, what? For anyone who has asked this question, the answer is Angus Wilson, whose first book, *The Wrong Set and Other Stories,* has just been published over here. In the England of Evelyn Waugh, everybody had plenty of money or managed to get the benefit of other people's having money; one was free to be as dizzy as one pleased, and the incidental brutality and swindling were hardly noticed in the general hilarity. In the England of Angus Wilson, the money has been giving out, and the clever upper-middle-class people are struggling, with a somewhat damaged dignity, to get hold of or to hang on to whatever income or position is attainable. In this struggle, though they keep up certain forms, they are always jeering and jabbing; they do not flinch from frank hatchet work. They all dislike one another, and the author dislikes the lot. It is hard to agree with the writer of the blurb on the jacket of this book that "beneath the surface brilliance of these stories there shines Wilson's deep compassion for humanity." Though he sometimes introduces a young person, unbroken to the ways of this world, who tries to take a stand against it, this character invariably turns out, like the girl in *Fresh Air Fiend,* to have played the role of a clumsy prig or, like the young men of *Crazy Crowd* and *Mother's Sense of Fun,* to succumb as helpless dupes. The gaiety is still going on that made the carnival of Evelyn Waugh—

Totentanz and *Saturnalia* are among Mr. Wilson's titles, as well as *Crazy Crowd*—but, as the first of these stories indicates, it is now a dance of the dying.

This point is made by *Totentanz* explicitly, and the story differs somewhat from the others. (It seems to have been the last written, since it recently appeared in *Horizon* and has been added to those included in the English edition of the book.) Mr. Wilson has allowed himself here, with his vampires and ghosts and fantastic wills, a certain satirical and poetical extravagance. The other stories keep the rules of realism, and they almost achieve plausibility as pictures of certain strata of the England that has been trying to readjust itself after the efforts and privations of the war—for even when the stories deal with earlier times, they seem to reflect the mood of the present, with its exasperated snapping and snarling disguised as exquisite malice, its vulgarization of the cultivated and learned (academic careerists and frauds are a specialty of Mr. Wilson's), its cruelty of comfortable people deathly afraid of losing their comforts, its sexual life turning sterile in the instinctive biological fear that the nation or the class may not survive. Yet these stories are fundamentally satirical. There is evidently in Mr. Wilson a strain of the harsh Scottish moralist who does not want to let anybody off and does not care if his sarcasm wounds. This is nowadays an unusual element to crop up in a British writer. The school of smart fiction in England, though it cultivates bitter implications and sometimes invokes religion, has come to perfect a cuisine of light appetizing dishes, agreeable for one dinner and easily digestible, which—much though it would have surprised George Moore or Henry James if anyone had prophesied it to them—almost rivals that of the French in the early nineteen-hundreds. And it is true that Wilson's stories, too, from the point of view of neatness and brevity and of the avoidance of emotionalism, are products of the same cuisine; but they are carried to lengths of caricature that prevent them from being so pleasantly assimilable as the usual British product. The book becomes a sort of thriller, for one goes on from one horror to another, beginning to hold onto one's seat as one wonders what uncomfortable ignoble thing Mr. Wilson will think up next. Yet one shares in the malevolent gusto with which he invents detail, for he is a master of mimicry and parody and is as funny as anyone can be who never becomes exhilarated. It is rather like a combination of Sinclair Lewis with the more biting side of Chekhov, and Mr. Wilson's dreadful people may affect us in the long run a little like the caricatures of Lewis (the up-and-coming museum curator of the story called *Realpolitik* is an incipiently American type who might easily have been imagined by Lewis). We end by being repelled and by feeling that it is not quite decent to enjoy so much ugliness and humiliation. There ought to be some noble value somewhere. Sinclair Lewis at least opposes, and not always ineffectively, to his bugaboos of rascality and cheapness the good old American virtues, upon which he still counts. Chekhov, who, like Mr. Wilson, plays the clinician for a failing organism, is sad as well as sardonic and has some sense of a human dignity that he hopes will emerge from the mess. But the things worth saving in *The Wrong Set* have been degraded almost beyond recognition; the victims of the people who are getting on have sunk almost out of reach of pity.

This may seem too severe a line to take with a book of short stories, a first book by a writer of thirty-six; but the talent displayed seems so firm and bold, so rich in invention and wit, that it stimulates these comparisons. Mr. Wilson may be capable of a great deal more, and even in this little collection the impression he makes is formidable. He seems, for better or worse, to represent something that is quite distinct from the well-bred and well-turned entertainment that we have lately been getting from England.

April 15, 1950

IS IT POSSIBLE TO PAT KINGSLEY AMIS?

"AFTER EVELYN WAUGH, what?" this reviewer asked six
years ago. The answer was Angus Wilson. Mr. Wilson is
still doing well. He continues to add to his album of tart
and trim little pictures of the English upper middle class,
shaken in its self-sufficiency and stinging itself to death.
But what is to be the next phase in England, and how
will it be written about? The answer, already, is Kingsley
Amis, the author of two novels: *Lucky Jim,* published in
1954, and *That Uncertain Feeling,* which has just come
out. These books are in the same general comic tradition
as those of Wilson and Waugh. Satirical and sometimes
farcical, they are derived from shrewd observation of
contemporary British life, and they occasionally imply
social morals. Yet between Kingsley Amis on the one
hand and Wilson and Waugh on the other, a definite
mutation has occurred. In the world of Angus Wilson,
the pressure is already felt of the Labour-run Welfare
State; a new social promiscuity has already begun. But
we have here hardly more than a glimpse of the survivors
of the war generation trying to make themselves a new
kind of life in an England where the class structure is
breaking up and the old orientations have been partly
lost. In the work of Kingsley Amis, we see everything
from the point of view of such baseless unoriented young
people. That uncertain feeling may be said to be the

theme of *Lucky Jim* as well as of the book to which it gives its title.

The effect of these novels of Amis's on the higher level of British journalism has, therefore, been curious to watch. They have become a subject of controversy, on which people sometimes fiercely take sides. *Lucky Jim* is extremely funny. Everybody was much amused by it, and since it is also a kind of male Cinderella or Ugly Duckling story, it left its readers good-humored and glowing. Jim Dixon, a young instructor in a third-rate provincial college, finds himself always out of key with its middle-class gentility and academic culture, and in mischievous embittered revolt against them. He is apparently as unlucky as possible. He commits every possible gaffe; his attempts to do what is expected of him invariably end in fiasco. The lecture on which his promotion depends turns into a comic debacle. Yet his honesty, vitality, humor, breaking through the taboos he has tried to observe, in the end win him every triumph, procure for him every prize. He knocks down his pretentious rival, obtains the devotion of a beautiful girl, is relieved providentially of a feeling of guilt in connection with another girl with whom he has gone rather far, and is rescued by a rich connoisseur from the failure of his academic career by being offered a job as his secretary. The reviewers were jolly about *Lucky Jim;* they patted him on his blond, bushy, rumpled head. But when the second Kingsley Amis book appeared, they began to become uneasy. I shall discuss this new book in a moment. In the meantime, it is enough to note that the element of loutishness here is made somewhat harder to swallow by being combined with an element of the sordid. The critics now held their noses and in retrospect complained that Lucky Jim, waking up in the morning with a hangover and hearing

someone singing Mozart in the bathroom, had murmured
to himself, "Filthy Mozart." Did not Amis, it began to be
asked, really share the views of his hero? Did he admire
the right things himself?

But this reaction to the second Kingsley Amis book had
already been anticipated on the strength of the first alone
by Mr. Somerset Maugham, writing in the December
25th issue of the London *Sunday Times*. Mr. Maugham
praised *Lucky Jim,* and he was the first to call attention to
its significance as a social document, but he regarded this
significance as "ominous": "I am told that today rather
more than sixty per cent of the men who go to the universities go on a Government grant. This is a new class
that has entered upon the scene. It is the white-collar
proletariat. Mr. Kingsley Amis is so talented, his observation is so keen, that you cannot fail to be convinced that
the young men he so brilliantly describes truly represent
the class with which his novel is concerned. They do not
go to the university to acquire culture, but to get a job,
and when they have got one, scamp it. They have no
manners, and are woefully unable to deal with any social
predicament. Their idea of a celebration is to go to a
public house and drink six beers. They are mean, malicious and envious. They will write anonymous letters to
harass a fellow undergraduate and listen in to a telephone
conversation that is no business of theirs. Charity, kindli-
ness, generosity, are qualities which they hold in contempt. They are scum. They will in due course leave the
university. Some will doubtless sink back, perhaps with
relief, into the modest class from which they emerged;
some will take to drink, some to crime and go to prison.
Others will become schoolmasters and form the young, or
journalists and mould public opinion. A few will go into
Parliament, become Cabinet Ministers and rule the coun-

try. I look upon myself as fortunate that I shall not live to see it."

This is much too black a picture of Jim, whose boorishness is partly the result of the recalcitrance of a homely sincerity against the frauds he is expected to practice. Though he is sometimes, in a youthful neurotic way, certainly spiteful and nasty, as when he destroys his fellow-lodger's life-insurance policies, he is capable in other connections of sympathy, courage and dignity. And Mr. Maugham's penchant for the trashy cliché has here served him even worse than usual in inspiring his remark "They are scum." The result of Mr. Maugham's article was to bring out a smart peppering of retorts in the correspondence columns of the *Sunday Times,* one of them from a grant-aided university graduate and another from a university teacher. Most of his students, this teacher says, "are not at a university to acquire culture but to get a job: this they share with the majority of students of whom we have record. A few are truly in search of culture and a few are 'mean, malicious, and envious': if one can judge from the university novels of the past hundred years, this means they are very like their predecessors. The main differences between them and the characters in *Verdant Green, Zuleika Dobson,* and *Tom Brown at Oxford* is that they have less money and work harder."

There is evidently a class issue here. The characters of Kingsley Amis are sometimes, to be sure, ill-bred in a peculiarly obnoxious way, and if Maugham had read the second of the novels, he would no doubt have expressed himself even more strongly. In noting the reception of this second book, one gets the impression that British opinion is beginning to gang up on Mr. Amis. A marked chill in the tone of the reviews has set in. The hero of the new novel does not seem to be patted on the head as

Lucky Jim was. A difference in the books themselves accounts for this. In the first, the repulsive people are the opponents of the hero and his beautiful girl, and the hero and his girl score. In *That Uncertain Feeling*, all the characters are more or less unpleasant, and the hero is telling the story himself, instead of, as in the case of Lucky Jim, being told about by the author, so we are never allowed to escape from the squalors of his personality. We see only so much of the world as he knows, and this seems to make it hard for some readers to correct the illusions and distortions of his limited point of view, and to lead them more easily to attribute the reactions of the character to the author, to suppose that the author is not aware of how disgusting his protagonist's life is and of how badly he and his friends are behaving.

John Lewis is assistant librarian in another provincial town, this time in Wales. He is married, and he and his wife, with a baby and a little girl, are living on his slender salary in unattractive lodgings. The young man, though he functions in the white-collar class, has originally come from the collieries, and he cherishes a contempt and resentment toward the "Anglicized upper classes" at the same time that he cannot resist their appeal. For him, this superior world consists of a desirable girl married to a well-to-do businessman and surrounded by a crowd of gay friends. This girl and her group are horrible—noisy, drunken, promiscuous and quarrelsome. But Mr. Amis is surely aware of this. It is a part of the satiric humor that these people should represent for Lewis the glamor of the privileged classes. The businessman's young bitch of a wife, for example, seems to me one of the most successful of Mr. Amis's comic characters. She seduces the young librarian and undermines his relations with his wife—assuring him, quite mendaciously, that her husband winks at her infidelities. This love affair is

all involved with her offer to persuade her husband to get
Lewis a better post that has just fallen vacant in the
library and that is due to be filled by a candidate who has
been chosen on his merits. A struggle goes on in the
young man's mind between his desire for the job and his
distaste at this method of getting it. The gradual involvement of Lewis in a sickening situation, his betrayal of his
caustic long-suffering wife and his relations with the hard-
drinking smart set, his concealment from himself of his
ignominy and his increasingly inflamed irritation with
both sides of his divided life—all this seems to me psychologically sound, and I get the impression that the author
knows exactly what he is doing. This book has no fairy-
tale ending, and, though not so enjoyable as *Lucky Jim*,
seems an attempt at a more serious study. *That Uncertain
Feeling* ends in a mess, and though the wires have been
successfully pulled and Lewis has been chosen for the
job, he refuses it and leaves the library, taking his family
away to the house of his father, a checking clerk in the
collieries, whom he very much likes and relies on and
who now gets him a job "in coal sales." "The money
wasn't bad:—not much less than I'd pulled in as an assistant librarian." This return to the collieries has a touch
of Lawrence, and the whole attitude of Lewis toward the
culture of the respectable world has something of a
Lawrentian ring. But the upshot is not melodramatic. On
this even lower social level, John Lewis is tempted again.
He receives what his father calls "an invitation to the
home of one of the premier hostesses in this part of
Wales. Mrs. Edith Rhys Protheroe requests the pleasure."
She is the wife of the big local butcher, and she has in
her drawing room "the latest Graham Greene and Angela
Thirkell lying, still in their jackets, on a copy of *Vogue*."
At the party, very much as before, the wife of a professor
at the local university makes a dead set for John, but this

time he avoids the trap. He leaves the party at once and takes his wife out to a pub.

The occasionally repulsive details of this book, the indecent outbursts of the hero in his moments of lechery or fury, do suggest a certain coarseness on the part of the author as well as on that of his hero; and it contains one extremely weak episode, the one in which John Lewis, disporting himself with his mistress, is caught in the house by her returning husband and resorts to all sorts of expedients of hiding, impersonating the plumber and finally disguising himself in a female costume. All this is so clumsily implausible that it reminds us of one of those sequences of grotesque and impossible gags in a second-rate movie comedy. In other ways, American influence plays in this book a conspicuous role. The author has evidently been reading a good deal of American fiction, and the tone of his hero owes something to this, as well as the conversation of the other characters. They are full of American wisecracks and of language picked up from the movies. To an American, this is rather depressing. These young Britishers seem to have borrowed some of the worst things we have to offer, and even things that are amusing at home come to seem to us rather dreary on the lips of an Americanizing British middle class. But it is a world that, even imitating America, still carries, in an eroded and degraded form, the skeleton of its class stratification. The great problem of John Lewis and Jim Dixon both is to resist the inherited impulse to invade a superior stratum and identify their interests with it. The only things they have behind them to brace them are the victory of the Labour Government in 1945, the ideals of the Welfare State, and they hold out as best they can, at the cost of much nervous strain, much confusion of social relations, much sacrifice of individual dignity. Jim advances himself; John Lewis loses ground, but, after once having been sent sprawling, he gets up and remains on his feet. These characters are not always attractive, but they interest me more than the people, also rather unattractive though presented with better manners, in the novels of Anthony Powell. Uncertain and perplexed though they are, they have still something to build, to win.

One of the features of the English *New Statesman & Nation* is a weekend competition. The subject set a few weeks ago was "an unprovoked attack by Lucky Jim on Mr. W. Somerset Maugham." The results were extremely amusing and showed, on the part of the contestants, a readiness to enter with gusto into the spirit of Amis's hero. The judge, by his tone, however, dissociated himself from this spirit: he referred to the winning entry as "a really outstanding bounderism," and this term points the issue involved. The word "bounderism" implies the whole system of standards against which Lucky Jim is revolting. If his boorishness and his infantile malevolence make him guilty of bounderism, what is the word for the obnoxiousness of Bertrand, the son of the professor of history in whose mediocre department poor Jim has been degrading himself in order to make sure that his appointment will be renewed? From the traditional point of view, of course, both these young men are bounders; but the difference is that Bertrand will have none of this, he aims at the best connections, while the strength of Jim Dixon resides in his not wanting not to acquiesce in being rated as a bounder. Like Alice, when she breaks out of Wonderland, he finds at last that he is prepared to assert himself, to vindicate his own reality, against a mere pack of cards.

March 24, 1956

CAVALIER AND YANKEE

THE LITERATURE produced in the American South before the Civil War is a field that few have explored, and even among specialists in Americana few people have any idea of how much of this literature there is. It is true that the literate class was small, that writing was not much encouraged, and that the ban on the discussion of slavery in the period just before the war had a further discouraging effect, yet the Southerners were far more articulate than one could learn from the old-fashioned literary histories, which were almost invariably written by Northerners. One knows about John C. Calhoun on account of his importance as a political figure, but how many have heard of George Fitzhugh or Hinton R. Helper, once famous and influential writers on politico-social subjects? A handful of readers of American fiction have heard of William Gilmore Simms as a sort of Southern counterpart of Cooper; but how many know even the names of those prewar Southern novelists George Tucker, Beverley Tucker, John P. Kennedy, William A. Caruthers and John Esten Cooke? It has even been rather difficult to find out about some of these writers; their books are mostly out of print, and though there have recently been biographies of a few of them, the events of their lives have been sometimes obscure. Vernon L. Parrington, in his *Main Currents in American Thought*, though he tried to do justice to the South, seems to have picked out his subjects a little at random. Jay B. Hubbell's *The South in American Literature, 1607–1900* has so far, I believe, gone further to cover this body of writing than any other work, and even it, as the author explains, is not meant to be comprehensive.

There is, however, from the point of view of the literary merit of these writers, good reason enough for this neglect: the mediocrity of most of their work. The reviewer, in connection with a book of his own, has recently had to acquaint himself with a certain amount of this literature, and he can testify that the irritation aroused by the crankiness of the publicists is only surpassed by the ennui produced by the insipidity of the novelists. Even Van Wyck Brooks, that alchemical transmuter of base or dull metals, hardly deigning to mention the publicists (he puts Helper and Fitzhugh in a footnote), is not able to do much for the novelists. When he tells us that Simms's *Woodcraft* is "certainly the best historical novel that was written in the South, or anywhere else, for that matter, at the time" or that Cooke's *The Virginia Comedians* "was a very good book indeed of the romantic type," the words have a hollow ring and scarcely disguise the fact that these romances are quite unreadable for anyone who is not under a scholar's obligation to allow himself to be steadily bored.

Yet these works have another kind of value: they reflect the mind of the South, its anxieties and consolations, its questionings and self-justifications, its reactions to social change. It is only from an historical point of view that this literature can be made at all interesting, and the most successful exploit as yet in turning it to historical account is undoubtedly *Cavalier and Yankee: The Old South and American National Character,* by William R. Taylor. Mr. Taylor has here tried to trace, by following the images that appear in this literature and the careers of the writers who created them, the early beginnings, the rapid growth and the finally more or less fixed identities of the two myths suggested by his title. For this purpose he has laid under contribution any document that throws light on his subject, but he has especially studied the work of the novelists mentioned above, and—since the vividly contrasting figures of the Yankee and the Cavalier were the result of a kind of collaboration between the North and the South—he has examined with equal interest the works and lives of three Northern novelists: Sarah Josepha Hale, the editor of *Godey's Lady's Book*, James Kirke Paulding, the friend and colleague of Washington Irving, and Harriet Beecher Stowe. He has explored this uninviting material with the thoroughness of a scholar and interpreted it with inspired insight; his presentation of his findings is so luminous that the book can be read by anyone not accustomed to systematic historical reading. Only rarely does he allow himself allusions that will not be readily understood by anyone not well acquainted with the details of American history—as when he refers, without explaining, to "the instruction of Senators" or to "the events at the end of [Patrick] Henry's life" that "had scarred his reputation." The style is quite free from the standard clichés of academic historical writing—though Mr. Taylor's vocabulary has its occasional ineptitudes, as when he evidently missuses *jejune* on page 233 and certainly misuses *transpire* on page 282, or when, on page 317, in speaking of two things, he says that one of them is "the least attractive." Let me say here that *Cavalier and Yankee* seems to me in its field an extremely important book, a brilliant and original contribution to America's understanding of itself.

The real theme of *Cavalier and Yankee* is the effort of the liberated Americans, after the Revolution, which had united them in a common aim, to decide what an American was, how he ought to think of himself, what image he should present to the world. Mr. Taylor begins with the correspondence between Jefferson and John Adams. They are wondering how their new democracy can be sure of producing men who will be able and intelligent enough to govern it. Jefferson believes that merit, regardless of social origins, will inevitably rise to the top and assume the responsibility of government; Adams is rather dubious and inclines to believe that there is something in maintaining, through family tradition, a high standard of public spirit and education. An early attempt to project an image of the ideal post-Revolutionary American was William Wirt's *Sketches of the Life and Character of Patrick Henry,* published in 1817. Neither Jefferson nor Adams approved of this book, for the reason, apparently, that the real Patrick Henry was entirely unlike themselves and did not at all represent their idea of what a superior American should be. Jefferson declared that Wirt had suppressed Patrick Henry's ignorance, his avarice and his vulgarity; Adams deplored Wirt's inaccuracy but said that he had enjoyed the book as he enjoyed romantic novels. That Wirt had falsified deliberately is shown by a letter to Jefferson in which he complains of Henry that "there are some ugly traits in [his] character" and that he was "verily as hopeless a subject as man could well desire." But the book made a great impression; it had run through twenty-five editions by 1871. What "Wirt wished to show," says Mr. Taylor, was "that during the early stages of the Revolution an epic struggle for preëminence had taken place between the old ideal of an aristocracy of birth and wealth and a new ideal of natural leadership." He believed that "the classical ideal was fading out of American life along with an aristocracy of birth" and that natural vitality was taking its place and would "emerge as a dominant cultural force."

But by the time of the deaths of these founding fathers who had always been thinking in terms of the United States as a whole, the Northern and the Southern groups of states were already somewhat pulling apart. Instead of producing an American type, imagining an American ideal that would be valid all over the country, they created two reciprocal myths, the Yankee and the Cavalier, which complemented one another. Mr. Taylor shows step by step how the dominating images were cultivated. He believes that the beginnings of the Southern one are to be found in Wirt's life of Henry—in its disparagement of acquisitive values and its idealization of old Virginia. There was nothing of the idealized plantation here, but this was not long in coming. It appeared in the eighteen-thirties with the novels of the writers I have mentioned. The myth of the Cavalier was the myth of the old plantation South. The Southerners had come to believe that the "ideals of the Revolutionary generation had been eroded away by a half century of democratic change and territorial expansion," and they "grasped for symbols of stability and order to stem their feelings of drift and uncertainty and to quiet their uneasiness about the inequities within Southern society." These symbols were usually drawn from the imagined conditions of plantation life before the Revolution. The serious rural depression that had lasted by 1830 for almost thirty years had depleted Tidewater Virginia by making its old families move West. It has been estimated that by 1830 "close to a third of those born in Virginia and Maryland around the turn of the century had crossed the Alleghenies. . . . The decline of plantation prosperity in the Carolinas came somewhat later, after the opening up of the Southwest." The literature of this period is nostalgic but also critical. The planters may be represented as bad managers or reckless wastrels who are failing through their own ineptitude.

In the meantime, the conception of natural vitality that appeared in Wirt's life of Henry was developing in an entirely non-classical way. We now have the crafty spy, the woodsman who is almost an Indian, the loyal down-to-earth retainer, more practical and slier than his master, who can come to his master's rescue. Mr. Taylor believes that this character for the first time becomes prominent and clearly defined in Cooper's early novel *The Spy,* in the person of Harvey Birch, "shrewd, acquisitive and mysterious in his movements," and of course Birch was followed by Natty Bumppo. The rough and uneducated man who is, however, full of courage and virtue and almost supernaturally skilled in all the arts of the hunter and the pathfinder was common to the novels of the North and the South, but he eventually emerges in the North as the Yankee par excellence. He will, at last, now rather more literate, arrive in King Arthur's court, and he will come to seem as alien to the Southerners as Mark Twain's hero was to the knights. The Southerners were living in a daydream of chivalry, and the Yankee had become the enemy—the materialist, the smart-aleck, the cheat, the boor. Wirt's ideal of natural vitality had by this time quite parted company from the gentlemanly ideal of the Old South.

In the creation of these two opposed figures, each group, as has been said, had a hand. The New Englanders, on their side, too, had misgivings about their Yankee. There was an element in the North—and it included a good many writers—who felt that, with the rapid growth of industry and the spreading ramifications of commerce, the Puritan stock was deteriorating. These people began to admire the South, not in its pre-Revolutionary phase but, without knowing it well, in its present one. James Kirke Paulding, who did visit Virginia and found it on the whole delightful, embodied in his *Letters from the South* of 1817, by way of contrast to the life that he found there, a nightmare of a mechanized country in which men constructed by machines were replacing "anatomical men." He regarded Andrew Jackson, a Tennesseean, as a triumphant example of the tough dynamic American, who, on the one hand, owed nothing to Europe, and, on the other, represented "a kind of success which had nothing to do with commerce and progress." He came to believe that the best hope for America would be a blending of the North and the South. "A mixture of the Cavalier and the Yankee," writes Mr. Taylor, "he appears to say [by implication in one of his novels], has produced a sturdy and tolerant race of men without the weaknesses of the former or the narrowness and bigotry of the latter."

It was actually true, says Taylor—though not in the way that Paulding hoped—that by the second quarter of the century the American North and South were not so different as they thought they were. The Northerners as well as the Southerners were worried about the direction that "progress" was taking, about the restlessness and instability of the new American society, and about the unscrupulousness and crassness of the self-made American man; and the Southerners and the Northerners both were far gone in speculation and trade; they were voting for the same national parties and pursuing the same social and political objectives. But from the time that the use of the cotton gin gave the cotton-growing states of the South a strong economic interest in slavery, the polarization of the opposite conceptions of the Yankee and the Cavalier became more and more extreme, till, at the time of the Civil War, they were exploited as the villain and the hero of reciprocal melodramas in which these roles were simply reversed. Mr. Taylor drops the story on the eve of secession, but one should mention that after the war the idealized Old South was moved up from the period before the Revolution, where the Southerners had originally located it, to the period before the Civil War, and that the Northerners, after defeating and ruining the South, feeling again the need for something in America to offset the by then, for many, even uglier industrial world, were again by the eighteen-nineties coming also to encourage this idealization.

It is a gift of certain historians to be able to put the reader back into the moment of the past they are dealing with, and to make him accept its assumptions, experience its fears and confusions, vibrate to its irrational impulses and follow its rational gropings, as if he did not know what was going to happen, had not yet heard the rest of the story. Mr. Taylor possesses this gift, and *Cavalier and Yankee* owes much of its effectiveness to this. One is made to feel the void of the early Republic, in which the successfully revolted but now somewhat battered ex-colonists have not really found themselves. What is going to take shape in that void? We are uncomfortable and self-assertive. We are supposed to have principles and purposes in common, but these principles and purposes are strained by the constantly intensifying conflict between differing social forms that are governed by different conceptions. To state the situation, however, in such an abstract and general way is really to misrepresent the effect of *Cavalier and Yankee*. The subject is here examined in terms of particular books and the people who wrote these books. It is lived through the lives of these individuals, and this leads one to realize more sharply how our national story has continued since the point at

which Taylor leaves us. Have we not really, to some
extent, always felt the blank of the void about us? Have
we not always been subjected to strain, to a strain which
is always taking different forms and arising from new
directions? Have we ever really known what we wanted
to be? Have we not always been rather nervous about
what we might be becoming? In our early post-Revolutionary boasts, in our later gigantic triumphs in technological and commercial achievement, in our present
huffings and puffings in competition with a supposed
potential enemy, have we not always been fearful of our
future?

This is what has made life in the United States—no
matter what one may have been doing: making money or
working in the laboratory or trying to promote the humanities—become always, in the span of a lifetime,
eventually so fatiguing. The Republic has always to be
saved, the wars in the name of democracy have recurrently to be won, the national standard of living has always to be rescued or maintained or raised; and although
we have always been as ready with official national slogans
as any advertizing agency, we have never been entirely
clear as to why all these things must be done, any more
than the founding fathers could be clear about what they
were founding. Mr. Taylor's *Cavalier and Yankee*, in
refusing to deal in large generalizations and in showing
the special pressures that our slogans have been meant to
relieve, has applied a fluoroscopic scrutiny to those early
and effortful days of the always inharmonious organism
in which we still struggle and squirm.

October 28, 1961

THE JAMES BRANCH CABELL
CASE REOPENED

CABELL IS OUT OF FASHION. He has been telling us this constantly himself, and he does not exaggerate. He has come nowadays to be fatally associated with all that was most meretricious in the twenties—the speakeasy sophistication, the half-baked provincial cleverness, the bad taste in dealing with sex that followed on liberation from the taboos of an earlier period. By the thirties, people sneered at the mention of *Jurgen;* by the forties, it was never mentioned. That Mr. Cabell himself came to share this disgust with his most famous book's reputation he explains in his new volume of memoirs, *As I Remember It: Some Epilogues in Recollection.* It was very embarrassing, he tells us, to find oneself admired and besieged by "hordes of idiots and prurient fools, of busybodies, of unpublished authors well worthy of that condition, of dabblers in black magic, of catamites and of amateur strumpets." The effect of the Cabell cult was eventually to leave the impression that its object was second-rate, and this is unjust to Mr. Cabell, whose distinction is real and of an uncommon kind.

It has, however, been something of a surprise for the writer of the present article to read Cabell, at this date, with pleasure. In the twenties I went through those new books of his that at the time were attracting attention in order to find out what they were, and what I found seemed for the most part so uncongenial that I did not go on reading him. It was only more than twenty years later that I took Cabell up again. A few years ago, a friend of mine—half-Northerner, half-Virginian: I am not sure that a one-hundred-per-cent Southerner would have found the book so sympathetic or that many Northern readers would have been so much interested in it—persuaded me to look into, as a document on the South, a then recent book of Cabell's called *Let Me Lie* (1947), described by the author as *Being in the main an Ethnological Account of the Remarkable Commonwealth of Virginia and the Making of Its History.* This book was so entertaining, so informative and so agreeably written—in contrast to what I remembered as the somewhat plushy overwriting of certain of the earlier books—that I have gone on reading the further collections of historical essays and personal memoirs that have followed *Let Me Lie,* and since I have lately been making an effort to understand the Southern point of view, I also went back to those novels of Cabell's (*The Cords of Vanity* and *The Rivet in Grandfather's Neck*) that take place in the Virginia of his youth, and so have been led to explore the more fanciful department of his work, which I had resolved, after *Jurgen,* to avoid—the novels that deal with Poictesme, the synthetic imaginary realm to which Cabell became addicted and about which, I must now admit, he has written some of his most successful as well as his most ambitious books. The result of this exploration I want to present here, and I have explained how it came to be made in order to bring out the fact that I am considering this author's work from a point of view somewhat different from that from which the critics of the late nineteen-tens observed him as an unknown luminary appearing on the Southern horizon, or from that of the readers of the twenties, greedily gulping him down as one of a variety of

novel intoxicants. There are already two notable essays on
Cabell that deal with his work as a whole, by writers who
are not superficial and who are not trying to beat the
drum for him, as his early admirers were—the essay by V.
L. Parrington in the third volume of *Main Currents in
American Thought,* a sympathetic and searching account
of Cabell's philosophy of life and art, and the section in
Alfred Kazin's *On Native Grounds,* which, written in
terms of the prejudices of the unsympathetic thirties,
gives, however, an intelligent and objective description of
the role Cabell played for the twenties. I shall, therefore,
try not to traverse again the ground that has already been
covered in these and in other studies but to deal with Mr.
Cabell's work by way of my own accidental approach—
that is, in terms of his regional and historical interest—
which has eventually led me to an appreciation of certain
aspects of his later work that I believe have not been
much brought out.

We Northerners do not, I believe—unless we have been a
good deal in the South—really grasp the state of mind of
the Southerners. We have always made a point, in our
relations with them, of disregarding what we call the
Civil War, they of remembering it and calling it the War
Between the States. We like to assume that the United
States is an integrated, homogeneous and smoothly functioning nation, and unless we are professional historians,
we succeed in forgetting completely that the former Confederacy was an occupied country to a greater or lesser
extent for twelve years after the War, and that it has still
a good deal of the mentality of a resentful and rebellious
province under some such great power unit as the old
Austro-Hungarian Empire. Except when an issue arises so
troublesome that it cannot be ignored—such as that of the
recent Supreme Court ruling against racial segregation in

the schools—we hardly realize how deep and how virulent, from a long-standing sense of grievance, runs the
instinct toward repudiation of any responsibility on the
part of the South to that federal government of states
which are by no means so completely united as the
Northerner likes to suppose. The Northerner does not
take account of the extent to which the Southerner—if
not overtly, at least among other Southerners and in his
own most intimate being—disassociates himself from the
North. For a writer, this has special consequences.

The commercial elements in the "New South" more
easily make common cause with the corresponding elements in the North and West. They do not worry about
the meaning of history, the philosophical values of life.
But the writer in or from the South is out of harmony
with his opposite number in the North in certain rather
serious ways. His education, to begin with, is distinctly
different. This is likely to be based on some acquaintance
with—or, at any rate, respect for—the Greek and Latin
classics, some knowledge of the English eighteenth century, a close familiarity with the romantic poets, and a
reading of Dickens and Thackeray. If it goes further, it
may run to an interest in memoirs of the French court.
The old-fashioned Southerner was steeped in Scott. The
newer kind picks up modern literature in its most non-
political phase—Joyce, Eliot, Henry James. The only
writer he much admires who has any sort of political
implications is W. B. Yeats, the spokesman of a long ago
subjugated but still insubmissive nation, who played
nobly, in relation to the non-Irish world, the role of a
defiant anachronism.

For both kinds of Southerner, the American republic
wears an aspect that seems strange to a Northerner, since
it is something already half-legendary, something that has
been valiantly fought for quite a long time ago in history,

like Christendom and Mary Stuart. The projects of the present-day United States—its hopes, its political devices, its role in the larger world—simply do not exist for these Southerners. For Jurgen, Hell is a democracy; for Allen Tate, the "great Dome" of the Capitol is a subject of crepuscular and gloomy reflections, and reflections assigned to Aeneas, who, from the point of view of the poet—since the Capitol is regarded as Roman—may without the least incongruity rejoin the classical tradition in Washington. When Faulkner departs from the South to write about the fliers of the First World War, we are as far from Woodrow Wilson as from Dos Passos and Eugene Debs and right back beside our gallant ally the Marquis de LaFayette, among exploits that ring with the mettle of Light Horse Harry Lee. What I am saying is, of course, not true in every respect of every Southern writer, but the Northerner is apt to underestimate the degree to which the Southern writer—however intuitive, intelligent, imaginative, well-travelled, well-read—may fail to accept our assumptions or to sympathize with our aims. We do not realize that he lives in a world in which planning, reform, progress, making the world safe for democracy, laying the foundations of a classless society, promoting the American way of life do not really mean anything at all. What makes his indifference possible, and even tolerably easy, for the Southerner is the fact that such phrases as these are often the merest cant and may disguise other interests less worthy. But the Southerner among Northerners, with his easy politeness and his discretion of minority status—and what with *our* being so sure of ourselves that we do not suspect others of doubting—is likely, in ordinary contacts, to conceal from us his lack of response, his complete non-participation. Yet the faith and the hope we cherish are definitely, inveterately, not there. The Southerner is quite cut off from our "*engagé*" preoccupations by an outlook that belongs to another world—a world with a feudal background—which combines a respect for this background, a certain nostalgia for it, with something more positive: an ideal of freedom—though a freedom, of course, demanded for no one else but the propertied classes.

This freedom had been gallantly won in a struggle with overlords beyond the sea, but the society that hoped to enjoy it has fallen victim to another tyranny; it has been beaten down in its flowering and kept from its natural growth, burnt over, pulled up by the roots, humiliated and impoverished, subjected to a cruel punishment by a group of those other American states beside which the South had once fought, under the leadership of a Virginian gentlemen, in behalf—as it had then supposed—of the rights of the men of substance. They are not in the same position, these contemporary writers of the South, as the Southern politicians who are working for Southern interests in Washington and who function as a part of the government. They still feel some pride in that capital to the founding of which General Washington, Mr. Jefferson, and other Southerners contributed after all, so much, but when they visit it, when they come into the presence of its actual administrators (see Felix Kennaston's lunch with Theodore Roosevelt in Cabell's *The Cream of the Jest*), it is with something of unpleasant embarrassment, of wistfulness, of alienation, of an undertone of sardonic hostility. The whole attitude of the Southerner toward the United States is admirably conveyed by Cabell in the section—an example, incidentally, of his least mannered prose at its best—called *Near a Flag in Summer* in *These Restless Heads*. Here he describes himself writing his books in a cottage on a mountainside, at a level with "the Republic's flag," "robustious" and "ever-busy," which he watches, now fluttering and flapping, as if boastful, indignant, or threatening, and now hanging limp like "a swollen leech." The writer works always in its presence, but he continues to remain quite detached from it, to remember "that these so large and impassive skies have seen over-many flags and far too many writers. With all the aforesaid national standards which but recently paraded through my mind, and with some thousands of other national standards, now forever evicted from human reverence into oblivion's scrap-pile and a pedant's occasional mention, I wonder that my friend Mr. John F. Atkins, the night watchman, should think it worth his while to be hoisting this doomed bit of bunting every morning and to be lowering it at sunset precisely."

Their history is not the same as ours—from, say, Buchanan on. They do not have the same Theodore Roosevelt—who invited a Negro to dinner and who scolded Owen Wister for idealizing prewar Charleston— let alone the same Lincoln. They do not even have the same national literature. It need not surprise us that Cabell should write of Lincoln as a sordid politician and of Harriet Beecher Stowe as an odious old tyrant and prig, but it does rather startle the Northerner to discover—in *Ladies and Gentlemen*—that the author is unable to believe that the literature of the United States has ever really amounted to anything. He will recognize only Poe as an authentic American "genius." He admits that there is a little of Mark Twain that is readable, but otherwise—the New England writers: Hawthorne, Thoreau, Emerson; the New Yorkers: Melville, Whitman, Henry James—the whole thing is a pretentious fraud. One remembers that Poe and Mark Twain were both more or less Southerners. Except for them, says Mr. Cabell, our letters are hopelessly second-rate, and he praises certain British writers—Arthur Machen, Stevenson, Saki—who may seem to the Northern reader much inferior to the native ones dismissed.

How, then, will the young Cabell nourish himself in a vanquished and ruined society, now subsumed under a system that he cannot accept, whose culture he considers null? Along what lines now can develop the career of a writer of remarkable gifts and unusual tenacity of purpose, born of the "quality" caste—he still always, though a little humorously, refers to a lady as a "gentlewoman"—in Richmond-in-Virginia (as he writes it), fourteen years after the Civil War and only two after the departure of the Yankees? This young man will begin by doing a good many of the traditional things for a cultivated person of the old stock. He graduates from William and Mary College, where he specializes in French and Greek; he has a period of newspaper work, first in the New York of 1899–1901, which he describes as "virtually village-like," then back home in Richmond; he goes in for genealogical research in a more or less professional fashion; he travels in England and France, partly to see the world, partly on a genealogical errand. He composes, in the taste of the nineties, many polished but indifferent verses—sestinas, ballades, rondeaux, which pretend to be translations from the French—and, inheriting the trappings of chivalrous romance so much beloved in the Old South, so delusive to the champions of the Confederacy (according to Mark Twain, the Civil War was partly caused by Walter Scott), he begins writing stories for the magazines.

His first ambition, he says, was to emulate the popular fiction of Anthony Hope, Henry Harland and Justus Miles Forman, and write novels "about beautiful fine girls and really splendid young men, and everything would come out all right in the end"; and for a time he is quite successful. His stories appear in *Harper's,* with pictures by Howard Pyle, and they are brought out as Christmas books, handsomely boxed, with the illustrations in color. But something is off-center in these stories. The editors of magazines are obliged to expunge certain kisses between persons not properly married, certain coarse references to Falstaff's "belly." When the heroine of a light little novel laid in contemporary Virginia makes use of the current American slang and, in a moment of crisis, says, "Damn you!," a controversy is stirred that goes on for months in the New York *Times Book Review*, as to how a young "gentlewoman" in fiction should be allowed to express herself. Cabell's illustrator, Howard Pyle, begins to complain that his stories "are neither exactly true to history nor exactly fanciful . . . that they are not true to medieval life, and that they lack a really permanent value such as I should now endeavor to present to the world." One of Cabell's medieval romances, the amusing and quite brilliant *Domnei* (then called *The Soul of Melicent*), a story of impossible prodigies of prowess and long-term fidelity, performed by a knight for his lady, seems almost—with its fairytale extravagances and its unexpected peripeties—to be getting out of hand. Cabell says that he had not known how to bring the book to a close, and we feel that he has stopped just in time to avoid an effect of comedy, since Melicent, finally deserved and won, could hardly have been worth all that trouble, and we are given the impression that her worshipper has become a good deal more interested in his semi-fraternal contests with his rival than in the object of these contests herself. Cabell points out, in this connection and in the case of others of his books, that he was always, in his earlier period, allowing his original hero, a conventional model of chivalry, to be played off the stage by a character—in *Domnei*, the ruthless rival—who makes hay of the chivalric code and eventually reduces it to absurdity.

In this South of the first decade of the twentieth century, intellectually so stagnant, the clever young man in his twenties is beginning to feel his superiority, to adopt a mocking tone toward his fellow-Southerners. He is obviously, just then, reading Wilde and Shaw, but his wit takes a line of its own, which is also a kind of development of one aspect of the Southern tradition. At college, he has written an essay on Congreve, always a great admiration of Cabell's, and he now begins to subvert or pepper the raptures and insipidities of chivalry with a cynicism from the eighteenth century. In two novels of contemporary Virginia—*The Cords of Vanity* (1909) and *The Rivet in Grandfather's Neck* (published in 1915 but finished, Cabell says, in 1911)—he makes a good deal of fun of the code of the Old South, and yet not in an un-Southern way. The three themes of his work, he tells us, are Chivalry, Gallantry and Poetry, and in the first of these books it is gallantry that completely gets the upper hand. This highly entertaining novel was received in its time with horror. The heroes of Bernard Shaw had their anti-Victorian morality, which no true moralist could easily dismiss, but Robert Etheridge Townsend—whose name invokes the Restoration Etherege—is not at all in earnest in *The Cords of Vanity,* and he is a good deal more "immoral," as morality was then conceived. It is curious to compare this novel with that somewhat similar book, F. Scott Fitzgerald's *This Side of Paradise,* which seemed scandalous in 1920. Cabell's Townsend has something in common with Fitzgerald's Amory Blaine, but he is more a man of the world, more literate, less easily excited, and, compared with his full-scale love affairs, the "petting" of Fitzgerald's young people—those truants from college proms—seems childish. Nothing, surely, could have been more inacceptable to the American taste of the early nineteen-hundreds.

What was worse, the unmaidenly maiden here appears in an even more frightening form than that of the young gentlewoman who said "Damn you!" in an earlier book. Robert Townsend amuses himself, during a summer at a Southern resort, by meetings in the woods with an attractive girl who is staying at the same hotel. He takes day-by-day notes on these meetings, and, once the summer is over, he proceeds—though with many qualms on the score of ungentlemanly behavior—to exploit the experience in a novel. This production he reads, in manuscript, to a sympathetic uncle, who tells him that it is all very well, but that he has just read the same story—exactly the same thing, "except in the names and in your messed-up purple language"—in a popular novel by a woman writer who uses a masculine name.

The Rivet in Grandfather's Neck appears to start out in a conventional way, but then performs surprising pirouettes and turns into—for Southern fiction—a new kind of rather Shavian comedy, in which the author pulls out rugs and chairs from under the Southern conventions. Yet Colonel Musgrave, the principal character—a professional genealogist and old-school Virginian snob—is made, in his outmoded way, to stand for something honorable and rather fine. The *Rivet* is a subtler and more serious, as well as more complicated, *Colonel Carter of Cartersville,* that once popular half-sentimental novel by F. Hopkinson Smith. The Colonel of James Branch Cabell is made to marry, with some condescension, a wife of inferior blood and loses her to an inferior man, but his loyalty, once given, cannot be withdrawn. He succeeds in getting her back, but soon loses her: she dies very young of an ailment connected with the birth of their son. After her death—though the husband has known very well of the element of the trashy in her and though he now has the opportunity to marry a woman who was his first love—he still remains faithful to the memory of his wife. At last, when he is dying himself, he imagines her returning to the house—inalienably, though changed, her home. He sees her go through the rooms, looking in vain "for her grandiose plush-covered chairs, her immaculate 'tidies,' and the proud yellow lambrequin, embroidered in high relief with white gardenias"—all of which have been weeded out by the Colonel's more fastidious daughter-in-law. He can see her doing all the domestic things, having all the housewifely reactions, that the Colonel knows she would; he hears her comment on the new colored maid; he imagines she has come into the sickroom, to the bed which was once hers. And with this vision the Colonel expires. This episode is, it seems to me, the first in which Cabell gives full proof of his powers. But these powers are not to find their fullest scope in presenting the contemporary South. He tells us that he was stopped, in this earlier phase, from dealing with some local subject by considering the fates of George W. Cable and other Southern writers when they tackled uncomfortable themes. The particular theme that made Cable an object of detestation on the part of his fellow-Louisianians—the difficult situation of persons of mixed black and white blood—is touched on by Cabell, though tellingly, only in *The Rivet in Grandfather's Neck*. One could not open up with impunity these old and sore scandals of the South, and it is quite impossible for Cabell to interest himself in the "New South." He cannot pretend to live in the accepted world of Southern legend; he is sure to give away the imposture. On the other hand, the Richmond of the Chamber of Commerce, the flourishing of which can bring nothing but a further *embourgeoisement*, is even more alien to him; it arouses distaste, and it bores him. The novelist hero of his next Southern book—*The Cream of the Jest* (1917)—gets away from this bourgeois Virginia by reverting in a series of daydreams to the fairy-tale world of *Domnei*.

The author of *The Cream of the Jest* will himself now remain in this fairy-tale world, but he will draw into it all his others. The Middle Ages, the seventeenth and eighteenth centuries, the inescapable mediocrity of modern life will now all be mixed up together and merged with the goblins and marvels of innumerable scrambled folklores. His mythological books of this period are undoubtedly Cabell's best, and they are also to become his most famous. So remote from the contemporary America which the writers of the North and the West were at that time intent on presenting in a satiric or pathetic light, how was it that these books emerged? How was it that they managed to attract so cordial a critical attention and at the same time to produce on the public such an exhilaratingly sensational effect? The attempted suppression of *Jurgen* had, of course, something to do with this. The younger generation in America were escaping from the genteel censorship that had become such a nuisance to literature, and they were rejoiced to find this heir of the eighteenth-century South who—in what now seems his rather old-fashioned, his sly and roguish way—had from the first treated taboos cavalierly. But the reactions to this libertine appeal did not entirely gratify Cabell. "The main trouble with my special sort of literary eminence," he explains in *As I Remember It,* "—not among the intelligent, I am so vainglorious as to hope, but among far too many other and more widely influential classes—was that I felt I had not earned my celebrity with fairness or through any personal achievement. It more or less troubled my conscience to reflect that after eighteen years of unsuccess I had become temporarily famous through accident." But the backing that Cabell did get from "the intelligent," who cast

him at that time in the kind of role that has come to be
known as "culture hero," was partly the result of their
recognizing that here was a conscientious craftsman who
had been sticking to superior standards through a discouraging period in our culture. He had, says Ellen
Glasgow in *The Woman Within,* "survived the blighting
frustration of every artist in the South."

But frustration for the artist, at the end of the century,
was not confined to the South. To go back into the American literature of the seventies, eighties and nineties is to
become aware that during this period (except in the case
of two preëminent, if imperfectly appreciated, figures:
Mark Twain and Henry James) those writers who were
aiming at serious work often labored in a kind of underground. They would sometimes attract attention only by a
book or two, sometimes remain hardly known; in some
cases, they are hardly known yet. Of the later crop of
writers, however, who were young at the beginning of
our century, a few possessed courage and conviction—
when the demand for a genuine literature began to assert
itself against the market of the "family" magazines—
found themselves, bewildered and blinking, in the full
day of newspaper fame. Cabell was one of these. Though
he had scored several early successes, he had made no
attempt to repeat them, but, developing an original line,
perfecting a personal art—quite incapable of breaking
down in the direction of the popular taste—he had gone
on producing books that must have seemed to the publishers and editors of the time almost perversely unpublishable.

This commanded admiration, but not merely this. In
his dismissal of the legends of the Old South, his disdain
for the projects of the new, in plunging for relief into a
fabulous dream that one could have as brightly colored, as
lively, as variegated as one pleased, Cabell had made him-

self free—refusing to take on the burden of the problems of America versus Europe, industrialism versus feudalism, the South versus the North, oneself in relation to one's neighbors—to find images for his personal sense of life. And the critical success of *The Cream of the Jest* and Cabell's other books, the attempted suppression of *Jurgen*, the failure of this attempt, and the excitement that accompanied the episode must have had the effect of arousing him to transcend his previous efforts. In the four major fantasies that follow—all written in the decade of the twenties and all part of the same cycle as *Jurgen*—Cabell called into play his full powers, put on his most dazzling performances, and established his most serious claims to be rated as a first-class poet. For it is perhaps less misleading to speak of these fantasies as "poems" rather than "novels." In creating a poetic convention, Cabell thus stands a bit aloof from the other Americans of his period, who for the most part—and even in the case of a writer so poetic as Hemingway—have always remained more or less loyal to the established conventions of realism.

Cabell himself, in his critical writings, has somewhat confused this question by rejecting what he refers to as "realism" with a certain superciliousness, apparently unaware that to glorify the "dream" as against the "real" is merely to express a preference for one kind of fictional convention rather than another. The convention, for example, of a Hemingway insists that an illusion be given of a consistency different from Cabell's, but his stories are waking dreams as much as Cabell's are. The work of Cabell differs also from that of most of the writers who were fashionable in the twenties in that he does not regard human destiny as tragic. Cabell is a *comic* poet, though one of—for modern times—almost unexampled splendor. Life, to be sure, he shows us, is full of discomfiting ironies, but they are rarely a reason for weeping. And life, in the long run, is scarcely susceptible of improvement. It is true that, at the end of *The Cream of the Jest,* he does go so far as to say that "it is only by preserving faith in human dreams that we may, after all, perhaps someday make them come true." (Cabell seems to confuse the "dream" as "ideal" with his other sense of "dream" as a non-realistic poetic convention.) But this has quite a different ring from the assurance, for example, of Anatole France—to whom Cabell is sometimes compared—that "Slowly but inevitably humanity realizes the dreams of the sages." Anatole France is a child of the Renaissance, of the Enlightenment, of the French Revolution, and this aphorism stands at the head of his collected political papers; we know the direction of those dreams of his that he believes will inevitably be realized. But in Cabell's case the Renaissance is a period of gorgeous costumes, lovely women and outrageous crimes, the age of Voltaire and Rousseau a carnival of wicked gallantries; and in his own country, itself revolutionary, he has been alienated from its progress in innovation. What *are* the "human dreams," for Cabell, that our faith in them may "make come true"? In these books, so crowded with heroes and gods, with adventurers, kings and enchanters, we may look for an answer in vain.

The key figure here ought to be Manuel, the protagonist of *Figures of Earth.* Manuel, Cabell tells us, is intended as a type of the man of action, in contrast to Jurgen, the man of intelligence, and, in taking account of what is likely to seem the relative unsatisfactoriness of Manuel, we come to realize the special conditions that limit his creator's dream. Manuel is meant to be sensual, unscrupulous, treacherous, brutal. He begins as a swineherd and ends as an emperor. We are shown first, in *Figures of*

Earth, Manuel as he lived; then, in *The Silver Stallion,*
the legend that is created about him after his death. He
has come to represent an ideal, and the people of Poictesme are made more virtuous as well as more civilized
through believing in his prowess and wisdom. They
expect him to return again to lead them to further
triumphs. Now, this in itself is a good idea. The author is
aiming to dramatize the process by which the beast who
has made himself what we call human may also—through
following his instincts, improvising his policies, taking
advantage of his happy chances—arrive at a position of
power over other men less pushing and lucky; to demonstrate how these, in their need for self-confidence, their
thirst to exalt themselves, may imagine him, once he is
gone, a faithful and fearless spirit, a past-master of state-
craft and strategy. But the trouble is that Cabell's Manuel
seems to offer too little basis for such a myth. In reading
Figures of Earth, we are likely to feel that we are following the adventures of a less sympathetic Jurgen. Yet the
author has tried to bring out from the first his hero's
strong will to power. "Will you remodel the world?" he is
asked. "Who knows? . . . At all events, I do not mean to
leave it unaltered." And he is made to repeat again and
again his undiscouraged intention of following after his
"own thinking and desires." One can see that there is
meant to be something more than a mere fairy-story
sequence in the episode of the three feathers, which,
though bogus, are believed to be magic and which exercise, by suggestion, a pseudo-magical influence—something about a great leader's power to communicate to
ordinary people his confidence in his own authority, as
Napoleon did with his marshals, Abraham Lincoln with
his Cabinet, Lenin with his commissars. But in following
the career of Manuel one finds no indications of greatness. It is true that he is made creative to the extent of

animating some figures of clay, which come out, however, more or less botched. But he is otherwise such a coward, such a double-crosser, has so little continuity of purpose that he seems to give little real ground for his eventual apotheosis. In order to grow a great reputation, do you not need the seeds of qualities that suggest nobility or mastery, and qualities at least in the direction of those with which reputation credits you? This man of action of Cabell's is given, to be sure, bursts of eloquence which sometimes turn into verse and the effect of which is half-ironic, yet which represent dreams of glory that are evidently meant to raise him above the common run. But if Manuel's deeds seem too rascally for a hero, these soliloquies seem too literary for a rascal.

A partial explanation, I think, of the unsatisfactoriness of Manuel is to be found in the epistle to John Wilkes Booth in Cabell's *Ladies and Gentlemen,* a volume of letters addressed to a variety of historical personages. The author here explains his conclusion that Lincoln, on the basis of no merit whatever, was entirely created as a statesman, a great leader and a noble person by his martyrdom at the hands of Booth, who is congratulated on producing this masterpiece. Now, there is certainly a myth about Lincoln, and Lincoln was, in some ways, certainly very unlike this myth, but one cannot go through the collected papers that chronicle the whole of his public career without becoming convinced that this extravagantly apotheosized President was, in character and intellect, actually a superior man who has been vulgarized rather than exalted by the popular myth about him. The Confederacy possessed no such able statesmen, or even—since the test of a military leader is bound to be ultimate success—any permanently impressive general. But the South also needed a myth, and it made one out of Robert E. Lee. Cabell respects Lee, but here also he rejects the myth, though he treats it more reverently than Lincoln's. He addresses to Lee, too, an epistle (this one in *Let Me Lie*), but we find that his regard for Lee is of very much the same kind as his attitude, half mocking, half affectionate, toward the archaic Colonel Musgrave.

This type appears again in the cycle in the story called *The Way of Ecben*, in which the true king, Alfgar, deposed by brutal gods—through fate, for no fault of his own—and humiliated by spiteful underlings for his irreducible majesty, remains loyal to his own superseded god. " 'He is but a little god, a well-nigh forgotten god,' said Alfgar. 'I retain no longer any faith in him, and that hope which he kindled is dead a great while since. Yet this god also is made holy by the love of his worshippers, whom I too loved.' " We can believe in the high-souled Alfgar, who wins to his moment of ecstatic vision just before the victorious gods of Rorn reduce him to a pinch of ashes. But it is one of the Southerner's handicaps that since his own attempted commonwealth did not succeed, he cannot admit successful action—at least, action on a high level—on the part of anyone else. No: Manuel must be a bluff. Yet, for a bluff, his prestige is incredible. Napoleon, like Manuel, knew that "the world wishes to be deceived," and he played on the French love of glory and exploited the idealism of the Revolution to defeat the Revolution's aims. One may consider him an odious character, one may find it difficult to understand how people can admire him, adore him, weep over his ultimate exile, spend their whole lives reading about him—till one remembers that he *was* an unusual being, capable of extreme concentration, irresistible up to a point as a never-flagging piston of purpose, unmoved by considerations of humanity or self-indulgence, who impressed the ordinary person by his habit, which so few possess, of fixing upon an objective and proceeding straight to the mark. For these powers, as

well as for the delusions he fostered, the French do Napoleon honor. But why was Manuel honored? His widow
and his aged mistresses come to pay their respects to his
empty tomb. They have no illusions about him. What
they are celebrating is simply his virility. Is this enough?
Surely not quite. And yet one must be wary in disparaging these volumes that deal with Manuel, to the seriousness of which an epigraph from Horace attests and which
the author has planted as a base for his work, calling the
whole thing a "Biography of the Life of Manuel"—since
Manuel's life is continued in his offspring, who comprise,
according to Cabell, all the other important characters in
his novels. It is one of those annoying productions, like
Flaubert's *L'Education Sentimentale,* that are likely to be
disconcerting by reason of the injuries they are bound to
inflict on our common human *amour-propre.* And it contains some excellent things—the whole episode at the
end, for example, of the Troubling Window in Manuel's
study. This window reveals a landscape that is not the
familiar one to be seen from the other windows and that
represents for Manuel, now elderly and successful, almost
at the end of his rocky career, the still unassuaged appe-
tites, the untried possibilities of life. One's present mode
of living excludes them and one ventures among them
now at one's peril.

If Cabell's Poictesme is lacking in the elements that
provide stability, it is marvellously happy in rendering the
unstable aspects of life—the fluidities, hoaxes, surprises;
illusions that conceal their opposites, ellipses of sleight-of-
hand that whisk away something important, inevitable
things that we do without knowing we are going to do
them, little incidents that seem to slip by and then later
return as obsessions; the desire, attained with difficulty,
that turns out to stultify or terrify; the summonings of
apparitions that result in nothing substantial, the annihi-

lations that do not destroy anything, the apparently significant episodes that are seen to have been purely subjective: one eventually wakes up from a dream; the bugaboos that turn out to be unsure of themselves, the ladies, long adored and hard won, from whom their devoted knights have in the end to flee for their lives; the amazing multiplications of gods or worlds, the unsettling changes of scale by which man becomes a titan or a pygmy in relation to his universe; the dissociation of personality—one finds oneself going away and leaving a simulacrum, the Sylan, apparently quite alien to one's inner self, performing one's usual functions; one recovers, as if nothing has happened, the woman one has forfeited to Death; one comes out at the other end of time and begins as a child again. All this quicksilver phantasmagoria—I take the phrase from Fernanda Pivano who refers to Cabell's work as "a great globe of scattering quicksilver"—is the author's "criticism of life." It is a unique artistic achievement, and one which it was possible to arrive at only by breaking through into a non-realistically conditioned world.

It is curious to compare these fantasies with a book written just before them—*The Certain Hour* of 1916, a collection of short stories dealing mostly with historical figures: Shakespeare, Wycherley, Sheridan and others. Here the felicity of the writing at its best—as we get it, for example, in *Olivia's Pottage*—seems quite out of proportion to the interest of the story, so implausible and so contrived; and the contrivances at their weakest—*Pro Honoria*—simply make us impatient with melodramatic reversals that verge on Gilbert and Sullivan. Yet as soon as the author, in his later books, has put aside any pretension of satisfying conventional requirements, the element of unpredictability comes to provide the real principle of life. What is delightful is the music of a counterpoint that is always betraying intention, outwitting expectation, through the play of unrecognized forces that nevertheless belong to the same harmonic system.

The poetry of these later creations does not, perhaps, present itself in quite a pure form. One should warn the prospective reader of a generation which does not know Cabell that his art is a little encumbered by ornamentations in an antique mode, which do not always make for lightness. Henry James, in his memoir of Turgenev, says that he once heard the Russian complain that the style of a certain French novel was too *"tarabiscoté"*; that is, that it "had on the surface too many little flowers and knots of ribbon." In this sense, the books of Cabell are among the most *"tarabiscotés"* ever written. The arch preciosity of the nineties was learned early and has never been purged. Cabell's writings are invariably prinked out with a passementerie of introductory verses, epigraphs, epistles dedicatory and citations from invented authorities. You can, of course, strip off these trimmings by skipping them, but you will then have to steel yourself to face such unnatural locutions as *no least, not ever* (Cabell never writes *never*), *dearliest, lateliest, futurely, a little by a little, to the other side* in the sense of *on the other hand, living* instead of *life,* and his device of a continuous present in such sentences as "But it is not of so-and-so I would be speaking" and "It troubled me to be seeing," which sounds as if it had been taken over from the plays of the old Abbey Theatre.

This is perhaps Cabell's own special remnant of the floweriness of old-fashioned Southern writing. But do not, in any case, let it put you off; you will soon forget about it. Hardly hedged by these arid frills lives the quicksilver world I have spoken of—a world of swift and witty colloquies, of vivid and enchanting colors, of continual metamorphoses. These fantasies are not logical allegories; it is one of their great virtues that they are not. They are closer to the psychology of dreams, and this gives them their uncanny effectiveness. The popularity of *Jurgen,* I believe, beyond the other books of its series, was due not to its superiority or to its publicized erotic interest—from this latter point of view, all these books of Cabell's are about the same—but to its being somewhat less elusive. If it is not a clear allegory, it has an element of the Odyssean and an element of the picaresque. And it is easier for the ordinary reader to understand and sympathize with the hero, to identify himself with Jurgen, than with Manuel or the heroes of the later books. These, however—*The High Place* (1923) and *Something About Eve* (1927)—seem to me more interesting creations. I agree with Mencken that *The High Place* is one of the best of Cabell's books. Here the dream evanescences and the images cast from mirrors reach a point of expert juggling that half conveys disquieting meanings. The element of the macabre increases. Is the author still pursuing his original aim—repeated so many times—"to write perfectly of beautiful happenings"? Most of the happenings in these books are not beautiful. It would surely be more accurate to say that he is here writing brilliantly of happenings that are awkward, embarrassing or bitter, and I suggest that there is a strong strain in Cabell's work of something I have not found suspected. Though Cabell himself is an Episcopalian, his father's family, he tells us, were Presbyterians, and, as in the case of a notable number of other American writers, the sulphur and brimstone of Calvinism can still, perhaps, be smelt on the premises after the Calvinist God has been forced to move out. Cabell often refers to his Scottish blood, and there is always something hard and sharp involved with his romanticism. There is a very strong Protestant sense of the importance of work, of accom-

plishment. "Patricia," he says of Colonel Musgrave's wife
in *The Rivet in Grandfather's Neck,* "was drawing her
own conclusions as to Lichfield's aristocracy. These people—for the most part a preposterously handsome race—
were the pleasantest of companions, and their manners
were perfection; but there was enough of old Roger
Stapylton's blood in Patricia's veins [her father had been
a successful banker] to make her feel, howsoever obscurely, that nobody is justified in living without even an
attempt at any personal achievement." There is also a
sense of morality, though this usually becomes explicit
only when Cabell is talking about his art. You find it
when he says that he fears he may not have earned the
reputation that came to him on account of *Jurgen;* you
have it when he says that the possession of talent imposes
the obligation to make of it the fullest use—a principle
that he is put to some trouble to reconcile with his other
statement that "the literary artist . . . labors primarily to
divert himself." There is even, on the next page to the
passage just noted—in the book of essays, *Straws and
Prayer Books*—a kind of non-literary self-castigation:
"No man," he goes on to say, "cares quite to face the truth
about himself." Looking back upon the past, he continues, he finds "much of what to the first glance seems
shirking and equivocation, so much of petty treacheries,
of small lies, and of responsibilities evaded, that I am
wholeheartedly glad to reflect my private observatory is
not, and never will be, open to the public." And though it
is true, as Alfred Kazin says, that there is something in
Cabell of complacency, it seems to me also true that the
supports upon which this complacency rests are always
made to seem rather dubious, and that what, in the long
run, he arrives at is a mastery in rendering the dubious.
These dreams are so very uncertain, and they are forever

leading their characters into such insecure situations—supremacies that make one uncomfortable, paradises that bore one or wear one out.

I had a very strong impression, in reading *The High Place* and *Something About Eve,* that they dealt with the theme of damnation, and I was surprised when I came, later on, to the preface of the first of these books, in the Storisende collected edition, to find the author explaining his intention in quite a different sense. In the latter of these books, Gerald Musgrave's long sojourn on Mispec Moor—surely, however, a dreary name, the first syllable of which suggests hatefulness*—with the amiable and domestic Maya, all his high curiosities muffled, his explorations forever postponed, was due not to the "beguilements" of Maya but rather to "his own nature." "Here are the woman and the child and common cordial human living: yonder in Antan is but ambiguity [this was the mysterious domain over which he had aspired to rule], it may be very glorious, it may be merely lethal. All news as to Antan, let it be pointed out, comes always to Gerald Musgrave from sources rather more than suspect. Meanwhile, here, upon Mispec Moor, stays that which is familiar and most dear. Man—being what he is—requires no persuading to remain where love attends him. The gods and the great myths go by, toward, it may be, concerns which are more lofty and more magnanimous: but man remains, of his own choice, and, be it added, because of all the wisdom that living has ever taught him. There are, it is said, those exceptional men who adventure very gloriously into Antan. Yet this rumor, too, comes always from ambiguous sources." No: nobody, perhaps, can ever

---

* I later learned from Mr. Cabell that Mispec Moor is an anagram for Compromise.

reach Antan. There may not even be any such place. (Note that the name of this realm where glory might or might not abide is evidently taken from Villon's refrain, "*Mais où sont les neiges d'antan!*," and assigns all true greatness to the past. With Cabell, the future counts for nothing at all, either as practical eventuality or projected myth.) But, in the meantime, the effect on the reader has not been at all such as the author says he intends. The reader—at least this reader—is not happy with Gerald and Maya on Mispec Moor, and when Gerald at last returns to his library in Lichfield to find the Sylan, his abandoned earth-inhabiting self, still industriously working at his table, compiling book after book—of an apparently scholarly kind—on the sexual habits of human beings, we feel that the two selves of Gerald represent the divergent elements of an essentially unsatisfactory experience. There is a conflict at the base of these books that makes them interesting as well as disturbing. May not such contentment as Gerald's be the drug of a moral stagnation, and may not stagnation, in Calvinistic terms, amount to the damnation against which hard striving— though it cannot by itself win Election—is regarded as a kind of precaution? The dizzy legerdemain of these stories results, for the reader, in sinkings and twinges. Read the chapter called *The Paragraph of the Sphinx,* in which Cabell is seen at his most adroit. It is a relief to discover that the author's "urbanity" is a poise never far from a precipice, that it can gasp at a momentary vision of the nullity or bafflement of human life. And the sadism that intrudes more and more in this series rather gets out of the range of "urbanity." This sadism reaches its climax in *The White Robe,* a formidable werewolf story. Here, too, we arrive at damnation, a damnation that the author intends, but which is at first disguised, in this case also, as a state of blessedness. The aim is, one comes to feel, for the author to appear "urbane" while the characters, and the readers, bite their lips.

To a younger generation, then, grown up too late for the Cabell boom, I would recommend, to begin with, the two books discussed above, and I would add to them a later production that seems to me among Cabell's best but that almost no one has read. Between the great depression and the second war—when few people were in the mood for him—Cabel published, in three instalments, with the titles *Smirt, Smith* and *Smire* (1934, 1935 and 1937), a work that—a further handicap—ought really to have been brought out in one volume, since the sections, if not read in order, can hardly be understood. This is a fantasy that differs from the earlier fantasies in being lighter and more consistently humorous, and also in being presented not as a fairy tale but explicitly as a dream. The dreamer is an elderly literary man whose popularity has recently declined and who is living in a Southern city, the life of which he finds rather dull. The author explains in a preface that he has had the idea of writing a novel which should consist entirely of an adult dream, and he expresses surprise that no one, not even Lewis Carroll, has ever attempted this. He forgets that Lewis Carroll *had* attempted it—though not with very great success—in one sequence of the complicated *Sylvie and Bruno,* and he is unaware that Joyce's *Finnegans Wake,* then appearing as *Work in Progress,* was precisely a single night's dream, composed in a Jabberwocky language of sleep. Cabell himself approaches this language when Smith is telling his nonsensical anecdotes, and he is quite close to Joyce at other points. Smirt-Smith-Smire attends his own burial, is embodied in his own grandchild, has children who are aspects of himself, and, revisiting them, now mature, finds he is invisible to them. The glorification of Smith, the eulogies of him delivered by his public, recall the apotheosis of Bloom in *Ulysses,* and these triumphs are likely to be followed by Joycean humiliations. But all the Cabellian motifs are here. Smith at one point is setting up shop with a comfortable woman named Arachne, and is hardly made nervous by feeling that eventually she may eat him up. He has a most friendly interview with God, in the course of which the latter apologizes for the Bible, written in His younger days and full, He confesses, of faults, and explains that He can now do much better and is writing another book. Smith cannot bear to warn Him that the new—and, no doubt, superior—work will not be at all well-received, since the only thing the reviewers will say of it is that He has failed to repeat His first great success. Smire finds himself at Carthage with Dido, but is prevented from making her his wife by realizing that if he should do so, the *Aeneid* could never be written—a concession in the interests of art; at Nazareth, he argues with Gabriel, come for the Annunciation, and explains the disasters it will launch, but again is obliged to yield— this time in the interests of "a superb dream, an ever-sustaining dream," the legend of Christianity. You have very much the same personnel—of deities, vampires and dragons, the adventurer, discomfited or gallant—as in the more elaborate series, but the events shimmer, melt and shift with an even more casual inconsequence.

In Italy, the three sections of *Smirt-Smith-Smire* have been brought out in a single volume, under the title *L'Incubo* (*The Nightmare*), with Surrealist illustrations by Fabrizio Clerici. A long preface by Fernanda Pivano, from which I have quoted above, is full of blunders about American literature and goes rather wide of the mark in attempting to relate Cabell to Surrealism and show that he does not run true to form. The Latins cannot understand that the Anglo-Saxon peoples have had always a poetic tradition of dreamlike and nonsensical fantasy—De Quincey, Poe, Dodgson and Lear—that is as natural to us as Surrealism for them seems bound to be self-conscious and synthetic. Yet this preface does have the merit—as when Signora Pivano says that the technique of *The Nightmare* represents a moral system that is an anarchy of allegories—of attacking the subject completely afresh, unencumbered by the old clichés of Cabell criticism. The main thing is that the book's three instalments have here been printed together. The same thing should be done for *The Nightmare* at home, with perhaps the same title, *The Nightmare*. We have hardly had a chance to enjoy or to judge this amusing and original book—of dream comedies the most opalescent.

Mr. Cabell's new collection of memoirs, *As I Remember It,* has a special place in his work. This volume—like its predecessor, *Quiet, Please*—is partly made up of reflections on the lapse of his reputation. The intellectual movement of the twenties put him in touch with the rest of the world and was evidently stimulating for him. Today that excitement has passed, and the citizen of Richmond has decided that such tumults, like love affairs, evaporate and leave no trace. The literary activities of that period can have, for Cabell, no permanent historical importance, since he cannot bring himself to believe that there is any such thing as American literature. He is even beginning to doubt that he would ever have seen anything in those books of the twenties if he had not happened to know the authors. The tide that crept even to Richmond has abated and left him again to his solitude and isolation, in which he continues to write when many of the stars of the twenties have fallen or flickered out—as he did before New York and Chicago had ever become aware of him. There is also in *As I Remember It*

a handful of memories of old friends and "collaborators"—Ellen Glasgow, Elinor Wylie, Hugh Walpole,
John Macy, Guy Holt. But what gives the book special
interest is Cabell's memoir of his first wife, with whom he
lived thirty-five years. They had nothing "in common," he
says, "except only a certain fondness for each other." She
never read his books, and he took very little interest in
her own so absorbing activities in connection with the
Daughters of the American Revolution and other organizations of the sort. But there seems to have been something of fatality in his marriage and in his relations with
his wife. One is struck, in reading this story, by its similarity to that of Colonel Musgrave and his not quite
accepted Patricia. Like the Colonel, the Colonel's creator—by providing Mrs. Cabell with a distinguished
genealogy—put her over on the very best people of Richmond, and like him, he came to love her for not behaving
quite as the very best people did. Cabell himself points
out this similarity, but he says that though *The Rivet in
Grandfather's Neck* was published after his marriage, it
had been written several years before. It would be obvious even if Cabell himself had not called attention to it
that Priscilla Bradley Cabell had sat for the whole series
of his excellent wives—Dame Lisa, Niafer, Maya,
Arachne. Yet, as he says of Gerald Musgrave, it must
have been his own nature that demanded her. If the
married state meant damnation, it was clearly the state in
which he was most at home. And his tribute to his companion of so many years is touching, convincing,
needed—an aspect of the story that had not yet been
filled in. The late Mrs. Cabell appears at last as a character in Cabell's fantastic drama as well as, so to speak, the
manager of the theater in which it was done. The most
curious feature of the story, the story of Cabell's life and
work, is that the book he has written about his wife

reproduces, after an interval of over forty years, the pathos as well as the situation of the last scene of *The Rivet in Grandfather's Neck*—the scene of the Colonel's death—imagined before he knew her.

April 21, 1956

JAMES BRANCH CABELL: 1879–1958

I DO NOT KNOW how many people will feel a special sense of loss at the death of James Branch Cabell. His old friends and admirers certainly will, but since the twenties he seems to have had few new readers. I myself rather scorned him in the twenties and came to be interested in him only much later. I published two years ago a long article about his work, so I shall not go over that ground again. But I may add that, since writing that article, the more I have thought about *Figures of Earth*— and its sequel *The Silver Stallion*—the more remarkable they have come to seem. Looking back, one can now understand the abrupt fluctuations of Cabell's fame. He began, in the early nineteen hundreds, as a writer of romantic short stories for the respectable magazines, but he put into them a tinge of irony which prevented them from being popular. He then gradually developed an ironic vein which gets its first clear and bold statement in *Jurgen*, published on the eve of the twenties, when its criticism of old-fashioned religion and nineteenth-century morality made it particularly welcome to the young. The book was gay as well as naughty, and the reader found it exhilarating to identify himself with the hero. But when Jurgen was followed by Manuel, this public was disappointed. It was not prepared for anything at once so bitter and with so little apparent bearing on contemporary life. Published when Cabell was forty-two, the chronicle of

Manuel the Redeemer was not a book for the young nor was it a book in the mood of the twenties. The story of the ambitious man of action who is cowardly, malignant and treacherous and who does not even enjoy very much what his crimes and double-dealing have won him, but who is rapidly, after his death, transformed into a great leader, a public benefactor and a saint, has the fatal disadvantage for a novel that the reader finds no inducement to identify himself with its central figure. Yet I am now not sure that this merciless chronicle in which all the values are negative save the naked human will, is not one of the best things of its kind in literature—on a plane, perhaps, with Flaubert and Swift.

Something About Eve was almost equally bitter, and also not for the young. By the time of the admirable *Nightmare* trilogy (*Smirt-Smith-Smire*), a somewhat more genial work, we were plunged in the turbulent thirties and, preoccupied with rescuing society, unprepared to pursue a dream-fantasy which though quite close at moments to *Finnegans Wake* was not at all of the school of Joyce. I had not at the time I wrote my article read the novels that followed the *Nightmare: The King Was in His Counting House, Hamlet Had an Uncle, The First Gentleman of America, There Were Two Pirates* and *The Devil's Own Dear Son*, which really constitute a group in themselves. The two that take place in Florida have their amusing or magical moments; but in general these stories are marked by a development, which becomes disagreeable, of the misanthropic sadism which was already a feature of the earlier work. *Hamlet Had an Uncle* especially is not merely inferior Cabell, it is also deliberately atrocious, the ugliest of all Cabell's works, and the atrocity here seems rather pointless. Hamlet and his uncle and the rest do not have the larger human implications of Manuel the Redeemer.

What, one wonders, at the time he was writing these books, had made Cabell's imagination so black? His non-fiction writings of his later years do not have this sinister quality, though one feels that he is bored by and chafes at the social and intellectual vacuum which Richmond seems to have become for him. He is also less in touch with the rest of the world, for the excitement of the twenties is long over, the literary friends of his own generation are either dead or inactive in retirement, while Cabell still survives and is active. One feels that a certain petulance is due partly to a lack of diversion, a cutting-off of communication. Aside from writing his memoirs— *These Restless Heads, Let Me Lie, As I Remember It,* the best of these later books—he seems to have little to occupy him but fretting about the neglect of his work and concocting too elaborate sarcasms about the people who pay him silly compliments or who write him stupid letters. Yet in this peevishness there is much of self-irony, and what is strong in him is a certain stoicism. In the letters I occasionally had from him, he always referred to the ailments which must have been making his life a misery—he had had a heart attack and was not allowed to climb the stairs to his study—in a characteristically de-tached and humorous way. "Meanwhile," he wrote last December, "I disintegrate with a variety that I find inter-esting. My latest and my most damnable acquirement in the form of maladies is arthritis, which since July has left me unable to get into a pair of shoes, and but hardly able to hobble about my own home with a cane's aid. So that leaves you at liberty to go ahead with a definite estimate of my career in letters since there now quite obviously is not going to be any more of it."

The theme in Cabell's writings which I have always found it most difficult to sympathize with is that of his persistent nostalgia for the ideal beautiful women of his adolescent imaginings. Yet this has its historical interest as a survival of the romantic and chivalrous dream that so dominated the Southern mind. The whole philosophy of Cabell, in fact, of the dream's being preferable to reality, is deeply involved with the history of the South. And his bitterness is the bitterness of the South at having had this dream proved a fiction, and then somehow having had still to live on it. The dignity of his life and work was also the dignity of the South in continuing to maintain its attitude. His career commands special respect by reason of the courage and consistency with which he pursued his course. In a period particularly unfavorable for any high standard of excellence, he developed a style that was sure to annoy, a point of view that was sure to outrage the readers of his own generation; then later, when his vogue with the young had lapsed, he continued for decades producing books that not only made no bid to recapture his audience but, becoming, as it were, more and more solipsistic, were calculated to discourage his publishers. I imagine that his steadfastness and self-respect will be more conspicuous to the future—in the history of our literature, which exhibits so many examples of acquiescence in mediocrity, of disaster and diversion of purpose—than it has recently been to us. In the meantime, his preciosity, so much out of fashion now, ought not to interfere with the recognition of his skill as a writer; nor the occasional coyness of his ribaldry disguise from us the mordancy of his restless inquiry into the meaning of his own life, the life of the defeated South and the processes of human history.

June 7, 1958

OO, THOSE AWFUL ORCS!

In 1937, DR. J. R. R. TOLKIEN, an Oxford don, published a children's book called *The Hobbit,* which had an immense success. The hobbits are a not quite human race who inhabit an imaginary country called the Shire and who combine the characteristics of certain English animals—they live in burrows like rabbits and badgers—with the traits of English country-dwellers, ranging from rustic to tweedy. (The name seems a telescoping of rabbit and Hobbs.) They have elves, trolls and dwarfs as neighbors, and they are associated with a magician called Gandalph and a slimy water-creature called Gollum. Dr. Tolkien became interested in his fairy-tale country and has gone on from this little story to elaborate a long romance, which has appeared under the general title, *The Lord of the Rings,* in three volumes called *The Fellowship of the Ring, The Two Towers* and *The Return of the King.* All the volumes are accompanied with maps, and Dr. Tolkien, who is a philologist, professor at Merton College of English Language and Literature, has equipped the final volume with a scholarly apparatus of appendices, explaining the alphabets and grammars of the various tongues spoken by his characters, and supplying their genealogies and chronological tables of their history.

Dr. Tolkien has announced that this series—the hypertrophic sequel to *The Hobbit*—is intended for adults rather than children, and it has had a resounding reception at the hands of a number of critics who are certainly grown-up in years. Mr. Richard Hughes, for example, has written of it that nothing of the kind on such a scale has been attempted since *The Faerie Queen,* and that "for width of imagination it almost beggars parallel." "It's odd, you know," says Miss Naomi Mitchison, "one takes it as seriously as Malory." And Mr. C. S. Lewis, also of Oxford, is able to top them all: "If Ariosto," he declares, "rivalled it in invention (in fact, he does not), he would still lack its heroic seriousness." Nor has America been behind. In the *Saturday Review of Literature,* Mr. Louis J. Halle, author of a book on *Civilization and Foreign Policy,* answers as follows a lady who—"lowering," he says, "her pince-nez"—has inquired what he finds in Tolkien: "What, dear lady, does this invented world have to do with our own? You ask for its meaning—as you ask for the meaning of the *Odyssey,* of *Genesis,* of *Faust*—in a word? In a word, then, its meaning is 'heroism.' It makes our own world, once more, heroic. What higher meaning than this is to be found in any literature?"

But if one goes from these eulogies to the book itself, one is let down, astonished, perplexed. The reviewer has just read the whole series aloud to his seven-year-old daughter, who has been through *The Hobbit* countless times, beginning it over again the moment she has finished, and whose interest has been held by its more prolix successors. One is puzzled to know why the author should have supposed he was writing for adults. There are, to be sure, some details that are a little unpleasant for a children's book, but except when he is being pedantic and also boring the adult reader, there is little in *The Lord of the Rings* over the head of a seven-year-old child. It is essentially a children's book—a children's book which has somehow got out of hand, since, instead of directing it at the "juvenile" market, the author has indulged himself in developing the fantasy for its own sake; and it ought to be said at this point, before emphasizing its inadequacies as literature, that Dr. Tolkien is not at all pretentious in regard to his fairy romance. In a statement prepared for his publishers, he has explained that he began it to amuse himself, as a philological game: "The invention of languages is the foundation. The 'stories' were made rather to provide a world for the languages than the reverse. I should have preferred to write in 'Elvish.'" He has omitted, he says, in the printed book, a good deal of the philological part; "but there is a great deal of linguistic matter . . . included or mythologically expressed in the book. It is to me, anyway, largely an essay in 'linguistic esthetic,' as I sometimes say to people who ask me 'what it is all about.' . . . It is not 'about' anything but itself. Certainly it has *no* allegorical intentions, general, particular or topical, moral, religious or political." An overgrown fairy story, a philological curiosity—that is, then, what *The Lord of the Rings* really is. The pretentiousness is all on the part of Dr. Tolkien's infatuated admirers, and it is merely these pretentions that I would here assail.

The most distinguished of Tolkien's admirers and the most conspicuous of his defenders has been Mr. W. H. Auden. That Auden is a master of English verse and a well-equipped critic of poetry, no one, as they say, will dispute. It is significant, then, that he comments on the badness of Tolkien's verse—there is a great deal of poetry in *The Lord of the Rings*—but is apparently quite insensitive through comparative lack of interest in this other department to the fact that Tolkien's prose is just as bad. Prose and verse are on the same level of professorial amateurishness. What I believe has misled Mr. Auden is his own special preoccupation with the legendary theme of the Quest. He has written a book about the literature of the Quest; he has experimented with the theme himself in a remarkable sequence of sonnets; and it is to be hoped that he will do something with it on an even larger scale. In the meantime—as sometimes happens with works that fall in with one's interests—he no doubt so overrates *The Lord of the Rings* because he reads into it something that he means to write himself. It is indeed the tale of a Quest, but, to this reader, an extremely unrewarding one. The hero has no serious temptations; is lured by no insidious enchantments, perplexed by no serious problems. What we get here is a simple confrontation—in more or less the traditional terms of British melodrama—of the Forces of Evil with the Forces of Good, the remote and alien villain with the plucky little home-grown hero. There are streaks of imagination: the ancient tree-spirits, the Ents, with their deep eyes, twiggy beards, rumbly voices; the Elves, whose nobility and beauty is elusive and not quite human. But even these are rather clumsily handled. There is never much development in the episodes; you simply go on getting more of the same. Dr. Tolkien has little skill at narrative and no instinct for literary form. The characters talk a story-book language that might have come out of Howard Pyle, and as personalities they do not impose themselves. At the end of this long romance, I had still no conception of the wizard Gandalph, who is made to play a cardinal role. I had never been able to visualize him at all. For the most part such characterizations as Dr. Tolkien is able to contrive are perfectly stereotyped: Frodo the good little Englishman; Samwise, his dog-like servant, who talks lower-class and respectful, and never deserts his master. These characters who are no characters are involved in interminable adventures the poverty of invention displayed in which is, it seems to me, almost pathetic. On the country in which the Hobbits, the Elves, the Ents and the other Good People live, the Forces of Evil are closing in, and they have to band together to save it. The hero is the Hobbit called Frodo who has become possessed of a ring that Sauron, the King of the Enemy, wants (that learned reptilian suggestion—doesn't it give you a goose-fleshy feeling?). In spite of the author's disclaimer, the struggle for the magic ring does seem to have some larger significance. This ring, if one continues to carry it, confers upon one special powers, but it is felt to become heavier and heavier; it exerts a sinister influence that one has to brace oneself to resist. The problem is for Frodo to get rid of it before he can succumb to this influence.

Now, this situation does create interest; it does seem to have possibilities. One looks forward to a queer dilemma, a new kind of hair-breadth escape, in which Frodo, in the Enemy's kingdom, will find himself half-seduced into taking over the enemy's point of view, so that the realm of shadows and monsters will come to seem to him, once he is in it, once he is strong in the power of the ring, a plausible and pleasant place, and he will narrowly escape the danger of becoming a monster himself. But these bugaboos are not magnetic; they are feeble and rather faceless; one does not feel they make any real threat. The Good People simply say "Boo" to them. There are Black Riders, of whom everyone is terrified but who never seem anything but specters. There are dreadful hovering birds—think of it, horrible birds of prey! There are ogreish disgusting Orcs, who, however, rarely get to the point of committing any overt acts. There is a giant female spider—a dreadful creepy-crawly spider!—who lives in a dark cave and eats people. What one misses in all these terrors is any trace of concrete reality. The preternatural, to be effective, should be given some sort of solidity, a real presence, recognizable features—as in Gulliver, as in Gogol, as in Poe; not like those phantom horrors of Algernon Blackwood which prove so disappointing after the travel-book substantiality of the landscapes in which he evokes them. Tolkien's horrors resemble these in their lack of real contact with their victims, who dispose of them as we do of the horrors in dreams by simply pushing them or puffing them away. As for Sauron, the ruler of Mordor (doesn't the very name have a shuddery sound?), who concentrates in his person everything that is threatening the Shire, the build-up for him goes on through three volumes. He makes his first, rather promising, appearance as a terrible fire-rimmed yellow eye seen in a water-mirror. But this is as far as we ever get. Once Sauron's realm is invaded, we think we are going to meet him; but he still remains nothing but a burning eye scrutinizing all that occurs from the window of a remote dark tower. This might, of course, be made effective; but actually it is not: we never feel Sauron's power. And the climax, to which we have been working up through exactly nine hundred and ninety-nine large close-printed pages, when it comes, proves extremely flat. The ring is at last got rid of by dropping it into a fiery crater, and the kingdom of Sauron "topples" in a brief and banal earthquake that sets fire to everything and burns it up, and so releases the author from the necessity of telling the reader what exactly was so terrible there. Frodo has come to the end of his Quest, but the reader has remained untouched by the wounds and fatigues of his journey. An impotence of imagination seems to me to sap the whole story. The wars are never dynamic; the ordeals give no sense of strain; the fair ladies would not stir a heartbeat; the horrors would not hurt a fly.

How is it, then, that these long-winded volumes of what looks to this reader like balderdash have elicited such tributes as those above? The answer is, I believe, that certain people—especially, perhaps, in Britain—have a lifelong appetite for juvenile trash. They would not accept adult trash, but, confronted with the pre-teen-age article, they revert to the mental phase which delighted in *Elsie Dinsmore* and *Little Lord Fauntleroy* and which seems to have made Billy Bunter almost a national figure in England. You can see it in the tone they fall into when they talk about Tolkien in print: they bubble, they squeal, they coo; they go on about Malory and Spenser— both of whom have a charm and distinction that Tolkien has never touched.

As for me, if we must read about imaginary kingdoms, give me James Branch Cabell's Poictesme. He at least writes for grown-up people, and he does not present the drama of life as a showdown between Good People and Goblins. He can cover more ground in an episode that lasts only three pages than Tolkien is able to in one of his twenty-page chapters, and he can create a more disquieting impression by a reference to something that is never described than Tolkien through his whole demonology.

April 14, 1956

BEES, WASPS AND BOMBERS

A RECENT BOOK on bees—*Bees: Their Vision, Chemical Senses and Language,* by Karl von Frisch—is sensational in its field, and, though not intended primarily for a popular audience, it ought to be widely read by people who are capable of being interested in what used to be called natural history. Herr von Frisch, a professor of zoölogy at the University of Munich, has for almost forty years been experimenting with bees from the point of view indicated by his subtitle. When the news of his remarkable most recent findings—of which he himself says that they at first "seemed too fantastic for belief"— reached this country after the war, his conclusions were received with some skepticism till his experiments were repeated and his conclusions confirmed by American entomologists as well as by those of other countries. He was then invited to the United States, and a lecture tour for him was financed by a committee of universities and scientific institutions. This small book contains his three lectures, delivered in 1949. They have the merit, rather unusual in scientific papers, of a simple, non-technical style and, with their drawings and photographs, are easily comprehensible to anybody.

Herr von Frisch began by investigating the color sense of bees, their ability to recognize shapes and their sensitivity to flavor and odor. He found out some very curious things, but he was led on to even stranger discoveries.

Bees, it seems, when they come back from foraging, if they have located a rich source of honey, can explain to their comrades at home exactly where to look for this source: how far it is, in what direction, and what flavor is to be expected. These data are mostly conveyed by movements, called "dances," that a home-coming bee executes for the benefit of his fellows. If the honey is within a radius of approximately a hundred meters from the hive, the returning bee does a "round dance," and the rest fly out in all directions and easily find the flowers. But if the honey is farther away, he performs what is described as a "wagging dance," which indicates by the number of turns in a given length of time *how much* farther away it is. He indicates also the direction by taking up a certain stance on the perpendicular wall of the honeycomb. If this stance points straight up and down, it means that they must fly toward the sun, wherever it happens to be at the moment, and an angle of deviation from this will indicate that a beeline to the honey lies at a similar angle from the line between the sun and the hive. If the bee is on a horizontal surface, he points straight toward the feeding-place, and if the hive is turned around, he keeps moving in such a way as still to point constantly, like a compass needle, in the direction of the honey. A highly developed sense of the polarity of light enables him to know where the sun is and hence maintain his sense of direction so long as any light is visible inside the hive. If this is shut off, however, he loses his orientation. There is much more to Herr von Frisch's findings, and presumably more to the language of bees than Herr von Frisch has yet decoded. It may be noted that the sweeter the honey, the livelier the performance of the dancers.

Insects in Your Life, by Dr. C. H. Curran, is a popular book by an authority, the Curator of Insects and Spiders in the American Museum of Natural History. The bees seem to be among the geniuses in the insect world, and there is nothing in Dr. Curran's volume quite so startling as the von Frisch revelations, but it is full of remarkable examples of the protective mimicry of mantises, the gyroscopic organs of flies and the complicated devices for protecting the young of wasps and other insects. The female botfly, it seems, will sit by a stagnant pool in which she knows mosquitoes are breeding and wait for the young mosquitoes to emerge from their pupal cases. While they are still too weak to make long flights, the botfly seizes them one by one, as they are resting on blades of grass and, taking pains not to injure them, lays her eggs beneath their abdomens and then lets them go. She repeats this about thirty times until all of her eggs are disposed of. The mosquitoes now fly away, looking for something to feed on. If they dine on cold-blooded animals, the fly eggs remain inactive. But the moment a mosquito alights on an animal with warm blood, they break open and the maggots pop out and burrow into the tiny hole that the mosquito has made by its bite. There they feed on the animal or human being, returning to the aperture to breathe and secreting a substance that protects them by preventing bacterial infection of the wound. At last, they come out and drop to the ground, where they enter the pupal stage and eventually become full-blown flies. *Insects in Your Life* is a combination of such curious and disconcerting facts with practical information on such subjects as the habits of clothes moths and methods for getting rid of them, the harmfulness of termites and ticks, and the uses of DDT.

Dragons in Amber: Further Adventures of a Romantic Naturalist, by Willy Ley, is the same sort of thing as his previous book, *The Lungfish, the Dodo and the*

Unicorn, but is even more miscellaneous. The first part deals mainly with fossils and with prehistoric animals: the history of amber, the footprints of the chirotherium, the emergence of the ichthyosaurus and the discovery of ancient mammoths deep-frozen in the Siberian ice. The second and third sections, though their titles, *The Last of Their Kind* and *Wanderers Across the Planet,* suggest systematic categories, seem really to serve to group in a more or less arbitrary way certain botanical, zoölogical and geological anomalies that happen to interest Mr. Ley and that he succeeds in making interesting to the reader: milu deer, pandas, sequoia and cycad trees, the queer life-cycle of the common eel, the prehistoric occurrence of camels in North America and their artificial reintroduction shortly before the Civil War, and the apocalyptic eruption of Krakatoa. I read Mr. Ley with enchantment. He has a considerable narrative gift and cannot tell about a scientific expedition or even a line of research or the development of a theory without investing it with excitement and creating dramatic suspense. (I do not believe, however, that it contributes to the romance of the ginkgo tree to say, of the first man who described it, that he studied, among other places, at Hamelin, "the town of the legendary pied piper.") Yet he always gives you the satisfaction of feeling that you are being supplied with a good deal of correct information and that no important links in the story are, as sometimes happens in popular science, perfunctorily being dropped out.

The acceptance of von Frisch's experiments was impeded, says Donald R. Griffin of the Department of Zoölogy at Cornell, who introduces the book on bees, by a reluctance on the part of biologists "to credit any claim that the reactions of lower animals attain a high degree of complexity, or what one might be tempted to call intelligence." But Dr. Curran admits that "some of the wasps show either intelligence or something that closely approaches it." Just as the anthropoid apes are now being found more human than they formerly were, at a time when human beings seem more bestial, so the insects are represented as more rational at a time when the activity of humans gives the impression of becoming more instinctual. The present is not one of the great ages of the self-dramatization of man. It is no age of authentic leaders in the departments of statesmanship or thought: Stalin and Hitler were produced by the swarm, in the manner of queen bees. Nor is it an age of great ideas. There is little left even of Marxism save a mask for a civilization that recalls the hill and the hive, and the remarkable achievements of our period—the new bombs and the planes that drop them—seem exercises in blind ingenuity turned out by mass production and operated by mass action. The nations fly out at one another, armed with these elaborate stings, often without even the justification of bees defending endangered hives. It is quite natural that Willy Ley, who began as a paleontologist, occupied with problems of brute survival, should have become an expert on rockets, about which he has also written (these animal books are merely his potboilers)—who, however, it ought to be added, left Germany for the United States when Hitler attempted to turn him from his researches on travel in space to devising new rockets for lethal weapons. And it is not surprising to learn that Dr. Curran has been studying the flight of flies, by means of high-speed moving pictures, for the Sperry Gyroscope Company, or that students of aerodynamics have been striving—as one can see from the shapes of bombing planes—to approximate the streamlining of the hawk moth. We are forced to recognize today that we resemble less the prophets and saints of the Old and the New Testaments, the heroes of

Plutarch's *Lives* or even the characters of Shakespeare, all self-conscious individuals, than the hardy individualized members of those flourishing insect species which, without the specialized brains of which we like to boast that they are "rational," perform such remarkable exploits of outwitting other insects in order to nourish their young, of organizing well-disciplined communities that never have revolutions and of perfecting delicate wings that never break off in the air.

July 14, 1951

MYCOPHILE AND MYCOPHOBE

Mushrooms, Russia, and History, by R. Gordon Wasson and Valentina Pavlovna Wasson is a somewhat troublesome book to review. Mr. Wasson is a Morgan partner and Mrs. Wasson is a pediatrician. They have no training as writers or scientists, and they make a point of calling themselves amateurs and being candid about their disqualifications. They have furthermore brought out their book in so unmanageable a format, at so high a price and in so limited an edition that it can scarcely, in any real sense, be said to be accessible to the public. It consists of two elaborate volumes, handsomely printed in Italy, which are embellished with eighty-two plates, that include a brilliant series of watercolors, never before published, of different species of mushrooms, by Jean-Henry Fabre, the once-famous French writer on insects. The set costs $125, and the edition consists of only 512 copies, and each of the volumes weighs a ton and is of a size and a shape so awkward as to make it extremely difficult, in any normal position, to cope with the voluminous text.

In spite of these obstacles, which seem calculated to occlude it from the reviewer as well as from the public, the work deserves special attention. Though sometimes inept and muddled, the authors have brought to light a good deal that is exciting and important. But, in view of the difficulty of acquiring the book, the critic must take as his aim to suggest how it may be reworked to present

what is valuable in it in a form available to the ordinary
reader rather than to suggest to this reader how he ought
to approach it in its present form. Yet one cannot write
an amateur review, one cannot, out of courtesy, assimilate
oneself to however confessedly amateurish a book. So
here is an account of the Wassons on mushrooms that
makes no allowance for their amateur status and assumes
that they offer their studies in the folklore and botany of
the subject as serious contributions.

In the first volume, then, of *Mushrooms,* etc., the Wassons are seen at their weakest. The first chapters, by Mrs.
Wasson, are bound to prove a stumbling block to no
matter how sympathetic a reader. These originally constituted, we gather, the opening of a quite different work—
a book about "the Russians and their food"—undertaken
by Mrs. Wasson before the book about mushrooms grew
out of it. For incomprehensible reasons, these chapters
have been incorporated in the work that eventually resulted and have carried along with them a title which,
besides being clumsy in itself, is entirely inappropriate to
it. This is properly a treatise on mushrooms, not on history or Russia. Though mushrooms, as the authors show,
are especially esteemed in Russia, Russian mushrooms are
no more important, for the general scope and purpose of
the book, than the mushrooms of any other country.

Mrs. Wasson's long summary of the history of Russia is
completely irrelevant to the subject; and her personal
reactions to mushrooms, as a patriotic Russian, strike a
somewhat false note in a book which—however ill-
equipped its authors in the discipline of botanical science—must be expected, from its very nature, to respect
scientific procedure. What Mrs. Wasson here mainly
gives us is what the Russians themselves call *klyukva.*
This originally meant synthetic Russian atmosphere pro-

duced by Russians for foreign consumption: a man in a Cossack costume, accompanied by an accordion or a bala-laika, singing *Ochi Chyorniye* or the *Volga Boat Song* in a New York or Paris night club. More recently, the Rus-sian exiles of long residence in foreign countries have been—innocently and understandably—producing a kind of *klyukva* intended for their own consumption. Mrs. Wasson writes: "This love of Russians for the earthy tribe of mushrooms, is, I suggest, a distinctive trait of the Slavs. In the face of an ever-mounting flood of printed matter and talk about Russia, that land remains for the English-speaking world as deep an enigma as ever. If among those who seek the key to the enigma there be some with an understanding heart and a poet's insight, let them lay aside for awhile most of what is written and uttered, and consider the lesson in Russian history and Russian ways that the mushroom has to teach. Here is evidence of our visceral attachment to the bounteous soil that is our Mother Russia. . . . With what astonishment my husband saw me, on our first walk [in the Catskills] dart with ecstasy to this fungus and that, and on bended knee strike what seemed to him poses of adoration! . . . To what a world of wonder and delight the fungal vo-cabulary of Russia transports us! . . . Close to forty years have passed since I last gathered mushrooms in Russia, and revelled in the mushroom lore that we all shared. As I reread the lines I have written, I became aware of receding planes of memory, on the periphery of my con-sciousness, strewn with visions of mushrooms that I can no longer identify by name, and with names of mush-rooms that are no longer attached to clearly defined images. What were those *belyanki** that refused to go to

---

* I am making the Wassons' transliteration consistent with the standard one.

war because they were aristocratic ladies?" And so on for a paragraph: "I recall another curious name—the *skripitsa,* or screeching mushroom: what could it have been?" etc. If Mrs. Wasson had looked in Dahl's Russian dictionary or in the old Brockhaus Russian encyclopaedia, she would have found almost all of these "fungal" mysteries identified by their Latin names; and, as a matter of fact, when we get to the end of the Wassons' own second volume, we find, in Appendix II, the *belyanki* ticketed as *Lactarius Pubescens.*

In any condensation of the Wassons' book, these obstructive preliminiary chapters ought certainly to be omitted. The one about the misuse of poisonous mushrooms in modern detective stories should be boiled down to a note. The only matter here that is valuable, the chapters on the Russian lore of mushrooms and the English antagonism to them, should be worked into the later chapter in which the curious contrast—brought out for the first time by the Wassons—of the attitudes toward the mushroom of the various nations is treated more comprehensively. Mrs. Wasson's own relation to the mushroom, emotional, national, personal, should be given its place in a foreword, which should also include the story of the conversion of the mushroom-fearing Mr. Wasson by the mushroom-loving Valentina Pavlovna and of the genesis in this conversion of their years of research and the present book—an odd episode, to be sure, which might have been made more interesting.

The remainder of the first volume is entirely occupied with etymologies, which may bewilder the nonphilological reader but are likely, in the long run, to cause him to lose confidence in the judgment of the authors. The Wassons have looked up the vocabulary of mushrooms and of ideas associated with mushrooms in innumerable languages and dialects, and they have established some sig-

nificant connections; but they have terribly compromised
these by entangling them in a web of improvisations that
have no basis in science or common sense. For example,
they have thrown some light on the association of mushrooms with toads, as in our English derogatory *toadstool*
and an old French term for mushroom, *pain de crapaud*;
but they have clouded this with new attempts at derivation and definition that run counter to scholarly opinion
and seem implausible if not impossible. They have discovered that an old French word for *toad* was *bot* and
that a current Italian one is *botta*, and they propose to
relate these terms to certain regional French words for
mushrooms such as *botet* and *boutarel*. Very well; let
us grant that the layman may accept this connection as
possible. But the authors want to get the Devil into it,
and they go about this in the following way.

The Wassons have scholarly authority for deriving
these French and Italians words for *toad* from an old
German word *buta*, which means *blunted, clumsy,
malformed;* and there is a French expression for *club
foot, pied-bot,* which is supposed to have the same
derivation. Now, the Devil is sometimes imagined as
limping, so the Wassons at once conclude that *le bot*
was "a euphemism for Satan"—though their only evidence for this consists of the Elizabethan "a bots on"
someone or something and the French exclamation *"Vrai
bot!,"* which occurs in Rabelais. But the first of these
refers to the cattle disease caused by the larvae of the
botfly—see the big Oxford dictionary: it is an expression
like "a pox" or "a murrain on"—and the second of them is
defined in Huguet's *Dictionnaire de la Langue Française
du Seizième Siècle* as a modified form of *vrai Dieu* (one
would hardly say *vrai Diable*). Yet Mr. Wasson assumes that his case is thus proved, and, in a paper more
recently published, asserts, as if on good authority, that

le bot in old French means "the Devil." And the
Wassons go on in their book to try to show that the
English word *bat*, the animal, equals *bot*, and hence
Devil, though the accepted derivation for *bat* is the
middle-English *bakke*, meaning *bat*, brought over by
the Scandinavians and ultimately deriving from *blaka*,
an Icelandic word for *flutter*. From this they take off in
a flight that explains Old Boots as a name for the Devil,
Puss-in-boots and the expression "Clumsy-Boots," used by
Bella to her husband in *Our Mutual Friend*, as based on
"le bot," the limping Devil, who has never been anything other than a philological invention of the Wassons.

They even go to the length of asserting that to describe
someone as "bats" is equivalent to saying he is possessed
by the Devil. The queerness of mushrooms and toads and
the fact that they are sometimes poisonous are enough to
account for their association in the minds of simple
people, and that the Devil was associated with both
mushrooms and toads is shown in a variety of ways: an
old Dutch word for mushrooms was *duivelsbrood*. But
the Wassons have overdone all this. In their chapter on
the *Amanita muscaria*, a mushroom which has been supposed to owe its name to its efficacy in killing flies—the
tradition has come down from the thirteenth century—
they go out of their way to demonstrate that this species
has been called "fly mushroom" for an entirely different
reason: its supposed connection with the spirits of evil.
The Wassons have had two sets of experiments made
with the purpose of finding out whether the "fly-killer"—
crushed in milk, with sugar, according to the old re-
ceipt—is actually fatal to flies; and one of these, performed in Oslo, gave only negative results, while the
other, performed in Paris, seemed to justify the ancient
belief: the flies that drank the milk did die. But even if
this *Amanita* is actually pernicious to flies, the Wassons—

apparently influenced by the mentality of the "New Criticism," with its napoleon-like "layers of interpretation"—contend that it is not improbable that the name "carries two layers of meaning, one for housewives and one for those initiated in sacred mysteries." This contention the two authors attempt to support by pages of far-fetched linkages between flies and the forces of evil—*bug, bugaboo,* etc.

The literary style of the Wassons is calculated to horripilate the literary as well as to alienate the scientific reader. Besides the examples already given, one may cite their delight in such phrases as "the gentle art of mushroom-knowing," their addiction to such dreadful words as *oft-times* and *unbeknownst,* and their concoction of such chapter headings as *Mucus and Love, The Riddle of the Toad* and *Other Secrets Mushroomic.*

But now, having cut our way through the etymological creepers of Volume I, let us go on to the revelations contained in the second volume. These chapters, besides being more interesting, are noticeably better written. The Wassons here are getting their hand in, and since the book itself has been published, the short articles they have been publishing in periodicals seem to show that they are becoming capable of presenting their ideas and experiences in a simpler and more clear-cut way. And they have here, in their expeditions in search of the "Sacred Mushroom," a remarkable story to tell.

When the Spaniards arrived in America, early in the sixteenth century, they found that, on festive occasions, the Mexican natives ate mushrooms which made them deliriously and dangerously drunk. Several species apparently had this effect. The mushrooms brought sometimes ecstatic visions, sometimes nightmares of doom; sometimes people laughed uncontrollably, sometimes they became suicidal, sometimes homicidal. The Wassons have collected and print here from the contemporary Spanish accounts, all the discoverable references to this phenomenon, and they have turned up a sixteenth-century drawing of a man sitting and eating mushrooms while an evidently divine figure, wearing a crenelated headdress and with clawed hands and feet, comes behind him and touches the back of his head. One species of hallucinatory mushroom was significantly known as God's Flesh. But these fungi were never encountered by any non-Indian again until 1936, when a traveling anthropologist, Mr. Robert J. Weitlaner, getting wind of a surviving cult in the remote town of Huantla de Jiménez, in the State of Oaxaca, Mexico, succeeded in obtaining some specimens, which eventually found their way to the botany department at Harvard. They were identified there as belonging to the genus *Panaeolus*, various species of which were already known in Europe and America. These have not ordinarily been eaten, but there is a record of one occasion, in 1916, when an American family who cooked and ate on toast what they believed to be *Panaeolus* mushrooms became wildly intoxicated. In 1938, another anthropologist and three other white people attended a rite in Huantla, at which the sacred mushrooms were eaten.

The Wassons decided to investigate Huantla, and in August, 1953, they went there with Mr. Weitlaner. An account of their adventures and researches in connection with the hallucinatory mushroom occupies about half of their second volume. They found that the natives believed that the god of the mushroom spoke to them, advising them about their affairs and prophesying the future. At a mushroom-eating ceremony at which the Wassons were present in Huantla but in which they did not take part, they inquired, since they had to pretend that there was something they wanted to know, about their eighteen-year-old son, from whom they had not heard since they left and whom they supposed to be in Boston. The priest of the mushrooms replied that the boy was in New York, that he was worried about some problem which he did not know how to deal with, and that "they" were reaching out for him to send him to war. His parents assumed that this could not be true, because the boy was exempt from the draft, but it later turned out that their son had actually been in New York at the time of the Mexican ceremony and that he had been going through a crisis about a girl and, as a result of it, had decided to enlist.

It occurred to the Wassons at about this time, though the connection had never been suggested, that the so-called "mushroom stones," found in quantities in Mexico and Guatemala—little statues of mushrooms with a human face or figure always embedded in the stem—must be images of the sacred mushroom, and that if this were true one could conclude from the archaeological evidence that the cult must have flourished from at least 1000 B.C. to about 900 A.D.

In June and July of 1955, the Wassons visited another Oaxacan village and attended somewhat different rites, at which for the first time they were permitted—and had the courage—to eat the sacred mushroom themselves. While the woman of the household, all through the night, under the influence of the drug, was performing a long ritual of chanting and dancing, the Wassons had hallucinations that fully convinced them that the mushroom deserved its reputation. Mr. Wasson saw a desert with caravans of camels and landscapes of "the estuaries of immense rivers brimming over with pellucid water." There were also "patterns" and "artistic motifs" that "seemed the very archetypes of beautiful form and color." The visions of Mrs. Wasson are not described in this book, but she has written about them in an article in the

This Week Sunday supplement of the New York *Herald Tribune* of May 19, 1957. She noticed at first that "my husband's red plaid sports shirt was glowing with a peculiar intensity. I stared at the crude wooden furniture. The cracks and knotholes were changing shape." She later found herself travelling through the caves of the Dordogne and delighting in their primitive paintings, which "seemed suffused with a crystal light." Then she was transported to France—to the Versailles of Louis XV—where she saw herself and her sister taking part in a great ball. "Hundreds of beautifully gowned couples danced the minuet in train and powdered periwig to the music of Mozart."

The Wassons' sixteen-year-old daughter who was with them and who also ate the mushrooms, first thought she saw "a nest of bright blue boxes piled up in the corner of the room," then cried out that she "felt like a chicken" (there were chickens straying through the house), then, in response to some remark of her father's, replied impatiently, "Oh Father, I'm having too good a time to bother talking to you!" In the meantime, Mrs. Wasson had visited a Spanish church, with a "towering crucifix," and an opera box at the Metropolitan, where that old favorite Chaikovsky ballet, *Les Sylphides,* was being performed; had "taken off through the skies with several of the dancers," and found herself "bending over a huge, deep blue Chinese vase, inspecting several handsome gold dragons crawling around at the bottom." Then she was carried to Holland and "exclaimed to myself, 'What nonsense—I wish to be in Russia!' I was in Russia. The tiles were framed about an old peasant stove. Children in colorful pre-World War I costumes were dancing around the room. Everyone was laughing and gay, singing old songs." But she could not stay long in Russia—not even to gather mushrooms. She was presently looking down on a map of China: "Cities, rivers and mountains were depicted in rubies, sapphires and emeralds."

They brought some of the mushrooms back with them and tried eating them in New York. "As we stood at the window and watched the gale tossing the trees and the water of the East River, with the rain driven in squalls before the wind, the whole scene was further quickened to life by the abnormal intensity of the colors that we saw. We had always thought that El Greco's apocalypic skies over Toledo were a figment of the poet's imagination. But on this night we saw El Greco's skies, nothing dimmed, whirling over New York."

In the meantime, they had visited still a third village, "in the coastal sierra of southern Oaxaca, a region almost unknown to travelers," and here they found the mushroom ritual mixed with Catholic rites. The mushrooms were always placed first before an image of the Virgin of Guadalupe, and the prayers for an abundant crop of them were addressed to a medley of deities—the Earth, God the Father, the Trinity, the Great Lightning Bolt that bred the mushroom and the Great Lightning Bolt that put blood into the mushroom. These last two especially interested the Wassons because they had discovered that in many parts of the world there was a uniform belief that mushrooms were engendered by thunderstorms. It would seem, however, that the Wassons exaggerate the value of this as proof of the divine or diabolic properties attributed to the mushrooms by primitive peoples. The feeling of the uncanniness of mushrooms must have been due to their suddenly appearing without anyone's understanding how they were able to seed themselves; and the idea that they were bred by the lightning is no doubt to be mainly accounted for by the fact that they are likely to push up after rain—an explanation that seems never to have occurred to the Wassons. The general avoidance of mushrooms among people who do not know them well must be due not primarily to a religious tabu but to accidents occurring from the poisonous kinds. One cannot argue from the thunder motif to the motif of divine provenance because the very few localities where mushrooms are eaten for divine inspiration do not necessarily coincide with those in which their sudden sprouting is supposed to be produced by thunder or lightning. In general, the Wassons' theory of the universal importance of the mushroom goes far beyond the actual evidence. "Our divine mushrooms," they say, "along with the secondary vegetable hallucinogens, may have played a role in the origins of human culture. . . . Yes, our mushrooms must have unlimbered the imagination of those first men who ate them, stirred their curiosity and speculative faculties. Our mushrooms could have sparked in them the very idea of God."

We now come, in Chapter 18, *The Anatomy of Mycophobia,* to the discussion of a very curious subject that the Wassons have apparently been the first to explore—the dichotomy of the people of the Western world into mycophiles, mushroom-lovers, and mycophobes, those who fear mushrooms. The Russians, as is well known, belong to the first of these categories; they are even, the Wassons claim, "mycolatrous." The Wassons invoke and quote the scenes of mushroom-gathering from *Anna Karenina,* and they might also have cited the excursions after mushrooms that occur in all émigré memoirs, usually in the same chapter that tells about the foreign tutors. The Russian vocabulary for mushrooms is enormous compared with most others, and the Wassons assert that, in some dialects of Russian, mushrooms are given the inflections appropriate to animate beings, and that some species have a form of the plural which otherwise occurs only in the case of young animals or human beings: *maslyata* and *oryata* like *tsypyata* and *rebyata*. The English-speaking peoples, on the other hand, distrust and dislike mushrooms. They employ, in general currency, only two words for these fungi: *mushrooms*, meaning harmless fungi, and *toadstools*, the poisonous kinds. A very few of the fungi, which do not look like mushrooms at all, have been given such names as *stinkhorns* and *puffballs*, and truffles, of course, though actually mushrooms, are thought of as something apart. We do have the word *morel* for the edible species of *Morchella*, although it is rarely heard, but we do not have any word for the edible *Boletus* which the French call *cêpe*. The writer of this article runs absolutely true to Anglo-Saxon habit (I hope that this has not affected the tone of my review) in being a lifelong and inexorable mycophobe. My prejudice has been strengthened by the disagreeable experience of once having been poisoned for days by a mess of *Something or other emeticus* which a Cape Cod neighbor had picked under the impression that it was an edible species. The Wassons make the point that in mycophile countries such accidents are very rare: the people know their mushrooms too well.

The French, the Wassons assert—leaving aside the South: Provence, traditionally a separate country, and Gascony, famous for *cêpes*—are not as yet truly a mycophile nation. The French Canadians did not eat wild mushrooms, and the taste for *cêpes*, truffles and *champignons* is of relatively recent date. Poisonings from mushrooms have been common in France. The same thing is true of the Germans, who, as late as the seventeenth century, were capable of insulting the Russians from the mycophobe point of view: "Our German people live like lords, eat fresh meat and drink wines and beer, while your people, like beasts and hounds, eat mushrooms and drink water and kvas." (This comes from a textbook of Russian for Germans, and it bears out the Wassons' contention, though they do not call attention to this, that the words for "mushrooms" in the Russian sentence refer to edible mushrooms, whereas in the German sentence the word is the contemptuous-sounding *Poggenstole* or *frog's stool.*) In Europe, the appetite for mushrooms is concentrated in a West Mediterranean patch, spanning the Pyrenees, which includes Provence and Catalonia. Both the Catalans and the Provençals have enormous mycological vocabularies; an authority on the Catalan mushroom has listed two hundred and twenty terms. Spain proper, rather strangely in view of this, has been inveterately mycophobe: its mushroom vocabulary is meager, and the same thing seems true of Portugal. The Arabs, with scanter resources, are "passionate mycophiles."

Here surely is a cleavage of peoples which should not be left unexploited by our passionate nationalists. The hostility which the United States and the Soviet Union have been working up against one another has had all too dubious an issue in the supposed incompatibility in the world at large of republican capitalism and totalitarian communism. We have now in the United States too many state-owned or state-subsidized institutions and too much government control of industry for this hackneyed antithesis to be plausible; and in Russia and its satellite countries, the unfortunate "proletariat," in the name of whom the government operates, has been repressed as completely and brutally as the workers in American steel towns ever were by the company's "Cossacks" and is in a far less advantageous position to demand and obtain what it needs than our organized labor is. The Russians have been as intent on imitating our farming and industrial methods as we have been on adopting the technique of their political heresy hunts.

Both they and we are now occupying or partly controlling considerable parts of the world where we are not necessarily welcome, and each is making it difficult for its citizens and for the citizens of the other to visit one another's countries or even one another's spheres of influence. The danger is, as time goes on, that the Soviet Union and the United States will get to be too much alike, and that the myths that are manufactured on both sides to keep up our reciprocal antagonism will all too obviously be seen to wear thin. But here, in the age-long antipathy between mycophobes and mycophiles, is something that we can get our teeth into. The struggle for power in our world lies clearly between clean-living mycophobes, disdainers of the foul-tasting fungi, and groveling mycophiles, who grub in the earth like pigs in search of these detestable morsels. The reviewer, though too old for combat, has never forgotten the horror of the effects of the *Something emeticus,* and he is ready to put his pen unreservedly at the service of the national propaganda. The British will be on our side; mycophilia in France and Germany is a mere affectation, skin-deep: these nations will be ranged with us, also. The notorious mycophilia of the Arabs can be used as a threat against them if they obstruct our free access to oil. Catalonia and Provence hardly count in any military way; they can easily be isolated and treated as a large concentration camp. Portugal and Spain will support us. And the mushroom-shaped pillars of smoke exploded by atomic bombs will acquire a symbolic significance. The competition in producing these weapons and the conflict to extinction which must follow will be given a moral meaning far profounder than any involved in the rival immoralities and moralities of the Soviet system and ours. Though the bombs and the smoke-shapes to which they give rise may seem to be almost identical, the ideals behind the two sets of weapons will be at opposite poles: the sinister mushroom of the Soviet Union will be the Marxist-Lenninist mushroom of mycophagy—Lenin, it seems, had a great love of mushrooms—while the towering American cloud will be the mushroom to end mushrooms. For the mushroom cult must be uprooted. It will not be enough in this contest merely to rename enemy foods, as we did in our first war against Germany when hamburgers became Salisbury steaks and sauerkraut victory cabbage. The treasonable consumption of mushrooms must be once and for all stamped out. A ban must be clapped on such dishes as beefsteak *aux champignons* and anything *aux truffes* or with sauce *Mornay*. (The Wassons must of course be interned even before hostilities begin.)

So, defenders of the American Way of Life; stout mushroom-despisers of Mother England; loyal members of the British Commonwealth speaking our common language, so free from the taint of the mushroom; brave allies of France, Spain and Germany, let us rescue from the menace of the mycophage the heritage of Christendom and the civilized West! Man your planes and unclench your bombs, release your unguided missiles, for the triumph of the Free World, where the favorable mention of mushrooms will be dealt with by prompt imprisonment and the eating or selling of mushrooms be visited with the heaviest penalties that emergency legislation can demand!

November 16, 1957

W. H. AUDEN IN AMERICA

IT IS INTERESTING to go back over Auden's books and to try to trace the effect on his work of his residence in the United States, to which he first came in 1939 and which, now an American citizen, he has made his headquarters ever since. Let me say at the outset that this influence of America does not seem to me in the least to have diluted the Englishness of Auden or to have changed its essential nature. Auden's genius is basically English—though in ways which, in the literary world, seem at present rather out of fashion. He is English in his toughness, his richness, his obstinacy, his adventurousness, his eccentricity. What America has done for Auden is to help him to acquire what is certainly today one of the best things an American can hope to have: a mind that feels itself at the center of things. It has given him a point of view that is inter- or super-national.

One can see now, in rereading Auden, that he had always a much more widely foraging habit of mind than most English writers of his generation. The chief theme of his early work was, to be sure, a British schoolboy conspiracy in which the Marxist crusade against capitalism was identified with the revolt of the young against schoolmasters and parents and their governments. The economic crisis of the thirties gave rise to such protests everywhere and inspired such subversive hopes, but the rebellion of Auden and his friends was so much in terms of the English world—of public school, university and Bloomsbury—in which they had grown up and been educated and in which they now felt themselves imprisoned—as scarcely to be intelligible elsewhere. A brilliant poem such as the *Last Will and Testament* of Auden and Louis MacNeice, included in their *Letters from Iceland,* will need eventually as many notes to explain its innumerable references to the Oxford-Cambridge-London group as the Testaments of Villon that suggested it (though it should always be able to speak for itself as the Testaments of Villon do). Yet there was more in this early Auden than the schoolboy loves and hates and the private jokes. The writer of this article, who first read Auden's poems at a time when he had seen very little of England since the beginning of the First World War in the summer of 1914, was largely unaware of their interest as a commentary on English life. It was only in 1945, when, returning to the United States after spending some time in England, he looked into these early poems of Auden again, that he found in them an illuminating picture of an England he had not known till he saw it, in a further phase, at the end of the second war: an England suburbanized, industrialized, considerably Americanized, impoverished and sadly crippled but pretending that nothing had happened. One could see how young men in England, in the years just before the war, might have thought they would be happier in the United States, where you had the whole thing on a bigger scale—the excitements of the machine age and its bankruptcies, the vulgarities as well as the freedoms of an era of social levelling—and with not so much of the past to act as a drag on new departures. Those who criticized Auden and his friends in the thirties for not outgrowing their schoolboy mentality should not blame them for breaking away and betaking themselves to a country where hardly half-a-dozen names in the Iceland Testament would even be recognized. They had already begun to explore: Spain and Germany as well as Iceland. Auden and Christopher Isherwood had made, in 1938, a journey to Hong Kong and Shanghai, then had crossed the Pacific to Vancouver and ended up in New York. They returned at that time to Europe, but the following year came back to live permanently here in the United States. With Auden the process of Americanization had already begun in England. He had been reading American writers, had tried his hand at American ballads, and had shown, in these and in *The Dance of Death,* published in 1933, that he had already—in rather a surprising way—got the hang of the American vernacular.

The first fruits of Auden's American period—especially *New Year Letter* of 1941, which contains the long poem of that title and the sonnet sequence *The Quest*—are already in certain ways quite distinct from anything he had written in England. The poet is more alone. "Derek" and his other allies as well as "the enemy" of *The Orators* have disappeared in *The Quest.*

> What is the greatest wonder in the world?
> The bare man Nothing in the Beggar's Bush.

These strange *dépaysés* sonnets seem to me unique and enchanting—their fairy-like phantoms that alternate with commonplace down-to-earth phrases, their images that dilate or wobble, the mysterious concluding poem with its blur of beginnings and endings:

> The gaunt and great, the famed for conversation
> Blushed in the stare of evening as they spoke,
> And felt their centre of volition shifted.

It was in connection with *New Year Letter* that the writer of this article first noticed a certain characteristic of Auden's writing. If one was baffled by a passage in one of his poems, one was likely to become aware soon afterwards that what the poet had been saying was something which, precisely, one had just felt oneself but which one had hardly expected to find expressed in poetry so promptly.

If the hero of *The Quest* seems stripped of his old friends, the longer poem, *New Year Letter*, addressed to a refugee from Germany, opens on a larger vista than those of the earlier poems:

> Across East River in the night
> Manhattan is ablaze with light . . .
>
> More even than in Europe, here
> The choice of patterns is made clear
> Which the machine imposes, what
> Is possible and what is not,
> To what conditions we must bow
> In building the Just City now.

The last lines of this poem give voice to the poet's exhilaration in moving about the world and the conviction of solidarity with companions in anxiety everywhere that was justified by such a response on the part of the foreign reader as, in my own case, I have mentioned above:

> O every day in sleep and labour
> Our life and death are with our neighbour,
> And love illuminates again
> The city and the lion's den,
> The world's great rage, the travel of young men.

He touches here on American history, but he makes no attempt to talk American. He speaks of "East River" without the article, as no New Yorker would do. One finds in the *Letter,* as in *The Quest,* an accent of loneliness. Yet one feels that the poet is now, as he was not in his earlier poems, a completely free-swimming organism; and he has created his extraordinary new language, a brilliant international English, which may drop into French or German or carry along bits of Latin and Greek, and which is presently to absorb much American. He is not here any longer rebelling against British institutions that have irked his boyhood. He is dealing with the whole modern world: its discomforts, its disquiets, its crimes, its myths—"the city and the lion's den"; with the problem of how to live in it, to get out of it what it can give, to avoid being paralyzed or bought by it. It may well be that this aspect of Auden is more intelligible to an American than to an Englishman, for this feeling oneself a member of a determined resistant minority has been now for nearly a hundred years a typical situation in America. Such people in the later nineteenth century were likely to be defeated or embittered. In our own, they have felt the backing of a partly inarticulate public who are not satisfied with the bilge that the popular media feed them in their movies and magazines, and who are grateful to anyone who will make a stand for that right to think for themselves which is supposed to be guaranteed us by the Bill of Rights and that right to a high level of culture which the framers of the Constitution—taking it so much for granted—would never have thought to include. These American writers of which I speak do not constitute a group, they do not frequent an official café; and on this account, the visitor from Europe is likely to come to the conclusion that, except in the universities, we have no intellectual life. He cannot conceive that the American writers are functioning in the crevices of cities, on the faculties of provincial colleges or scattered all over the country in the solitude of ranches and farms. This kind of life was now to be Auden's lot, and he must have had some desolating experiences:

> Some think they're strong, some think they're smart,
> Like butterflies they're pulled apart,
> America can break your heart.
> *You don't know all, sir, you don't know all.*

But I have always been struck by the naturalness with which Auden took things here for granted and—though I thought there was a good deal he did not understand—with the perfect propriety of his being here. One felt this especially when one noticed how easily he was able to incorporate the American colloquial speech, American allusions and customs, into the marvellous amalgam of his language, along with his foreign quotations, his technical vocabulary of botany, psychology and metallurgy (that sometimes derail the reader) and all those toothsome old British words—such as *mawmet, faffle* and *balter*—that turn out, when you look them up, to be Prov. Eng. or Dial. Eng., Archaic or Obsolete. It is not a question here of a successful American impersonation, as in the case of those stories of Kipling's that are supposed to be told by Americans or of those parts of Isherwood's *The World in the Evening* in which the narrator's American aspect is supposed to be uppermost. Such performances are *tours de force,* in which the least slip will jar. But in Auden an "East River" or two does not matter, since it is not an imaginary American who is speaking —and even when Auden has assigned his lines to some invented being (he has little dramatic sense)—it is the language of Auden that is speaking, and this language has breathed in its Americanism as easily as its Oxford gossip, its country talk of *leats* and *eagres,* its Horatian and Anglo-Saxon metres. The poem called *The Un-*

known Citizen, contributed to the *New Yorker* at an early stage of Auden's American residence, was a satire on standardization of a kind of which we had already had a good deal and which it did not take Auden to give us; but by the time he wrote his Phi Beta Kappa ode for Harvard in 1946, he had a quite intimate knowledge of the special world to which he was addressing himself, and had something of his own to tell it.

It is curious to compare Auden in his London dress of the *Poems* of 1930, published by Faber & Faber, one of their thin and distinguished volumes that all the smart people read, with Auden in American homespun—or at least, in a New York suit—the *Collected Poetry* of 1945, published by Random House. Hardly can we recognize here the young man, just up from Oxford, who appeared, under Eliot's patronage, in company with a few select friends. The friends are no longer present; the poems that seemed to herald the British revolution—including some very good ones—have for the most part been pitilessly scrapped. We find a volume printed on not good gray paper, of over four hundred pages, in which the pieces are all run together, not beginning on separate pages, and in which old poems have been given new titles of a colloquial, even folksy kind: *Please Make Yourself at Home, It's Too Much, Something is Bound to Happen, Venus Will Now Say a Few Words.* Here are most of our favorite old friends, along with a lot of new ones, sitting around in New York or strolling on the college campus. One saw with surprise that Auden—so far from being a rarity that could only be appreciated by a few—was the old-fashioned kind of poet, like Browning or Henry Wadsworth Longfellow (not that I would compare him with the latter), who is at his best when printed and read in bulk. He amuses us, converses with us, does his best to give us good advice; he sings us comic songs, supplies us with brilliant elegies on the deaths of great contemporaries; he charms us, he lulls us to sleep; he lifts us to a moment of inspiration. In metrics, in architectronics, as well as in his handling of language, he is, of course, an incredible virtuoso—the most accomplished poet in English since the great nineteenth-century masters; Tennyson, Browning and Swinburne; he does not call attention to this, and many people who read him do not even know it. If he is not precisely a "family poet" like Longfellow, Wordsworth and Tennyson, the fact that he is one of the most edible, one of the most satisfactory of contemporary writers in verse is proved by the sales of the *Collected Poetry,* which have reached, in the United States, the almost unprecedented figure for poetry of over thirty thousand copies.

I have had lately a little the feeling that the interest for Auden of the United States is not now quite so lively as it once was. His last book, *The Shield of Achilles,* seems less localized than any of its predecessors. One of its most attractive features is the sequence of lovely *Bucolics* that consist—under such bald titles as *Mountains, Lakes, Islands* and so on—of generalized pieces about landscape, about landscape presented in a novel but very characteristic way that is at once geological and subjective. Since becoming an American citizen, the poet has not ceased to explore, to roam—he has covered more ground in this country than most Americans do, and he now spends his summers in Italy. This spring he returns to England to be lecturer on poetry at Oxford. It is a part of his role to go everywhere, be accessible to all sorts of people, serve interestedly and conscientiously in innumerable varied capacities: on the staff of a Middle Western college; at a cultural congress in India; on a grand jury in New York City, deciding the fate of gangsters; on a committee of the American Academy, making handouts to needy writers.

He has above all withstood the ordeal of America through a habitation of seventeen years; he has even "succeeded" here. And he has made all these exploits contribute to the work of a great English poet who is also—in the not *mondain* sense—one of the great English men of the world.

June 9, 1956

"MISS BUTTLE" AND "MR. ELIOT"

LAST SUMMER a number of literary people in England and the United States received copies of a book called *The Sweeniad*, which purported to have been written by one Myra Buttle. Myra Buttle, as the preface explains, is "a very ordinary girl," who is "kept pretty busy" in the shop, "what with my grandmother being bedridden," but who does manage to read a certain amount of modern poetry and has been getting rather depressed about it. "The underlying message of the 'Main stream' poets seems to be that life is a sorry business anyhow, but that it might just be worth losing if, as an interim measure, we could undo the Renaissance and restore the Middle Ages, thereby making everybody as miserable as ourselves. Being a healthy girl with a good appetite, engaged to be married to a judo champion, this was too much for me to swallow and I was kept awake at night worrying about it all." These anxieties give rise to a dream, the subject of the long poem that follows—which turns out to be a satire on T. S. Eliot (Myra Buttle, My Rebuttal).

This book has now been regularly published in both England and the United States, and it is an open secret that the author is a Cambridge professor named Victor Purcell, a lecturer on Far Eastern affairs, who has previously published—in 1944—only one book of verse, *Cadmus: The Poet and the World*. Curiosity about the author of *The Sweeniad* has led the reviewer to look up this earlier

volume and to discover, in the contrast between the two,
a literary case so odd that one cannot think of anything to
match it. *Cadmus,* like *The Sweeniad,* is a long varied
poem, which covers a good deal of ground and involves
frequent changes of meter, but it is seriously, not humorously, meant, and, far from showing any talent, as *The
Sweeniad* sometimes does, it is incredibly hilariously
awful. The unintentional comedy of *Cadmus* is as funny
as anything in *The Sweeniad,* and before going on to the
satire I want to give a few examples of passages from the
earlier poem and discuss their relation to the later one.

Now, *Cadmus* is a kind of epic, which aims at nothing
less than to cover the whole history of Western poetry.
The first canto prepares the way by describing the origin
of the earth and the evolution of life:

> The shallow threshold of the sounding sea
> Was floored with crumbled layers of debris,
> A liquid mud of silicates and lime,
> And with this mud was other mud, a slime,
> A viscous ooze, a dimly vibrant plasm,
> A pungent, flowing mass—Great God's orgasm! . . .

> The chapter closes in climatic rigour
> Which tests the mammals' balance and their vigour.
> The orbit of the earth was now elliptic,
> Its axis heeled towards the new ecliptic,
> And age by age the length of winters grew
> While summers shortened. . . .
> America as south as Ohio
> Was overwhelmed by ice, and rocks, and snow.
> And when this chill and rigorous age began
> The hidden scene was being set for man.

The second canto traces the rise of ancient civilization
to its climax in the glory of Greece, which is treated in a

burst of Greek meters—hexameters, alcaics and sapphics. In the third canto, Rome takes over:

> But there was a nation
> Which sucked as it could its mighty exhalation
> Into its blood and then outbreathed a breath
> Redeeming Europe from a cultural death.
> The shape of Rome was never of a piece
> With the fine pattern of defeated Greece,
> But though to the better part it had no claim
> It still had solidarity of aim,
> Forming the structure of society
> Upon the most rigorous filial piety.

But,

> Goths and Visigoths, Vandals, Huns and Franks
> Bore down upon the weakened Roman ranks
> In crushing avalanches, Rome was sick,
> Effete, diseased in body politic.

Then Christianity, the Crusades, the cathedrals—arriving at the Renaissance.

The fourth and the fifth cantos present a whole costume pageant of European poetry through the ages. Here the poet further exercises his virtuosity by composing the section on Dante in mediocre *terza rima*. Dante is followed by

> Petrarch with his beauteous Laura.
> He beckoned me to throb within her aura

and by Villon, who frankly confesses that

> We womanized, we cheated, and we stole.

Eventually we come to Tennyson whose advent is introduced by a passage on the industrial revolution:

From the remotest ages up to now
That great and basic instrument, the plough,
Was king and overlord among machinery,
And fields and pastures formed the social scenery

but

Factories and mills began to block the view
And unseen powers began to interact,
Obscuring the basic agricultural fact.

with the result that Tennyson is forced to take refuge in
the world of Arthurian legend. He figures as

the Poet Laureate,
A royal servant, pillar of the state,
A metrist of the very first ability
Whose muse had no superior in fertility.

We end with Kipling and Eliot, the latter of whom is
treated with a certain respect:

Defence of the ancient tragic viewpoint with
Imaginative restatement of a myth,
Dispensing with all the logic of narration,
Inventing a symbolical notation,
Like a new scale, a revolution planned
And brought to fruit in Eliot's "Waste Land."

There are moments when it is difficult to believe,
through all this, that the author does not *mean* to be
funny. Besides the metrically awkward and the anticli-
mactic lines, we stumble over false rhymes of which one
would say that they can only have been planted to bring a
laugh:

No weed or tare
Can prosper there,
No bat, no faun with cloven heel,

> No worm or snail
> Or serpent's scale
> To mar this idyll and ideal!

> A variant of the solar chemistry
> That made the splendid earth—for men
> And worms, and light, and rocks are brethren.

> This age was Nicolette a trull, Aucassin
> By turns a pimp, a poet, and assassin.

When the poet turns his hand to a lyric interlude, the result is close to Gilbert and Sullivan:

> As nature ranges my measure changes to follow its pattern of life and mood.
> My down-beats follow the darting swallow, my upbeats soar with the falcon's brood.

But the case is not so simple as these passages suggest. Mr. Purcell is not merely inept; he is not merely a bad poet. The curious thing is that though his purpose is undoubtedly lofty, his accent seems naturally, invincibly, involuntarily satirical. When these verses are at all well turned, they fall into the prosaic wit of a respectable eighteenth-century versifier, and when not, they sound like the specimens in "Martinus Scriblerus's" comic treatise, *The Art of Sinking in Poetry*. Now, in cantos six, seven and eight, in which the poet is dealing with contemporary England, he becomes deliberately satirical both in tone and in form, and though these sections are not really successful either, they are a good deal better than what has gone before. But when we come to *The Sweeniad*, we find that the qualities of *Cadmus* have surprisingly been transposed in such a way as to achieve a vein of knockabout burlesque. The bathos, the reckless rhymes, the tendency to drop into doggerel, the ready hand at improvised parody, the Gilbert and Sullivan touch all contribute to an effect of an opposite kind from that at which *Cadmus* aims. What is peculiar in Purcell's case is that, following his true bent, he should have been able to turn into intentional humor his unintentional humor, and make people laugh at his subject instead of himself. And it is even more unexpected that the often clumsy metrist of *Cadmus* should, now that he can clown at his ease, appear as so accomplished a versifier that, before the secret of its authorship was out, it was natural to guess that *The Sweeniad* had been written by somebody as technically proficient as Robert Graves or C. Day Lewis.

The "argument" of *The Sweeniad* is as follows. A Prologue shows a darkened "Ghost Theatre"—

> This vast unlighted room
> Is the symbol of the tomb
> And likewise of the womb—

in which reigns a general confusion of mind created by modern science, in its whole range from physics to psychoanalysis:

> Who's that up the gallery? What's he trying to convey?
> The Second Law of Thermodynamics, did you say?
> "When the position and velocity of molecules are distrib-
>   uted absolutely at random the entropy is complete."
> Bravo, my boy! Your obfuscation is a treat,
> The words are in the dictionary; the syntax is correct—
> *Reductio ad absurdum* of the "Indirect"!
> But though your talent cannot be denied,
> Some may think you would be better occupied
> Sitting in the kitchen doing your philately,
> Or in the WC, re-writing *Lady Chatterley*.

The atmosphere is somewhat enlivened by what appear to be the voices of Louis MacNeice and John Wain, but inspissated by the presence of Empson. Then,

But hark! I hear the distant tread of Him,
Of Him, the Twentieth Century's undisputed Cham
Of Poetry, and Britain's brightest gift from Uncle Sam!
(There comes a hush:
All traffic stops from Russell Square to Shepherds' Bush.)

And

Now to the roll of muffled drums
To us the fabled Sweeney comes.

The dictator Sweeney begins by delivering a parody of *The Waste Land*—a little late in the day, perhaps, since *The Waste Land* has already been much parodied; but the quotations at the end are amusing, including as they do a line of Egyptian hieroglyphics, which is explained in the notes as

"Literally, Thy breath of life is sweet in my nostril—Life here is an occult symbol for death"

followed by

. . . — — — . . .

"The famous Morse signal of distress sent out by the *Titanic* on 14 April, 1912. Here it is sent out by the inhabitants of the Unreal City. No one answers it."

and

"A message in manual code from Microcephalos, the deaf-and-dumb soothsayer of Thebes, to Tiresias (who was blind anyway)."

The poem is expounded at length, and this is followed by the main action of *The Sweeniad*—the trial of the

"Blessed Sweeney," whose

> cult is authorized in person or by proxy
> By all the cardinals and priests, the ruling
> laity, and the acolytes of orthodoxy,

before the Tribunal of the Republic of Letters, the citizens of which insist

> that a writer should receive his meed of praise
> Not as a halo but a crown of bays.

To decide whether Sweeney deserves one "as poet, critic, sociologist, and man," in terms of "good and evil," not of "'grace' and 'sin,'" his case is argued before a "Pope" by a Postulator and a Devil's Advocate. The speeches are in prose but are interrupted by a variety of rhymed choruses. The Devil's Advocate concludes as follows, "That he [Sweeney] is, or originally was, a genuine poet is not contested by me, but I do assert that he has for altogether different reasons been 'beatified' while still on earth." He recommends Sweeney's exclusion "from the communion of Humaner Letters."

The "Pope" invites Sweeney to speak, and the voice of the invisible poet is heard to reply in parody:

> Because I do not want to think again
> Because I do not want
> Because I do not want to think
> Desiring the blessed fame and saintly crown
> I no longer want to want what you want me to want
> (Why should the baptized infant want the font?)
> Why should I plead
> To Gentiles branded with the mark of Cain?

DEVIL'S ADVOCATE

He means, your Holiness, that he denies the jurisdiction of this court.

THE "POPE"

Just as I thought.

The parodies here are never quite so good as Henry Reed's *Chard Whitlow*, but they have their amusing moments. Sweeney, for example, is made to speak of

> An experience so ecstatic
> That it makes a good dinner
> Seem like a bad one.
> (I sometimes wonder whether this is what
>   Krishna meant.)

The verdict, in the humanist court, goes against the saintly Sweeney, who is heard intoning as follows:

> Between the mystification
> And the deception
> Between the multiplication
> And the division
> Falls the Tower of London
>
> Many Nouns in *is* we find
> To the Masculine assigned:
> Amnis, axis, caulis, collis,
> Clunis, crinis, fascis, follis . . .
> Take away the number you first thought of . . .
> Stop breeding . . .
> Stop breathing . . .
>   *Pop!*

And *The Sweeniad* ends with a chorus that declares war on "Anti-Lifemanship."

In all this, there is much that is unjust to Eliot. It is incorrect to represent him as hostile to Gibbon of whom he has put on record his appreciation. It is silly to be outraged by his criticism of Shakespeare, Milton and

Shelley—especially in the case of the first, whom he can hardly be accused of underrating. And it is hardly a novel heresy to believe, as Eliot does, and as the reviewer agrees with him in doing, that Dante—whom Yeats calls in one of his poems "the chief imagination of Christendom"—produced in the *Divina Commedia* a work of art that transcends any of Shakespeare's plays, or even all of them taken together, in its philosophical grasp, its criticism of moral experience and the perfection of its execution. As for the predominance in Milton of the auditory over the visual sense—Eliot's emphasis on which brings loud protest from "Myra Buttle"—one would think this so perfectly obvious that nobody would venture to question it. And although one may like Shelley's poetry better than Eliot seems to, his criticism of Shelley's loose writing has been very much to the point in connection with the spare and compressed kind of style which Eliot himself has practiced and which, with Pound, he has been trying to teach. Especially, the "Pope's" final summing-up of the case against "Sweeney" is weak:

> But we, a court of men, have other tests—
> Whether or not the Claimant manifests
> A talent for credulity or revels
> In lice, or fasts, or fisticuffs with devils,
> Is quite irrelevant. We do not care
> Whether he's nude or wears a shirt of hair
> Or, like St. Simeon, lives up in the air.
> We proffer questions of a different grain—
> Whether he's enlightened or humane,
> How would he pleasure a wench or drive a spigot?
> Is he of tolerant mind or just a bigot?
> Has he the zest for life of Rabelais
> (Accepting, of course, the standards of our day)?

Is he as joyous as Boccaccio?
In both these cases we must answer "No."
Would Falstaff choose him as a drinking pal?
How would he fare with Bardolph or Prince Hal?
Has he the quiet detachment of Montaigne?
Can he compete with Milton's epic strain?
Would Dryden praise his satire, or would Pope
Approve his riddles or his narrow scope?
Has he a touch of Browning's lyric gift,
Or *saeva indignatio* of Swift?
Has Blake's compassion taught his heart to sing?
Has he the lift of Shelley's heavenly wing?
Has he the humour that would save his feet
From falling in the pitfalls of conceit
Waiting to trap the clerical élite?

These questions are completely irrelevant. Why should Eliot, an artist in his own right, be expected to do or be any of these things? He should, in fact, not be expected to duplicate the qualities of anyone else. As for the question about Dryden and Pope, they would not have approved his "riddles"—if any such speculations make sense—but they might well have admitted his skill with words, which at moments is quite close to their own. Nor has the supposed austerity of Eliot's habits anything to do with the matter. There *is* certainly a cult of Eliot, but it has never—so far as I have known—been based on any such assumption. How this cult has come into being I shall in a moment attempt to explain. But in the meantime I want to return to the somewhat obtuse author of *Cadmus,* who appears, in the passage just quoted, rather embarrassingly from behind "Myra Buttle." That *The Sweeniad* should be unjust is something to be taken for granted; all satirists are unjust to their subjects. And that the author should be something of a Philistine may be also an essential feature of the successful satirist's role, as in the case of W. S. Gilbert, or even of Aristophanes. Mr. Purcell, with far less ability, really has something in common with such writers of fantastic comedy; and on the whole he has handled his Philistinism cleverly by inventing the anxious young girl who is occupied with Grandmother's shop and is about to marry a judo champion, and using her as a mask for his outburst. It is a part of the comedy, its mainspring, that a limited and well-meaning person should give voice to a long resentment. Myra Buttle has the crude common sense of one of Molière's servants who cannot swallow the pretensions of their masters, who laugh at the bourgeois gentleman or rebel against the precious ladies.

And why is it possible to some extent to enjoy "Myra Buttle's" reaction? Why is it that one finds in the advertizing material put out by the publishers of *The Sweeniad* quite a number of delighted comments by distinguished contemporaries of Eliot, who are, nevertheless, one imagines, neither unfriendly toward him nor unappreciative of his merits? I shall try to answer this question, but since the subject is rather complex, the inquiry will not be simple.

To attempt at the beginning, however, to formulate a useful distinction, I would suggest that there are two personalities involved—T. S. Eliot, the author of *The Sacred Wood, The Waste Land, The Cocktail Party,* and other excellent things, and "Mr. Eliot," the public figure, the pillar of British culture, and the remote inscrutable deity who presides over the American academic guild of what its members like to call criticism. The point is that Eliot is a genuine person, whose work is of exceptional interest, but that the public "Mr. Eliot" is a fictional character, a creation of T. S. Eliot's, almost as truly as "Myra Buttle" is a creation of Victor Purcell's.

The situation is further complicated by the fact that "Mr. Eliot" wears two aspects—one British and one American—and we have to distinguish between the two. The English, with their sense of hierarchy, always like to have a grand master of literature, a kind of Archbishop of Canterbury, a privileged veteran who has received all the possible honors. Thomas Hardy, after the death of Meredith, was lifted to this position, and, after Hardy's death, Bernard Shaw. To pay a visit to Meredith, Hardy or Shaw, once they had attained this eminence, meant almost in the literary world what it meant for a débutante to be received at Buckingham Palace. When Shaw died, there was no one of his stature to accede to the vacant throne. E. M. Forster was magnified, but his work had not the weight of these others', and he did not care to be a great figure. The result was a kind of triumvirate, with the much-respected Forster in quiet retirement in the upper rooms of the palace, Eliot very much to the fore as the well-groomed head of the literary state who presided on official occasions, and Somerset Maugham installed in a comfortable reception room to make contact with that part of the public which was not up to "Mr. Eliot." As a consequence of his occupying this princely position, it seemed for years impossible in England to write any serious criticism of Eliot's work. A visitor from the United States was astonished at the extent to which Eliot had those hypercritical old Britishers buffaloed. There had been nothing to prepare one, for example, for the feebleness of his comedy *The Confidential Clerk,* which was running with immense success and which one made a point of seeing—only to find that the author's researches into the secrets of the dramatic art, about which there had been some publicity, had resulted in the careful exploitation of a few rudimentary tricks, and that his upper-class English characters (that dutiful old retainer! that vague but compelling lady!) seemed like somewhat faded memories of some Galsworthy novel that the author might have read in crossing, on the occasion of his first visit to England. I found, when I discussed this play with people in London, that everybody seemed to agree with me, but I gathered that respect for Eliot had made it impossible for anyone to commit himself by printing a sincere opinion. There was as yet no Victor Purcell, as there was not as yet any Lord Altrincham.

The triumph of the British "Mr. Eliot" was also illustrated, at about this time, by a pamphlet called *The Literature of Politics,* by "T. S. Eliot, O.M., with a foreword by the Right Honourable Sir Anthony Eden, K.G., M.C., M.P.," published in 1955 by the Conservative Political Centre. This is a lecture "delivered at a Literary Luncheon organized by the London Conservative Union," with "The Rt. Hon. D. Heathcoat Amory, M.P.," in the chair, and a self-parody of an exquisite absurdity that "Myra Buttle" could never achieve. The discourse commences with the usual note of abysmal self-deprecation: "Not today, for the first time, but for some time past, have I been aware how very rash it was of me to accept your invitation to address this Literary Luncheon: my acceptance is only one more illustration of a truth that I should have learned from experience, that one can face nearly any danger intrepidly, and even court it wantonly, so long as it is far enough off. My foolhardiness, on this occasion, was twofold. While I do not suppose that everyone in this room is an accomplished public speaker, I take it for granted that those who are not are at least seasoned listeners, with pretty high standards of what they expect in the way of oratory. And a man of letters, far from being thereby licensed to the platform and the rostrum, is more likely than not to be a poor speaker, relatively at ease—but only relatively—when he has prepared, as I have today, not only his thoughts but his words. Second, I was rash in consenting to appear in an unfamiliar role and context. That, of course, may have increased the size of my audience: you are, very likely, at this moment experiencing the thrill of a crowd gathered to watch a man take a very high dive, when the rumor has been put about that he does not know how to swim. I hope you will be disappointed: but I do not know myself whether or not, after the splash has subsided, my head will emerge from the water." This goes on for over two pages of the fourteen pages of the "lecture."

He then asks himself the question "What is the literature of Conservatism?" and answers, "There are four names which we could all, without any prompting, repeat in chorus, for they constantly turn up together. . . . They are, of course, the names of Bolingbroke, Burke, Coleridge and Disraeli." What, he inquires, have these four writers in common? "I am inclined to believe it a good thing that we should find the question difficult to answer. If, in my attempt to give grounds for my belief, you find me descending to platitude and commonplace, I hope you will attribute it to my simplicity and inexperience; if, on the other hand, you convict me of uttering nonsense, I ask for no quarter at all." He now tells us that there are two types of political development: one that starts with "a body of doctrine" and goes on to try to "realize a programme" based upon this doctrine, and another that begins with a practical party and goes on to an attempt to discover "what its fundamental tenets are." "When a party committed to an unalterable doctrine finds itself in a position of power, two things may happen." On the one hand, the leaders of the party will try either to "postpone the part of their programme that they see to be

impracticable" or, fraudulently, to make it appear that
they are actually carrying it out; or, like the Jacobins,
they will try to be logical at the expense of the social
realities. The two opposite dangers—of opportunism and
fanaticism—make the substance of another paragraph.
This is followed by an approving reference to somebody
or other's statement that in the United States "the true
conservatives . . . in recent times" have been not "political figures" but "philosophic observers and moralists,
often in academic positions," such as "Paul More" and
Irving Babbitt who have no direct influence on politics.
But this is not as it should be. The "legislator" and "the
man whose business is merely to think and write" should
keep in closer touch with one another. A further platitude on the opposite dangers of excessively doctrinaire
theory and excessively opportunistic adaptability, a plug
for Charles Maurras, a snubbing of Bernard Shaw, and
you've had it.

The American "Mr. Eliot" appears in a quite distinct
role—less official and social than academic. Though "appears" is perhaps not the word. The American "Mr.
Eliot" is the constant all-pervasive presence that was
characterized by whoever made the joke about "The
Blessed Thomas Eliot Considered as the Air We
Breathe." I would not hold Eliot responsible for everything his adorers have done, but I think it is undeniable
that the aridity of our literary monthlies and quarterlies
partly derives from the old *Criterion*. This review—so
elegant in format—used to seem to me, from the very
beginning, rather dreary and disappointing, as if put
together by Eliot without much discrimination, or even
any very great enthusiasm, and always with too wary an
eye on the people who might be put off by rowdy or
erratic writings. There was an effort to establish an interchange between the cultural activities of the various

countries, but remarkably little real contact, even in the
literary field, with what was going on in the world during
the period between the two World Wars. The *Criterion's*
format and tone were imitated by Lincoln Kirstein in his
quarterly the *Hound & Horn,* which was founded in
1927 and ran till 1934, and several other such periodicals
carried the tradition on. The pages of these reviews were
always peppered with "Mr. Eliot," "in Mr. Eliot's
phrase," "as Mr. Eliot has pointed out." They have been
so peppered for now three decades. (The first number of
a new one, the *Texas Quarterly,* exactly like all the
others, has just reached me as I have been writing this. I
open it and find, in an article on Baudelaire and Poe,
"Now, that Mr. Eliot knows French well, no one will
deny. But to assess the value of a translation of this magnitude is not easy." The next article is called *Baudelaire:
The Question of His Sincerity, or, Variations on Several
Texts by Eliot.*) Though Eliot's name has been mentioned as often and with the same kind of awe as that of
the Hebrew Jahveh, it is not sacrilegious to pronounce it
and its vowels have not been disguised; one is even permitted respectfully to register small differences from "Mr.
Eliot"; yet his name has come to stand almost as much as
Jahveh for a remote and faceless protector, for an unapproachable power, and it has evidently, in the long run,
had the result of making Eliot feel that he has been put
by his admirers into a false position. His address *The
Frontiers of Criticism,* delivered before a vast audience, in
1956, at the University of Minnesota, and now included
in *On Poetry and Poets,* his recent collection of essays,
represents a natural impulse on the part of the authentic
Eliot to dissociate himself from "Mr. Eliot" in the special
tutelary aspect under which he has been worshipped in
the United States: that of patron of the "symbolic"
analysts and the inquirers into literary sources who deso-

late the pages of these journals. He has even, in the lecture just mentioned, gone to the length of regretting his notes to *The Waste Land* and implying that he would like to suppress them. But he is obviously speaking too late. His last poem, *The Cultivation of Christmas Trees,* a pale little self-parody of thirty-four lines ($1.25 in cardboard covers, $2 in cloth), was snapped up at once by one of these experts and subjected to a long going-over.

The point is that Eliot's work is fatally suited to the needs of American teachers of courses in English. In the first place, there is very little of it: you can get through it all in the evenings of a week. Those English professors are lazy. They rarely know anything but English Lit., and they rarely read anything in English that they do not have to read for their degrees and their courses or to get themselves a little credit by writing in some critical organ about one of their accepted subjects. In American schools and colleges forty or fifty years ago, there was a canon of English poets that did not extend much, I think, beyond Tennyson, and a canon of English prose that, so far as I remember, stopped short with Carlyle. Contemporary literature was never mentioned, and American writers were completely ignored. Today there are courses in the modern novel and officially recognized American classics; yet the scope of the English departments seems in other ways even more limited. You need not acquaint yourself now with even so many books as the old generation did. You talk about a few books at greater length and in a far more specialized way. It is almost like Talmudic *pilpul,* that method of rabbinical exegesis of which the criterion of excellence came to consist in the degree of farfetchedness that could be compassed by subtle argument. (A recent issue of an academic quarterly, *Modern Fiction Studies,* contains essays arguing intricately that in Henry James's story *The Jolly Corner* there are not one but *two* ghosts, and that *The Turn of the Screw* is a religious allegory.) For this kind of exegesis the poetry of Eliot has provided the ideal text. Not only is it small in bulk; it presents in the shortest space a maximum of out-of-the-way references that the researcher may hope to run down, of apparently symbolic images that the interpreter may hope to illuminate and of often unavowed quotations that, working in some other connection, one may joyously stumble upon.* The commentators have been preying on Eliot's work, like sandpipers pecking for sand fleas, so persistently for so many decades that they seem to have been getting on Eliot's nerves and to have goaded him into telling them that they have unearthed more revelations than the poet had buried secrets.

So much for "Mr. Eliot's" public and its need to accept him, to invent him. This invention is not, however, entirely the work of the public. The poet has himself collaborated; he has, in fact, given his public its cue. But just how has he produced this result, and why? We must realize first of all that Eliot is essentially a dramatist. This was plain from his earliest poems. Some of these were dramatic monologues in which the speaker was given a name—Gerontion or J. Alfred Prufrock—but the speakers in *The Waste Land* and *Ash Wednesday* are hardly

---

* I contribute my own suggestion that *The Love Song of J. Alfred Prufrock,* first published in 1915, may owe something to *Wet Magic,* a children's story by E. Nesbit, first published in 1913. In this story, a captured mermaid, exhibited in a tank, is described as "a mass of something dark that looked as if it were partly browny-green fish and partly greeny-brown seaweed," and a sister mermaid who pleads for her rescue as "something white and brown and green." The children who effect this rescue are rewarded by an underwater visit to the King and Queen of the sea, but are made to forget this visit when at last they are returned to the earth.

less dramatic masks. In the case of *The Waste Land*, the many quotations—of which so much complaint was once made and of which "Myra Buttle" is still complaining—are a part of the dramatic situation: they are simply the kind of thing that goes on in the head of a troubled man who has drunk deep at the best universities and is half-drugged with literature, who has studied a little Sanskrit at Harvard and done a certain amount of travelling in Europe—as *Ash Wednesday* is the broken soliloquy of a man who is trying to resign himself to some prostrating disappointment and who is groping to revive his spirit by establishing some relation with God. It is not necessary, in the first of these cases, to understand all Eliot's literary references, or, in the second, to share his hunger for religious experience: all that is necessary here is a willingness to be interested in the character. And the lines that Eliot wrote for these characters rang so roundly in the ears of contemporaries as to make quite absurd the objections of those critics who asserted that he spoke only riddles and did not convey any real meaning. "Myra Buttle," too, protests against this, but the very attack in *The Sweeniad* on the influence of the poet on the literary world is evidence that he did convey something, an emotion that others shared. Actually, T. S. Eliot has been one of the great phrasemakers of our time and has provided almost as many book titles, chapter headings, epigraphs and clichés for editorial writers as Kipling or the "Alice" books.

It was obvious from the beginning that Eliot would or should write plays, and as early as 1926 he began, in the first instalment of *Sweeney Agonistes*, experimenting with the dramatic form. This play he never completed, but he later went on to write others, and the best of them were extremely effective. He also became an actor in his own person, developed his public self as a theatrical character, or characters. This process no doubt began with his original transformation of the American into a Britisher; but his roles have not, I think, been entirely British: he has something of a repertoire. There is, for example, *the Anglican clergyman,* one of Eliot's most successful, if not most exhilarating, impersonations. You can hear how the voice is handled in the droning and monotonous recording he has made of the *Four Quartets,* but to see him do this in public is to succumb to the same kind of illusion that is evoked by one of Ruth Draper's monologues. Eliot makes clergyman's jokes, he laughs a clergyman's laugh; you could swear he wore a turned-around collar. Another of his masks is *the formidable professor,* who gives ignorance and error short shrift. This seems to me American rather than British and to have probably been acquired at Harvard from old-fashioned snobs and pedants like George Kittredge, Barrett Wendell and Irving Babbitt. This is the personage who dismisses large subjects with casual but blighting comments—sometimes, as in the case of Russian literature or of certain American writers, on matters about which, as was likely to happen with those caustic old cocks of the classroom, he obviously knows very little. That, however, goes down well with his followers, who feel at once that they are relieved from the necessity of ever bothering to look into these subjects. This is also the "Mr. Eliot" who says of the Haidee episode in Byron's *Don Juan* that it "deserves pretty high marks," and who talks of the enjoyment of poetry in such a peculiar way: "Unless we are able to enjoy the work of Pope, we cannot arrive at a full understanding of English poetry"; "I find myself in agreement with Herr Holthusen: and indeed, if he is wrong and Dr. Heller is right, then I can only enjoy the poetry of Rilke under a misunderstanding"; "Where there is the continuity of such a positive personality [as Yeats] and such a single purpose, the later work cannot be understood, or properly enjoyed, without a study and appreciation of the earlier."

This professor merges with *Dr. Johnson,* which seems to me one of Eliot's less satisfactory characters. The manners and physique of Johnson make a genuine impersonation incompatible with Eliot's public presence, yet he has a real cult of Johnson, and the example of the author of *The Lives of the Poets* has evidently counted for something in the tone and the tenor of Eliot's pronouncements. But when he tries Johnson's own line of criticism—the attempt to check logically on literal meaning—this carries him off his own track. Certainly Dr. Johnson would not have liked Shelley's skylark, but he would have liked Eliot's own poetry even less. It is true, of course, that Eliot uses words as precisely as Pope did, and more precisely than Shelley, but his free flight of Symbolist metaphors would have set off the thunders of Johnson, so that his Neo-Johnsonian procedure, directed against the Romantics, does not really come out right as a parallel to Johnson's against the Metaphysicals, whom Eliot regards as kin spirits and whom he has done so much to bring into fashion.

As a Neo-Johnsonian dictator, however, throning it in old London and laying down the rules of taste, Eliot has made an impression, and in the this role I find him as irritating as "Myra Buttle" does. What *is* this "Main Stream" of poetry that he is always talking about, which he apparently identifies with Pound and himself and with the poets who more or less derive from them, and the price of the divergence from which, as Eliot seems to imply, is irretrievably to be lost in the sands? Who have been the best English poets of the generation following Eliot's? Let us say Auden, Thomas and Betjeman. And what have these three in common? Auden has learned something from Eliot in his semi-colloquial style. Auden and Thomas both make tangles of metaphors. But John Betjeman is quite outside the fashion. Is he, then, like the lady in his poem—not being in the Main Stream—destined to be left stranded and lonely on "the shining fields of mud"? Are the successful poems of Spender in the Main Stream? Is the fluent virtuosity of MacNeice and Day Lewis? They do all more or less use colloquial language. But is Yeats in the Main Stream? He is the greatest poet in English of his age, but his remarks on Eliot's poetry show how alien to him it seemed. The realism of his later poems is as much in a traditional grand manner as the romanticism of his early ones. It is true that—it is said, under the influence of Pound—he moved from the vagueness and fluency that sometimes characterized his early poems to a style that was harder and terser; but what has this style in common with Auden or Dylan Thomas? One feels that the Main Stream, though it sprang from aesthetic heresy, is now regarded by Eliot as something like the "Main Line" that runs west from Philadelphia and on which all the well-established and well-thought-of people are supposed to have their residences. The other chief function of Eliot-Johnson is instructing the readers and writers of the present as to which poets of the past, and to what extent, it is permitted them to read and admire. Here the accepted position and the authoritative tone are all. Every directive is at once accepted: "Yes, yes, as Mr. Eliot has said"; "Mr. Eliot has pointed out that Mother Goose at her most surprising has something in common with Blake." It should be said in justice to Eliot that he has frankly—in *The Frontiers of Criticism*—described his early essays as "a by-product of my private poetry-workshop; or a prolongation of the thinking that went into the formation of my own verse." Later, he changed his mind about some of the poets whose tendencies had at that time seemed inimical to his own and Pound's. But there was still always something of the dictator in the way in which he went about this. Now we need not any longer snub Milton; we need not any longer be shy—if we realize that what he wrote was not exactly poetry but only excellent verse—of indulging ourselves a little in Kipling. (His followers have seemed strangely inattentive to one of his latest cues: that we may now also look into Longfellow.)

Then—analyzing the components of the public Eliot— we come to *the genteel Bostonian*. Of this race, in his earlier days, the poet, of course, made a certain amount of fun. There were Aunt Helen Slingsby, in her "small house near a fashionable square," and Cousin Harriet, who every evening read the Boston *Evening Transcript*. Mr. Prufrock and Burbank with a Baedeker were the male counterparts of these. But though Eliot is finely ironic at the expense of their decorums and their inhibitions, he has to some extent shared these and has used them for one aspect of his public personality. His dramatized anti-Semitism is really, I think, a part of this, as is his dramatized Anglophilia. They are the prejudices of old Tory gentility, which Eliot has liked to preserve as self-conscious anachronisms. The Jew in *Gerontion* is a Shylock "squatting on the window sill," and the Jews in the Burbank-Bleistein poem are the vulgarians of ancient caricature. One of its most skilful witticisms depends on the assumption that there is something inherently ridiculous in a man named Klein's being given a title. It does not occur to Eliot that Bleistein, who looks at pictures with "a lusterless protrusive eye," may possibly be a better judge of Canalettos than Burbank with his Baedeker. In his anthology of Kipling's verse, he makes a point of including *The Waster*—surely Kipling at his most hateful worst—which manages at the same time to be anti-

Semitic and anti-German. In *After Strange Gods*, he writes that in the kind of society he regards as desirable, "reasons of race and religion combine to make any large number of free-thinking Jews undesirable"; and then, amusingly, in his speech at the Conservative Luncheon, in checking off his four great conservative writers, he allows that "Disraeli also [one imagines a brief pause] deserves a pass degree, though churchmanship is the one point on which I feel more sympathy with Mr. Gladstone." One free-thinking Jew is all right if he is working for the interests of the Tories.

In any case, however, it must not be imagined that Eliot, as the Advocatus Diaboli asserts in *The Sweeniad*, "is utterly incapable of laughing at himself." The truth is that there is a rascal in Eliot. It is, I believe, the recalcitrance of this rascal that has convinced him of the reality of Original Sin: he has identified himself surely as much with the unregenerate Sweeney as with the ineffective Prufrock. It was the young rascal who wrote the disturbing poems, full of ironies and moral shocks; it is the old rascal who puts on the public show with which we are here concerned, and it is plain enough that Eliot is sometimes irreverent toward the attitudes of "Mr. Eliot." Three anecdotes may illustrate this. Two of them have come to me at second hand, and I cannot be sure of their accuracy, but they represent the kind of thing that we have come to expect from Eliot. At the conclusion of a lecture or a reading of his poetry at some town not far from Boston, an enthusiastic lady is supposed to have expressed surprise at his radiant and youthful appearance and to have asked him how he ever managed it. "Gin and drugs, Madam—gin and drugs!" the poet is supposed to have replied. The other stories are more ambiguous. When Eliot had been awarded the Nobel Prize and was flying from the United States, a reporter is said to have asked him which work of his had won him this honor. He answers, "Why, I think the whole corpus," and the reporter returns to his office and writes that it was not *The Waste Land* that had made Eliot a Nobel prizeman but a work called *The Whole Corpus,* which must have sounded to the reporter even grimmer. Was this a joke on Eliot or a joke on the reporter and the public? Years ago, at the New School for Social Research, I heard Eliot read *Sweeney Among the Nightingales.* He prefaced it by explaining that the action took place in a dive, and added, "Not, of course, that I have ever been in such a place!" This seems to me very typical. The respectable persons in his audience—of whom Eliot is always very much aware—would have taken him at his word; the others would have known he was joking. He has been able thus to have it both ways. He hedges his bets on "Mr. Eliot" by an undercurrent of self-irony and his bets on the old rascal by always maintaining a decorous front. He has himself depicted this duality in his frontispiece to *Old Possum's Book of Practical Cats,* in which an old-fashioned dude in a silk hat and white spats is roller-skating arm in arm with a dubious-looking character in a bowler and a false beard.

In this character of Old Possum, who plays dead but pursues his own ends and indulges his private ribaldry, Eliot seems to run true to a familiar New England type. This type may be an excellent businessman—as Eliot is said to be—or professional man or banker; he will enjoy a solid position, and he appears to be completely conventional; but he will preserve, through all the shrewdness of his worldly dealings, a certain indestructible vein of idealism, the allotropic version, in modern terms, of the Puritan's sense of righteousness. Such a man rarely sticks out his neck in any very hazardous way, but he may go to unconventional lengths—as Thomas Wentworth Higginson did by financing and backing John Brown—in promoting the crusades of others. (Ezra Pound and Wyndham Lewis have been Eliot's John Brown.) If the respectable Bostonian is cagy about not letting himself be caught, his fidelity to moral principle cannot easily be caught, either; it will not be corrupted by commerce, it will form and reserve its own judgments in the transaction of professional business, it will crop up after eclipse. Unlike Pound and Lewis, his old allies, Eliot has never agitated in the interests of the school he belonged to, and he has never, under the influence of political fanaticism, allowed himself to become a scandal; but he has always stood up for these old allies, and he has never, in the field of literature, allowed himself to let down the movement of which Joyce is the greatest name. An example of this was his effort—frustrated though it was—to correct the disparaging obituary given Joyce by the London *Times*.

As for Eliot's political opinions, this brings us to the whole heat-provoking question of his non-literary views and their relation to his literary ones. Can these views—religious, social, political—really be said to exist, and if so, in what sense?

To begin with the religious position, this, at least, has been made fairly explicit. We know from Eliot's essay on Pascal that "among religions" he "finds Christianity, and Catholic Christianity, to account most satisfactorily for the world and especially the moral world within," and that he accepts the miraculous element in the Gospels; and we know from his essay *Religion and Literature* that he believes in the existence of "a supernatural order" which holds a position of "primacy . . . over the natural life." We know that he is a practicing Anglo-Catholic. Yet what one seems to find in his writings is a darkness which imposes a need to believe rather than the light of belief. It seems to me that Eliot's religious impulse is stated most strongly and clearly in the scene in *The Cocktail Party* in which Celia interviews Harcourt-Reilly and describes to him the cause of her self-discontent:

> It's not the feeling of anything I've ever *done*,
> Which I might get away from, or of anything in me
> I could get rid of—but of emptiness, of failure
> Towards someone, or something, outside of myself;
> And I feel I must . . . *atone*—is that the word?

Isn't this closer to Protestantism than to Catholicism, a question of keeping one's accounts right with God by taking some appropriate action? For Celia will end by finding that she has to *do* something effective: she joins a "nursing order"—"very austere," we are told—and is crucified, on a savage island, on which she has been nursing converted natives, in an uprising of the unconverted. So Harry, in *The Family Reunion*, when his feeling of guilt has been exorcised, announces that he is headed for

Somewhere on the other side of despair.
To the worship in the desert, the thirst and deprivation,
A stony sanctuary and a primitive altar,
The heat of the sun and the icy vigil,
A care over lives of humble people,
The lesson of ignorance, of incurable diseases.

This evidently represents Eliot's ideal of virtue, of saintliness—an ideal of Spartan good works that may lead to a perfect martyrdom. But in its context in Eliot's work, there is something a little wrong with it. It makes one think of what used to be known as "entering the field of foreign missions," which is what the other characters in *The Family Reunion* assume—not perhaps, one gathers,

wrongly—that Harry is going to do; of the minister announcing the sum that has been raised for converting the
heathen and the sum that is still needed, out of the
pockets of his comfortable congregation, who enjoy a
vicarious sense of propagating the Christian faith and,
when a missionary is eaten by cannibals, of vicarious
sacrifice. And then there is a kind of snobbery that is
rather disagreeable. Celia is made so much better than
anyone else in the play, made to exist on so infinitely
superior a level, that we discount, don't quite swallow,
her crucifixion, and react in the direction of sympathy for
the characters so invidiously contrasted with her and
supposed to be so hopelessly second-rate. Both *Murder in
the Cathedral* and *The Cocktail Party* are intended to
exalt humility, which the author, in an essay on Baudelaire, describes as "the greatest, the most difficult, of the
Christian virtues," but in both cases the moral snobbery
does a good deal to discredit the humility. It is fatal to
combine the two—can you really, in attempting to be
humble yourself, explicitly *exalt* humility?—and the im-
propriety of this has, in the case of "Mr. Eliot" in his role
of *the Christian,* been more obvious than in his writings
for the stage.

You will find if you consult *Who's Who* that "Mr.
Eliot" has the following distinctions: He is a D.Litt. of
Oxford; a Litt.D. of Harvard, Yale, Princeton, Columbia,
Bristol, Leeds, and Washington; an LL.D. of Edinburgh
and St. Andrews; a D. ès L. of Paris, Aix-Marseille, and
Rennes; a D. Phil. of Munich; an Honorary Fellow of
Merton College and of Magdalen College; an Officier de
la Légion d'Honneur; and a Foreign Member of the
Accademia dei Lincei of Rome. And he has received the
Nobel Prize—as the photographs from Stockholm
show—with the Order of Merit around his neck. Yet we
know that the speeches which Eliot delivers on such occa-

sions begin almost invariably—like his speech before the Conservative Luncheon—with protracted expressions of humility; and Eliot is too much of a showman, too self-conscious and too accomplished, to persuade us to believe for a moment in his highly successful self in this character of an apologetic humble person. His tone is actually that of one who feels quite sure of his own superiority and regards himself as a person of consequence—in which he is perfectly justified; but why must he deluge us with humility? Bernard Shaw, another great showman, had a much less dangerous pose: his line was that he knew he was wonderful, that nobody could hold a candle to him. One might find this good fun or a bore. But we do not know how to react to "Mr. Eliot's" self-deprecation, which seems actually a form of pretentiousness. He will speak of his "meagre poetic gifts" and announce that in his opinions on anything but poetry he is ready to stand corrected, and even in poetic matters we find that he is prepared to revise his opinions. Yet, in doing this, he manages to talk about himself almost as much as Shaw. Even in his very brief speech under the auspices of Anthony Eden, he took time to explain to his audience that Coleridge "was rather a man of my own type, differing from myself chiefly in being immensely more learned, more industrious, and endowed with a more powerful and subtle mind." Can an authentic humility be acted, and can a professional oracle be humble? For "Mr. Eliot" is also an *oracle*—the last of the six aspects between which I have been trying to discriminate. He knows that every tiny poem, every slender pamphlet of an essay that he drops into the literary world, will be received with profound respect and read with devoted attention. Being an oracle is a natural vocation for which certain people are gifted; it may not have, necessarily, anything to do with wisdom, anything to do with prophetic insight. André

Gide, who—unlike Shaw and Eliot—had nothing of the public performer, was an enormous success as an oracle, and yet he had little of importance to say. He, too, could command attention by sending to press his least gleam of thought, his feeblest imagination, and seemed to have the whole literary world in France hanging on the successive instalments of his rather dry and trivial diary. It is all in the timing, the presence, the silences, the timbre of voice. "Mr. Eliot" is a master of this and has created a solemn hush whenever he has made a pronouncement on the problems of contemporary society.

"Myra Buttle" has dug out some queer ones: " 'Education has to be from top to bottom religious,' he said in an article in a Church newspaper. The control of education, he went on, must be by priests and 'the educational hierarchy should be a religious hierarchy.' He advocated a strong reaction against the secularization of the universities, and recommended reintroducing the religious tests. Government, he said, should be conducted by those 'whose responsibility is inherited with affluence and position.' While careful to concede that education should be open to individuals with exceptional talent who have been properly 'screened' and who are willing to swear allegiance to the Establishment, he insisted that it should be confined generally to the well-born and wealthy, 'since to be educated above one's station leads to unhappiness and social instability.' . . . He considerd that 'tolerance was greatly overestimated.' 'I have no objection to being called a bigot myself,' he declared. 'The Church's business,' he insisted, 'was to *interfere* with the world': there could be no nonsense of 'live and let live.' . . . 'If you want a Christian Society (he said) you cannot allow congeries of independent sects'; they must be eradicated. The Church, he added, has to speak 'with final authority in mortal matters and on the conduct of foreign affairs.' "

I do not know when these passages were written, and I do not know whether the satirist may not have distorted their meaning in the satirical use he has made of them—as I find that he has somewhat distorted the passage in which Eliot compares Shakespeare and Dante. But up until about twenty years ago Eliot made no attempt to give a systematic account of his views. In 1928, he delivered one of his most tremendous oracles, the announcement in the preface to *For Lancelot Andrewes*, that he had "in preparation a trilogy: *The School of Donne; The Outline of Royalism*; and *The Principles of Modern Heresy*." These books were never written, but they became very influential, and thus achieved a triumph for the oracle. The followers of Eliot assumed that he could explain all these matters if he would, and that in the meantime they did not have to worry about the poetry of the Romantics, the politics of bourgeois republics or the philosophical points of view of persons who, accepting no orthodoxy, were unable to recognize a heresy. The non-followers of Eliot caught echoes of Charles Maurras and Babbitt and More. The American "Humanists" are distinctly audible in one of "Myra Buttle's" quotations: "I have no more sympathy with the purely humanitarian attitude towards war than the humanitarian attitude towards anything else. I should not enjoy the prospect of abolishing suffering without at the same time perfecting human nature." And one wonders with "Myra Buttle" whether all this was not "just an act," a mere flourishing about of old properties. It was always so hard to pin Eliot down and find out exactly what he believed. He was likely to be evasive when challenged. There was a curious correspondence last August and September in the London *Times Literary Supplement* between Eliot, the writer of a leading article called *Classic Inhumanism* and several other correspondents. Eliot denied the accuracy of certain statements about his career and opinions, but his opponents were able to demonstrate that in most cases these statements had been correct. What was strange was that Eliot himself should, in this connection and others, have shown himself so offhand and vague about matters on which he had once expressed himself so positively and even sharply. The discrepancy between his stern authoritarian tone and his subsequent readjustments has ended by leading one to disregard his occasional fee-fi-fo-fum. One might for a moment have wondered how he proposed, in his Christian society, to deal with a possible surplus of non-Tory free-thinking Jews—a quota for each country, perhaps, and the rest of them sent to Israel?—or what sort of supervision of the press would be exercised in this society, since, although he had made it plain that he did not approve of the current kind of censorship, he evidently believed that, in the interests of religion, some curb on free expression was needed. What would he do, for example, about Lawrence and Hardy, whose influence, in *After Strange Gods*, he seems to regard as dubious? What exactly would happen to the promulgator of heresy in Eliot's Christian society?

But these questions did not trouble us long, for Eliot cares much more about literature than he does about anything else. The heresy-hunting appendix in *After Strange Gods* is taken so lightly by the author that it is made to seem almost a parlor game, while the literary criticism of contemporaries, no matter how suspect as moralists, is as usual acute and interesting. No one who has ever met Eliot or followed his career as a publisher and editor could regard him as genuinely intolerant. He is as sensitive in his response to literature and as generous in encouragement of talent as anybody of our time. This is where his real modesty comes in and, fortunately, works against Johnson-Babbitt, Cousin Harriet and Aunt Helen

Slingsby. The "liberalism" he scoffs at in politics he displays—though he seems to think he shouldn't—in the field of literature, and in this he is quite different from Babbitt and More, who made it one of their principal objects to try to knock contemporary talent on the head. He evidently had no inhibitions about inviting free-thinking Jews to contribute to the *Criterion,* and he sometimes praises the work of writers whose attitude toward religion is hostile. If he failed to formulate a system, it was simply, one came to conclude, that he knew that if he did so he would land himself—in his essay *Second Thoughts About Humanism* you see him trying to guard against this—in some such all too simple-minded, some such aesthetically stupid philosophy as that of Babbitt and More.

One would have been willing to let it go at this. But more recently—perhaps under pressure of the crisis of the second war—T. S. Eliot has at last made an effort to give us something like an ordered exposition of his general social ideas. This is to be found in *The Idea of a Christian Society* of 1939 and *Notes Towards the Definition of Culture* of 1948, and these books must be tackled as primary documents by anybody dealing with Eliot. I wonder whether "Myra Buttle" has read them, for the kind of thing *The Sweeniad* ridicules in the passages quoted above is here presented in a soberer, more temperate and better-considered form. My own reaction, however, to these more conscientious books is that once the fee-fi-fo-fum is dropped and the ideas are brought out into the open and disciplined by Eliot's common sense, they are seen not to count for much. In the domain of contemporary problems of the social and political kind, the author's shift of his residence from the United States to England, as well as his habit of dwelling in the highest intellectual realm of the pre-Enlightenment classics, has rather disqualified him. Though these books are full of references to specific countries with their special problems, the whole thing seems to hang in the void. He is sound enough on the negative side—the bleakness of industrial life, the stunting of artistic production in an age of commercialization, the lowering by popular education of the standards of humanistic culture. But he seems to have no grasp of the social realities of which these deficiencies are aspects. The standard of living of the working class has risen in industrial society; the literary production of the United States has had in the last few decades—Eliot himself is a part of this—its most fertile and brilliant period since the fifties of the last century; scientific and technological education has equipped the human race for triumphs that were only being dreamed of a few hundred years ago, when the ideals of humanism dominated. There is always the danger, of course, that the human race may wipe itself out; but, in view of the murderous record of almost two Christian millennia, I do not understand how Eliot can hope that this religion may save us. It is difficult even to understand how Eliot envisages his Christian society. What precisely are to be the relations between the Church and the State? What kind of controls will be exercised over literature and education? How will the "dissident sects" be confined, as he says they should, to a "marginal" status? And one cannot find any hint as to how the conditions we know, the processes in which we participate, could ever be made to lead to the society that Eliot has projected. Does he imagine that the Communist countries, even with modified regimes, can ever be converted to enthroning the church in any official way, or that the countries with a variety of sects will agree on an established church? Does he imagine that in countries where the classes are fluid, such as Russia and the United

States, you can ever get people pinned back into the compartments of a stabilized hierarchy of classes? But there is so little insight here as to what people are like or how they live in the middle of the twentieth century that the picture of the future is virtually blank. The Christianity of Eliot itself is made neither impressive nor plausible—that is, it is not made real. What would it do for society? How could people be induced to accept it? In these pages it appears as a phantom that gives out neither heat nor light.

The Eliot family of New England has been prominent for generations in religion and education, and the truth is, I suppose, that Eliot's impulsion to establish himself in these fields as a responsible public figure is a piece of pure atavism. The fact that this particular Eliot happens to be a dramatic poet makes the exploit come out rather queerly, and his functioning in another environment—where the background for keeping up the classics is no longer the American wilderness and the church is the Church of England instead of the Congregational or the Unitarian—displaces the teacher and preacher to a social and political vacuum, in which, although he earnestly desires, like any other Eliot, to provide instruction and guidance, he does not have to deal with the immediate problems of a particular time and place.

But now, having spent so much time in trying to show that "Myra Buttle" on "Mr. Eliot" is not due entirely to the Philistinism, and possibly the embitterment, of the author of *Cadmus*, I must not leave the subject without making it clear that the high prestige of T. S. Eliot is not entirely due to the idiocy of the hungry sheep who look up and do not know that they are not being fed. I have been rereading Eliot's poetry in connection with this article, and it seems to me as good as it ever did. Not only is Eliot a master of "phrasing," as Clive Bell said years ago, not only is his workmanship as a poet perfection, but his verses have an emotional vibration, a curious life of their own, that seems almost to detach them from the author. Of no other poet, perhaps, does a bon mot of Cocteau's seem so true: The artist is a kind of prison from which the works of art escape. The verses of Eliot lodge in one's head without one's ever having learned them, and remain with one all through life. I do not, however, mean to imply that it is impossible for Eliot in person to make this vibration felt. On the contrary, in his public readings he is able to give his poetry all its value. The acting here goes into the poetry. My experience in hearing him has been that he is a good deal better on the platform than in any of the recordings he has done. He seems to need to feel his audience. I have heard him make of *Difficulties of a Statesman* a wonderful little dramatic soliloquy, bringing out all its changes of mood and pace, and working up to a climax of desperation. He can even produce this vibration through the medium of some essay on a poetic subject. I was present a few years ago when he read one of his later papers on Milton among the marble halls of the Frick Museum. I did not care in the least about his "message" that it would now not necessarily be harmful to make contact with the poetry of Milton; but he communicated so intense an excitement that I found myself later regretting, when I saw the essay in print, that he had dimmed this a little by dropping out some rather colloquial phrases more appropriate to the platform than the page. Yet this passage was simply a tribute to the masterly skill of Milton in manipulating great masses of words. It is the power to produce this vibration—which cannot be disregarded— that has made the author of *The Waste Land,* for all his funereal tone and the mummeries of "Mr. Eliot," one of the live nerves of modern literature.

It is only in the case of the *Four Quartets* that the lines of his verse—for this reader, at least—have not vibrated with quite the highest frequency. The best of Eliot's poetry, as he explains in one of his essays, is mostly of the "compulsive" kind; it imposes itself on the reader because it has imposed itself on the poet himself; but one feels in the *Four Quartets* that he is patiently spinning out verses which in some cases are close to prose. It is all too much a long muttering, with few flashes of vivid speech. The first of the quartets, *Burnt Norton,* seems to me the most successful. The passage about the Chinese jar (with its echo in *The Dry Salvages*) are among the best lines he has written:

> Words move, music moves
> Only in time; but that which is only living
> Can only die. Words, after speech, reach
> Into the silence. Only by the form, the pattern,
> Can words or music reach
> The stillness, as a Chinese jar still
> Moves perpetually in its stillness.
> Not the stillness of the violin, while the note lasts,
> Not that only . . .

The Dantesque movement in *Little Gidding,* which has been a good deal admired, is a fine imitation of Dante—Mr. Purcell might compare it with his own in *Cadmus*—but is it really very interesting Eliot? If, however, a certain amount of energy has gone out of Eliot's poetry, it seems to have been picked up by his theater. I have spoken disparagingly of *The Confidential Clerk,* but my theory has come to be that every other one of Eliot's plays turns out well. *Sweeney Agonistes* plus; *The Rock* very minus; *Murder in the Cathedral* plus; *The Family Reunion* minus; *The Cocktail Party* his highest point; *The Confidential Clerk* one of his lowest. At this rate, the next of Eliot's plays might well be a masterpiece. Its title has been announced: *The Elder Statesman*. A very promising subject!

May 24, 1958

1965. This play was a disappointment.

WORDS OF ILL-OMEN

ANYONE WHO HAS BEEN READING the more literate departments of the British and American press in the period since the last war must have been becoming aware, in the case of certain English words, of a recent change in usage which sometimes amounts to a change in meaning. I have been making a collection of such words and trying to discover the implications of the roles which they have lately been made to play, and I present here a list of conspicuous examples—some British, some American, some both—with the best that I can do in the way of explanation.

1. *Womanize, womanizer* (British). This word, as one learns from the Oxford English Dictionary, meant originally *to render effeminate* or *to become womanlike*. Later, however, it came to mean *to consort illicitly with women*. The first illustration of this latter meaning is quoted from the slang dictionary of Farmer and Henley of 1893; the next is from Compton Mackenzie's *Sinister Street* (1914): "The bad men [among Oxford students] went up to London and womanized"; and under *womanizer*, of which a similar definition is given, the only example is from Galsworthy's *The White Monkey* (1924): "Somehow . . . I feel he's a womanizer." But this word, in its twentieth-century sense, has lately become much more common. In *Six Proust Reconstructions*

403

by Pamela Hansford Johnson, we find, for example, ". . . she'd never be safe with an old womanizer like you"; and in Victor Purcell's epic poem *Cadmus* (1944), an amusing use is made of it, which makes one suspect that the word is coming to mean something more than *to consort illicitly with women:* that it implies a disparagement of the sex itself. Purcell makes François Villon confess that "we womanized, we cheated, and we stole"; and we have only to imagine how Villon would actually have described his activities to see the absurdity of this and how far away Villon is from the England in which *Cadmus* was written. Nor would the French lady in Miss Hansford Johnson's pastiche of Proust have used any word equivalent to *womanizer:* no such word exists in France. She would have said *'vieux satyre'* or *'vieux coureur'* or some other such more lively word. In English, the older words would have been *whoring* or *wenching* or *chambering* or *seducing,* all of which have different nuances, social or aesthetic or moral, and a *womanizer* would have been particularized as a *libertine,* a *rake,* a *Lothario,* a *Lovelace,* a *gallant* or a *ladies' man* (in America as a *Casanova,* a *heartbreaker,* a *great lover,* a *skirt-chaser* or a *swordsman*); but *womanize* seems to reduce all intimate intercourse with women to the same insipid-sounding level. Since *Cadmus,* this tendency has been carried farther, till one feels that, from the point of view of the contemporary British intelligentsia, not only would Byron have been a womanizer but also Tracy Tupman and Nathaniel Winkle in their flirtations with the ladies at Dingley Dell. The playing-down of the importance of women—in the role at least of charmers or idols—has been long, of course, an English trait. *Uxorious* is another English word which, I should think, does not have an equivalent, at least a common equivalent, in any other modern language: it is used always in a derogatory sense to refer to a husband who cares too much for or who spends too much time with his wife. And *womanizer* seems sometimes in England to have come to be used simply as a derogatory epithet for a man who likes women. The word has, in fact, become disgusting.

2. *Religionist* (American). The OED's definition of this is, "One addicted or attached to religion; one imbued with, or zealous for, religion. Sometimes in bad sense, a religious zealot or pretender." The examples here given show that through the seventeenth and eighteenth centuries in England religionists were contrasted with atheists. Webster's dictionary echoes the English definition and does not go beyond; yet lately in the United States *religionist* has taken on a new and definite meaning. When *religionists* are referred to in the current press, it is clear that this term includes anyone who is professionally occupied with religion, of whatever church, movement or status—that is, anyone from Billy Graham to Reinhold Niebuhr. This is, like *womanizer*, a word that destroys distinctions. Here again one has only to remember the words it is used to displace—*priest, minister, rabbi*, etc.; *churchman, divine, man of God, evangelist, religious teacher, parson, preacher; sky-pilot, hot-gospeller*—to see that it is now as generic as *businessman, farmer* or *artist*. The contrast with *atheist* is no longer implied. A religionist is merely someone who professionally works at religion as an industrialist works at industry. Religion is the religionist's "line."

3. *Massive*. This word has become one of the worst bores and nuisances of both British and American journalism, and what seems to have been its sudden and rapid emergence is a phenomenon which ought to be studied. It has no doubt been given special prestige by the declara-

tion of Mr. Dulles in his speech to the Council on Foreign Relations of 12 January, 1954, that "Local Defense must be reinforced by the further deterrent of massive retaliatory power," but the word had already begun circulating. It is now to be found everywhere, and one even has an uneasy feeling that it may announce the presence of radioactivity. In the course of a few weeks I have been able to pick up a whole pile of examples.

Let me establish the word first in its earlier sense by some quotations from *David Copperfield*: "an office that ought to have been on the ground floor of the Tower of Babel, it was so massively constructed . . . sundry immense manuscript Books of Evidence taken on affidavit, strongly bound and tied together in massive sets. . . . His gold watch-chain was so massive, that a fancy came across me, that he ought to have a sinewy golden arm, to draw it out with, like those which are put up over the gold-beaters' shops." These all apply to inert materials, but you have also a human massiveness not devoid of moral implication: "There was a fine massive gravity on his face, I did not venture to disturb." The definitions of the word in the OED mostly deal with this sort of mass, though there follow examples of *massive* applied to "immaterial things" (massive thought, massive character), to disease (massive gangrene, massive swellings), and to volume of sound (massive bass, massive chorus). Ruskin, it seems, spoke of clouds as "massive or striated," but added, "I cannot find a better word than massive, though it is not a good one, for I mean it only to signify a fleecy arrangement in which no lines are visible." Note Ruskin's apology for extending the meaning.

Now, the single use of *massive* among the recent examples I have gathered which comes under the first of the old definitions occurs in an article by S. J. Perelman in the *New Yorker*. He speaks of "a massive fireplace";

but this is probably to be explained by his penchant for writing parodies of various old-fashioned styles. Sir Harold Nicolson, in a review of Belloc's letters in the *Observer,* just manages to remain within the old definition when he writes of Belloc's "querulousness—so distressing in a massive, mighty man"; and T. S. Eliot, in his introduction to a volume of selections from Joyce, *Introducing James Joyce,* is also just within the old definition when he refers to *Finnegans Wake* as "that massive work." *Finnegans Wake* is not massive by reason of bulk —a novel by Dickens is much longer—but its density does perhaps make it massive. The *Times Literary Supplement* provides another example of *massive* applied to books: "All these biographies are monumental in a sense beyond the merely massive and the physically weighty"; and Pamela Hansford Johnson, in the book already mentioned, applies the word to style: "He informed her, in a style as steady and massive as Cicero's." But isn't Nicolson stretching it a little when he speaks, in a review in the New York *Times Book Review,* of "the fourth volume of Winston Churchill's massive *History of the English-Speaking Peoples*"; and, in the *Sunday Times,* of de Tocqueville's "massive studies of the *ancien régime* in France or the development of young America"? Maybe not: it is a matter of relative scale. But what adjective have you left for Gibbon? In a second use of *massive* in the Churchill review, this writer does, however, depart from the older uses of the word: the American Civil War, he says, was "a cosmic clash between strong men and massive principles." (I do not care for *cosmic* here either. I have always regarded this loose use of *cosmic* as a particularly undesirable Americanism.)

The tendency to make *massive* a substitute not merely for *enormous, immense* and *huge* but even for *large* and *extensive* as applying to all sorts of phenomena, social, financial, political and psychological, is illustrated by the following examples:

"It is easy and proper for the American Ambassador to Canada . . . and for Canadian economists to argue that massive American investment, at this stage, is essential to Canada's growth." (An article in *Harper's Magazine* on *Why Canadians Are Turning Anti-American*.)

"The Marxists claim, of course, that colonialism invariably represented a massive and cruel exploitation of the colonial peoples. . . . It is small wonder that it has all added up to a massive anti-Western complex." (George Kennan: *Russia, the Atom and the West*.)

"There was a massive creation, consumption, and disposal of goods." (Dan Jacobson in *Encounter*.)

Here are a number of examples—all from recent issues of the New York *Times*—that have been obviously inspired by Dulles: "A massive wave of Soviet, Chinese Communist and East European criticism has been directed at Yugoslavia. . . . Under Virginia's so-called 'massive resistance' laws, no Negro has been integrated in a public school. . . . While somewhat inconclusive, the first report of the United Nations observers in Lebanon failed to support the Lebanese Government's charges of massive intervention. . . . The United States Embassy here announced early today that 'a massive airlift' of petroleum products for Jordan would be started within the next few hours. . . . Dr. Malik replied a few days later that 'massive intervention' was continuing." . . .

You find also now a frequent use of the adverb: in the *Times Literary Supplement* editorial already quoted above, for example, "the realism of massively accumulated detail," and in a novel by John Wain, " 'I've had my breakfast,' I said, bringing his organizing power massively into play." In a notice of a volume of reporting pieces in the *Times Literary Supplement,* the anonymous reviewer writes, "individually, they are massively observant." In *Inside Russia Today,* John Gunther says of Marx that he "was massively influenced by several French thinkers." (*Vogue* referred to this volume as "a massive book.") In the *Letter from Paris* in the *New Yorker,* one finds, "This is a call for the saviour that has not been massively heard in the Paris streets."

"No one, certainly not Lord Altrincham, we feel, would decry the massive difficulties confronting the young woman who is called upon to combine the personal and institutional qualities demanded of the Monarch today." (Lord Altrincham and Others: *Is The Monarchy Perfect?*)

. . . "for several minutes the three of us waited with bowed heads . . . while he built up a massive edifice of bad language." (John Wain: *The Contenders.*) The use of *massive* here is possible under the old definition but provides another example of the fashionable addiction to the word.

"He could then argue that the Russians with their massive conventional forces and their interior lines cannot be contained without nuclear weapons." (Walter Lippmann.)

. . . "he felt that his work was misunderstood on a massive scale." (*Adventures of a Pacifist* in the *New Yorker.*) "In around a thousand pages, Max Lerner . . . has undertaken . . . a massive attempt to describe the main characteristics and currents of American life and thought." . . . . (A review in the *New Yorker.*)

"Instead of the weekly issue of *Punch* or the *New Yorker,* subscribers will receive a small phial (wrapped, of course, in massive quantities of advertising matter), with instructions on how and when to inject its contents, thereby giving rise to fits of healthy, invigorating laughter." (Malcolm Muggeridge in *Esquire.*)

Some of these phrases—John Gunther's, for example—seem to me inexact, even if the meaning of *massive* is extended. Russia might perhaps be said to have been massively influenced by Marx; can you say that Marx's thought was massively influenced by earlier thinkers? But even when the words are properly used in the more limited old-fashioned senses, they are certainly used far too often. *Massive* and *massively* occur only four times in the whole of *David Copperfield,* but in short articles like the Nicolson review and the *TLS* editorial, the writers have slipped into using them twice. Now, why has the word become so popular? It may be that the Marxist *masses,* in the sense of the working classes, has—in the last case above, for example—a little something to do with it. But what are undoubtedly most important, from the strictly material point of view, are the immense modern buildings and power plants, our machines for transportation and industry and war; and from the point of view of range or effect, our modern commercial enterprises and military operations. And there are also, of course, the great power units. Mr. Dulles's "further deterrent of massive retaliatory power" is also an inexact use of the word, but it is evident that Mr. Dulles was thinking both of the power of the United States and of the effect of the modern bomb. We are awed and yet stimulated by our awareness of size, weight, explosive force and expanding governmental domination, and these feelings have their expression in our use of *massive.*

4. *Superb* and *fabulous.* These words are, too, being terribly overworked and applied in inappropriate connections. Someone, for example, wrote somewhere of Bernard Baruch's "superb plan for atomic control." Now, *superbus* in Latin meant *proud,* and hence *magnificent, splendid.* Webster gives as its first meaning, "noble,

stately, lordly, majestic"; then "rich, elegant, sumptuous."
A statue may thus be superb; a palace may be superb; but
how can a proposal by Mr. Baruch be properly praised as
superb? Of course, Webster adds a third definition:
"supremely good of its kind." Does this cover the Baruch
plan? It seems to me that even in this more general use
anything described as *superb* ought to possess some special magnificence of a physical or moral or aesthetic kind.
But the word has come to be applied to almost anything
one thinks rather good. It is especially a reviewer's cliché.
For examples you have only to run your eye down the
columns and advertizements of any paper or department
devoted to books. In a non-literary context, a curious
example occurs in *Amid the Alien Corn: An Intrepid
Englishman in the Heart of America,* by Hugh Wil-
loughby. In a description of American football in a
Middle-Western college, he says that "lavatory paper
thrown high with an end loose makes a superb streamer."

This writer notes the American use of *fabulous* in the
sense, as he says, simply of *marvellous.* This is a similar
case of a word which has been robbed of its real implications. This indiscriminate use of *fabulous* has been probably brought on by such publishers' titles as *The Fabulous Clip Joint, The Fabulous Comedian, The Fabulous
Wilson Mizener.* I am told that in Hollywood the degrees
of excellence are *good, fabulous, fantastic.*

5. We come now to certain common words and
phrases that have acquired a peculiar force in the better
class of English weeklies: the *New Statesman,* the *Spectator,* the *Listener,* the *Sunday Times,* the *Observer,* etc.
The object of these little clichés is quietly to disparage.

One may mention here a mocking use of *massive,* of
which I have no example to hand. When Nicolson
applies *massive* to Churchill's history, he is making it look

more important than it is; but if H. R. Trevor-Roper, say, were to apply it to Arnold Toynbee's *A Study of History,* the intention would probably be to make the book look less important.

Unhappily, unluckily. These words are among the most damaging that a writer of this kind can employ. I have collected no examples, so improvise:

It is evident that Mr.——— has some first-hand acquaintance with the Balkans, and when he attempts nothing more than farce, he sometimes succeeds admirably; but he has also tried for pity and terror, for which, unhappily, he has little talent.

Mr.———, with an intrepidity which cannot but command respect, has sought to show that Lucrezia Borgia was by no means the monster we imagine, but "affectionate in her family relations" and "one of the most delightful women of her day." Unluckily, the evidence of contemporaries fails to support his thesis.

In America, we more often say *unfortunately,* which may on occasion be sharper, but is usually less patronizing.

Alas. Here are some actual examples of the British use of this word. From a review by John Raymond in the *New Statesman:* "The French, who are inclined to forget that he [Montaigne] was of English extraction, split him up mostly into '*l'homme*' and '*le philosophe.*' We non-Latins know that things cannot (alas!) be divided so easily." The exclamation point and parentheses here make this instance rather exceptional; the usual procedure is to enclose the word simply in commas, to slip it in in the most unobtrusive way, with no emphasis or change of accent to indicate a shaking of the head.

"She never ceased to speak of her employer with an admiration that, alas, was genuine." (A review by Raymond Mortimer of *The History of Fanny Burney* in the *Sunday Times*.)

This casual use of the word has also had some currency in the United States. Thus we find in a review by M. L. Rosenthal of the *Variorum Edition of the Poems of W. B. Yeats* in the *Nation*, "One can almost, alas, foresee the revolt of the young against the 'oppressive' idioms of his phrasing and rhythm" . . . But it seems to us somewhat affected and may even provoke resentment. I understand that, in response to the indignant complaint of a well-known American writer, the use of *alas* in letters of rejection has been banned in the *New Yorker* office. We occasionally, in the United States, put *alas* at the beginning of a sentence with perhaps an exclamation point, and thus give it emotional force. The first British instance quoted above does show a nuance of emotion, though we are not told exactly what prompts it. As a rule, the unemphasized British *alas* is the hallmark of modest smugness.

Contrive. Apart from its mechanical sense, this word has long been employed in a contemptuous or humorous one. Examples from *David Copperfield*: "Of Sophy telling us when she saw Traddles (whom I had entrusted with the license) asked for it, she almost fainted, having been convinced that he would contrive to lose it, or to have his pocket picked. . . . We had not sat here many minutes, when Mrs. Markleham, who usually contrived to be in a fuss about something, came bustling in."

But this use of *contrive*, in England, has recently become a good deal more common. An example from *Is the Monarchy Perfect?*: "At best, this kind of work-juggling contrives to create only a vague feeling, which is beyond logic and defies analysis." And it has been caught over by us. Mr. Harry Levin writes, in *Modern Language Notes* of 2 February, on a book about literary criticism, "Messrs. Wimsatt and Brooks avoid this dilemma by contriving another." That *contrive* should be so often substituted for *manage* or *arrange,* or used in cases where it would formerly have been natural to say *has succeeded in doing so-and-so* would seem to indicate that this quietly disparaging tone has in certain quarters become so habitual that its appropriateness to the subject is never questioned. All of these now fashionable words imply a certain unwillingness to take one's subject too seriously or to become too much excited about it. It may be that in the case of *contrive* our mechanical civilization has something to do with its common use. The false reasoning or whatever one wants to condemn is conceived as a cheap or amateurish device which does not function as a real machine.

Almost certainly, though it is not disparaging, belongs to the same level of British journalism and may also be listed here. This phrase—which is somewhat less common in America—is usually what Stephen Potter would call a gamesmanship ploy. It is used to bring pressure on the reader to induce him to accept the writer's view on a question which cannot be settled without some definite evidence but in regard to which such evidence is lacking. One may write, say, of the Casement diaries that they are "almost certainly genuine (or forged)."

The most amusing use of this phrase that I have seen gives it, however, a different force. Geoffrey Gorer in his book *The Marquis de Sade* writes of one of his subject's exploits with three prostitutes and his valet that Sade "was almost certainly exploring conscientiously and practically all possible extensions of sensual pleasure, from which he was to draw his theory and criticism some years

later. Both his physical and mental courage were adequate
to the task." Now, anyone who knows anything about
Sade can hardly be in any *uncertainty* as to what the
Marquis was up to. The purpose of the *almost certainly*
here—as well as of the British emphasis on the stamina
and pluck of Sade—has been evidently to create for this
scandalous affair an atmosphere of respectability.

6. *Committed, commitment. Committed* is the English
equivalent for Jean-Paul Sartre's *engagé,* as in the phrase
littérature engagée, and I believe, though I cannot be
sure, that the use of the word in this sense of someone's
being dedicated to, or interested in advancing, some political or social cause came later than *engagé* and was an
attempt to transfer the latter idea to English. Everybody
is so well aware of the currency and meaning of *committed* and *commitment*—which are common to the "intellectuals" of Britain and the United States—that one
need not give many examples. In the *New Statesman*
one finds an article by Walter Allen called *All Out
on Sunday: Commitment in the Thirties,* which
contains the following passage: "The literature of the
Thirties seems to me today to have been primarily social
in its implication rather than political. It was a socially
committed poetry." It may be noted that the writer says
further on: "it was the rise of Fascism that turned social
concern on the part of many young writers into direct
political involvement for some of them." This use of *involvement,* too, is new. *Involvement* differs from *commitment* in implying some active kind of responsibility.
What is shown, I believe, by the emergence of these
words with this special new significance is a general
despair of politics and indifference to social questions. To
devote oneself to a cause or even to try to further some
non-personal end has become so uncommon since the war

that we have found we need special words to refer to the exceptional people who do so.

7. *Communicate, communications.* These words are very interesting and important. They are, I believe, American products—certainly they have been hardest worked in the United States; but they seem to be spreading to England. I do not know how *communications* first came to be extended from the telegraph and telephone to the periodical press and the whole network of popular mechanical amusement—moving pictures, radio and television—nor how the fine arts came to be lumped in with these. There was a time when the *Saturday Review of Literature* talked constantly of "communications," which seemed to include everything from Homer to the latest be-bop record. To call everything "communications" was evidently intended to produce the effect of dignifying the dope purveyed on the movie screen, the radio and TV by pretending that it had been concocted by people who wanted to convey some message to their fellow men and at the same time, by including the fine arts in the same category with film and comic-strip, of making them appear less esoteric. At this time there were menacing complaints in the *Saturday Review* and elsewhere against certain modern poets and novelists on the ground that they did not "communicate," and so deserved to be banished from this category. A humorous echo of this is to be found in a letter to the editor of *Encounter:* "Either I have failed to communicate, or Mr. Braine read February's *Encounter* on a merry-go-round and then wrapped it round his fish and chips." And the idea that literature ought to be expected to "communicate" is involved in the following passage from an interview by Art Buchwald with Allen Ginsberg in the New York *Herald:* "Unfortunately," said Mr. Ginsberg, "another poet was reciting

some uncommunicative junk, and we didn't like it." This ideal of communication appears also in more serious connections. "It is no shame to the original writer," says Joyce Cary in *Art and Reality*, "that he wants to be read, to communicate." And Orson Welles in an article in the *Observer*: "If man cannot communicate, can he be expected to control his destiny?" A review by David Stevenson in the *Nation*: "Mr. Brooks finds that he can give us a clear and definite answer to this question, and thereby keep his novel within the limits of communication appropriate to his third report."

It seemed difficult, at first, to understand why so much should be made at that particular moment of the idea of communication. Certainly communications have never been so easy as now, and the things to be communicated do not seem to be of any more importance than usual. Was this recent use of the word really stimulated by a special sense of urgency?

One gets, however, more light on "communications" by approaching it from the practical non-literary direction. In the *Bulletin of Information* of Columbia University for 1957, we find listed two courses in "Communications." One of these is called "House publications and other employee communications." This course, says the *Bulletin*, "will deal with those communications media, both printed and spoken, that enable an employer, whether government, institution, or company, to seek among its employees a better understanding of its policies, products, services, and general operation. The media to be considered include house publications: magazines, tabloids, and newspapers; supervisory employee bulletins, manuals and annual reports; letters; advertising; motion pictures; exhibits; open house; and oral communications." The other course is called "Research in public opinion and communications." "The public opinion survey: research techniques, analysis of data. Research into mass communications media: newspapers, radio, magazines, movies. Content analysis and audience effect. Recommended for the students who plan a career in public relations, radio, or advertising." It would seem that "communications" is here simply a handy name for the various techniques of propaganda. In reply to a letter on the subject, Mr. Jacques Barzun of Columbia has written me as follows: " 'Communications' in the sense you describe is used throughout the academic world, high schools included. It covers different subjects in different places and sometimes (I think) it covers the void. The usage is faintly justified by two things—first, people's awareness that they do not understand one another, from which they infer the existence of a technique for reducing Babel; and second, the need to describe the new, electrical means of addressing large groups. At various times I have tried to prevent the use of 'communications' and, worse still, 'communications arts,' to designate courses in radio, television, and the rest. But it is a lost battle, at least until someone fashions a new word. Meantime, the confusion persists. Is *writing* included in communications? Are motion pictures a communication art? etc." It seems to me that the new blanket use of the word implies not merely a need that is felt on the part of people in general to understand one another and hence to coöperate, but also a drive on the part of the directors of political and business enterprises to manipulate large groups more effectively and, on the part of our ever more centralized governments, to bring the population into line. The two motives of course go together; they are aspects of the same process.

8. *Tension* and *relax*. These words are now much used in the United States; the implications are all too obvious. *Relax* is more colloquial than literary: people tell one

another to relax. *Tension* has been taken over by the literary magazines and given a special meaning: one talks about the 'tension' in a novel or poem, which means anything from a conflict between personal forces to an opposition of ideas, usually referred to in terms of "symbols." Example: "His first [novel] . . . was a report on the tensions and conflicts of personality on the staff of a weekly news magazine." (From the *Nation* review quoted above.) The word has come also to play a great role in sociological and psychological literature.

9. *Kudos*. Something very peculiar has been happening to this word in the United States. *Kudos* is a Greek word (singular), which means "glory, fame, renown." It must owe its currency in English to the British public schools and universities, with their tradition of classical learning. But it is now turning up in the American press as an English plural, ending in s, the singular being presumably *kudo*. Granville Hicks, for example, in the *Saturday Review*, says "Cheever has been writing excellent short stories for twenty years or more with comparatively few kudos" . . . Now, *Time* magazine has lately had the habit of listing, every June, the recipients of academic honors under the simple rubric "Kudos," and one wonders whether this has been misunderstood as a plural meaning public honors—perhaps on a false analogy with *kilos* or with Ernest Hemingway's *kudus*. In any case, the first missteps have been made, and *kudos* may take its place—along with the stubborn false meanings of *jejune, demean* and *transpire* and the false derivation of *sacrilegious*—as a plural applied to honorary degrees, Oscars, prizes in beauty contests and the rewards for winning the 21 Quiz contest.

September 6 and 13, 1958

DOCTOR LIFE AND HIS
GUARDIAN ANGEL

IN DEALING WITH *Doctor Zhivago*, the novel by Boris
Pasternak, the reviewer—not to end on a dampening
note—proposes to reverse the usual procedure and discuss
the translation first. This translation was made in England by Max Hayward and Manya Harari (though the
poems which compose the last chapter are translated by
Bernard Guilbert Guerney); the copyright page of the
American edition shows that it was revised over here; and
a lack of coördination between these several hands may
be part of the explanation of the unsatisfactoriness of this
English version. But, comparing it with the Russian text,
one gets the impression that a project which, if properly
carried out, might well have taken many months has been
put through in too much of a hurry and without the
translators' having beforehand sufficiently studied the
book.

This is said with full recognition that the problems of
translating Pasternak are exceptional and must be peculiarly daunting. This writer has an enormous range of
idiom—he makes all kinds of people talk, each in the
language of his milieu and time—and an immense literary vocabulary. He is also an extremely idiosyncratic
writer, a "difficult" modern poet who has taken to prose, in
which medium, despite his eloquence, his brilliance and
the exactitude of his observation, he is somewhat less at

home than with verse. There are passages of subjective impressionism in the early part of the book, where the characters are children or adolescents, which present the translator with difficulties of a somewhat similar kind to those which would be encountered in translating, say, Virginia Woolf.

There is also always the difficulty that—since the syntax of the language is so different from ours—the translator from Russian, if he wants to be read smoothly, must always do a good deal of paraphrasing. He must give himself a free hand to improvise a kind of equivalent, and Pasternak is one of the writers who must tax the translator to the point of torture. It is a feature of Pasternak's poetry that he likes to begin his stanzas with a predicate and not arrive at the subject till the final line, and this method may become rather clumsy when employed in a sentence of prose, especially if the subject at the end is preceded by a long parade of modifiers. This preliminary procession of modifiers, is a peculiarity of Russian style that it seems to me Pasternak abuses. Turgenev and Chekhov avoided it, but Tolstoy defiantly overdid it,* and Pasternak—who in various ways shows traces of Tolstoy's influence—lays it on in a remorseless way. It is nerve-racking to the foreign reader—and somewhat annoying, I learn, even for Russians—to find piled up in front of a substantive a variety of carefully chosen adjectives and of long participles that whistle and hiss, or bump like old-fashioned trunks, and that are sometimes submodifiers of one another, all of which the reader must hold in mind without knowing what they are being applied to till he comes to the noun at the end. When he does finally reach this word, he may have to reread the

---

* I have found that Turgenev complains of this, in connection with some of Tolstoy's earliest writings, as an instance of his natural clumsiness.

sentence backwards. For the translator, this phenomenon must be even more exasperating. He is obliged to sort out these modifiers, put some of them *after* the noun and assign some of the participles to relative clauses. Constance Garnett, in translating Tolstoy, when she found too many of these on her hands, recklessly adopted the method of simply leaving some of them out. The English translators of *Doctor Zhivago* have resorted to the same practice, but have treated their text even more casually.

To cite a relatively mild example: one passage, if the order of the words were followed, would read in translation, "The sun's rays, reflected from the golden cupolas of the Church of the Savior, fell on the paved with four-cornered cut stones, in the cracks grown with grass, square." The translators give us: "Sunshine glancing off the golden domes of the Church of the Savior played on the square below where grass was growing in the cracks between the paving stones." Very well: this sounds natural enough. Let the squareness of the paving stones go; if the translators had tried to fit it in, they would have found themselves embarrassed with a repetition of "square" in two different senses. But a couple of paragraphs further on, we find them making it, "They applied for premises and obtained the use of some shoestore or flower shop, which had been empty and closed down since the first days of the Revolution, and there they sold out their small haphazard collections." (The presence of "store" and "shop" side by side in one sentence would seem to show a lack of harmony between the American and the British hands.) What Pasternak wrote was: "They would apply for premises of this kind. They would obtain the use of some warehouse for shoes which had been empty since the first days of the Revolution or the greenhouse of some florist whose business had been closed down, and under their wide vaults they would sell their meager and haphazard collections of books." Why make shops of the warehouse and the greenhouse, and why leave out the incongruity of the wide vaults? In many other passages of this translation the omissions are far more serious. Of the heroine on a hot spring morning, in a moment of depression and letdown at the time of her first love affair, Pasternak writes, "From the grassy smell and the young greenery her head ached, as at Shrovetide from the vodka and the frying of pancakes." All we get of this in the English translation is "The grassy smell of earth and young leaves made one drowsy as on the morning after a Shrovetide feast." Being drowsy is quite different from a headache, and the vodka and pancakes of Shrovetide are especially important because they turn up again later in the section called *Varykino* and are connected with Pasternak's all-pervading theme of death and resurrection.

The translators also, in some cases, carelessly obliterate metaphors that could perfectly well have been preserved. One of the sections, which describes a winter day, begins with a terse two-word sentence that means something like "The weather was struggling to recuperate." This expression is not, I think, an invention of the author's, but it is more interesting than "The weather was unseasonable," which, besides, conveys a wrong idea. A similar crisp two-word statement about the playing of a work by Chaikovsky, "The trio began to sob," is rendered as "The music rose plaintively." The intent observation of Pasternak is constantly sacrificed. The rich soil "which shows brown in the sun with varying shades of chocolate and coffee" is turned into "the black soil . . . shimmered with rich golden browns," which gives a different picture. It is one of the characteristics of Pasternak's style that, somewhat as in the case of Proust, a regard for realistic accuracy often pushes him, at his most poetic, to images and details that surprise one by their departure from elegant convention; but the translators are sufficiently insensitive to drop many of these touches out or to substitute for them something banal—as when in the case of the description of the nightingale's song in the Varykino chapter, in which the surrounding vegetation is said to "shake the dew off and preen itself, quivering as if it were being tickled," all we get of this is "trembled with delight." And why should "Again the day passed with an insane slowness," an unconventional phrase in Russian, be rendered "Another day went by like a dream?" Further evidences of haste are inaccuracies of a rudimentary kind. "The gold balls on fire towers" become "The golden tops of belfries," and when the author tells us of one of his characters that "he rounded out his historical-philological education by studying mathematics by himself," this is rendered as "after taking his degree in the humanities [he] trained himself in science and mathematics," which is inept as well as incorrect. In a discussion of Pushkin's poetry, the translators mistake a mention of the Arzamas Literary Society, to which Pushkin belonged in St. Petersburg, for a reference to some imaginary residence in the town after which the society was named—a mistake that could have been averted by consulting any life of Pushkin or any history of Russian literature. On page 25 of the English version, the heroine is correctly described as having "fair hair," but on page 46, with no justification whatever in the Russian, we are told that her hair was "dark." Кузнечики are not crickets but grasshoppers or locusts, etc.

These criticisms may be boring, but since no one else has yet made them, they ought to be put on record. The reader of the Pantheon translation should be told that *Doctor Zhivago* is a richer, a solider, a subtler and a much more intense work than he will be able to find out from this version of it. So much of the detail has been scrapped, so many of the descriptions have been dismantled, and so many of the conversations have been telescoped that there are moments when one could almost imagine that the translators have been doing a job for the *Reader's Digest*. That abridgment is not inevitable, that the difficulties of the text are not insurmountable, is shown by the Italian translation, which cuts very few corners and quite faithfully follows the text.

All this is not said, however, to discourage you from reading the novel, which is one of the very great books of our time. Tolstoy and Turgenev first made their impression in translations that were sometimes far less competent than that of Harari and Hayward. The good thing that can be said for this version is that it reads well, it does not sound translated. And it is the triumph, in any case, of the literary genius of the Russians, master storytellers, master moralists, that they have been able to leave their language and a good deal of their style behind, to submit to be stripped of so much, and yet to hold the world spellbound.

Doctor Zhivago has no doubt been much read—like other books that promise to throw some light on the lives of our opposite numbers in the Soviet Union—out of simple curiosity. But it is not really a book about Russia in the sense that the newspaper accounts of it might lead the reader to expect; it is a book about human life, and its main theme is death and resurrection.

Dr. Zhivago is the hero of the story, and though Zhivago is a real Russian name—there was a nineteenth-century painter called Zhivago—it is obvious that Pasternak wants to suggest живой, *alive, living* (to one form of which it almost corresponds), as well as жизнь, *life,* and жить, *to live.* These words are constantly used by Zhivago in his arguments against the deadness of political abstractions and the tyranny of government control. One is reminded, in reading *Zhivago*, of Yeats's constant insistence on the importance in literature of "the crooked way of life" as distinguished from "inorganic, logical straightness." One may not at first notice this dominant theme, though it is first announced on page 9 (of the translation) and repeated on page 67. One is likely to be so much surprised at finding a book from the Soviet Union which pays no deference to the official ideology, which has been written completely outside it on assumptions that have nothing in common with Marxism, that one does not at first quite know where one is. Then one realizes that where one is with Pasternak is exactly where one is oneself, at home in the great literary tradition of bold thinking and original art.

Pasternak is as much an example of the intellectual man of the world as Pushkin or Turgenev or Tolstoy, yet he is saturated with Russian life and language in a way that makes most Soviet writing look like diagrams drawn up in offices. His father was a painter, his mother a musician; he studied philosophy in Germany, and he evidently, like Zhivago, before the first war, lived a good deal in Eastern Europe. At the time of the Revolution, he was twenty-seven—that is, his mind was already formed. That this mind should have continued to function for forty years in the Soviet Union, judging the events in Russia and continuing to think in terms of the whole sweep of human history, is likely to seem as astonishing as that the mammoths preserved in Siberian ice should still have their flesh intact. We find that we are reading a contemporary and peer of Faulkner, Malraux and Auden, and we are so eager to see how such a mind will deal with the Bolshevik seizure of power, the dictatorship of the proletariat, the Civil Wars, the Soviet state after Lenin's

death, the purges, and the war against Germany that we
may not notice at first that his interest in such matters is,
in a sense, incidental. For though he touches on all these
events and though his comment on them is breathtak-
ingly explicit, and as enlightening as it is unexpected,
there is developed throughout the novel, consistently and
step by step, a point of view that is universal, that does
not cater to Soviet officialdom or even to Russian patriotism and from which war and revolution are seen as
striking local occurrences that have made Russia loom
larger to the rest of the world as well as to the Russians
themselves but that must be taken in a wider perspective
as the transient phenomena they are. It will be well, then,
before coming to the story itself, to try to give some
account of Pasternak's general view as it is gradually built
up for the reader in conversations between Zhivago and
the other characters.

It ought to be explained at the outset that Pasternak—
though his parents were Jewish—seems to have been
drawn to the Greek Orthodox Church, that the ritual and
the doctrine of the Church have come to represent for
him the fundamental moral realities. Yet his religious
position is peculiar. It is as if his Jewish authority had
somehow made it possible for him to reinvent Christianity—which, to this non-religious reviewer, is made here
to seem a good deal more impressive than in the works of
the literary converts: a force of regeneration that has
given Pasternak the faith to survive and the courage to
write this book. Since it is usually Zhivago or his uncle,
whose line of thought the nephew is supposed to be following, who develops this point of view, I shall not, I
think, be misrepresenting it if I summarize it by putting
together the utterances of several characters at different
ages and in various circumstances.

It is possible, then, we are told at the beginning, "to be

an atheist, not to know whether God exists or why there should be one," and yet to believe that Jesus has brought to man the supreme revelation. By displacing the moral emphasis from the society, from the nation, from the people in the sense of the *populus Romanus* to the individual soul, to "the idea of the free personality and the idea of life as a sacrifice," he for the first time rescued man from the matrix of nature and inaugurated a society that was truly human. It has been the great mistake of the Jews—it is a Jewish character who makes this point— not to recognize this revelation, which has been their own chief gift to humanity. The doctrine of the salvation of the individual disregards, supersedes nationalities, yet the Jews, with all their social idealism, have remained professional nationalists and have paid for this with unnecessary suffering.

But Jesus also brought immortality. One must be "faithful to immortality, which is another word for life, a somewhat intensified word." The resurrection of all humanity in another world is unthinkable and ridiculous. We should be animals still craving our animal life, and our removal from the continuum of the universe would leave it and God without meaning. But life, which pervades the universe, does incessantly renew itself in its innumerable different forms. Our birth is a resurrection, and we shall rise again in our children as well as in our work.

The approach to human problems of the official Soviet philosophy has been based on a crude misconception. It has always talked about "remaking life," but "people who can talk in this way—even though they may have seen a good deal of the world—have never known life at all, have never felt its spirit, its soul. For them, human existence is a lump of raw material which has not been ennobled by their touch, which has never been worked

over by them. But life is not a material, it is not a substantial thing. It is something that eternally renews itself,
a principle that is always taking different shapes; it is
always remaking and recreating itself; it is away out of
reach of our stupid theories." The Communists are always
thinking in terms of "building new worlds, transition
periods. . . . That is all they have been taught, and it is
all they understand. And do you know why they make all
this fuss about these eternal preparations? From sheer
lack of any definite competence, from the absence of real
ability. Man is born to live and not to prepare to live.
And life itself, the phenomenon of life, the gift of life is
such an absorbing and serious matter! So why try to substitute for it this childish harlequinade of immature
fantasies," such escapades as that of the schoolboys in
Chekhov's story, who decide to run away to America but
who never get farther than the nearest Russian town.
(The translators have omitted this amusing reference.)

As for Marxism: when a provincial lawyer who professes the official creed while continuing to carry on his
bourgeois business tells Zhivago that Marxism is "a positive science, the study of reality, the theory of historical
conditions," the doctor answers, "Marxism a science? To
argue that with someone one hardly knows is of course
rather imprudent—but never mind about that. Marxism
is too little in control of itself to be considered a science.
The sciences are better equilibrated. Marxism and objectivity? I don't know of any movement more completely
shut in upon itself and remoter from the facts than
Marxism. Everybody is preoccupied with proving himself
in practice, and the people who are in power are compelled by the fable of their infallibility to exert their
utmost efforts to keep their eyes averted from the truth.
Politics mean nothing to me. I cannot care for people who
are indifferent to truth." The whole attempt on the part

of Marxism to see everything in terms of classes, to force
people into social camps and to align them against one
another—Reds against Whites, peasants and workers, on
the one hand, against nobility and bourgeoisie, on the
other—is contrary to the real character of human nature.
It disregards the fundamental Christian truth: that the
vital unit is the individual. The very self-discipline, to
some degree heroic, which has transformed the railroad
worker's young son into an uncompromising commissar
imposes a false mold which in the long run would prove
fatal. The thing that redeems him as a human being is
that he cannot quite submit to this mold. When Zhivago
confronts him, the Doctor discovers that this young man
is not quite what his formidable reputation has led
Zhivago to expect to meet. "It is a good thing," Zhivago
says, "when a man fails to live up to your expectation,
when he is different from your previously conceived idea.
To run true to type is the extinction of a man, his condemnation to death. If he cannot be assigned to a category, if he is not a model of something, a half of what is
needed is there. He is still free from himself, he has
acquired an atom of immortality."

But now let us proceed to the story itself to see how
this immortality is realized.

The first chapters—except for the poetic impressionism—sound rather like Dos Passos's *Manhattan Transfer*.
You are quickly switched from one to another of several
groups of characters: a little boy attends his mother's
funeral and spends the night with his uncle in a monastery; a little Jewish boy, travelling with his lawyer father,
sees a man throw himself out of the train; a little girl
comes to Moscow with her French mother, a widow in
reduced circumstances, who takes over a dressmaking
business; a railroad workers' strike on the eve of the 1905

revolution; a big Christmas-tree celebration in a well-to-do
Moscow home. All these characters are interconnected,
but one does not at first get the hang of them. In childhood and adolescence, we do not yet know whom we see,
where we stand in relation to one another; we are simply
a lot of young people together. But the pattern of the
narrative soon changes with the coming of the First
World War. Young Yury Andreyevich studies medicine
and becomes Dr. Zhivago; he marries the daughter of a
chemistry professor whose grandfather was an industrialist and landowner. Larisa, the daughter of the impoverished Frenchwoman, marries the studious son of a railroad worker who has been exiled for his political activities. The narrative now concentrates on Zhivago and
Larisa; they emerge as the hero and heroine. Though
married to others, they are separated from their families
and thrown together at intervals by the vicissitudes of the
war and the Revolution, and their intermittent, inescapable and mutually inspiring love affair provides the
vitalizing central charge that makes them resistant to
pressures and clairvoyant in the midst of confusion.
When the great social crisis comes, the background of
their cultivated bourgeois world melts away, with many
of its figures; other figures fall into place in the drama of
the Civil Wars and the establishment of the new society;
but Yury Andreyevich and Larisa Fyodorovna are both at
once too much individualists, too much naturally immune
to the materialistic doctrine and too much products of the
old education—and Larisa is not even a Russian—to
accept the Communist creed and that method of dealing
with human problems which it suggests to uneducated
men recently risen to power.

It should be noted in this connection that one of the
most startling features of the book is Pasternak's abstention—in spite of the sympathy with which he presents

them—from any idealization, of either Tolstoy's or
Lenin's kind, of the peasantry, "the toiling masses." Not
that the bourgeoisie is flattered. Nobody is flattered, nor is
anyone condemned on the basis of office or class. There
are no caricatures and no glorifications. The author never
departs from his Christian ideal of taking every individual seriously as a soul which must be respected.
Komarovsky, the shady lawyer, who stands for the worst
of the old bourgeoisie, who has been more or less responsible for the suicide of Zhivago's reckless father (the man
who threw himself from the train), who sets up Larisa's
mother in business and then seduces the daughter, is
shown struggling against a real love for Larisa. And Pasha,
the railroad worker's son, whom Larisa afterwards marries,
is first made to seem sympathetic by reason of his diligence
and ambition; then arrogant and unpleasant when, having
taken the name of Strelnikov (which suggests shooting
people), he appears as the formidable commissar the very
mention of whose name creates terror, and baits Zhivago
in a menacing way as a potential counter-revolutionary;
then made a pathetic figure when the Party authorities
are after him and he takes refuge in the same house as
Zhivago.

There is a wonderful scene here: "They had been
talking a long time, for hours, as only Russians in Russia
talk, as talked particularly the frightened and anxious, the
frantic and raving people that all Russians were at that
time. . . . He was unable to stop talking, he held on as
tightly as he could—in order not to be alone—to his conversation with the Doctor. Was he afraid of the gnawing
of conscience or of his load of depressing memories, or
was he burdened by the self-dissatisfaction in which a
man becomes unbearable and hateful to himself and
ready to die of shame. . . . This was the malady of the
age, the revolutionary madness of the period. What really

went on in their minds was quite different from their words and their outward appearance. The conscience of no one was clean. Everyone had good grounds for feeling that he was as guilty as possible, a secret criminal, an unmasked impostor. As soon as any pretext presented itself, there would burst forth and rush to extravagant lengths a debauch of self-torturing imagination. People would run on into fantasies, they would falsely denounce themselves, not merely from the working of fear but as the result of a morbid destructive impulse, deliberately, in a state of metaphysical trance and that passion for self-condemnation which cannot be stemmed when once it has been given way to."

The commissar, now under suspicion, has hoped to clear himself of the charges against him, but he knows from his own methods with others that he will not be given a chance to defend himself. The interesting point is made that he has elicited so many confessions of counter-revolutionary guilt that he is tempted by the guilt of his own inhuman acts to make a "self-unmasking" confession not of these but of political offenses which he has actually not committed. He shoots himself in the morning, but not before, in the talk of the previous night, he has poured out—it is the first time in the novel that we have had a full statement of this—the whole apologia for his generation. This passage is too long to quote, but in its insight into the sources of the Communist faith of the early days of the Revolution, it is as important as the negative passages of Pasternak's political commentary which are currently being printed in the press, out of context and in a way that is quite misleading. Doctor Zhivago, Pasha-Strelnikov begins by telling him, cannot understand his point of view: he has grown up in a different world from the one that Pasha came out of; and Pasha describes this world of overcrowding and dirt and privation, and the animus it gave the young people, who had always been aware of the indifference to them of the rich in the smart streets, to turn the social world upside down. Marxism has shown them "the root of the evil and where to find the remedy for it." This resentment had been seething all over Europe through the whole of the nineteenth century, and the great revolutionary movement—with "its pitiless instruments devised in the name of pity"—had found its full expression in Lenin, with the result that "the immense figure of Russia, impossible to disregard," had "suddenly risen before the eyes of the world, blazing up like a candle of redemption for all the slackness and the misfortunes of humanity."

Pasha has been wrecked as a human being by his attempt to play a Marxist role. Zhivago and Larisa, who do not attempt roles, will outlive him, but they, too, are to be destroyed. Life in Moscow becomes so difficult in the days after the Revolution that Yury Andreyevich decides to get as far away as possible, to take his family to the Ural Mountains, where his father-in-law had had an estate and where he hopes to find some peace of mind. But the East, he finds, is even more disrupted and dangerous. He is kidnapped and pressed into service by a band of wandering partisans who are fighting the White leader Kolchak in Siberia. He has come upon Larisa again in the nearby town of Yuratin, in which, before Pasha's enlistment, she had been living with him and teaching school. She had married her young proletarian out of a kind of feeling of duty that she ought, on account of her own disadvantages, to identify her interests with his, yet her natural "affinity," her deep understanding, is all with Yury Andreyevich. Pasha had already become aware that Larisa could not really love him—"he was jealous of her very thoughts, of the mug from which she drank, of the pillow on which she lay"—and he goes away to the war to prove himself to himself, to impress her, to compete with what she represents (and this in spite of the fact that his original revolutionary impulse has been spurred by his desire to protect her, a finer nature than his, from the indignity of her early helplessness). Missing in action and supposed to be dead, he has escaped from his German captors and recreated himself as "Strelnikov"—also, as Larisa knows, partly to build up something so strong that she cannot refuse to admire it. But he has never—for all his impressive exterior—succeeded in getting his inner morale to the point where he dares to come back to her. And in the meantime, Yury Andreyevich, escaped from the partisan band, *has* returned to Larisa. His wife, as the result of his disappearance, has made her way back to Moscow and so to Paris. He had already been having a love affair with Larisa, and he now begins living with her in Yuratin. But they both now come under suspicion, she as "Strelnikov's" wife, he on account of his original thinking. While working in a local hospital, he lectures on evolution, and his views about the adaptation of organisms to environment are not sufficiently mechanical for the provincial Marxists. Though he is valued as a diagnostician, he finds that when he talks about intuition, they begin to shy away from him: they are afraid of a heresy, a trap. He and Larisa do not have "the right attitude." A counter-revolutionary group with a hidden store of arms is discovered at this point in Yuratin, and they know that they may be pounced upon at any moment. They get away to the place in the country—the estate of his wife's father—in which Yury Andreyevich has lived with his family.

This episode of their life in the country—the last desperate phase of their love—is unlike anything else in fiction: full of the tension of anguish and terror, yet also of nobility and exaltation. It is winter; the house is freezing. Zhivago has to keep the stove going; Larisa has to clean up the rooms. Larisa's little daughter is with them. Her mother tries to give her lessons, and sometimes, when she is out with her sled, the lovers' hands happen to touch, and they drop their time-consuming housework for interludes of passionate tenderness. (The translators have weakened the force of this passage by omitting "the minutes ran into hours" and by changing its whole rhythm.) They know that it is only a question of time before the police will find them. Yet Zhivago, when Larisa has gone to bed, returns to his early poetry, and in the course of these nocturnal sessions, his creative activity renews itself. "After two or three stanzas that came pouring and several metaphors by which he was himself surprised, the work took possession of him, and he began to feel the presence of what is called inspiration. The correlation of the forces that govern artistic genius had as it were been turned upside down. It is no longer the man and the state of his soul, for which he is seeking expression, that are in the ascendancy now, but the language with which he seeks to express it. This language, which is the place of origin and the repository of beauty and meaning, itself begins to think and to speak for the man and is completely transformed into music, not in terms of outward audible sonorities but in terms of the impetuosity and the power of its inward current. Now, like the great rolling mass of the torrent of a river, by its own movement turning as if on a lathe the stones that lie on its bed and revolving the wheels of mills, the onrushing speech itself, by force of its own laws, molds in its course, in passing, the music and the rhythm of the poem, and a thousand other forms and configurations which are even more important than these but which have not yet been recognized or taken into consideration, which have not as yet even been given names. At such moments, Yury

Andreyevich felt that the main work was not done by him but somehow somewhere above him, that it had found him and taken control of him—the poetry and thought of the world in its present phase and that which is coming, that which is following in orderly progression, the next step which has become inevitable in poetry's historical development. And he felt himself only the occasion, the *point d'appui,* for it to get itself into movement." He looks at the girl and Larisa asleep side by side in their bed. "The cleanness of the linen, the cleanness of the rooms [the achievement of the *women's* work], the purity of their features, fusing with the purity of the night, the snow and the stars" make him "exult and weep with a feeling of the triumphant purity of existence." Then, at three o'clock, he is torn from his concentration by a plaintive and dismal sound. He sees far off, over the wild waste of snow, four shadows that make little marks on it. Starved wolves have smelled the horse in the stable.

This chapter, at the end of which Zhivago is to lose Larisa, is the emotional climax of this extraordinary book, in which everyone is degraded or ruined or crushed but in which the positive values—Christianity and love and art—are presented with such overwhelming power that the barbarities against which they must assert themselves seem lacking in long-range importance. But Komarovsky, the indestructible rascal who has been both Larisa's and her mother's lover, and whom Larisa has once tried to shoot, eventually turns up in Yuratin, and Zhivago—to save Larisa's life—allows him to take her to the Far East. To induce her to go, he has promised her to follow, but when she has left, he makes his furtive and difficult way—mostly on foot—back to Moscow, where it is possible for him only to a limited extent to pick up his former life. His old friends have managed to adapt themselves. One of them has been arrested, imprisoned and exiled for his unorthodox opinions, and he sickens Yury Andreyevich by telling him how much good has been done him by a brainwashing at the hands of the examining magistrate. Zhivago has lost first his family, then Larisa; though he continues to practice medicine, he has no chance for a real career, and though he publishes, in a semi-private way, a few papers on historical and scientific subjects, and though these papers make a certain impression, his work cannot be freely accepted. He marries the daughter of his former servant.

It is impossible, however, to summarize, in an article such as this, what happens in *Doctor Zhivago*, and any attempt at a thorough analysis would be likely to reach almost the proportions of the studies devoted to Joyce. The story itself is so long and complex—it covers so much ground—that a mere recapitulation would be impossible within the scope of a review, and one finds, threaded in and out of the story, a phase-by-phase chronicle of Soviet policy, and a discussion of the development of Russian literature which touches on almost all its great figures from Pushkin to the school of modern poetry which is represented by Pasternak himself. There is also involved in the story an historical-political fable—see Larisa's relations with Zhivago, Komarovsky and Pasha—of the kind that since the time of Turgenev has been traditional in Russian fiction, as well as (what for Pasternak is far more important) a kind of religious parable. The reader will not at first notice this, though it constitutes the core of the novel. The incidents succeed one another with so much invention and vivacity, with such range of characterization and description, each submerges us so completely in the atmosphere of its moment of Russian life, we are carried along so absorbedly by the vodka parties, the unexpected encounters, the journeyings (the chaotic interminable train-trip of Zhivago and his family to the Urals that occupies a whole long chapter), the campaigns (the adventures of the partisans in the forest is a whole story in itself), the conversations (the nocturnal talks, both comic and desolating, between Zhivago, bored, irritated and sleepy, and the fervent young partisan leader, who shoots his men for distilling vodka but has discovered the virtues of cocaine as an ideological stimulus and is depleting the Doctor's medical store and keeping him awake at night with his hopped-up pep talks), and the intensely personal love affairs, at once so exciting and so dolorous, that are always being broken up by public events—we have so much the illusion of following life that we only come gradually to realize the poetic significance of these happenings. For if Gogol's *Dead Souls* is, as he called it, a "poem," *Doctor Zhivago* is also a poem. Though we may think, when we begin it, that we are entering again the familiar world of social fiction—the "group" novel of intertwined strands, such as Sartre's Existentialist series, *Les Chemins de la Liberté,* which has now been bogged down for so long, simply, it would seem, for the reason that Sartre has changed his political line, or Leonov's *Road to the Ocean,* in which a real Russian talent falsifies and nullifies itself by submitting to a Soviet formula—we presently become aware that *Doctor Zhivago* is more like an epic than even *War and Peace,* that the landscapes, the personalities, the tragic outbursts, the comic anecdotes (usually as much horrible as comic) are poetic in their relief and their meaning. This book, in which everything seems real, is not at all "realistic." It exhibits, in fact—as a whole as well as in individual episodes—in spite of its immediacy of detail, of all the costumes and accents and jargon and paraphernalia and living conditions of twentieth-century Russia, something of the technique and the spirit of the *skazka,* the Russian folk tale. The narrative is full of coincidences, each of which is in itself quite plausible but the repeated occurrence of which might shake our "suspension of disbelief" if we were not so much under the spell of what is really a legend, a fable. We are no more surprised or put out by the fact that the characters of *Doctor Zhivago* are always meeting one another again in different guises and changed states of mind than we are in a fairy tale when the wretched old crone whom the youngest of three brothers has been the first to treat with courtesy turns out to be a powerful spirit who can determine success or failure.

The most *skazka*-like element in the story is Zhivago's half-brother Evgraf, who is really a supernatural figure. Evgraf is introduced so unobtrusively that we do not at first pay attention to him, and we have to go back later to look him up. Zhivago's unreliable father has left his wife for a princess with the hybrid name of Stolbunova-Enrici, by whom he has had a son. The half-celestial personality of the son is evidently adumbrated when we are told that the mother is a «мечтательница и сумасбродка», "a dreamer and rather mad (or erratic)." Yury Andreyevich's mother is characterized with similar brevity as «мягкая мечтательница», "gentle, a dreamer." (The translator has muffed this significant repetition by combining the two epithets of the first of these descriptions into the single blank word "eccentric.") The Princess and her illegitimate son live far away, on the outskirts of Omsk, in Siberia. The Princess never goes out, and nobody knows what they live on. Yury Andreyevich has seen a photograph of their house, with five plate-glass windows and stucco medallions, and has felt that it was staring at him in a hostile way across all the thousands of versts and that sooner or later its glance will be fatal. Partly out of fear of this, partly out of contempt for litigation, he refuses to contest the claims to his father's estate of this princess and another of his father's mistresses, and he is rewarded for his renunciation by the strange intervention in his favor at critical times in his life of his mysterious half-brother from the East. At the time of the victory of the workers in the fighting of the October days and the transfer of power to the Soviets, the Doctor walks out at night in the midst of a heavy snowstorm and buys a paper which carries the news. In order to get light to read it, he goes into the entrance hall of an unknown building. An eighteen-year-old boy comes downstairs in a Siberian fur coat and fur cap. He has narrow Kirghizan eyes but something aristocratic in his face—"the shy ray, the hidden delicacy, which is sometimes found in persons of mixed and complicated stock and which seems to have been brought from afar." Zhivago does not know that it is his half-brother Evgraf, but the apparition afterwards haunts him. This is the moment of his most wholehearted enthusiasm for the success of the Revolution. He feels that there is something characteristic of Russia in the drastic directness, the rude courage, of the sweeping away of the old order—"something of the uncompromising clarity of Pushkin, of the unevasive fidelity to facts of Tolstoy." One imagines at this point that Evgraf is meant to represent something sound, at once popular and noble, in Russia, and as the story goes on one suspects that he may even be intended to embody the old conception of "Holy Russia." One becomes more and more aware that Pasternak's book is studded with the symbolism of the Orthodox Church. The five barless windows of the house in Siberia are the five wounds of Jesus. (The number five elsewhere appears, and always with sinister significance: the five-o'clock train from which the older Zhivago throws himself, the five conspirators in the forest who try to murder the partisan leader.) Evgraf is a guardian angel, but he is also, with his dark face, the angel of death. And yet death is always followed by resurrection. Three times, like the fairy in the folk tale, he comes to Yury Andreyevich's rescue: first when, before Zhivago has taken his family away, he collapses in Moscow with typhus; again, when he is marooned with his family in the Urals, before he has been kidnapped by the partisans; and finally when, returned to Moscow, unwanted and unassimilable, he is on the point of petering out. On this last occasion, Evgraf induces him to leave for a time his devoted lower-class wife and provides him with lodgings in which to write. We never know what Evgraf is or how he accomplishes his miracles; he is always an important person whose authority is felt at once, never questioned; he can always produce food, secure for his half-brother conditions of leisure. Yet we do not know what office he holds, why he is always so sure of himself, how he has managed to escape the purges. On his third intervention, he brings death in the flesh. The Doctor, now hidden from his family, does not survive his last creative liberation, but Evgraf preserves his manuscripts, the poems in which Yury lives again. Since "Yury" is a Russian equivalent for "George," the Russian reader will have guessed by this time that Zhivago is St. George, the martyr, who is supposed to have paid with his life for his audacity in arguing Christianity with Diocletian. He has written in the Urals, with the wolves on the horizon, a queer poem with an unexpected ending, about the battle of St. George with the Dragon, which we shall read in the final chapter. (One suspects that the legends of St. Larisa and St. Eugraphos, after whom the heroine and Evgraf are named, would reveal further connections between the characters and the hagiography of the Orthodox Church. A mythological Larisa is supposed to have been the wife of Poseidon, and Pasternak's Larisa is associated with the sea by Zhivago.) Evgraf, a general now, appears for the

last time toward the end of the second great war to rescue the daughter of Larisa and Yury, born after her flight
with Komarovsky and abandoned with a peasant family,
who has been partially reduced to the level of a peasant
and yet knows that she is something else. Evgraf will see
that she is educated (the importance of education is emphasized all through the book).

By this time, we are quite aware that the theme of
death and resurrection, slipped into the first pages, is
central to the whole book, repeated in all sorts of variations and with ever stronger positive force. Again and
again the characters are entombed and rise from the tomb.
Evgraf is the angel at the grave. The father, enmeshed in
the financial ruin entailed by his emotional instability,
has thrown himself out of the train; Yury Andreyevich,
the son, with sclerosis of the heart, is suffocating on a
crowded tram, tries to get a window up, then forces his
way out and drops dead on the curb. And in the interval
between these two deaths, the incidents that join them
together are now seen to compose a sequence of images,
sometimes physical, sometimes spiritual, of the cycle of
extinction and survival. The vodka and pancakes of
Shrovetide—which in Russia is dedicated both to the
dead and to the renewal of life by marriage—are a ritual
symbol of the theme. The second of these references is a
herald of Evgraf's second intervention. The Jewish boy in
the station who is thinking about "what it means to be a
Jew" and paying no attention to the man who has just
then committed suicide—he later adapts himself to the
Moscow regime, though not with the same enthusiasm as
the non-Jewish friend who has been brainwashed—is
meant to illustrate the author's conception of the too self-
centered role of the Jews. The book begins with the
burial of Yury's mother and the night in the monastery,
in which no special ray of light is yet seen; and we have

afterwards the escape from the train of the prisoners condemned to forced labor; the shooting, on the edge of a
precipice, of the vodka distillers and other offenders, of
whom one, a backward boy, survives; the burial of the old
woman by her murderer in the pit in which she has been
hoarding potatoes, and the escape, through taking refuge
in an underground cave, in the raid that follows the
murder, of a boy who is suspected already of having
committed it; and the trapping in the cellar of the murderer of the husband of the peasant woman with whom
the daughter of Zhivago and Larisa has been living. Pasternak keeps too close to real life to perpetrate a monotonous allegory. In this last-mentioned instance of
burial, there is no resurrection for the brute. He is held
prisoner by the woman whose husband has been killed,
and she allows him to strangle her little boy, whom he
has taken down with him as a hostage. The abandoned
daughter of Zhivago and Larisa flags a passing train—the
husband of the woman was a signalman—and the train-
men bring out the murderer, tie him to the tracks and
run over him. The woman, as a result of all this, goes
mad. Here it is the girl who escapes from the household
which has been for her a tomb.

The last chapter is composed of Zhivago's poems,
which have been published after his death. The reader,
when he faces this chapter, may be somewhat puzzled and
dubious as to why what is ostensibly a story should be
prolonged by what looks like an appendix; but by the
time we have finished these poems, we see that they are
needed to complete the book, that the theme only now in
this chapter gets its full triumphant statement. These
poems fall into two series, which alternate and echo one
another and merge. One sequence recapitulates certain
incidents of Zhivago's life and grows darker with the
parting from Larisa and the darkness of the oppression of

Stalin: "For this in early spring my friends and I gather together, and our evenings are farewells, our feasts are testaments, in order that our hidden stream of suffering may warm the cold of existence." The other of these sequences commemorates the holy days of the Church and the main events of the life of Jesus. The gloomy poem quoted above is followed by *Evil Days,* the entrance of Christ into Jerusalem and the giving him up for judgment to the dregs of society by "the dark forces of the Temple," and his memory at this moment, of his bounty at Cana and his bringing Lazarus back from the tomb; then two poems on Mary Magdalene, with whom we have already had some intimation that Larisa is to be identified (after all, she could never get away from Komarovsky, whom she has married in the Far East). The last magnificent poem of this somber yet affirmative series gives us Jesus in the Garden of Gethsemane. "I shall descend into the grave," it ends, "and on the third day I shall rise again, and as rafts float along the river, so the centuries, like the barges of a caravan, for my judgment will float down out of darkness."

I assume that by this time everybody knows that *Doctor Zhivago* has not been published in Russia, that the manuscript was brought out of the Soviet Union by the Italian leftist publisher Feltrinelli, that Pasternak was awarded the Nobel Prize and that the anti-creative bureaucrats who are allowed in the Soviet Union to interfere in matters of literature—sounding much like those Mississippi newspapers which raised a howl against Faulkner in the same situation—have compelled him to refuse this reward. I do not, however, in paying my respects to the official mediocrities of Moscow, want to adopt the self-righteous attitude toward Russia which has become official in the United States. On hearing of this literary crisis, Secretary Dulles said that "it illustrates what I said last night. The system of international Communism insists on conformity not only in deed but in thought. Anything a little out of line they try to stamp out." *Doctor Zhivago* is not merely a little out of line with the assumptions of the Soviet Union; it presents a radical criticism of all our supposedly democratic but more and more centralized societies. The criticism of Pasternak's novel is directed at conditions and tendencies which are in evidence all over the world and which have lately become pronounced in the United States. Here is a quotation from Pasternak which might equally well apply to ourselves: "It was then," says Larisa of the First World War, "that untruth came to the land of Russia. The first disaster, the root of future evil, was the loss of faith in one's own opinion. They imagined that the time had passed for them to pay attention to the promptings of moral feeling, that one now had to sing with the general voice and to live by the general notions that were being thrust upon one."

Doctor Zhivago will, I believe, come to stand as one of the great events in man's literary and moral history. Nobody could have written it in a totalitarian state and turned it loose on the world who did not have the courage of genius. May his guardian angel be with him! His book is a great act of faith in art and in the human spirit. As for his enemies in his fatherland, I predict that their children, over their vodka and tea, will be talking about the relations between Larisa Fyodorovna and Pasha and Yury Andreyevich, as their parents, and I don't doubt they themselves, have talked about Tatyana and Lensky and Evgeni Onegin, and Natasha and Prince André and Pierre.

November 15, 1958

LEGEND AND SYMBOL IN
DOCTOR ZHIVAGO

WHEN I WROTE a review last November of Pasternak's *Doctor Zhivago,* I was aware that the main theme of the book was death and ressurrection, which was constantly turning up in the images, the situations and the religious references, but I was only just becoming aware that the characters, all of whom were named—as was customary in Russia under the old régime—after saints of the Orthodox calendar, were partly to be understood in terms of the legends of these saints. The more one studies *Doctor Zhivago,* the more one comes to realize that it is studded with symbols and significant puns, that there is something in it of *Finnegans Wake,* and something of the cabalistic *Zohar,* which discovers a whole system of hidden meanings in the text of the Hebrew Bible. This kind of thing, of course, is fashionable, and it is sometimes emphasized by critics at the expense of the more important aspects of some work of literature or discovered in works in which it does not exist; but the more one reads *Doctor Zhivago,* the more one becomes convinced that it is really pervaded by a poetic symbolism, and from the moment one begins to get the sense of this, the story gains another dimension.

I have not studied the book carefully from this point of view, but two friends, Miss Barbara Deming and Mrs. Dimitri Lehovich, have been giving special attention to certain elements in *Doctor Zhivago* and have pointed out implications which are likely to be missed by anyone who is reading it for the first time without yet having picked up the clues. I am very much indebted to the findings of these readers, which will in some cases be given in their own words. Here are some notes on the leading motifs.

I have already mentioned, in reviewing *Zhivago*, that the name of the hero "almost corresponded" with the genitive and accusative singular of the adjective живой, living: живого. I did not know that the old Church Russian form of this was spelt *zhivago*, and that the opening lines of the novel recall to the Russian reader certain passages from the Gospels and the prayer book. By means of a play on words, the main theme of death and resurrection is sounded in the second paragraph. The cortege of the funeral of Yury's mother is on its way to the cemetery. People ask, "Whom are they burying?" The answer is simply, "Zhivago." At the beginning of the twenty-fourth chapter of Luke in the text of the Russian Bible, the scene in which the women come to the grave and find the stone rolled away, the angels are made to ask them, "Что вы ищете живого между мертвых?" "Why do you seek the living among the dead?" Two variations on this passage occur in the Russian liturgy: "Why do you think the living is among the dead? For God is arisen from the sepulchre"; and "Why seek ye the living among the dead? Why do you mourn the incorruptible amidst the corrupted?" The *g* in the accusative singular of *zhivoy* is ordinarily pronounced as *v*, but in the Biblical form as *g*, so the identification is complete.

The Russian name Yury is a form of George, and a reference to the legend of St. George throws much light on the role of Zhivago, who specifically appears as this saint in the poem about slaying the dragon.

St. George is supposed to have died three times, and three times to have been resurrected, as happens with Yury on the three occasions when he feels himself going under and is revived by his half-brother Evgraf. But the parallel between the legend and the life of Zhivago seems to be further complicated by a parallel with Pasternak's own career. We find in the history of St. George—as recounted in Voragine's *Golden Legend*—that he put off "the habit of a knight" and "took that of a Christian man" as a result of the martyrdom, under Diocletian and Maximian, of twenty-two thousand Christians, which caused some to renounce their faith. Now, Pasternak's interest in Christianity is said to date from 1936, when the great purges were getting under way. St. George, according to the legend, was subjected, as a result of his persistence in preaching Christianity, to a series of terrible ordeals: beatings, drinkings of poison, slashings by sword-bristling wheels and immersions in molten lead, from all of which he recovered; and that he was finally compelled to "make sacrifice to the idols"—as Pasternak, who is known in some cases to have refused to sign petitions for the death of Stalin's victims, is said on one or two occasions to have been forced to sign denunciations. St. George, when brought to his knees in submission to the pagan deities, was not deterred from making his prayer to his own God, whereupon "fire descended from heaven and burnt the temple and the idols and their priests," and "the earth opened and swallowed all the cinders and ashes that were left." We now hear of an official called Dacian, "the provost," who is evidently Maximian himself, since Maximian came from Dacia and since we know that his wife, "Queen Alexandra," was attracted or converted to Christianity (as was also Diocletian's consort). This personage, according to Voragine, was so angry over the blasting of the temple that he exclaimed to his wife, "I shall die for anger if I may not surmount and overcome this man." "Then said she to him, 'Evil and cruel tyrant! Seest thou not the great virtue of the Christian people? I said to thee well that thou shouldst not do to them any harm, for their God fighteth for them, and know thou well that I will become Christian!' Then was Dacian much abashed and said to her: 'Wilt thou be Christian?' Then he took her by the hair and did beat her cruelly." Dacian now ordered that George should be beheaded. Alexandra was also a martyr, and her day in the Orthodox calendar is the same as St. George's: April 23rd.

This story suggests two correspondences. There is the relation, on the one hand, between Larisa and her husband, General Strelnikov, who is carrying out the official line with a severity that turns into terrorism, and, on the other, between Larisa and Zhivago. But there is also a curious possible connection with the life of Pasternak himself. The relations between Pasternak and Stalin are discussed in an article in the December issue of the Russian periodical *Novy Zhurnal*. The author, Mr. Mikhail Koryakov, shows that Pasternak, even in the dangerous years of 1936 and 1937, appeared at literary conferences and gave expression to independent non-official views. His opinions became so abhorrent that his speeches were no longer printed, and one can only get an idea of what they contained from the things that were said condemning them. Yet never in these years of suppression was Pasternak even arrested. Mr. Koryakov comes to the conclusion that there can be no explanation of this, at a time when almost every other Soviet writer of any talent or principle was imprisoned or exiled or shot, except that the word had been given by Stalin that Pasternak was not to be touched. But why, conceivably, should Stalin have protected him? Pasternak published in 1935 a volume of translations from the Georgian poets, but could this have been enough to exempt him? Mr. Koryakov believes that he has found out the reason:

"This is connected with the death of N. S. Allilueva, Stalin's wife. Those who knew her say that she was beautiful. 'She was elegant and had a good figure. She wore a simple dark blue dress with a white blouse,' it is said of her in certain memoirs. 'Her hair was combed back smooth with a straight part and a well-arranged knot at the back. She had a natural refinement of manner. Her hands were especially beautiful—one's glance involuntarily lingered on them. It is only in Bryulov's portraits that one can see hands of such classic shape.' . . . There is no doubt that Stalin loved her very much. There are various stories of how she died: one is that Stalin shot her; another that she killed herself; while the official version has it that she died from peritonitis. And there is also the story that the peritonitis had been brought on by a serious wound in the abdomen, and that the shot had occurred at the moment when Stalin was wresting the revolver from her.* It is a fixed rule of the Soviet papers that they never give any publicity to anything that happens in the family of a 'party or government leader.' But when N. S. Allilueva died, the papers were full of letters and telegrams expressing sympathy for Stalin. Among these was a letter from the Soviet writers, and this of course was an organized affair, as all such

---

* The story I used to hear was that on some occasion when guests were present at dinner, Stalin kept flicking bread pellets at his wife, and that she afterwards went out and shot herself. There has also been current a legend—significant in this connection—that she defied Stalin's brutal policies by attempting to protect her friends.

expressions of sympathy were. It was signed by thirty-three writers, who included B. Pilnyak, M. Koltsov, S. Dinamov, A. Selivanovsky, L. Averbach, all of whom were to perish in the Yezhov terror. The letter was routine and vulgar, as all such letters were:

" 'Dear Comrade Stalin!

It is difficult to find the right words of condolence. Please accept our grief at the death of N. S. Allilueva, who devoted all her strength to the effort of freeing the millions of oppressed humanity, that effort of which you are the leader and for which we are ready to give our lives in affirmation of its indestructible vital force.'

"Boris Pasternak was not among these thirty-three writers. Though the letter was brought him, he had refused to sign it. The proof of this is that just below the letter, as printed in the *Literaturnaya Gazeta* of November 17th, 1932, appears a special postscript by Pasternak, in which he says that he has read the letter, but that rather than sign it, he has added a postscript. Here it is, enigmatic and striking:

" 'I associate myself with the feeling of my comrades. I had been thinking, the evening before, deeply and persistently of Stalin; for the first time from the point of view of the artist. In the morning I read the news. I was as shaken as if I had been present, as if I had lived it and seen it.

Boris Pasternak.'

"Whatever were the circumstances of Allilueva's death, it was for Stalin a great misfortune. I heard in Moscow that he would often in the evening drive out to the Novodevichye Cemetery and for hours sit on her grave. It is possible that Pasternak's unconventional and rather mysterious postscript may, if not have shaken Stalin, at least have got under his skin. He could not, in the first place, have failed to be struck by the fact that Pasternak had refused to sign the banal routine letter and had expressed his feeling in his own words—which implied that he did have some feeling! And what did it mean: 'I had been thinking, the evening before, deeply and persistently of Stalin,' and 'in the morning I heard the news'? What mysticism, what 'devilry' was this? Stalin was a rough man, but he was not without his 'depths.' . . . These lines might have set him brooding. And, furthermore, what did it mean that Pasternak, in November, 1932, had 'deeply and persistently' thought of him—'for the first time from the point of view of the artist'? Did that mean as a prophet, as a clairvoyant—who might in some sense have 'been present' at the moment of Allilueva's death and have 'seen' how she died? May we not guess that Stalin had a cold shudder [literally, that ants ran over his body] when he read these lines of the poet? May we not guess that at that moment there was roused in him the traditional oriental tendency to see in the poet a 'dervish'? We may remember what Pushkin said about this in his *Journey to Erzerum*: 'Pushchin gave me the title of poet. The Pasha folded his hands on his breast and bowed, after saying to me through an interpreter: "That hour is blessed when we meet a poet. The poet is brother to the dervish. He has no country nor is he blessed with the things of this world; and while we, poor creatures that we are, are worrying about fame, about power, about riches, he stands on a basis of equality with the powerful of the earth, and the people bow down before him." '

"Did not Stalin see such a 'dervish' in Pasternak? . . . If one did not have to bow before him, he at least deserved defence and protection. . . . I believe that, from that moment, from the 17th of November, 1932, Pasternak, without himself being aware of it, had entered into Stalin's personal life, had in some sense come to figure in his spiritual landscape, so that one could not touch Pasternak without personally affecting Stalin."

These, of course, are merely speculations, but in an article that followed Koryakov's in the *Novoe Russkoe Slovo,* Gleb Struve recalls that it had already been thought that "Pasternak had inspired Stalin with some mysterious fear," and he tells one version of the much-circulated story—supposed to date from about 1931—of Stalin's having called Pasternak on the telephone. The poet Osip Mandelstam had been arrested for a satirical epigram about Stalin, and Pasternak, on an appeal from Mandelstam's wife, had asked Bukharin to try to get him off. Stalin is supposed to have rung Pasternak up and asked him whether Mandelstam was a good poet, and then to have asked Pasternak why he never came to see him. Whatever the reason may have been for Pasternak's unique immunity, the fact that he was thus immune suggests the unexplained authority and the similar inviolability of Yury's half-brother Evgraf in the novel. Evgraf remains mysteriously free: he is always in a position to come to Yury's rescue and to the last he escapes the purges. I believe that Mrs. Lehovich has discovered the key to Evgraf and to his fairy-story relationship with Zhivago.

It seems fairly clear [Mrs. Lehovich writes] that Yury Zhivago represents the thinking and idealistic part of Russian society before and after the revolution, which included members of the upper and middle classes, intellectuals and students, merchants and professional people, whose striving for justice and freedom expressed itself in the most varied ways. One might say that Yury was a composite of all the characters who had influenced his childhood and youth, notably of his uncle Nikolai Niko-layevich, a religious philosopher "who was a free man . . . who had a nobleman's feeling of equality with all the living"; of his future father-in-law Alexander Gro-meko, a chemistry professor and an enlightened member of a good Moscow family ("We Gromekos outgrew the passion of covetousness a generation ago"); of his friends and contemporaries: the student Misha Gordon, who is interested in philosophy, theology and philology, and Tonya, who appears as the embodiment of the positive traditional values in these people's way of life.

One half of Doctor Zhivago is all these people. He is Yury-George, the idealistic but still down-to-earth man who, at one point in the book, accepts with such joy the simplicity of living by the labour of his hands: "What happiness to work for oneself and one's family from sunrise to sunset, building a home, cultivating the earth." In the Church calendar, the name George means "culti-vator" [Greek: *georgos,* farmer]. The other half of Doc-tor Zhivago, the element that makes him unique among all these "men of good will," that saves him as an indi-vidual, is embodied in the person of Evgraf.

Evgraf is Yury's *alter ego,* his creative, his poetic self. What are Evgraf's characteristics? He has just come, on his first appearance, from his birthplace or home in Siberia, to which he subsequently returns several times. Siberia seems in general, in the novel, to figure less as an actual locality than as an expression for "lying low" or "going underground," a place to which the various char-acters withdraw when they have to leave the center of events. (Larisa "goes to Siberia" after the revolutionary outbreaks die down in 1911, and again after the Bolshe-vik coup, as do Yury Zhivago and his family when, later on, conditions in Moscow become impossible, etc.)

Whenever Evgraf appears, he seems—like inspiration—to descend upon Yury from some higher realm. The first time that Yury sees him is at the moment when he (Yury) is reading the news of the Bolshevik insurrection in the entrance hall of the strange house in Moscow. "He heard footsteps overhead. Someone was coming downstairs." When Evgraf turns up in Varykino, Yury writes in his journal: "And there, as if fallen from the clouds, appeared brother Evgraf." In the concluding chapter, Yury meets Evgraf in the street: "As usual, he seemed to have landed out of the sky." Evgraf, thus, arrives unexpectedly, nobody knows from whence, but always from somewhere above, and when he has given his helping hand, he vanishes. Is it possible for an artist to understand whence or how his creative genius comes?

"Strange," writes Yury, "he is my half-brother and bears the same name as I, and yet I know less about him than I do about anyone else."

The advent of Evgraf, however, may apparently be also invoked by writing of a more prosaic kind. It is when Yury has started giving vent to his gloom in his notes called *Playing at Being People,* in Moscow, and afterwards, in Varykino, when he is writing his journal, that Evgraf makes his first two appearances.

Evgraf comes into Yury's life at precisely those times when ordinary living is becoming too hard to bear and when the effort of the struggle to survive is threatening to overwhelm him. He is able to help Yury materially by providing food, leisure, an apartment; and, what is more important, he saves Yury as a human being by making it possible for him to escape into, to right himself by, creative work. Thus, just before Yury's illness, when Evgraf will come to his rescue, the hardships of the Zhivagos have reached a peak. All their thoughts have been concentrated on procuring the bare necessities of life, and

Yury is "walking home along the endless stretches of
Meshchanskaya Street" when he feels himself coming
down with typhus. Later on, when they are living in
Varykino and all Yury's energy is being expended on the
tasks of keeping his house heated and his family fed, he
wishes that he could find time to write. "The nightingale's
song 'Wake up! Wake up!' sounded almost like the pre-
Easter prayer: 'Arise my soul, cease slumbering, awaken.' "
Evgraf arrives at this moment (as Yury notes in his journal) and promises "to facilitate our household duties so
that Tonya would have time to see to Shura's education,
and I should have time for my medical and literary work."
Finally, at the end of the book, Yury, who has been finding the air of Moscow more and more difficult to breathe,
is "seeking to change his fate"; and Evgraf, who has descended again, "bypassing the minor obstacles of living . . .
conceived a practical plan for helping his brother and
saving him. The disappearance and seclusion of Yury
Andreyevich were Evgraf's idea and invention."

But Evgraf's most important function is actually helping Yury to write. It is surely not a coincidence that the
name Evgraf in the Russian calendar means *writer*
[Greek: εὔγραφος]. Yury's and Evgraf's collaboration is
described at the time of Yury's illness in Moscow when,
in the course of his delirious dreaming: "Tonya brings
the glowing, penetrating, orange light of the lamp closer
to him. . . . Work becomes possible. He is writing fe-
verishly and with extraordinary felicity that which he
should have written long ago but never could. And now
it all comes out perfectly. He was distracted only from
time to time by that boy with the slanting Tartar eyes and
the Siberian coat of deerskin. Quite obviously that boy is
the spirit of death, even simply his death. But how can
he be that if he is helping him to write a poem? Can death
be useful, can it help?" And further on: "I must awaken.

I must awaken and arise. I must be resurrected." Has not
Yury given the answer already at an earlier point in the
story when he is musing in the cemetery after Anna Ivanovna's funeral?: "Now as never before it was clear to him
that art is always, incessantly occupied with two matters.
It is constantly meditating on death and, in doing so,
constantly creating life."

That Evgraf is Yury's creative genius is made even
clearer by the description of their final meeting: "His
brother's support lent wings to Yury Andreyevich. Now,
as always before, the secret of his power remained unexplained. Yury Andreyevich did not attempt to penetrate
it."

When Zhivago is dead and his family and friends have
gathered in the room where he lies, two people, Evgraf
and Larisa, stand out from all the rest: "They did not
claim any closer tie with the dead man than the others.
. . . Their composure was remarkable, and it produced a
strange impression, as if they were involved not only in
the funeral but also in the death. . . ." These two,
though immortal, *were* Yury. One was his creative
genius, the other the life-giving force which for a time he
had made his own.

This brings us to the question of Larisa: who she is,
what she represents.

I had noted, when I reviewed the book, that she sometimes has an aspect of Mary Magdalene and that she is
often associated with the sea, but I had not yet grasped
the significance of this latter association. I have learned
since from the Orthodox calendar that Larisa means *sea
gull, sea bird;* from the *Encyclopædia Britannica* that the
shrine of St. George was built near the legendary scene
of Perseus' rescue of Andomeda from the sea-monster,
and that the slaying by St. George of the dragon is sup-

posed to have been derived from this. A letter from a correspondent has added the information that the worship of St. George on the coast of Lebanon is connected with temples to Poseidon. Now, a mythical pre-Christian Larisa is supposed to have been the wife of Poseidon. But why is the Larisa (Lara) of the novel identified with the sea?

Miss Deming, in clearing this up, has brought out what is seen at once to be one of the main poetic themes of *Zhivago:*

Is Lara [Miss Deming writes] not associated with the sea because it is an image of the free, the spontaneous—the truly alive? Zhivago says, "Life is not . . . a substantial thing. It is something that eternally renews itself" (which might also describe the sea). He speaks of the "sea of life, the sea of spontaneity." On page 391 [of the English translation], Zhivago asks himself: "What was she (Lara) to him? . . . Oh, that question he could always answer. . . .Oh, how sweet to be alive! . . . Oh, the ever-present longing to thank life, thank existence itself, to thank them as one being to another being. This was exactly what Lara was. You could not communicate with life and existence, but *she was their representative, their expression,* in her the inarticulate principle of existence became sensitive and capable of speech." (Italics Miss Deming's.)

Is Lara not also associated with the sea—and I would add with wind—because it is "life's storm" that casts Lara and Zhivago together? Zhivago does not choose Lara, he says; does not prefer her to Tonya, his wife. "Ineluctable reality" joins them:

> In years of hardship, in the days
> Of an unthinkable existence

> She had been cast up from the depths
> By a high wave of destiny.
>
> (*Parting*)

Lara is associated with the sea—and with wind—in the following passages:

On pages 150–51, in the middle of a stormy night, after she has left Melyuzeyevo, there is a knocking at the door of the house where she has been staying, and both Zhivago and Mlle Fleury go downstairs, hoping to find Lara, who has for some reason returned. There is no one at the door. A gust of wind showers them with cold raindrops. They find that a branch knocking on a window has broken a pane, and there are huge puddles on the floor— "and the same thing in what used to be Lara's room— there was a sea, a real sea, an ocean." They go back to their beds, but both continue to imagine Lara outside the house "in the form of a watery wraith." On page 304, Zhivago, living in anticipation through a meeting with Lara, dreams that: "A dark muffled figure will open the door, and the promise of her nearness, unowned by any-one in the world . . . will reach him like the first wave of the sea as you run down over the sandy beach in the dark." And on page 452, after he and Lara have been separated, Zhivago muses: "I'll trace your features on paper, as the sea, after a fearful storm has churned it up, traces the form of the greatest farthest-reaching wave on the sand. Seaweed, shells, cork, pebbles, the lightest, most imponderable things that it could lift from its bed, are cast up in a broken sinuous line on the sand. This line, endlessly stretching into the distance, is the frontier of the highest tide. That was how life's storm cast you up on my shore, O my pride. . . ." One could also note that when Zhivago first visits her, in Yuryatin, he finds her drawing water from the well. It is again very windy.

I suggest, then, that the sea represents for Pasternak the principle of life itself, which is indicated by the name Zhivago. One finds that Yury himself is associated by Pasternak with water imagery. On pages 89–90, at Anna Ivanovna's funeral, he walks on alone, ahead of the other mourners, and, "In answer to the desolation brought by death to the people slowly pacing after him, he was drawn, as irresistibly as water funnelling downward, to dream, to think, to work out new forms, to bring beauty into being. Now, as never before, it was clear to him that art is always, ceaselessly occupied with two matters. It is constantly meditating on death and, in doing so, constantly creating life." On page 502, when Lara takes leave of him in his coffin, she addresses him, "Farewell, my great one, my kin, farewell my pride, farewell, my swift deep little river, how I loved your day-long splashing, how I loved to plunge into your cold waves." The association of Zhivago with a river is followed here by the association of Lara with rain: her tears "seemed to hold her words together in a tender, quick whispering like the rustling of silky leaves in a warm windy rain." Lara and Zhivago are cast together because they are kin—water flowing to water.

On page 229, Pasternak describes a stream-bed, tucked up in the snow like a child in its cot, which in spring will rush down to the viaduct below. Both Lara and Zhivago, like water under snow, persist through the winter of the period, remain alive in an exceptional sense, while so many others "play" at being people, give up "the habit of thinking and judging for themselves," "idiotically pompous with each other." Lara's "greatest defeat in life" is in her marriage with Pasha, when she, too, succumbs to the general pomposity, fails to be natural with him. But in the main, both Lara and Zhivago, heroically and with each other's help, remain free individuals—manage not to lose the "immortal part" of themselves.

The large theme of *Doctor Zhivago* is death and resurrection, and the image of the sea is a part of this. On page 12, Pasternak speaks of the freedom resulting "from the feeling that all human lives . . . *flowed into each other* [italics B. D.]—a happy feeling that all events took place not only on earth, in which the dead are buried, but also in some other region which some called the Kingdom of God, others history, and still others by some other name." In the passage in which Lara says farewell to Zhivago, she loses all feeling of helplessness in death's presence, musing on the fact that their joyful sense of being part of a greater whole is just what had always united her with Zhivago. She feels suddenly as if she has lived twenty lives, lost Zhivago countless times (feels their lives flow into the "general stream of life"). "Communion with others is immortal," Nikolai says. (In the final chapter, Zhivago's life and his words flow into the lives of Dudorov and Gordon—reclaiming them from the dead, from those who merely "play at being people.") The sea, then, for Pasternak, is the sea of life—and, one could add, of immortality, "a stronger word for life."

Imagery of the sea or of water appears in a few further connections. There is, for example, the passage (page 437) in which Zhivago feels the approach of inspiration, and language itself begins to think and speak for him, its inward flow, "like the current of a mighty river polishing stones and turning wheels by its very movement," creating, in passing, meter and rhythm and countless other relationships. Here again it is really the "stream of general life" that is referred to, for "at such moments Yury Andreyevich felt that the main part of the work was being done not by him but by a superior power which was above him and directed him, namely the movement of universal thought and poetry in its present historical stage and the one to come."

In his first "rash enthusiasm" about the revolution, Zhivago speaks of it in similar terms (page 146): "Everyone was revived, reborn, changed, transformed. . . . It seems to me that socialism is the sea, and all these separate streams, these private individual revolutions, are flowing into it—the sea of life, the sea of spontaneity." Later, of course, his charge against the revolutionaries is precisely that they deny to life its true quality—try to treat it as a substance that can be moulded.

There is still another passage that is important to mention: the beautiful section in which Pasternak describes the thaw and the spring floods in the mountains, when all the various waters rush out with a roar and spread themselves, and rain leaps from clouds—and then four prisoners escape from the train. As Zhivago says, "They just broke free like the water" (page 238). One has the feeling that the floods have actually prompted the escape of the prisoners. Throughout the book, Pasternak notes the power of nature to communicate to human beings the impulse towards freedom, towards rebirth. (It is, for example, a sudden storm, sweeping the smell of rain into the school-room where she sits, sending the papers flying about, that rouses Lara to her decision to escape from Komarovsky—page 72.) Those who are truly alive, in Pasternak's eyes, feel themselves part of the "general stream of life" (see the poem *Dawn*: "I feel I am melting, even as the snow melts . . .").

Mrs. Lehovich agrees with this and points out that the name of Yury's second wife, Marina, also suggests the sea, and that Zhivago goes to her for water. The idea [Mrs. Lehovich writes] represented by the heroine Larisa is the most elusive in the whole book, although it is perhaps the one for which we are given the largest number of clues of different kinds and at different levels.

In the Russian Orthodox calendar many names are given a definite meaning. Larisa is supposed to mean *sea gull,* and this evokes two expressions frequently used in Russian: "free as a bird" and "boundless as the sea." Larisa has her own climate, a rather windy one. Her appearances are heralded by an abundance of fresh air and a feeling of spaciousness: "The flower-scented air of these open spaces . . . was dearer to her than her father and mother, better than a lover, wiser than a book." "When she entered it was as if a window were flung open. The room filled with light and air." When Larisa is far away, a muggy, depressing atmosphere often prevails, and never more so than when freedom has fallen to its lowest ebb. There is something elemental about Larisa.

Does Larisa personify the Revolution? This can hardly be possible, for in that case she would have remained in the center of events after October, 1917, and in the years that followed, when revolution swept the capital and the country, and she does not do this but withdraws and conceals herself in a remote Siberian town. This identification, also, seems too simple, and Larisa is not at all simple. The point here is probably that Larisa represents the spirit of freedom (the ideas of liberty, freedom, and franchise are all contained in the Russian word *svoboda*), and that once the new system has been got under way, she prefers to be free of that, too. But Larisa's exact meaning will always escape us; she will assume different aspects as the novel unfolds, though her image will remain constant and her direction, under changing conditions, will always remain the same.

It should also be noted [E.W. writing] that the Larisa of the novel may possibly have some connection with

Pasternak's admiration for Larisa Reisner, a writer and Socialist worker of the early days of the Revolution. Here is a brief account of her career from a German anthology of Russian short stories—*Dreissig Neue Erzähler des Neuen Russland*—published in 1929:

"Larisa Reisner was born in Lublin in 1895, the daughter of a professor. Her early years were spent in France and Germany, where her father had gone to study. In Western Europe he became a Socialist, and it was possible for him to return to Russia only after the 1905 revolution. At the Gymnasium Larisa wrote her first play. In 1914, after the outbreak of war, she founded, together with her father, a magazine called *Rudin*, in order to fight against the betrayal of international solidarity. As soon as the February revolution broke out, she began to be active in the workers' clubs, took part in the appropriation of art treasures, joined the Communist Party, and went to the front. In 1919, she was staff commissar of the Baltic fleet. In 1920 she became the wife of Raskolnikov, the Soviet envoy to Kabul. She was in Germany in 1923, soon after the Cuno strike, at the time of the Hamburg uprising. On returning to the Soviet Union, she travelled as a reporter through the great industrial regions. At the same time, she studied economics and revolutionary history, and lectured. She died of typhus in 1926."

Pasternak's poem about Larisa Reisner, written at the time of her death—*In Memory of Reisner*—is almost an apotheosis. She is presented, like the Larisa of the novel, in association with water imagery: the floodings of spring thaw, the boilings of life in a still.

(An article by Mr. Yury Bol'shukhin in the *Novoe Russkoe Slovo* supplies some further details: Larisa Reisner was a Trotskyite: her husband has been described as

having a character like that of Saint-Just, and he was
purged in the thirties during the Stalin terror.)

"Moreau and Vetchinkin. *Seeders. Threshers.*" This
sign appears five times in *Doctor Zhivago,* when Yury
either sees it or thinks of it.

I was puzzled by it when I first read the book,
but assumed that it merely stood for the eternal problem
of agriculture that has pressed upon the new Russia as it
did upon the old. I believe that this is one of its meanings, but I recognized later that the seeders and threshers
contained the death and resurrection motif. Miss Deming
pointed out to me further that since the sign makes its
final appearance (page 305) at the branch of the road
through the forest at the time when Zhivago is unable to
decide between his wife and Larisa, and just at the
moment when he is about to be kidnapped by the
partisans and is saved from making this choice by being
thrust into a life of action, the persistently recurring
billboard must have some connection with the crisis. Mrs.
Lehovich reminded me that *vetchina* means *ham,* and
that *vetchinka* would be its diminutive, *hamlet,* and
it may be that the sign is related to the Hamlet of the
first poem of the last chapter. This Hamlet—who, in the
language of Jesus in Mark 14.36, begs that his cup may
pass—has been called to play a role in the drama of his
age, but knows, in his solitude and darkness, that he is
cast for another play, his own. For Yury it is equally impossible to escape from the Revolution or to follow the
clear line of his will, which itself, between Larisa and
Tonya, is balked by a bifurcation. The partisans drag him
off to take part in their eager campaigning, which is entirely irrelevant to his purposes, and to preach to him their
infantile bigotry, which can only exasperate and bore
him. The most striking thing that met his eye on his first

arrival at Yuryatin had been a great trail of smoke from "the giant illusion," which was burning down. (This is perhaps another of Pasternak's plays on words that do not come out in English: in the early days of the cinema, moving picture houses were sometimes called "illusions," as shows with magicians and freaks had been. The Russian phrase here is "иллюзион Гигант.")

When Yury escapes at last from the partisans, and Tonya has got away to Paris, and there is no longer any obstacle to his living with Larisa, he passes by the signboard again on his way to Varykino with her, but though he looks for it, it is now too dark to see it: there is now, in the darkness of the terror from which he and Larisa are fleeing, no longer any problem of choosing. Later on, just before his death, when Evgraf has again intervened to give him an interval of freedom from his family life with Marina, and he is trying to bring some literary order into the confused materials supplied by his past, in the moments when "his imagination failed and he could not get on with his work," he would draw branching roads in his margins, with the Moreau and Vetchinkin sign, and also intersections of city streets, like the one at which he had first read the news of the success of the Bolshevik *coup d'état*, just before the first descent of Evgraf was to lead him to take the right turning.

If, bearing all this in mind, we now scrutinize the obsessive billboard, we find that in its French form the name Moreau is compounded of *mort* and *eau*, death and water, and that in its Russian form, Moro, it suggests the word *more*, pestilence (the typhus which Yury comes down with in the winter of the Bolshevik Revolution?), which is the root of the verb морить, to exterminate, starve or exhaust, as well as the word *more*, sea. With these references on his left, and on his right the seeders and threshers, Yury's Hamlet, in great embarrassment,

finds himself—"to be or not to be?"—solicited both by life
and by death, which, however, like the buried seed, like
the compact ambiguity of the word *Moreau*, embody a
single process: the unimpedable continuity of life.

This sign with its prism of meanings is very much in
the manner of Joyce, and it seems likely that Pasternak
has been influenced by *Finnegans Wake*.

Zhivago, the "living man," is simultaneously Hamlet,
St. George and Jesus, just as H. C. Earwicker, "Here
Comes Everybody," is Adam, Tristram, Finnegan, etc.;
and he is also, just as Earwicker is split in two as the
brothers Shem and Shaun, divided into the two personalities of the half-brothers, Evgraf and Yury. Larisa—
the feminine principle, as is shown by what her name has
in common with Marina's—is given, like Anna Livia, the
essence of the liquid element. As Anna Livia, at the end
of *Finnegans Wake*, is flowing away from her household
and slipping out to her father, the sea, leaving her daughter to flow in her stead, so Larisa eludes those who love
her: Pasha, Yury, Komarovsky, and leaves her daughters:
one by Antipov, who is studying for the protean profession of actress, and one by Yury, who also seeks freedom
and has been proving elusive, too.

Such a method on the part of a novelist may, of course,
when detected by his commentators, give rise to a certain
amount of nonsense. One can hardly, for example, accept
all the conjectures of Mr. Mikhail Koryakov, the author
of the article quoted earlier on the relations between
Pasternak and Stalin. Mr. Koryakov, in another article,
in the *Novoe Russkoe Slovo* of February 8th, has tried to
show that Yury's competence as an oculist—which is
never, as Mr. Koryakov notes, mentioned after his gradu-
ation from medical school—is picked up towards the end
of the book when Zhivago, on being told by Dudorov,
who has served a term in jail, that he feels he is a better

man for the brain-washing given him by the magistrate, has the melancholy impression of listening to a horse who is telling about breaking himself in. The breaking-in of a horse, Mr. Koryakov points out, implies the use of blinders, the partial suppression of the use of the eye, and he manages, by an argument I shall not trace, to discover in these two widely separated passages a "polemic with Mayakovsky."

Yet symbols and parallels do evidently exist in *Zhivago*. They are deliberate and very important: the whole story is organized around them; they lie at the center of the meaning of the book; and once we have become aware of them, we see it composed as a harmony.

Certain criticis who have made the objection that *Zhivago* is a social novel, conceived in an antiquated mode and not very well contrived, have completely missed the spirit and the shape of the book. These critics have been misled, I believe, by the English and Anglo-American translations, which—partly, perhaps, inevitably, but to some extent unnecessarily—have eliminated so much of the poetry and ignored the significant emphases. *Doctor Zhivago* is not at all old-fashioned: in spite of some echoes of the Tolstoyan tone in certain of the military scenes, there is no point in comparing it with *War and Peace*. It is a modern poetic novel by a writer who has read Proust, Joyce and Faulkner, and who, like Virginia Woolf or the Lawrence Durrell of the Alexandria series, has gone on from his predecessors to invent in this genre a variation of his own. We may early in our reading of the book come to see that the most salient incidents are intended to stand for something—as in the case of the masterly episode of the journey in the train with the deaf-mute, who figures the insulation from reality of a certain type of *exalté* in the first phase of the Revolution. But we may still be disposed to wonder, at the beginning of one of the divisions of a chapter, why the author has chosen to describe at such length some aspect of the weather or the landscape or to concentrate upon some scene involving a set of characters to whom we have not yet been introduced and whom we do not expect to meet again.

I am puzzled still by some of these passages. Why, for example, at the beginning of *The Highway,* do we spend so much time in the merchant's house in the little Siberian village? That this opening has some special significance is shown by the fact that it is saturated, in a very Joycean way—I was quite unaware of this till Mrs. Lehovich called my attention to it—with ecclesiastical references: words, objects, colors and sounds. (It is Holy Week, to be sure: death and resurrection again.) But in most cases it soon becomes clear that the apparently random description or scene is a metaphor for some moment of history, some facet of the social situation, some state of mind of the characters, which forms the real subject of its section.

And so, we come finally to realize, the whole book is an enormous metaphor for the author's vision of life. The personalities of Yury and Larisa stream back into wider reaches, a realm in which their contours and features are lost, in which they become indefinables, unclassifiable poetic elements that can only be conveyed by imagery; and it is not only the imagery of these metaphors but their rhythms of recurrence, their alienations, their confluences and interfusions that express the real sense of *Zhivago.*

April 25, 1959

1965. In the *Nation* of September 12, 1959, there appeared an important interview with Pasternak by Mr.

Ralph E. Matlaw, a professor of Russian at Princeton. Pasternak told Mr. Matlaw that *Zhivago* had "nothing to do with Joyce," and that he knew only vaguely of *Finnegans Wake*. He had, he said, no use at all for the kind of symbolism suggested in my articles. "The name Zhivago has no special significance, it is just a name." But when the interviewer raised the question of the significant recurrence of windows, the poet said, "Ah, you noticed that, did you?," and in another connection, replied, "Certainly, there are several such organizing centers or principles in the book." In other cases, Pasternak "maintained that none of these images was more than a description, and none was symbolic, but he was willing, if not eager to entertain the idea. . . . I concluded that while a great deal of the symbolism . . . is conscious, there is also much that is valid if not conscious or intentional. . . . [Certain of his] remarks on procedure seemed to me guarded or at least reticent. But the flashes of interest in new questions and pleasure in the discovery of new details . . . point to the thought, skill and love lavished on *Doctor Zhivago*. At the same time, they strongly suggest that its structural and symbolic ramifications, while consistent, far exceed Pasternak's conscious efforts."

I believe that two factors are involved in Pasternak's statements in this interview and in certain of his letters to foreigners. First, as Mr. Matlaw suggests, it seems to me that Pasternak was not always aware of the poetic implications of his apparently realistic imagery. His poetry proper—that is, his verse—is full of metaphors not immediately identifiable and unexpected associations of ideas, which must have gone straight to the page from the poet's mind without his having reasoned about them. Second, that he knew it would be very unwise to make all his meaning explicit. For his relations with the Soviets and the outside world, he had to practice in connection with *Zhivago* a constant and skilful duplicity. This began when the Soviet government forbade him to publish the novel after the manuscript was already in Italy in the hands of Feltrinelli, and he was obliged to send the publisher a telegram declaring that the novel was immature and he had decided that it ought not to be published. A little while afterwards, Feltrinelli received a smuggled-out letter saying something like, "I took special pains to word my wire in such a way that you would understand it in the opposite sense." He thereafter wrote to people abroad that his confessions of error in the Soviet press were not to be taken seriously, and, in a similarly smuggled letter, he wrote to Stephen Spender, near the end, that his life had been made a hell. He could hardly have admitted publicly in an officially atheistic state that his book had a Christian base. In one of his public utterences, he says that his use of the Gospels is merely so much paraphernalia, and it is difficult to be sure to what extent Pasternak had become a believer; but the impact of the final poem, with all that has gone before it, gives certainly a strong impression of resulting from true Christian conviction, and Pasternak was buried at the last with the rites of the Greek Orthodox Church. He never denied that, in the novel, the careers of Yury and Larisa offered parallels to the legends of their saints. This question seems never to have been asked him, but it is hard to see how he could have answered it. And it may be that the same considerations prevented him from admitting the reasons for his choice of the name Zhivago.

DONMANSHIP

IT IS ASTONISHING that Stephen Potter should have been able to sustain this joke so long. *Supermanship, or How to Continue to Stay on Top without Actually Falling Apart,* the fourth volume of the series that began with *Gamesmanship,* is in no respect inferior to the others. It begins with a report on the progress of the Lifemanship Correspondence College of One-Upness and Gameslife-mastery. The college has now a new building, "actually smaller" but "infinitely more modern," which "partly derives from the Chapel of the Secondary School at Ausverfleischenhültz." There have also been changes in personnel. G. Odoreida, whose "unethical" practices had always presented a problem, was, it seems, dropped four years ago, and has started a spurious school of his own. On the other hand, three new members have been added to the Lifemanship staff. C. Sticking has a "primary attack," "extraordinarily difficult to counter," which mainly consists of a laugh, "big and Falstaffian, blowing away cobwebs," "a happy guilt-free laugh—'gloriously sane,' little Effie Weeks called it." He was able to remain "top man" for fourteen months till deposed by the Law-renceman, who is "small, pale, intent, serious, with rather large plastic features in a small face, and a big dark beard, round and soft and soggy." They never knew whether he had actually read Lawrence (D. H.), but he had some-how picked up from him a formidable method. It was found that he could stop Sticking dead in his tracks by shifting the conversation to a level where one found oneself groping with primitive symbols and profound psychological insights. Both, however, were put to rout by J. Cannery—who seems to combine something of Angus Wilson with something of John Betjeman. Cannery was invariably delighted with everything that was said and done because—a specialist in the history of lift styles—he was a connoisseur in the ideas and architecture of the middle class day-before-yesterday. If Sticking said, "Progress . . . ," for example, the Lawrenceman would say, "In what sense?" But Cannery would block them with, "It's dead right for period." One thing that makes these books so good is the brevity and compactness of the presentation. As in any practical manual, the principles are stated and concisely illustrated. Nothing goes on too long.

This opening section is followed by discussions of the Lifemanship of Babies; "How to be good at the piano without being able to play much really"; "How to be Top Christmas"; Reviewmanship; Carmanship; and the ploys and counterploys in use among lecturers and chairmen. The chairman, to undermine the lecturer, may have little notes sent him from the audience and reply with distracting signals; or, in sitting down after his introduction, cross his legs in such a way as to reveal that his right sock does not extend much above the shoe, thus diverting the attention of the audience to "this large white naked ankle." The lecturer may resort to the Distinction gambit by waiting till the house is quiet and "taking one small tablet out of a green glass bottle from which a very long tail of cotton-wool has to be pulled before the tablet will come out, and then be stuffed back after," thus suggesting that he is "plucky to be there at all" and that it is only the burning spirit that gives him the strength "to raise the chalk to the blackboard." There is, also, a ploy-by-ploy guide to the ways in which Supertown and Supercountry may score off one another when playing host.

I had supposed that the kind of covert dueling which Potter has been satirizing—though of course it goes on everywhere—was a phenomenon that, in this virulent form, was particularly characteristic of English life in the period since the last war—in which a fierce competition of pretenses has been stimulated by the recent lapsing of actual prestige and wealth. But a rereading of Thackeray's *Book of Snobs* has shown me that this habit is of very long standing. The fakery of Supercountry as well as other themes of Potter's appear here in more pompous and brutal terms. Of the pretenses that are satirized by Thackeray, winemanship survives in Potter; but in Potters' more impoverished and less feudal world, there can hardly be any question of having the grocer brought in to play butler.

There is one aspect of Potter's subject which I have been looking to see him deal with but which he has so far unaccountably neglected: one-upmanship in academic circles. This seems strange in view of the fact that Stephen Potter began as a scholar and must know the academic life. It is to be hoped that he will eventually deal with it; but, in the meantime, since he has not done so, I should like to add here a few notes that I have collected in this department.

The commonest and most primitive kind of competition that goes on among American professors is to top one another in reading. I was once told of a conversation between Irving Babbitt and someone else of equal competence in the field of romantic literature which soon reduced itself entirely to an exchange of the titles of books. In this game, the opponent is supposed to show by a brief appropriate comment that he has read the book named by the other. Of course it is easy to cheat if one's opponent does not press one too far. One may know something *about* the book without having actually read it, and so risk a non-committal response that cannot be too wide of the mark. But if the question is cleverly put and searchingly followed up, it may reduce the opponent to a confession of ignorance. One of the high scores is driving one's opponent—this is quite difficult to do—to a confession that he has not only not read the book but has not even heard of it. The highest points of all—and I have heard of this happening at Harvard—are scored by inventing a non-existent book and getting the other man to pretend he has read it. The most reliable way, I should say from my own experience, for the non-academic person to counter a well-equipped scholar, who has scrutinized and read more than he has, is to cut in with some opinion, offhandedly and freely expressed, which is quite outside the scholar's gambits and will cause him to gasp and sulk. I discovered this, entirely without malice, through a series of incidents in conversing with professors. In talking to the late Tucker Brooke, at the time he was working on Marlowe, I referred to T. S. Eliot's theory that *The Jew of Malta* was meant to be comic. It turned out that Eliot on Marlowe was completely out of bounds. When, later, I had been reading John Ford, I expressed to another Elizabethan expert what seemed to me the harmless opinion that Ford, when he strove to be fancy and fine, was imitating the later Shakespeare. This elicited the sharp rejoinder that this had never been said by anyone, that no statement of any such opinion could be found in the literature of the subject. I now exploit these shock tactics deliberately.

But all this is crude enough work in comparison with

the refinements of one-upmanship which are practiced in the English universities. A book can be banished from the conversation by saying, "Oh, do you really?" and changing the subject. John Strachey has an excellent story of meeting in the street at Cambridge, in his undergraduate days, his older cousin Lytton, to whom he expressed his enthusiasm for Freud. Lytton soon put an end to this by saying simply, in his high voice, "Does that interest you?" There is also the more piquant method of behaving in such a way as to suggest that for reasons too vile to mention, the author in question is a pariah. Either ploy is effective in preventing one's opponent from knowing whether the author has been read or not. There is also the more commonplace trick of concealing one's ignorance of, say, Wells's novels by admiring his scientific fantasies (which one may well not have read either) or of Shaw's plays by praising his dramatic—or even better, his music criticism.

But the feats I admire most are the Oxford-Cambridge devices for remaining inexpugnably on top of one's subject. I used to be told that the approved procedure was to go on being known all one's life as an authority on some subject without ever publishing anything. You were supposed to know so much about it that no one dared to bring it up in your presence. Then you died, leaving nothing but notes, which you bequeathed to some scholar, who would never do anything with them. But I believe that this quiet method is now rather out of date. Instead, they have a marvellous new double ploy. You work a long time on some aspect of, say, Milton, of whom—to the consternation of people who think highly of him and are eager to hear about him—you speak with utter contempt: "A randy old Puritan who hated women"; or of Voltaire: "A professional cad." But then when your book appears, it turns out that you have treated your subject with deep reverence and perfect discretion. You have thus, very effectively, scored twice: first by shocking people, then—after the shock has worn off—by doing what they hadn't expected.

September 26, 1959

THE ALBUMS OF EDWARD GOREY

I FIND THAT I CANNOT REMEMBER to have seen a single printed word about the books of Edward Gorey, but it is not, I suppose, surprising that his work should have received no attention. It so far consists of four small volumes —never running to much over sixty pages—of drawings accompanied by captions. I do not think that this neglect is entirely due to its macabre or Surrealist character, for this is a quality that is now rather fashionable and that other artists have been able to cash in on. Gorey's drawings have something in common with one aspect of Ronald Searle and with such a book of Philippe Jullian's as *Le Cirque du Père Lachaise*. But Searle works for *Punch*, and both he and Jullian are illustrators of other people's books, while Gorey, except for designing the covers of certain of the paperback Anchor series, has done little commercial illustrating. He has been working quite perversely to please himself, and has created a whole little personal world, equally amusing and somber, nostalgic and claustrophobic, at the same time poetic and poisoned.

This world, in which costume and furnishings are always very important, is sometimes late Victorian: balustraded and panelled great houses, in which the cups hang on hooks in the china closet and the master may be found chewing the bell rope; sometimes of the early nineteen-hundreds, where young men in peg-top trousers and boaters and young ladies in sailor blouses become involved in sinister incidents while rowing or playing croquet; sometimes, though more rarely, of the twenties, in which girls with short skirts and cloche hats may be subjected to upsetting experiences.

The first of Mr. Gorey's books, *The Unstrung Harp; or, Mr. Earbrass Writes a Novel,* was published in 1953. In this chronicle of thirty drawings has been concentrated the boredom, the monotony, the impermeable solipsistic confinement of the life of the professional writer. When Mr. Earbrass is first revealed to us, he is standing on his snow-covered lawn, fur-coated but holding a croquet mallet as he broods over the balls and wickets of a game left unfinished at the end of the summer. Mr. Earbrass lives alone in the country in a decorous old-fashioned house, and he seems to get along without servants. He has short legs and a long, bald flat head, with no forehead, and the portraits and statuettes with which his rooms are sparsely ornamented all look exactly like him. He always begins a new novel on November 18th every other year, and since it is snowing this year on November 18th, he starts his story with a blizzard. We follow him through the months of the writing of the book, the rereading of the manuscript with sharp disgust, the laborious rearrangement of material, the preparation of the final clean copy. We see him looking up an epigraph and making some notes for a landscape. One day, at the head of the stairs, he meets one of his minor characters, who in appearance closely resembles himself. We find him at a literary dinner among his fellow-authors, "few of whom he recognizes and none of whom he knows," but all of whom look very much like him. We see him going through his galleys; examining the sketch for the jacket; reflecting on the number of copies that it is appropriate to send out to friends; loitering at a shop-window and "having made certain, out of the corner of his eye," that his own book is there, going on, "in a state of extreme and pointless em-

barrassment," to take account of all the other titles; then
when the reviews come in, trying not to be too eager to
read them. He finally "stands on the terrace at twilight.
It is bleak; it is cold; and the virtue has gone out of everything." We last see him waiting for the boat that is to
take him to the Continent for a holiday. He expects to be
horribly seasick, but though he knows "he is a person to
whom things do not happen, perhaps they may when he
is on the other side."

The next album, *The Listing Attic* (1954), is a collection of illustrated limericks, which makes something of a
new departure in this form. The note is struck on an
opening page by an anguished and writhen figure who
cries, *"O rage! O désespoir!"* The incidents described in
these verses are sometimes horrible and always uncomfortable. Brilliant though many of the inventions are,
they are sometimes allowed to suffer from the lameness of
Mr. Gorey's verse. Such things should be polished and
perfect. It is annoying that the effectiveness of certain of
the best should be seriously impaired, as they are, by an
awkwardness of meter and phrasing:

> The sight of his guests filled Lord Cray
> At breakfast with horrid dismay,
>> So he launched off the spoons
>> The pits from his prunes
> At their heads as they neared the buffet.

> An indefatigable woman named Bavel
> Had often occasion to travel;
>> On the way she would sit
>> And furiously knit,
> And on the way back she'd unravel.

She has evidently knitted a sweater for an octopus, and
she eyes with a kind of fierce defiant smirk the man who
is sitting beside her and who is evidently somewhat dismayed. The limericks written in French have the handi-

cap that the author has not grasped, or chooses to disregard, the metrical importance of a final mute "e" when
the next word begins with a consonant. (And there is no
such word as *"estropiéments."*)

These books were followed by *The Doubtful Guest.*
Here we get a fuller picture of the morbid Edwardian
household of which we have had glimpses in *The Listing
Attic*. The young men with high collars are timid and
pale; the ladies are domestic and modest. The head of the
family, the Master, has become the most impressive figure
in Mr. Gorey's world of heavy draperies, flowered wallpaper and cavernous staircases. Black-bearded, towering
and usually clad in a thick fur coat or a corded and
wadded dressing gown, below which appear narrow,
patrician feet, he is evidently domineering, probably a
little cruel. But his authority is to be shaken by the
Doubtful Guest. This being, who invades the household, first appears on the terrace, perched on a stone urn.
It is a kind of flat-headed bird, with short legs and
penguin wings, which looks rather like Mr. Earbrass, the
novelist. It is wearing a muffler and tennis shoes—the
latter, with Gorey, a recurrent motif. It runs quickly into
the house and stands at first "with its nose to the wall,"
but in the morning it joins the family for breakfast and
eats up all the syrup and toast as well as part of a plate.
The family are helpless against it, and it becomes a permanent nuisance.

It wrenched off the horn from the new gramophone,
And could not be persuaded to leave it alone. . . .

At times it would tear up whole chapters from books,
Or put roomfuls of pictures askew on their hooks. . . .

It would carry off objects of which it grew fond,
And protect them by dropping them into the pond.

But this creature is not merely mischievous; it seems also distinctly unhappy; and no "adjustment" to it is ever made: there is no outcome to the story of the Doubtful Guest. The conflict is never "resolved." At the end of the sequence, the tennis-shoed penguin has been living with the family for seventeen years. The small boy has grown to manhood; the parents are now gray.

The next album (1958), is called, ominously, *The Object-Lesson*. Here you have another such family, but their adventures are entirely Surrealist and remind one a little of such books of Max Ernst's as *La Femme 100 Têtes*. The "story line" is always shifting; the situations are never explained. One of the most delightful sequences is expounded by the following three captions:

"He descended [from the top of a tower] destroying the letter unread,

and stepped backwards into the water [a black-mustached massive figure, wearing a plaid Scotch cape].

Heavens, how dashing! cried the people in the dinghy. . . ."

These seem to me the very best drawings that Gorey has so far done; he is really becoming a master. In the first—"It was already Thursday"—an anxious-faced black female figure, lightly balanced at the right by a potted plant, is thrown into rigid and sharp relief by a long expanse of curly-patterned wallpaper. In a scene on the top of the tower, another lady clad in black, with her high heels and feather boa, makes an exquisite silhouette as she throws herself over the battlements. In the sequence

"On the shore a bat, or possibly an umbrella.

disengaged itself from the shrubbery,

causing those nearby to recollect the miseries of childhood . . . ,"

the spare delicacy of the the trees and the queer flying
object contrast, on the barren landscape, with the almost
monumental forms of the heavily upholstered persons. At
the end—"Farewell"—three silent figures, the Master and
two of his ladies, face a long expanse of darkening sky, a
background like the wallpaper in the first of the pictures,
balanced by a remote little moon, which, in its place in
the composition, has the value of the potted plant.

These albums give me something of the same sort of
pleasure that I get from Aubrey Beardsley and Max Beerbohm, and I find that I like to return to them.

December 26, 1959

MAX NOMAD AND WACLAW MACHAJSKI

THE SPECIALIST IN REVOLUTIONARY HISTORY who writes
under the name of Max Nomad has published a new and
important book called *Aspects of Revolt*. Max Nomad,
whose first book, *Rebels and Renegades*, appeared in
1932, has occupied a unique position in the intellectual
world of New York. Though working exclusively in the
field of reformist and radical politics, he has had no affili-
ation, during this period of literary activity, with any
political party, nor has he written to promote any cause.
He has been critical of the leaders of all the movements,
and this has not made him popular with the Left. Far
from sharing utopian illusions, he is skeptical alike of the
capacity of the masses to improve their own condition and
of the capacity for sustained disinterestedness of those
who claim to represent them. What, then, is the fascination that revolution exerts for Max Nomad? What has
made him a connoisseur of radicals? In order to understand his point of view, you must know that he was born
in Eastern Galicia and educated mostly in Vienna, and
that, as he tells us in the preface to this latest book, he
was "a Socialist in my high-school days, an Anarchist as a
college student, a Syndicalist *sui generis* during the years
of my romantic and not-so-romantic vagabondage, and
finally a Soviet sympathizer some forty years ago when
Lenin and Trotsky were still glorious legends, between
1917 and 1920." But at some point—what was cardinal

for his thinking—he came under the influence of Waclaw Machajski, an heretical Polish radical whose ideas
are calculated to eat away the convictions of any school
that has pretended to have for its object the establishment
of a Socialist state which will realize a dream of equality.

Waclaw Machajski (pronounced "Vátzlav Makhígh-
ski"), who was born in Russian Poland, began as a Polish
nationalist and then became a revolutionary Marxist.
When Machajski was twenty-six years old, in 1892, he
made an attempt to smuggle into Poland a provocative
manifesto, prepared by Polish and Russian students in
Switzerland, that was intended to support a rebellion of
the factory workers of Lodz. He was caught and sent to
Siberia, where he spent eight years in the extreme north-
east, on the edge of the Arctic Circle. He had, however,
as was possible in those days, when the censorship was
easy to evade, an excellent opportunity to acquaint
himself with Socialist literature, and this literature had
upon Machajski an entirely unintended effect. It led him
to certain conclusions quite contrary to Socialist theory
which he expounded first, while still in Siberia, in a
small treatise called *The Evolution of Social Democracy*,
published under a pseudonym and circulated illegally.
This he later, after leaving Russia, incorporated in a
larger work, called *The Intellectual Worker*, which was
printed in Russian in Geneva.

The most important feature of the theory of politics
which Machajski propounded in these writings was the
discovery that the Socialists, who had put themselves
forward as the spokesmen and agents of the working
class, in reality belonged already, without their being
aware of it, to a class of an entirely new kind, whose
interests they would eventually defend at the expense of
the interests of the manual workers. This class was
composed of technicians, intellectuals, professional men,

and middle-class clerks and officials who had had a good
education. It was a group that had enormously increased
in the course of the eighteenth and nineteenth centuries,
and it had now become impossible for its members to
depend, as they had formerly done, on aristocratic or royal
patronage. They did not recognize themselves as a class,
but, conscious that their value to society was increasing in
proportion to the decline of the feudal regime, they felt
also the impulse toward power, and they reached out—
having no other possible allies against the remnants of the
old society and the strong and commercial bourgeoisie—
for the support of the working class. In the case of the
Socialist parties in the countries west of Tsarist Russia,
Machajski decided that, no matter how Marxist they
pretended to be in their objectives, they were not moved
by any real intention of overthrowing the capitalist system: they merely wanted to have a share in directing it;
and as for Russia itself, when its rebels should have got
rid of absolutism, they would eventually behave in the
same way. These reformers did not really aim at what
they called the "classless society," which was just as much
"pie in the sky" as their American Socialist successors
were to call the rewards of religion. It was a lure to win
adherents from the working class. Their true unavowed
aim was gradually to supplant the private capitalists, and
for this they needed first not violence but democratic
processes of government, which would enable them to get
into office, and then government ownership of industries,
which would make them the supreme masters. They
would absorb certain former capitalists and certain able
self-educated workers, and they would function as an
administrative hierarchy, with larger salaries than the
working class, and in consequence wider freedom and
superior education. They would soon forget the interests
of the working class when its help was no longer needed.

Now, this theory of Machajski's falls in with a number of striking predictions—inspired by hopes or by fears—that had already been made by others. One remembers the ideal of the Comte de Saint-Simon, who, in the early years of the nineteenth century, proposed a great "Council of Newton"—since he believed that it was Newton who had been chosen by God to convey the divine revelations—to be composed exclusively of scientists, writers, composers and painters, which was to organize and run society in accordance with social laws corresponding to the physical ones that governed the heavenly bodies; and one remembers that the followers of Saint-Simon emphatically disavowed any interest in promoting equality among the properly unequal grades of men. It is significant in this connection that the last leader of the Saint-Simonist movement should have begun as an engineer and ended as a railroad director. And Max Nomad quotes some other prophecies by political thinkers that point in the same direction. The Anarchist leader Mikhail Bakunin, in 1873, predicted that the Marxist state, if it ever came into existence, would be dominated by a "privileged minority. . . . That minority, the Marxists say, will consist of workers. Yes, perhaps of *former* workers. And these, as soon as they become rulers or representatives of the people, will cease to be workers and will look upon the entire world of manual workers from the heights of the State. They will no longer represent the people, but themselves and their own pretensions to rule the people. . . . They will establish a single State Bank that will concentrate in its hands all commercial-industrial, agricultural and even scientific production; and the mass of the people will be divided into two armies, the industrial and the agricultural, which will be under the direct command of government engineers who will constitute a new privileged scientific political class." Herbert Spencer, in 1884, in his *Man Versus the State,* said that "the machinery of Communism, like existing social machinery, has to be framed out of existing human nature; and the defects of existing human nature will generate in the one the same evils as in the other. The love of power, the selfishness, the injustice, the untruthfulness, which often in comparatively short times bring private organizations to disaster, will inevitably, where their effects accumulate from generation to generation, work evils far greater and less remediable; since, vast and complex and possessed of all the resources, the administrative organization, once developed and consolidated, must become irresistible. . . . It would need but a war with an adjacent society, or some internal discontent demanding forcible suppression, to at once transform a socialistic administration into a grinding tyranny like that of ancient Peru, under which the mass of the people, controlled by grades of officials, and leading lives that were inspected out-of-doors and indoors, labored for the support of the organization which regulated them, and were left with but a bare subsistence for themselves." Max Nomad might also have cited Flaubert's prophetic creation, in his *L'Éducation Sentimentale,* of Sénécal, the mathematics teacher, who is first an intransigent Socialist, then a merciless factory foreman, then a policeman putting down the workers in the revolution of 1848. Thorstein Veblen, who was not intransigent but who made certain radical criticisms of the American economic system, departed from conventional theory by arguing, in *The Engineers and the Price System*—the book that gave rise to the Technocracy movement—that if any sort of Socialistic society was ever to be realized in the United States, the transformation would have to be effected not by the working class but by the concerted action of the engineers. The cold contempt of Marx and Engels for most of their working-class collaborators, although this was not shared by Lenin, set an example to the later leaders of the Union of Soviet Socialist Republics, who have confirmed the worst apprehensions of Bakunin and Herbert Spencer. The forecasts of James Burnham's book *The Managerial Revolution* are in process of being confirmed by the tightening grip on the United States of the armed forces, the engineers (the Corps of Engineers is of course itself a part of the Army), and a host of professional bureaucrats, often the products of our "schools of administration," who are rapidly and alarmingly getting into their hands more and more of the business of the government, the foundations, the universities and the various public institutions—to which group, as Max Nomad points out, the officials of the labor unions also belong.

In regard to the fundamental principle involved in these recurrent phenomena, so subversive of Socialist assumptions, Machajski was certainly right. There is a category of class here implied that has never been recognized in quite the same way by the analysts of "class structure." Mussolini and the Russian Communists and the bureaucrats of the Pentagon Building, though they speak in different-sounding dialects, wear uniforms of different design and mutually denounce one another, do undoubtedly have nevertheless a professional managerial interest in common. But Machajski's announcement of this law by which the managers and intellectuals first enlist the support of the manual workers and then drop them to consolidate their own position did not, as one might have expected, put an end to his radical activities. If the leaders of the Socialist sects had invariably, in the past, let the workers down, he himself would prove an exception by continuing to defend their interests; he would stick by them to the end. He would not only fight

to increase their wages but would insist, after the advent
of the bureaucratic state, on reducing its managers' salaries to a parity with the workers' augmented pay. But
how was this to be accomplished? By a revolutionary
dictatorship—for it was figuratively in very small type
that Machajski admitted this. He spoke of it in print only
once, and his followers mistakenly assumed that he had
later abandoned this idea. In his post-Siberian phase, he
never mentioned the seizure of power but spoke exclusively of the strategy of strikes as a way of enforcing the
workers' demands. But even though he does not go
further than the pressure to be brought to bear by striking, there is implied here, as Max Nomad says, a serious
inconsistency with Machajski's general thesis. For would
not the end result of the policy of continual strikes be not
merely equalization of income but also nationalization of
industry? The employers could not be expected to consent
to reduce their own incomes to the level of the manual
workers, and if they declared a general lockout, the
government would have to take over. If the educated
followers of Machajski then took over the government,
they would soon become a specialized group and would
award themselves special privileges. When Machajski's
disciples asked him why they themselves, not coming
from the laboring class, were working against their own
class interests, he would answer that they were working
in the interests of their "revolutionary career"—that is,
they were the only revolutionists who would be able to
sustain their loyalty to the working class and who would
thus effect a true revolution. When they asked him how,
assuming their eventual success, it would be possible for
the uneducated workers not to continue to be deceived by
the educated people who governed them, he would answer that the means of deception would by that time have
become exhausted.

Machajski and his Russian followers, who called themselves the Workers' Conspiracy, took a small but active
part in the 1905 revolution, concentrating on public
works for the relief for the unemployed, rather than on
the struggle for political democracy. But the group was
broken up by arrests, and Machajski again went abroad.
He was able to come back to Russia after the Bolshevik
Revolution and to publish one issue of a paper called
Workers' Revolution, in which he warned the industrial
workers who were supposedly now the masters of Russia
that it was really the intelligentsia who would rule *them*
through their workers' deputies. He told them that they
must equalize incomes (which, consistently with the
teaching of Marx, had never been an aim of the Soviets),
otherwise they would never be allowed to have access to
the higher grades of education. "When the working class
strives for its own rule, it means that it strives for revolutionary domination *over* the government. Through its
revolutionary pressure, through the expression of the will
of the toiling millions, the working class ought to dictate
the law to the government." But how was this to rescue
the situation from Machajski's own vicious circle? Nobody, in any case, paid much attention. Some of his followers had joined the Bolsheviks. But, later on, the predictions of Machajski began to trouble the minds of the
manipulators of the Soviet ideology. In the twenties, they
went so far as to prohibit the republication of Machajski's
books and pamphlets which had been written in Siberia
and Switzerland twenty years before, and the more the
Soviet society came to justify Machajski's thesis by
producing a privileged officialdom that coerced and ha-
rassed the "peasants and workers," the more savage
against him this officialdom became. Trotsky made a
point of attacking him, because almost to the end, in
exile, he persisted in denying that the Soviet bureaucracy

was really an exploiting class. When Machajski died, in 1926, *Pravda* printed four columns of denunciation, and twelve years later, at the time of the purges, when the bureaucracy had become a despotism, it devoted six columns to him. These blasts, says Max Nomad, must have seemed to it the only revenge it could take. He was dead, and no doubt his few followers had either also died or left Russia, so they could not be made to confess that they were counter-revolutionary Trotskyists in the service of Wall Street and Hitler.

The story of Waclaw Machajski is told in Max Nomad's new book, and he is present in all its thinking, as he has been in that of Nomad's earlier works. Max Nomad is to this extent a loyal disciple: that he still stands up for "the masses" and believes that their condition has been actually improved by the struggle of organized labor, though—with the exception of "a few pure idealists"—their leaders continue to behave in the way Machajski said they would. As we have seen, he shows Machajski's inconsistencies, but he also elaborates Machajski's themes and supplements Machajskis' findings with a good deal of new material derived from his own research and observation.

One of the chapters of *Aspects of Revolt, The Elusive Ideal,* discusses equality of income and seeks to show that it can never be realized, since there must always, at the outset of any society that is aiming to establish Socialism—as Marx was forced to admit and as the Soviet Union has demonstrated—be categories of public servants who need to live in greater comfort and who may claim for themselves higher incomes than the citizens on lower levels of culture and responsibility. These begin with a great advantage over the general run of the population because they are better educated. Now, suppose that, by some miracle of disinterestedness, these exceptionally well-equipped officials make an attempt to give everybody else the benefit of a training equal to theirs. Long before the general level has been raised to the point at which the former illiterates have shown themselves capable of this higher education, the program to improve them will inevitably have lapsed; the official technicians and managers will so have consolidated their group position that they will have made such higher training their monopoly. This happened in the Soviet Union, where at first the children of the Red Army officers and of the other upper strata were sent to superior schools; but this grading of education is now said to have been abolished or disguised. In any case, the student who could qualify for higher education must be sound in his attitude toward the Soviet State and may be expected, if able enough, to take his place in its upper ranks; and something of the kind must also have happened in the case of the families of our union officials, who can afford to send their children to better schools than are possible for the ordinary members. Differences in education will be always, says Max Nomad, unavoidable, and they will always make equality impossible. Another chapter, *Why and How They Changed,* presents a whole parade of cases of Left statesmen and labor leaders—Weitling, Lassalle, Clemenceau, Briand, Pilsudski, Ramsay MacDonald, Mussolini—who illustrate Machajski's thesis in a variety of ways. We learn that even Norman Thomas, who has been surely one of the most steadfast of Socialist leaders, has finally been brought to the conclusion that "the messianic hope which consciously or unconsciously inspired most of us to become Socialists is scarcely tenable in America or elsewhere in the world. . . . History and our better knowledge of our human psychology have destroyed or profoundly altered that particular scheme of earthly salvation. We have learned much about the temptations of power, and we know that there is no messianic working class nor any sort of élite that we can trust automatically to save 'mankind.'"

Another chapter, *The Pedestal*—particularly dampening—consists of examples of the recurrent stupidity of the uninstructed masses in voting against their own interests: "the docility," for example, "of the millions of American organized workers who, save in the case of almost monumental scandals, permanently reëlect their dictatorial rulers, even if—not satisfied with their fabulous salaries—they are disposing of the union treasuries and welfare funds as if they were their own property"; the action of the British lower classes, after the victory of the Labour Party in 1945, in subsequently restoring the Conservatives, for the reason, according to Nomad, that they believed themselves to have risen to the middle class and now to owe it their class allegiance; and the voting out of office by the Milwaukee electorate of their Socialist municipal government, after what Mr. Nomad says was "an unimpeachable twenty-four year record of a graftless administration," under the influence of "a young and charming demagogue whose only plank was 'Clean out City Hall and oust the Socialists.'"

Has Max Nomad perhaps himself been a little inconsistent here? Might not this administration, in its twenty-four years of office, already, in conformity with Machajski's law, have been alienating itself from its constituents, so that these latter were correct in repudiating it? And what about the British Labour government in the country in all the world in which Sorel's law of "social capillarity" is supposed to operate most rapidly? There is also an amusing chapter, *Dead Dogs and Holy Falsehoods,* which discusses the uses of slander in the revolutionary struggle for power, from John Quincy Adams's description of

Jefferson as "double-dealing, treacherous, and false beyond all toleration," through Marx's nasty attack on
Bakunin for the purpose of getting him out of the First
International, to *Pravda's* characterization of Gandhi as "a
flunky of British imperialism." But this kind of slander is
by no means confined to the politics of revolution. What
about Lyndon Johnson on Kennedy just before the latter's
nomination? What about Kennedy on Nixon just afterwards?

One gets a distinct impression that Max Nomad keeps
a filing case in which he puts away, as he happens on
them, examples of the various types of paradox involved
in Left Wing politics—which paradoxes themselves form
a kind of collection. Thus in chapters such as the two last
mentioned there are moments when *Aspects of Revolt*
seems a little like a mere cabinet of curiosities of revolutionary behavior. There are also a chapter on *Bandits
with a Philosophy*—Pancho Villa, the American Anar-
chists, the Bolshevik "expropriators," of whom Stalin was
one and at whose "expropriations" Lenin winked—and
another on *Angry Amazons*—Frances Wright, the early-
nineteenth-century social reformer; Sofia 'erovskaya,
who assassinated Alexander II; Emma Goldman, the
Anarchist; Rosa Luxemburg, the independent Marxist;
and Beatrice Webb, the British Fabian Socialist—as to
whom Max Nomad seems to feel that they cannot be
assigned to the same category as his masculine figures and
whose careers he makes little attempt to analyze in the
Machajskian terms. Yet *Aspects of Revolt* is an effort in
the direction of an "anatomy" of revolution. It is, so far,
Nomad's best book, and one stops oneself from saying
what a pity it is that it was not written earlier, because
when one compares it with his earlier books—*Rebels and
Renegades* of 1932, and *Apostles of Revolution* of 1939—
one sees that before the last war Max Nomad, though

quite non-utopian, had still retained a little more of his original radical faith. At the end of the second of these, he expresses the hope that "out of this bloody welter may emerge a European Union of Democratic Socialist Republics, equally remote from the jungle of capitalist chaos and from the graveyard of Fascist or 'Communist' totalitarianism. For all its economic inequalities, for all its never-ending class struggles between the higher and the lower income groups, such a Union would point the way toward a new civilization. A civilization combining the security of a planned socialized economy with that freedom of expression which is the only guarantee of progress."

A new phase for Max Nomad had, one sees, begun when, in 1953, he published his *A Skeptic's Political Dictionary and Handbook for the Disenchanted*. This mordant and amusing volume is described by the author in a foreword as a work of "melancholy radicalism." "My own modest ambition," he concludes, "is merely to help those few decent people, in the words of Chamfort, who may be hiding somewhere, to see clearly through the political double talk of yesterday, today, and the threatening tomorrow." Here is his definition of "Communist": "1. A man not to be judged hastily. He may turn out to be a stoolpigeon for the F.B.I. rather than a spy for the M.V.D. 2. One who believes that political liberty, though granted by non-Communists to Communists, should not be granted by Communists to non-Communists. 3. One who believes that a full dinnerpail is better than the right of free speech, and that therefore those who get impatient about the absence of the former under 'Communism' should be deprived of the right to complain about it." And here is his definition of "American Democracy": "A system under which the voters invariably elect the candidates presented to them by the political machines of one of the two big office-holders' and office-seekers' trusts. The result is a government of the people, by the people, for the people, carried on by politicians and office-holders in partnership with those owning the wealth of the country and holding it in trust for the people."

But he has not allowed himself to become a cynic. In the preface to *Aspects of Revolt,* which is, I suppose, his real testament, "I have no use," he says, "for those snobs, whether Nietzscheans or plain Babbitts, who look down with contempt upon the crowd; yet I cannot help realizing that the masses are hopelessly benighted and gullible, ready to submit to any form of servitude, either sanctified by tradition or ushered in by demagogues and adventurers after the long overdue collapse of the old regime." And the book, although also "disenchanted," is the most impressive example he has given us of his good will and his fundamental humanity as well as his immense multilingual learning and his inquiring comprehensive intelligence.

In the last chapter of *Aspects of Revolt*—called *Changeless America?*—Nomad speculates on the future of the United States. "The indifference," he says, "of the American workers toward anti-capitalist ideas has given America the unique status of a country which, for all its anti-Communist hysteria, is not threatened by either Socialism or Communism." But suppose automation and mechanical brains result in mass unemployment? Might not this result in violence of the characteristically American kind? Might not this rebellion necessitate the organization of "a super-New Deal that would combine the advantages of the Welfare State with those of a semi-socialized economy and full employment—while maintaining the traditional vocabulary of 'free enterprise,' dear to rich and poor alike in the United States, as are the myths of monarchy, pseudo-democracy, Socialism, Communism, and Fascism to the illusion-hungry denizens of other sections of the globe?" Or might not "an overproduction of the technical intelligentsia" result in the engineers' strike that Thorstein Veblen thought a possibility and the assumption by the engineers of the direction of American industry? "All this," Max Nomad concludes, "may or may not happen in the more or less distant future. However, for the time being it looks as if the comforts and benefits enjoyed by the great majority of those who in other countries are included among the underprivileged were a guarantee against any attempt—peaceful or violent—at a thoroughgoing change in the American way of life, all its injustices, inequalities, and prejudices notwithstanding." But "the center of gravity," he thinks, may "shift from the big shareholders to the engineers, the economists and the intellectual workers in general, whom the other sections of the population may have to restrain from becoming all too powerful."

The last time I saw Max Nomad was some years ago in Webster Hall, at a debate between Peter Viereck and Corliss Lamont, with Norman Thomas presiding. He was sitting in the first row of the balcony, regarding the speakers with the round dark eyes that combine a certain irony with blandness, and I wondered what had brought him out. Norman Thomas and Corliss Lamont were perfectly familiar to him; he must have known exactly what they would say; and I decided that it was the neo-conservatism of the Metternich-admiring Viereck which had piqued the curiosity of this expert. When I greeted him after it was over, he said nothing about the debate, but simply raised his eyebrows and smiled—the equivalent of a gentle shrug.

October 15, 1960

GEORGE F. KENNAN

GEORGE F. KENNAN's new study of international relations—*Russia and the West Under Lenin and Stalin*—is
surely one of the most valuable books that have appeared
in the United States since the end of the last war. To
describe it as simply a study of international relations is,
in fact, to give no idea of the nature of its singular
importance. This phrase suggests something academic,
and Mr. Kennan is anything but academic; nor, in spite
of his long years of service in the consulates and embassies
of Europe, is he at all readily recognizable as what is
called a career diplomat. Mr. Kennan has a quite independent and a deeply inquiring mind; his knowledge of
Western Europe and Russia is based upon long first-hand
experience as well as years of systematic research, and his
books are, I believe, in their field, coming to mark a
distinctly new phase in American political thought. He
has not merely mastered the languages and the histories
of the countries with which he deals; he has observed
them with a combination of sympathetic comprehension
and critical objectivity that must be rare in our State
Department. Together with a strong sense of fact and an
always realistic grasp of the practical problems of statesmanship, he has a sensitivity to personal relationships and
to the influence of national atmospheres as well as to the
literature and art of the foreign countries in which he has
lived, and our own national characteristics are subjected

to the same cool scrutiny as those of these other countries. The result is an overall view which transcends the provinciality of so much of our foreign policy and embraces the whole immense area from Washington to Peking. No one but an American could have written this book. It is one of the hopeful signs of a contemporary American consciousness that is finding itself at home in a larger world and bringing to it a new intelligence.

These chapters were first delivered as lectures at Oxford and Harvard Universities, and before a discussion of their content it may be worthwhile to say a word about their form. In view of the amount of ground covered and of the extreme complexity of the subject matter, the book is a triumph of presentation. The reviewer heard some of the lectures at Harvard, and as lectures they could hardly have been better. Though the succession of events was so close, the pace of narrative never telescoped them in such a way as to make them hard to follow, and though the argument had to be condensed, the language never failed to reach the listener through becoming too dry or abstract; the lucid and well-thought-out sentences were framed with a pleasant colloquialism that put the speaker and his audience quite at ease with one another. These qualities make the book always readable, but from the literary point of view the texts could have stood some revision. Mr. Kennan, though so careful a scholar, with so fine an appreciation of literature, is in some ways rather careless as a writer. He habitually uses *transpire* as if it meant *occur* and *disinterestedness* as if it meant *lack of interest*. He makes "a series of demands" plural and uses wrongly a plural "protagonists" (you can have only one protagonist in any given situation). He writes, "The country was *rampant* with hardship and disease" and "He finally succeeded . . . in licking the heavy financial problem which the depression had *spelled* for the German gov-

ernment." In the matter of colloquialism, he is sometimes
very happy, and sometimes, perhaps, not so happy, as
when he says that a "definition of peaceful coëxistence"
made by Chicherin at the Genoa Conference was "one
which Khrushchev could buy today." And there are
occasionally sentences that have quite gone wrong in
idiom or in grammar. It may well be that Mr. Kennan,
with his new official duties, had not time to attend to
these matters, but his publishers ought to have done so.
They have left Mr. Kennan's expression sometimes limping behind his intellect.

It would be sterile to attempt to summarize a work that
is itself a summary. But it ought to be said that, in the
period covered—from the Russian Revolution to the end
of the Second World War—many gaps are here filled
that, to the ordinary reader, had presented only confusion
or mystery. The reviewer spent several months at the end
of the First World War at the GHQ in France of the
American Expeditionary Force, in what was called the
Department of Exterior Fronts, sticking pins in a wall
map of Russia. These pins had different-colored heads
and were supposed to show the operations, as they were
conveyed by routine dispatches, of the various Allied and
White Russian forces engaged with the Soviet armies.
The dispatches, of course, told us nothing as to why these
Allied troops were out there in Archangel, Murmansk
and Siberia, and no real further light was thrown by the
bulletins of Chicherin, the Soviet Foreign Minister, that
strange nobleman among the Bolsheviks, who is well
described by Mr. Kennan. These bulletins were cast
entirely in a vague and eerie Marxist phraseology that
seemed to emanate from a disembodied spirit, diffusing its
thin voice through airwaves from the unknown transmuted realm that Russia had now become. I did not at

that time understand what French and British and Czech
and American troops were supposed to be doing in those
places. I had never, in fact, understood till I read Mr.
Kennan's book precisely what was involved in their various exploits. Mr. Kennan has looked up all the scattered
sources and disentangled all the anomalous situations,
showing just what was done by whom, and what they
hoped they were accomplishing by it, which was often
something quite different from the results that their
actions had. We Americans have been made by the
Soviets the archvillains in the foreign intervention on the
side of the Russian Whites, but Mr. Kennan—and he is
no special pleader—is able to show that Woodrow Wilson
did his best to keep us out of these doomed operations.

In regard to the behavior of Stalin toward the Western
countries, Mr. Kennan attempts a full explanation that,
to this reader, is partly novel. He believes that Stalin
hated the West for the same reason that he jumped at
any pretext for liquidating the Westernized Bolsheviks—
because he himself, uneducated, untravelled, knew nothing about the West and could not bear to get out of his
depth. Mr. Kennan dismisses the notion that Russia is a
great enigma. (One remembers Franklin Roosevelt's in-
souciant statement that he must someday try to find out
"what makes the Russians tick.") He reminds us that the
Western democracies, preoccupied with winning the
war—which seemed to them of paramount importance—
did not have any real comprehension of what was then
going on in the Russia that had suddenly dropped out of
it. We knew little about Russian society and we had no
realistic conception of the crisis it was going through.
Though Wilson, unlike the governments of England and
France, was in general sympathetic with the revolution,
the sole concern of the Western alliance was to make sure
that Russian armies were kept in action against the

Germans. The Russians and the West were, Mr. Kennan says—as in the case of our mechanical dispatches and the euphoric air vibrations of Chicherin—really "talking past" one another. Nor have we ever, officially, since then, learned to face and to accept Communist Russia. For this there is now no excuse. (I here paraphrase Mr. Kennan rather freely.) We must take cognizance of the Soviet Union with intelligence and equanimity. It is not dignified to keep denouncing a country with which one is technically at peace (let alone, as Dulles used to do, keep announcing that its regime is about to fall); leave that to *its* propagandists. And we should take account of the fact that, with our swift alternations between panicky vilification and applause for a gallant ally, our pretensions to be the sanctuary of civil rights and our outbreaks of violent repression, we may seem as enigmatic to the Russians as they have ever seemed to us.

On the subject of the Far East, Mr. Kennan declares himself less competent, but, treating China on a lesser scale, he is equally convincing in triangulating it in relation to the West and to Russia. The United States and the Soviet Union both, not understanding one another, were also in their respective ways mistaken about China. If the West assumed ignorantly that Russia, once it had got rid of the tsardom, would establish a parliament and a constitution, and if Russia expected that the West would almost immediately take its place in the Marxist picture by imposing the dictatorship of the proletariat, the first of these powers went wrong in supposing that there existed in China a responsible central government with which it would be possible to negotiate and the second in supposing that the Kuomintang, a local nationalistic movement, could be depended on as a Communist instrument. It would have been impossible for Stalin to manipulate amorphous China. It was the weakening of Europe by the two world wars, the subjugation of China by the Japanese, and their removal as a result of the second that eventually "created vacuums into which the Communists were prepared to flow," just as it was Hitler who, by wrecking Eastern Europe, laid it open to the Russian occupation. (This is true enough, and yet, in the case of China, it seems to me that Mr. Kennan should a little more take into account the logical appeal of Communism for a country that has adopted a program for the construction of an industrial society but has no money with which to finance it.)

These reciprocal misunderstandings derive, of course, not entirely from different systems, different ideologies, but also from geographical remoteness, and it is Kennan's consoling belief that this geographical remoteness is bound to prevent in the future any one of these apparently formidable powers from achieving world domination. The Russians have not been able really to dominate China, so how, the implication follows, can either they dominate the United States or we the Soviet Union? "There is no magic by which great nations are brought to obey for any length of time the will of people very far away who understand their problems poorly and with whom they feel no intimacy of origin or understanding. This has to be done by bayonets, or it is not done at all. . . . There are geographic limits to the possibilities of military occupation." Mr. Kennan does not mention the possibility, which seems to be obsessive for the official mind, that one power may damage another in such a way as to provide a "vacuum" so immense that the victor may occupy it and impose a domination more drastic than that of the Russians in China. It would, in that event, be a question not merely of bayonets but of a permanent threat of destruction, with a press that printed only Marxist jargon or a people that drank Coca-Cola and bought only quickly obsolescent goods, and there is also the possibility that the problem of the overpopulation of the world might be solved by the filling of two vacuums with the colonists from an overpeopled China.

Mr. Kennan, however, believes that "universal world dominion is a technical impossibility," and this disbelief seems to derive from a fundamental disbelief in the possible extensibility of any strongly centralized agency, even when it aims at being international and promoting the interests of peace. One has to look in this connection for the answers to certain questions—as to which this new book leaves one wondering—to an earlier set of lectures, *American Diplomacy 1900–50*, published in 1951. Here one finds that Mr. Kennan has little faith in a League of Nations or a United Nations. A great power can always defy them, and the voting by national units, regardless of their size or importance, encourages the inflamed modern nationalism that such organizations are supposed to check; one should rather encourage a fluidity that would not take national divisions too seriously, since these are often arbitrary and unrealistic. Even, besides, if one can act in a military way against the kind of aggression that is overt, how can such an international tribunal prevent—as in the case of Russia with its satellites of Eastern Europe—a quiet taking-over by penetration? The American faith in such agencies is the result of the tradition in the English-speaking countries of reliance on legalistic methods—a tradition that hardly exists except in America and Western Europe. Nor can "summitry," he concludes, prove of very much use. When the heads of great governments meet, they are obliged to make such serious compromises that what emerges from a summit conference is likely to be something as incoherent and as unworkable as the Treaty of Versailles, and the statesmen who conduct the conferences are invariably so hurried and so overtaxed by the number of the problems that they have to consider, so pursued by the Klieg lights of publicity, that it is almost impossible for them to accomplish anything. They are quite inadequate for "the task of diplomacy—which is really one of style, of perseverance and of ceaseless vigilance."

This brings us to recommendations which to some may come as unexpected. Mr. Kennan falls back on a method that seems to have something in common with the old-fashioned "balance of power." If there is danger of a dislocation of a stabilized status quo, let steps be taken to forestall it. By a single great power? By an alliance *ad hoc?* This seems to be left a little vague. And by whom are such decisions to be taken? Mr. Kennan makes very clear—though he does not have much hope of obtaining it—the procedure he would recommend. It is one of his strongest complaints that the direction of our foreign policy is too often deflected and confused by the pressure of public opinion. One may feel that perhaps Mr. Kennan, in this as in other respects, underestimates the ever-growing powers of the centralized modern government, that he here fails to recognize to what degree—as in the case of the last war—American public opinion is itself coming to be manipulated by systematic official propaganda. (As we shall see in a later quotation, he seems to identify the propaganda, once the country has gone to war, with the pressure of public opinion itself.) But let us assume that our foreign policy is distracted thus by popular pressures and ask how he proposes to avoid it. The answer—as he gives it in *American Diplomacy*—is by making "more effective use of the principle of professionalism," by developing "a corps of professional officers superior to anything that exists or ever has existed in this field . . . by treating these men with respect and drawing on their insight and experience." He fully recognizes the difficulty of realizing such an ideal—that to depend upon such professionals "runs counter to strong prejudices and preconceptions in sections of our public mind, particularly in Congress and the press, and that for this reason we are probably condemned to continue relying almost exclusively on what we might call 'diplomacy by dilettantism.'"

One sees what Kennan wants to avoid and one sympathizes with his wish to avoid it: the oscillations between abject terror and moist-eyed sentimentality that characterize our relations with foreign countries; our tendency to imagine them as heroes or villains. Up to the time of the First World War, the United States adored Germany. We went there to study music, philosophy, medicine and classical philology; the Kaiser and Theodore Roosevelt were regarded as opposite numbers. But from the moment of the invasion of Belgium, the Germans became "Huns" and the Kaiser "the Beast of Berlin." At the time of the war between Russia and Japan, the Japanese were "a wonderful little people," who were sling-shotting the Russian Goliath, the despotic oppressor of millions, but when we ourselves went to war with Japan, the Japanese became hissing little reptiles that it was now our duty to exterminate. When our up-to-date reptile-killer had worked on Nagasaki and Hiroshima, we made Japan our favorite pet till our favorite pet bit us. In the case of the Russians, we hailed them as allies in the struggle against Hitler without stopping to take account of the objectives of the Soviet government. Then, confronted, as Kennan says, with the kind of thing they might naturally have been expected to do, we transformed them into a menace to the "free world." What is needed, says Mr. Kennan, is to arrive at some understanding of what alien civilizations are up to. We should totally dismiss from our minds any assumption that they ought to resemble ours or what we like to imagine ours to be, that they should imitate our own institutions. (One remembers in this connection the small but significant fiasco of our attempt, when we occupied Germany at the end of the last war, to put an end to duelling at Heidelberg.) We should intervene only to obviate any move that might seriously upset the world's equilibrium, and we should do this without indulging in public professions of righteousness.

Mr. Kennan is at his best when he is criticizing national mythologies. The first chapter of *Russia and the West—Conflict of the Two Worlds*—contains a brilliant examination of the delusions, on the one hand, of the Soviet Union and, on the other, of the Western democracies. The pretensions of the former as saviors of the world through the rescue of an insurgent working class by a privileged class of bureaucrats and the theology of Dialectical Materialism, which is supposed to make this inevitable, have by this time become quite familiar, but Mr. Kennan, as usual, approaches the subject in a somewhat original way. He has a calmly deflating comment on the prophetic vision of Lenin and his early followers that was to supply the official Soviet stereotypes: "The image of reality against the background of which the political fanatic plays his part is always largely artificial. He creates it for himself; but he believes in it implicitly, and in part he generally succeeds in making it seem real to others as well. And his role, as he plays it, may be none the less heroic and impressive for this artificiality of the scenery." The falsity of our own pretensions has not, however, been so often exposed by writers who do not, as Kennan does not, also follow a Socialist line in attributing all our own shortcomings to the vices of a capitalist society. It is therefore perhaps more important to call attention to his comment on our own delusions:

"There is, let me assure you, nothing in nature more egocentrical than the embattled democracy. It soon becomes the victim of its own war propaganda. It then tends to attach to its own cause an absolute value which distorts its own vision on everything else. *Its* enemy becomes the embodiment of all evil. *Its* own side, on the other hand, is the center of all virtue. The contest comes to be viewed as having a final, apocalyptic quality. If *we* lose, all is lost; life will no longer be worth living; there will be nothing to be salvaged. If we win, then everything will be possible; all problems will become soluble; the one great source of evil—*our* enemy—will have been crushed; the forces of good will then sweep forward unimpeded; all worthy aspirations will be satisfied.

"It will readily be seen that people who have got themselves into this frame of mind have little understanding for the issues of any contest other than the one in which they are involved. The idea of people wasting time and substance on any *other* issue seems to them preposterous. This explains why Allied statesmen were simply unable to comprehend how people in Russia could be interested in an internal Russian political crisis when there was a war on in the West. Did the Russians not realize, it was asked in Paris and London, that everything depended on the defeat of the Germans, that if Germany was successful, no one could ever conceivably be happy again, whereas if Germany lost, everyone would somehow or other receive what he wanted?"

The fatal result of this habit of diabolizing the current enemy is that we always condemn him to the penalty of "unconditional surrender." We, the American Union, began this, of course, in our own Civil War, and we are now paying the penalty for it in the new conflict between the South and the federal government over the desegregation of Southern schools—a conflict that a great many Northerners, now quite unaware of what we did to the South in the war and the Reconstruction, regard with the same self-righteousness in respect to the obstinacy of Southern resistance that accompanied our struggle against it of a hundred years ago. Mr. Kennan does not deal with the Civil War, but he shows how, by pursuing a similar policy at the end of the First World War, by behaving as if the Kaiser were a Hitler, the Allies were rewarded, only twenty years later, by the horrors of a genuine Hitler—just as, earlier, by ruining the South and outlawing its governing class, we gave rise to the Ku Klux Klan and prepared for the bestial hoodlums who have perpetrated the bombings of Negro homes and the anti-Negro school and bus riots. If, says Kennan, we meant what Woodrow Wilson said—that we had no quarrel with the German people but wanted only to liberate them from their militaristic masters—we should not have attempted to crush them, should not have subjected to ostracism the representatives of the Weimar Republic. Mr. Kennan reports that at the Genoa Conference of 1922 the Germans were hardly admitted to intercourse with the English and French delegations and so were driven to make a pact with the Russians, and that at Geneva as late as 1927 "the thought of a German appearing on the . . . golf links still threw consternation into the hearts of ex-Allied officials serving at the League of Nations." (The relations between Russia and Germany from the peace of Brest-Litovsk to the Nazi-Soviet pact—neither of which ought to have come as a surprise—are another department that the Western democracies have been likely to disregard, but upon which Mr. Kennan throws a great deal of light.) If, on the other hand, the peace of Versailles was intended to be punitive for the

Germans, we should have done better "to leave the Kaiser and generals in power, to bear the onus of this situation and to reap the responsibility they had invited." Woodrow Wilson was in this case frustrated by the vindictiveness of Clemenceau and by Lloyd George's politic hedging, just as Lincoln's generous program for readmitting the South to the Union was destroyed by his assassination and by the vindictiveness of the Radical Republicans. We should get rid of the idea that the enemy, no matter how badly we may think he has behaved, must "deserve" the worst we can give him. "I find this word 'deserve,'" says Mr. Kennan, "when applied to an entire people, too vague to have historical usefulness." It is, in fact, not a question of "not being beastly" to the Germans, however beastly they may have been, but of not preparing new disasters.

The urgent advisability of dissociating moral judgments from the conduct of foreign policy is perhaps the chief burden of Mr. Kennan's book. This habit of regarding our opponent as a culprit has, he believes, been unfortunately encouraged by the conception of a world supercourt that has authority to try a nation, to find it guilty and to condemn it to punishment. What does it mean to call a nation guilty? The modern nations are political entities which are continually recombining, undergoing constant alterations in purpose, importance and size. No relations among these entities can ever be perfect; there are always conflicting interests. Relations with Russia in particular have always been annoying and difficult. (Mr. Kennan quotes a statement by Theodore Roosevelt, at the time of the Russo-Japanese War, on the "contemptuous effrontery" of Russian diplomacy, which sounds as if it had been written today.) In our differences with foreign powers, we must give up our melodramatic ideas of absolute right and absolute wrong. We ourselves have not been wholly guiltless, wholly benevolent in intention, as we like to believe we have, and we disguise from ourselves what we are, not by the formulas of Marxist ideology but, as Mr. Kennan says, by "self-idealization and the search for absolutes in world affairs: for absolute security, absolute amity, absolute harmony." He goes on: "We are a strong nation, wielding great power. We cannot help wielding this power. It comes to us by virtue of our sheer size and strength, whether we wish it or not. But to wield power is always at best an ambivalent thing—a sharing in the guilt taken upon themselves by all those men who, over the course of the ages, have sought or consented to tell others what to do. There is no greater American error than the belief that liberal institutions and the rule of law relieve a nation of the moral dilemma involved in the exercise of power. Power, like sex, may be concealed and outwardly ignored, and in our society it often is; but neither in the one case nor in the other does this concealment save us from the destruction of our innocence or from the confrontation with the dilemmas these necessities imply. When the ambivalence of one's virtue is recognized, the total iniquity of one's opponent is also irreparably impaired."

When Kennan's lectures were delivered at Harvard, they were received with the enormous enthusiasm with which the undergraduates there have been showing their gratitude to anyone—from J. R. Oppenheimer to Angus Wilson—who evidently knows what he is talking about and is giving them not showmanship or official cant but an honest account of something. That this approval was not, however, quite unanimous was made plain to me by an encounter, after the last of Kennan's appearances, with a middle-aged acquaintance from Boston. When I expressed my admiration for the lectures, I saw that they had left him aghast. The lecturer's exhortation not to cultivate moral absolutes was so far from having found a sympathetic response that he replied, after a moment to get his breath, that Mr. Kennan did not seem to have grasped the difference between right and wrong. So the favorable response to the book on the part of the press and the public has surprised me and seems to me encouraging as a sign perhaps of a stirring in the direction of relativistic intelligence.

September 9, 1961

THAT SUMMER IN PARIS

THE SUMMER OF 1929 was spent by Morley Callaghan in Paris. He had already, at twenty-six, a reputation as a writer of short stories and had just published his first novel. His work had been introduced to Max Perkins, at Scribners, by Scott Fitzgerald and Ernest Hemingway, and he had left his native Toronto and given up the practice of law to go to Europe, as they had done. Hemingway Callaghan had known before, when they had both been reporters on the Toronto *Star,* and though he had never met Scott Fitzgerald, he eventually got to know him in Paris—as well as Joyce, Miró, Allen Tate, Michael Arlen, Ford Madox Ford and many other famous émigrés of the period—and he has now written a book called *That Summer in Paris,* which recreates that last moment of aesthetic exuberance just before the Great Depression set in. It deals mainly with Fitzgerald and Hemingway, and it has something of the fascination of Trelawny's *Recollections of Shelley and Byron.* Since Callaghan was four years younger than Hemingway and seven years younger than Fitzgerald, he approached them with a certain awe, and there are moments when one is reminded less of Trelawny with his two illustrious friends than of the Dormouse at the Mad Tea-Party, between the March Hare (Fitzgerald) and the Mad Hatter (Hemingway). But Morley Callaghan was never asleep, and they could not get him into their teapot. His powers of obser-

vation, so quiet but so alert, were never blinded by the
dazzling performances that these two great actors of the
twenties spent so much of their time putting on. Fitzgerald and Hemingway were both romantics; they lived
in semi-adolescent fantasies. Each of them was rather a
poet who put himself at the center of his poem than, as
Morley Callaghan was, an inquirer into what went on in
other people's minds; but in Callaghan's less brilliantly
imagined world, as we know from his excellent novels,
the man himself is not at the center as a self-assertive self-
conscious ego which must force the world to come to
terms with it and, whether in success or failure, to recognize its incomparable importance. Who *is* the writer
Morley Callaghan, the reader of his books might well ask,
as he could not possibly ask of Hemingway or of Fitzgerald. Callaghan is so much interested in moral character
as exhibited in other people's behavior that, unlike his
two exhibitionistic friends, he never shows himself at all.
The people in his stories do not burst upon us as they do
in Scott Fitzgerald or incise themselves as they do in
Hemingway; gently but very surely they lay hold on the
reader's attention and gradually become more interesting,
become something often startlingly different from what
we had at first supposed, and the situations seem to
unfold almost without the author's manipulation. Morley
Callaghan has nothing of the lyricism that intoxicated the
readers of his two older colleagues, and the rhythms of his
prose, though they carry one, do not stimulate the same
kind of emotion, but his unobtrusive art is more subtle
and his intelligence more mature than those of either of
the others. It is thus of particular interest to see what
Morley Callaghan, at sixty, will make of himself at
twenty-six and of his two fellow-writers who shared with
him a devotion to good writing but practically nothing
else. Little did he know, he says, when he arrived with

his young wife in Paris, what a drama of "fierce passions" awaited them there. "Fierce passions" is perhaps too strong for the highly competitive touchiness of three ambitious young literary men—for the young Callaghan himself, it seems, had something of the pugnacious Irishman; but the story does have the tensity that Callaghan gets into his novels, a tensity always of personal relations, which implies no melodramatic assumptions but depends on the involvement with one another of men of different aims and "conditionings." What he has written is so very different from anything that either of his friends could conceivably ever have written.

The reviewer, who knew both of these friends, may begin by assuring the reader that their old companion's account of them seems to him perfectly accurate. And the memoirist has performed here a feat rather uncommon in literary circles: the gift of moral objectivity that I have spoken of above has enabled him to include in his portraits their unpleasant and outrageous traits and yet never to indulge himself in malice. He sometimes resented them extremely, as no one could fail to do, for they were both, at relatively slight and often unexpected provocation, capable of becoming insufferable, and he is still a little annoyed at the memory of certain incidents; yet his attitude is fundamentally a friendly and admiring one. It is possible that his picture of them, nevertheless, may offend some members of a public that has known Fitzgerald and Hemingway only from their books and their reputations. The careers and personalities of both—apart, I mean, from their work—have become so idealized and aggrandized that the popular conceptions of them have no longer very much connection with the improbable human beings themselves. It is true that in Fitzgerald's case so much has been written about him since his death that no one who has read this material will be surprised by, for example, Morley Callaghan's account of his first meeting with him. Fitzgerald, on this occasion, read aloud from the manuscript of *A Farewell to Arms* that now famous *cri de cœur,* "If people bring so much courage to this world the world has to kill them to break them," etc., and asked him, "Isn't it beautiful?" Callaghan said, "Yes, it is," but then added a characteristic criticism, "But maybe it's too deliberate. Maybe the rhythmic flow is too determined, and the passage emerges as a set-piece." "All right," said Fitzgerald, "it doesn't impress you." "If you ask me," said Zelda firmly, "it sounds pretty damned Biblical." Later, when the Callaghans were leaving and Fitzgerald was arranging a lunch, he asked whom they would like him to invite—Clive Bell, who was then in Paris? When Callaghan, who had read Bell's *Art,* did not seem sufficiently enthusiastic, Fitzgerald, reflecting, said, "No. No, I don't think he impresses you enough"; then, "Who does impress you, Morley? . . . Would this impress you, Morley?" "Suddenly," writes Callaghan, "he got down on his knees, put his head on the floor and tried to stand on his head. One leg came up, and he tried to get the other one up and maintain his balance. . . . Then he lost his balance and sprawled flat on his face. I got up and helped him to his feet. 'You're a little drunk,' I said. 'No, not at all,' he said, and he was almost convincing. . . . Untroubled, he walked us to the door and shook hands politely."

But the situation with Hemingway was different, for Hemingway was performing in his own imagination an entirely different drama. Fitzgerald liked to clown in public, but the character that Hemingway was playing had always to be heroic. He, too, was capable of nonsense and could be an amusing companion, but his joking was rather ill-natured and likely to take the turn of sneering at possible rivals, of a ribbing that, as Callaghan records, came close to or amounted to insult. About himself he had little sense of humor. By his tendency to create the impression that he was many kinds of an athletic champion and by his enlistment in exploits of gallantry that were not what he thought they were, he sometimes made himself a comic character, and this, among friends and non-friends, gave rise to innumerable anecdotes in which it was all too easy to make him appear absurd. Morley Callaghan tells at length the true story of the once famous boxing-match between Hemingway and himself, during which Fitzgerald, who was supposed to be keeping time, became so absorbed in the spectacle that he let a round go on too long, and Hemingway was eventually knocked down. The story, as we read it, is extremely funny, but Hemingway was furious at losing face and allowed the small mishap to rankle and later to put an end to good relations between the three friends. It should have become an old joke among them, but Hemingway was incapable of seeing a joke in which he himself was made ridiculous. Any undertaking in which he had fallen down, any contest in which he had been worsted, was immediately, as Callaghan says, transformed in his own mind into an episode that illustrated his prowess, and any rumor that might have got abroad of his not having come out on top was somehow to be blamed on the double-crossing or the cowardice of his opponent, and by the time that the incident got into his books, it had been charged with such intense emotion that the reader found it irresistible and went on, if not otherwise enlightened, to accept the superman legend that, collaborating with his press, he was to project onto the public imagination. Morley Callaghan has stated his own view of this with his usual sympathetic insight in commenting on Hemingway's preposterous remark "My writing is nothing. My boxing is everything." Callaghan had reason to know that

Hemingway was not much of a boxer, and when this remark was repeated to him, it made him laugh. "That a great artist like Ernest could have such a view of himself seemed incredible. Yet in the strange dark depths of his being he had to pretend to believe it. For the sake of the peace of their own souls most men live by pretending to believe in something they secretly know isn't true. . . . I had discovered that Ernest's attitude to his boxing was related to the source of his power as an imaginative writer. His imaginative work had such a literal touch that a whole generation came to believe he was only telling what he, himself, had seen happen, or what had actually happened to him. His readers made him his own hero. As he grew older it must have had tragic disadvantages for him." Thus the world failed to get from Hemingway a Falstaff or a Don Quixote, but it did get the extraordinary short stories that really constituted, in English, a new kind of poetry.

By the strange law that seems to govern the convolutions of such personalities, it would seem that though Hemingway, in regard to his own feats, was given to exaggeration, he was capable also of concealing the truth about actions that were genuinely admirable. The late, brilliant Harold Laski was in the habit of improvising freely historical data, quotations from books and interesting conversations which he claimed to have had with celebrities whom he had actually never met, and those who knew him were always on their guard to discount these too apt inventions. I have told in an earlier piece how when Laski came back from a visit to the United States at the time of the second war, he described his adventures at length to a friend but never mentioned Franklin Roosevelt. As a result, the friend came to the conclusion that Laski had had a meeting with Roosevelt—which turned out to have been the case. So Scott

Fitzgerald once told me that, in all his acquaintance with Hemingway, he had never been able to find out from him what had actually happened in Italy when Hemingway was shell-shocked and wounded, and that it was only when he ran into somebody who had been there and knew about it that he learned that Hemingway had been peppered by a shell while performing an act of gratuitous bravery—he had gone back to rescue a man who was too badly wounded to move. I suppose that for such a mind the incident which has been transformed thereafter belongs to a fictional world: it is intended, like any made-up story, not to supply information but simply to excite or amuse, while the things that really happened and that are all to one's credit are even less to be given out than the things that are not to one's credit: they are guarded by a decent discretion; it would embarrass one to talk about them. It is quite common for imaginative writers, when they have made use of actual material in producing a work of fiction, to find afterwards that they no longer quite know what was actual and what was invented— they remember the stories they have written but have forgotten what the raw materials were—and in Hemingway's serious writing his use of his raw materials does not in the least count in connection with the power and the beauty of his work. That he had shown unusual courage, that he had undergone trying ordeals, that he had been brought to the verge of madness is, from his early work, not to be doubted, and it does not detract from this that he tried in his later years to reënact these experiences in travesty. But one does have to discount this travesty in dealing with the Hemingway legend.

I remember—to give a few reminiscences of my own— how, seeing Hemingway only rarely, on his visits to New York, I noted the gradual progress of this dramatized public personality. When I first met him, he was quite unknown; he had only had published, in Paris, two small *plaquettes* of stories and poems. He had come down to New York from Toronto, and I thought that he was one of the glibbest and slickest and most knowing young newspapermen I had ever met. On a later trip, to see his publishers, when his first books had made him famous, he had put on a certain amount of weight and was cultivating a gruff, laconic and youthfully mock-modest manner: he was, in fact, beginning to talk like a Hemingway character. I spoke of this to Elinor Wylie, at one of whose parties he had been, and she said that she had noticed it, too: he was, she said, "playing the butcher's boy." The last time I ever saw him I had dinner in New York with him and Scott Fitzgerald. Hemingway was now a great man and Scott was so much overcome by his greatness that he embarrassed me by his self-abasement, and he finally lay down on the restaurant floor, pretending to be unconscious but actually listening in on the conversation and from time to time needling his hero, whose weaknesses he had studied intently, with malicious little interpolations. On this occasion Hemingway told me of a recent trip through the South that he had made in a car with his young son. He had at one point suddenly become aware that he had entered the state of Mississippi: "I realized that we were in the Faulkner country." At the country hotel where they spent the night, he had had the boy go to bed, then had sat up all night himself, with his "gun" on the table in front of him. Two ideas, I believe, were revealed by this story, which he told me with the utmost seriousness: the assumption that Mississippi was inhabited by Faulkner characters and the assumption that Faulkner was a dangerous rival, who would take the same view of Hemingway that Hemingway did of him and, now that he had invaded Faulkner's territory, might well send some of these characters to do him violence. I thought this was rather queer, but no queerer, perhaps, than some other things that came out in drinking conversations. The inflation after this of the Hemingway legend, the magnification of the he-man Hemingway, hard-drinking, hard-loving and hard-fighting, so obviously encouraged by himself, rather discouraged me with him, and I did not see him again. But I had some direct evidence of what was happening to him when he succeeded in delaying for several months the publication of a book of mine by getting out an injunction against the publishers. The book contained an essay about him which had already appeared in the *Atlantic Monthly* and which, as a whole, could not possibly be called either unfavorable or unsympathetic. But I had prodded the publicity Hemingway, and the publicity Hemingway was bellowing. When I found out that he had written his lawyer a letter of many pages, in which he claimed that about every other sentence was libellous (the publishers had sent him proofs), I concluded that he was not quite sane. His objections were eventually all boiled down to two trivial errors of fact and one error about an incident in one of his books, which of course I should have been glad to correct if he had simply written me about them. My first contract for the book had been with Scribners, but they had not hesitated to break it, because they had correctly guessed the effect that publishing this essay would have on their most popular author. He had already made them an indignant scene, in which he had accused them of letting him down, when he discovered that the sales of *For Whom the Bell Tolls* had not outdone those of *Gone With the Wind,* which he had learned was the best-selling novel ever published in the United States. I should add that I had with him years later some perfectly amiable correspondence, as if nothing unpleasant had happened. When I referred to the fuss he had made about my book, he said that he had really forgotten about it, and, not knowing I had seen his letter, blamed the incident on the Scribner office.

This false public personality to the creation of which Hemingway lent himself—for it is exploited in his magazine articles of this period as well as in the reports of the press—had its source in the ancient tradition that the ideal American hero must conform to a certain type: he was supposed to be virile to the point of brutality, a crack shot and a keen woodsman, indifferent to danger and unflinching under pain, an indomitable endurer of hardship, and always a man's man, not—except when he "truly" loved—entirely at home among women. In the case of a sickly and sensitive man who deliberately sets out to achieve this role, he may end by producing a "persona" that seems rather forced and overdone. Francis Parkman, Theodore Roosevelt and H. L. Mencken were all in their various ways examples of this, and Hemingway was also an example, but a much more precarious and a tragic one. I never could understand how so many people imagined from Hemingway's books that the author was a hardboiled character who was interested only in crude inarticulate characters. Except in an occasional story about gangsters or pugilists, his heroes are invariably sensitive men who are on the verge of cracking up, or who have already been defeated, or who pay for their honor or their love by being robbed of what they have won or being crippled or demoralized or killed. And even in *Green Hills of Africa,* in which Hemingway himself takes the stage and features himself as his own first person singular, the theme of an ominous self-distrust is allowed to give him a certain affinity with the fatally disintegrated heroes of his short stories of hunting in Africa, *Francis Macomber* and *The Snows of Kilimanjaro.*

Yet, in view of the success of the legend, it is probable that Callaghan's book will surprise and shock the Hemingway fans. Such admirers must, however, have already been shocked by Hemingway's final breakdown, and Callaghan's account of the high-strung young man—rather unreliable in his loyalties and always afraid of failure, who, as Callaghan says, "kept death in his work as a Medieval scholar might have kept a skull on his desk," the scrupulous craftsman who lived poor for his work (when Fitzgerald could only live expensively) but who worried about his "career," alternately a delightful companion who could hypnotize by his talk and would go out of his way to be kind and a spiteful opponent who could harbor a grudge—will help them to understand this breakdown, and to imagine the life of acute moral strain that gave a sharp edge to his sensuous enjoyment; of delusions, euphoric or frightening, that made his personal relations erratic; of deep malaise when the true and fine artist found the early success that he had earned in Paris turning into a kind of success that in the long run could only be degrading—to imagine the difficult life which brought him to such a death.

February 23, 1963

DAWN POWELL: GREENWICH VILLAGE
IN THE FIFTIES

WHY IS IT that the novels of Miss Dawn Powell are so
much less well known than they deserve to be? This is, I
believe, partly due to her complete indifference to publicity. She rarely goes to publishers' lunches or has publishers' parties given her; she declines to play the great
lady of letters, and she does not encourage interviews or
the appearance of her photograph on book jackets. No
effort has been made to glamorize her, and it would be
hopeless to try to glamorize her novels. For in these
novels—another reason that they have not been more
popular—she does nothing to stimulate feminine daydreams. The woman reader can find no comfort in identifying herself with Miss Powell's heroines. The women
who appear in her stories are likely to be as sordid and
absurd as the men. There are no love scenes that will
rouse you or melt you. It is true that in her more recent
books she has been relenting a little. In *The Locusts
Have No King,* she did close on a note of enduring affection, though an affection sorely tried and battered—"In a
world of destruction," the author concludes, "one must
hold fast to whatever fragments of love are left, for sometimes a mosaic can be more beautiful than an unbroken
pattern"—and in her last book but one, *A Cage for
Lovers,* there are actually a young man and a young

woman who, though kept apart by an ogress, are benevolently united at the end.

But love is not Miss Powell's theme. Her real theme is the provincial in New York who has come on from the Middle West and acclimated himself (or herself) to the city and made himself a permanent place there, without ever, however, losing his fascinated sense of an alien and anarchic society. Like Miss Powell, who was born in Ohio, these immigrants find themselves vividly aware of elements of Manhattan life that the native of New York takes for granted, since he has usually no very intimate experience of anything else to contrast with them. To such recent arrivals in town, the New Yorkers seem giddy and unreliable, their activities confused and often pointless; yet once the transplantation has taken root, they may enjoy in the very amorality of this life a certain relaxation and freedom, a certain convivial comfort in the assurance that, whatever you do, no one—though lovers and spouses may occasionally make themselves disagreeable—is really going to call you to account. Such a world has great comic possibilities if one has enjoyed it on its own terms and yet observed it from a point of view that does not quite accept these terms as normal, and Miss Powell has exploited these possibilities with a wit, a gift of comic invention and an individual accent that make her books unlike any others. The mind, the personality behind them, with all its sophistication, is very stout and self-sustaining, strong in Middle Western common sense, capable of toughness and brusqueness; yet a fairyland strain of Welsh fantasy instils into everything she writes a kind of kaleidoscopic liveliness that renders even her hardheadedness elusive.

Miss Powell has explored several New York milieux. In *A Time to Be Born,* she was dealing with a successful

uptown world of big journalistic publishing and insati-
able careerist women; in *Angels on Toast,* with a somewhat lesser world of delirious advertizing men and their
equally unstable mates; in *A Cage for Lovers,* with a
mansion on the Hudson and the dead weight of inherited
money. But in her new book, *The Golden Spur,* she
returns to a favorite field, which has figured in others of
her novels: the Bohemian downtown world of writers,
painters and professional drinkers, with their feminine
consorts and hangers-on, which has its center in Greenwich Village. She has given us already, in other books, the
Village in several of its phases. Of the earlier romantic
and radical phase, which was certainly the most creative,
she has had little first-hand knowledge, and she has not
attempted this, but she has condensed the atmosphere of
its later ones in images that do not always keep their
contours yet that live as they are blown down the wind;
and it is a proof of her quality as a literary artist that she
does not depend directly on gossip and never writes a
roman à clef. The reviewer has been pretty well acquainted with a good many people of the kind that have
provided Miss Powell's material, yet he has almost never
found Miss Powell exploiting a personality among them
whom he was able to recognize. She has imagined and
established for her readers her own Greenwich Village
world, which is never journalistic copy and which possesses a memorable reality of which journalistic fiction is
incapable. Her chronicle extends from the days of such
old-fashioned resorts as the Brevoort and the Lafayette,
with their elegant and well-served French restaurants and
domino-playing cafés, which encouraged the dignity of
love and art and afforded a comfortable setting for leisurely conversations; the days of those small cheap and
decent hotels in which thrifty conscientious craftsmen
and cultivated ladies of slender means could go on living

for years and decades without having their habits disturbed—her chronicle, perhaps rather her poem, extends
from the era of this tranquil quarter, now almost entirely
destroyed to make way for huge apartment buildings, to
the era of those noisy abysmal bars, which, though graded
from better to worse, have all a certain messy turbidity. In
these hangouts, the hack writer, the talentless artist, the
habitual cadger of loans can drift on in a timeless existence of lamplit emboothed drinking, with a backdrop
of bright-labelled bottles standing by like a smartly cos-
tumed guard against the mirror that expands the room
beyond its crowded narrow limits in space, and in the
casual but dependable companionship of the bartender
and the other habitués, while the girls who inspire
speculation by their constant exchange of partners and
their possible availability laugh and brighten after leaving
the office or perfunctorily keeping house in the studio,
and thus provide a fitful play of romance.

In *The Golden Spur* we see the Village at a point of its
decline that is rather squalid: bearded beatniks and abstract painters have seeped in among the Guggenheim
fellows, the raffish N.Y.U. professors and the adult-edu-
cation students. It is a phase with which Miss Powell is
evidently not so intimate and not so sympathetic as she
was with the Village of an earlier time but which she
nevertheless accepts as still more or less cozy and more or
less fun in the good old Village tradition. If one does not
have the benefit at one's favorite bar, as one sometimes
did with the cafés of the past, of a lobby with a telephone
girl who always knew whom everybody was looking for
and who would never be indiscreet, one can still give this
bar as a mailing address or a place where one can be
reached by telephone and be granted a certain latitude in
the matter of hanging up tabs.

The Golden Spur is such a bar, which dates, however, from an earlier period. Jonathan Jaimison, of Silver City, Ohio, has learned from an aunt at home that he is an illegitimate child, the son of his now deceased mother by someone she had known in New York during a legendary time in her youth when she had had a brief fling in the East. She had supported herself by typing and thus had met distinguished people of whom she was to talk ever after. But she had never told anyone who her lover was, and the boy has come on to find out, with no clues save a few names and the knowledge that the Golden Spur had been a place that his mother had frequented. Gradually he makes connections with her former employers and friends: a clever alcoholic professor who leads rather a miserable life between a wife who has tricked him into marrying her and a mistress who wants to marry him; a successful, somewhat stuffed-shirt lawyer with a wife who has taken him over and set him up in suburban Connecticut; and a demoralized best-selling novelist whose pride receives a serious blow when the wife whom he has ridiculed and neglected runs away on a yacht with a title. None of them has a son, and when the first and the last of the three come to understand that Jonathan is looking for a father, the novelist and the professor both try to imagine that they may have begotten him in some now forgotten moment: this would give them a new bond and interest, help to bolster up their disappointing lives. The boy is good-looking and bright, a fine upstanding product of Ohio, as different as possible from themselves. The rich lawyer has always known what he was doing and cannot cherish any such delusion, but, having only one daughter, in whom he is quite uninterested and who is quite uninterested in him, he would be glad to attach to himself such an evidently able young fellow, whom

he would train in his own law office and who would thus
become dependent on him and succeed him in his profession. Jonathan, admiring and gratified, hopes greatly
that he has now found his father. I ought not to reveal
whose son the boy unexpectedly turns out to be, but Miss
Powell, who has sometimes been criticized for the form-
lessness of her novels and their inconclusive endings, has
constructed here a very neat plot, and for once in her
career played Santa Claus and made her hero a generous
present. She then has him reject, however, the privileges
of the social position to which he is now entitled and flee
from the opening of an uptown gallery that he has undertaken to subsidize, in company with an erratic and much
esteemed painter—you never know in Miss Powell's novels
whether the painters are really any good—who has become its principal star but who prefers to the patronage of
the affluent a lodging in a rickety warehouse near Hous-
ton Street, on the lower West Side. Jonathan escapes to
the Golden Spur, to which by this hour, as he knows,
"the old crowd must be heading . . . for post-mortems
and wakes." In the cab with him and the painter is the
lawyer's unappreciated daughter, who has succeeded in
persuading her parents to let her live in New York on her
own, and who has even managed to go on the stage
without their knowing about it; who has, in fact, been
leading a double life between suburban correctitude on
the one hand and abandoned Bohemianism on the other.
Jonathan, who has met her in both of her roles, has fallen
deeply in love with her, and he doesn't really care at that
point that she has also been sleeping with the painter and
lying to him about it: "The truth had no part in love
anyway, except for the truth of finding each other at the
right moment."

I have said that Dawn Powell must be less at home in

the "beat" than in the old Village, yet it is interesting to find that in *The Golden Spur* she has succeeded in modulating without too much strain from the charming Lafayette café to its so much less distinguished successor, and that the beatnik's dread of the "square" comes to seem here the natural extension of the old Greenwich Villager's attitude toward the traditional artists' enemy: "uptown."

I hope that the tone of this article—sociological and somewhat nostalgic—will not obscure the fact that Dawn Powell's novels are among the most amusing being written, and in this respect quite on a level with those of Anthony Powell, Evelyn Waugh and Muriel Spark. Miss Powell's success in England shows, I think, that she is closer to this high social comedy than to any accepted brand of American humor—and the English do not insist on having the women in their fiction made attractive. Miss Powell's books are more than merely funny; they are full of psychological insights that are at once sympathetic and cynical, and they have episodes that are rather macabre, which seem to hint at something close to embitterment. The recurring types in these books—with whom the innocent provincial is confronted—are the discouraged alcoholic, the creepy homosexual, the unscrupulous feminine "operator" and the tyrannous woman patron, and Miss Powell can make them all look very gruesome. All are present in *The Golden Spur,* but not in their most repellent forms, and here as elsewhere one can always be sure that some sudden new comic idea will give a twist to the situation, which has seemed to be irretrievably uncomfortable, and introduce an arbitrary element that will lend the proceedings a touch of ballet. There are few real happy endings in Dawn Powell's novels, but there are no real tragedies, either. These beings shift and cling and twitch in their antic liaisons and ambitions, on their way to some undetermined limbo out of reach of any moral law. But don't those wide-eyed boys and girls from Ohio survive and redeem the rest? Don't be too sure of that.

November 17, 1962

AN INTERVIEW WITH
EDMUND WILSON

INTERVIEWER. What brings you to England, Mr. Wilson?

WILSON. I wanted to dine at the Café Royal. I have never been able to get any English friend to go there with me. They always say that it isn't what it used to be. But I want to see it all the same. That's one reason, and another is that I want to get a set of Ackermann's *London* at a somewhat cheaper price than they ask for it in the United States. I feel that when I'll have achieved these two objectives, I need never come to London again. Not that I don't enjoy it, but it's so hard to live through the London Sunday, and such a nuisance having to go to Paris on Saturday. Besides, I'm afraid of finding that the old London I used to like isn't really there any more.

INTERVIEWER. May I ask you for your opinion of some of our English writers?

WILSON. Certainly, if I've read them.

INTERVIEWER. How do you feel about Sir Charles Snow?

WILSON. My only objection to his novels is that I find them almost completely unreadable. But I always stand up for him in opposition to the virtually united front against him of the London literary world. He does have "something to say"—put that in quotes. He's been bold enough to disregard the literary rules and to open up a whole new geography of the intellectual world, so everybody is furious with him. I like to read him when he's not writing novels, though I think he has to some extent created a false issue in the matter of the "Two Cultures." Perhaps not in England, where there seems to be a sort of social barrier between science and the humanistic studies, but in the United States everybody who goes to college— or at least they did in my time—has to take a certain amount of science. Snow insists that it is just as absurd not to know the Second Law of Thermodynamics as not to have read any Shakespeare. I once knew about the Second Law, but I couldn't tell you what it is now—I don't think I really need it—and I imagine that there are many scientists who would get little or nothing out of Shakespeare.

INTERVIEWER. How do you feel about the Snow-Leavis controversy?

WILSON. Why, I believe that I'm rather on Snow's side. I don't actually know much about Leavis. I'm told that he's a stimulating teacher—such people sometimes are: Irving Babbitt at Harvard, for instance—the fanatical literary moralists—and that parts of his books are brilliant. But I haven't read these books, and when I have read him, he was always railing against somebody. He's the kind of dogmatic person who inevitably antagonizes me. I can't understand making a life-or-death issue out of one's preference for this or that writer. Why try to cast an anathema on somebody who doesn't like George Eliot? I detested *Silas Marner* and *Adam Bede* when I had to read them for school, and I've never got around to *Middlemarch*. And why regard Max Beerbohm as trivial? He seems to me to have been one of the best writers of his period. Leavis tries to be scathing about Snow's style, but if this lecture is a fair sample of Leavis's, I'd say that he didn't express himself nearly so well as Snow. Still, it may be that something of importance is involved in the

Snow-Leavis controversy. I think that Leavis has one real point—one that I had raised in my own mind: that Snow seems to take it for granted that technical education and technical advances are desirable in themselves. This naturally gets Leavis's back up, because his interest in literature is passionate and moral—almost, I suppose, religious. For Leavis, Snow, I suppose, is committing the sin against the Holy Ghost.

INTERVIEWER. What do you think of Kingsley Amis?

WILSON. His last novel is by far his best—*Take a Girl Like You*. The use of language is wonderful, and he has made a kind of squalid but delightful poetry out of—one doesn't know what to call it: not lower-middle-class life, but something that I suppose is new in England, a kind of world that is more like America, where people meet and drink and make love and have flip conversations without belonging to any class at all. I felt in reading this book, as I had not done in reading his verse, that Amis is really a poet. *Take a Girl Like You* is, I think, the best humorous poem that has come out of England since Betjeman has been Poet Laureate.

INTERVIEWER. You are mistaken; John Betjeman is not Poet Laureate. Masefield is still—

WILSON. Nonsense. I've been much amused by the way in which Betjeman has been handling the Royal Family. They had already been made to look middle-class by the English press and its public. Betjeman has made them suburban.

INTERVIEWER. And Anthony Powell—have you read him?

WILSON. I don't see why you make so much fuss about him. He's just entertaining enough to read in bed late at night in summer, when his books usually reach me. If Evelyn Waugh is the Shakespeare of this school, Powell is the Middleton or the Day. It's a pity he ever dipped into Proust—and that goes for Durrell, too, though of course Durrell did more than dip, he saturated himself completely. Durrell is even better to read in bed. He creates such an atmosphere of sinister suspense, heavy odors and colors, and fantastic sexual didos, and the Alexandrian series is full of extraordinary descriptions of a kind that few people can do. He has a real mastery of language at a time when so much English prose is self-conscious, impoverished and pale. But the trouble with this series is that—along with the trick of astonishing the reader by revealing new aspects of his characters—he took over Proust's preoccupation with disabling and distressing illness and the torments of frustrated love. With Proust these obsessions are neurotically real, but in Durrell's case you feel that he is a strong healthy fellow who immensely enjoys himself, and that all this is artificial. He mutilates all his characters or gives them perversions or diseases. By the time he gets to the end, practically everybody has been crippled in one way or another, and we don't much believe in any of it. And then the real big surprise comes—which is also a giveaway—when the whole grotesque carnival of horror and lust turns out to have a happy ending. Boy and Girl go off to Paris together, and there is nothing to prevent us from supposing that they will live happily ever after. She has lost her right hand, to be sure, but she has learned to paint with an artificial one, and for some reason this has made her the great painter that she couldn't be before.

INTERVIEWER. You spoke of Evelyn Waugh. Have you been reading his later books?

WILSON. I regard *Gilbert Pinfold* as the greatest Protestant allegory since *Pilgrim's Progress*, and the military series is also good—it is the first time he has succeeded in getting into any of his books a suggestion of Christianity, *Helena* was his weakest novel: it turned out that the mother of Constantine came from a good English county family and that the heretics were horrible underbred people whom one wouldn't care to know.

INTERVIEWER. Angus Wilson?

WILSON. I think that he interests me more than any other English novelist I read. No nostalgia for the twenties or the old institutions. He concentrates on the present, on the new social types that have appeared since the war, and the changed situation of the old ones, and I feel that I am getting a great deal of light on what is happening at the present time in England. His last book is one of his best—*The Old Men at the Zoo.* He is always particularly good when he impersonates a character who is telling the story. *For Whom the Cloche Tolls* is one of the best of his shorter things—and the most unappreciated. It was not even published in America. The subject of *The Old Men* is rather like one of Snow's. The relations between men in an institution—it is, in fact, a Snow novel written by someone with more talent for fiction. The reviews of it in England that I read mostly sounded as if they had been written by the imaginary narrator himself—the slightly intelligent civil servant who is always saving face and carrying on. I almost suspect Angus Wilson of having forged these reviews himself—like the archeological controversy in the appendix to *Anglo-Saxon Attitudes.*

INTERVIEWER. You follow the English press?

WILSON. Oh, yes. I subscribe to the *New Statesman* and regularly read the *TLS, Encounter,* the *Observer* and the *Sunday Times*—sometimes the *Spectator* and the *Listener.* My house is full of these weeklies; when I go down to dinner I find them. Hence, I suppose, this interview. As for the *Observer* and the *Sunday Times*—since I rarely read the editorials, I can't detect much difference between them. One has Kenneth Tynan and the other Cyril Connolly. Tynan is still young, with, I hope, the best of his career before him, but I can never read Cyril Connolly without wishing he were doing something that was better worth doing than most of those reviews. But why mention it? I think that he rather enjoys having this kind of thing said about him. And then there is Harold Nicolson—I don't know whether he irritates me or amuses me more. He works up so much moral indignation about the writers whose biographies he reviews: Montesquieu, Goldsmith, the Goncourts. He began it years ago in his book about Verlaine. As I remember, he reproved Verlaine for his lack of moral backbone, when the substance of Verlaine's poetry is entirely a matter of fleeting impressions, quickly varying moods and the pathos of emotional instability. If Verlaine had had moral backbone, his poetry would never have existed. And how can you scold someone like Goldsmith or worry because Montesquieu, in some connection, is supposed to have "behaved badly"? The only writer on whom I have read Nicolson who seems to me somewhat to deserve this peevish kind of disapproval is William Beckford, whom I have always thought very unpleasant; yet V. S. Pritchett, in one of his best reviews, writing about the same biography, shows a sympathetic comprehension that made me feel I knew Beckford better. I am glad to see, however, that the staggering contradictions of Dostoevsky have forced Nicolson to yield a little. In the most recent review of his I've read, he concludes, "In some ways this collection of letters shows us how petty a great man can be. In other ways it teaches us never to condemn a genius for the way in which he behaves."

INTERVIEWER. Would you care to express an opinion of Sir Winston Churchill as a writer?

WILSON. A romantic American journalist infatuated with English history. And this reminds me that I'd like to

say something about someone I know you're not going to
ask me about: the writer that nobody—in London, at
least—takes seriously. He had an American mother, like
Churchill. I mean Compton Mackenzie. He makes a
mistake nowadays, I think, in always describing himself
as an "entertainer." A good many of his books, actually,
since his early period, are meant to convey "a message"—
put that in quotes. For years he has been trying in his
work to plead for the rights of small nations and cultural
minorities, as against all the forces which are driving us in
the direction of centralized power that tries to process or
crush them. His rather odd long novel *The Four Winds
of Love* is all—and somewhat irrelevantly to the career of
the hero, who is a playwright and not an editorial writer,
though, to be sure, he is a Scottish nationalist—it all
amounts to a defense of oppressed and recalcitrant
groups: the Greeks, the Poles, the Jews, the Irish, the
Scottish, and even the Bretons and the Cornish. But I
never remember to have seen a review of one of these
later novels that gave any indication of what Mackenzie
was driving at. The trouble is that he is both a professed
Scot and something of a crypto-American, so he is always
at an angle to English society. They don't understand him
or don't want to understand him, and I suppose they
resent such a comic portrait as that of Captain Waggett
in the Scottish series—which is so lightly done but so
deadly in intention—more than anything in Bernard
Shaw. And nobody is able to bring himself to give
Mackenzie credit for being the fine artist that at his best
he is. Most of his recent novels have not even been published in America, and I can't imagine why. In my youth
he was extremely popular. But now people—not I, however—laugh their heads off over P. G. Wodehouse and
pretend to take him seriously as a writer and speak with
respect of Somerset Maugham, a bad writer with none of

Mackenzie's distinction, when they have often never heard of Mackenzie. Since nobody else is doing him justice, I'm going to have to write about him myself, so I shan't give you a lecture on the subject.

INTERVIEWER. I am sure that Ackermann and the Café Royal are not your only reasons for coming to England. There must surely be other reasons.

WILSON. No other reasons. My English friends I see when they come to America—and, as a matter of fact, I'm not really in England. The question is, am I really anywhere? I'm not really in America either; I take so little part in what is happening there, and have so little sympathy with it. I say that I'm afraid of finding that the London I once knew isn't there any more, but the New York I used to know has disappeared long ago. Why, there's hardly a house in New York where I ever lived or went in my youth that is still even standing now! There are times when I'm not even sure that I'm real. Would you say I was real?

INTERVIEWER. I can't be sure.

WILSON. Are you real?

INTERVIEWER. I'm afraid not.

WILSON. Are these people we're talking about real?

INTERVIEWER. I don't think they quite know. Sir Winston, perhaps.

WILSON. In a sense, I suppose, I'm in Cambridge, Mass., imprisoned in an upstairs room, with the complete works of Swinburne and the six volumes of his correspondence and a lot of books about him on my desk, on the windowsill, on the bureau and on the empty bed next to mine. I sleep with them, work with them, eat with them. It's a possible mode of escape. But Swinburne himself is a little unreal, and outside I can see nothing but a narrow Cambridge street—the gray snow and ice or slush are all over the sidewalks and road. There are ugly

frame-houses opposite, all crowded up against one another. In the mornings the garbage collectors bang around
the big garbage cans that always stand in front of the
houses—it's a feature of Cambridge life. Later on, you
hear the gaspings and barkings of the cars that people are
trying to start, trying to get them out of the snowdrifts—
the streets there are never cleaned. This sometimes goes
on for hours. But if you don't look out of the windows,
it's like a long voyage on a boat that never gets to
Europe—when you just lie in your berth and read. I feel
sometimes that I'm getting to the proverbial point when
good Americans die and go to Paris. But of course if one
went there alive, one might be killed by a plastic bomb.
And then there are Anouilh's plays.

Interviewer. You don't care for Anouilh's plays?

Wilson. I abominate them. It's a kind of fraudulent
cleverness that I hate to see them getting in France:
forced whimsey—the French should never be whimsical—implausible improvised shocks, interminable *tirades*
that pretend to mean something. Other people are doing
it, too—Françoise Sagan, for example. Jean Cocteau
began it when he became meretricious in his later plays;
Giraudoux carried it on. Anouilh made an industry of it,
and now his plays are being done everywhere—in England, America and Germany as well as in France. Yes,
one of the chief problems of modern life is to avoid seeing
Anouilh's plays.

Interviewer. What is your opinion of the British
theater?

Wilson. Very high at the present time. I used to
think, after the First World War, that our theater had
become very good and the London theater—after the big
Shaw-Barker period—relatively uninteresting. Now it is
the other way around. New York isn't any good—except

for an occasional off-Broadway production—and London is very strong. The best of your actors are wonderful: Gielgud, Olivier, Guinness, Peggy Ashcroft, Pamela Brown, Edith Evans. We have no such actors in America. Even Noël Coward is not to be sneezed at.

The Interviewer sneezes.

WILSON. But *Blithe Spirit* is an excellent comedy. If *The Importance of Being Earnest* survives, *Blithe Spirit* ought to survive—though, of course, Coward's style isn't as good as Wilde's. In any case, we have no such actors in America as the ones I have just mentioned. Lunt and Fontanne are the nearest thing. The only Broadway event of any importance that I have seen in many years is Mike Nichols and Elaine May. I've been to their show four times, which I can't imagine doing with any other recent Broadway production. I think that they are serious artists and have all kinds of possibilities, but they have been written about as if they were trivial—in connection with sick jokes and so forth. Every one of their sketches, no matter how brief or funny, creates a real dramatic tension, and they sometimes come close to the tragic: the Teen-Agers and the Pirandello and the sketch about the little girl whose father is going to prison. This season I have heard it said that the Little Players at Central Park West is the best thing in the theater in New York, and now that Nichols and May are not doing their show any more, I don't think that is far from the truth. It is a theater of glove puppets—that is, not marionettes but the kind of puppets you put your hands in. I've been an amateur Punch-and-Judy operator myself, but I never could have believed that this kind of thing could be raised to such a point of perfection. Everything is done by one man, whose management of the movements and gestures is absolutely astonishing to me, and as an impersonator of voices and accents he rivals Peter Sellers. The whole thing has an elegance and imagination which must make it unique in this kind of entertainment.

INTERVIEWER. To go back to the bombs you were speaking of—would you care to express your views on nuclear warfare?

WILSON. I have been very pessimistic. There is nothing really serious at issue between us and the Soviet Union, and we are becoming more and more alike, but the more we become alike, the more we glare and square off at one another. It's just an animal rivalry—a couple of gorillas beating their breasts. I try to look on the cheerful side, and to tell myself that there's no real way of getting rid of the horrible American cities except to have them vaporized, so I am not in favor of those weapons which exterminate the human beings without destroying the buildings. And it is something of a consolation to remember that if New York, for example, were bombed, Nelson Rockefeller and Henry Luce and Cardinal Spellman and Robert Moses might be quickly eliminated; and then if Washington got it, the Pentagon, the C.I.A. and all the rest of the government bureaucracy would go. But I hope that as between us and Russia the destruction would be reciprocal. Moscow is a dreadful place, too—also swarming with bureaucrats.

INTERVIEWER. You don't see any hope, then?

WILSON. Not much—but then I'm getting old: I am constantly riddled with gout and I have almost no teeth in my lower jaw.

INTERVIEWER. You seem to me very vigorous.

WILSON. It's these drinks that produce the illusion. Can't I give you another?

INTERVIEWER. No, thank you.

WILSON. I'm also allergic to the dust from old books— an occupational hazard that I'd never heard of till last winter in Cambridge, when I was coughing and sneezing for months, and finally went to a throat-and-nose man and found out what was the matter with me. I'd had to read a lot of old bound periodicals and things for my book on the Civil War. It seems that this allergy is a common complaint. One of the librarians at Harvard had to retire on that account, and a girl who does research for a friend of mine has to wear a gauze mask in the stacks. There's also, it seems, an allergy to calf bindings, which I'm told has a slight prestige value in academic circles.

INTERVIEWER. Interesting. . . . Your book on the Civil War. That's the American Civil War, isn't it?

WILSON. Yes: the North and the South—Lincoln and Lee and all that.

INTERVIEWER. Do you remember the Civil War?

WILSON. Oh, very well. I was a drummer boy at Gettysburg, one of the big battles. But later on I came to realize that the South ought to have been allowed to secede from the Union—that was the great issue for the North rather than slavery, you know—and I deserted and took refuge in upstate New York, which had always been rather disaffected. I became what is called a Copperhead.

INTERVIEWER. We haven't talked about American writers. What contemporary American writers do you think most highly of?

WILSON. Well, I don't read them very much nowadays. I have been trying to keep up my English. I've had to read foreign writers, and, in connection with the Civil War, so many inferior books of that period that I feel I've been losing my hold on good literary English, but, as I say, I don't think that current English prose is especially exhilarating. I feel that my own prose is getting as "pale" and "impoverished" as anybody's. It has been a great relief to me lately to read some of the Elizabethans I hadn't read before. But I can't write my articles in Elizabethan.

And the various American styles are no good to me. I can't write Hemingway. I can't write Mencken. I can't write the jargon of the critical quarterlies. This is always something of a problem in America. If you are not doing a play or a novel in which you make people talk the way they do, you have no standard American medium in which to express yourself. I am giving myself a vacation from the kind of language I usually write by concocting a sort of farce-melodrama of academic life, in which the professors and students talk like professors and students, and one of the professors, who is something of an old ham, forges an Elizabethan play which he pretends to have discovered in England and which he gets produced in the college, with himself in the role of the Duke. A performance of a part of this play takes up the whole of the second act, and this is giving me an opportunity to write some Elizabethan. The villain is a New Critic, who methodically takes Yeats's poems apart and discovers homosexuality in *The Wild Swans at Coole*—note the "Wilde" swans, and of course the swans are really young men. The hero is a young instructor, boorish but brilliant, whom the English Department is trying to eliminate. They are competing for the hand of the Professor's daughter. The Professor himself represents the spirit of creative scholarship, which always has to more or less forge the works of its favorite subjects.

But you asked me what writers I admire. Well, the only American fiction writers I always read are Salinger, James Baldwin, Edwin O'Connor. There is nothing invidious about this; it is just that I haven't got around to reading most of the others. (I'm not speaking of the older ones, like Faulkner, Dos Passos and Dawn Powell.) James Baldwin I think most remarkable. He is not only one of the best Negro writers that we have ever had in this country, he is one of the best writers that we have.

He has mastered a taut and incisive style—which is what Negro writers often lack—and in writing about what it means to be a Negro he is writing about what it means to be a man. No one is more concerned with the Negro problem, and yet no one so far transcends it by intellect and style. He concentrates on himself or his principal character an intense kind of isolating spotlight, which makes him stand out against his sordid background—or, rather, he makes this individual seem to shine and throw everything else into shadow.

As for poetry, aside from the older poets, the only one I really read is Robert Lowell—I mean, the only American poet. He has done something very extraordinary; he has made poetry out of modern Boston. He spares nothing of its dinginess and ugliness and vulgarity. You have all the constriction and agonizing of the Puritans and the puritanism and parochialism of the Irish Catholics; you can feel behind his work the cramped frame, the straining energies, the sloppy icy winters, when everybody has a cold and the cars can't make it up Beacon Hill on account of its being so slippery—even in Boston they don't do much about the streets in winter. He even writes about those garbage pails. But the poetry never ceases to be noble, and the imagery, which is spiky and dark, is also in its way rich and brilliant. He is, I think, the only recent American poet—if you don't count Eliot—who writes successfully in the language and cadence and rhyme of the resounding English tradition. In some way that I find it rather hard to define, he and W. H. Auden stand distinctly apart from the other contemporary poets. It is a matter of stature, I suppose. They are not playing a game or amusing themselves or trying to make an impression or occasionally giving expression to some more or less poignant emotion. They have higher and more serious ambitions and they also have big enough talents to achieve

poetic careers on the old nineteenth-century scale. Lowell's recent book of translations, called *Imitations,* is, so far
as I know, the only book of its kind in literature. I have
always said that the best translations—the *Rubáiyát,* for
example—are those that depart most widely from the
originals—that is, if the translator is himself a good poet;
otherwise the result may be horrible. Now, Lowell, who
has used material from a variety of other writers, all the
way from Homer to Pasternak, has produced a volume of
verse which consists of variations on themes provided by
these other poets and which is really an original sequence
by Robert Lowell of Boston. It has, in general, it seems to
me, been stupidly received. It is absurd to complain, for
example, that he has not followed Baudelaire literally
when he has made a point of explaining in his foreword
that he has taken every possible liberty—has changed the
order of stanzas, invented stanzas of his own and contributed his own new images. He has also in many cases
transmuted the whole tone and color of the poem which
he has taken as a point of departure. A pretentious reviewer in *Time* magazine tried to take him to task in this
way, and then went on to be patronizing about his
handling of Leopardi's *L'Infinito,* which the reviewer
calls "one of the supreme sonnets in all literature." But
L'Infinito is not a sonnet!

Oh, and I ought to mention Elizabeth Bishop. She's
not a poet on Lowell's scale, but her poetry is perfectly
delightful and quite unlike anyone else's. She is never
self-conscious or aware of the fashion but simply ripples
out her poems like fluid diaphanous scarves.*

---

* 1965. I did not include John Berryman, because I could not
at that time refer to him as someone I habitually read. He had
published his remarkable long poem, *Homage to Mistress Bradstreet,* so astonishing an advance over his earlier work, but since
then he had published nothing. In 1964, however, he brought out

INTERVIEWER. And now, if you don't mind, a question about yourself. To what do you attribute your success as a writer?

WILSON. Am I a success as a writer?

INTERVIEWER. I suppose so, or they wouldn't have sent me to interview you.

WILSON. Well, then, I attribute such success as I have had to the use of the periodic sentence.

INTERVIEWER: Surely that is not the whole story.

WILSON. And to my use of the colon and the semi-colon. Writing so long for the *New Yorker* may have led me a little to overdo the comma.

INTERVIEWER. What else?

WILSON. My invariable habit of writing in pencil on those "legal-size" yellow pads—the kind that are ruled with blue lines. I believe that composing on the type-writer has probably done more than anything else to deteriorate English prose.

INTERVIEWER. Well, I mustn't take up any more of your time. Thank you very much.

WILSON. It's I who am grateful to you. I might be boring somebody with all these opinions, but you don't really exist, as you say, and when they're printed, people can skip them.

---

his 77 *Dream Songs,* which carry a good deal further the highly individual language of *Mistress Bradstreet.* These new poems may puzzle and even repel; but the more one gives oneself up to reading them, the more they impose themselves, the more intimately their broken accents speak to us. This is not a new set of tricks but a new poetic personality. These poems are the utterances of a writer who has arrived at his own idiom to express his self-mockery and panic, his moments of lyric grandeur and his relapses into infantilism: noble openings that give way to clowning, the babble of baby talk that disguises an inner writh-ing, disgust at what he reads in the papers, admiration for the masters of his craft.

INTERVIEWER. Goodbye. Thank you.

WILSON. Goodbye. What horrible weather. It's equally bad in London or Cambridge.

The Interviewer disappears; Wilson floats up to his study.

WILSON. I must make an effort not to evaporate.

June 2, 1962

NEWTON ARVIN'S *LONGFELLOW*

At the time this reviewer was in college (1912–16), there were, so far as I know, only three men in the Eastern universities who had occupied themselves seriously with American literature—George E. Woodberry at Columbia, Thomas R. Lounsbury at Yale and Barrett Wendell at Harvard. Barrett Wendell had published in 1900 a short *Literary History of America,* but his book was characterized by an almost complete disregard of contemporary American writers as well as a somewhat cavalier attitude toward even the New England classics, to which he was closest in sympathy. At Princeton, that indomitable buffalo the Scottish-German Duncan Spaeth was considered to have made himself rather ridiculous by including in a course on nineteenth-century English poetry a lecture on Walt Whitman and summing up the poet's career with "Walt Whitman—born on Long Island, died in Camden—found life beautiful!"

Today it is all very different. The old writers have been reread, and a new hierarchy has been established among them. The writers of the turn of the century have been taken more seriously than they were in their time. Discoveries have recently been made, not only of interesting writers who had been completely forgotten after never having been much read but even of writers of merit who had never or hardly been published at all. Much valuable work has been done in the way of biography, bibliography, documentation and scholarly editions, and much still remains to be done. Since J. A. Harrison's Poe and the old Boston-published collected works of Emerson and Hawthorne and the other New Englanders, we have had no complete up-to-date edition of any important nineteenth century prose writer. With all the fuss about Melville and Henry James, there is still no satisfactory edition of James, and the only collected edition of Melville was published in England in the twenties and has long been out of print. Several really distinguished writers, such as Kate Chopin, Frederick G. Tuckerman, Harold Frederic and Henry B. Fuller, are only just beginning to get proper attention. But if the work of excavation and appreciation has not yet been carried far enough, the academic exploitation of "American Lit." has been carried a good deal too far.

In the American universities today, the teaching of and writing about the national literature has become an immense academic industry. So far from being scorned, as it was in my youth, the concentration on American authors seems now to have become a sure way of arriving at a berth in the English Department. I have written "American authors," but really all that seems to be necessary is to stake out some claim in a very limited area—let us say (I am improvising) the "Hartford wits" or the South Carolina poets—and to write a huge book about it, or to lay hold on some minor figure—say, Freneau or Charles Brockden Brown—and attempt to make him seem important. The scholars then persuade their university presses to reprint some work or works of their author, sometimes indiscriminately selected, to which they write long introductions. In this field all perspective is lost. These specialists are often quite unable to distinguish between what is fine and deserves especial attention, what has an interest merely social and historical, and what is mediocre or worse and of little interest from any point of view. Inside this academic domain you apparently get credit for your articles and books irrespective of critical capacity. There seems to be a tacit understanding that judgment and taste should not count and should not even be brought into discussion. And it seems to be a special qualification for writing about American literature that one should be wholly and incuriously ignorant of the literatures of other countries—sometimes even of the literature of England—so that anything one finds in the author or group to whom one has attached oneself may be regarded as purely American and therefore as possessing for scholarship a peculiar and compelling prestige. The sexual situations described in American fiction could only have taken place in America; the typical trappings of Romanticism, the stock plots of Victorian novels are profoundly significant of tendencies characteristic of the United States. And at the same time, since Christian doctrine has now become all the thing, it is a trick to find religious symbols and allegories in even such extremely non-religious writers as Henry James and Stephen Crane. One is reminded by this branch of interpretation of the technique of Jewish *pilpul,* that purely intellectual exercise which consists in explaining some passage from Scripture in a fantastically farfetched way and then in justifying this interpretation by a well-woven web of reasoning.

In all this writing about American literature, there has, in any case, been very little that can itself be called first-rate literature. Leon Edel's biography of Henry James, which presents the results of exhaustive research and acute psychological insight with so much lucidity and elegance, will undoubtedly stand as a literary classic. But otherwise, among the writers who have really devoted their lives to the study of our literature—I hope that I am not doing anyone an injustice—I can think of only two who can themselves be called first-rate writers: Van Wyck Brooks and Newton Arvin. When I speak of them as first-rate writers, I do not mean merely that they write literate English (many writers on literature do not) or merely that their work is not tainted by the jargons of the various "critical" schools. They both belong to the pre-jargon period, when literary history and criticism were themselves a department of literature. Van Wyck Brooks, in his *Makers and Finders,* with its various prolegomena and addenda, is one of the top American writers of our time. One encounters in the academic world a rather grudging respect for Brooks and sometimes an overt hostility, which may seem strange unless one realizes that he was the first modern literary historian to read through the whole of American belles lettres, to make discoveries, to readjust proportions, and to round out the old-fashioned summaries, which seemed usually to have been produced by the latest of the professorial summarists' simply following the summaries of his predecessors. Mr. Brooks carried out his own inventory and—while more or less excluding the literature of ideas: theology, philosophy and politics—he covered the whole ground and brought to light our half-buried resources. Our debt to Mr. Brooks for thus opening up the field is enormous, but one suspects that the coldness of the academics is partly due precisely to the magnitude of his labors, to his not having limited himself to some special figure or corner, to his not having become the big Emerson man or the big James Kirke Paulding man—this and Brooks' out-of-bounds range and the fact that he is also a literary artist and that his work is an imaginative creation which belongs to a tradition that differs from the local academic one: the tradition of the literary historians of Europe, of such writers as De Sanctis and Taine. If one needs any further explanation for the academic attitude toward Brooks: some of his books have sold tremendously well.

Newton Arvin, a younger man, is, I suppose, to some extent a follower of Brooks. His new book is dedicated to him: *Longfellow: His Life and Work.* He, too, has a charm of style—a curious kind of radiance, which is a personal emanation—and the ability to renew stale subjects, so that, in this case, the old household word of Cambridge, Massachusetts, is made to yield a more delightful book than one could ever have believed possible. But Mr. Arvin's way of doing this is different from Van Wyck Brooks's. He is more interested in the psychology of his subjects than Mr. Brooks has ever been since his studies, published in the twenties, of Mark Twain and Henry James. He has no revelations to spring about Longfellow's personal life, but makes us feel that we have travelled with him and lived with him in the Craigie House, and that we know what kind of man he was. Mr. Arvin also differs from Mr. Brooks in that one of the most valuable features of this book is the skill with which he is able to trace in Longfellow's earliest poems the motifs that express the moods of the real lyric poet in Longfellow as distinguished from the inspirational moralist, and to take note of the lyric devices by which he expressed these moods. At a time when so much attention is devoted to symbols and images without regard for music or feeling, this kind of connoisseurship is rare. It has been one of the virtues of Eliot that he was able to criticize comparatively the poets about whom he wrote, bringing into one field of vision the poets of different countries and age and calling attention to passages in which the flavor and movement of any given poet were shown to their best advantage. Van Wyck Brooks has hardly attempted this;

he is most interested in extracting from a writer's work, no matter how coarse in texture or how insipid in tone, a sort of precious quintessence, in imparting to it the sheen of his own fine prose. But Newton Arvin is interested in the style of his author, also, in a way that Mr. Brooks is not. Appreciatively but not too indulgently, he can take us through Longfellow's work, poem by poem, sometimes line by line, in the manner of a Saintsbury or an Arnold, in the days when poetry was still judged as an art rather than claimed as a profitable field in which to find texts to "explicate," and can show us how his style has developed and his degrees of success in this style.

Mr. Arvin understands metrics—a subject in which the younger poets, despite their imitations of Auden, seem not to feel very much interest—and Longfellow was a metrical virtuoso, as much an innovator as Swinburne or Browning. Mr. Arvin is able to analyze, with expert skill, the classical hexameters of *Evangeline* and the use in *Hiawatha* of the Finnish epic meter, to show how Longfellow competes in *The Saga of King Olaf* with the Swedish poet Tegnér by writing a long Norse saga with every canto in a different meter (with the exception of the opening and the close), and to point out how he invents new patterns, in measure and stanza form, appropriate to the effects that he wants to convey. (Since the reviewer must never fail at some point to put himself one up on the author, I may, however, note that I do not believe that Mr. Arvin ought to feel, as he says he does, that the poem called *The Golden Mile-Stone* seems "to cry out for rhymes." It is surely a kind of imitation of Horace's version of alcaics—like Tennyson's poem about Milton and Auden's somewhat freer equivalents—but with a third line of only four syllables, such as does not occur in the Odes.)

The true personal lyric vein of Longfellow as distinguished from his practical and exhortatory one—"Life is real! Life is earnest!," etc.—is, as Mr. Arvin finds, rather minor, wistful and brooding: the sadness of New England twilights, the silence of New England winters, the "sands damp and brown" of the New England coast, and the tumult or waste of the desolate sea. The neutral shades of these mezzotints seem to imply, though Mr. Arvin does not emphasize this, a certain indifference to color. Even Longfellow's summer landscapes have nothing of the glare of the New England sun; even their greenery seems somewhat grayish. And his longer pieces, once so much read—*Evangeline* and *The Courtship of Miles Standish*—seem today like rather fine steel engravings of the decorous historical or pastoral kind, such as used to hang in old-fashioned houses. The dramas and the other long pieces—except for *Hiawatha,* which for me has still a certain charm—I have never attempted to read, and I am grateful to Mr. Arvin for reading and reporting on them, though the chapters in which he discusses them are the only ones in his book in which his subject does a little let him down. It is actually depressing to read of the feebleness and dullness of *Christus: A Mystery* and *Judas Maccabaeus.* Mr. Arvin finds considerably more interesting the late unfinished *Michael Angelo,* in which Longfellow makes the Master, now like Longfellow himself grown old, express his thoughts about death and art, and his forebodings about the future of a Florence that has lost her freedom—forebodings that, as Mr. Arvin says, undoubtedly reflect Longfellow's own in regard to the United States of the seventies:

> Ah, woe is me!
> I hoped to see my country rise to heights
> Of happiness and freedom yet unreached
> By other nations, but the climbing wave
> Pauses, lets go its hold, and slides again
> Back to the common level, with a hoarse
> Death-rattle in its throat. I am too old
> To hope for better days.

I am ready to believe Mr. Arvin when he concludes that the *Tales of a Wayside Inn* is by far the most successful of the poet's large-scale productions. I was astonished when, a few years ago, I read them aloud to my daughter—following the tradition of *The Children's Hour,* a poem Mr. Arvin appears to detest—to discover how lively and varied they were. But these have to be read thus consecutively, so that it is possible to be entertained by their metrical and narrative skill, which can hardly be illustrated by excerpts. Beside Browning, whom, in this department, Longfellow rather resembles, he of course looks thin and superficial, with no such passages of dramatic emotion, no such impact of verbal power; yet certain of Longfellow's ballads are effective and unforgettable. I still feel, having memorized it in childhood, that *Paul Revere's Ride* is one of the very best of the New England ballads, and was much interested by Newton Arvin's discussion of it. He shows how important to the poem is the use that the poet makes of his characteristic moods and landscapes: the view from the North Church belfry of the spooky and moonlit harbor, with the menacing "huge black bulk" of the British man-of-war, and the churchyard, in which lie the dead "in their night-encampment on the hill"; the gallop through the sleeping countryside, with "the barking of the farmer's dog, the damp of the river fog," "the meeting-house windows blank and bare" that gaze on Revere "with a spectral glare," all the nocturnal hush that precedes the explosion of conflict; and the climax of the next-to-last stanza, which dramatizes all the more effectively for failing to describe it at length the outbreak of the April fighting.

Mr. Arvin has dealt at length with Longfellow's travels abroad and his knowledge and adaptation of foreign literatures. The young man from Portland, Maine, went to Europe at the age of nineteen, in order to train for the

new chair of modern languages to which his alma mater,
Bowdoin College, had rather daringly, at that age, appointed him. He spent a little over three years (1826–
29), mostly in the Latin countries, where he learned
French, Italian and Spanish; on a later trip (1835–36),
he did the Germanic end—Germany, Switzerland, Holland and the Scandinavian countries—improved his
knowledge of German, learned Swedish, Danish and
Dutch, and took lessons in Icelandic and Finnish. He
taught foreign literature first for six years at Bowdoin,
then for eighteen at Harvard, and by his lectures, translations and essays he distinguished himself as an educator
for our then very limited provincial culture. It is another
of Mr. Arvin's qualifications, rare among specialists in
American literature, that he is well-equipped to cope with
all this. He has a first-hand acquaintance with the literatures of the chief European countries, and he has been
able—getting expert opinion on writings to which his
range did not extend—to explain the use made by Longfellow of the Continental writers he read and the fidelity
of his many translations.

The banality and the lack of intensity which, as Mr.
Arvin admits, are elements of weakness in Longfellow's
work should not be allowed to obscure his distinction as
both a local poet and an international scholar, and the
bourgeois domesticity he celebrated was combined in a
not unattractive way with a liking for a rather princely
style of life—a large mansion, handsome books, the best
wine. Though Longfellow's poetic style could hardly have
contrasted more antipodally with those of Eliot and
Pound, he was closer to these modern successors as a
bringer of news from abroad, an importer into English of
foreign arts, than any intervening poet.

Mr. Arvin has summed Longfellow up—on the basis of
his shorter poems—in a paragraph of perfect taste and

justice: "For these reasons and others, one could wish away perhaps half the short poems of Longfellow's Harvard years. The rest, unequal as they may be in value, are worth preserving in some ideal anthology of verse of the second order. His art, with some ups and downs, was to go on refining and enhancing itself perceptibly to the very end, but already the poems down to *The Seaside and the Fireside* furnish pretty much the measure of his capacities as a lyrical and narrative poet. There are states of feeling that remain this side of either ecstasy or despair—sadness, weariness, a half-pleasurable fear, elation, the simple apprehension of beauty—that Longfellow could express with a veracity that has nothing in it of falseness or the meretricious. Moods of the weather, seasons of the year, divisions of the day or night—to these external states he was delicately sensitive, and they often become the expressive equivalents of his emotions. The physical *element* of his imagination, as Gaston Bachelard would say, was water, not earth or air or destructive fire, and the sea was for him a symbol that, in its allurement and its menace, had the primordial power of a symbol in a dream. He had something like a genius for narrative poetry—not, to be sure, of the psychologically or philosophically interesting sort, but in the popular and romantic sense—and he could almost always draw, to happy effect, on legend or literary tradition. His sense of form was fallible, but at his best he is an accomplished, sometimes an exquisite, craftsman, like a master in some minor art, a potter or a silversmith; and his command of his materials, at such times—language, meter, rhyme, imagery—though it is not that of a great artist, is wholly adequate to his purposes."

March 23, 1963

A POSTSCRIPT TO FOWLER: CURRENT CLICHÉS AND SOLECISMS

1. *Based upon.* There has come to be a habit of using this phrase as a floating past particle that depends on no substantive. It seems now, in the United States at any rate, to have become an accepted usage in political speaking and writing. Here is a sentence from an article by Walter Lippman: "I would in fact go a bit further, based not on what he said but on the general tone of his remarks, that in his book it is natural for a great power to undermine an unfriendly government within its own sphere of interest." And here are two examples from utterances of Mr. Kennedy at the time of his campaign for the presidency: "I would hope that all ambassadors would be chosen, based upon their skill and ability to represent the United States in the country involved." "But based on my observation of him in 1952 and in 1956, and last Saturday, Mr. Truman regarded an open convention as one which studies all the candidates, reviews their records and then takes his advice." In a form letter from the Princeton Club of New York, I find the following sentence, which in other respects as well as in its misuse of *based upon* is a poor advertizement for Princeton: "Based upon these prior inquiries, we believe that appropriate club quarters can be provided in one or more conveniently located clubs in the Grand Central

area for the period when we will not have our own club facilities."

2. *Crucial.* This word, which means properly *decisive, critical,* has come to be used, and used constantly, in writing as well as in conversation as if it meant merely *important.* Here are two examples from an article in *Commentary* by Philip Roth on *Writing American Fiction:* "But what is crucial, of course, is that these books aren't very good. . . . Of course it is of crucial importance, I think, that the regeneration of Henderson takes place in a world that is thoroughly and wholly imagined, *but does not really exist"* . . . Wouldn't *fundamental* be better here? (While I am fault-finding, I may as well mention that "of course" and "I think" should not be written together.) From a review by Keith Waterhouse in the *New Statesman:* "It is only 200 words long, but it is one of the most crucial chapters in the book." Can a chapter be more or less crucial? From a review by M. I. Finley, also in the *New Statesman:* "It is crucial that here the picture section, including the extensive caption material, was 'the responsibility of the publishers,' not of the scholars who give the book its cachet." But here is an example of the use of *crucial* which seems to me correct because it denotes an event upon which a sequence turns, instead of as in the one above, merely the most important factor in a situation. From an article by Sir Robert Watson-Watt, *The Truth about Churchill's Aid,* in the *Saturday Review:* "Without radar the crucial preliminary airdrops of parachute troops in Sicily and Normandy would have been impossible."

3. *Deceptively simple.* This has become one of the commonest and most tiresome clichés of current literary journalism. From a review of the *Judgment at Nurem-*

berg film by Bosley Crowther in the New York *Times*: "This issue, deceptively simple in basic moral terms but highly involved and perplexing when set against hard realities . . ." From an article called *The New Waugh* in the *Times Literary Supplement*: "A last joke from the riches of this deceptively simple-reading book." From an article called *Poet in a Wilderness,* also in the *TLS*: "He never in the whole of his 214 *Meditations* writes two lines as moving and as deceptively simple as Herbert's," etc. From a review of a book called *Ancient Israel* by Nelson Glueck in the literary section of the New York Sunday *Times* ". . . the significance of the sacrifices and the nature of ritual are examined in a deceptively simple but deeply erudite fashion." A review in the *New Statesman* of *The Penguin Book of New Zealand Verse*: "R. A. K. Mason's deceptively simple lyrics." I regret that I must also give an instance of the use of this inane cliché by one of the most delightful writers in England, Cyril Connolly, who, in a review of Louis MacNeice's *Solstices,* describes two of these poems as "deceptively simple." Just who, in any of these cases, is being or is likely to be deceived? Evidently not the reviewer. What is the meaning of *simple* here? A clear unpretentious style? Brevity of formulation? Why should it be assumed that the former may not involve subtlety or the latter erudition?

4. *Kudos.* I have already spoken of this misunderstood word in a previous article in these pages. It seems now to be well established as the plural of a word meaning *honorable mention* or *prize* or something of the kind.* An Australian correspondent has sent me a clipping of a

---

* 1965. It is still used by *Time* magazine to announce commencement degrees, and in the issue of December 20, 1963, we were told that Marian Anderson was the "possessor of a score of honorary degrees and countless other kudos."

heading "Kudos Are in Order" from a newspaper article on "business trends," and tells me that the word *media* is now appearing as a singular. *Protagonist* has become another classical casualty. I find a typical example of its reckless misuse in an essay by Louis Auchincloss on Edith Wharton's novels: "The change, if change it really is, comes with the infiltration of the other protagonists of the drama, the Spraggs, the Wellington Brys, the Gormers, Tim Rosedale, the Van Osburghs, people who can spend a thousand dollars to Mrs. Peniston's one." These people are parvenu intruders engaged in an "assault on the brownstone citadel of old New York." *Protagonists* here is used to mean simply important characters. But the original meaning of *protagonist* was the chief actor in a Greek drama. There are thus hardly any real protagonists in the society novels of Edith Wharton, in the sense in which Oedipus or Othello or Brand or Saint Joan is one, or in fiction, perhaps, Don Quixote or David Copperfield or Captain Ahab. And, in any case, in referring to a single work, you cannot have more than one protagonist. [I find that the misuse of *protagonist* has already been dealt with by Fowler.]

5. *Massive.* I have also written before of this stupid and oppressive word, which seems to have become since then even more common as a ready cliché that acts as a blackout on thinking. One now meets it in every department: literary, political, scientific. In a period of moral impotence, so many things are thought of as intimidating that they are euphemistically referred to as "massive." I shall not present further examples except to register a feeling of horror at finding this adjective resorted to three times, and twice in the same paragraph, by Lionel Trilling in *Commentary,* in the course of an otherwise admirable discussion of the Leavis-Snow controversy: "mas-

sive significance" of *The Two Cultures;* "massive intention" of *The Two Cultures;* "quite massive blunder" of
Snow in regard to the Victorian writers. Was Snow's
essay really that huge and weighty? If it was, perhaps
then it might follow that any blunder in it must also be
massive. I myself, I am sorry to say, have lately been
described as massive: in an article called *Fitzgerald's
Grand Illusion* by David Littlejohn in the *Commonweal,*
I am referred to as "the massive Johnsonian 'father-
figure.'" And, apropos, let us not only scrap *massive;* let
us be careful about using *Johnsonian,* which has been so
inappropriately applied to so many people from G. K.
Chesterton to Alexander Woollcott. And I much object to
father-figure even in quotes. It makes me feel as if I
resembled that colossal wooden statue of Hindenburg that
the Germans used to hammer nails in.

6. *Saga.* The vulgar use of this word for any kind of
history or story is enough to turn one's stomach. The
ordinary casual use is illustrated in a recent review by
Edward Lucie-Smith in the *New Statesman:* "One suspects . . . that she would have figured in one of Flook's
sagas, if Flook had only met her." One of the very worst
examples of the misuse of *saga* is to be found in a
competent enough little book, the volume on Henry
James by Douglas W. Jefferson in the *Writers and Critics*
series: "He developed a connoisseur's interest in the
points of the English social saga . . . In [James's later
novels] . . . he returned to his early theme of the American in Europe, and one of the minor pleasures of reading
these books is that of seeing the familiar points of the saga
recurring in more refined or somewhat disguised form."
Now, even if one extends the word *saga* by applying it to
some modern story, it should still have at least the connection with the ancient Icelandic legends that it refers to

something epic or heroic. It is impossible, from the passages above, to know what Mr. Jefferson imagines a saga to be. What on earth does he mean by "the points of the English social saga"? The usages of English society?

7. *By any standards*. This is one of the sloppiest of the current clichés. What are these standards supposed to be? I find that I have saved only one example—again from the pages of the *New Statesman*—which does not, I am happy to say, show this phrase at its idiotic worst. In reviewing a play called *The Devils*, Roger Gellert writes as follows: "In my view, [it] is, with all its faults, easily the nearest English drama has got to a great tragedy for 300 years or more. There hasn't, remember, been much competition. But the range of Whiting's play, the sustained imagination of its highly personal style, the fluidity of its kaleidoscopic action, the irony and audacity of its conception, are thrilling by any standard." Mr. Gellert specifically limits the setting of this standard to the Elizabethans, which is to say, one supposes, to Shakespeare; and he does not venture any adjective more committal than a subjective "thrilling." But the phrase is often used more loosely, as when a new novel is described as "of major significance" or "a superb achievement" "by any standards," without one's knowing whether the standards invoked are supposed to include Tolstoy and Flaubert or whether it merely means that the reviewer does not happen at the moment to remember that he has ever read any novel that seemed to excite him more.

8. *Transpire*. This belongs to a group of words that are in process of losing their original meaning, a group which includes also *disinterested, jejune, demean, flair* and *fey*. The misuse of Latin derivatives began, I suppose, in

England when the old kind of journalism, rather ponderous in style and composed by university graduates with a classical education, began to be supplemented by the daily press, in which very much less literate writers carried over the old tone and vocabulary without necessarily knowing what their language meant. In America this debasement probably went faster and further. Is the cause of all these words, then, completely lost? I gather that the editors of the newest Webster have written most of them off. The habit of thinking in a Latin vocabulary does seem to be disappearing. I discovered a few years ago in giving a seminar at Harvard that one of my ablest students, who knew Latin extremely well, was capable of writing *mitigate against* for *militate against,* as William Faulkner habitually did; and in reading to my not yet teen-age daughter, I found that the Latin derivatives which Dickens liked to use facetiously and which it seems to me I understood before I had studied much Latin had usually to be explained to her. Today one does not like to use *jejune* for fear of its being mistaken to mean *callow* instead of *arid,* though *transpire* has still held up to the extent that one can distinguish two classes of writers: those who do and those who do not know what it means. I suppose that the mid-century facetious use of some of these learned words really marked the linguistic moment when these fundamental errors began to be made. The illiterate use of *chronic*—"I suffer from chilblains something chronic"—has left intact its proper meaning, and the misuse of *promiscuous* for *casual* has more or less killed off the adjective but left *promiscuity* current, used in its proper sense in connection with sexual relations; but the vulgar use of *demean* to mean *degrade* instead of *behave,* once exploited like *chronic* for comic effect, as when a landlady would be made to say something like, "I wouldn't demean myself to associate with her!," has become so generally accepted that one rarely sees it used correctly. *Demean,* however, though thus wrongly used, is at least made to convey something definite, whereas in the case of *flair,* few writers, in the United States at least, seem either to know what it means or even precisely what meaning they attach to it. They do not connect it with the French *flairer,* and one sometimes finds it written *flare.* As for the non-Latin *fey,* the meaning ordinarily assigned to it is equally vague and mistaken. It seems to be used as if it meant *somewhat whimsical, in touch with a supernatural world* or even simply *a little cracked,* instead of—I quote the Shorter Oxford English Dictionary—"1. Fated to die, doomed; also, dying; 2. Presaging death; 3. Accursed, unlucky; 4. Feeble, timid, weak." Thus Lincoln might be said to have been fey, but not J. M. Barrie or his characters. I suspect that a part of the trouble here has been caused by a confusion of *fey* with *fay,* a fairy. Here, I take it, is a curious example of *fey* in the sense of *absurd.* I find it in the text on the back of a record album of comic folk-songs: "The arrangements . . . are full, rich and authentic . . . which of course makes the fey lyrics all the funnier."

9. *Tribute.* Another casualty of careless writing. It is often used for *testimony to* or *proof* or *evidence of.* One can say, "It is a great tribute to Professor X's eminence in his field that his colleagues are still speaking to him"; but one cannot say, "It is a great tribute to the shrewdness of the Board of Trustees that the University is still solvent." A tribute has to be an acknowledgment that somebody does honor to somebody. Here are some examples of this common misuse. From a New York *Times* editorial: "It is, unfortunately, no tribute to the 'wisdom of the East'

that India and the United Arab Republic sided with the Soviets." From an article by Earl Miner in the *Nation* on *C. P. Snow and the Realistic Novel:* "It is a tribute to C. P. Snow the writer that one of his novels, and that not his best . . . gives a more convincing and satisfying treatment of the problems of integrating our civilization." And I quote with regret from that brilliant little book *The Legacy of the Civil War* by Robert Penn Warren: "Perhaps, as some other historians say, the gusty vigor of the heroes of the period from Grant to McKinley is a tribute to the American character" . . . [This has also been dealt with by Fowler.]

In the matter of clichés, of course, none of us literary journalists is guiltless. Many years ago Robert Littell contributed to the *New Republic* an article on this subject called *Vivid and Its Pals,* and I never fall back on *vivid,* when writing about a literary subject, without feeling a twinge of conscience.

Compassion, compassionate, perceptive and *significant,* the last in the vague sense of *striking* or *important,* I abominate and never use. I should say, from my own experience, that the dependence on political or literary clichés is almost certain to increase with long journalistic practice, and in the long run may make one's writing quite colorless. New fashions in clichés have, of course, come in since I started writing articles, but I have hardly learned to use them. I have done nothing with *mystique* or *resonance* or with the fancier use of *context.* I have noted my opinion of *massive.* *Wry* is now much in vogue and being overworked. The reaction to the massive is, naturally enough, the wry. *Permissive* and *reductive* are now popular, but I shall never be able to use them. I have not even been able to make out exactly what *reductive* means. *Abrasive* is coming in, in application to literary qualities. This is not bad perhaps, but it will soon, I fear, become as common as *sensitive* and *perceptive*.

> In that grey realm, where never firedrake burned,
> Not even grey at last could be discerned.

February 8, 1963

1965. I have been horrified to find William Faulkner's favorite error, *mitigate against* for *militate against* in an article by Roy Fuller in the *London Magazine* of November, 1964.

MORE NOTES ON CURRENT CLICHÉS

1. *Massive* once again. After writing on this subject last February, I decided to make a collection, over a period of a few weeks, of all the sentences in which *massive* occurred; but I found that it was now used so often that this involved too much trouble, and I presently gave it up. "A massive demonstration"; "a massive Labrador retriever"; "the remarkable migration of Norwegian lemmings which was so massive that . . ."; "McNamara as he worked in shirtsleeves behind his massive Pentagon desk"; "the massive success of *The Ten Commandments*"; "a massive adornment to any library" (*The Letters of Oscar Wilde*); "He [Henry James] cultivated a massive indirectness of language"; "the whole massive drama" [Russia and China]; "a massive all-day protest in downtown Nashville"; "the more massive understanding of his [Bosch's] greatest follower, Peter Brueghel"; "a plan by the Communist bloc to introduce a massive fifth column into Greece"; "a massive movement of non-coöperation by European Catholics"; "Massive Search Begins for the Killer"; "finally came the job of filing the massive report"; "a massive engineering project"; "the latest massive instalment of Pope John's plan"; "his [C. Wright Mills's] massive shoulders"; "that massive trilogy *Die Schlafwandler*"; "four massive myths of the Gutenberg transformation of society"; "a massive stunning blow which only the United States could deliver"; "his [Walt Whitman's]

massive faults"; "all achieved massive notoriety"; "thus massively increasing the property's value" (both on the same page of a book on the Profumo scandal).

But this is enough. It has now become impossible to pick up a paper or a magazine without encountering this word. I wonder whether any other adjective has ever been so monotonously overworked. Sometimes it is properly used, but even its appropriate use seems a part of the curious run on it. It has been suggested by Mr. Harry Levin that this run was originally started by the announcement that Franklin D. Roosevelt died from a "massive cerebral hemorrhage." Here the language, one supposes, was technical; but for the layman the adjective was striking: it attracted public attention. Later on, John Foster Dulles attracted attention to the word again with his "massive retaliation."

2. *Stylish*. What is the meaning of this word at present? Here are current examples of its use: "Marcel Marceau shows himself to be a stylish musician of motion"; "*Landru* is a French film . . . which stylishly but puzzlingly details the career of the French murderer"; "There are stylish small performances by" so-and-so; "Beckford's literary output, from the youthful skit, *Biographical Memoirs*, etc., to the mellow and stylish *Recollections*," etc. Now, the word *stylish* in my youth was always slightly vulgar and comic:

> It won't be a stylish marriage—
> We can't afford a carriage . . .

It meant being in the fashion. But it is no longer used in this way. Has it come to mean having style in the purely aesthetic sense? Or in the sense of a personal style? I ask honestly for information. I find that I am annoyed by this use of the word because it fails to convey to me anything definite. The following comes perhaps closer to the old-fashioned usage familiar to me: "a Brazilian film whose theme of social injustice is wisely—and stylishly—dressed in the clothing of a thriller."

3. And what has *vintage* come to mean? "These [letters to Fenner Brockway from Bernard Shaw] range from vintage mock-modesty . . . to a genuinely modest gesture." A publisher's advertizement announces *Vintage Thurber*. Why "vintage"? Does the writer mean merely characteristic or does he mean that we are familiar from of old with Thurber's humor and Shaw's mock-modesty? In other cases, this word seems to be used to indicate especial excellence. Vintage wine is the wine of a certain year, and there is an assumption that such wine is particularly good—although, of course, all vintages are not so. Does "vintage" therefore mean that the work in question was produced during the writer's best period?

4. *Conversation piece.* A conversation piece is a picture of a group of people conversing. From Cyril Connolly's introduction to *Les Pavillons:* "Nothing helps us better to understand the past than a small conversation piece." But when did it come to be used, as one finds it in the women's magazines, to mean an object—a queer ornament or a startling picture—that may stimulate conversation?*

5. *Reportage, novella.* The first of these is an instance of the kind of unnecessary foreign borrowing that George Moore wanted to see eliminated. Why not simply *reporting?* In the case of the second, it is true that we do not have in English any single word for the narrative that is

---

* In an article in *Time* magazine, I find a pet vulture on a chandelier described as a "conversation piece."

longer than a short-story but not so long as a novel. But why go so far afield for it? Saintsbury and Henry James were in the habit of using *nouvelle,* and this seems to me better than *novella,* for which I have a special dislike because I think it was introduced by the American *Story* magazine and was an ignorant affectation.

6. *Galère,* which means *galley,* not *gallery.* When the father in Molière's *Les Fourberies de Scapin* is told that his son has been tricked by a Turk into going aboard a galley and has been carried off for ransom, he exclaims, *"Que diable allait il faire dans cette galère?"* ("What the devil was he doing in that galley?"), and in the dialogue that follows he repeats this five times. The line became a saying, and it may have been made more popular by what is perhaps an echo of it by Voltaire. When Candide finds Pangloss and Thunder-ten-Trouckh as galley slaves in Constantinople, he first exclaims, *"Est-ce un songe? veillé-je? suis-je dans cette galère?"* Then, *"Et pourquoi êtes-vous tous deux aux galères en Turquie?"* The phrase has been carried over into English, and the galley has been turned into a gallery. Examples: Edward Crankshaw in the *Observer,* "The world . . . did not stop to ask why on earth Albania should be in that gallery at all"; Harry T. Moore in the *Saturday Review,* "For instance, what the devil is Gore Vidal doing in this gallery. . . .?" This is evidently an error of fairly long standing, for I find it included in Fowler.

7. *Breakthrough.* This word has now become very fashionable. My theory about it is that we are up against so many insoluble problems that we like to think of breaking through something. The current use of the word has been burlesqued by Mr. Connolly in an account of an imaginary operation of the pretentious pseudo-scholarly

kind conducted on *Finnegans Wake* by a group of contemporary critics. When the "breakthrough" finally occurs, it is not clear that anything has been accomplished.

8. *Naked force.* This is something that the other side resorts to. Thus, according to the United States State Department, Fidel Castro uses naked force in Cuba; but the kind of force that the United States makes use of in Vietnam or Laos is presumably fully uniformed.

9. *Thoughtful people.* This seems to me one of the most depressing of the clichés of liberal journalism. When I meet it, I have a vision of a man very palely cogitating and coming to the sober conclusion that something or other perhaps presents a problem. But there is no such person. This figure is a myth. "Thoughtful people believe," "Thoughtful people are beginning to ask," simply mean that the editor has some opinion or other which he wants to make impressive in this way; but instead of conjuring up these phantoms, he would do better to state it himself.

10. And do let us scrap the *love-hate relationship!*

December 6, 1963

EVERY MAN HIS OWN ECKERMANN

EDMUND WILSON. I'm delighted to hear about your new magazine.

THE VISITOR. We hope that it's going to be good.

WILSON. God knows that some such thing is needed. The disappearance of the *Times* Sunday book section at the time of the printers' strike only made us aware that it had never existed. Apart from Norman Cousins's campaign for peace and an occasional article on popular science, the *Saturday Review* is interesting only for its reports on new phonograph records. And those quarterlies are still mostly wandering in the vast academic desert of the structure of *The Sound and the Fury,* the variants in the texts of *The Scarlet Letter* and the religious significance of *The Great Gatsby.*

But where did you get the money? Not from a foundation, I imagine.

THE VISITOR. That's where we were very lucky. We tried the foundations first, but of course there was nothing doing.

WILSON. The big ones, so far as I can see—in the literary and scholarly departments, at least—are run by second-rate professors who have found that they can make more money out of that kind of bureaucratic job than out of mediocre teaching. I've been trying for many years to get really good complete editions of the American classics printed—like the French Pléiade series, you know. When a publisher friend of mine who has been trying to do something about it went to the Rockefeller Foundation, he was told that it would first be necessary to have a study made in order to find out whether the books were available—which everyone who has done any work in this field could have told him at once they are not—and then the foundation man remarked that there was really no point in reprinting any author complete: who ever read all of Shakespeare? At the Ford Foundation, he was told that the whole of their cultural budget had been allotted to provide two planes to fly over the Middle West, broadcasting educational programs. The people on these foundations do not seem to have any competence to make judgments on the projects submitted to them—I except the Guggenheim Foundation, which is an older and quite different thing—and they feel free to formulate projects themselves in fields they know nothing about, with no relevance to the applicants' aims. A middle-aged anthropologist who had devoted many years of his life to a group of Australian aborigines or a tribe of Mexican Indians or something of the sort was told, when he applied to one of the foundations, that it had been re-ported in their offices that very little anthropological work had as yet been done on the Turks, and that they might recommend him to investigate this subject, of which he was totally ignorant. A scholar friend of mine who is an expert on the numismatics of the Graeco-Roman world had, when I last saw him, been trying without success to get a grant which would enable him to do research on the coinage of Alexander the Great—of special interest, it seems, as the first really international currency. I have just read that he has been made chairman of the American School of Classical Studies in Athens. I hear of nothing but such stupidities on the part of the big foundations.

I have just had a letter from the Ford Foundation inviting me to recommend candidates—let me read it to you—for "a one-year program designed to enable a limited number of poets, novelists and short story writers to spend a year with professional resident theater companies. The intention of the program is to bring established writers in non-dramatic forms into formal association with the theater and, by acquainting them with stage problems and the requirements of dramatic writing, ultimately to improve the quality of plays and scripts available to American directors, actors and producers." What nonsense! A typical foundation project, obviously thought up by somebody who knows nothing about the theater. What are these prospective playwrights supposed to be actually doing? The way to learn about the theater is to have a play put on or to act in one, and a grant from the Ford Foundation can hardly help one much to do either. A man who really wants to write plays is sufficiently enamored of the theater to get into it at any cost. If a poet does not write plays, why encourage him to hang around theaters? There are some very good people here who are listed as having had grants, but what a farfetched pretext for giving them money to work! In the case of the universities, I don't know whether the grants that they obtain from the foundations are for projects originated by the bureaucrats, which the university devotes to some other use, or whether the university, knowing how these things are done, dreams up some grandiose project which it knows will appeal to the foundation mind and then uses it for something else; but I have seen a certain amount of evidence that these subsidies do not always go for the purposes for which they were granted.

Well, tell me how you did get your subsidy.

THE VISITOR. It all comes from one backer.

WILSON. An old-fashioned patron?

THE VISITOR. Yes.

WILSON. You don't think he'll interfere with you?

THE VISITOR. I don't see how he can. He's unshock-able—about politics or religion or art or sex or anything. He doesn't want his name made public, but he's a culti-vated European who married a rich American woman. She died and left him all her money, and he doesn't know what to do with it. He's a collector of various things, but his collections are now practically complete, and are beginning in fact to bore him. He says that, first of all, he would like to see a review that he himself can read, and, second, that a country as big as this and as powerful as we are now supposed to be has enough nearly literate people to make it perhaps important to establish a cultural journal which will not have to worry about money and so will be free to set its own standards and to get only first-rate writers who are allowed to say anything they please. He himself was something of a figure in the cultural life of his country before the Russians took over.

WILSON. Won't we want to contribute himself?

THE VISITOR. He comes from a country with a mi-nority language—only spoken by a few hundred thousand people. He has always read English but he doesn't write it. German was his second language.

WILSON. One of those Baltic barons?

THE VISITOR. I'm not allowed to tell.

WILSON. Well, I congratulate you!—You say "cultural journal." So you won't be dealing only with books.

THE VISITOR. No, with all the arts—and that's what I wanted to ask you about. You've written so much about literature but not much about painting and music. We wondered if you wouldn't contribute some opinions about graphic and musical subjects.

WILSON. Gladly: I know nothing whatever about them.

THE VISITOR. But in the twenties you used to do articles on concerts and exhibitions.

WILSON. Oh, that was in the days when I was cultural man-of-all-work for the *New Republic*. I wrote about everything from burlesque shows and circuses to Stravinsky and Georgia O'Keeffe. I'd never dare to write such stuff today.

THE VISITOR. An informal interview perhaps.

WILSON. That's what I thought you meant.

THE VISITOR. I'm sure you must have some ideas on current tendencies in the musical and artistic worlds.

WILSON. I never think much in terms of tendencies even in the literary world. I have preferences in music and painting, of course, but there wouldn't be any point in enumerating, for example, my favorite painters. In my case, such preferences would be of no interest. If I should say that I like Edwin Dickinson but don't very much like Rouault, it would be like announcing in public that I like shad but don't like lobster. In order to talk critically about an art, you have to have some inside knowledge of it, and as I'm neither a musician nor a painter even in an amateur way, I don't really know how those things are done, so, in any technical sense, I don't know what these artists are doing.

THE VISITOR. It would be interesting to hear your preferences.

WILSON. It wouldn't be at all interesting for painters or musicians, I'm afraid. But if you want some unauthoritative opinions, here goes. There's one great phenomenon of modern painting about which I seem to be in a minority of one. That's Picasso. I can't really feel much interest in him. Of course, I see the brilliance of his work, and even at times the beauty. I'm willing to believe that Picasso is the greatest draftsman since Raphael—that he's a prodigy of inventiveness, "resourcefulness," virtuosity, variety, all that. And yet somehow the whole thing bores me. I can't help feeling that the man himself is shallow. The deliberate ugliness of his women that are seen simultaneously in fishlike full-face and profile seems to me in its way just as facile as the pathos and charm of the acrobats that he was doing in his early period, or the cubism that he played with and abandoned. He goes on doing one thing after the other without ever becoming any more impressive. It's all on the same level! His idea of tragic bitterness at the time of the Spanish Civil War! He could only make Franco grotesque and humanly unbelievable, and those horses with tongues like spikes and eyes like little dots on the sides of their heads—that he said represented the Spanish people—and those caricatured classical women with their thick necks and wooden faces and their fingers and toes like sausages— you can't imagine them suffering anguish. Picasso was much more interested in his cleverness in putting over women and horses that looked like that than in anything connected with Franco. You know that popular print that belongs to the Guernica period: the little girl holding a candle and confronting the monstrous Minotaur? Once years ago my wife was going to buy it as a Christmas present for me, but was dissuaded by Clement Greenberg, the art critic, who assured her that I'd very soon get bored with it. So I bought it for myself and hung it in my office, but Greenberg's prediction turned out to be correct. I usually enjoy the horrific, but I couldn't believe in that Minotaur, and eventually I gave it away. Put Picasso beside Goya and he's nowhere. In Goya you do feel the horror—a desperate tortured contempt—of the cruelties of war and the Inquisition, of Saturn devouring his children. And his drawings are dark and corrosive, they leave a scar on the mind, whereas—in spite of his calculated outrageousness—Picasso merely startles and

amuses. I never get tired of Goya, who is one of the artists
that I find most congenial.

I have always had a very strong taste for the satirical
and the rather sinister; and I am under the impression—
which artists tell me makes no sense—that I am much
more sensitive to line than to color. I like things to be
rather dry and drawn incisively instead of fluently. I particularly admire Degas, and Matisse means very little to
me. My first great admirations were Hogarth and Dü-
rer—I used to have them up on my walls at college. Then
I discovered Callot, who is of course a lesser artist but
who has for me a special personal interest. I was stationed
in France during the First World War near Nancy in
Lorraine, where Callot was born, and when the city was
threatened by the Germans, an old print dealer there got
out and set up shop in the town where I was. I bought
from him a number of Callot prints, some made from the
original blocks, and a copy of the eighteenth-century
engraving copied from Callot's most popular plate, *La
Tentation de Saint-Antoine*. These stood me in good
stead. They fell in with my mood of those years and they
gave me a certain support. I had some of the series of *Dé-
sastres de la Guerre*—which inspired Goya's series—and I
took acrid satisfaction in the irony and objectivity of Callot's detailed picture of the life of his time. I still like to
have these prints around me. Later on I got Lieure's
"Catalogue" of Callot, which reproduces the whole of his
work. It is fascinating. It seems to unroll through its many
fascicules the whole life of the seventeenth century: wars,
fairs, landscapes, cities, beggars, commedia dell' arte actors, the ceremonies and fêtes of the court—with the people seen as sharp tiny figures, almost on the scale of
insects. It is characteristic of Callot that when he gives us
a closer view of them, they are likely to be less satisfactory:

their features are so much less distinct than these prickly little midgelike figures.

I like picture books in general of the comic or fantastic kind: Gilray, Rowlandson, Fuseli, Spitzweg, Cruikshank, Phiz, Edward Lear, Beardsley, Toulouse-Lautrec, George du Maurier, Phil May, Max Beerbohm, Sem, Max Ernst, Marc Chagall, Peggy Bacon, Saul Steinberg, Leonard Baskin, Edward Gorey—to mention people of very different magnitudes. But a would-be ironist that I do not like is that half baked Belgian, Ensor. I believe that Sem, the great French caricaturist, is a much underrated artist. He is one of those people that the French consign to an inferior category—like Yvette Guilbert, who was certainly one of the great French artists of her time, but when she went back to France in the twenties—having greatly extended her range during the years she had lived in New York—she was not taken seriously in Paris, where they spoke of her rather disdainfully as *"une chanteuse de café chantant."* So Forain is taken seriously, is supposed to belong to legitimate art— I suppose because he painted as well as drew—though he is certainly a second-rate artist and was apparently a detestable person—Sem's caricatures of Forain are interesting from this point of view—whereas Sem is somehow still a mere journalist, though he is actually a far more interesting and a far more distinguished artist. He had a whole very remarkable artistic development. He began with an album of the prominent people of his native town of Périgueux, where his father was a grocer; then he did one of Marseille; then he came on to Paris, where he caricatured year after year the whole social, artistic and literary world, with all its changing fashions in costume and restaurants and dances and sports. And he steadily improves as an artist. There is even an advance in draftsmanship between the album which shows all his Parisian characters mad about dancing the tango and the one in which they are dancing the Black Bottom. The one about the Black Bottom contains some of Sem's best work. He is a master at showing action. How would Elsa Maxwell and the Aga Khan and Barry Wall and Cécile Sorel disport themselves when madly possessed by the spirit of the Black Bottom? Everyone will dance it differently, and the album is a tumult of movement. And everybody is dressed characteristically. Sem was a contemporary of Sargent, and he has something of Sargent's virtuosity with fine fabrics and well-cut garments: the silk hats and smart clothes of the men, the great cloaks and long skirts of the ladies, in the era before skirts were lifted. There is never any touch of idealization. Sem's art is astringent but rarely brutal, and the people are usually enjoying themselves. Proust's favorite, Robert de Montesquiou, was also a favorite of Sem's, and it is curious to compare Sem's caricatures of him with the character of Proust's Charlus, to which Montesquiou is supposed to have contributed. Charlus is temperamental and uncomfortable, humiliated, venomous, doomed, whereas Montesquiou according to Sem is always having the time of his life—dining with his friend Yturri, who always applauds and adores him, or strutting through a recital of his poems to an audience of delighted ladies. I don't know why the people who write about Proust don't illustrate their books with Sem's caricatures. He and Proust knew one another, and they were dealing with the same society. It is said that Sem used to stay up till all hours in fashionable restaurants waiting for the moment when some fashionable lady would drop her social mask—which seems to me very Proustian. But Sem rarely aims to degrade as Proust so often does. His drawings have often a peculiar beauty—those of the actress Marthe Brandès, with her flat yellow

pompadour, her skull-like face and the gestures, at once
sinuous and angular, of her long-boned body and arms;
the old Rothschild couple taking a walk along the beach
at sunset, she briskly moving ahead with her positive para-
sol and her salient determined chin, he strolling behind
with his half-closed eyes, his black suit and his long white
dundrearies; and even the dandiacal figure of the professional decadent Jean Lorrain—with whom Proust once
fought a duel—vulgarly precious and weakly supercilious,
his fingers loaded with rings.

THE VISITOR. Daumier?

WILSON. For some reason I don't enjoy Daumier nearly
so much as certain other people that I know are his in-
feriors as artists. I think that the trouble is that a kind of
classical sculpture somehow blunts the effect of his satire.*
Gavarni I don't like at all—it's a proof of the Goncourts'
dubious taste that they make such a fuss about him. I
suppose that on account of his being so unimaginative
they thought he was naturalistic. The drawings of Henri
Monnier are feeble enough in this satirical vein, but his
little one-act dramas or dialogues are really biting *eaux-
fortes* in prose. They anticipate Flaubert and Maupassant.
Well, people sometimes tell me—though I don't think it's
entirely true—that I mainly go to pictures for the qualities of literature, that what I really like are illustrations.

THE VISITOR. But a good deal of the work of Picasso
has also illustrational interest.

---

* 1965. In his *Voix du Silence,* André Malraux attempts to
show that Daumier was one of the precursors of modern art in
tending to depersonalize his figures and to turn them into purely
formal compositions. He reproduces a first study for a painting,
Avocats en Conversation, which does give this almost Rouault-
esque, though more structural, impression. I believe that this explains my reaction. I can admire Daumier from this point of
view; but he does not really fall into the category of the more
grotesque caricaturists.

WILSON. Yes: he turns out innumerable albums, but I never buy these albums. I look through them in the houses of friends.—Oh, I forgot to mention George Grosz: I think one of the greatest of the satirical artists— quite in a class with Hogarth. There has lately been an excellent film made out of his drawings and paintings. It brings out the concentrated life that Grosz has put into all those middle-class German faces: their coarseness, stupidity, meanness, complacency, debauchery, cruelty. It is a vitality less diffused than Picasso's. The faces of all these creatures, no matter how brutelike they are, have expressions of the fiercest intensity: they reflect the intensity of the artist. Then, Grosz, too, is a master draftsman. The stock thing to say about him, after he came to America in 1932, was that his work was no longer so interesting; but this was not at all true. He had a straight non-satirical side, which he mainly developed in the United States: the sand-dunes, the nude figures, the portraits of friends, all as solidly constructed as Dürers. And when he went back to satire at the time of Hitler, his Nazi butchers and miserable "Stickmen" were as powerful as anything he had done in his youth and were remarkable for a new use of color. It is true that when he first came to this country, he somewhat relented in his harshness, so that his work seemed less characteristic. There was a German admiration for America that was not merely chic as in France but was based on the obvious features that Germany had had in common with us: energetic activity, mechanical skill, urban building and middle-class comfort. I had never really understood how far this admiration had gone in George Grosz's case till I asked him once what he thought of American painting. He said that he didn't think much of it but that American commercial art was something new in the world, which did interest him. It created a whole ideal of the desirable and attainable life:

handsome men and beautiful women, with their spic-and-span smiling children, all eating the most excellent food, traveling in the smoothest-running cars, basking and getting tanned on the most enjoyable beaches, housewives relieved of drudgery, husbands coming home from the office and relaxing in adjustable chairs while the comely and comradely wives revive them with a well-iced martini. It had never occurred to me before that the pictures in our advertizements might be of interest to subsequent civilizations, like Greek statues or Cretan murals. They certainly made a startling contrast to George Grosz's representation of life in Berlin, but since I did not much believe in the ideal they depicted and thought that the realities of American life offered plenty of subjects for satire, I was surprised to discover that George was more or less delighted with America. In his account of his return to Germany in his book about himself, it is plain that he is full of pride at exhibiting himself as an American. He says that he bought for the occasion one of the most ostentatious of those gaudy American ties that were popular a few years ago—which he would never have worn in New York. The same thing seems to have happened in the case of Kurt Weill. Behind the revolutionary satire of *Mahagonny,* for example, which is supposed to take place in the United States, where neither he nor Bert Brecht had ever been, you feel an admiration for America, and when Weill did come over here, it was astonishing to find that he was able to get quite away from that German turbidity and sullenness, and to turn out such pretty poignancies as *September Song,* which appealed so successfully to the popular taste, and the delightful lyric numbers of the musical *One Touch of Venus.*

In any case, George Grosz had swung himself quite out of the orbit of the great central Paris market, which had operated with such shrewdness and assiduity in building up Picasso and the rest. It seems to me that he and Chelishchev—and please *don't* spell it Tchelitchew, though he let it go that way himself: he said that he did not sign his pictures, nobody else could have painted them—Chelishchev and George Grosz, it seems to me, were always at a disadvantage in not belonging to the Paris club. Chelishchev was a brilliant painter, who started out as something of an imitator of Picasso but arrived at an originality less extraverted, rather morbid but extremely imaginative—with his pathetic gallery of freaks, his trees that turn into children and his anatomical paintings of desquamated human heads, all in queer iridescent harlequin colors, that it seems to me no one but a Russian, with a Russian's love of gorgeousness and lack of chastened taste, would ever have thought of combining. And there is a Russian ingenuity that goes with these rather garishly assorted colors. Those prestidigitating paintings of Chelishchev that seem to be trees or portraits but turn out to conceal other things have a kinship with the novels of Nabokov, who loves to perform the same kind of tricks and to juxtapose gemmy colors, as both are very much in the tradition of the precious mechanical peacock that Catherine the Great gave Potyomkin and those very fancy Easter eggs manufactured for the Russians by Fabergé. I suppose there's something Byzantine about it. The rich many-colored vestments of the old Greek Orthodox Church, with their Fabergé gold and silver, make the same sort of impression on me. It may well be that Pavel Chelishchev was actually, as he seemed to believe, the greatest Russian painter since the ikon-makers. He used to say that Peter the Great had destroyed the tradition of Russian painting by suppressing the Old Believers and so ruining ikon art—and that he had been appointed to revive it. In any case, Chelishchev, like George Grosz, came to the United States, and neither of them has ever attained to the same international currency as the members of the organized Surrealist group, all of whom it seems to me—except perhaps Dali—were very much inferior to them. But they did not belong to a group and they were never the darlings of the dealers.

THE VISITOR. I should imagine that you don't care much for abstract painting.

WILSON. In regard to the abstract painters, I have only a coarse jest: they might be useful as designers of linoleum if they were capable of the necessary discipline.

THE VISITOR. You were speaking of Kurt Weill. Have you similar prejudices in music?

WILSON. I'm afraid that my taste in music is influenced as much by my interest in the drama as my interest in the graphic arts is influenced by their literary content. To me, such composers as Verdi and Wagner are primarily great dramatists, and I have had a good deal of pleasure in getting complete recordings of their operas and following their libretti line by line, which since I'm not able to read the scores and since you can't really follow them in the opera house, I hadn't been able to do before. Also, *Boris Godunov*. When I first saw it at the Metropolitan and tried to make sense of the Italian libretto, I couldn't understand what it was all about. It was only when I read Pushkin's play and got to know more about Russia that I could see how tremendously dramatic it was. Musorgsky's libretto, which I had never seen till I got a Soviet recording, is one of the best ever written. Musorgsky wrote this himself. He based it on Pushkin's tragedy—which is not one of his most successful works: an attempt to write a Russian *Macbeth*—and converted it into a masterpiece. He added elements from Russian folk music—like the ballad of the Siege of Kazan. The Soviet version has restored it to Musorgsky's original arrangement. The Idiot

is given his proper importance in the scene where he says
to Boris: "The nasty boys took my kopek. Give orders to
have their throats cut as you cut the little Tsarevich's
throat"; and then he reappears at the end. They sometimes in Western productions have it end with the death
of Boris, but this is all wrong. Musorgsky had made it end
with the army of the rebellion marching off and the Idiot
left behind, sitting alone on the stage, as the snow begins
to fall. He sings again his ominous song that he has sung
after his scene with Boris:

> Flow, flow, bitter tears
> Weep, weep, Christian souls.
> Soon the darkness will fall,
> A darkness terribly dark,
> Which we shall not be able to see through.
> Woe, Woe, Russia.
> Weep, Russian people,
> Hungry people!

—with its little twitching accompaniment—I hope you
don't mind my singing. This is one of the greatest
moments in opera. It could hardly have been done that
way when Stalin was alive. But everything in Musorgsky
is dramatic. Compare the sound of the bells in *Boris* and
in *Khovanshchina*—in the first, they are mocking at Boris,
evidently making him uneasy, at the same time that they
are celebrating his coronation; in the second, they are
pounding an assertion of power. And the *Songs and
Dances of Death*: the dialogue between Death and the
mother of the dying child, with the spine-chilling voice of
Death chanting a lullaby while the mother grows more
and more frantic; the peasant dying in the snowstorm
while the voice of Death sings the trepak and reminds
him of old moments of jollity.

THE VISITOR. How do you feel about contemporary opera?

WILSON. I very much admire Britten—though I am told by musical friends that I shouldn't admire him so much. He, too, has the dramatic sense to a degree that is very rare. The interludes in *Peter Grimes* which so intensify the drama of the action, the shadowy buildup of *The Turn of the Screw*, with its children's voices and nursery jingles that are always made shadowy, too. Britten's *Turn of the Screw* is altogether an original creation, quite distinct from Henry James's story. Menotti of course, too, has the dramatic instinct highly developed; but he is sometimes more a man of the theater than a first-rate musical artist. Berg's *Wozzek* and *Lulu*, too—though I've only heard the latter on records—are most effective in their creepy way. *Lulu* is a very strange performance. Berg sets out to turn into opera the whole of Frank Wedekind's long play in two parts that deals with the destructive career of the simpleminded but irresistible *"Erdgeist"* Lulu, and through hours of grayest recitative the more or less repulsive characters discuss their sordid affairs, financial as well as artistic and amorous. The play itself is always in danger of becoming unintentionally funny—so it presents a considerable challenge—but Berg has put into it, it seems to me, more real pathos than Wedekind was capable of, and at the end the terrible shriek of the Jack the Ripper scene has been led up to with as much suspense and comes with as much horror as the murder of the wife in *Wozzeck*, with the ripples spreading out on the water when the murderer throws his knife into the pond. I wonder whether the monochrome of *The Turn of the Screw*—not particularly characteristic of Britten—doesn't derive from the tonelessness of *Wozzeck*. The nursery rhymes of the children and the boy's piano exercise are flattened and deprived of their

melodic fulness like the song of the woman at the
window and the military march in *Wozzeck*. It is all like
a discolored photograph—very effective in its melancholy
ghostly way, but it makes one long for something more
ringing.

THE VISITOR. Have you heard Schoenberg's *Moses
and Aaron?*

WILSON. Only on records, again. It is impressive, but,
in spite of its leaning on Wagner, it did not seem to me
very dramatic—though I'm told that the orgy of the
Golden Calf, which needs a ballet, of course, is quite
terrific on the stage. But what a disagreeable orgy, so full
of reminders of death!—though this is, of course, just
what Schoenberg intends. The Wagnerian romanticism
that Schoenberg began with was reduced, as he developed his later method, to more and more of a starvation
diet; and I felt about *Moses and Aaron* that it was too
moralistic and didactic—very much a lugubrious mono-
logue of the somber and stern Jewish leader, who is never
to arrive in the Promised Land. Moses goes up on the
mountain and is handed the laws of the twelve-tone row.
It takes him some time to master them, and while he has
been away, the people have been getting dissatisfied.
They are longing to dance and to sing, and Aaron—who
is somebody like Stravinsky or Bartók or Hindemith, who
is weak enough to make use of melody—agrees to let
them have their fun. At the end of the Golden Calf
revelry, Moses comes down from the mountain and is
furious at what has been going on. The Golden Calf
vanishes, and the people complain that he has robbed
them of their *joie de vivre*. Moses rebukes Aaron, who
has proved disloyal to his leader by giving them *"das
Bild"* and *"das Wunder"* instead of waiting for Moses to
bring his *"Gedanke,"* which transcends these meretricious
attractions. Aaron defends himself on the ground that

ordinary people are only able to comprehend a part of the all-inclusive *"Gedanke."* "Shall I debase *der Gedanke?"* cries Moses—that is, abandon the serial system. He smashes the Tables of the Law and begs God to relieve him of his mission. For the very queer and arrogant last scene, Schoenberg never wrote the music. His difficulties and doubts about it appear from passages in his letters. It was as if he, too, had broken his tables, as if he, too, were becoming discouraged, were losing his grip on his mission. But he had written the libretto for this scene, and here Aaron-Stravinsky is brought in in chains, and Moses-Schoenberg bawls him out for stooping to please the people instead of consecrating his gifts to the *Gottesgedanke.* "Shall we kill him?" the soldiers ask. "No," says Moses. "Set him free, and let him live if he can." But Aaron is by this time so crushed by shame that when the soldiers release him, he falls down dead—which is not the case in the Bible, where he continues to coöperate with Moses and take orders directly from God.

THE VISITOR. What do you think of twelve-tone music in general?

WILSON. I can't follow it, so I don't really know. But I've found it reassuring to learn that accomplished musicians can't follow it either—that is, simply from hearing it without a score. I was talking about it the other day with one of the most distinguished American conductors, and one who is particularly notable for his catholicity of taste. I asked in what way the serial system was an improvement on music that was simply atonal. He said that it had two advantages. *One,* that it gave to the analysts of scores and the writers of program notes more scope for their technical explanations and made their explanations more necessary; and *Two,* that a man like Schoenberg, so exacting and puritanical, having completely made hay of the conventional harmonies, felt constrained to impose on himself a difficult gratuitous discipline. Debussy had not felt the need of any such theoretical structure, and Webern, though he followed Schoenberg, could have achieved his effects without it. But the serial system has, in any case, by this time become something of a cult. I'm told that in the schools of music, the Schoenberg technique is now so much the thing that the students have to withstand a strong pressure, and even to risk something like ostracism, if they don't want to become twelve-toners. A friend of mine who has seen a good deal of these students tells me that it is almost like the pressure of a homosexual group—though he didn't mean to imply that there was any connection between homosexuality and serial music. Except, of course, that they're both *culs de sac*. It strikes me that—in America, at least—the composers are the most ingrown group of any in the major arts. Their audience is so limited, and it is almost as if, finding themselves doomed to this, they take pride in defying the neglect of them by making it more limited still. They feel safer in the Kafka-esque burrow of the dark and hidden twelve-tone row.

But I'm afraid that the Anglo-Saxons are no longer a musical people—though they seem to have been in the past. Shakespeare is full of music, and the poetry up through the seventeenth century continues to show the influence of music to a degree that you don't find today. It may be that the Cromwellian attack on the Church and the theater and on gaiety in general blasted music so it never recovered. In any case, the Anglo-Saxon world has not for several centuries been musical. In Germany and Italy and Russia, the people were always singing and playing on some instrument or other. But I don't think we have much music in us. Prokofiev, for example, may not have been a great composer, but he was certainly full of music. So was Richard Strauss, who was certainly not a great composer. We have no such composers as this. Of course our popular music is brilliant, and it goes all over the world. But a good deal of it has been derived from materials provided by the Negroes, with their supreme African sense of rhythm, and much of the best of it has been written by Jews. I don't know why the Jews should be so musical. Perhaps they brought their love of music from Russia and the German-speaking countries, and they could cultivate music in the synagogue at a time when a Jew was not free to cultivate the plastic arts, and when his full self-expression in literature was still hampered by difficulties of language.

It seems to me, besides, that the problem of a market has affected non-popular music more perhaps than it has done even painting. Music is not a parasitic art, but in order really to flourish, it seems to need to be supported by some well-established institution that will enable it to reach a large audience: the theater, the Church, the dance. The symphony orchestras can keep it alive, but they cannot—even by way of recordings—make the music of the concert hall a part of the life of a people. The dramatic element is very important. Aside from church music and opera, you find that even in concert-hall music Beethoven was a one-man drama, as was Brahms in his quieter way, and Richard Strauss, when he was not doing operas, was composing his programmatic "tone-poems" which couldn't be more theatrical. A Menotti can make money by writing for the stage, a Copland by writing for ballet or the movies, but a non-dramatic composer, unless he has private means, has to depend on grants from foundations or get a job in the music department of some university. How great would be Stravinsky's reputation or how widely would his work be played, if he had not in his early career made connections with Dyagilev and been able to go on writing ballets all his life? His non-theatrical works are as delightful as everything else he writes but they are only very rarely played—you have to get them on records.

THE VISITOR. You *do* admire Stravinsky?

WILSON. Tremendously. Unlike Picasso, Stravinsky *has* meant a good deal to me—more than any other contemporary artist in any non-literary art. It is inspiring for any kind of craftsman to have the spectacle of such a sustained career—the artist always himself and always doing something different, but always doing everything intensely with economy, perfect craftsmanship and style—so different from Picasso's diffuseness that sometimes seems almost mere doodling. Stravinsky has kept going through his eighties with such tireless pertinacity and vivacity that I feel he has helped *me* to keep going. I'm not in the least religious, but I think it's significant and admirable that Stravinsky should begin every day with a prayer.

—Well, I guess that's enough. When people get to talking about subjects that they don't really know inside out, you are likely to get a combination of banalities, naïvetés and what I love to have my critics call "gross errors," and I expect I've been guilty of all of them. I hope I haven't given the impression that I think that Sem's caricatures are more important that Michael Angelo—though I really don't care much for Titans—or that I don't admire the poignant and skeletal Schoenberg of *Pierrot Lunaire* or the scrolling black steel shavings of the *Five Pieces for Orchestra*.

THE VISITOR. Thank you very much.—Now, what doo yoo theenk of thees keend of myooseec?

A prolonged even whistling is heard.

WILSON. It doesn't sound eeree or loopee enough for electronic myooseec.

THE VISITOR. Electroneec? Noo: Electrooloox—a keend

of myooseec freequeentlee heerd een thee oordeenaree Amereereecan hoosehoold.

WILSON. Yes: eet soonds veeree fameeliar. Noo, tell mee, what are yoo going too call yoor magazeen?

THE VISITOR. The seem neem: *Eelectroloox,* and thee poorpose weel bee the seem.

WILSON. Woon't yoo reeveel, pleese?

THE VISITOR. Eeee—eesee, eeesee does eet. Thees weel geeve yoo soom ideee of the keend of mateereeal that wee are hooping too coollect and preesent.

The sound suddenly ceases. Wilson awakes. The maid has stopped the vacuum cleaner in order to empty its contents.

Spring, 1963

MY FIFTY YEARS WITH DICTIONARIES
AND GRAMMARS

I HAVE ALWAYS BEEN GREEDY for words. I never can get enough of them. I love Elizabethan plays, dictionaries of slang and argot, lists of Americanisms. I am always studying foreign languages, though my grasp of them is likely to be literary rather than practically colloquial. I suppose that it is partly that I like to recapture the excitement I felt in childhood when, attacking for the first time on my own a greenish primer with myrtle on the cover, I found that the sentences ran on into meaning; and partly, I think, that I get from this exercise the same sort of intellectual relaxation that other people get from crossword puzzles and chess problems. I have come to depend for a kind of consolation, in circumstances trying or boring, on the quiet unexacting support that is afforded by lexicons and grammars; and I have discovered that reviewing conjugations and declensions is a very effective device for putting oneself to sleep. A foreign language commits you to nothing: by amusing the mind, at first, with technical problems of grammar and the accents of a new vocabulary, it frees one from one's pressing immediate problems and from the tone of one's own community (though, in the case of a modern language studied with contemporary apparatus, one does not, to be sure, as I shall presently show, find it possible, under present circumstances, entirely to detach oneself from these). And in the meantime one is getting new insights—always, I find, surprising—into the way in which other people live, or have lived, in other parts of the world, and the infinite variety of ways in which they conceive their existence. As was said to me once of Welsh by a friend who was born in Wales, "A language is a way of life."

My first linguistic passions were French and Greek. Greek was then far more attractive to me than Latin. In its elegance and flexibility, it seemed to have more in common with French than the Latin from which French was derived. The false-naïve of the irony of Plato—so completely deflavored by Jowett—was not far from Anatole France. But one had to adjust oneself, much more than with French or Latin, to a different set of feelings and habits. What nuances were conveyed by those particles, what moral-aesthetic values were implied by the Greek abstract words that denoted human qualities? One could not really pin these down by consulting the lexicon and grammar. They were likely to be rather elusive. It was one of my chief pleasures at college to read such delightful writers as Homer, Aristophanes and Plato in those usually thin red volumes, printed on India paper, stamped with gold on the covers and with gilt edges on all three open sides, which at that time were published by the Clarendon Press. (These texts are still available, printed from the same clear plates, but produced in a coarser and more textbooklike form.) I passed on from the old abridged dictionary handed down to me by my father to the huge complete Liddell and Scott, and I remember my triumphant feeling of being now at last fully equipped to cope with this enchanting literature when, throwing myself off balance on my bicycle by swinging the book with one hand, I brought it back from the University Store. Those broad columns, with their dark-faced Greek that threaded the light-faced English, seemed fine-spun for all their compactness. And I wrote a little poem at this time, which I am quoting here not for its merit but as an example from my earlier years of my sentimental relations with dictionaries. (The dictionary in question was, however, of course, the old one, not the brand-new Liddell and Scott.)

On a Rose Found in a Greek Dictionary

In what dead summer came her petals here?
By what dead fingers dropped to mark a page,
Among the little words that live so clear
Beside such dimness and decay of age?

This heavy tomb, whose walls can only bleach
Her hue, shall make the lightest leaf to spring
From the full-petalled flower of ancient speech,
The frailest epigram, a fadeless thing.

When I later found a copy of Donnegan (referred to in the poem below), the predecessor of Liddell and Scott, and could see what its unattractive format and its relative inadequacies had been, I understood what a valuable aid to the study of Greek in the English-speaking world had been rendered by these two English scholars through the dictionary to which they had devoted a decade and which they went on improving as long as they lived. They have stood behind scholar and amateur, shedding light on the text before them, opening up for them that great philosophical, scientific, artistic and civic world, so bright and live still though long buried, which seems so far beyond probability. They brought Hellas to modern Britain, or, rather—coming after the period when the language was still a commodity sufficiently inaccessible for Dr. Johnson to declare that Greek was like lace: everyone got as much of it as he could—they put it within easier reach of the literate. After figures like Bentley and Porson, the geniuses of textual criticism, came the poets and the imaginative prose writers (the earlier of whom, of course, did not have the benefit of Liddell and Scott)—Shelley, Landor, Browning, Arnold, Swinburne, Pater, Wilde and Compton Mackenzie—whose youth had been nurtured on Greek. The place held by Liddell and Scott in the literary consciousness of England is given touching and quaint expression in a late poem of Thomas Hardy's. (In order to make the rhymes come out right, one must pronounce the Greek words in these verses in the old-fashioned British way.)

LIDDELL AND SCOTT

On the Completion of Their Lexicon

(WRITTEN AFTER THE DEATH OF LIDDELL IN 1898. SCOTT HAD DIED SOME TEN YEARS EARLIER.)

"Well, though it seems
Beyond our dreams,"
Said Liddell to Scott,
"We've really got
To the very end,
All inked and penned
Blotless and fair
Without turning a hair,
This sultry summer day, A.D.
Eighteen hundred and forty-three.

"I've often, I own,
Belched many a moan
At undertaking it,
And dreamt forsaking it.
—Yes, on to Pi,
When the end loomed nigh,

And friends said: 'You've as good as done,
I almost wished we'd not begun.
Even now, if people only knew
My sinkings, as we slowly drew
Along through Kappa, Lambda, Mu,
They'd be concerned at my misgiving,
And how I mused on a College living
   Right down to Sigma,
    But feared a stigma
If I succumbed, and left old Donnegan
For weary freshmen's eyes to con again:
And how I often, often wondered
What could have led me to have blundered
So far away from sound theology
To dialects and etymology;
Words, accents not to be breathed by men
Of any country ever again!"

    "My heart most failed,
    Indeed, quite quailed,"
   Said Scott to Liddell,
   "Long ere the middle! . . .
    'Twas one wet dawn
    When, slippers on,
   And a cold in the head anew,
    Gazing at Delta
    I turned and felt a
   Wish for bed anew,
   And to let supersedings
   Of Passow's readings
   In dialects go.
   'That German has read
   More than we!' I said;
  Yea, several times did I feel so! . . .

"O that first morning, smiling bland,
With sheets of foolscap, quills in hand,
To write ἀάατος and ἀαγής
Followed by fifteen hundred pages,
What nerve was ours
So to back our powers,
Assured that we should reach ὠώδης
While there was breath left in our bodies!"

Liddell replied: "Well, that's past now;
The job's done, thank God, anyhow."

"And yet it's not,"
Considered Scott,
"For we've to get
Subscribers yet
We must remember;
Yes; by September."
"O Lord; dismiss that. We'll succeed.
Dinner is my immediate need.
I feel as hollow as a fiddle,
Working so many hours," said Liddell.

H. G. Liddell, who had been headmaster of Westminster School, was later Dean of Christ Church, Oxford. When errors in the dictionary were brought to his
attention, he would humorously blame them on Scott.
He was the father of that pretty little girl, so much
photographed by Lewis Carroll, to whom the celibate
tutor in mathematics, on a boating excursion at Oxford,
first told the strange fairy story that later became *Alice in
Wonderland*; and the dictionary of Liddell and Scott still
sometimes evokes for me Oxford and the neo-Oxonian
atmosphere of Princeton: my humanistic studies there,
with an infinite leisure to pursue them; early-summer

canoe trips or moonlight skating through the level country solitudes of Stony Brook; and late evenings of study at
a roll-top desk by the light of a gooseneck lamp, in a
solitude only disturbed when the singing of old college
songs by upperclassmen who had been to "the Nass"
made a jarring and yet lyric accompaniment to the fluting
and fluttering of *The Birds* or the weavings of Platonic
dialogue. When the bawling of the revellers came closer,
I felt that I could perfectly sympathize with that great
lexicographer of legend who, interrupted at his table
by a knock on the door, opened it, strangled the stranger
and then returned to his work; but who inspired such
respect as a scholar that he never was called to account. I
have several times encountered this story, but the scholar's name is never given. It can hardly have been Liddell
or Scott; but since he seems to have been an Englishman,
I like to think that this winking at his involuntary crime
was one of those gratuitous indulgences which the English do sometimes grant in the interests of talent or
learning—as when Porson, whose dissipations and refusal
to subscribe to the Thirty-nine Articles as well as his
habitually ungentlemanly conduct had cost him a fellowship at Cambridge, was rescued by a life annuity provided by a group of distinguished friends.

I did not study Hebrew until a good deal later, and I
never went anything like so far with it as I had with
Latin and Greek, but I was able, in plodding through
parts of the Bible, to appreciate another great monument
of scholarship, and, I suppose, a more original one:
Gesenius's *Hebrew and English Lexicon of the Old
Testament, Including the Biblical Chaldee.* My edition,
also inherited, in this case from a great-uncle and a
grandfather who had been at the Princeton Theological
Seminary, was published in Boston in 1844; but the

lexicon, in an edition brought up to date, has remained through all these decades the standard work in use by non-Jewish students. Gesenius is, in fact, it seems to me, not only one of the most satisfactory but one of the most historically suggestive of the dictionaries with which I have worked.

Its compiler, Heinrich Friedrich Wilhelm Gesenius, was already in 1810, at the age of twenty-four, the "professor extraordinarius in theology" at the University of Göttingen. The next year he transferred to Halle, where he spent the rest of his life. There had never existed through the Middle Ages, outside the Jewish world itself, any tradition of Hebrew scholarship. When, in the fifteenth century, with the Renaissance, an interest in the subject was roused, it was found that it was not always easy for a Gentile to get access to Hebrew. On the one hand, the learned Jews were sometimes reluctant to teach Christians, and, on the other, many Christian churchmen believed, as a matter of religion, that Jewish learning ought to be suppressed. The curiosity of a Christian humanist, Johann Reuchlin of Pforzheim, precipitated a strange crisis which lasted for ten years (1506–16). An accomplished classical scholar, Reuchlin became fascinated by Hebrew, which opened up to him a whole new realm both mystical and philological, and he succeeded in mastering the subject to an extent that made it possible for him, in 1506, to publish a book, *De Rudimentis Hebraicis*. He even got as far as the Cabala, and believed that its doctrines could be invoked in the defense of Christianity. This unheard-of conjunction of religions provoked a violent reaction on the part of a fanatical converted Jew, Johann Pfefferkorn, of Cologne, who had attached himself to the Dominican order. He obtained from the Emperor Maximilian of the Holy Roman Empire an order that authorized the destruction of all He-

brew books except Bibles then to be found in the possession of the Jews of Cologne and Frankfurt. The Jews
appealed against this, and Reuchlin, who held at that
time a judicial office in Tübingen, was appointed to give
an opinion. He decided that, except for books which
actually blasphemed against Jesus, the order should be
rescinded, and the edict was accordingly withdrawn, but
the Dominicans would not accept this. They started a
trial for heresy before the Grand Inquisitor at Mainz; but
Reuchlin appealed to the Pope, through the latter's physician, a Jew, to let him be tried in his own diocese,
Speyer. The Pope consented to this, and the Bishop of
Speyer decided in Reuchlin's favor. There were larger
issues here involved than the mutual antagonism of Jew
and Christian. Johann Reuchlin represented humanism;
the humanists were on his side, and the Reformation was
under way. (Martin Luther studied Hebrew in Reuchlin's grammar in order to read the Bible for himself.)
Against them were aligned the clergy and certain of the
universities. They persecuted Reuchlin for years and
pretty well succeeded in impoverishing him.

But the battle for Hebrew was won. Luther learned it,
and Calvin learned it. The Buxtorfs, father and son
(1564–1629 and 1599–1664), were to make great further
progress in Hebrew studies. But it remained for Gesenius
to free it from theological preoccupations and to subject it
to the discipline of comparative philology. His linguistic
enthusiasm and his gift for lucid exposition made him the
most popular scholar in the field of Semitics in Germany,
where his contemporaries the brothers Grimm were carrying on the researches that laid the foundations of modern
philology; and in the later years of his life his lectures at
Halle were attended by almost five hundred students.
One can understand this in studying his lexicon, which is
remarkable for a high sensitivity to words and a faculty of

imaginative conjecture, when Gesenius is able to throw light on the meaning or derivation of hitherto obscure expressions by referring them to possible analogues in other tongues, among which—ancient and modern, Romance and Germanic, Greek, Semitic and Oriental—his range in his age must have been unsurpassed. His dictionary has also the value of being virtually a concordance to the Hebrew Bible. It enables you to run down almost any word to the passages in which it occurs. And it is a dictionary also that "reads." Gesenius's evident feeling for the poetry and drama of the Bible, his virtuosity of reference in time and place, the recapitulation of the uses of a word and the attempt to determine its meaning, which may vary in different contexts, give the articles a vivid interest.

The difference in quality of this lexicon from the dryness and meagerness of the textbooks that provide the irreducible minimum needed by Christian students in order to meet the requirements of such seminaries as still demand Hebrew was strikingly illustrated for me when I bought a small pocket dictionary that I hoped would be a convenience but that turned out to be too limited to be of much use. One day, when I was trying to find something in it, my eye was caught by a verb of which the brief definition given seemed curious and rather comic: שָׁבָה , "wandering about lasciviously." When I looked this up in Gesenius, I discovered that it occurs only once, in Jeremiah V:8, and that the passage may be taken to mean either "Like fed horses do they [the young men] roam about" or "They are like fed horses in the morning"—in either case, "inflamed with lust." The verse in the King James Version goes on as follows: "Every one neighed after his neighbor's wife." And Gesenius notes passages in other books which contain somewhat similar ideas.

The original Gesenius was written in Latin, and it is considerably less ample than the English version. This translation was the work of an American, Edward Robinson of Union Theological Seminary, New York, who, after Gesenius' death, improved the original text "with corrections and large additions, partly furnished by the author in manuscript, and partly condensed from his larger thesaurus." It was thus, at the time of its publication, the best version of Gesenius in circulation. It is also most attractive in typography and format, with the Semitic words standing out in their bigger and blacker type and set off by the wide white margins, in columns of which the print—as is not always the case with dictionaries published in the middle of the nineteenth century—is not too small and dense to be easily read.

To compare, in this field of grammar, the textbooks written by Christians with a textbook written by a Jew is immediately to be made aware of a lack of adaptability of the two mentalities to one another. They tend to pull against each other. I always find a pleasure almost sensual in attacking a new language, especially if it has a strange alphabet whose barrier I find I can penetrate. But Hebrew resists penetration. It does not want to be violated. I believe that it is possible, for practical purposes, for a non-Jew to be a sound enough Biblical scholar and yet somehow to remain outside Hebrew. The yeshiva and the synagogue are needed as well as the dictionary and the grammar, and the Christian is as unlikely to have studied rabbinics as the professional Jewish scholar is to have made himself an expert on Christian theology. Reuchlin was altogether exceptional in having explored the Cabala, as is the great Harvard scholar H. A. Wolfson in going on from Spinoza and Philo to deal with the Fathers of the Christian Church. It is harder for the non-Jewish student to accept the conventions of the Semitic

mind—to which, however, he remotely owes his alphabet
—than to accept the conventions of the Greeks or Romans.
When Spinoza made an attempt to compose a Hebrew
grammar for Gentiles, he had to write it in Latin, and
he tried to fit the Hebrew inflections into the paradigms
used for Latin, to which they do not lend themselves. It
is not merely that Hebrew reads from right to left instead
of from left to right (that is not in itself a great impedi-
ment), but it is necessary for the non-Jewish student to
work at the language with explanations that run in the
opposite direction. I have sometimes been made quite seasick by being obliged to turn to and fro between the text
of the Hebrew Bible, which is of course paged from what
we think of as the back of the book to what we think of as
the front, and Gesenius, which, though the Hebrew runs
from right to left, is paged the other way; or by using an
Israeli lexicon in which the English-into-Hebrew is paged
one way and the Hebrew-into-English the other, so that
there are two different title pages, at opposite ends of the
book. A curious example of this head-on—or, rather, tail-
on—opposition is an *Essentials of Biblical Hebrew,* which
I studied at a Christian seminary. It was intended to
make everything as simple and as easily assimilable as
possible, but the grammarian had retained the Hebrew
paradigm in showing the conjugation of the verb, which
is presented, from our point of view, wrong end up—that
is, you begin with the third person and proceed through
the second to the first. The reason for the primacy of the
third person singular is that this is the form which—instead of the infinitive—you look up in the Hebrew
dictionary; but once the non-Jewish reader knows this,
there does not seem to be any good reason that the
conjugations should not be learned in what is for him the
natural order. I once put this up to the professors of
Hebrew at a Christian theological seminary, but they

evidently regarded it as unthinkable that the traditional procedure should be reversed. The real reason was, I felt, that though the Hebrew-English dictionaries are allowed to run from left to right, it would seem to be something of a sacrilege to upend the Hebrew paradigm. One's hand would be stayed by the same kind of awe that prevents even Jews who are not very religious from pronouncing the "tetragrammaton," the unpronounceable name of God, for which Adonai, "My Lord," is substituted and which is also, I understand—except for the Bible itself— even in Israel unwritable and unprintable.

For the prestige of the Bible as a sacred work, quite different from other books, may even today be felt by even a non-Jewish student of no religious faith from the moment he attacks it in the Masoretic text. The Jews do not worship images but they do really worship this text. It is primarily on this account that the orthodox Jewish scholars were often so much disturbed by the finding, in the Dead Sea caves, of texts that had variant readings. Such texts had already been known to exist—such as that of the Samaritan Bible, that used for the translation of the Septuagint, that used by St. Jerome for the Vulgate, and that quoted by Justin Martyr in his dialogue with the Rabbi Trypho. But the rabbis who at some undetermined date, perhaps in the ninth century A.D., established an authoritative version did their best to suppress all the differing ones, and this version has since been accepted as final and not to be questioned—as virtually, in fact, divine. The discovery of other texts, which sometimes make better sense than the Masoretic and thus clear up some of its puzzles, could shake the whole foundation of Judaism. "The omission or the addition of one letter," says the Talmud, "might mean the destruction of the whole world." All that is unreliable, that is superfluous or now unintelligible in the Masoretic Bible has become so distilled to holiness, so imbued with a kind of mythology, that it can hardly ever be known by the Gentile grammarian or student what is really experienced by the orthodox Jew when he reads the Masoretic Bible. I was once asked by a young Jewish student who had specialized in Hebrew literature what on earth a Gentile could make of what he found in this literature. It does not help to explain that the early New Englanders were always identifying themselves with the scriptural Children of Israel and thought habitually about what they were doing in terms of their own version of the Law and the Prophets. All this to the orthodox Jew seems so different from his own traditions that he cannot for a moment take it seriously.

I had before been made aware of the difference between the Torah and the Gentiles' Pentateuch when I turned from my dreary *Essentials* to examine an older grammar, a much more elaborate one in two volumes, written by a Dr. Isaac Nordheimer, whom I assumed to have been a Jew, acting professor of Hebrew in the University of the City of New York, and published in 1838–1841. Here I found for the first time an analysis of the mysterious signs called "accents" that hover above the Bible text and that confuse one in reading the vowels. All that I had known up to then was that if you were able to spot the right squiggle it would show you which syllable to stress, and these signs are for the most part, I found, disregarded in Christian seminaries and have been treated with a certain contempt by even the accomplished Renan. But I learned from Dr. Nordheimer's grammar that they constitute a personalized hierarchy of "Rulers," the "disjunctive accents" that show how the words are to be spaced apart, which are Emperors, Kings, Princes and Officers, and the inferior "conjunctive accents," which are Servants or Attendants to the others. These accents

appear to have been introduced to indicate the structure
of the verses, then later to have come to serve as a musical
guide for the chanting. In any case, they are sometimes
important for the correct interpretation of the text. They
were once believed to be of divine origin, to have originated in the legendary "Great Synagogue" to which the
prophets were supposed to have transmitted the Torah. It
has even been imagined that these accents, as well as the
"pointings" that indicate the vowels, were already written
in the Pentateuch when Moses received it on Sinai.
Then, besides this, the characters of the alphabet have,
like the Roman ones, been assigned numerical values,
which have also symbolical and mystical meanings and
thus add a new dimension to the interpretation of the
Bible, as an ingenious contrivance of anagrams was made
to give a deeper significance to proper names and other
words. The Cabalists carried to extreme lengths the
elaboration of both these devices and made of the numerical calculations a complicated science called "ge-
matria"—so that, for anyone aware of all this, the text of
the Bible is loaded with ideas that do not appear on the
surface. According to the Cabala, the alphabet itself is
made up of twenty-two "dynamic powers." Even today, in
The Bridal Canopy, by the contemporary Hebrew novelist Shmuel Yosef Agnon, there is a ballad in which the
alphabet is represented as a group of men, each of whom
marries a wife with a name that begins with his letter and
goes to live, in the land of Israel, in a place whose name
also begins with this letter.

The Hebrew language—as distinguished from its characters, which are used also for Yiddish and Ladino, the
German and Spanish dialects spoken in modern times by
the Jews—is by some regarded as sacred, so that it cannot
be used for everyday speech. In Jerusalem, the fanatically
orthodox sect who call themselves the Guardians of the

City refuse to speak anything but Yiddish and have never forgiven the Israelis for making Hebrew the national language. Not only does the Hebrew of the Bible present barriers to the ordinary Gentile student—the consonants that look too much alike and that in sound (since, in certain cases, the old pronunciation has been lost or dropped) seem sometimes to duplicate one another, the relatively low visibility of the vowels, the unaccountable anomalies of grammar—but the language seems sometimes recalcitrant even to the Gentile scholar who specializes in it. It may be noticed, for example, that Renan, before he wrote his religious histories, brought out the first volume of an *Histoire Générale des Langues Sémitiques,* which, though now, I believe, superseded, makes excellent reading for the layman, since it treats the old Semitic languages in terms of the habitat and history of the various peoples who spoke them. Renan announced a second volume, which was to present a grammatical analysis, but he never carried out this project, and one wonders whether it may not have been the grammatical anomalies mentioned above that baffled his orderly mind.* It is amusing, in his *Histoire du Peuple d'Israël,* to find him urbanely attenuating the so often astonishing statements of Scripture as doubtless exaggerations due to the grandiose tendencies of the Hebraic imagination; but Jewish grammar had hedged itself in from even Renan's searching mind. And the language is still hedged in, even as written in Israel. The difficulty of printing Hebrew

---

* Since writing this, I have been told by M. André Dupont-Sommer, the distinguished French Semitic scholar who is Renan's successor at the Collège de France, that Renan never really accepted the decipherment of the cuneiform script, and that the probability is that his failure to go through with the second volume of his *Histoire Générale* was due to the difficulty of his coming to terms with another Semitic language, Assyro-Babylonian, which was at that time imperfectly understood.

with the "pointings" that indicate the vowels and identify certain of the consonants is so formidable, and entails so much extra expense, that, for ordinary purposes, it is not very often attempted. Only one or two newspapers, intended for newcomers, and books of poetry, in which it may be possible to mistake one word for another, will supply these aids to the foreigner. When I visited Israel some years ago, I found that the comment of the non-Jewish journalists in connection with any notable Israeli achievement was likely to be the catchword "And they do it all without vowels!" The language, by reason of its very obstructions, has been probably, for the modern Israelis as it has been for the Jews in the past, a source of inbred strength and cohesiveness. There is now, I understand, a project, backed by one of the Rothschilds, to have all Hebrew printed with pointings, or even in Roman characters. It will be interesting to see what comes of this. It will certainly encounter a determined resistance.

II

In 1935 I spent five months in the Soviet Union, and I took with me the only Russian grammar that I had been able to find at Brentano's. This proved to be the very oddest work of the kind that has ever come into my hands. It was one of a series called Method Gaspey-Otto-Sauer, published in Heidelberg, apparently under the general editorship of someone called Pietro Motti, "Knight of the Crown of Italy, formerly professor of Modern Languages at the Royal Piacenza Technical Institution." This volume is supposed to be by Motti himself, but he more or less confesses in his preface that his knowledge of the language is limited: "My good-will and patience were often sorely tried; special works were at every moment to be consulted and information to be got from Russia." In this preface, he asserts quite falsely that "it will soon be seen that Russian is a very methodical language," and that "great simplification is afforded by a constant application of the law of permutation"—whatever that means. He is even brazen enough to declare that "the Russian sentence is on the whole so like the English, that all details have been disregarded as a work of supererogation"; but the next moment he gives the situation away by saying that "such [details] must be left to practice and reading, unless beginners are to be utterly disheartened." Actually, the Russian sentence is very unlike the English: on account of the six Russian cases, which indicate syntactical relations, there is a good deal more freedom in the order of the words, and if it is true of the German sentence that you do not know what anybody is doing till you come to the verb at the end, it sometimes happens with a Russian sentence that you do not know who is doing it till you come to the noun at the end.

If it were not for this solemn preface, one might have a suspicion that the grammar which follows is intended as a sly burlesque of the classical Ollendorff manuals, and one cannot be altogether sure that the Russians with whom Signor Motti says that he has been corresponding may not have been pulling his leg. The whole thing has a flavor of parody of the kind to which Russians are tempted when confronted with the culture of the West. Every lesson in this grammar, for example, includes a set of English sentences—called, delightfully, "Promiscuous Exercises" —that the beginner is supposed to convert into Russian, and these exercises seem designed for the purpose of confounding this beginner at once with a maximum of difficulty and a maximum of absurdity. I quote a selection from Lesson 30: "Are you right? No, I am wrong. What bull have you? I have the bull of the good Russian proprietor. Have I the sugar or the honey? You have nothing. What sort of tea have you? I have not the tea, I have the coffee of my father. [The articles here make no sense, since no articles exist in Russian; you can only say, in Russian, "I have no tea." The last sentence quoted above is thus not really possible either in English or in Russian.] Does the prince possess a beautiful horse? He has no beautiful horse; he has an ugly ass." This, although somewhat grotesque, is not so far from the familiar old-fashioned routine of *le parapluie de ma tante*. But there is also a strange vein of fantasy: "To whom does this officer give his lion? He gives it to his father. . . . Did you see the miller's ass? I saw it and I saw the tall horse of the little prince. Of which prince? Of that of whom you always speak. . . . Which do you prefer, veal or mutton? I like neither veal nor mutton, I like coffee and tea. . . . Have you my weasel? I have my weasel. What weasel has he? He has the weasel of your cousin." After "weasel," Signor Motti kindly helps the student out by inserting, in parentheses, "(хорёкъ)," but хорёкъ means a polecat, not a weasel, which is properly ласка—so that a traveller who tried this gambit might well be thought offensive, if not demented. "Of what emperor did you speak? I spoke of the emperor who has many brave warriors. Why did you speak neither with Alexander nor with Constantine? Because they did not speak with me. . . . Did you see on those high trees the nests of the old nightingales?" This exercise works up to the following anecdote: "GIRL AND PHILOSOPHER. At the moment, when a learned philosopher was very busy in his study, a little girl came to ask him for some fire. 'But,' says the doctor, 'you have nothing to take it in.' And he was going to fetch (и онъ собрался принести) something for that purpose, when the little girl stooped down at the fireplace, and, taking some cold ashes in [one] hand, with the other she put burning embers on them. The astonished doctor threw down (бросилъ въ сторону) his book, saying: 'With all my learning, I never should have found out that expedient.'"

Later on, by way of other, more practical manuals, I arrived at Nevill Forbes's *Russian Grammar,* an elegant and scholarly work, at that time, as far as I know, the most comprehensive thing of its kind that had ever been attempted in English. Nevill Forbes was Reader in Russian and the Other Slavonic Languages at Oxford, and he wrestled in this book with the formidable, the finally impossible task of presenting Russian grammar to his countrymen in a lucid and logical way. Yet I have never shown this book to a Russian who did not cry out and insist on corrections. An English-speaking reader, on the other hand, finds Nevill Forbes most sympathetic and appreciates the slight tone of irony that occasionally touches his elucidations. Of the *g* in the masculine genitive singular, which is pronounced as if it were a *v,* he remarks that "it is a good instance to quote when Russians accuse English of being written one way and spoken another," and in explaining the diminutives he says that when "the conductor in a train . . . asks to see your билетики [little tickets], this does not imply that the tickets are small, but merely that the conductor would not refuse a drink." I once read this statement to a Russian, who received it with protestations. It is true, as Nevill Forbes says, that though "in many cases the diminutives are really meant to imply smallness," they are also "very frequently used merely as a means of express- ing affection, politeness, or good humor, and in such they are difficult, if not impossible to translate in English"; and I think that my Russian friend's point was that the conductor's calling the tickets билетики was really an expression of deference, not of familiarity. At one time I spent several weeks in quarantine in a hospital in Odessa, and I found that this use of diminutives—which seemed to me infantile—had an exasperating effect on my nerves, but when I cited them to the same Russian friend, I was told that, as Nevill Forbes says, these diminutives in different connections have different connotations. The grammarian or the translator who is trying to put Russian into English has constantly to struggle with such problems, as to which he can sometimes find no real assurance even in applying to Russians. I once complained about Constance Garnett, the translator of so many Russian novels, that she never seemed to have taken the precaution of reading her translations to a Russian who was holding the Russian text; but Mr. Max Hayward, the co-translator of *Doctor Zhivago* and probably the best-equipped of the English translators of Russian, replied—what is confirmed by my own experience—that if you try some dubious passage on several Russians, they may all give you different explanations.

The trouble here—and the inevitable difficulty of attempting to learn Russian from a grammar—is that the language is a tissue of idioms, which has never been systematized, as French or English has been. It is a language produced by illiterate people. I do not, of course, refer to Pushkin and the great literature that he did so much to launch, but this literary language, though Pushkin refined it and partly, in fact, invented it, was produced from a linguistic chaos and was to remain, from the point of view of grammar, one of the most intractable of the major languages. Old Slavonic was a scholarly concoction, derived from a dialect of Bulgarian but written in an alphabet based on the Greek and provided with a set of tenses that were partly made to follow the Greek ones.

This was devised for the use of the Greek Orthodox Church, and it was written and read at first only in the churches and the monasteries. The people spoke their Slavic language, which had little in common with this; but the Cyrillic alphabet—the Greek alphabet with two Hebrew characters and several other additions—came gradually to be used also for secular purposes: legal and administrative documents, diplomatic and private correspondence. Then the priests and the monks got to writing Russian, and they produced, during the seventeenth century, some extraordinarily hybrid chronicles. It was not till the middle of the eighteenth century that a standard usage emerged. This was more or less the modern Russian language, which was praised, in a famous passage, by Lomonosov, the eighteenth-century scientist and poet. It was a mixture of language elements. Old Slavonic accounts for some of its curious features, such as the g pronounced as v which I have mentioned before. It had been pronounced as g in Bulgarian, but the Russians pronounced it as v and never bothered to change the spelling. There had also got into this language some Tatar from the Tatar invasion; some Polish in the seventeenth century, when the Russians were beginning to require a vocabulary for European things and ideas that they had to get from further West; some German and Dutch under Peter the Great; and a sprinkling of French under Catherine. This language, so rich in vocabulary, was immensely expressive as a literary medium, but it was a language all made up of special locutions, and its wildly irregular inflections would have been hopelessly recalcitrant to any such discipline as the European languages had undergone. When you add to this, borrowed from Marxism, a German philosophico-political jargon, you get a barrier to communication between the West and the East that has undoubtedly, in recent years, had a good deal to do with our difficulties.

I am told by teachers of Russian that though a class may start off with enthusiasm and even a certain exhilaration at discovering that the queer-looking alphabet is really not at all difficult and—since the scrapping of five useless characters at the time of the Kerensky revolution—far more logical (in spite of the illogical g) than our alphabet for the spelling of English, there inevitably comes a moment when a good many students drop off; and anybody who sticks to Russian is likely from time to time to feel that he has reached a point where he seems not to be making satisfactory progress and that he must give himself perhaps a brief respite and then jack himself up again. To anyone with an appetite for words, the rewards of persevering are enormous. The verbs, though annoyingly complicated, come to exercise a certain fascination, with their nuances of implication and their unexpected shifts of meaning. I once asked Mr. Vladimir Nabokov if my impression that these Russian verbs which mask and unmask themselves with prefixes—prefixes that, sometimes remaining the same, may affect the stems in quite different ways—and that transform themselves, also (the verbs), through various internal changes, behaved differently from non-Slavic verbs and had something uncanny about them. Mr. Nabokov was taught English in childhood and has so intimately the sense of that language that he perhaps regards Russian with a certain detachment uncommon among his countrymen. He said that yes, he had always been delighted by what he called the "magic world of Russian verbs." (I have never got over an impression that Latin, German and English verbs are much more energetic and forceful, much more verbs of positive action, than the Greek and

the Russian ones, which convey rather ways of proceeding, modes of feeling and distinctions in thinking. I do
not know how far this is fanciful.) But for the student
who wants to learn Russian and is no connoisseur of
language, who therefore may not be susceptible to this
magic of the Russian verbs, I believe that the teacher of
Russian should begin by explaining what the student is
faced with—a language quite different from the languages that he is likely to have studied before. He should
know something of the history of Russian; he should have
it made clear to him that the development of Russian has
been different from the development of the languages of
the West; and the news should be broken to him that he
cannot depend upon the kind of student's grammar to
which he is already accustomed to anything like the same
extent as in the case of the Western languages.

The more scholarly kind of grammar that makes a real
attempt to cover the subject is a work the student cannot
cope with until after he has already made considerable
progress. Nevill Forbes died tragically and prematurely,
so he did not live to bring his grammar up to date in
spelling and changes of usage and the dropping of certain
inflections. It was impossible to republish or even to revise
his once uniquely valuable book. But he was later succeeded at Oxford by Mr. B. O. Unbegaun, and Mr.
Unbegaun has now written a grammar of his own, which
supersedes Nevill Forbes's and which seems to me something of a masterpiece. Mr. Unbegaun explains in his
preface that he has aimed to present "only the minimum
necessary for the understanding of the mechanism of
modern literary Russian," and that he will make no
attempt to provide the historical explanations—so revelatory of primitive habits of mind—of which Nevill Forbes
gives us glimpses. But Mr. Unbegaun's "minimum," for
the foreigner, will be likely to tell him more than he has

ever known before about the untamed behavior of the Russian tongue. His book will not, as I say, be of very much use to a student who is not quite advanced, and might indeed scare him out of his wits, but by the more experienced student it may be read with much profit and interest. Here they are, all captured and sorted out, clearly listed and their tricks exposed—those elusive Russian words that are always changing their faces and appearing in unexpected company and assuming or losing tails. Nevill Forbes is a British explorer who has brought home some interesting specimens and mounted them for home inspection as if they were butterflies and beetles; Mr. Unbegaun has stocked a zoo that seems to cage the whole wild fauna.*

In the matter of Russian dictionaries, I have always, in ordinary reading, used the popular Russian-English handbook, first published in 1936, of Professors V. K. Müller and S. K. Boyanus, but I very soon discovered its peculiar defects as an aid with pre-Communist literature. The anticlericalism of the Soviet Union has excluded from it or buried obscurely a number of ecclesiastical terms, so that some non-Soviet lexicon is necessary where Tolstoy or Dostoevsky or Chekhov is describing the life of the priesthood or some ceremony of the Orthodox Church. There are also touches of quaint Soviet cockiness. Under совать, a saying of Stalin's is listed as an example of its use—"not to poke one's swinish snout in our Soviet

---

* Forbes's *Russian Grammar* has now been brought out by the Oxford University Press in a new edition prepared by J. C. Dumbeck of the University of Manchester. Dr. Dumbeck has adapted it to the new spelling and brought its usages up to date, and he has enlarged it and made it much more complete. It was inevitable, one supposes, that he should have dropped Forbes's little pleasantries, which gave the book a personal accent.

garden." Professor Boyanus, it seems, got away on some pretext to England and never returned to Russia, so his name had to be banished from the title page—which was then, however, left to read as follows:

Русско-Английский
Словарь
составили
проф. В. К. Мюллер

But составили, "compiled," the plural form of the third person past of the verb, no longer now corresponds with the singular Professor Müller. It is hard to be perfectly sure when a Soviet citizen is winking.

I eventually succeeded in acquiring, through the kindness of a Russian friend—for, though this work has been lately reprinted, it was then hard to find and expensive— a fine pre-Revolutionary set of Dahl's great compilation in Russian, *An Explanatory Dictionary of the Living Great-Russian Language,* introduced by a portrait of the author, with a beard like a long pair of lungs, in a huge old-fashioned high-backed chair. Vladimir Ivanovich Dahl (1801–72) was, like Gesenius and Dr. Johnson, one of the pioneering masters of lexicography. He was originally a physician, and in the course of his service as an Army doctor had travelled a good deal in Russia and had talked with all sorts of people. He was remarkably many-sided in his interests. He published manuals of zoölogy and botany as well as medical papers; but his principal work was in the field of linguistics and popular Russian culture. He is said to have been able, like Professor Higgins, to detect the place of origin of anyone he met as soon as he opened his mouth, and he wrote a set of stories and sketches intended to illustrate the peculiarities of various localities and milieux. He published an immense collection of thirty thousand Russian proverbs, which may well be on Khrushchev's shelves, and made a collection of four thousand folk tales, which he turned over to Afanasyev, the Russian Grimm, as well as collections of folk songs and popular prints. But the most important work of Dahl's life, to which he brought all his varied learning, was the dictionary mentioned above. Together with a wide knowledge of literature, he had, like Mencken, a voracious appetite for colloquial and vulgar speech, which was, I should suppose, unique among the dictionary-makers of his period. His dictionary is wonderful in its wealth of examples as well as in its lists of synonyms and its identification of flora and fauna by their correct scientific names.

Though the old encyclopedia of Brockhaus and Efron (published before the Revolution) insists—in doing Dahl, however, full honor—that "he remained to the end of his days a self-taught dilettante," his book has the attractiveness, the personal flavor, of the man with a passion for his subject who has explored the whole field for himself. He made errors, and his modes of procedure were sometimes mistaken or impractical, but a later Russian scholar, I. Boduen-de-Kurtene (a French name which looks queer in Russian), brought out in 1904 a revised and enlarged edition, to which he also had devoted an immense amount of labor. Boduen-de-Kurtene even went so far as to include all the Russian *gros mots* (what have come to be known in English as "four-letter words") which Dahl had felt he had to omit—a step that was, as far as I know, then unprecedented (save for dead languages) in the history of lexicography. The English four-letter words relating to sex have not even been admitted to the great Oxford English Dictionary—inaugurated in 1858 though not finished till 1928—of Murray, Bradley, Craigie and Onions. (These omissions have since been repaired—though with asterisks standing for the vowels—by Mr. Eric Partridge in his *Dictionary of Slang and Unconventional English*.) One is startled, in the 1904 Dahl, to discover, under the Russian equivalent of a word to which D. H. Lawrence has especially attracted attention by featuring it in *Lady Chatterley's Lover,* a conjugation of what is, euphemistically, sometimes referred to as "the mother oath"—an exploit which has its scholarly justification in the circumstance that this verb is irregular. But when Dahl was reprinted in the Soviet Union, the prudish authorities reverted to the pre-Boduen-de-Kurtene policy.

To take on thus, without inhibitions, the whole range of colloquial speech was possible for Russian scholars of the nineteenth century for the reason that the Russian language had never been regularized to the point at which such practice would have been felt to be improper. The language had never been purged to the same degree as seventeenth-century French or eighteenth-century English. It has been more or less stabilized at the opposite extreme from the purified classicism of French at the period when it was possible for a critic, embarrassed at being informed that the word *dog* occurred in Homer, to lay it down that "if the word *dog* occurs in Homer, you may be sure that that word is noble in Greek." Tolstoy, in *War and Peace,* makes great play with this contrast between Russian and French and produces ironic or comic effects by allowing his characters to relapse into Russian after talking the language of the court: in Russian they sound homelier and blunter, their true old Russian selves are revealed. In the time of Dahl and Kurtene, it would have been quite impossible in Russia to attempt to establish a standard of vocabulary, style and usage as was done by the dictionary of the French Academy, and the Russians were thus able to anticipate the kind of all-inclusive dictionary that is now felt to be needed for the languages of the West.

This tendency toward all-inclusiveness is seen in its extreme form in the new edition of the American Webster's, which has recently provoked so much controversy and which has already been treated at length in an article in the *New Yorker* by Mr. Dwight Macdonald. I shall not deal here with English dictionaries, and I have not examined the new Webster's, but I gather that it has made a departure from tradition in listing colloquial and illiterate usage side by side with literary English and the language of educated people, without indicating, in many cases, any preference in favor of the latter. And even the French are yielding. The latest edition of the Petit Larousse contains words that would not have been admitted to any of the previous ones and for which one would have had to resort to one of those dictionaries of argot that were never retrospective or comprehensive. I used to read Huysmans in my youth with the aid of Delvau's *Dictionnaire de la Langue Verte*. When Flaubert wrote to Huysmans, in 1879, about the latter's novel *Les Sœurs Vatard*, he reproached him for making use, not merely in the dialogue of his lower-class characters but also in his narrative prose, of vulgar colloquial expressions, *"énergiques et souvent grossières,"* with which Flaubert was unfamiliar (*"un tas de mots qui ne sont dans aucun dictionnaire"*), and indeed these expressions, which Huysmans found so flavorsome, are imbedded in his tight-pressed prose in exactly the same way as the out-of-the-way technical and literary terms that he also so greatly relished—which is to say, like the truffles and pistachio nuts in the pâté of a rich French meat loaf. But Delvau collects examples from *Les Sœurs Vatard*, and he includes all but one of the words and phrases cited by Flaubert as unintelligible:

maboule, poivrots, bibines, godinette, du tape à l'œil.
The exception, *maboule,* is now to be found in a Petit
Larousse of 1948, as well as *du tape à l'œil,* though the
latter is somewhat differently defined; and the newest
edition of the Petit Larousse is more helpful than you
might expect if you are reading Jean Genet or *Zazie dans
le Métro.* But the distinctions in usage are here made
quite clear, as they apparently are not in Webster's; the
colloquialisms and vulgarisms are designated as "Fam." or
"Pop."

A queer example of this crisis in lexicography is an
ambitious and rather pretentious work in two large volumes, English-German and German-English, published,
respectively, in 1938 and 1953 and dedicated to *"der
Völkerverständigung."* It was conceived by Dr. Karl
Wildhagen of Kiel, who completed the first volume and
sketched the second but did not live to carry his project
through, and the German-English volume was undertaken by Dr. Will Héraucourt of Königsberg. "The object of this book," as Dr. Héraucourt explains in a preface
somewhat showily written in English, "is to represent, in
the whole diversity of its social and individual structure,
the vocabulary and usage of present-day German, i.e. of
the 19th century and 20th century, including standard
speech (as basis), the conversational language of the
educated classes, colloquial speech [Fam.], the poetical
language, dialect, and slang. In order to provide space for
the living language we have deliberately refrained from
dealing fully with the vocabulary of earlier centuries.
. . . The dictionary is not intended exclusively for school
and university nor even for science, industry and commerce but also for the 'man in the street.' It will serve
alike those who read the classics and those who read the
illustrated weeklies. Where the rule is 'gentlemen only' it
will serve its purpose just as well as amongst 'ladies only.'

The guiding principle has always been 'Proper words in proper places'; as an English colleague remarked 'I call a spade a spade; some call it a b....y shovel.' Consult in this connection e.g. *A-a, Baba, Heia, Piepvogel, Wauwau,* etc.,—*prima, knorke, edel;—Mords-, Pfunds-, Heiden-, Scheiss-,* etc. It makes a world of difference whether the peasant or his wife has 'Holz vor der Hütt 'n' (→Holz), or whether he or she wears the trousers. The 'unmention-ables' of the 19th century have their place in this dic-tionary just like all forms and varieties of the word *Hose,* from the substantial *Arbeitshose* to the flimsy *scanties* (honi soit qui mal y pense! → Knigge)." He goes on to explain that the dictionary is intended to cover fully "technical and industrial terms": "The latest scientific and technical advances from ballpoint-pens to television sets and from atomic research to synthesis of vitamins are represented." He declares that "German slang is in no sense less picturesque than the English and the Ameri-can," and he invokes, as an exemplar, Eric Partridge.

I do not know about the English-German volume, which is the work of Dr. Wildhagen alone. I bought the German-English one with a view to reading the German classics, but in spite of what is said above I found it not well suited for this purpose. The decision to refrain "from dealing fully with the vocabulary of early centuries" has prevented it from being useful to anyone whose German is as weak as mine, and I did not at first do it justice as an exploit of an unconventional kind. The attempt to trans-pose expressions of colloquial German into English col-loquial equivalents has sometimes produced bizarre re-sults, not easily recognizable: "He is great on the piano" is hardly possible as a rendering of *"Er spielt famos Klavier,"* nor is "To be flossy *oder* gay with a person" admissible as the American for *"Sich jedem gegenüber Frechheiten erlauben."* The desire to exhibit a knowledge

of English colloquialisms is in some cases indulged unnecessarily, as when *"Er schlief den ganzen Tag"* is
translated as "He slept the clock round," and the virtuosity of topical allusion sometimes leaves the actual meaning obscure, as in such a laconic entry as *"Knigge: kennen
Sie—nicht?* [mm] have you read Emily Post?" (One
learns from the list of abbreviations that "[mm]" means
mutatis mutandis.) Yet the command of colloquial
speech—German, English and American—is actually
rather impressive, and the book may, for its purpose, have
some practical value. It is, in any case, of a certain importance as indicating the current interest in recording
the vocabulary of the common speech.

III

I received from Budapest a couple of summers ago a small
and attractive volume containing translations of two of
my plays. I learned from a biographical note and from
reviews which were later sent me that I was known in
Hungary only as a dramatist, in which capacity, I was
happy to hear, I was rather highly regarded—perhaps as a
kind of Molnár with an up-to-date social conscience. I
therefore examined these translations with interest, referring to the English text, and decided that the least I
could do for the so generously appreciative Hungarians
was to learn the Hungarian language. I had already felt a
certain curiosity about it, since it belongs to the so-called
Finno-Ugric group, the origins of which are somewhat
obscure but which are supposed to have been left in pools
in certain parts of Europe and Russia from the flood of
some early oriental invasion. I was stimulated further by
the fact that in the region in upstate New York in which
I spend my summers I have several Hungarian neighbors,
who could help me in studying the language, and by the

fact that a literary Hungarian friend had for years been crying up to me the brilliance of Hungarian poetry—especially that of Endre Ady, the translations of whose work into German and French which this friend induced me to read had seemed to me rather flat but who, now that I have read him a little in his own so very different tongue, does impress me as deserving the enthusiasm that is felt for him by most of his compatriots.

I must say that I set out on this exploit with a slightly uneasy memory of the senile Baron Hulot in Balzac tottering up to the attic to embark on his last liaison. I found it at first very difficult to obtain a full-length scholarly grammar. The dictionaries available were quite first-rate. The two volumes compiled by László Országh, which can be obtained from Budapest, are ample for the needs of the beginner and admirable in their presentation, besides which—what is rare with such lexicons—they have a certain aesthetic attractiveness and are pleasant to handle and have around. They are fat but well proportioned in format, five and a half by eight. The Magyar-Angol is bound in a sober gray, with the lettering stamped in blue, the Anglo-Magyar in a luscious deep rose, with the lettering stamped in gold; in each case, the color is appropriate to the language that is being revealed.* (The bindings of Hungarian books have a special kind of richness and gaiety that has something, I think, in common with Hungarian cuisine and music. A recent volume of Sándor Petőfi's collected poems is bound in bright-scarlet silk, with gold trimmings, pale-yellow page tops, and a matching pale-yellow silk book-

---

* Dr. Országh, I afterwards found, has published also two much more comprehensive dictionaries, English-Hungarian and Hungarian-English. His knowledge of English idiom, even at its most colloquial, American as well as British, is to an English-speaking student astonishing.

mark; and the edition of Molnár's plays, as they came out one by one, during his lifetime, in small, rather squat volumes, the pages of which are enclosed in a delicate frame of red lines, may still be found in appetizing bindings of purple, gray, blue and red.) But a practical grammar is a different matter. A new one has, I believe, just been published, but at the time I began on the language there was no such work in print, and I started with two handbooks of colloquial Hungarian—one evidently intended for British tourists or for Britishers with business in Hungary, *Colloquial Hungarian,* by Arthur H. Whitney, first published in 1944, and the other, *Spoken Hungarian,* prepared by Thomas A. Sebeok in 1945 for the use of the American armed forces at the time, at the end of the last war, when there seemed to be a possibility that our armies might go into Hungary. Both these works are unsatisfactory, and I was told by the Hungarians with whom I was working that the exemplary conversations concocted in them were sometimes not natural or idiomatic. In the Whitney book, the exposition—perhaps partly from exigencies of space—is hurried and not very clear; the declensions and conjugations are all run together in the text or diagrammed too densely in the back of the book, and the lesson-by-lesson vocabulary is administered in a jumbled and indigestible form. The exercises in reading are labored instalments of a narrative that is boring to the last degree. A Mr. and Mrs. Szabó (Taylor), apparently from somewhere in the provinces, arrive in Budapest by rail, in company with a Mr. Fehér (White), who lives in Budapest and whose acquaintance they seem to have made on the train. The Szabós put up at a respectable hotel, while their friend Mr. Fehér, a bachelor, goes home to his three-room flat. Mr. Fehér is attentive to the Szabós. He shows them the sights of the city, takes them out to cafés, restaurants and theaters. Remembering the comedies of Molnár, I kept expecting Mr. Fehér to show an interest in Mrs. Szabó. In Lesson 9, "A Hölgyek," "The Ladies"—which Mr. Whitney translates as "The Women"—I hoped that a drama was starting. I quote from Mr. Whitney's own translation:

"Suddenly, everyone looked in the direction of the lift. A woman came out of it, in a white evening gown. She was very beautiful and still young. She was not hurrying, because she knew everyone was looking only at her. Three women who were chatting, suddenly became silent, but they were looking only at the gown.

"After the young woman a gentleman emerged, in black clothes, but nobody looked at the gentleman, but everyone was admiring the lady, as she went across the vestibule and out of the big glass door.

"Both White and Taylor looked at her, and then both thought better of it and turned round. Just in time, because Madame was coming down the broad staircase. Our friend White thought to himself that she, too, was beautiful, with her black hair and white skin. The dark evening gown suited her no longer young years very well."

But the beautiful lady in white never appears again, nor does anything further come of Mr. Fehér's admiration for Mrs. Szabó. The little group are very bourgeois. Mr. Szabó is an "architectural engineer," Mr. Fehér is a businessman and works in an office. The Szabós get a letter from their son, talk about a postcard they have had from a young couple who spent their honeymoon in England, and exchange domestic pleasantries. These Hungarians are themselves somewhat British: "Mary will bring the tea in," says a Mrs. Szakács (Cook), the wife of "a writer-friend" of Mr. Fehér's, to whose flat Mr. Fehér takes the Szabós. "And give me the timetable,

Mary, dear [*Marikám*]! It's on the sideboard." Then she turns to her guests. "How do you like your tea, Helen, dear? Is this strong enough? Do you take sugar?" "Please. My husband drinks tea without milk."

In the end, the Szabós simply depart. "We haven't had," remarks Mrs. Szabó, as they are taking a last stroll on the Danube embankment, "such a nice summer holiday for a long time. Isn't the sky magnificent?" "Magnificent certainly," says her husband, "but there are a lot of holes in it, don't you think?" "Jack!! I don't know what's wrong with you. What a thing to say!—to spoil my mood with such a stupid joke!" "Forgive me, my angel, I'm in such a wonderful mood, that I hardly know what I'm saying."

When the Szabós are settled in the train, and Mr. Szabó has lit his pipe after buying his wife some chocolate, Mr. Fehér rushes up to say goodby. They thank him for his friendly offices and invite him to come to visit them.

One must not, of course, expect entertaining fiction of the authors of colloquial manuals.* Their problem, and rather a difficult one, is that of telling some sort of story while illustrating the principles of grammar explained in

---

* The dramatist Eugène Ionesco, in an interview in the *Listener* of December 24, 1965, explains that his play *The Baldheaded Prima Donna* was inspired by studying English in a manual of conversation and becoming at first irritated then charmed by the dialogues between a Mr. and Mrs. Smith and a Mr. and Mrs. Parker, "who met in the evening and talked of all sorts of things, such as, it is nice to live in the town but the country is quieter." "This world," he says, "seemed so banal and yet so improbable, strange and bizarre." The play was taken as a satire on the English, and people who saw it and knew England "said to me. 'You must have lived a long time in England,' whereas in fact I had never been there."

the current lesson and without giving the student words and forms that have not as yet been explained. But these manuals reflect the mentalities of the grammarians who have prepared them and who are usually aiming at the guidance of some particular kind of student, whose needs they may not merely want to meet but whose ideas they may also want to influence. The manual for our armed forces takes the ordinary American to Hungary. Here we follow the adventures of a soldier arriving in a strange country and making contacts with the young people there. He must be able to get around and to order food. He must not be guilty of boorish behavior, and he must be able to get himself a girl. Says a G.I. of this imaginary occupation to the headwaiter from whom he has just ordered dinner: "One moment! That beautiful girl over there at the table, does she work here?"

HEADWAITER. Yes, she works in the restaurant making out the bills. She is my younger sister.

SOLDIER. Really? Say to her that I don't want to speak to her because maybe she doesn't talk to people with whom she's not acquainted—but if you would introduce me. . . .

HEADWAITER. I don't know, respected sir; my sister doesn't much like soldiers, because they only stay a short time in Budapest. But you are from the United States. . . . Eva, come here a minute! I should like to introduce this soldier gentleman to you.

EVA. Good evening. I see that you are from the United States.

SOLDIER. Yes, miss. Won't you please sit down. Wouldn't you like some dinner, or perhaps a little wine?

EVA. No, no—just a little hot milk please. And a cigarette. Thank you. Have you got a match?

SOLDIER. Tell me, Headwaiter, what time do the movies begin?

He asks her to go to the movies with him, and she answers, "But you're an entirely unknown soldier! No, thank you, but I don't like soldiers. And I work here in the restaurant till 9. How long will you be in Budapest?"

SOLDIER. I think three or four weeks, maybe two months. And then I go back to Texas.

EVA. Oh, really? What do you do in Texas?

SOLDIER. I'm a farmer, I work with my father. I haven't got any friends or relations in Budapest, and I'd like to go to the movies this evening—do come with me.

EVA. I can't go this evening. But tomorrow night I'm not working, and then perhaps I might go with you.

This is clearer and simpler than Whitney, but it will not any more than Whitney provide a real survey of Hungarian. Even for its limited purpose, it has one extremely ill-advised feature, in common with other such manuals for American soldiers and with the courses in foreign languages prepared for them at the time of the last war. Some official or committee—I assume—had at that time the absurd idea of teaching pronunciation not by using the alphabet of the language in hand or its version of the Roman alphabet but by substituting for it an adaptation of the version of the Roman alphabet so inconsistently employed for English. Thus the student had to learn a system that had nothing in common with the system according to which the language was actually written. In the case of Hungarian, this "Spoken Hungarian" demands that the American soldier learn *"Kösönöm, nem akarok kaaveet"* alongside *"Köszönöm, nem akarok kávét"* ("Thank you, I don't want any coffee").

What is the advantage of this? In Hungarian, the pronunciation does not present very much difficulty, and the use of the Roman characters with their diacritic marks is logical, whereas the use of them here in the manual is quite different from their use in English. It produces, in fact, a language which is superfluous and artificial, a language which does not exist. We have no *aa* combination in English, and a double *e* in English is sounded as in *seen,* which is not at all the same as the Hungarian *é*. In the teaching of Russian at the time of the war the distortion became fantastic. Instead of learning the Cyrillic alphabet, one of the few easy features of the language, the students were compelled to master what was really an imaginary Slavic language written in Roman characters, which disqualified them from recognizing real Russian. I hope that this foolish system—a typical product of American pedagogy—has now been allowed to die and will never be adopted again.

But the Americans did not take over Hungary. The Soviets, as we know, did, and they have not been idle or incompetent in providing apparatus for their people to learn Hungarian. They have published two excellent beginners' grammars, to which I eventually resorted—one in German and one in Russian—as well as a bang-up scholarly work in Russian in two comprehensive volumes.* These grammars are also of interest in revealing a third point of view, that of the Soviet Union, from which

---

* I have since seen *Esquisse de la Langue Hoagroise* in the series *Les Langues et Leur Structures* (Paris, Librairie Klincksieck) by Aurélien Saurageot, Professor of Finno-Ugric Languages at the École Nationale des Langues Orientales. This is not a book for beginners but a lucid and interesting treatise by a foreigner who has studied the language and come to his own conclusions. There are many illustrative passages chosen from Hungarian authors.

Hungary may be approached. The grammar in German, which starts off with one lesson of farmyard vocabulary, is otherwise—although Hungary has always up to now been predominantly an agricultural country—largely occupied with factory workers and party congresses and foreign students from the satellite countries who are invariably working their heads off; and although it is useful, of course, to learn the names of the various trades and of the nationals of these countries, it is depressing to be confronted with an exercise which is all made up of this kind of thing:

"Look! There are the Hungarian fellow-workers!"

"I am Kovács József [Joseph Smith], an ironworker. These men here on the right are Hungarian miners and on the left textile workers. Are you ironworkers?"

"No, I am the only ironworker, they are miners. This comrade is a Soviet journalist."

"No, I am not a journalist. I am a Romanian textile worker."

"Where are the Chinese? Are there no Chinese workers here?"

"Why, yes, they are here."

"Where are the Albanians?"

"They are over there on the right."

"How many Romanian delegates are there?"

"Two Romanian delegates, four Poles, five Czechoslovaks, four Albanians."

No matter whether we find ourselves dealing with Mr. and Mrs. Szabó, the boy from Texas and the headwaiter's sister, or the Romanian textile worker and the five Czechoslovak delegates, we are here equally far from the weasel of your cousin, the nests of the nightingales in the high trees, and that prince of whom you always speak.

But this grammar is to be recommended (in the series *Tanuljunk Nyelveket*). Some such large-scale treatise, it seems, was needed for the students who have been coming to Hungary as a way of getting out of East Germany, and the book has a German completeness which seems to leave no point unexplained. It has, however, been compiled by Hungarians and is enlivened by attractive features which have an air rather Magyar than Germanic: a colored plate of the principal colors, which is an aid to remembering the words for them; a great many little drawings which help to fix actions and objects; and with each lesson a pinch of proverbs, a joke with a comic illustration, and, following the tradition of Kodály and Bartók, a little folk song, with its music given, which the student is supposed to learn. One feels, also, by Lesson 19 that the obligatory Soviet façade is beginning at last to give way before the impact of the intractable Hungarian patriotism. A brief history of Hungary here ends with nothing more propagandistic than the statement that after the Nazis had left Budapest in ruins, the reparation of the damage was carried out "successfully in a short time under the leadership of the Communist Party and by the arduous labors of the population."

If one wants to find the Russian formulas applied in their most uncompromising terms, one may examine an English grammar prepared in the Soviet Union and first published in 1959: a *Manual of the English Language*, by M. Galinskaya and Z. Tsvetkova. In the first half of the grammar described above, the authors, to be sure, were obliged to assume that Hungary was wholeheartedly a Communist society. Not only do we read about delegates from all the satellite countries but the visitor who wants to go shopping is immediately directed to the Állami Áruház, the State Department Store, "where you can get so much of everything," and Lake Balaton, formerly a smart resort, where people went to spas to "take the waters," and now, it seems, still a place, like Cape Cod, where writers, artists and other "intellectuals" go to spend their summers, is presented as exclusively a kind of preserve in which the workers and students are permitted to enjoy their brief holidays. But the Soviet manual for English is forbidden, of course, to assume that we are all contented workers together; it can never be allowed to deviate from the official line of the Cold War. From the moment that the rudiments of English have been explained to the beginning student, there is nothing in the reading exercises but an idealized representation of Soviet society and a denigration of the "capitalist system," which is aimed at both England and the United States. On page 227 we find the following dialogue, in which, it should be explained, the pidgin English is mostly intentional, since the student is supposed to supply the correct English forms of the verbs for the incorrect ones in parentheses:

IN THE READING-HALL OF THE INSTITUTE
(*Petrov is reading. Stepanov enters.*)

STEPANOV. Hello, Boris. What you (read)?

PETROV. I (read) *Sister Carrie* by Dreiser. And what will you do? Why you (take) so many books and magazines?

STEPANOV. I (read) them for my report.

PETROV. What report?

STEPANOV. Next week I (speak) about unemployment in capitalist countries.

PETROV. Oh, it's an interesting subject. You (get) much material?

STEPANOV. Yes, I (have). I already (read) many books and magazines on the subject, but as I have some time I (want) to read more.

PETROV. You (read) *Sister Carrie*—the book which I (read) now?

STEPANOV. I (read + not) it yet. (Be) there anything about unemployment in it?

PETROV. I (can not) tell you for sure because I (finish + not) it yet. It is not written especially on unemployment, but it (give) you good pictures of American life. And, as you (know), there (be) always unemployment in any capitalist country.

STEPANOV. Yes, the life of the working people (be) very hard there. Thank you, I (read) the book as soon as you (finish) it.

PETROV. I (finish) it tomorrow. What other books or magazines you (read) already?

STEPANOV. I (read) a lot of them. There (be) something about unemployment in almost every book about capitalist countries. I think I (get) much material. I (read) these books and magazines today and tomorrow, and the day after tomorrow I (start) writing the text of my report.

PETROV. You (read) *Chronic Unemployment in Capitalist Countries* by Ivanov?

STEPANOV. Yes, it (be) the first book that I (read). Well, the librarian (look) at us. Let us stop talking. Good-bye.

PETROV. Good-bye.

Thereafter the Soviet student is insulated against the West by a series of loaded selections from English and American books, including Galsworthy's *The White*

Monkey and the ballad of *Barnacle Bill the Sailor,* retitled *The Awakening of Barnacle Bill,* which illustrate the miseries of unemployment, the class conflict in the merchant marine and the manifestations of color prejudice. The most curious of these exercises for reading are two juxtaposed selections about railroads—one a Soviet encomium of the Soviet railroads built since the Revolution and the other an episode from *Three Men in a Boat,* by the English humorist Jerome K. Jerome. Jerome was very popular in Russia before the Revolution, but the comrades who wrote this grammar have found a new use for *Three Men in a Boat.* The selection included here is an exaggerated British joke about the vagueness of the officials at Waterloo Station, but in this case it has been exploited for the purpose of demonstrating the ridiculous inefficiency of capitalist railroads in contrast to Communist ones. (When I visited Russia in 1935, the railroads must have been among the vaguest and the most unreliable in the world; I do not know how much, subsequently, they may have improved.) The corruption of true art by commercialism is also illustrated by apt quotations, among them the following poem:

In My Garret

At the top of a lodging-house
I sit with burning heart,
And think of the age-old saying—
In a garret is starving art.

And tho' my guts are sore
And my feet are icy cold
I'm very glad that I can say
My mind has not been sold.

The working-class is rising,
It needs its poets all;
And here is one who's waiting for
The Revolution Call.

by Patrick Rowe (abridged)

These failures and abuses are offset by exercises intended to impress upon the student the superior oppor-
tunities provided in the Soviet Union for the diligent and
earnest and obedient and modestly ambitious young man—
for example, a chronicle called *Victor's Biography,* which
runs through several lessons: "I was born in 1930 in the
small town of Perov. Both my father and my mother were
workers. My father was a welder and my mother was a
tanner." Victor wants to be a worker, too, but his mother
says he must study and go to a kolkhoz. When he is
fourteen, he joins the Komsomol. His father fights
bravely against Nazi Germany. "His letters were always
interesting. I read them at our Komsomol meetings."
Victor, when he finishes school, decides to become "a
historian," so he has to go to Moscow to study. We next
see him on his way to a teaching job in a model provincial
town, which has "some big plants," "some smaller plants"
and "also many cultural institutions."

There is, of course, nothing here that would help one
in finding one's way around in Britain or the United
States—in ordering a meal or a drink or in getting to
know the natives—nor is there any description of these
countries except that they are capitalist prisons, where the
only choice for the worker is between exploitation and
unemployment.

But, on the other hand, it cannot be said that an old
Hungarian grammar, written in Hungarian for immigrants, which I borrowed from one of my New York

State neighbors, gives a much more attractive picture of life in the United States. The title page has been lost, so I cannot be sure of the date, but it must have been not long after 1913, since Woodrow Wilson is the last President listed, and only the date of his first inauguration is given. Here is the rather bleak prospect which, according to this manual, the American city offered to the newly arrived immigrant:

Are you the foreman? Yes, sir, what do you want? I am looking for work. . . . Can you tell me where I can get some work? There in that building is a free employment office. . . . How much wages do you ask? Twenty dollars a month. I will pay you ten dollars a month. . . . I want a situation as a cook, Sir. . . . Is your family large? No, there are only four persons. . . . Do you expect high wages? No, Ma'am, I care more for good treatment. . . . Where have you been in service last? At Mrs. Kovács, 184 Woodland Ave. How long were you there? Three months, Ma'am. Why did you leave that place so soon? Because I did not like it there. Where did you serve before you came to Mrs. Kovács? Nowhere, Ma'am; I had just arrived from Hungary. . . . Has the grocer's wife paid all she owes? She owes me a year's rent and has only paid a quarter's. . . . Can every citizen become President? No. He must be a native born American, must be over 35 years of age, and must have been 14 years resident of the United States. . . . This country is the United States of America. It is the land of freedom and liberty, because the people govern themselves. All citizens love their country, because they know that this freedom was earned by men who gave their lives for it. . . . The American flag means liberty and justice for everybody. . . . It is not the money you earn that will make you rich, but the money you save. You should save some money out of your earnings to put in the bank. In the bank, the money is safe. If you keep money at home, you may lose it or spend it. . . . [A letter of appeal to the landlord] Sir,—For ten years past I have been your tenant, and you are aware that I never failed to pay my rent when it was due; but now, owing to sickness and the general business depression, which has prevented me from seeking regular employment, I am reluctantly compelled to ask your indulgence. . . . Leave me alone [presumably a woman speaking]. . . . Widow of 38 would like to correspond with a good, honorable gentleman, with intention of matrimony; no triflers.

If Russian is a language of idioms, illogical and partly primitive, originally developed at random by more or less illiterate people, Hungarian is an orderly language, established in its present form by highly literate writers and scholars. That it belongs to an "agglutinative" linguistic group is likely to scare people away from it: the adjective sounds so unpleasant. But an agglutinative language is merely one in which the syntactical relations that the more familiar languages express mostly by prepositions, personal pronouns, adverbs and auxiliary verbs are attached to the main parts of speech and written as a part of the word. In the case of Hungarian, this need not result in the long polysyllabled units of its now remote cousin Finnish. If clumsily written, it may tend to these, but, written well, it is neat and terse. There are relatively few irregularities, and its units are constructed in an orderly way. One reason for this is undoubtedly that it was disciplined and codified in the modern age. In old Hungary, it was simply a folk language, seldom spoken by educated people. The upper classes spoke Latin (which was sometimes still kept alive for university

examinations and even dinner-table conversation well up
into the present century), and when once, in the early
nineteenth century, a delegation of Hungarian nobles
visited Rome to confer with the Vatican and were received by the fabulous Cardinal Mezzofanti, who was
fluent in fifty or sixty languages and addressed them in
what he thought was their habitual tongue, only one of
them was able to answer him. But Hungarian had been
and remained the tongue of the original settlers, which
had been brought by them from somewhere in the East
and which had always been spoken by the people, and a
lexicon and grammar had been compiled as early as the
thirties of the sixteenth century. When the great Magyar
nationalist movement against the Austrian domination
began seriously gathering steam, toward the end of the
eighteenth century, the Hungarian language was cultivated, and the writers became ambitious to produce a true
native literature. An Hungarian Academy of Sciences
was founded in 1830, and a good deal of work was now
done on the language. It was necessary to create a vocabulary for many conceptions and inventions that the folk
language had had no words for, and to systematize and
regularize the grammar. Jacob Grimm, the great folklorist
and philologian, who lived long enough to see this development, asserted of the new Hungarian that it was a
model of a planned language and might appropriately be
used for international diplomacy. In 1839, it was made
the official language of Hungary.

An Hungarian grammar, then, if the subject is properly presented, can pretty well cover the ground, and
cover it without confusion, for one who wants to study
the language. The grammatical principles may be new to
him, but, though complicated, one gets the hang of them,
and to follow their exposition is an agreeable intellectual
exercise. The manual intended for American soldiers of

which I have spoken above has pages that look rather like logarithm tables, from which it is possible to calculate what almost any given noun in any relation will be. The vocabulary is also strange, though it contains a considerable Slavic element, derived, I suppose, from the period when the original Magyars resided in Russia before they came further West and from the Slovaks and Slovenes who are still their neighbors. There is far less German than one might expect, though the language of politeness and honorifics seems partly to consist of translations of the conventional German formulas. The built-in tenses and modes of the verbs result in a pleasant compactness; one can usually see at a glance what the meaning of any verb is. When written and printed, Hungarian has a kind of full-flavored nuttiness that makes in poetry for a tight condensation, quite alien to the European modes of expression and not recognizably soluble in transposition into languages more liquefied. Yet it does not sound clipped in the speaking. The spoken language has a soft sing-song cadence.

The Magyars, in their migration from the East—their origins are still mysterious, and a meager historical record only begins at the end of the ninth century A.D.—dug themselves into the Danube Valley, so fertile with its black alluvial soil and walled in by the Carpathian Mountains and the Transylvanian Alps, and bred themselves as a strong well-knit people, tough, truculent and self-assertive as well as imaginative and dashing, capable both of barbaric wildness and of poetic and intellectual brilliance, and their language embodies all this: it is solid and tight-muscled yet lyric. It is limited—developed too late and, in spite of Grimm's admiration, hardly suitable for general use—but, as was said to me by a Magyar friend, it is like the Hungarian cuisine: the materials are rather few, but one can make of them a marvellous dinner.

I sometimes find it disquieting to reflect that the variety of the languages, so interesting in itself, is bound, to a certain extent, to keep human culture shut up in compartments. The art of Kodály and Bartók can be easily enjoyed by anyone who is capable of listening to music. Munkácsy's enormous painting of the blind Milton dictating to his daughters, which is now in the New York Public Library, has lodged itself in our minds almost like that of Washington crossing the Delaware; but how, short of learning Hungarian, can we know the art of Endre Ady, who is regarded by many Hungarians as the greatest Hungarian poet, and how can the Magyars themselves know precisely how to estimate his genius in relation to that of more widely known and more easily approachable writers? I have been told by a Hungarian friend that when he once asked Béla Bartók whether he really thought that Ady was as great as they liked to believe, the great composer countered with "What do *you* think?" It seems much like the case of Pushkin, but, with the increase of interest in Russian studies, Pushkin is at last coming through to the West. My own impression is, from a meager enough knowledge of Ady's work, that the poet's position in Hungary has been rather like Yeats's in Ireland. Ady went to Paris in his youth and was influenced by Verlaine and the Symbolist poets; then he became, from the beginning of this century, a sort of spokesman for Hungarian nationality. He was never a public figure, but his work became a rallying point. An Hungarian who was young in that period once said to me that Ady was a "state of mind." Though tempermentally very different from Yeats—his life was rather reckless and riotous, and he died tragically of syphilis at forty-two—he identifies himself with his country and is very much preoccupied with his ancestry, half Magyar and rootedly rural; and his poems are full of allusions, geographical and mythological, that, like Yeats's, can only be explained by one who knows the country well. He had a wide range in meter as well as in mood, and he produced a large body of work. Like Yeats, he invented a personal idiom, and, like Pushkin—one is told by his countrymen—he contributed to the creation of the literary language. But Yeats was not obliged to write Gaelic—his poetry was accessible to anyone who read English—and Pushkin was inaugurating a literature which was immediately to lead into prose fiction and, in translation, to travel all over the world; the moral insight and the story-telling genius of the Russians were to plunge through the barriers of language. But what is to be the future of Hungarian literature? Even with the Russians on their necks, one of their best writers in jail and others driven into exile, the imaginative genius of the Magyars has never yielded to bullying, and it is reported that in Budapest the literary journal of the Communist press, called *Élet és Irodalom* (*Life and Literature*), is usually—on the ground that it has nothing to do with either—referred to as simply *És*. The Hungarian national spirit is evidently still represented by the old slogan *"Nem, nem, soha!"* ("No, no, never!") which was adopted when the country was broken up at the end of the First World War, and by the staggering agglutinative stunt-word *legeslegmegengesztelhetetlenebbeknek,* "to the most and most irreconcilable ones" (in which only the *engesztel,* "conciliate," represents the root idea), which, before this dismemberment took place, when Fiume was still under the thumb of Hungary and the Italian-speaking officials were ordered to learn Hungarian, the natives in defiant ridicule wrote up on the city walls. The capacity for resistance to alien domination, which had already been demonstrated by Hungary at the time of the invasions of Genghis Khan, of the Turks and of the Austrian Empire, was awakened again against Russia in the rebellion of 1956. In this uprising, the writers of Hungary played a very important role, as they had always done in the past in the Hungarian nationalist movement. Sándor Petőfi, the great poet of the early nineteenth century, disappeared—either killed or captured—in the uprising of 1848, when he was fighting against the Russians, whom Franz Josef had called in to defend him against the insurgent Hungarians.

And yet the reverbations of Petőfi's fame have only faintly been heard outside Hungary. Mór Jókai, a popular novelist, was in my youth somewhat read in English, but he now seems completely forgotten; Ferenc Molnár, once popular on Broadway, survives only in adaptations of *Liliom*. The influential Hungarian scientists are obliged to write either in German or in English in order readily to exchange ideas with fellow-workers in their various fields. But it is nevertheless true that such of these cultural minorities as have remained self-assertive and determined still stand for us against the monotony, the desolating anonymity of the bureaucratic centralized state, which has come more and more to be based on the international language of science. I am all for international coöperation in political arrangements and cultural exchange as well as in the sciences. The nearest things we have had in the West to real international languages—Latin and French and English—have, of course, been immensely valuable. It does, from one point of view, seem impractical to have so many different words to represent the same things. Yet what a word really represents is the relation of the speaker to the thing. I have spoken of the difficulty for a modern Anglo-Saxon of grasping the moralities of the ancient Greeks—Jowett's translation of Plato, with its capitalized Christian "God," is a conspicuous example of this—and of the reciprocal difficulties of Russian "Marxists" and American "democrats" in understanding one another. And as Henry James remarked, the Anglo-Saxon *love*, the French *amour* and the Italian *amore* all represent different conceptions. Certain of our Indian groups have a whole set of different words—indicating, as I remember, the sex, the age, and the season and color of coat—for the animals among which they live; the Arabs have innumerable words for "camel," while we have only one. The close intimacy of these people with their animals is peculiar to their "way of life."

Well, how much simplification is to be desired? In the realm of ideas, a good deal. The Communists and the Western politicians have each their own brand of cant with which they disguise the actualities of the societies they attempt to govern. But they have certain problems in common, and they must eventually come to recognize what these problems in common are. When they do so, they will have to arrive at a new interlingual vocabulary, or at least a set of common basic concepts, which can deal with these actualities. But as for the minority languages, you cannot, in the meantime, destroy them, try to break them down or wipe them out—as every empire and federation does—without a certain violation of the minority man's individuality and of the corporate life of his group, which will be likely to make trouble later on, when he has you at a disadvantage and does the same thing to you or takes it out on a weaker party or simply resorts to some despairing revenge. You cannot beyond a certain point "process" or "brainwash" or "educate" the speaker of another language by compelling him to learn your own language, for you cannot destroy his relations with his environment and with his own kind. The sacred language of the Jews is still braced to resist the *goyim;* the Russian language, the old Russian language that Lomonosov praised, is still a highly inappropriate medium for conveying the mechanics of Marxism; the Hungarians, threatened with German, consolidated their non-European language, so rebarbative to all their neighbors, and made it the symbol of their national identity—and then reversed the situation by ramming it down the throats of the reluctant Slavs and Romanians who were living within their boundaries. The modern grammars I have mentioned above—the Hungarian one for the American soldier, the Russian one for the Russian studying English, the Soviet one for the German student who wants to study Hungarian, and the American one for the Hungarian immigrant—all have one fundamental aim in common: they are trying to impose the standards of an industrial civilization which insists upon uniformity, and though they all may to some slight extent serve as aids to international understanding, they are all rather desolating documents. What they all except the German one lack is any suggestion of a language's greatness.

A language that has once borne the impress of the masters of thought and art is impregnated forever after with the genius and authority of these masters. Greek and Latin have outlasted their papyruses, and Hebrew through three thousand years has never lost the imprint of the "word of God" that has been stamped upon it as deeply as those characters incised in the two copper scrolls discovered in one of the Dead Sea caves, which, before they were cut into strips, could be read in relief through the outer layer and which have turned out to be directions for finding a treasure, presumably that of the Temple, hidden away, to keep them from the Romans, in those barren inaccessible hills. The pictured tapestry of English poetry, the fine even weave of French prose have had wide currency and withstood long wear. The great flow of Russian song and talk, now withdrawing and hushed, now hissing and pushing the shore, was made to pour itself at last into well-blown transparent containers that would make its volatility portable, as if it were possible for a substance to be crystalline at the same time as fluid. And the stanzas of Petöfi and Ady may still throb and darken and flare wherever, among alien tongues, an Hungarian struggles in exile.

James Joyce said of *Finnegans Wake* that he had written the night's dream of his Dubliner in a mixture of tongues from all over the world for the reason that the emotion and the imagery of dreams antedate all the other languages and are the realm from which the others have sprung; and yet English, outlandish though he makes it look, is the basic linguistic medium through which, in *Finnegans Wake,* these other languages reach us. We cannot get away from our languages, and from the content that their common people as well as their men of genius have in the course of the centuries given them. We may hope that there will yet be a medium by means of which all the peoples can communicate with one another, but we cannot forecast what such a language might be, we can hardly as yet even speculate as to which linguistic elements will predominate; still less can we concoct one synthetically. And in the meantime we find a variety of admirable literary media, molded to forms of beauty or charged with intellectual power, and I hope, to the best of my ability, to keep on exploring these.

April 20, 1963

THE GENIE OF THE VIA GIULIA

THE REVIEWS OF THE ENGLISH TRANSLATIONS of Mario Praz's books have often been written on a false assumption. The reviewers tend to suppose that Praz is a literary critic like any other and to complain that they do not find in him what they get from T. S. Eliot or F. R. Leavis or whomever they most respect, while at the same time he does not supply them with an academic scholarly work of the kind that has been begun as a Ph.D. thesis and then expanded into what aims to be a definitive work on its subject. Signor Praz's best-known book in English is *La Carne, la Morte, e il Diavolo nella Letteratura Romantica,* translated as *The Romantic Agony,* a study of the influence of the Marquis de Sade on the Romantics, from Shelley to D'Annunzio, a book which cannot be ignored by anybody who is interested in modern literature. Aside from this book, Signor Praz is chiefly known as perhaps the leading authority in Italy on English literature. He spent eleven years studying in England and teaching Italian literature at the Universities of Liverpool and Manchester, and he is now Professor of English Language and Literature at the University of Rome. He has written much on English literature in English as well as in Italian, and has published in English an interesting book: *The Flaming Heart, Essays on Crashaw, Machiavelli, and Other Studies of the Relations Between Italian and English Literature.* I do not know of anyone else on the Continent who is capable of such competent reviewing of current English and American books or from whose journalism it would have been possible to compile such a readable and reliable selection as the two volumes of his *Cronache Letterarie Anglosassoni*. Yet to think of Mario Praz as primarily an English expert and a literary critic is largely to misconceive his role. He should be considered as primarily an artist—and I do not even say literary artist, for the results of his activities as a collector of furniture, pictures and *objets d'art* are as much a part of his *oeuvre* as his books. He is an artist and a unique personality who expresses himself through his art in connection with any subject he is treating. Two of his books, which have just been translated—as *The House of Life* and *An Illustrated History of Furnishing*—really for the first time make it possible for English-speaking readers to acquaint themselves with this personality.

Before dealing with these books, however, I want to discuss a little some of the writings, mostly unread in English, which have led up to these recent works. Praz's first characteristic book that I know (published in 1925) is *Secentismo e Marinismo in Inghilterra*, a study of those seventeenth-century poets, English, Italian and Spanish, who cultivated farfetched "conceits" and who combined the erotic with the pious. The inclusion of a reproduction of a photograph of Bernini's Santa Teresa in her anguished and equivocal ecstasy is typical of Praz's method, since he devotes as much attention to the visual arts as he does to literature, and it strikes the note of his peculiar quality, for which I have found it inevitable to invent the term *il prazzesco*. The next important step, it seems to me, is his account of a trip to Spain—*Penisola Pentagonale*, published in 1928, and translated as *Unromantic Spain*. I take a special delight in this book—a delight that is entirely malicious. I, too, like Mario Praz—as he explains in a new edition of 1954—have been bored by Hispanophiles, and I have also been bored by everything, with the exception of Spanish painting, that I have ever known about Spain. I have made a point of learning no Spanish, and I have never got through *Don Quixote*; I have never visited Spain or any other Hispanic country. But Mario Praz does know Spanish and *has* visited Spain, and his report on it confirms me in my prejudices. He says that at the time he lived in England he heard Spain so much raved about as "geniune, profound, etc." that he decided "to investigate that genuineness, to take soundings of that profundity." What he produced when he returned was, he says, "substantially a polemical book," for which he is now a little apologetic and which he explains he has somewhat toned down (I should like to see the original edition). He found the religion depressing, the landscape and the cities monotonous, the people very pleasant but indifferent, the whole country "delicious to live in"—this was 1926, he reminds us—"if life were, as, alas, it is not, a continual Sunday holiday." As for literature: Calderón is as repetitive and boring as St. John of the Cross. He does not even care much for the painting. Contrast, he invites the reader, the Italian with the Spanish rooms in the London National Gallery. "In the former, a resounding gaiety of color, like triumphant banners flying over the turquoise of the lagoons, all of the hues of the rainbow pressed till they have yielded the refinement of their essence, an exuberance of ungirt heavens, an opulence of fine clothes, cf juicy fruits, of magnificent flowers . . . But if in the Italian rooms the color of the heavens dominates, it is that of the earth that reigns in the Spanish ones. It is almost as if the Italian painters had acquired their education by lifting their eyes to the eternal azure while the Spaniards, dazzled by their yellow sun, had kept them constantly fixed on the brown fields, the burnt ochres of the dry plateaux. . . . Take away the sulphurous lamp of the canvases of Greco [who was, of course, not really a Spaniard] and the rest of the Spanish collection will seem to be tuned to a single note, an earthy note of cork and pumice."

We have already in *Penisola Pentagonale* what are to become some of the most striking features of this highly idiosyncratic writer: his brilliant powers of description, his lyric interludes which are really prose poems, and his Proustian reflections on life (which, however, have not been, I think, derived from Proust), as when he speaks of the difference in our attitude toward people casually encountered in our native country and people observed abroad, who seem to us attractive or romantic because we cannot really know about them. And we have also his saturnine humor. His description of a bullfight he witnessed has given me as much satisfaction as anything of the kind I have ever read. Mario Praz attends this spectacle, during Holy Week in Seville, with an American couple and their daughter, and it is difficult to tell which he dislikes the more—the idiocy and cruelty of the bullfight itself or the reactions of the American family. The father is so much disgusted by the death of the first bull that he takes the mother away. In a spirit of American progress—to the astonishment of the Spaniards—he points at the carcass of the bull being dragged by mules from the ring and, seizing a bystander by the arm, exclaims, "Yesterday!"; then, pointing at a plane which is flying overhead, *"Mañana!"* The daughter stays on and is disappointed; she had hoped to see somebody killed, but what happens seems much less exciting than a movie in which Douglas Fairbanks had thrown himself out of an airplane and landed on top of a train which at that moment was crossing a burning bridge above a cataract. The second bull, pricked by the banderilleros and stabbed in the neck by the matador, goes off to lie down in a corner and pacifically "meditates on his fate." Goaded into getting up, he accepts the final thrust "with stoical resignation." The third bull "seems to contemplate with a detached amusement the tarantella of the dancing banderilleros. The picadores put the bellies of the horses practically on top of his horns, but, disdainful, he barely grazes them and turns his head in the other direction." At this point, due to some accident, two heifers escape from the bull pen, and the bull who is supposed to be fighting breaks away and simply follows them, "just as in England, the husbands follow the wives who have come on Saturday night to drag them out of the pubs."* The need is felt for something more spirited, and with the fourth of the bulls, the matador goes through a "series of acrobatic contortions and complicated kneelings under the nose of the bull," but the animal will take only a few steps forward, then stop and take a few steps back, "with the chronometric regularity of a mechanical toy." This bull, however, is killed by the first thrust, to a chorus of ecstatic *olés!* and a shower of caps into the bull ring. The fifth wants to jump over the barrier where the arena attendants are sitting; the sixth bull turns out to be cross-eyed, to the great indignation of the public; and the last one shows so much fight that the espada gives the thrust as he is running away, thereby rousing cheers for the bull and boos for the matador.

"Now," the author begins his next chapter, "do not imagine that the bullfight described above is a caricature. On the contrary, it is typical. Except that, ordinarily, the spectacle is considerably more monotonous." An ideal

---

* Signor Praz has written *giovenchi,* bullocks, instead of *giovenche,* heifers, but, in the light of other evidence, is now inclined to believe that these animals must have been females.

bullfight, he says, was described by Gautier in his book on Spain, which has been plagiarized by another writer, but about this exploitation Gautier could hardly complain, since he had got the story from a Mme d'Aulnoy of the end of the eighteenth century, who had herself taken it from someone else. There follows an hilarious discussion of the foreign aficionados who make literary capital of bullfights. The author summarizes a novel by Henry de Montherlant—*Les Bestiaries*—in such a way as to make it sound like a parody, but since he quotes actual passages of incredible absurdity, it cannot be merely Praz being amusing at Montherlant's expense. The first symptoms of the Hispanophile disease for which Praz has invented the word *"pantaurismo"* are that the sufferer begins using a comb of lead in order to blacken his hair, that he covers his fingers with rings, takes to wearing a cordovan felt hat, is continually having his shoes shined, and goes to *Carmen* at every opportunity. He cultivates passionate love and insists on being brutal to his women. "Up to this point, one might suspect that it was a question of a variety of sadism. But sadism is too obvious and common," and it may have unpleasant consequences. Encouraged by remembering that in Latin *torus*, not far from *toro*, means bed, he identifies his love affairs with bullfights. Sometimes, when by himself, he flourishes a muleta at his bed and plunges a sword into the feather-stuffed coverlet. He has never yet attended a bullfight, but he is conscious of the taurine aspect of everything: crocodiles, motorcycles, trams. He feels the need for "creative murder." Eventually, he comes to see the bullfight as fundamentally a religious rite. The corrida is a kind of Mass: the matador and his bull are symbols of the priest and his God. Are not all important holy days in Spain celebrated with special bullfights? "The canonization of Saint Teresa alone cost more than two hundred bulls their lives, since every convent founded by her put on a corrida." The better a Christian one is, the more one should love bullfights. The author goes on to Maurice Barrès, another intemperate Hispanophile, who, according to Praz, associated the voluptuousness of the bullfight with that of the auto-da-fé, the Inquisitional burnings at the stake (of which a picture is pointedly included). (*Death in the Afternoon* had not yet appeared when *Penisola Pentagonale* was written, but Praz does not neglect, in the new edition, to tell Hemingway off in a note.)

This chapter, so pleasantly deflating, seems to me a little marred by one quality of Mario Praz's which occasionally gets out of hand: a malignity which tends sometimes to coarseness. At the end, he slightly queers his effect, which ought to be one of controlled exasperation, by a kind of angry hounding of Barrès. As I have said, he apologizes, in this second edition, for the polemical character of the book, but one cannot put this quality down to the aggressive perversity of youth. One strikes it from time to time in all of Praz's writing. Reading at random in his volume of essays, *Lettrice Notturna,* I find one, written in 1945—*Sul "Demonico"*—in which he writes of Mussolini's death, the gruesome manner of his execution, in a way that, however much the Italians must have suffered from this bumptious charlatan, I feel to be a little too gloating. One of the features of Spain that Mario Praz found least congenial was the ceaseless preoccupation with death—a kind of worship of death—that is characteristic of Spanish religion. With this feeling, too, I sympathize, though never having been in Spain, I have encountered this cult of death only in our own Southwest, with its skeletons sitting in chariots dragged along in religious processions and its self-flagellating and self-crucifying survival of the Franciscan sect of Penitentes. Yet, as Praz explains in his foreword, the chapter from which I have quoted—called *Sangue, Voluttà, Morte*—contained the germ of his most famous book, which diagnoses "the Romantic Agony" and which is entirely characteristic of the author. Why are these subjects, then, here not abhorrent to him as they were when he encountered this combination during Holy Week in Seville? Why are they not repulsive to the reader? Because what is arid and dull in Spain is, like the paintings of Italy that he celebrates, presented in the later book with so rich an Italian palette, recreated with so loving a gusto. Though Praz is saturnine, even somber, he is also in his way buoyant.

But before we meet Praz in his happiest form, let us further take stock of *il prazzesco*. If the macabre is one element of this, there is also the element of sheer oddity. He loves the grotesque, the incongruous, and his books, among other things, are cabinets of curios. There is nothing that Praz enjoys more than a bit of unexploited monstrosity. There are the images of Marini and Góngora; there are the demons and witches of the Romantic Agony. There are the Renaissance "monsters of Bomarzo," giant human figures and animals carved out of stone, why and by whom no one knows, for the garden of a villa which is now a wilderness. There is that book of mysterious authorship, the *Polifili Hypnerotomachia* of 1499 (partly translated into English a century later as *The Strife of Love in a Dreame*), with the strange symbolism of its primitive woodcuts and its ornate and polyglot style, the influence of which Praz traces down through Swinburne and Beardsley, and of which he notes that Thomas Griffiths Wainewright, the poisoner-painter celebrated by Wilde, boasted of possessing a copy. There is *The Hero in Eclipse in Victorian Fiction*, a study of the mediocre ideal of contentment and respectability which came to dominate English novels in the nineteenth century—a work that is illustrated, however, by a selection of photographs of paintings which are calculated to bring out the morbidity, the eccentricity and the sensuality that this enveloping blanket masked. On a visit to the United States, on the mission, itself rather incongruous, of studying our neo-classical architecture, he succeeded in discovering *il prazzesco* where a native would never have suspected it. He was delighted to have it pointed out to him that the Pilgrims' Monument in Provincetown was a replica of the Torre del Mangia in Siena, and he somehow became aware—what very few Americans know—that a little creek called the Tiber runs under the city of Washington, a fact which he at once connected with what he supposed were the pretensions of our capital to be regarded as the new Rome. His most remarkable achievement in this line—described in his book of travels, *Viaggi in Occidente*—was his discovery in Connecticut of what he calls "the most romantic house in America"—though I have never known anyone else who has visited it or even anyone who has ever heard of it—which, as in the case of the monsters of Bomarzo, has to be searched for in a kind of jungle. "I found it with difficulty in the woods near New Haven. It was the house of a Prix de Rome sculptor. When the artist had grown old, he abandoned the place one day, took with him his personal belongings, and went to live in a boarding house ten miles away, without ever setting foot in it again or even bothering to close the door. The vegetation twined about the statues, and it may be that vandals have completed the work of disintegration by nature and time, for the limbs of certain marble dancers seem disfigured by hammer blows. Or was it the artist himself who, in a crisis of exasperation, had mutilated them before giving up his house and his art? This house, which I should call the House of the Bankrupt Sculptor, dates only from yesterday, yet it seems more remote in time and longer dead than any of the houses of the two-thousand-year-old Pompeii."

I have been emphasizing the elements in Mario Praz of the mordant, the macabre and the queer, but this will give no idea of either the beauty or the range of his work. His reading in belles-lettres and his knowledge of the arts are enormous. To the training in the Greek and Latin classics that most Italian men of letters have he has added a competence in French, German and Russian as well as in English and Spanish. *The House of Life* is, I believe, his masterpiece—a book unlike any other, and a much more complete expression of Mario Praz's sensibility than any of his other books. It must be explained that "the House" in question is the apartment in a palazzo on the Via Giulia, in Rome, in which Praz has been living since 1934. His rooms house a huge collection of furniture, mainly Empire, books, pictures and curious objects— though none, I think, of the objects is not attractive as well as curious, or rather, perhaps, is not, by arrangement or association, made to appear attractive. The apartment is not like a private museum, because it composes a unit, because, like the book which describes it, it is the intimate integument of Praz himself. The apartment is "the House of Life" because it is the house of Praz's life, and the description of his collection here is inextricable from the memories of his life. A common acquaintance of Praz and mine once told me of seeing him when the acquaintance had been much depressed by the suicide of a friend, and of Praz's saying to him, "One must attach oneself to objects." This is one of the themes of his book. "Mine, alas," he writes of the English wife from whom he is separated, "is one of those temperaments that are lazy in human relationships, too content to take things for granted, to consider as fixed, once and for all, the thing which for others has to be a fresh conquest each day, the delicate balance of living forces in continual motion. It is perhaps for this reason that I have put so much of my mind into the cult of things which to most people seem devoid of life, such as furniture, why I have sinned by 'bowing down to graven images.'" And, speaking of the ability of public men to remember people's names and faces: "This gift I do not possess, or only in a very intermittent fashion, with regard to people; whereas I am capable of remembering, with great precision, the appearance and whereabouts of objects of art, pictures, furniture, and things of even less importance. Things remain impressed in my memory more than people. Things which have no soul, or rather, which have the soul with which we endow them, and which can also disappoint us when one day the scales fall from our eyes; but people disappoint us too often, for it is only very rarely that we come to know them, and when we think we know them and feel ourselves in unison with them, it is because it is the thickest scales of all which then cover our eyes—the scales of love."

In its literal material aspect—that of memoirs of the obsessed collector—we have, in *The House of Life,* stories of pure detective work, such as that of the differing portraits, one of which Praz possesses, of Caroline Murat and her children, and stories of the prolonged pursuit of some coveted piece of furniture, which display a passion almost amorous, as in the case of a marble-topped table which, when he first saw it, he could not afford—with its Egyptian terminal figures and its frieze of cupids on dolphins—and which was bought up by someone else: he had been "proposing, on one of my returns from England to Florence, to go into the shop and open negotiations—like a crusader coming back from the Holy Land to betroth himself to the girl he has so long dreamed of, when she, unable to go on waiting, has given herself to another." There is also the story of the writing desk, so dear to him for so long, which, finding a more desirable one, he discarded like a cast-off mistress. He gave it away to a friend, who, himself finding one he liked better, traded it in to a dealer. But the table proved to be unsalable and may perhaps, says Praz, "still be languishing, dust-covered, in the warehouse of the dealer, who told me he was proposing to cut it in two to make two small console-tables, which are apparently easier to sell." For the converse of the fixation on objects is that the objects are endowed with life. I have always, in visiting Praz's apartment, as soon as I came into the entrance hall, with its charming statue of Cupid, which he says one of his maids used to kiss, and passed by the portraits of the anteroom, been made to feel that there were presences lurking about me, and I am interested to find, in his *History of Furnishing,* the reflection that "for a soul that loves order and cherishes experience, numerous delicate affinities are established between itself and the things of its outward abode, so that finally there is no longer any distinction between the outward and the inward." These presences—artists long passed into eclipse, craftsmen no longer famous, vanished families, faded myths—have been somehow brought to life, refreshened, by proximity to Mario Praz.

In this book, *The House of Life,* he escorts us around his apartment, room by room and piece by piece, with occasional learned digressions. "The style of the rosewood sofa-table on which the little bust of Shakespeare reposes" reminds him of Keats's relation to the decorative art of the Regency, and he demonstrates the close connection between this art and the literature of the period: "The composite Romantic product beneath a seemingly Classic form." In this kind of connoisseur's perception, Mario Praz, as a critic, is at his best. But the objects also carry him back to his family, to his youth in Florence, to his marriage and his love affairs; the Aubusson carpet reminds him of a night when the June moonlight fell on it, and he and a friend were talking, perhaps for the last time, during the horrible days of the war—the friend a soldier on his way to North Africa, Praz, with his wife and daughter, living in fear of bombardment. But more often, landscapes, enchanting moments; memories of Liverpool and an English Doris, whom he idealized and did not understand; interesting people who shared his tastes: Maurice Baring and Vernon Lee.

The translation of *The House of Life* by Angus Davidson seems to me one of the best I have ever read. Davidson is such a good writer himself that if it were not that Praz is speaking about himself, it might pass for an original work. But it is a pity that it had to be abridged— the illustrations as well as the text. The chapter on "Lucia's Bedroom" has been denuded of so much fine *prazzesco*: an extensive section on dolls' houses; a discussion of antique bidets, of which the author owns a curious specimen; some account of Jules-Émile Saintin, a forgotten late-nineteenth-century painter, one of whose pictures is hanging on Praz's walls: a stubborn French non-Impressionist who ran true to Praz's tradition of incongruity both by filling his canvases with minute detail and by his having at one time in America painted pictures of frontier action, such as *The War Path* and *The Pony Express,* and then in Paris chic tableaux of fashionable ladies, surrounded by furniture and ornaments, like scenes from the novels of the period; and a lyrical love affair with a beautiful Florentine Letizia, "with a long body like the sheath of a sword, the head a little heavy on the narrow shoulders, but a slim and graceful body, of the elegance of a bronze Sardinian statuette," in which, however, characteristically, the youthful summer gaiety is seasoned with a description of a ward of syphilitic children which he visited in Letizia's company. I suppose that, in making these cuts, it was thought that the English-speaking public, not really being accustomed to Praz, would not be able to take him in all his voluminous richness, yet without the dimension of the excessive there is no true Mario Praz.

An Illustrated History of Furnishing from the Renaissance to the 20th Century—is in a sense an extension of *The House of Life*. In 1945, Praz published a little book called—after Poe's *The Philosophy of Furniture*—*La Filosofia dell' Arredamento*. This essay has now been revised and enlarged, and it appears as the introduction to the *Illustrated History of Furnishing*, a book of four hundred illustrations—sixty-three pages in color—with a commentary by Praz. One could hardly do justice to this book by attempting to cover its contents. One can only explain that it is an enormous collection of paintings, drawings and engravings of all kinds of rooms in all kinds of dwellings, from royal palaces to taverns, collected from all over Europe as well as from Russia and America. There are usually people in these rooms, so the book is a history of social life as well as a history of furnishing. I have found it inexhaustibly interesting. It provides such a variety of entertainment that one cannot take it in by merely setting out to go through it. One should have it around on the table and give it an hour from time to time. It is, in any case, a wonderful volume that nobody but Praz would have undertaken. The translation by William Weaver is not nearly so good as Davidson's of

The House of Life. It is not infrequently clumsy and sometimes even ungrammatical.

Mario Praz, in one of the last essays of *Lettrice Notturna,* speculates as to what posterity would make of him if his works should be lost or forgotten and the only traces of his existence be personal mentions of him in the writings of contemporaries. In a letter of Edmund Gosse's, he is referred to, it seems, as "an interesting young professor . . . a great Swinburnian." Charles Du Bos, in his diary, tells of meeting him and says that he is "a great friend of Vernon Lee and that he is working in the British Museum on the seventeenth-century poets." In an account of a convention of the P.E.N. Club, he figures, distorted to "Marco Pron," as one of "the great animators" of that organization. (In every case, he points out, he is something "great.") In a book by Derek Patmore called *Italian Pageant,* he is referred to as "Dr. Mario Praz, so long a staunch friend of Great Britain." Now, suppose that, together with these references, there should survive of Mario Praz's writings only a translation of his *Gusto Neoclassico* done in Hungary without his permission and adapted to the official Marxist line, according to which "Comrade Praz" is made "to denounce with heavy irony the aristocratic and capitalistic society which produced the neoclassic taste." Then suppose the researcher should find in Charles Jackson's *The Outer Edges* the statement that "the best reading in the world for a sexual delinquent is provided by Mario Pratz [sic] and Bertold Brecht." Would this student not come to the conclusion that he was reading about different people?

No: the situation is quite unthinkable. Mario Praz will need no such identification. He will come to be known to posterity—so far as a foreigner can judge—as one of the best Italian writers of his time. Born in Rome, to which he has returned to live, he is a genie who brings us Rome in huge armfuls—its cosmopolitan culture, its accumulations of the ages, its happy freedom from narrow prejudices, its conviction of being at the center of the world, its appetite for rich materials: literature to be relished, colors to sate the eye, soups, pasta and fruits to be tasted, flesh, fabrics and ornaments and marbles to be pored upon and cherished and prized.

February 20, 1965

INDEX

INDEX

An asterisk indicates a reference to an author whose work is mentioned without his being named.